THE DEVELOPMENT OF THE
GERMAN PUBLIC MIND

THE DEVELOPMENT
OF THE
GERMAN PUBLIC MIND

*A Social History
of German Political Sentiments
Aspirations and Ideas*

BY

FREDERICK HERTZ

The Age of Enlightenment

LONDON
GEORGE ALLEN & UNWIN LTD
RUSKIN HOUSE MUSEUM STREET

PRINTED IN GREAT BRITAIN
in 10 pt. Pilgrim type
BY EAST MIDLAND PRINTING CO. LTD.
BURY ST. EDMUNDS

TO THE RIGHT HONOURABLE
LORD BEVERIDGE
IN GRATITUDE AND ADMIRATION

PREFACE

THE Public Mind, which this book attempts to trace consists in the wide variety of political sentiments, aspirations and ideas held by the different social sections of a people. The word 'political' implies not merely the striving for, and the exercise of, collective power but also the aim of a legal order without which the use of power does not make politics. The concept 'public mind' includes both views and feelings apt to inspire groups of people but it excludes speculations of abstract thinkers too difficult or unpopular to play a rôle in politics. Nor can the public mind be completely identified with 'public opinion', which is a rather nebulous idea, and, in my view, should be applied only to sentiments which fluctuate on the surface of politics, but not to deeply rooted convictions.

The study of history and politics requires not merely the ascertainment of what happened, and of the immediate causes of these actions, but also the explanation of the wider background, particularly of the general valuations or norms obtaining in a group involved, in a nation or an age. It is certainly of the greatest importance to scrutinize the official documents in the archives but it must not lead to the view: Quod non in actis, non in mundo. Though individuals sometimes had paramount influence in bringing about momentous events, they could not have achieved this without the response of groups of a congenial mentality. Each group mind is directed by a combination of ideals, traditions and interests, of historical legends and vulgarized philosophy, now commonly known as an ideology. A nation includes numerous groups imbued with very different ideologies which largely contradict one another, and besides countless people of indeterminate type.

This concept of the public mind is obviously entirely opposed to the widespread habit of ascribing to nations, classes and other groups a unitary, unchangeable mentality such as the alleged national character, racial spirit or class interest. These concepts have largely been discarded in serious research but they still play a very powerful and disastrous role in politics. Hitler's racialism was the peak of this mania though there have also been many similar aberrations in various other nations. In the last war Lord Vansittart, 'Chief diplomatic adviser of the British Government', wrote a book in which it was maintained that 'the German has not really altered since Tacitus' day. He has always been a barbarian and warlover, the enemy of humanitarianism, liberalism and Christian civilisation, and the Hitler régime is no accidental phenomenon but a logical fruit of German history. To mankind as a whole Germans have brought nothing but misery in all its forms.' This kind of opinions has certainly had a great share in bringing about the present condition of the world.

The principal object of this book consists therefore in shaping a history of the ideas which determined the political opinions, feelings and actions of the German-speaking peoples in the age of Enlightenment, primarily the development of views on religion and toleration, right and wrong, government, war and peace, rank and honour, freedom and equality, labour, property and welfare, the task of the state and its organization. In many cases there is a great contrast between the opinions and actions of politicians, and to bridge it is one of the aims of an ideology. In this book both fields must be considered, theory as well as practice.

The age of enlightenment sought to found state and society on human nature which, rather optimistically, was often identified with reason. Jurists and legislators made the attempt to ascertain the law of nature, philosophers taught a natural religion, or a natural social order, and poets sung the beauty of nature. Various branches of learning were created, or received new foundations, to explore the nature of man. This task primarily required the study of the development of human valuations.

Our presentation, on the one hand, excludes many subjects which are usually treated in the conventional history, because their investigation does not shed much light on political psychology. On the other hand, facts are sometimes included which are seldom discussed in detail, for example conditions of foreign peoples. The reason is partly the fact that their doings brought about reactions of German peoples which to understand requires a closer knowledge of the situation on the other side. Partly, however, a comparison between German and foreign conditions is needed to illuminate the question of national peculiarities which is often obscured by deep-rooted prejudice.

Our investigation does not presuppose the existence of a German political nation which hardly was a reality in the old Empire, but refers to the German speaking peoples, of which, however, a few can be treated in some detail only. The realm of ideas, moreover, has no fixed frontiers. In the 18th century the French language had a dominating position at the German courts and in the aristocracy while outside the German Empire wide circles of non-Germans used the German language as the international language of communication. French and other foreign writers were therefore read by many Germans with enthusiasm while among non-Germans the educated people were also reading German books and adopted their ideas. The latter expansion of culture is less widely known than the former, and it is a merit of the late Professor Fritz Valjavec to have described in various important books the German influence upon the South East of Europe.

A*

CONTENTS

1

THE EMPIRE, ITS FRONTIERS AND STRUCTURE
AND THE SPIRIT OF PARTICULARISM

TERRITORIES AND MEMBERS OF THE EMPIRE

THE official name of the old German Empire up to its end in 1806 was 'The Holy Roman Empire of the German Nation'. This title referred to the predominantly German parts of the greater Empire founded by Charlemagne and restored by Otto I. But already many centuries before its formal end, the nature and extent of its wider range were controversial. It gradually became little more than a phantom sometimes evoked in ancient ceremonies, or in academic disputations, to arouse awe. But even the concrete Empire, as it existed after the Peace of Westphalia, had in many places and in certain respects, rather vague frontiers and a political structure difficult to define. The modern national State has fixed frontiers, its ruling organs and members have definite rights and duties, and it is supposed to possess the ability of forming a common will. But the old German Empire showed strange anomalies in these respects indicating that its inhabitants were lagging far behind many other peoples in the development towards nationhood. The cause of this was the strength of territorial separatism, or particularism, and the relative weakness of the central power. As a consequence it was sometimes unclear whether, or how far, a territory belonged to the Empire. There was an official list of its territories, the Matric, which was, however, incomplete. All the princes and Free Towns had a seat and vote in the Diet of the Empire, the Reichstag, and were called its Estates. But there were also Estates without land in the Empire, for example the Duke of Savoy, and there were princes who had possessions inside and outside the Empire, and were Estates only for their German territories. Quite a number were both vassals of the Emperor and independent kings of a foreign realm. This double position easily led to a conflict of rights, duties and interests. It might happen that a prince was, as a foreign king, at war with the Empire, but, as a vassal of the Emperor, had to furnish him with a contingent of troops for this war. Besides the princes there were also many rulers who had the same rights but were not Estates, because they had no seat and vote in the Reichstag. Most of them belonged to the category of Knights of the Empire (Reichsritter).

Uncertainties about how far a territory belonged to the Empire sprang from the feudal origin of the relations between Emperor and princes. The relation between a lord and a vassal was a contract capable of great modifications, and did not mean the absolute submission of a subject to his sovereign. Many territories had in the course of time received such exemptions from their duties to the Empire that their status was questionable.[1] The Bohemian countries and the Austrian Netherlands were not subject to the legislation and jurisdiction of the Empire. The Austrian territories were exempt from its jurisdiction and whether they were subject to its legislation was uncertain. The Burgundian circle was on the one hand a part of the Empire, on the other a fief granted to the Crown of Spain and later to Austria. As part of the Empire it had a claim to its protection, which was bound to involve Germany in wars between Spain and France. There were still 75 principalities in Italy, which were fiefs of the Empire, but did not form part of it. Their princes recognized the Emperor as overlord and paid him feudal fees, regarding him as their protector against aggressive powers; otherwise the overlordship was merely nominal. Nevertheless, in the Thirty Years' War the claim of the Emperor to the right of intervention in the succession to the throne of Mantua caused the entry of France into the war, which had most disastrous consequences for Germany. In general, the French-German antagonism developed out of the enmity between France and Spain, and the unclear position of fiefs of the Empire in the possession of Spain.

TERRITORIAL STRUCTURE AND SIZE OF THE EMPIRE

The politics of the Empire suffered not only because of the vagueness of certain frontiers and allegiances, but also from the extraordinary multitude and irrational configuration of its territories. In 1521 the Matric listed 415 territories, and in the late 18th century

[1] Cf. the list of territories of uncertain membership in Bornhak, p. 54.

314, but many were not included. Many rulers possessed several lands, differing in laws and institutions. In the beginning of the 18th century, the number of ruling princes and self-governing Free Towns was 234, and there were, moreover, 1475 Free Knights, who were also rulers, though not Estates. The excessive splitting up of Germany was mainly due to the fact that the fiefs had gradually assumed an hereditary patrimonial character, and could be acquired sold, pawned, and divided, like any other property. Since the 16th century, however, the striving of princes to prevent partitions in the interest of the greatness of their house began to emerge. The first-born son alone was to succeed. But it took two centuries till this principle prevailed everywhere. The princes also tried to increase their lands by dynastic marriages, succession pacts, purchases, etc., and it was in their interest to build a unitary state out of these acquisitions. The Estates of these lands, however, were usually entirely opposed to the integration of their own small land into a wider state, but political and economic progress certainly demanded this integration. The small territories had mostly quite impracti-cable frontiers, they often comprised enclaves belonging to another State, and not seldom a ruler possessed lands widely distant from one another between which there was no connection. The dynasty then strove to acquire territories filling the gaps and this caused much strife between rivals.

The Empire surpassed all European states in population, except Russia, but its structure diminished the advantages of a large popula-tion. The number of inhabitants was difficult to ascertain. Only Prussia and Austria frequently took a census while most of the other states were content with estimates. Statisticians often tried to calcu-late the population of the Empire but their results differed widely; towards the end of the 18th century, however, many of them agreed on a figure between 26 and 28 millions. The latest and most reliable statistics, referring to this time, are contained in Friedrich Leopold Brunn's work, which has been revised by the director of the Prussian statistical bureau. Brunn estimated Germany's total population at 28 millions, but regarded a higher figure as possible.

The greatest German power was that of the Habsburgs; according to the census of 1784 the Austrian and Bohemian countries had 7.9 million inhabitants, their Swabian lands 0.2 million, and Belgium over 1.8 million. The Habsburgs therefore ruled over 9.9 or 10 millions within the Empire. In addition, however, they had foreign dominions which were not included in the German Empire, in particular Hungary and her associated Southern Slav countries, Galicia and Bukowina, and Lombardy. The total population of the

Habsburg's Empire was, towards the end of the century, estimated at between 22 and 24 millions.

The next largest realm was that of Prussia which in 1786, the year, when Frederick II died, had 5,277,281 inhabitants, and inclusive of the army 5,630,850.[2] This also included the Duchies of Prussia and Silesia, which were officially considered outside the Empire. The size of the other states of the Empire, exclusive of the Burgundian Circle (Belgium and Luxemburg) was the following:

Size of States in inhabitants	1 mill. or more	500.000 to 1 mill.	300.000 to 500.000	100.000 to 300.000	under 100.000
Number of States:	2	2	5	14	ca 290
Total of population, millions	4,18	1,52	1,76	1,65	2,58

This table shows that there were only two States with more than a million inhabitants, namely Bavaria-Palatinate (2.07 million) and Saxony (2.10 million). The next class comprised Hanover with 873.000 and Wurttemberg with 650,000. In the lowest class the average population was less than 10.000. The table does not, however, include the Free Knights who towards the end of the Empire, amounted to ca 1475 persons ruling over 450,000 inhabitants in all. On the average one Free Knight therefore ruled over ca 300 subjects. The table includes 64 ecclesiastical rulers with 3,04 million people and 51 Free Towns with 733,900. The rest were lay rulers with different titles such as King, Duke, Landgrave, Margrave, Count, etc.

The antagonism of Catholicism and Protestantism still played a very great rôle in Germany's politics. According to Meusel there were—15 million Catholics, from 11 to 12 million Lutherans, 2 million of the Reformed Church (Calvinists) and ca 182.000 Jews. If the non-German Belgians, Slavs etc, who were Catholics, are deducted, the Protestants were slightly more numerous.

The distribution of States according to their population had many implications of political significance. On the one hand the figures illustrate the strength of the decentralizing tendencies, known as particularism. On the other they imply also a centralizing factor. The numerous small rulers, and the Catholic prelates, both great and small, inclined to the side of the Emperor, in whom they saw their protector against aggressive neighbours. For the same reason the Free Towns, though mostly Protestant, usually sided with his party.

[2] According to the census, the figures of which are quoted in Behre's book. The often quoted figures given by Hertzberg are less accurate since they were estimated according to Suessmilch's method.

The princes of larger states had often ambitions incompatible with the position of the Emperor and opposed to the development of a common German nation.

THE SPIRIT OF PARTICULARISM

The splitting up of Germany into numerous States contributed much to the evolution of a specific mentality known as particularism. It shaped Germany's fate more than anything else and for a long time prevented the rise of a strong national sentiment. Group separatism is a striving deeply rooted in human nature and it can only be more or less overcome by a wider solidarity, if natural and historic conditions are favourable. The foundations of larger states and nations were everywhere laid by conquerors and a national sentiment developed much later. But in Germany many factors worked against the development of a unitary nation. The great conflicts between Emperors and Popes in the Middle Ages brought about an increasing decline of the central power and a rise of the Emperors' vassals to the position of princes. This process led to a spirit of dynastic, territorial and social separatism, aggravated by rivalries for power and prestige, by tribal traditions, religious struggles, and by the intervention of foreign powers. France, in particular, did everything it could to make the territorial princes as strong as possible in order to weaken the Imperial power. This policy was represented as a defence of German Liberty against Habsburg Imperialism. A certain national feeling was not entirely absent, but it was vague or dormant, and awoke only in reaction to strong provocation. Publicists sometimes deplored national calamities, reminded the public of Germany's glory in the past, and pleaded for greater unity or for more loyalty to the Emperor. Yet a movement for political centralization and a unitary nationality did not exist.

From the point of view of our present, highly developed, all-powerful national state this is difficult to understand, but in the old times the economic and cultural advantages of such a state could no more be foreseen than its terrible aspects. But it may at least be noted that many evils of little states became a burden upon the people only when the example of Louis XIV created a new type of monarch which the German princelings wanted to imitate. Previously most German rulers were not much different from other noblemen. They mainly lived on the feudal returns of their domains, they did not have to care for the upkeep of a splendid court nor had they to bear the expenses of a large army and a great staff of officials. Many of them were very popular.

PARTICULARISM AND FOREIGN COUNTRIES

Though the great majority of the Germans clung to their small homelands, there was often considerable emigration. Soil and climate of the German countries were then mostly less favourable than those of many other European countries, natural catastrophes, bad crops, wars, the scarcity of soil, and social or religious oppression induced numerous Germans to leave their homelands in order to gain a better living. Apart from such causes there were also many gifted or ambitious people who found their native countries too small and their conditions too narrow to make a great career, and they sought better opportunities abroad.

The number of Germans in foreign armies was particularly large. A considerable part of the French army consisted of German mercenaries commanded by German officers. They never hesitated to fight against the troops of the Emperor, the German Empire or German princes. One of the greatest generals of Louis XIV was Marshal Count Schomberg, whose German name Schoenburg was frenchified in France. He served also in the Swedish and Dutch armies, and successively became a fieldmarshal of France, Portugal, Brandenburg and England. As a strict Calvinist he left France after the Revocation of the Edict of Nantes and became William's III foremost military leader. He was buried as Duke of Leinster in Westminster Cathedral. The military success of William's III expedition to England was largely due to him. Another prominent officer of King William was Landgrave George of Hesse-Darmstadt who, in different armies, fought in many countries of Europe, and in 1704 proposed the attack on Gibraltar which he then conquered for Britain. The Marshal de Saxe, an illegitimate son of Augustus the Strong of Saxony, was also one of the greatest generals of Louis XIV. Count Johann Mathias von der Schulenburg, a Saxon fieldmarshal, later entered the service of Venice and won splendid victories over Turkish armies far superior in numbers which aroused enthusiasm all over Europe. The grateful republic erected a marble statue of him on the island of Corfu in his honour, and after his death another was put up in Venice. The princes of Waldeck also had a martial tradition which they could not exercise at home. Their name appeared therefore among the fieldmarshals of the Netherlands, Portugal, Venice, Austria etc. Russia too had many generals of German origin, and Count Muennich was the originator of Russia's military prestige.

At that time the aristocracy everywhere showed a strong international spirit, but in Germany this feature was particularly pronounced. The noble officers of all armies regarded themselves as a sort of brotherhood. It was not considered dishonourable to serve the enemy of one's own country or to change sides in a war, provided this was not connected with treason. The fact that before the battle of Fonteney the French and English officers exchanged polite salutes was not an isolated case. On the eve of the battle of Malplaquet, for instance, generals and other high officers of the German and French troops met between the fronts for a friendly talk and payed their respects to one another.

The prestige of the German princes made them and their relatives particularly eligible for intermarriage with foreign royal houses. If a royal house died out, one of them also was sometimes elected king by the Estates. The Habsburgs had shown the world how to bring together a great Empire by a far-sighted policy of dynastic marriages and by standing for election by the Estates. Many other German princes followed their example. Christian of Oldenburg was in 1488 elected King by the Danish Estates, later ruled also in Sweden and Norway, and founded the present Danish dynasty. Sweden was from 1654 to 1818 under the rule of German kings, and three dynasties succeeded one another. Frederick Augustus I of Saxony was elected King of Poland in 1697, and in 1734 was succeeded by his son. The Dutch national anthem still celebrates "Wilhelmus of Nassauen, a prince of German blood"—the leader of the revolution against Spain, and ancestor of a long line of Dutch rulers up to our time. William III, who was of the same house, played the decisive rôle in the 'Glorious Revolution', and was elected King of England. In 1714 George I of Hanover ascended the English throne, and his descendant Queen Victoria married in 1840 Prince Albert of Saxe-Coburg-Gotha. The Hohenzollern obtained in 1701 the title of King of Prussia, a country outside the Empire. Peter III of Holstein-Gottorp became Tsar of Russia in 1762, but shortly was murdered and succeeded by Catherine II, surnamed the Great. Her father had been prince of Anhalt-Zerbst, one of the smallest German states. Of the Palatine branch of the Wittelsbachs Frederick V was elected King of Bohemia, and of the Bavarian branch Charles Albert became Emperor. Other princes of this house nearly became kings of Belgium and Spain. The acquisition of a foreign crown by a German prince was a factor diminishing the German central power since the Emperor had to be very chary in handling a vassal who was also a foreign king. The achievement of German nationhood was thereby made very difficult.

The German kings and queens on foreign thrones brought many nobles with them and links between the aristocracies of both coun-

tries much increased. Many German noblemen became prominent
statesmen or generals in foreign countries. In Denmark, for
example, Count Johann Hartwig Ernst Bernstorff and his nephew
Andreas Peter Bernstorff were admired in all countries for their
policy which made Denmark, though an absolute monarchy, the
most liberal and progressive state in Europe. Andreas Gottlieb
Bernstorff played a very important rôle as a minister of George I of
England.

A very great number of Germans became famous abroad as
scholars, artists, composers, industrialists, merchants and bankers.
They particularly liked to settle in England.

INTERNAL CONSEQUENCES OF PARTICULARISM

The fact that the Empire comprised so many small states divided
by interests and jealousy made it often very difficult to combine
their forces for a common cause. German history demonstrates the
evils of political particularism on every page. The following chapters will give ample proofs of its disastrous consequences. Nevertheless it did sometimes have favourable results too, especially in
cultural matters. A good-natured and able prince could in a small
state often do very beneficial work, since he could more easily be in
touch with the people and see conditions in the right light than in a
large state. Apart from the personality of the ruler, however, the
mere fact that there were so many of them was not without its
benefits, because it stimulated a rivalry in cultural activities. Princes
who had a bad reputation as spendthrifts or libertines may have had
merits as patrons of art. They embellished the towns of their resi-
dences with beautiful buildings, and parks, created art galleries and
theatres, or introduced industries making luxury goods. Others
furthered science and learning, education or humanitarian institutions, or agriculture and trade. Germany's extreme decentralization,
which was an evil in politics, had therefore the advantage of spreading cultural benefits more widely than in a strictly centralized state.

Almost every major government particularly wanted to have its
own university. About 1780 their number in Germany was 37, and
in all German-speaking countries 42. Half of them were Protestant,
and half Catholic. Moreover, there were many other institutes for
higher education, such as academies for noblemen (Ritterakade-
mieen), Jesuit Colleges with chairs of theology and philosophy, and
so on. Learning was widely spread, scholars were numerous and the
production of books large. The greatest achievement of many small
rulers was the initiation of universal elementary education of the

people. Their motive was mainly religious and the wish to lift up the common people. Protestant princes were the first, Catholics followed later. In Wurttemberg and Saxony attempts were made in the 16th century. Ludwig V of Hesse decreed in 1619 that every child, even in the rural districts, should attend school under penalty of a fine for absence. In Gotha Duke Ernest the Pious introduced obligatory education and an excellent school system in 1648. Similar plans were made in Weimar (1612), in Brunswick (1647), Wurttemberg (1649), Saxony (1713), Baden (1750), Prussia (1717), and so on. The practical realization, however, took time. There was often resistance, which had to be overcome, opinions wavered whether the Church or the State was competent, attendance was often not compulsory, teachers had to be trained and schools built. It was said of Ernest of Gotha that under his reign the peasants were better educated than the noblemen were elsewhere.

It is interesting to compare this striving of small German princes with the policy of great centralized states which were focussed on the aims of power, glory and splendour. Cardinal Richelieu, who enabled Louis XIV to attain supremacy in Europe, stressed in his Political Testament (I.ch.2, sect. 10) that too much spreading of education was a grave danger to the state. It would damage trade, ruin agriculture, and deprive the state of soldiers who mainly came from the rude and ignorant people. It would fill France with troublemakers and endanger public order. Numerous teachers and masses of children instructed seemed to Richelieu a malady, a poisoning of the mind. He wanted the number of colleges to be reduced and instruction for most people to be restricted to the minimum necessary for soldiers and traders. Cardinal Fleury, a successor of Richelieu, expressed similar opinions.[3]

TOLERANCE AND INTELLECTUAL FREEDOM

The fierce religious struggles of the 16th and 17th centuries brought about an increase in religious, political and cultural in-

[3] A great French scholar, Professor Daniel Mornet, has shown in his work Les origines intellectuelles de la Revolution Francaise, 1933, p. 420, that most of the famous French writers of the age of enlightenment wished that the common people should learn in school merely the minimum necessary for their work, but not so much that they would begin to think about great problems, which appeared dangerous to these philosophers. In the fifth year of the Revolution the universal instruction of the people was enacted, but this law was not carried out. Real progress was made not before the year of 1833. The German princes wished their peoples to be able to read primarily for studying the Bible. They thereby showed more confidence in the common man than the philosophers mentioned since the Bible raises the greatest problems and its study has very often had revolutionary consequences.

tolerance, and a severe censorship. Yet the multitude of regimes in Germany tended to weaken fanaticism and persecution. Among the hundreds of rulers there were always also tolerant ones either because of their religious thought, or of their mild character, or owing to their indifference or enlightenment. Already Erasmus had advised a French scholar, Louis de Berguin, who was persecuted in France, to flee to Germany where he would be entirely safe. He did not follow this advice and was burned at the stake. Bold thinkers had in decentralized Germany a better chance of finding an asylum than in a centralized state. In many places of Germany intolerance and persecution were severe, in others not. With the progress of enlightenment the number of countries increased where the censorship was lenient or hardly existed The antagonism between the religious parties, the dynasties and the peoples worked in the same sense, since sharp criticism of one of these was often tolerated in a country where this agreed with public opinion. The absence of national unity contributed much to Germany's political weakness but it had a great share in paving the way for the advent of her golden age in the realm of the spirit. The favourable tendencies of German particularism mentioned here, however, must not be praised too highly. Its cultural advantages were often more than outweighed by its political shortcomings.

PARTICULARISM AND MONARCHICAL ABSOLUTISM

Most German territories had a sort of parliamentary representation exercised by the Estates consisting of prelates of the Church and delegates of the universities, the landed nobility, the towns, and sometimes the peasants. They, or their delegates, assembled in Diets composed of three or four colleges. They had more or less rights of a parliament and mostly possessed also great influence on the administration of their country. Resolutions were passed by each College, and then an agreement was sought between the Colleges. The greater towns within a principality had not only a seat in the Diet but also a considerable autonomy and a town council managing the municipal affairs. The Free Towns were separate states. In the second half of the 17th century, however, the princes began to establish their own unrestricted power, and to this end tried to suppress the rights of the Estates, to curtail the autonomy of their towns, and to incorporate Free Towns in their state. The Diets were not abolished but were no longer convoked, or in some form deprived of their powers. Louis XIV was the model of these princes, they tried to introduce his absolutism, militarism and luxurious court life in their states, often with the assistance of the French King, and many of them became practically his vassals.

This policy of the princes aroused the resistance of the Estates. Its crucial point was the setting up of a standing army instead of the obsolete feudal service of the nobles, or the hiring of mercenaries when a war was already imminent. The Estates, however, usually opposed the raising of permanent troops, even when the country was threatened with becoming involved in a war. They feared that a standing army would undermine their influence on politics. But they defended an untenable position. In a world swayed by power politics on a large scale, the idea of the Estates to keep their little country unarmed and neutral was a dangerous illusion. Germany did not have a bulwark like England which was protected by the sea and a strong navy, and therefore had, as a rule, no need of a standing land army, or, if the need did arise, could easily hire troops from continental rulers because of her financial strength.

Particularism facilitated the achievement of the princes' aims. They usually ruled several small territories and could overcome the resistance of their Estates one after the other. When Frederick II, surnamed the Great, became King of Prussia, his countries had together a population of two and a quarter millions with 13 different Diets of Estates. Brandenburg was one of his countries, it was divided into five districts of which each had separate Estates. Hanover, with a population of 850,000, had six provincial Diets which assembled at different places. G. Kuentzel points out[4] that the various Estates of the parts of Prussia had no feeling of solidarity, and that in most parts the Diets were split by fierce struggles between the colleges, and even within these between sections such as lords and knights, nobles of old and new title, great and small towns etc.

If the German territorial Estates often failed to maintain their power, this was partly due to the fact that the princes often were the progressive element and had the support of the middle and lower classes. In France, too, the bourgeoisie stood on the side of the King against the nobles, as the last Estates General (1614) had shown. Another example was the establishment of monarchical absolutism in Denmark (1660). In Germany, the nobles in the Estates laid great stress upon maintaining and extending their feudal rights over the serfs while the princes tended to protect the serfs against the lords. The towns stood in the Estates largely for suppressing industries in the rural districts, or safeguarding rights of the guilds at the expense

[4] Cf. G. Kuentzel, Staendetum und Fuerstentum, vornehmlich Preussens, im 17. Jahrhundert in Festschrift fuer Schmoller 1908.

of the lower classes while many rulers favoured the latter. In religious questions the Estates usually defended the orthodox point of view while many princes had more enlightened opinions. The Estates were further opposed to the plans of princes to unite small territories to a great state. On the other hand, they also rejected a complete partition of their country between heirs, insisting that at least common Estates must be maintained. It therefore happened that two, three or even four states had a common Diet. But it also occurred that heirs ruled a country together or in alternation.

Yet, the Estates too sometimes defended public interests, in particular by blaming arbitrary acts of the prince or by declining the laying of new financial burdens on the people. Some of the Estates included also representatives of the peasants, especially in Wurttemberg, the Tyrol, Vorarlberg, East Friesia and several other small lands.[5] Furthermore, the Estates did not everywhere lose their influence. They retained it in some of the greater states such as Saxony, Wurttemberg, Hanover, Brunswick, Mecklenburgh, Hesse-Cassel and Hesse-Darmstadt, and in many of the small territories. In many cases they elected a small committee to take over their functions, and invested it with the right of co-opting new members. On the whole, the power of the Estates declined. Far-sighted men often thought that conditions demanded the dictatorship of an enlightened prince but did not renounce the institution of the Estates for ever.

THE DARK SIDE OF GERMAN ABSOLUTISM

The evil sides of absolutism, even of the enlightened type, are generally known and will be illustrated in many places of this book. In Germany, moreover, they were often aggravated by specific factors, in particular remnants of feudalism, patrimonialism, and particularism. Many rulers could not afford a modern administration and get rid of feudal and other obsolete institutions and ideas. They regarded their state as a patrimony, a property inherited from their ancestors. Actually, many states had to a large extent originated by the accumulation of lands and rights by means of private transactions—a process very similar to the gradual bringing together of a big fortune. The mainstay of many princes was their private domain which for a long time was not distinguished from state property. The Estates often declared the prince must live and govern on the returns of his domains, inherited tolls etc and taxes

[5] In the 18th century J. J. Moser indicated about 20 territories where the peasants were represented. Most of them were very small.

could only be voted in quite exceptional cases, such as war. Particularism with its multitude of little states had many consequences. In a small state the prince, together with a few advisors, could manage affairs himself, a large state required a large staff of officials who often became the real rulers. Many of the princes have left a very bad record,[6] though it also happened that a prince whose life was scandalous had ministers who were careful and expert administrators.

The courts in the small states were often a heavy financial burden on the people and a source of universal corruption. They were full of intrigants, adventurers and courtesans exploiting the prince by stimulating his baser instincts. The ruler was often entirely in the hands of the courtiers and did not hear the truth about conditions in his country. The wastefulness of the court ruined finances and forced the ruler to resort to the selling of posts and similar measures. Frederick II already jeered at the princelings who all wanted to have a Versailles and to play Louis XIV. Though their little state had no need of an army, they kept one because the prestige of a monarch demanded it. A prince who had not the money to keep more than a very small number of soldiers, had at least a stock of uniforms so that the soldiers could appear at parades several times clad in different uniforms thus creating the illusion of a great army. They also appointed an excessive number of generals and colonels because their gorgeous uniforms increased the splendour of the court. The *Journal von und fuer Deutschland* in 1784 reported that a certain ruler had not the means to pay officers for his little army. Instead he employed the clerks in his government office. When the drummer called to the parade they laid down their quills, donned uniforms, pigtails and sabres and appeared on the parade ground dressed as officers.

It sometimes happened that the Estates turned down the proposition of their prince to vote money for the establishment of standing troops but had no objection to his keeping mercenaries at his own expense and hiring them out to foreign powers, which would cost them nothing and even bring money into the country. Many princes found this profitable, they therefore kept a staff of recruiting officers in order to enrol mercenaries, who were drilled and then hired out to other governments wanting them for their wars. The best customers were the rich commercial countries, such as the Nether-

---

[6] Cf. the works of Biedermann and Boehn. Vehse's work on the history of the German courts is to-day antiquated, as regards the larger states. Many new sources have been opened since this work appeared. But large parts are still valuable in illustrating the atmosphere of the courts.

lands, England and Venice. This system aroused much bitter criticism and discredited the German name abroad, but its defenders replied that the soldiers had entered the service voluntarily and were paid for it. In reality a great proportion of them were brought in by shameful tricks or by slightly veiled force. Soldiering was despised by respectable people, and it often happened that, if a soldier took place in an inn, other guests stood up and left it. Recruiting was therefore not a simple task. Tall and strong men were offered high bounties for enlisting. Many recruiting officers lived in inns where they tried to make contact with suitable people. Others let a band play merry music on a public place to attract lads. These were then offered gratis drinks till they were sufficiently tipsy to sell their freedom. Methods were often employed which were little short of kidnapping. Convicts, vagabonds etc. were put in the army without much ado. The south west and west of Germany with their numerous tiny 'states', consisting often only of a few villages, were the best places for this business. They were swarming with people who were ruined or dishonest. These miniature states could not afford a proper police force and thieves or robbers could be over the frontier very quickly. The lending of soldiers to foreign powers was often defended with the argument that it was the best way of getting rid of the worst elements of the people and even receiving a good price for them. But a great many of the soldiers had only enlisted because they could not find another post or had been more or less forced to do so. J. G. Seume, a distinguished writer, became a victim of unscrupulous recruitment. Moreover, in a few cases people were even conscripted. German princes often permitted foreign governments to recruit soldiers in their territories themselves. Sometimes the Estates voted for the lending of troops in order to use the payment for restoring the public finances. The large states, especially Austria and Prussia, considered the hiring out of troops beneath their dignity, and also needed recruits for their own armies. In any case, Germany became the greatest market for this disreputable trade.

It is a significant fact that it was on the whole not considered justifiable for a government to force its subjects to serve as soldiers, except in order to defend the country against a menacing invasion and then only with great limitations. Prussia first introduced a measure of limited conscription, because the brutal recruiting methods of Frederick William I had aroused the greatest indignation. General conscription was first introduced by the French revolutionary government in its aggressive phase.

2

THE EMPEROR AND THE ESTATES

RIGHTS AND MIGHT OF THE EMPEROR

THE extraordinary power of the princes greatly restricted the constitutional position of the Emperor. Formally, the princes were still his vassals, but their solemn investment by the Emperor with their lands as fiefs, and their oath to be loyal and obedient to him, had become little more than a ceremony. The princes were usually represented at it by an envoy and some even omitted to do this. The policy of many of them was often actually contrary to their oath. The Emperor could not take any important measure without the assent of the Electors or the Diet of the Empire. The revenues connected with his dignity had become trifling. There were also princes and publicists wishing to make the Empire a loose federation and the Emperor the president of a republic of princes.

In reality, however, the power of the Emperor was very substantial; not because of his imperial dignity but because he was the strongest of the princes and within and without the Empire possessed much greater territories and had among the German rulers many more supporters than any other ruler. Many princes did everything to prevent the increase of his position in all regards. Before his coronation the Emperor had to promise under oath that he would not make his dignity hereditary. But in reality it was nearly hereditary. Through almost four centuries, with a minor exception, it was always a Habsburg who was elected Emperor. This certainly had disadvantages, especially because the dynastic connection between the Spanish and Austrian Habsburgs provoked France's enmity. Yet without the power of the Habsburgs the Empire would surely have fallen to pieces and large parts would have been annexed by strong rulers. If there had no longer been

Habsburgs the other potent dynasties would never have consented to the lasting elevation of a rival house to the imperial dignity; they would rather have returned to the policy of electing Emperors from changing and preferably weak dynasties, which had had disastrous results in the 14th century. The great military powers, France in the West and Turkey in the East, would have had a free hand to conquer large tracts of land, and the European Balance of Power would have come to an end. Since France would have dominated the Netherlands and extensive German, Spanish and Italian territories, a British world empire could not have arisen. Without the means and the leadership of the Habsburgs the Empire could not be defended. Even if an Emperor from another dynasty had been elected, his position would have been as precarious as that of the elected King of Poland. The small princes of the Empire and the Free Towns saw in the Habsburg Emperors their protectors against the aggression of strong neighbours and therefore formed a sort of imperial party in the Reichstag, which as a rule comprised the majority among the princes and the towns.[1]

THE REICHSTAG

The Diet of the Empire had a very ample competence but its activities were often paralysed by the lack of national solidarity, the rivalry between its members and their quarrels about questions of prestige. It consisted of three Colleges, that of the Electors, that of the Princes, and that of the Free Towns. The Electors had the right to elect the Emperor. Their original number was seven, three ecclesiastical and four lay princes. The Bohemian Electorate was for some time dormant. The Peace of Westphalia added a new Electorate and in 1692 a ninth one was created, though it was generally recognized only in 1708, when the Bohemian Electorate was also restored. There had for some time been an equal number of Catholics and Protestants in this College, but later the former obtained the majority through a change of religion by Protestant Electors. The College of Princes comprised, towards the middle of the 18th century, Estates with 95 votes, and towards its end with 100 votes. Of the latter 37 were ecclesiastical and 63 secular. The small rulers, however did not have a full vote but formed sections called benches, of which each had one vote only. In this College, too, the Catholics

---

[1] It is surprising that even a far-sighted historian like James Bryce wrote that the Habsburgs had never regarded the Empire as anything other than an instrument for their personal or dynastic purposes. This judgment shows the influence of the Prussian school of history.

were in the majority. Lastly, there was the College of the Free
Towns which had 51 members, of whom 34 were Protestant, 13
Catholic and 4 mixed.

Within each College the majority of votes was decisive. When a
bill was proposed, each College deliberated and voted separately,
and then they tried to work out a common proposition. If this succeeded, it was submitted to the Emperor and by his sanction became
law. Whether the Emperor might ratify the resolution of a majority
of the Colleges against the resolute opposition of the third one was
controversial.

The crucial question for our specific problem is whether the
Reichstag may be considered as a form of national representation,
besides representing dynastic interests. There is no doubt that sometimes situations occurred, which aroused widespread feeling of
national solidarity against foreign aggressors. Apart from such
exceptions, however, the Reichstag neither expressed national
aspirations of the German people, nor did it do much to promote
them.

The paramount question was still the antagonism between Catholics and Protestants, though it was often not raised for religious
reasons, but because Protestantism served as a symbol of a policy
opposed to the Emperor, who was regarded as the head of the
Catholics. As mentioned already, these formed the majority in two
Colleges and also in the population as a whole, though the latter
difference was small. The Protestants, however, largely lived in the
more advanced parts of the Empire, they possessed great commercial cities, famous universities and countries with a good system of
schools. The publishers, booksellers and editors of journals were
mostly Protestants.[2] The antagonism between the denominations
was perhaps often determined less by religious than by other
reasons.

The Peace of Westphalia had laid down that in the Reichstag
and in the High Courts the representatives of a religion could not
outvote the other side. This was called the Principle of Parity.
Whenever Protestants and Catholics were of different opinions, a
decision could not be reached by the majority but only by an
amicable settlement. The Protestants in the Reichstag were
organized in a corporation designed to maintain the Parity, to repel
Catholic encroachments and to exercise the veto against bills

---

[2] It is noteworthy that in the Golden Age of German thought and poetry,
in the second half of the 18th century, all the great poets and philosophers
were Protestants. They ascribed this to the greater measure of intellectual
freedom in their territories.

violating their interests. This certainly was an effective weapon against anti-evangelical fanaticism. But it was also sometimes used in a way incompatible with any parliamentary procedure. In 1717, for example, the Free Town of Cologne petitioned the Reichstag to decrease its contribution to expenses because trade and wealth had much declined. But the Evangelical Corporation declared that the town had brought this about by unjust oppression of its Protestant citizens, that it was therefore an Evangelical interest and not liable to a decision by the majority.

Among the numerous princes represented in the Reichstag, there was a great variety of rank, power and prestige. In consequence, points of precedence and ceremonial were constantly raised, hindering serious deliberations. This mentality also affected the republican Free Towns, which carried on long quarrels about precedence. Once the Turks had penetrated deep into Austria, while the discussions of the Reichstag were for many weeks blocked by an altercation between Saxe-Gotha and Saxe-Weimar about which of them should have precedence in voting. In 1748 a question of etiquette led to a long, acrimonious strife. The question at issue was, who was entitled to lead the wife of the Emperor's representative to table. The conflict soon became one about whether the ecclesiastical or the lay princes were of higher rank, and no less than ten pamphlets about this affair were published.

The Free Towns had little understanding of the national importance of the Reichstag. Their number, wealth and power had much declined. In 1521, the Matric of Worms had registered 84 of them, but at the end of the Thirty Years War their number had sunk to 62, and it was soon further reduced by the French annexation of ten Alsatian towns. Princes, whose territories surrounded Free Towns, harassed them by economic blockades and other vexations. The legal position of many towns was unclear owing to the ambiguities inherent in feudal privileges. Ever more towns had to give up the struggle for their freedom and to submit to the rule of princes. After the terrible ordeal of the great war, they were particularly unwilling or unable to assume burdens for the Empire. Many of them were practically bankrupt. Towns often stayed away from the Reichstag because of the expense of sending an envoy. They preferred asking a burgher of the town where the Reichstag was held to represent them. Soon the deputy from Regensburg was also the delegate of most Protestant towns, and in 1707 it happened that he was the only member present.

Even towns which were in a better financial position did not show much national spirit. Commercial interests, internal party politics and the pride of municipal independence were often stronger than loyalty to the Empire. Sometimes the claims of princes hindered a town from sending a deputy. The greatest and richest Free Town was Hamburg. It had been called to the Reichstag since 1460, but the King of Denmark in his capacity as Duke of Holstein claimed to be her Lord, and though the Reichstag and the Kammergericht rejected his claim, he insisted upon it and often besieged or blockaded Hamburg. At last the King and his relatives renounced their claims but only for great financial compensations (Treaty of Gottorp, 1768).

The towns subject to a prince were not represented in the Reichstag, but in the territorial Diets. In some of them they played a considerable role, in others not. In Saxony, for example, 128 towns had the right to send deputies to the Diet. Towns like Leipzig, moreover, had an almost republican autonomy. The deputies to the Diets were nominated by the town councils.

In every country with a parliamentary life it was the knights or the gentry who formed the most active element. In Germany, however, the knights, who were subjects of princes, sat in the territorial Diets, not in the Reichstag. The Free Knights, who were subject to the Emperor alone, and were also rulers of small territories, had seats neither in the Reichstag nor in any Diet. In the 15th century Emperor Sigismund had harboured the plan of forming an alliance of the towns and the knights under his leadership against the princes, in order to strengthen the central authority. This might have transformed the Reichstag into a real Parliament. But both the towns and the knights were reluctant from aversion to paying taxes. In 1687 the Free Knights wished to enter the Reichstag, but most princes were strongly opposed to it, because this would have increased the power of the Emperor, and the plan failed. The Free Knights were of the greatest value to the Emperor, providing him with numerous statesmen, officials and military leaders.

Conditions deteriorated still more when, in 1681, the Reichstag began to sit permanently. Before this event, the Emperor and the Estates had to a great extent taken part in the Reichstag themselves, and had been able to cultivate personal relations, and thus to overcome differences. But when the sessions became permanent this was no longer possible. The Emperor was now represented by a commissary of high rank, and the Estates sent envoys. These were mainly lawyers of middle class origin, who had risen in the service of their princes and had been ennobled. Foreign kings often sent envoys too, and some of them had seats in the Reichstag because of their German possessions. The Reichstag assumed the character of a congress of diplomats. Many of the lawyers who were in the service of rulers showed their professional tendency of stressing legal points to the utmost, dwelling on formalities and points of honour, and putting the smallest interest of their patrons before the greatest ones of Germany. It was also a serious weakness of the Reichstag that the envoys had often to wait for instructions from their governments, or used this as a pretext for protracting deliberations, if this seemed to serve their interest.

A few examples may illustrate the ways of the Reichstag. We have already mentioned the principle of Parity between Protestants and Catholics, laid down by the Peace of Westphalia. In 1672 the Reichstag had to appoint generals for the army of the Empire, and made two Protestants generals of cavalry, and two Catholics generals of infantry. But the Catholics vetoed this decision on the ground that the parity of religion had thereby been violated, since a general of cavalry was commonly considered of higher rank than a general of infantry. The ability of a general was therefore considered of less importance than his religion. Until the end of the 18th century the veto was exercised another eight times, always by the Protestants.

Already in 1653-54 there had been discussions whether matters of taxation might be decided by majority. The Emperor, most Electors, and the Catholic Estates answered in the affirmative. But the majority of the Protestant princes were only willing to allow it in really necessary cases, though it was difficult to say who should decide whether there was a necessity for it, if not the Reichstag. The Elector of Brandenburg, a Calvinist, and the Protestant Free Towns were quite against it. The question whether taxes might be voted by the majority, and whether in that case the opposing minority had to pay them as well, was never definitely settled.

Even if a bill had been voted by the Reichstag and sanctioned by the Emperor, however, it was often not properly carried out because the Empire had no executive organs of its own. If a ruler refused to obey, the Emperor could only instruct the Circle of the Empire, to which he belonged, and possibly others also, to take measures in order to enforce the law. In practice, this meant that some of his neighbours were expected to act as executive organs. Usually they did so, especially as they could expect advantages from it. But what could be done to force a powerful German prince, who possibly was also the King of a foreign realm, to obey the Reichstag? Nor could the Empire have its own executive organs, because the Estates were opposed to their establishment, and because there was no money available to pay them. Its only permanent tax was a contribution for the maintenance of one of the two High Courts of Justice, the Reichskammergericht, and many Estates were so reluctant to pay it that the Court was always in the greatest financial straits.

Further the Empire had no diplomatic service, because the money was lacking. But the Emperor had ambassadors abroad on behalf of his own countries, who often acted for the Empire also. The army of the Empire was equally stunted for financial reasons. There was a list of the contingents of troops which the Estates had to provide when the Reichstag declared war, but it was so faulty that Estates often had a good pretext to decline the fulfilment of their obligations. In the 17th century and later, French aggressions led to various reforms designed to establish a serviceable army of the Empire. In 1681 a contingent to be provided by every circle was fixed, each circle subdividing its contingent among its Estates. The plan to set up a standing army failed. In consequence the army could only be enlisted when war had been declared. The results were most unsatisfactory. The troops were differently equipped, and badly officered, and had never been trained together, if at all. Often large sections were never organized or available. The military value of this army was very low, and if the Emperor and some of the greater rulers had not provided their own troops, the Empire would have remained practically undefended.

THE HIGH COURTS OF THE EMPIRE

The only important function of which particularism could not deprive the Emperor was that of being the highest judge. It was a fundamental idea of German law that the king was the fountain of all justice and though in the course of time the administration of justice had mostly fallen into the hands of princes, nobles and towns, the head of the Empire still retained far-reaching rights as the supreme judge, which he exercised through two High Courts, posessing the same competence. One was the Kaiserliche und Reichskammergericht (Chamber Court), the other the Reichshofrat (Aulic Council). Details apart, they had to decide: 1) lawsuits between rulers, namely princes, Free Towns and Free Knights; 2) appeals against the judgments of territorial courts, though with the exception of certain minor cases or such requiring expeditious treatment; and 3) lawsuits of subjects against their rulers, not only in civil, but also in criminal and political cases. Their jurisdiction forms a subject of the greatest significance.[3]

[3] I shall shortly publish a study of it in the Mitteilungen des Institutes fuer oesterreichische Geschichtsforschung.

B

The organs of the Chamber Court of the Empire were mainly chosen and paid by the Estates, though a few of them were chosen by the Emperor. The Aulic Council of the Empire was appointed and maintained by the Emperor. The former Court resided at the Western frontier of the Empire, at the end in Wetzlar, the latter at the Eastern border, in Vienna. The countries of the House of Austria were exempted from their jurisdiction. Every claimant could choose to which Court he wanted to appeal. Both Courts had an organization and rules of procedure carefully safeguarding the juristic qualifications, integrity, independence and political and religious impartiality of their members. Both were, on the whole, distinguished by a very high standard of jurisdiction.

The High Courts were often violently decried by enemies. Princes who had set might over right were furious if a High Court declared that this was against the law and decreed their making amends or paying penalties. They also greatly resented it when a High Court proclaimed that a judgment of one of their own Courts was a perversion of justice and therefore null and void, or if the Court accepted a law-suit from one of their subjects against their own person, and found that the subject was right. The idea that a prince was, in the eyes of the law, on the same level as a common man and could be sued and sentenced, was so repulsive to princes imbued with the spirit of the age of Louis XIV that they were bound to resent it deeply. Both courts, moreover, also had faults which could justly be criticized, though their extent must not be overestimated. Though the judicial organs were prohibited from accepting gifts, custom found nothing wrong with this if they were not made expressly for the perversion of justice.[4] The assessors of the courts were not well paid and largely depended on perquisites paid by the parties. Some of them accepted gifts. Furthermore the Chamber Court was particularly hit by the animosity of many princes, who frequently refused to pay adequate contributions for the expenses of this Court, as they were obliged to do. It was therefore constantly understaffed, the salary of the assessors was too low and they had often to wait a long time for it. In consequence great arrears of actions accumulated, without any prospect that they would be dealt with. This discredited the Court in spite of its otherwise good work. The Aulic Council was paid by the Emperor, it worked with fewer formalities and more quickly, and so the number of actions it treated became much greater than that at the Chamber Court. A defect of this court, however, was that among its members there were usually some young noblemen in order to

[4] Cf. E. Doehring, Geschichte der Deutschen Rechtspflege, 1953.

be trained in affairs of state who often had not taken their studies very seriously, and regarded this post merely as a stepping-stone to the post of an ambassador or minister.[5] Yet the great majority of the counsellors were well versed in the law and did splendid work.

The High Courts played a great part in maintaining internal peace. Among the nearly two thousand rulers of the Empire there was always much bitter strife, which to a great extent sprang from the countless family pacts between dynasties and the extremely unclear legal conditions concerning the succession of a ruler who was the last of his line. If the courts had not intervened, the Empire would have been the scene of unending internal feuds, in which the strong would have devoured the weak. Further, the great majority of states were very small and little able or disposed to maintain courts of justice with properly qualified judges and other personnel. The greater rulers could afford well-trained organs of justice, they had courts of appeal and often possessed an Imperial privilege exempting minor cases up to a certain amount from the jurisdiction of the High Courts. In complicated questions of law rulers also consulted the law faculties of universities. Nevertheless, numerous courts of the small states often committed grave errors of justice. This evil was further aggravated by the belief of despotic princes that they were not bound by the rules of law, but could arbitrarily interfere in a court case, a procedure known as cabinet justice.

The High Courts very frequently declared such judgments as invalid, forbade their execution and not seldom also decreed that the prince concerned had to engage competent lawyers as judges. Sometimes the ruler was also sentenced to a penalty for miscarriage of justice. In any case he had to report within a fixed, short term that he had obeyed the orders of the High Court.

As mentioned already, there was no appeal in certain cases, but this privilege, which not many Princes enjoyed, was invalid if the rules of fair trial had not been observed. In cases of the denial or undue procrastination of justice, if the defence had been impeded, or the plaintiff or witnesses had been threatened by the government, etc., the High Court was always competent to redress the wrong. If there was danger that a government accused by a subject might arrest him or hinder him from collecting evidence, the High Court put him under its protection. Poor persons received special facilities enabling them to bring an action. The High Court further often ordered the prince of a neighbouring state to investigate

5 J. J. Moser gives examples of the scandalous ignorance of public law which he experienced in his intercourse with some of these aristocrats. Lebenslauf IV, pp. 8, 21.

matters impartially and to report about them. The execution of its
judgment was entrusted to one or more rulers of the circle in which
the country was situated.

Though an action at a High Court was expensive, not only rich
people made use of it, but also ordinary men. At the Imperial Aulic
Council alone between 2,000 and 3,000 new lawsuits were brought
every year. Peasants and other people of small means collected
funds to employ a solicitor. Many farmers, and serfs too, sued their
rulers or landlords because rents or other dues had been arbitrarily
raised. Simple burghers, and particularly many Jews, demanded
through them the payment of debts or for goods supplied, officials
took legal actions against their princes to get their wages paid or to
obtain redress of injuries which they had suffered.

The High Courts, moreover, also heard cases in which princes had
violated constitutional rights. It often happened that the Estates of
a country, or a section of them, or a number of subjects, complained
that their ruler had levied illegal taxes not voted by the diets, that
he had not convoked the Estates, or had not given account of the
use made of taxes collected. The belief that the power of the prince
was unlimited was progressing and ever more rulers no longer
convened the Estates, but decreed taxes themselves. The High
Courts, however, did not recognize the abolition of an institution
like the Estates in this way. In numerous cases they decided that
princes were not entitled to levy taxes not voted by the Estates and
forced them to repay them if already collected. An exception was
made of contributions to the defence of the Empire voted by the
Reichstag or the diets of the circles. But the princes had no right to
demand more money for themselves, they might only demand
amounts for the public benefit and must let the Estates inspect the
accounts.

It is clear that it was also the policy of the Emperors to maintain
the rights of the Estates against the striving of the princes for
absolute power and full sovereignty. In 1670, the Reichstag resolved
that subjects should be obliged to pay contributions for all military
purposes which would have been a blow at the roots of the Estates.
But the Emperor vetoed this proposition of the Reichstag.

In Mecklenburgh-Schwerin the Estates carried on a long struggle
about their rights with three successive Dukes who wished to
establish a despotism. Duke Charles Leopold even married a Russian
princess and induced Tsar Peter I to send an army of 50,000 Russians
into his country in order to support him. The Imperial Aulic Counsel defended the cause of the Estates in many decrees and in 1728,
the Emperor, on its advice, deposed the Duke. His successor had in

1755 to conclude a pact with the Estates, recognizing their rights.

Prince Hyacinth of Orange-Nassau-Siegen, a near relative of King William III of England, ruled his country in a very arbitrary way and once when his subjects resisted, ordered a peasant, whom he regarded as a rebel, to be executed without a judicial procedure. The Aulic Council investigated the case and Emperor Joseph I deposed the Prince, who had to go into exile.

The High Courts often decided a case not according to the letter of the written law or following the authority of old customs, but on reasons based on the idea of a natural law or the rights of man. In 1631, the Aulic Council had to decide on the appeal of some men whose wives had been accused of witchcraft at the Court of the Bishop of Bamberg. The High Court ordered the Bishop, under the threat of a high penalty, to mitigate the confinement, to permit a defence of the women, and to observe the rules of lawful trial. The confiscation of the property of the women was declared unlawful. The Prince-Abbot of Corvey in 1777 permitted Austrian troops to recruit inhabitants of the town of Hoexter compulsorily. The Chamber Court, however, decided that this was only permissible in an emergency, to defend the country. Professor Puetter, the greatest expert in public law, had put forward this argument on grounds of natural law.

Princes could also be accused of crimes. Several such cases happened under Joseph II : Count Carl Magnus had raised loans in the name of some of his boroughs, forging signatures, and had used the money for himself. The Aulic Council in 1775 sentenced him to ten years imprisonment 'with only the barest sustenance'. Another small ruler had to serve two years in prison because he had appropriated land of peasants, and a third one died before he was sentenced.

3

RELIGION AND ENLIGHTENMENT

THE IDEA OF ENLIGHTENMENT

SINCE the middle ages the spirit of the age had shown several momentous variations. As always, this spirit comprised many different currents struggling with one another. After the great religious conflicts and the subsequent wars of the 16th and 17th centuries, however, a current later called Enlightenment set in, and soon attained great strength. Its principal feature was the belief in the supreme authority of reason in contrast to the belief in divine revelation laid down in the Bible and ecclesiastical dogmas, which had also had great influence on the laws and usages of state and society. The striving for enlightenment sprang from man's self-confidence, his wish to liberate himself from numerous shackles of the past and to build a new order based on human nature. In this respect enlightenment has achieved most beneficial results and has laid foundations of the modern world. Yet its thought has not created a generally accepted system of principles, but led to the emergence of many schools. The enthusiasts for enlightenment were not exclusively actuated by reason, but also by irrational sentiments and they were not at all in accord as to the system of morality, politics and social order prescribed by the voice of reason or nature. This was due, no doubt, to the fact that human nature itself is full of contradictions and can be interpreted in many different ways. Many believers in enlightenment even had so little confidence in reason that they regarded only the intellectual and ruling classes as fitted to live according to its standards. Voltaire, Bolingbroke and Frederick II were convinced that the common man, when enlightened, could no longer be governed.

The first activities of Enlightenment were directed against religious fanaticism and the witch-mania.

THE WITCH-MANIA

In the old times the Church considered the belief in witchcraft a pagan superstition. But this later changed; a bull of Innocent VIII of 1484, and subsequent decrees of other Popes sanctioned proceedings against witches and sorcerers. The Protestant Churches followed this example. Even after the Reformation there were one and a half centuries filled with countless trials, mainly against women accused of intercourse with the devil. In many cases the women themselves related such acts, believing their dreams or hallucinations to have been reality, or a small incident aroused suspicions which turned into mass hysteria. The suspects were horribly tortured till they confessed and were then burned. The number of victims became enormous.

In the second half of the 16th century, Johannes Weyer (1515-1588) made a bold stand against the raging mania. He was born in Flemish-Brabant, but regarded himself as a German. Weyer became one of the most famous physicians of the time, and in 1550 entered the service of Duke William III of Juelich, Cleve and Berg, who was an enlightened ruler and protected him against enemies. In 1563 Weyer published a Latin book against the persecution of alleged witches who, he declared, were mostly mentally deranged and not responsible for their doings. He further pointed out that the witch-hunt was mainly due to the illusions of the mob. The book caused a great sensation, was five times reprinted and translated into various languages. It was dedicated to Emperor Ferdinand I, who expressed his acceptance and approval. The author continued his fight vigorously for about twenty years, and quite a number of other writers published similar books referring to him as their leader. Several rulers prohibited the persecution of witches in their territories, and, as Weyer reports, many courts began to acquit persons accused or adopted a reasonable procedure. But he was also much attacked by opponents. The greatest French jurist, Jean Bodin, abused him in a book though the author was otherwise an enlightened thinker and a friend of religious toleration. The learned king of England, James I, too, in a book against T. Weyer and R. Scot defended the belief in witches, though he was for caution in trying them. The Jesuit Martin Delrio violently combated Weyer. At last, obscurantism and fanaticism triumphed. The mass trials of witches became worse than ever, especially in Germany during the Thirty Years' War. In England the mania raged particularly during the Puritan revolution, though less than in Germany. Scotland too was a fertile ground for it.

The fact that this persecution was particularly widespread in Germany had many reasons. The endless theological struggles intensified the fear of satanic powers, and the Thirty Years' War seemed to convert the country into a hell, breeding cruelty, superstition and hysteria. The excessive particularism of Germany aggravated the evil. Witch-trials were especially numerous in the small ecclesiastical and secular territories. The governments of large States usually had enlightened princes, counsellors and judges, and more power to resist the pressure of public opinion, often backed by the Estates, though there were exceptions. In Saxony, where Lutheran orthodoxy was very strong, conditions were as bad as in Bavaria, the main seat of Catholic bigotry. The highest authority in criminal law was Benedict Carpzov, a Saxon, who gave full support to the witch-trials. He boasted that he had read the whole Bible fifty-three times and had signed 20,000 death sentences. In small territories financial interests also played a rôle since the possessions of the convicts were often confiscated and the judges profited from this. Emperor Ferdinand II strictly prohibited any confiscation, and the High Courts tried to secure a fair hearing, but with little success.

There were always theologians, jurists and others who had great misgivings about the trials, and a number of books critical of them appeared, though often without the name of the author. General Count Tilly in 1618 declared of the Jesuit University of Ingolstadt that most of the jurists there disliked the trials and regarded depositions confirming witchcraft as springing from illusion. Among the Jesuits, however, opinions differed. Many of their prominent theologians advocated witch-trials. But the general of the Order, Vitelleschi, was for keeping aloof from them, and quite a number of eminent German Jesuits, especially Adam Tanner and Paul Laymann, criticised the main cause of the atrocities, namely the unfairness of the trial, such as torture. A fair trial would in most cases have shown at once that there was no real evidence, but that the charge sprang either from mental insanity, or from personal enmity, or from gross distortion of the facts. In 1631 the Jesuit Friedrich Spee published, anonymously a book against the trials under the title 'Cautio criminalis de processibus contra sagas' (Caution in trials against witches), which became a landmark in the history of the persecution. Johann Philipp von Schoenburg, who later became Archbishop and Elector of Mainz, in his youth asked Spee how it came about that he had entirely white hair, though he was still young. Spee replied that the witches had done this, since of all the witches whose confession he had heard, and whom he had accompanied to their execution, there was not one of whose guilt he was convinced. Schoenburg was the first ecclesiastical ruler who suppressed witch-trials in his territory. In 1680 the Dutch theologian Balthasar Bekker, a Calvinist, brought out a book which was particularly efficient in destroying the belief in witchcraft. Among the German jurists Christian Thomasius had the greatest merit.

The degradation of justice to barbarism under the pressure of mass fanaticism and maladministration of justice was definitely abolished with the rise of monarchial power. Louis XIV and Elector Frederick William of Brandenburg-Prussia did much to put an end to it, and Austria followed suit. In England a woman was sentenced for witchcraft in 1712, but the king pardoned her. In Scotland the last execution took place in 1722. There were still a few executions in German Catholic States in the second half of the 18th century, the last one in 1775, and in the Calvinist part of the Canton Glarus there was even one in 1782.

INTOLERANCE AND TOLERANCE IN GERMANY

In Germany religion played a very great part in politics though it was often more or less a mask for other aims. The Peace of Westphalia had laid down so many exceptions from the principle that the ruler could decide which religion was permitted in his country, that there were many territories where more than one denomination enjoyed a certain freedom, or at least the private exercise of its cult. Even at the worst, the ruler was compelled to grant dissenters the right to emigrate and to take with them their belongings and the value of their real estate. Catholic intolerance, often instigated by the Jesuits, was worst in Austria, Bavaria and the states under a prince-bishop. But there were also Lutheran states where the people were very intolerant against other religions. In Augsburg the shoemakers put a mark on the shoes indicating whether they were made by a Protestant or a Catholic. F. K. Moser remarked that there were among the Lutherans such who would rather go bare-footed than wear shoes made by a Catholic. The Calvinists were perhaps less intolerant than the others.

Yet the spirit of tolerance was spreading irresistibly, largely for economic reasons. All governments became convinced that the prosperity of their countries demanded a large population and a flourishing foreign trade. Both reasons spoke for toleration which had made Holland rich. Many governments, however, feared that different religious communities could not peaceably live side by side, but that constant friction between them must inevitably lead

B*

to civil war. In cases where this seemed improbable the ban on other religions was often dropped.

Toleration was more advanced in Protestant Germany than in France where Protestants were considered enemies of the state and cruelly persecuted. Great numbers of them fled to Germany, and wherever they were admitted they contributed much to the development of industries, commerce and learning. Lutheran Wurttemberg, however, denied them asylum because they were Calvinists. In Catholic Austria Protestants were not tolerated, but many exceptions were made for traders and soldiers, and others were transported to Transylvania where there was religious freedom. In England the Catholics were widely considered enemies of the nation and subject to discrimination and in the great struggles of the 17th century temporarily other denominations also were persecuted.

In the 16th and 17th centuries nobles had often fought princes under the banner of Protestantism and had thereby aroused the opinion that their creed contained an anti-monarchial tendency. The Jesuits understood how to exploit such facts for their propaganda. In the 17th and 18th centuries, therefore, an extraordinary number of princes, nobles and scholars adopted the Catholic faith, partly from religious, partly from political reasons. At the Westphalian peace conference the three most prominent representatives of the Emperor had all once been Lutherans and then become Catholics. The same applied to many of the statesmen who built the Austrian Empire.

ORTHODOXY AND ITS OPPONENTS

All the German Churches were ruled by their orthodox sections. But the Augsburg Confession, as the Lutheran Church was officially called, was particularly dogmatic. Luthers epigones regarded every word in the Bible as sacrosanct, though their master had often been considerably less rigid in this respect. In general, the Church, which he had founded, had already during his lifetime greatly changed from its original free spirit to the character of a state Church, with a privileged priesthood, highly intolerant, and involved in endless bitter altercations about abstruse questions of theology. It is further now often believed that Luther prepared the ground for the evils of monarchial absolutism, but this view is an exaggeration. Luther followed in this respect the true Christian doctrine, which was also shared by Calvin. He most vigorously condemned princes oppressing and exploiting the people in order to lead a life of luxury and glory at their expense. Aggressive wars were to him an abomination.

Moreover, it was not the countries where Lutheranism reigned that the territorial Diets lost their liberties. The Catholic Wittelsbachs and Habsburgs, and the Calvinist Hohenzollerns suppressed their Estates, but they retained their powers in Lutheran countries such as Saxony, Hanover, Brunswick, Hesse-Darmstadt, Wurttemberg, the small Saxon principalities etc.

Far-sighted princes often made attempts to bring about a union of the warring Christian Churches, in particular the followers of Luther and of Calvin. But all these efforts foundered, mainly on the rock of Lutheran orthodoxy, to which the Reformed Church appeared as the devil incarnate. This antagonism was not exclusively due to dogmatic differences, but also to the fact that the Calvinists showed a warlike spirit and had the greater share in the responsibility for the Thirty Years War. The Lutheran Church, however, stood for peace, and in this respect remained nearer to the spirit of Christ than her rival. For a considerable time Lutheran preachers made also efforts to guide the conscience of their princes according to Christian principles, sometimes not without success.[1] They often warned the prince against a life of debauchery or dissipation. With the rise of absolutism this often changed.

The Reformed (Calvinist) Church had its bulwark in the Netherlands, and the Dutch theologians were in close relations with their German co-religionists. Though orthodoxy had a very strong position in the Netherlands too, there was also a considerable measure of religious freedom and the country became the main seat of free thought. Its republican and commercial character encouraged toleration and Calvinism had a strong note of rationalism. Many prominent French and English thinkers found asylum from persecution there. The country had also a very high standard in science and learning. In Germany studies grievously suffered through the Thirty Years' War while in the Netherlands Descartes wrote his works which brought about an intellectual revolution. Grotius, Spinoza, Hobbes, Bayle and others too were foremost in spreading the seeds of enlightenment all over Europe. Balthasar Bekker's book already mentioned was particularly effective in destroying the belief in a devil, in demons and witches.

The philosophy of Benedict Spinoza (1632-77) appeared to the orthodox theologians as the worst kind of atheism. However this may be, his philosophy was certainly incompatible with fundamental Christian beliefs. Yet he was quickly appreciated in Germany. Elector Charles Lewis of the Palatinate offered him the chair of

[1] On Lutheranism cf. W. Elerts admirable work Morphologie des Luthertums, vol. II, 1932.

philosophy at the University of Heidelberg in 1673, but he refused.
There is no doubt that the Thirty Years' War had widely spread
religious indifference, scepticism and unbelief. Examples could be
found from all classes. There was, for instance, Matthias Knutzen,
who had studied theology but could find no post, and who, in 1674
founded in Jena a sect called the Conscience People (Gewissener),
since he considered conscience the only source of religion. He taught
that there was neither God nor Devil; the magistrate is nothing to
be esteemed, neither are priests or churches. Instead of magistrates
and priests conscience, knowledge and reason shall govern our life.
Marriage and free union are the same. There is no immortality,
heaven or hell. The Bible is self-contradictory. It is enough if men
live honestly, do not injure anybody, and give each his own.[2]
Knutzen was expelled from Jena and nothing is known of his further
life.

Soon scholarly books appeared inspired by Spinoza's teachings,
though mostly without the name of the author. Among them were
writings by two high officials, F. W. Stosch and T. L. Lau. Others
went less far. Professor J. F. Ludovici, a privy counsellor, professed
it was sufficient to live according to the spirit of Christ; the Bible,
sacraments and clergy were superfluous. J. C. Edelmann's life and
work are particularly illuminating for Germany's spiritual development in the first half of the 18th century. He was first a Pietist, then
embraced Deism, and at last become a follower of Spinoza. The
apologists of orthodoxy complained in the beginning of the century
already that Germany was even more infected with atheism than
Holland, though they understood by it every radical criticism of
the dogmas. The rise of freethought was particularly stimulated by
the increasing influence of English thinkers. The striving to base
religion and philosophy not on the Bible and dogmas but exclusively
on reason had, in England, inspired great thinkers as early as the
17th century. The school of Deism taught a religion without revelation, dogmas, rites and priesthood. A great section of the English
clergy, too, was critical of the orthodox beliefs and favoured an
outlook known at Latitudinarianism. Some thinkers, however,
rejected also the striving to derive religion and morality from ideas
inborn in the human mind, and advocated scepticism and agnosti-
cism. David Hume, who completed this development, wrote : 'Last
century our ancestors were inflamed with the most furious
enthusiasm, and are now settled into the most cool indifference,
with regard to religious matters, that is to be found in any nation

[2] On Knutzen and other freethinkers of the 17th century cf. Robertson
II p. 296.

of the world.' When he wrote this, however, a new wave of religious enthusiasm was already approaching in the form of Methodism.

The rise of religious freethought also had implications with regard to the idea of morality. Hobbes held that morality consisted in rules established by the state in order to prevent its subjects from robbing and killing one another. Locke and many others regarded morality as a striving to promote the happiness of mankind. Shaftesbury considered it a harmony of the mental faculties, a parallel to the sense of beauty. His strongest opponent was Bernard of Mandeville, a London doctor and psychologist, who put forward the view that morality taken seriously would be detrimental to state and society : morality was mainly a mask for egoism and vanity; it was the passions and vices which made a nation rich and strong. There were now people, he wrote, who were founding schools for the poor. But would it not lead to disaster if the common people were educated? He ascribed the foundation of charity schools merely to the vanity of men from the middle classes who wanted to be somebodies.[3]

THE RISE OF PIETISM

The power of narrow-minded orthodoxy was not only criticized by scholars on grounds of reason alone, but also by numerous others who found it incompatible with the true spirit of Christianity. This movement, too, comprised many different schools, and may be called Pietism in the wider sense. Thinkers of this type appeared in all Churches and countries, especially in the Netherlands, France, England and Germany. During the Thirty Years' War George Calixtus (1586-1656) was one of the most prominent Lutheran theologians. He revived the conciliatory spirit and the humanistic tradition of Melanchthon, and laid stress not on dogmatic subtleties, but on love of God and one's neighbour, and the old tradition of the Church. His studies and long journeys in many countries had taught him that other creeds had their noble sides too and he wished to promote love and toleration between them. This aroused the greatest wrath of the orthodox, who accused him of harbouring no less than 88 dogmatic errors. Calixtus and his school paved the way for Pietism.

The founders of German Pietism were two Lutheran clergymen, Philipp Jacob Spener (1635-1705) and his disciple August Hermann

[3] On the idea of schools for the common people in England cf. the excursus page 58.

Francke (1663-1727). They by no means intended to put forward new theological doctrines, always emphasized their loyalty to the Augsburg Church, and disliked being called Pietists, as that smacked of a sect. In their view, it was not the Church with its dogmatic beliefs and its rites which was essential, but the inner life of the individuals. A complete change of heart was needed, a spiritual re-birth. True Christianity consisted in piety, humility, purity and love. Every Christian was to be a priest in his way of living and in serving his neighbour, in particular the poor and helpless. Spener and Francke formed small conventicles of men and women for reading and meditating the Scriptures together. All ranks and classes were admitted, and were considered equals. They observed a rigorous morality and shunned entertainments and luxuries. Spener was a quietist, and his followers were often called 'die Stillen in Lande' (the quiet in the country). Francke was much more of an activist, a fiery and energetic worker, and more puritanical than Spener.

The first important post held by Spener was that of a preacher in Frankfurt. In this position he elaborated a project to help the poor and orphans. After much opposition the town council accepted it (1679). The results were so good that many towns and governments followed the model of Frankfurt and created similar institutions. Spener did much to awaken the social conscience. He was later also accused of holding communist opinions, though his views were merely those of the Gospel and Fathers of the Church.

Spener was then called to Dresden as the principal Court Preacher to Duke Johann Georg III of Saxony. But he lost the duke's favour when he admonished him to give up heavy drinking. Moreover, he and Francke got into trouble with the orthodox theologians who suspected them of striving to undermine the Church. The University of Wittenberg later announced that Spener had committed 263 deviations from the true Lutheran faith. The tension became so great that Spener and Francke left Saxony and went to Branden-burg. Margrave Frederick was very tolerant and gave posts to them and many other Pietists. Spener continued his social work, and had a prominent share in devising the plans for a thorough-going reform of the Poor Law (1695); the cost was to be covered by a poor rate and entertainment taxes. The law became fundamental for the development of relief to the poor.

A. H. Francke became a professor at the newly founded University of Halle and taught Oriental languages and theology. He lectured mainly in German instead of in Latin, as was then usual. But he and his school were not keen on theology. They declared that they wanted to awake the conscience, not to make scholars. Frederick William I, the soldier king, sympathized with the Pietists and in 1729 decreed that all students of theology had to attend lectures at Halle for two years. In this way the Prussian clergy became imbued with the spirit of Pietism. It penetrated other universities also, and in spite of the strong opposition of the ortho- dox party it gradually won predominance. Most governments became favourable to Pietism and supported its rise. Francke used his knowledge of languages to improve Luther's translation of the Bible. He also founded an institute for propagating it, and by means of cheap editions achieved an enormous increase in the sale of copies. Now at last everyone could have his own Bible.

The most famous work of Francke was an orphanage, various schools and other institutions which still exist in Halle. He intro- duced important educational reforms, though their puritan spirit had the disadvantage that the pupils were surfeited with Bible reading and praying and denied sufficient recreation, games and sport. When Francke died his orphanage harboured 134 orphans and his schools had 2,207 pupils and 175 teachers. His work gave the impetus to the foundation of numerous orphanages in Germany and other countries. The Pietists tried also to provide schools for the country people, and their patron Frederick William I took this up. Another work dear to Francke was the sending out of mis- sionaries to the heathens. King Frederick IV of Denmark wished the Gospel to be preached in the Danish colonies in the West Indies. Francke provided the missionaries and also visited the West Indies himself.

Pietism soon greatly impressed numerous German princes, noblemen, statesmen and high officers. Under its influence not a few court preachers exhorted their princes to mend their ways. Frederick William I accepted such admonitions patiently in spite of his violent temper. The preacher Freylinghausen was once a guest of the King and used this opportunity for telling him that hunting, in which he took great pleasure, was a sin because the animals were terribly tormented by it, the King's confessor, Roloff, told him on his deathbed that he doubted whether his soul would go to heaven because his mind was not Christian. He blamed him for his irascibility, for his oppression of his subjects, the laying of new burdens on the peasants and the aggravation of death sentences. Other preachers, too, sometimes reprimanded him frankly.

Owing to pietism toleration made progress and charitable work was undertaken. Disciples of Francke also obtained influence at foreign courts. One of them was A. W. Boehme, who became Court

Chaplain to Queen Anne and King George I, and worked in Francke's spirit. In Denmark the Kings Frederick IV and Christian VI did this, too. Among the German people the class of artisans was particularly receptive to it. But the tradesmen disliked its rejection of the commercial spirit, and the broad masses were reluctant because of its ban on popular entertainments. In general women, Jews and poor people loved it. In Wurttemberg prominent theologians, especially J. A. Bengel, cultivated a specific form of Pietism which penetrated a wide section of the people. Among the Reformed Church a modified Pietism was spread by J. Coccejus, a German preacher living in the Netherlands, and by the French theologian Labadie. There were also corresponding movements among Catholics.

ZINZENDORF AND THE COMMUNITY OF BRETHREN

Francke's schools at Halle included also a college for young noblemen. One of his pupils was Count Nikolaus Ludwig Zinzendorf (1700-1760). His family originally lived in Austria, but had left it at the time of the Counter-Reformation, and settled in Lusatia. At school already Nikolaus showed a fiery enthusiasm for the aims of Pietism. But he had to read law, and enter the legal profession, and could only devote himself entirely to his religious ideals after several years. In the meantime, he had permitted a group of Moravian refugees to settle on his land, and to found a community called Herrenhut. Now, he began to concentrate his energy on this venture, and to develop it with enthusiasm, generosity and genius. It was not, however, his intention to found a new Church or sect, but he wished to create an independent section of the Lutheran Church, and to work for brotherhood between all Christians whatever their denomination. All of them were admitted, not only Lutherans. Zinzendorf's religion consisted in a passionate and sometimes eccentric cult of Christ's personality, particularly of the suffering on the cross. This seemed to him the only essential point in religion, the only way to make men love each other, and the common ground on which all denominations could meet. Zinzendorf was an impressive personality, he possessed the fervour of a prophet and the imagination of a poet, and disposed of immense energy. He wrote about 100 tracts, but his greatest force was in his spoken addresses, which were taken down by his disciples. There are still 10,000 addresses preserved in manuscript, and 500 in print. Besides that he improvised religious songs of which 2,000 are extant.

The community founded by Zinzendorf was known as the

Brethren Unity, and in some countries as Moravians. Pietists and mystics from all parts of Germany joined it. Most of them were skilled artisans, who by their probity, peaceableness and diligence acquired a great reputation, but many noblemen and scholars also became members. The Brethren laid no stress on theology and ritual, but concentrated upon meditation on Christ's life and death, and on achieving their own moral rebirth. Every trace of egoism, ambition, pride, discord and anger was to be exterminated, and instead humility, concord, friendliness, patience, veracity and helpfulness were to be features of the regenerated character. The Brethren lived in communities separated from the world on the model of the Apostles and the first Christians. No exaggerated puritanism was demanded; life should be joyful, and community singing and harmless fun were much practised. The mystical contemplation of Christ's wounds often had a strange sexual note which modern psychoanalysts have discussed. Zinzendorf's advocacy of religious toleration had the result that orthodox theologians considered him a dangerous enemy of the Church, and fired broadsides of obloqy upon him. But Zinzendorf willingly submitted to investigations of his activities by competent authorities. They led to the verdict that his work was in conformity with the Augsburg Confession.

The Brethren had no hierarchy. Christ was considered their head, and doubtful questions were decided by drawing the lot. The administration was conducted by lay elders, and lay preachers were numerous. Though the community also comprised many nobles, rank was of no account among them. Zinzendorf later renounced his title of count, though a certain aristocratic element in his mind never disappeared.

A section of the community wished to found a separate Church, in which it saw the continuation of the old Bohemian and Moravian Brethren, who had been suppressed by the Counter-Reformation, and whose last bishop had been Comenius. Zinzendorf was at first against this proposal because it might arouse the hostility of other Churches. But at last he complied with this wish, and for some time even became bishop of the Moravian Church. In Prussia, England and some other countries, the Church was officially recognized under this name. Elsewhere, however, the Brethren remained an independent section of the local Protestant Church. The Brethren did not wish to make proselytes at the expense of other Churches, but worked for their reconciliation.

The educational aspirations of the Brethren led to the establishment of a number of schools of various types, which had a remarkable success. Zinzendorf had original ideas on education and the psychology of children. In contrast to the severity of the Pietist schools, which in his opinion must lead to hypocrisy, he stressed that children should be educated with love and in freedom. Nothing should be forbidden or prescribed for them, but they should be left to educate themselves. 'Children,' he wrote, 'are little majesties,— and they should not be treated differently from born kings.'

In 1736 the intrigues of the orthodox party and the intervention of the Austrian government induced the government of Saxony to expel Zinzendorf, and this banishment lasted eleven years. He continued his work in various other countries, especially in the territory of a small Pietist ruler in western Germany, and later in England, and made numerous journeys founding groups of Brethren in many countries. He had already, three years before, started missionary work among the heathens. This task had hitherto been neglected by the Protestant nations, while the Catholics had under-taken it on a grand scale. The Protestant powers, in particular England and the Netherlands, and their chartered companies en-gaged in colonial trade, were indifferent or hostile to missionary work because they feared that it might jeopardize their commercial interests. In the 17th century John Eliot, an English Puritan, became a missionary among the American natives, but his work was wrecked by wars and other events. Francke therefore opened a new field, and Zinzendorf followed his example. At that time extra-ordinary hardships and risks were involved in these activities. The expeditions of the Brethren were, moreover, often faced with particularly dangerous tasks, for example missions to lepers in Africa and Christians enslaved by Algerian pirates. Zinzendorf not only organized and financed the missions, but also himself under-took three journeys to the Red Indians, who received him in a friendly way. In 1741 he landed in America and spent Christmas Eve with a Brethren Settlement in Pennsylvania, who were building the first house in a primeval forest. They assembled in a room which was to be the cowshed, and in commemoration of Christ's birth they called the place Bethlehem. This settlement was organized as a communist society, following the example of the Apostles. It greatly flourished and expanded, but after twenty years communism was abandoned, merely because the number of Brethren had become so great that a life on the model of the Apostles was no longer practi-cable. Bethlehem is still the main seat of the Brethren in America, and also that of one of the greatest iron and armament works.

Many other expeditions followed. At the time when Zinzendorf died (1760) the missionary success of the Brethren surpassed every-thing that had been done up to then by the Protestant world for the conversion of the heathens. By that time they had sent 226 missionaries to all parts of the world, except Australia. In addition, the Halle Pietists, co-operating with Denmark, in the 18th century trained and sent out 60 missionaries.[4] Later Britain became the leading missionary country, employing many German missionaries also.

When Zinzendorf was in America he advised the Brethren not to undertake superficial mass conversions of the Red Indians, but first to win them for a life based on regular work, to civilize them and to educate missionaries from their midst. The Brethren followed this advice, they opened schools for the natives, learned their language and treated them as equals. But this greatly displeased many white frontiersmen whose aim was to rob the land of the Indians and to exterminate them. In 1782 a large gang of frontiersmen led by Colonel David Williamson attacked a settlement composed of German and Red Indian Brethren. These offered no resistance but kneeled down in prayer. They were all clubbed to death and scalped —men, women and children, altogether 93. The murderers put fire to the houses and celebrated their victory by an alcoholic orgy. This catastrophe put an end to the missionary work of the Brethren in those parts.

THE FURTHER DEVELOPMENT OF PIETISM

The Pietists, and in particular the Brethren, had certain traits in common with the Quakers,[5] who were in their early days widely regarded as dangerous enthusiasts. To the German orthodox theologians they were long a bogey and the former used the word Quaker as an insult which they constantly hurled at the Pietists. William Penn twice travelled in Germany and founded groups there. Robert Barclay and George Fox too visited Germany. On the other hand, German pietists early extended their activities to England where they founded various societies. The Moravian Brethren also exercised considerable influence on the origins of Methodism. John and Charles Wesley met a group of them on a journey to America and were deeply impressed by them. In 1738 John Wesley was in close contact with another group in London, especially with their spiritual leader Peter Boehler, to whom he confessed to have owed his re-birth. Later he visited Zinzendorf in Herrenhut.

Another off-shoot of Pietism was the thought of Gottfried Arnold (1666-1714) who experienced his spiritual re-birth through Spener.

[4] Cf. on these early missions Hagenbach V.I. p 545.
[5] But there were also differences. Cf. Hagenbach vol. V. 2. p. 313.

Arnold's most important book is his History of the Church and the Heresies (1699). This very learned work tries to show that the Church early lost her divine character owing to the intrusion of Greek philosophy, her alliance with the Roman Empire, and moral decay; henceforth true Christianity was mainly to be found among heretics, inspired by mystical piety. Throughout the course of history, Arnold said, such men appeared again and again, wishing to restore the purity of the Church, but they were all persecuted and crucified by her; Luther started the Reformation under the inspiration of Tauler's mysticism, but soon became false to his principles. Arnold wrote and edited also mystical books and wrote great hymns, comparable to the poetry of his contemporary Johann Scheffler, known as Angelus Silesius, a Catholic. Arnold's pessimism reminds one of Sebastian Franck. His great work made a deep impression on many of the best Christians, but aroused the hatred of the orthodox party. King Frederick of Prussia, to whom the work was dedicated, protected the author.

While many Pietists had great merits in spreading a sense of religious freedom, toleration, charity and human brotherhood, many others fell into aberrations. The experience of the sectarian movement at Luther's time repeated itself. The identification of one's subjective Inner Voice with the Spirit of God brought about the emergence of ecstatic visionaries marked by radical idealism but lacking any common sense. Churches and states appeared to them as the Babel of the Apocalypse and they believed in the imminent second advent of Christ. Great numbers cultivated an excessive puritanism, shunning even harmless pleasures and entertainments. Life seemed to them nothing but sin. A little girl of six, from a noble family, prayed to God that He should not let her become a whore. Many fell into ecstasies, with convulsions, groaning and whimpering. There were sectarians preaching complete sexual abstinence, even in marriage, while others indulged in sexual licence, both kinds putting forward religious arguments. Had not Spener said a man re-born could not sin? Social inequality, owning property and the existence of a government were often condemned by reference to the Scriptures. No wonder that many governments came to the conclusion that Pietism, or certain sections of it, might endanger public order. Prohibitions and restrictions were decreed, and certain Pietists were expelled.

Pietism had an affinity with mysticism, but also with Enlightenment, which was to succeed it. Both disliked fanaticism, superstition and intolerance, and stressed the worth of the individual and the value of freedom. Both abhorred war, persecution and cruelty.

In a time when the spirit of Louis XIV elevated the monarch almost
to the rank of God, and filled the ruling classes with an extravagant
lust for luxury, dissipation and glory at the expense of the poor
people, Pietism inspired not a few German princes and noblemen
with a sense of their duties towards their subjects and awakened the
social conscience in wider circles. Spener, Francke and Zinzendorf
all gave practical emphasis to the idea of human brotherhood. The
legal diversity of ranks was recognized, but among the Brethren all
were equal. The common people, too, were to have schools and the
opportunity of rising to a higher intellectual and social level. The
despised savage and heathen, too, was regarded as a brother, and
missionaries went out to bring him the Gospel, and to open for him
the way to civilization and equality. While European traders became rich by shipping Negro slaves to America, the missionaries
spread the spirit which eventually led to the abolition of slavery.

In internal politics the Pietists abided by Luther's principles,
which were identical with the old Christian ones. But they prepared
the rise of the common man to a greater share in politics by giving
him influence in Church life, spreading education and the use of the
German language and ignoring differences of rank and class. A
nationalism based on the idea of the superiority of one nation over
others, however, was utterly alien and contrary to Pietism. Zinzendorf's estate was situated in Lusatia, where many Slavs (Wenden)
still lived. He told them they should remain loyal to their nationality
and preserve it in order to be useful to their people. He also wished
that the Red Indians should, after their conversion, have their own
State and preserve their nationality.

Though Pietism and Enlightenment had for some time pursued
certain common aims, their road soon parted. Many Pietists were
greatly disturbed by the impression that the development of the
belief in reason alone, seemed to undermine the belief in God and
in morality. Not a few of them now appeared to become defenders
of orthodox theses. Christian Wolff's philosophy conquered the mind
of the German intellectual youth. But when he taught that the
Chinese, who did not believe in a God, had a better morality than
the Christians, Francke turned against him, and the king expelled
the philosopher. This aroused an outcry in the academic world and
discredited the Pietists. Sections of them had also lost their enthusiasm and sincerity. The Pietists had taught Puritanism and had condemned entertainments, among them the theatre, merry music,
dancing, playing cards or ninepins, smoking tobacco, reading fiction,
the use of hair-powder etc. But when Puritanism became a mass
movement it unavoidably led to the spread of Pharisaism among

its adherents. The rejection of literature and art by the Pietists further estranged them from the mind of the young generation. Frau Gottsched, the wife of the most influential literary critic and herself a much admired writer of comedies, published. in 1736, a revised version of a French play written by a Jesuit against the Jansenists. She altered it, however, into a satire against the hypocrisy of the Pietists. Other attacks followed.

THE DEVELOPMENT OF BIBLE CRITICISM
THE CLERGY IN THE SERVICE OF
ENLIGHTENED ABSOLUTISM

The rule of orthodoxy was further increasingly weakened and undermined by the progress of the critical study of the Scriptures. It showed that the Bible was not a work imbued with one spirit, that of God, but a collection of books greatly differing in outlook. Large parts could not have been written by the authors to whom they were attributed. It also became clear that many passages had not the sense hitherto attributed to them. On the whole. the Bible appeared as a product of historic development, which had gradually gone through various phases of religious thought. The results of this study seemed not incompatible with religion as such, but in any case contradicted the traditional dogmatic assumptions and demanded their revision.

An important criticism of the Old Testament had been put forward by Spinoza in 1670. Christian thinkers too, had taken exception to certain passages of the Bible. Zinzendorf had found that the Bible was full of faults. But the first systematic critical investigation of the whole Bible was made in two books by a French Catholic priest, Richard Simon (1678-1689). His writings were condemned by the Catholic Church. Several prominent Protestant scholars carried on the study of the Bible and also revised the history of the Church and her dogmas. Johann Salomo Semler (1725-1791) alone wrote 171 studies on this subject, and opened a new epoch in the development of this branch of learning. He came to the conclusion that the very core of Christianity could assume numerous different forms of belief and that everybody should be free to have his 'private' religion. Radical critics such as Reimarus and Bahrdt went much farther, they rejected any revelation, denied that Christ was God, and even disparaged his and the apostles' character. Many great thinkers took part in these controversies. It is not our task, however. to follow them in all respects but to show only how they influenced political opinions.[6]

The struggles of enlightenment were concerned with several issues which were interconnected. There was the antagonism between orthodoxy and other forms of Christian beliefs. Then arose the question of religion as such. Was there a God, and what was his attitude to the world? Lastly, the Church was faced with the claim of the state to exclusive external power within its frontiers. The decisions on all these questions might also have moral and political implications though this was partly controversial.

The struggles between state and Church will be related in other places. They were not necessarily connected with the questions of religion. Maria Theresa and Joseph II were pious Christians but went farther in intervening in the affairs of the Church than the unbelieving Frederick the Great. Law and administration increasingly became the prerogative of the state and the ecclesiastical influence was eliminated. The clergy was largely transformed into organs of the state. It became their task to make the subjects loyal, useful and contented citizens. They had to inform them from the pulpits of the decrees of the rulers and to exhort them to be obedient.

THE CATHOLIC CHURCH AND THE JESUITS

The Church of Rome was less disturbed by religious strife than Protestantism. It had maintained its unity and supra-national character better than the new creed, which had soon divided itself into numerous national Churches. In consequence of the Reformation the Catholic Church had been purged of many serious abuses and the morals of the priesthood had improved. The Jesuits provided the Papacy with an army excellently organized and trained to defend the faith against all adversaries.

The Papacy, the monks, and particularly the Jesuit Order, were widely regarded as the greatest enemies of enlightenment. They were violently denounced for superstitious practices, intolerance, political intrigues and moral corruption in countless writings of Protestant authors. The cleavage between Protestants and Catholics was one of the greatest obstacles to the development of Germany's unity and nationhood. The charges against the Catholics certainly contained a good deal of truth. Yet it must be kept in mind that the antagonism of two great religious parties, aggravated by numerous deep-rooted traditions and interests, naturally poisoned the atmosphere and was most unfavourable to any mutual appreciation.

[6] An excellent presentation of these struggles is in Fritz Valjavec, Geschichte der abendlaendischen Aufklaruno 1961.

In spite of many unquestionable faults, the Jesuits were popular in wide circles of Catholic Germany and exercised an outstanding attraction on many Protestants, too. The form of religion which they cultivated corresponded to the feelings and longings of the people. They did not preach the terrible doctrine that God had irrevocably predestinated most men to eternal damnation, nor did they enter in their sermons into abstruse dogmatic speculations, or prescribe a rigorous puritanism, banning even harmless entertainment. The churches were not stripped of everything appealing to the emotions such as music, pictures, sculpture and impressive rites. On the contrary, the Jesuits laid stress upon elevating the soul by the fine arts, and their churches, built in the baroque style, were full of presentations of Christian heroism, and passionate love of the Divine. Jesuit missionaries even adapted themselves to the beliefs and rites of the Hindus and Chinese in order to win their confidence. A certain adoption of pagan customs for this purpose was one of the oldest traditions of the Church, but naturally involved great risks. Confession became one of the main instruments of the Jesuits to guide the life of the believers. They also developed a way of judging sin very mildly, known as probabilism. This theory could easily be misused, and, no doubt, was often applied in this way. But was it wrong in itself? Had not Christ said we should not judge our neighbour and forgive him again and again? Did not modern jurists increasingly take account of extenuating circumstances in assessing responsibility for crimes?

The Jesuits further practised charity in manifold ways. The poor, sick, weak and oppressed were cared for, comforted or assisted by them. They were eager to attend those affected by the plague, they looked after wounded soldiers, prisoners of war and convicts, helped Christians enslaved by infidel enemies to regain liberty, and rescued fallen women. Their preachers and publicists often castigated the upper and landed classes for exploiting their serfs, domestic servants or workers. Jesuits were foremost as missionaries among primitive tribes in most parts of the new world, they spread Christianity and civilization, and many of them sacrificed their lives. Their missionary activities laid the ground for the study of the mind and the languages of these peoples, they became pioneers in exploring new countries, and in South America they organized a kind of socialist welfare State among the natives. Their position in oversea countries led to the foundation of plantations and commercial enterprises owned by the Order, which had great profits from them. Emperors, kings and others made vast donations in land and money to the Order, which were mainly used to build splendid

Churches and colleges. Great stress was laid on science and learning, and there was no branch of them in which Jesuits were not among the most distinguished scholars. Equally great were their merits as schoolmasters. In the Catholic countries the ruling and intellectual classes were educated by them, and trained for life. One of the reasons why Catholicism at the beginning of the age of Enlightenment made such astounding progress among the ruling and upper classes was that a great many Catholic noblemen became priests in the Jesuit Order, while Protestant noblemen very seldom chose the profession of clergymen. This seemed to show that the former took religion more seriously than the latter.

Further many Jesuits early showed understanding for the ideas of Enlightenment, and were in close contact with Protestant scholars such as Leibniz and Wolff. An important feature of the Order was its drastic opposition to every kind of nationalism.[7] In their schools the teachers and pupils were, on principle, drawn from different nationalities, and language was no difficulty, since fluent Latin was one of the main aims of instruction.

The grandiose development of the Order, however, aroused acute jealousy and enmity against the Jesuits, even among the Catholics. It was remarked that their General wanted to be superior to the Pope, though the Order had been foremost in defending the absolute power and infallibility of the Papacy. In the course of time there were numerous bitter quarrels between the Jesuits and all the other orders and organs of the Church. The Order had also become very big, and at last had about 23,000 members. So large a group must have comprised undesirable elements also. Yet there is evidence that as a rule the Jesuits did not misuse their wealth and power for a life of pleasure.

The founder of the Order and its successive leaders made every effort to prevent the members from being involved in politics. They knew the risks inherent in it. Politics were often bound to breed a spirit incompatible with Christianity, they might lead to conflicts between rulers and between peoples equally important to the Order, and the Jesuits invested with political power might become corrupted by it. If a ruler, therefore, asked the General to let him have a father as a confessor, this was only granted under the condition that he should be concerned with questions of conscience, but not assume the functions of a political adviser, at least not officially.

This distinction, however, could not be implemented. The most important political questions were often ones of conscience, and

---

[7] Nevertheless Jesuits have played a great part in preparing and fostering the national revival of peoples subject to foreign masters.

the rulers insisted upon consulting their confessors in almost every question of significance. Jesuits became confessors to many Catholic rulers, and some of them exercised the greatest influence on politics. They were also frequently infected with the political tendencies dominant at the court of the ruler, and were thereby estranged from the true Christian spirit. The experience was confirmed that great power breeds its own misuse.

The involvment in politics at last brought about the suppression of the Jesuit Order, first by Portugal, and then by the governments of Paris, Madrid, Naples and Parma. These latter states, which were all under the rule of members of the French dynasty of Bourbon, in 1773 forced the Pope to dissolve the Order. The governments mentioned carried out the suppression of the Jesuits with a brutality for which there was no justification. This act was widely celebrated as a triumph of enlightenment though its motives hardly fitted this concept. In the German and Austrian countries, with the exception of Prussia, the Order also came to an end, but here the governments proceeded in a fair way.

The Jesuits were often rightly condemned for their encouragement of fanaticism, obscurantism and superstition. But there were also many Jesuits whose attitude to religion, philosophy and politics was reasonable, who were famous scientists, good educators and active enemies of despotism and social or national oppression. The monumental work of the Jesuit B. Duhr on the history of the Order in the German-speaking countries gives numerous important examples, and also one of the greatest Protestant theologians of recent times, H. Boehmer, has in a masterly book appreciated their activities with great fairness.

EXCURSUS ON THE IDEA OF POPULAR
EDUCATION IN ENGLAND. (CF. P. 45)

In Britain education for the people was mainly propagated by the Charity School Movement, on which Mrs. M. G. Jones has written a most informative book. But many regarded it as a social danger if the lower classes should be educated. The most bitter and poisonous opponent was B. de Mandeville.

In 1807 Samuel Whitbread introduced a bill in the House of Commons proposing a general national education, though without compulsion. He pointed out that in Scotland every parish had a school and that this had had the best results. In reply D. Giddy, M.P., said: 'Howsoever specious in theory the project may be of giving education to the labouring classes of the poor it would in effect be prejudicial to their morals and happiness; it would teach them to despise their lot in life, instead of making them good servants in agriculture and other laborious employments to which their rank in society has destined them; instead of teaching them subordination it would render them factious and refractory, as was evident in the manufacturing countries; it would enable them to read seditious pamphlets, vicious books and publications against Christianity; it would render them insolent to their superiors' and so on. The bill was rejected by the House of Lords.

As late as 1833 William Cobbett, the great tribune of the people, opposed the idea of a general education of the people 'on the ground that education was not improving the condition of the country and did nothing but increase the number of schoolmasters and school-mistresses, that new race of idlers'.

4

GERMANY'S SOCIAL STRUCTURE AND ECONOMIC
CONDITIONS

THE CONSEQUENCES OF THE THIRTY YEARS' WAR

IN the 17th and 18th centuries the Netherlands, France and England entered a period of vigorous economic development, they were rivals for world supremacy in trade, commerce, shipping and colonisation and great wars were waged for this aim. Their economic development also had most important political and cultural consequences. Germany, however, was excluded from these struggles and their successes, because of her economic ruin through the Thirty Years' War. The times had passed when the bankers of Augsburg, the industrialists of Nuremberg and the merchants and shippers of Lubeck, Hamburg and Cologne were leading in international trade and traffic. This marvellous development of the Western nations was largely due to their national unity and power. But Germany was farther from nationhood than ever, and the army which the Reichstag could raise was unable even to defend the frontiers on is own. A German navy did not exist.

The greatest and most urgent task for Germany was the rebuilding of its economic structure, which the Thirty Years' War had to a great extent destroyed, and this had to be done under the impact of many new wars forced upon Germany by Louis XIV and others. As regards the losses in population through the Thirty Years' War, many local records have been preserved and experts in economic history have used them to assess average figures for Germany as a whole : G. Franz estimated them at 40% of the rural population and 30% of the urban one. Some regions suffered less, but in others the loss was between 50 and 70%, and F. Luetge thinks that the whole of Germany may have lost at least 50% of its people. At the beginning of the 17th century, Bohemia had according to Gindely's estimate 2 millions inhabitants, and one and a half centuries later the country had not yet reached this figure again owing to the war. Wurttemberg had 444.552 inhabitants in 1622, and 425.030 in 1730. Other territories too took a century or more to attain their former state of population. But there were also regions which had not been theatres of war, such as the Alpine countries, and which therefore had only suffered its indirect consequences, like the plague or famine.

Besides these losses in population the other factors of production and trade had also been largely destroyed or damaged, such as the buildings, the implements, the cattle and the fertility of the soil. War, famine, pestilence and demoralisation had rendered large sections of the people unfit for regular, strenuous or skilled work. There were countless invalids, beggars, robbers and vagabonds. Moreover, there was much land whose owners had vanished and to which nobody laid claim or could prove his title. Agricultural prices were low since demand was lacking, and wages were high because the supply of labour was scarce. The birthrate was high, but this was more than outweighed by the great mortality. It therefore became the main principle of economic policy to increase the population by all means. This need was partly fulfilled by the settlement of soldiers, of refugees and immigrants.

The war had in many territories created conditions which made it impossible for numerous individuals to restart work in a desirable way. Antiquated privileges, lack of capital, backwardness in methods of production and aversion to innovations etc. formed great obstacles. Economic reconstruction therefore demanded far-sighted planning which a strong government only could undertake and direct. In various territories rulers and statesmen fitted for this task actually came to power. They primarily laid great stress on increasing the population and this had far-reaching implications. Human life and health were more highly estimated by the governments than before. The demand was raised that capital punishment should be restricted to the gravest cases, and that minor offenders should be spared to do work useful to the community. Religious intolerance was waived in favour of foreign dissenters or Jews who might bring new industries or economic improvements. Parents with many children got premiums or were to pay lower taxes. Girls with illegitimate children should not be put to shame. The people's health was to be furthered by measures of hygiene. Governments collected statistics in order to obtain information on the basis of

which a policy could be framed. Feudal and other obsolete privileges hampering economic progress were to be abolished. The spirit
of the age was favourable to a strong monarchy which alone seemed
to be able to suppress religious strife and to secure peace. In Germany vital economic interests too were speaking for it

THE PEASANTS

The peasants formed the greatest part of the population. They
had suffered most throughout the long war and many of them were
also seriously hit by its consequences. The majority were unfree or
more or less subject to the landed nobility. Many were called
Leibeigene (serfs) but this did not mean a sort of slavery, as unin-
formed people believe. The sense of the word was that they owed
their lord dues and services, and needed for certain acts his permission, not because he had let them ground on lease, but because
he was supposed to protect their persons.[1] This was the legal sense
of the word, but it was very usual to call peasants serfs whose
obligations to the lord were onerous, irrespective of whether the
burdens rested on the soil or on his person. The lords were in no
case owners of the serfs as in Russia. The peasants mostly cultivated
the soil of their lord and had to pay him for its lease a rent, and to
perform services, they were subject to his jurisdiction in lesser
cases, sometimes also in graver ones, and had to ask for his permission if they wanted to leave their farm, take up a trade or marry.
The soil let to them could not as a rule be arbitrarily taken from
them and on their death went to their heirs. The lord usually could
not arbitrarily increase the rent and services and owed his serfs help
when they fell ill, in old age or when hit by natural catastrophes.
The legal situation of the peasants showed countless variations.
Professor Luebke has described five regions showing typical conditions but within each there were also many differences in the
obligations of the peasants. Some were much restricted in their
freedom or greatly overburdened, others were much better off. We
have descriptions of the misery of numerous peasants, but there
were also many who had a good life or were rich.

[1] The status of the peasants was often unclear. In the Swabian county of
Hohenzollern the peasants maintained that their former serfdom had
vanished by immemorial custom and raised further claims, in particular the
right to freely hunting in the woods of the country. For two hundred years
they fought for these claims with the utmost pertinacity and, in frequent
rebellions and by appeals to the High Courts of the Empire, which issued
many judgments, partly for, partly against them. Cf. J. Kramer, Die
Grafschaft Hohenzollern, ein Bild sueddeutscher Volkszustaende, 1873.

The legal and economic conditions of the peasants were, for example, favourable in Wurttemberg, on the middle Rhine and on the Mosel, in Thuringia, Saxony, Nether-Saxony, parts of Hesse and Franconia, the Tyrol and other Alpine lands of Austria etc. In Bavaria the peasants were mostly unfree by law, but could buy their freedom for a very small fee, and hardly differed from freemen. In many territories the monasteries had large estates. The Church was usually a mild lord, but her peasants were not very productive because of the numerous holidays, pilgrimages and similar religious obligations. Princes who did not depend on the nobles tried to protect the peasants against exploitation by them. But where Estates dominated by the nobles had power, the latter tried to increase the subjection of their serfs. To this end they were only willing to vote taxes to the ruler if he granted them larger public rights over the peasants. It is noteworthy that legally unfree peasants were often in better economic conditions than free ones. Not seldom the peasants were serfs voluntarily because this brought them advantages. In many territories where the peasants were free, they suffered under the lack of sufficient soil and the smallness of their plots. On the Rhine they were often exposed to devastation of their farms because of the numerous wars waged by France. In the East they suffered under the inroads of the Turks. One of the worst scourges for the peasants was the passion rulers and nobles had for the chase. They kept much game, prohibited the peasants from protecting their fields against it, and compelled them to act as beaters even when they were occupied with the harvest. The hunt often swept over the fields like a hailstorm.

East of the Elbe the nobles were mostly farmers themselves, while in the other parts of Germany they merely let their land to the peasants for rents and services. In the middle ages the peasants had been settled in the east as free men and under favourable conditions. But when the knights were no longer much occupied with defending the country, and when the Baltic trade in grain became profitable, they began to enlarge their estates at the expense of the peasants, who were depressed to the status of labourers on the farms of the knights. The Thirty Years' War and the subsequent time gave many opportunities for these changes. The Hohenzollerns later broke the political power of the nobles, but left them the authority over the peasants, since they needed the knights as officers; when sections of the peasants were later enrolled in the army, the Hohenzollern rulers began to protect them and to ameliorate their lot on their domains.

In the Bohemian countries and parts of Hungary the peasants

were grievously oppressed. Before the Habsburgs these countries were reigned by weak kings of Polish origin who granted the nobles every enlargement of their power over the serfs which they demanded. In 1620 the Venetian ambassador in Vienna wrote that the Bohemian peasants gave the impression of slaves. The long war brought them indescribable sufferings. True, there were always lords inspired by humane feelings. The greatest Bohemian landowner, Prince Johann Adolf Schwarzenberg wrote in 1673 to the director of his estates: 'One must help the poor in every possible way and consider that God will punish injustice done to them and reward those who do good to them'. But the majority of the high nobility did not care much for the welfare of the peasants, nor did they bother about the management of their estates. They left this, as a rule, to stewards who were intent on squeezing the serfs not only for the profit of the lords, but also for their own pockets. The Bohemian peasants were often driven to desperation and there were frequent riots.

Nobles of strong religious convictions early began to doubt that serfdom was legitimate. In 1688 Count Christof Rantzau emancipated his serfs, declaring that serfdom was against nature, reason and Christianity. His heirs, however, restored former conditions. In the 18th century Count Christian Guenther von Stolberg was the first in Germany who set his serfs free and many other nobles followed his example, which was also in their own interest.

In the age of Enlightenment criticism of serfdom increased. But it was long doubtful whether an instant, complete liberation was in the interest of the peasants. Christian Garve described the uncanny, threatening mentality of the peasants. Joseph II eventually took energetic action in his territories but his reforms could not be completed owing to the resistance of his enemies and his early death. The living conditions of the peasants were, however, also depressed by their primitive way of cultivating the soil. They stubbornly clung to their old ways and resisted every innovation. But in the second half of the 18th century great improvements were initiated, mainly by three men: J. Ch. Schubart, A. Thaer and J. N. Schwerz. None of them came from the rural classes or was actuated mainly by selfish interest. They were largely inspired by humanitarian zeal and were much assisted in their work by progressive noble landowners. They succeeded in introducing greatly improved methods into agriculture, following the model of farming in England, Belgium and Lombardy. These reforms not only improved the living conditions of the peasants but also transformed their whole mentality. As long as the peasant was subject to feudal exploitation and to the power of old customs he worked in a lazy, careless way. But the new agriculture demanded knowledge, observation and the belief in progress. Under Frederick II the Prussian serfs were long against cultivating potatoes, and other innovations, and often had to be forced to adopt improvements. But gradually they learned that the new ways were a great benefit. The spreading of elementary schools for the people contributed much to the rise of their intellectual level.

TRADE AND COMMERCE

The Thirty Years' War had also been a catastrophe for trade and commerce. Apart from individual losses, Germany as a whole appeared to be depressed to economic servitude. The highways of trade were the great rivers, and all their estuaries were now in foreign hands. After the war Sweden controlled the mouth of the Oder, Elbe and Weser. Half of her revenues came from tolls on Germany's Baltic trade, which, however, was also liable to Danish tolls. The Rhine, the Maas and the Scheldt flowed into the sea on Dutch territory, and this was used by the Netherlands to prohibit German navigation into the sea, and to levy tolls on German traffic on these rivers. The mouth of the Danube was under the domination of the Turkish Empire which also possessed most of the countries through which it flowed nearly up to Vienna.

The commercial policy of all powers was at that time guided by the principles of mercantilism. This system aimed at developing all the economic forces of a country by drastic protectionism and government regulation. Special attention was given to the development of export industries which would bring money into the country. Though Germany exported linen, woollens, iron, metal goods, timber, and other articles, the imports were considerably greater in value. Many German governments therefore made great efforts to found new industries. First of all they tried to replace the luxury goods imported from France and mainly bought by princes and the aristocracy. Many princes founded factories for making porcelain, silk, mirrors, etc., and also such making cloth, foods, armaments etc. for the soldiers. Gradually many other industries were started. In the towns industrial production was mostly under the control of the trade guilds whose principal aim was the safeguarding of their local monopolies. They also wished to prevent any producer from earning more than the others, and therefore opposed the introduction of machines. Their petty egoism was injurious to the rise of production and to the welfare of their workers and the

C

consumers. The Reichstag and some rulers tried to overcome their obstruction to progress by legislation, and the latter also by licences to industrialists, exempting them from the control of the guilds.

On the whole, the spirit of the urban middle class was unfavourable to large-scale enterprises, nor did they possess the means and experience for them. Rulers, great landowners, foreign technicians and businessmen played a more active role in promoting the foundation of new industries. A very important contribution was further made by foreign refugees from religious persecution, such as Netherlanders, and French Huguenots, and by Jews. In many other countries, too, these categories were equally significant for industrial development. The reason seems to have been the specific mentality of these circles, particularly their freedom from the local conventions antagonistic to capitalism. This matter has been much discussed by sociologists.

To a great extent the development of new industries took place either in new towns founded by princes for this purpose, or in rural areas where wood, other raw materials and labour were plentiful and cheap, and where the guilds had no influence. But in these regions good roads and other necessities of industrial production were lacking and had to be created. On the existing roads, on rivers and at town gates there were numerous tolls. Particularism was often a grave obstacle to the building of roads designed to cross several territories. Moreover, the rise of industries was faced with very considerable general difficulties such as the low purchasing power of the people, who produced nearly all necessities themselves, the lack of capital and credit, the multitude of currencies, weights and measures, the frequent depreciation of currencies for fiscal reasons, obsolete privileges, and so on. Many industries founded at that time with the support of governments could therefore not take root, and had later to close down. Those founded by private enterprise in Saxony, Silesia, the Rhinelands etc. were healthier and prosperous. But the primary condition for production on a large scale was a wide market. Germany's excessive particularism, however, and the fact that many rulers at that time embarked on a policy of mercantilistic seclusion resulted in narrow markets. For Germany mercantilism could not have the same success as for the maritime powers because she had little access to the overseas markets.

THE LABOUR QUESTION

One of the principal aims of mercantilism was to use the whole manpower of the country for productive work. But almost everywhere in Europe the striving to found industries was faced with the difficulty of finding sufficient workers, though a great proportion of the people was unemployed and destitute. The reasons for this strange fact are controversial. It may be that nascent industrialism was not congenial to the people because of its discipline, its mechanical nature, lack of rest, and so on. In Germany conditions were particularly bad. Through the great war a large proportion of the people had lost the habit of regular work, and they had first to be compelled to it, if necessary by force.

Where the lords had still great power over numerous serfs as in Bohemia or Silesia, they often set them to work in cottage industries, factories or mines. The rulers of Prussia and other countries laid stress upon recruiting soldiers for their armies mainly from outside their realms in order not to decrease the number of workers available for industries. In Prussia even the soldiers had to do industrial work, if they were not engaged in military exercises. Their barracks therefore looked like factories. Numerous technicians and skilled workers were imported from abroad. Many princes and towns further established workhouses where tramps, beggars and convicts were employed in industrial work. Orphanages provided juvenile workers for factories. In all these matters the German governments followed the way shown by the industrially advanced countries such as Italy, the Netherlands, France and England, who all had difficulties with the problems of poverty, unemployment and finding workers for industries. Sombart in his work on Capitalism gives numerous examples (1.2. chap. 54). The methods used led to the revival of compulsory labour, a sort of new serfdom, even in 'England. Queen Elizabeth already had made a law 'to banish idleness' providing that all unmarried persons under 30 years, versed in an occupation, but without property and employment could be forced to become workers. Low wages were fixed by the Justices of Peace. A sort of serfdom further existed in coal and salt-mines, especially in Scotland, until 1775. In England an Act of 1662 provided that every parish might refuse admittance to a poor man likely to become a burden on the rates, who thereby was tied to a place, and could there be forced to work at low wages. In Germany many governments dealt with the poor in a similar spirit.

THE FINANCIAL SYSTEM

In the earlier part of the epoch the revenues of the State consisted mainly of the returns of the domains of the rulers, of a land-tax or property tax, and certain customary dues. The expenditure largely depended on the greatness and style of the court, and the cost of the army. The income of the ruler and the state were not yet clearly separated. With the rise of absolutism, revenues and expenditure underwent considerable changes. The excise was introduced because, according to the opinion of the time, it was not dependent on a vote of the Estates. Foreign subsidies and also payment for German troops hired by foreign powers were a considerable income.[2] One of the worst points in the finance of the age was the exemption of the nobles and the clergy from taxation, which in most countries was the rule, though there were some exceptions. In the course of time the scope of State activities grew and accordingly also the bureaucracy and its cost. State finance was increasingly separated from that of the ruler. In many territories the rulers possessed a great part of the land, and this accentuated the patrimonial character of the State. The standpoints of a ruler and a landlord were often difficult to separate. It was therefore a great advance when it was laid down whether a domain was the property of the prince or the state. Though the collection of revenues was often farmed out to financiers, this system never reached the same proportions as in France, where it was one of the main reasons for the terrible misery of the people. Nor was the selling of posts so widespread as in France, where it had ruinous consequences.

EMIGRATION AND SETTLEMENT ABROAD

In the middle ages peasants who wanted to improve their lot could migrate to territories with vast uncultivated lands, or to a town, where they received freedom, if their lord had not reclaimed them within a year. Later such migrations were made more difficult, but this could be overcome by paying a fee to the lord, or by running away without his permission. Governments welcomed immigration of useful people. In parts of Germany with numerous little territories it was usually easy to pass into another state. Their rulers often had not even the means to prevent it. The multitude of small states therefore facilitated the overcoming of hard serfdom and the spread of freedom. On the other hand, conditions in the little states

[2] According to Guelich's careful studies the subsidies paid to German States for soldiers hired amounted to about 550 million Thalers from 1700 to 1790. Cf. Guelich, Geschichtliche Darstellung des Handels, II. p. 208.

were often unfavourable owing to maladministration, lack of defence against the invasion of enemies and so on. In consequence, many people sought to emigrate abroad, and German farmers and artisans were appreciated for their efficiency in most countries.

William Penn on his travels in Germany made contact with various sects related to the Quakers and invited them to come to America, where he planned to create a commonwealth. In 1682-83 he began this work in Pennsylvania and Philadelphia was founded. Many Mennonites followed his call, especially from Crefeld. In 1682 a Society for emigration to Pennsylvania was set up in Frankfurt. Its leader was Franz Daniel Pastorius who landed at the mouth of the Delaware with a number of emigrants and founded German-town, near Philadelphia. In 1688 these German settlers published a protest against negro slavery, the first of its kind. This group of Germans were Quakers, but in the course of time many others immigrated, belonging to similar sects. They all hoped to found a new Jerusalem.

The people of the Palatinate, in German called Pfaelzer, were particularly eager to emigrate and this word was therefore often also applied to emigrants in general. A constant stream of them took place; most of them went to Pennsylvania, but considerable numbers settled in other countries, too. In 1709 another mass exodus set in, partly under the stress of a particularly severe winter. Queen Anne, advised by Marlborough and her German chaplain, invited Germans to come to England and from there to emigrate to America. The result surpassed every expectation. Soon a vast number of Germans had assembled near London. Estimates of their number varied, the highest was over 32,000. Ships for so many were not available. The Queen, the Quakers and many others supported them generously, but hostile voices were also heard. At last the Catholics were sent back to Germany, several thousand others went to Ireland to work there as weavers, others got work in England, a great many perished, and the rest reached America.

Another mass exodus took place in 1717. Pennsylvania and other places were gradually to a great extent settled by Germans. About the middle of the century the governor of Pennsylvania estimated them at three-fifths of the population. German settlers had a great share in the cultural and economic development of the United States. In the War of Independence they gave great support to the cause of national freedom. Many of the immigrants became famous in American history : in 1723 Johann Peter Rockefeller came from Germany and settled in New Jersey; J. J. Astor, born in Waldorf near Heidelberg, arrived in 1783.

Many other great emigrations of German peasants occurred to the countries on the lower Danube, when Austria had liberated them from Turkish domination, to the Banat, Bukowina and Galicia, but also to Russia, Spain etc.

THE NOBILITY

In former times the attitude of the nobles had often compelled the rulers to seek the support of the middle class, and they had chosen their chancellors and counsellors largely from its ranks. But with the rise of absolutism the princes no longer had to fear the nobles, since they now had their standing armies and officials, instead of the quite obsolete military and administrative organs from the nobility. The rulers could now safely employ aristocrats as ministers, diplomats and officers. Many nobles had in the meantime acquired the qualifications for their new rôle. They studied law and politics, then visited foreign countries and were introduced at courts there. In many cases able men from the middle class could still make a career, and were ennobled, but the sons of noble families had better chances. Well-paid posts went mainly to aristocrats. If they had large debts the prince often graciously paid them, nobles were mostly exempt from taxes, and if they committed crimes they were not seldom treated much more mildly than commoners.

The cleavage between the upper and the middle classes was deeper in Germany than in England, where a strong royalty, the Church and the power of money had early brought about the end of feudalism and a certain national and social unity. German particularism bred not only national but also social disintegration. Every rank and class was split into different sections imbued with mutual jealousy. The high nobility did not regard the lower as being of equal blood and did not intermarry with them. The lesser nobles usually behaved in the same way towards commoners. English and French law did not recognize the legal principle of equality of birth (Ebenbürtigkeit) Haughty exclusiveness could be found in all aristocracies, but in Germany it was particularly pronounced. The old families looked down on those of younger titles, there was animosity between the urban and rural nobles, and so on. A factor fostering excessive consciousness of rank was that most German nobles were not wealthy.[3] Many a poor nobleman sought to counter-

[3] Towards the end of the 18th century there were about 1475 Free Knights who had the rights of rulers, though their title was usually only baron, and in some cases count. They had 2,870 landed estates, ca 450,000 subjects, and an income of 2,400.000 Gulden. The average income of a knight was therefore

vail his financial straits by stressing that his pedigree was much more exalted than that of other nobles possessing more money and power, especially if they had bought their title.

The lack of means also induced many nobles to abstain from attending the diets of the Estates. They feared the expenses and tended to transfer the functions of the Estates to small committees composed of nobles who were better situated. This suited the rulers well since they could more easily deal with a few wealthy magnates than with numerous poor knights.

It would, however, be a great mistake to overlook that the German nobility comprised many different types. Nobles who in the Thirty Years' War had served as generals or colonels sometimes brought home fortunes, mostly the result of ruthless plunder, and used it to buy estates. Others had received large donations from the Emperor for their service, or had bought confiscated possessions of rebels at a cheap price. Some regions had been little affected by the war while in others the manor houses of the nobles had been sacked and burnt down, and their land had been devastated. There was also a great proletariat of noblemen which already existed long before the war, and which went back to the old robber knights. Gustav Freytag has given a description of the life of the Krippenreiter, as they were called. They lived by extorting money, victuals etc. from squires, burghers and peasants, by means of violence and fraud.[4] In certain regions there were also many noblemen who were farmers and did not differ much from well situated peasants. The Emperor ennobled many of his leading officials, or sold titles to rich upstarts. The rise of absolutism originated standing armies, large bureaucracies and extensive courts, and with them new types of aristocracies. In many Catholic territories the bishops and other prelates were elected by noble canons, who mostly chose a local noble.

The Imperial Court of Vienna attracted nobles from most countries of Europe as well as Austria, and had an international character. Many of the aristocrats were very rich, possessing large estates in Bohemia, Hungary etc. A considerable number distinguished themselves as statesmen or as military leaders, and there were not a few who showed a keen cultural interest. They built splendid palaces, collected art treasures, cultivated the theatre and music and were patrons of scholars and artists. There were mag-

ca 1600 fl or 160 Pound Sterling. The average number of subjects per knight was ca 300. The income per head of the population was therefore not quite 11 shillings in English currency. This was already a section of the nobility which possessed wealth.

[4] Similar conditions existed also in Swabia. Cf. K.H. v. Lang, Memoiren 1842. I, p. 31.

nates who did much to promote agricultural and industrial progress on their land while others found this beneath their dignity. In many Austrian territories, however, sections of the nobility had a good record both in public affairs and in cultural matters. Adam Wolf, and recently Otto Brunner, have given us most informative studies of the personalities of Austrian lords. It is surprising to learn how many of them possessed great libraries, made serious studies, and wrote remarkable books. Some also devoted themselves to great causes, sacrificing their personal interest to their ideals.

From numerous examples the following may be quoted.[5] Count F. A. Sporck (1662-1738) was the grandson of a Westphalian peasant who was unfree but wealthy. This serf had a son who rose to the position of a general in the imperial army and became a count. His son, F. A. Sporck, promoted cultural interests in a grand way and also was an always helpful friend of his peasants and a philanthropist. Among the numerous patrons of art Prince Eusebius Karl Liechtenstein was particularly prominent and the picture gallery collected by him and his successors is still the greatest private one in Europe. Count Leopold Berchtold dedicated his whole life to humanitarian aims. He did not only make donations for them but undertook many travels to countries where people were suffering in order to find means of relief. In England he was called 'the German Howard'.

The publisher Friedrich Nicolai, who played a great rôle in the literary life of his time, also studied conditions in various parts of Germany. Though he was very prejudiced against Austria he admits in the book on his travels (V. p. 289), that the Austrian noblemen showed less pride and haughtiness towards the middle class than the nobles in many other parts of the Empire and that, in particular they treated non-Nobles of merit with the greatest politeness. The memoirs of the time relate many facts confirming this, though this observation must, of course, not be generalized. There were certainly many other types too.

F. W. von Taube, a senior Austrian official of North German descent, ascribed the great rôle of Austrian noblemen to the fact that landed estates yielded from 5 to 6%, and even 7%, in Austria, but only the half in Northern Germany. Moreover, he said, the Austrian nobles live mainly in towns while the North German ones reside in their estates in the country. French aristocrats often remarked that the Prussian Junkers accepted posts which were beneath the dignity of a nobleman because of their poverty.

[5] For details see the books indicated in the bibliographical notes.

THE NOBILITY AND CULTURAL DEVELOPMENT

Similar examples could be found in many other parts of Germany though the nobles with cultural aspirations certainly formed a minor section everywhere. A large proportion were either indifferent to higher interests, or imbued with class prejudice and egotism, or more or less corrupted by the ways of life in high society, in particular cultivated at numerous courts. Yet there were also rulers and nobles of better dispositions. Just before the outbreak of the Thirty Years' War, in 1617, several princes and aristocrats from Anhalt and Weimar founded a society named Fruchtbringende Gesellschaft (Fruit-bearing Society) or Palmenorden (Palm-Order). Its aim was the maintenance of morality and good manners, and particularly the cultivation of the German language and its preservation from corruption by foreign elements. Prince Ludwig of Anhalt became its president, and his successors were also princes. A few years later already it had 200 members, mainly princes, noblemen and scholars from the middle class. When, in 1648, the proposition was put forward to admit only nobles as members, Prince Ludwig turned it down, saying that in the thirty-one years since the society's foundation it had always been assumed that scholars were noblemen. Quite a number of similar societies was founded. Many untitled scholars and poets belonged to them, and important work was done for the improvement of the language and literature. In the 17th century, and later, a remarkable number of nobles wrote poetry themselves, or were in close touch with poets. Many authors were ennobled for their merits. This tendency would have been still greater if a very large section of the aristocracy had not been exclusively attracted to French literature, which then was, indeed, on a much higher level than the German, and had attained its golden age. Moreover, the prestige of Louis XIV had made the adoption of the French language, civilization and customs the ruling fashion in high society.

These remarks show that the German nobility was not entirely prevented by pride of rank from mixing with non-nobles in cultural activities. Other examples of freedom from aristocratic prejudice were given by the numerous nobles who joined the Pietists or became Jesuits. In the age of Enlightenment movements stressing human brotherhood, such as Freemasonry, Philanthropism and the Illuminati attracted a large proportion of the nobles.

C*

THE COMMERCIAL AND INDUSTRIAL CLASSES

A wealthy and united middle class was missing in Germany and this had great political consequences. Individual men of substance existed, but no class comparable to the English or Dutch merchants or the gentry. The urban patriciate had partly kept their capital, especially if their grandfathers had in time withdrawn from business and invested their money in land. The experience that many of the great bankers of Augsburg and Nuremberg had been ruined because the kings to whom they had lent money defaulted, was not forgotten. Most urban patricians, however, regarded trade as beneath their aristocratic dignity, though others were less prejudiced. In Frankfurt, for example, there were two patrician gilds, Limpurg and Frauenstein. The members of the former did not trade, the members of the latter might be wholesale merchants. The Hanse towns were anti-aristocratic. In Hamburg, Luebeck and Bremen titled burghers were not elected town councillors. In South Germany, however, it was often complained that merchants who had become rich soon bought a title and retired from business, wishing to be recognized as equals by the nobility. Large fortunes were earned by contractors or financiers in times of great wars. Most rulers, even the greatest, were then compelled to take loans at very high interest rates. They did not even spurn borrowing a small amount from one of their officials or a professor. But the great contractors were mostly Jews who had many international contacts and were able to get money from abroad, which they lent to princes. The Court-Jews played then a very great part in finance.[6] All these and other facts show how scarce liquid capital was.

The middle classes, too, were divided into sections separated from one another by privileges and mutual animosity. The town governments were usually in the hands of old families who like the princes and nobles regarded their powers as patrimonial and therefore used them for their own enrichment. This led to many quarrels of these classes with the artisans and small traders. These and the workers were full of spite against the privileged sections of the burghers. Internal strife also contributed to the decline of the position of the Free Towns. The old walls were no longer a protection against artillery and, moreover, were usually in a very bad state owing to financial straits. This helped the princes to establish their sovereignty over certain towns whose status had long been

---

[6] Schnee's great work on the Court-Jews gives a most interesting picture of their activities, which prepared the way for the emancipation of the Jews.

controversial. They also founded new towns, partly in order to attract industries.

Yet there were still towns which were free and prospering. Hamburg greatly increased her trade, though largely as an entrepôt of English and French commerce. Leipzig and Breslau, though legally subject to rulers, had great autonomy and profited from the trade with Poland and Russia, Frankfurt was the chief financial centre and shared with Leipzig the trade in books. Most of the towns were small. The larger ones had between 30,000 and 50,000 inhabitants. But there were Free Towns comprising no more than 1,000 or 2,000 people. Some of the larger ones, however, possessed also a rural area whose population was shown separately from that of the city. The largest town was Vienna, the seat of the imperial government. Its population towards the end of the 18th century was stated as 268,000, including the suburbs outside the walls. Berlin had ca 145,000. Among the Free Towns Hamburg was the largest with about 100,000 inhabitants. In 1700 London already had 674,000 and Paris half a million inhabitants. Towards the end of the 18th century, Paris had about 670,000 and London 865,000. But it was not the mere number of inhabitants which was decisive for shaping the public mind. What was missing in Germany was primarily a great centre of intellectual life and politics such as Paris and London. The growth of such a centre was prevented by the power of particularism. Its absence, however, was not widely regarded as a misfortune. In England and France the growth of the capitals aroused great misgivings, and several kings tried to check it, mainly because of the risk of a revolution. In Germany no town included the elements needed for a revolution, and even if there had been one, it could not have swept the country with it. As regards Vienna, her social structure was adverse to such an event. She was situated at the periphery of the German Empire and was remote from the Protestant German towns which were the main seats of trade and learning. Vienna's intellectual life was more dominated by Italian and Spanish models than by French, Dutch and English ones as in Protestant Germany. Her trade looked eastwards, not towards Germany. Berlin, too, could for obvious reasons not become a national centre.

The lack of social unity among the middle classes was paralleled by a similar condition in the lower classes. It has already been shown that the peasants who formed the great majority of the people were divided into a very great number of sections differing in legal status and in interests. They did not by any means form a class with a feeling of solidarity and the same was also the case among the industrial workers. There were, further, sections which were practically outcasts. Even the common man could look down on people still more despised than he. The development of customary law had led to the separation of numerous groups of people from the normal life of the community. They were regarded as unrespectable and were subject to manifold disabilities, especially exclusion from the guilds. Their descendants, too, were branded with legal or social inferiority. Among them were illegitimate children, shepherds, millers, bath-keepers, linen weavers, hangmen, knackers; many public employees of low rank, such as beadles, summoners, night-watchmen, customs men, gravediggers etc. But also comedians, gleemen, and certain musicians were not considered honourable. Some of the categories were even untouchable. If someone shook hands with the hangman he was regarded as being as infamous as the latter. The Reichstag, the Emperor and other rulers often tried to abolish or mitigate discrimination against some of these groups. But the common man stubbornly clung to his superstitious prejudices. Soldiering too was a widely despised occupation.

THE INTELLECTUAL CLASSES

It has already been mentioned that the division of Germany into numerous states caused the foundation of a very great number of universities, academies and colleges though many of them were small. In the 18th century England had two universities only and they were in a bad state.[7] The great number of German universities sometimes had favourable consequences because it encouraged competition in research and also enabled scholars ahead of their time to put forward their views. The foundation of the universities of Halle and Goettingen, for example, opened an epoch in the history of German learning, as they introduced a new spirit into the study of many branches. But the abundance of universities fostered adverse tendencies also. Students had always and in all countries been an unruly element, although in the middle ages they had lived in colleges and hostels and were subject to a certain discipline. In Germany, however, this system disappeared while in England it survived, safeguarding discipline. German particularism led to constant jealousies and rows between the students from different German territories, who were organized into fraternities according to their homelands. This state of things was then called nationalism.

[7] Cf. G. M. Trevelyan, *History of England*, 1952 p. 521. Nevertheless English thought and learning were flourishing. Scotland had 4 universities.

Each little territory was regarded as a nation in the mediaeval sense of the word.[8] In English university life this kind of division had never played a great rôle, though there had often been fights between the Northerners and the Southerners. In Germany, however, it was one of the factors which rendered the relations between students very turbulent. Students from different territories looked upon one another as enemies and were eager to provoke clashes and fights. Duelling was not a German custom and was unknown in the middle ages; it originated in France where the aristocracy practised it almost as a sport, and this habit then spread in Germany also, and particularly among the students. Heavy drinking had always been a widespread vice in Germany, even at the courts of princes and among the clergy. The students too were addicts and they framed a system of rules enforcing an excessive consumption of alcohol.

Already at the beginning of the 17th century the conduct of a large section of students aroused the gravest complaints, and the Thirty Years' War increased the evil to the utmost. In the war many universities, libraries etc. were destroyed or plundered, the revenues vanished, numerous students and also professors were forced to become soldiers to earn a living, and acquired the habits of the soldiery of the time. The result was that many universities became the seat of the worst demoralization and brutality, though not all of them were equally bad. At the Catholic universities the Jesuits kept discipline and when Pietism gained influence in the Protestant universities conditions improved there, but many others were blemished by the grossest dissoluteness and brawls between sections of the students, who also terrorized the others. The rector and the senate could incarcerate rowdies. But often they preferred to be lenient because the fraternities threatened that otherwise they would migrate as a whole to another university, which would have greatly damaged the financial interest of the professors and the town. The large number of universities facilitated this blackmailing. The government had often to intervene. If a duel resulted in the death of one of the students the other was legally liable to be executed as a murderer but he often escaped this penalty. Sometimes the rulers had to call up the Burgher guard against the rioting students. However, with the progress of enlightenment many students formed

[8] Buesching, the greatest German geographer, relates in his description of Germany that the Germans consisted of many nations and showed great differences of character and customs. Nicolai emphasized how difficult it was for a North German to understand an Austrian, and that the Austrians often could not understand the Bavarians. He also pointed out that the difference of religion led to a great diversity in the character and even the physiognomy of Catholics and Protestants.

clubs in order to cultivate a better spirit and this had some results. But often the old evil spirit got the upper hand again.

The universities still resembled states within the state. The Rector was entitled to princely honours, and in some places the soldiers presented arms when he appeared. Among the faculties the theological had the highest status. In the 17th century Protestant princes consulted the theological faculty of their university in the most important political questions. In Leipzig a theologian was addressed as Excellency. The jurists formed the second category, they were legally equal to the nobility, were often asked by the princes for advice in questions of public law, and frequently had to decide difficult cases of law. The students of the humanities formed the lowest faculty, and the nobles looked down upon the 'schoolmasters'. The salaries of professors were usually low, but they had perquisites, in some places for example the right to brew beer for their own use. The earnings from books were also very low, and frequently a professor had to pay the cost of printing. Yet we know of scholars who possessed very large libraries, comprising 10,000, 30,000 or even 50,000 volumes, or who had their private observatories, laboratories etc. This seems to show that wealthy men, too, became professors. A characteristic feature of the age was the number of 'polyhistors', who possessed great learning in many fields. They often had incomes from various different sources. The fact that many expensive books could be published shows that there was a public interested in them and able to pay the price. The publisher Johann Heinrich Zedler of Leipzig brought out an enormous Encyclopedia in 68 volumes folio, comprising 67.325 pages (1732-54). It was published by subscription, and besides had the financial assistance of a wealthy Leipzig merchant J. H. Wolff. A staff of professors edited it, and it became an accumulation of knowledge unparalleled in any country. Its general outlook was progressive.

The prospects of members of the professions depended on the wealth of the public. In England a lawyer or writer could earn much money since the country was rich and its wealth was rapidly increasing. But in Germany the chances were not good, except for a section of the lawyers. The multitude of states and the complexity of social and legal conditions gave many lawyers the opportunity of endlessly protracting a law-suit for their own profit but to the detriment of their clients. Rulers wishing to reform the law therefore laid great stress on setting an end to this practice. An author, however, could before the second half of the 18th century hardly live on the returns of his books, at least not in poetry and fiction. If one scans the names of the German poets in the earlier part of the age one finds that they were either rich patricians or nobles, or had a secure post leaving them sufficient free time, or had a prince or nobleman as patron. The others starved. Most books are preceded by a dedication to a high personality, full of flattery. The purpose of this custom was to maintain the favour of a patron.

The chance of getting a post in the service of a ruler or town or nobleman was comparatively not bad. The organization of the new type of state demanded a greatly increased number of officials, especially of lawyers. The old Schoeffen (jurymen) were replaced by judges learned in the Roman Law, and appointed by the ruler. But the governments also needed every other kind of people with higher qualifications. The fact that each State was still divided into provinces with separate laws and institutions necessitated a much greater number of officials than in a centralized state. The pay was usually very meagre, the officials had long no claim to a pension, and could at any time be dismissed. But a young man in search of a post had no great choice. The German intellectuals therefore to a great extent depended on the chance of finding employment in the service of a prince. This naturally also had a great influence on their political attitude. Many officials, professors and writers showed a spirit of great servility towards princes and nobles. Yet the belief in the necessity of a strong monarchical power did not exclude the striving for liberal reforms. Enlightened rulers were the hope of the progressive elements. When, towards the end of the century, the striving for freedom and nationhood made headway, it was mainly noblemen, civil servants and scholars who were its spokesmen.

THE JEWS

The Jews had, in the middle ages, been much persecuted in all countries of Europe, and had been completely expelled from the states where the government was centralized as in England, France or Spain. In Germany they were never driven out as a whole, but in many Free Towns they became often the victims of frenzied mobs and were robbed, slain or forced to flee. A great proportion found refuge in Poland, but in Germany too there were always territories where they were admitted and could exist. Popes, bishops, emperors, kings and princes were on the whole much more tolerant than the artisans and traders of the towns, who hated them as usurers or for alleged crimes, such as spreading the plague or ritual murder. But in many cases the town authorities soon found that the Jews were needed for financial reasons and admitted a number again, though

under great restrictions. In the four centuries following the middle
ages princes gradually replaced the feudal institutions in their
countries by those of a modern state, they created standing armies
and large numbers of officials, maintained splendid courts, and
waged great wars. For these purposes much money was needed and
the Estates were everywhere unwilling, and often unable, to vote
the amounts required. These conditions gave many Jews the opportunity to play a paramount rôle in financing the new policies, and
soon there was hardly a court without its Court Jew, or close relations with Jewish bankers. They advised the rulers how to raise
money from their countries without the consent of the Estates, they
advanced them large amounts on securities, they used their contacts with capitalists in many countries to arrange large loans; they
also delivered supplies to the armies, took over the mint, and so on.
The Habsburg Emperors were foremost in making use of their services, but soon all the other dynasties followed their example.
Fmperor Ferdinand II even ennobled the Jewish banker Jacob
Bassevi in Prague with the title 'von Treuenberg' which means
'mountain of faithfulness'. Many Court Jews served their princes
well. But there were naturally also many who cared more for their
own profit than for that of their masters. In any case they made
themselves many enemies, and not a few were later prosecuted
and sentenced to death, or became bankrupt, since the government
was unable to pay its debts or raised counterclaims. Yet certain
Jewish families became so outstanding, not only by their wealth
but also by unshakeable reliability, that they formed a kind of international aristocracy. Ruling princes treated them accordingly. A
similar position was held by the great Jewish merchant bankers of
Hamburg, who in the 17th century had come as refugees from
Portugal and had greatly contributed to Hamburg's commercial
development by their knowledge of the markets for colonial products. Many Jews also obtained a great reputation as physicians and
scholars. Count Palatine Karl Ludwig even offered the chair of
philosophy in Heidelberg to Spinoza.

This position of a narrow circle was, however, in glaring contrast
to that of the great majority of Jews, who lived in the most unfavourable, insecure and humiliating circumstances. In most German
territories the Jews were in principle excluded from settlement and
from almost all sources of making a living except such despised by
most people. They could obtain permits to exercise certain trades,
if the government regarded it as in the public interest, and they had
to pay for the privilege. In any case the government wished to prevent any considerable increase in the number of Jews. Jewish

beggars were expelled. But the danger often arose that all Jews from a certain region, or of a certain state, would be driven out. In Austria this happened three times within 74 years but was always revoked quickly, because it turned out to be prejudicious to the state finance. Frederick II too once threatened a mass expulsion. In many places Jews had to pay a toll on entering a town. Sometimes princes put obligations on the Jews for which there was no reasonable justification. Frederick William I ordered that the wild pigs killed during court chases must be bought by the Jews, obviously only because their religion forbade them pork. Frederick the Great ordered that Jews must, when they married, buy products of the state porcelain factory and they were forced to buy such which otherwise were not saleable.

The Jews were generally considered an alien people, and shared this opinion themselves. They usually lived separated from the Christians in ghettos, which often consisted of a single street, overcrowded and filthy. They were only permitted to leave it in certain cases and were not allowed to mix with Christians on promenades etc. Their communities had a great autonomy. The rabbis were often called in from Poland where orthodoxy was particularly rigid. Among themselves the Jews spoke their own jargon, and the learning of literary German might be punished with expulsion from the community.

Under all these circumstances it was easy to understand that a great number of the Jews indulged in dishonest practices to earn a living, and that there was also among them a considerable criminal element. Jews played a greal rôle as receivers of stolen goods, as robbers, leaders of gangs, smugglers etc. Numerous cartoons showing their criminal activities and final execution contributed towards exacerbating public opinion against them.

Nevertheless, a great number of Jews gradually succeeded in overcoming all the barriers keeping them aloof from other people, and in making valuable contributions to economic and cultural development. In particular, they engaged in new industries and trades in which there was little competition, and where the government encouraged newcomers. They formed the mainstay of the Leipzig trade fair, where they were foremost in carrying on trade with Poland, Russia and other eastern countries. In the textile trade too they were very active. The economic rise of the Jews prepared the way for their emancipation.

ECONOMIC CONDITIONS AND POLITICAL OPINIONS

Political aspirations are largely determined by economic and social conditions, and it would therefore be desirable that we should give a picture of Germany's development in these respects. In spite of much information being available about local and regional facts, however, it is not possible to integrate them to a whole. The statistics of the age show too many gaps and data which cannot be combined. As regards the two large states of Austria and Prussia, there is no doubt that their economic resources increased considerably in the second half of the 18th century. Their governments settled great numbers of people on land which previously was not, or little, cultivated. They also made every effort to improve the methods of production and to promote industries and commerce. How far they succeeded in improving economic and social conditions is difficult to say, because the methods of the dominating system of mercantilism sometimes showed fallacious results. Its statistics recorded the increase in the output of certain industries subsidized but not the decreases in other productions which were the victims of the policy of mercantilism. We can therefore only give a few statistical data likely to show the general tendency of development.

When Frederick II died Prussia's total industries had 150,155 workers. At that time in the Austrian provinces of Bohemia and Moravia the textile industries alone employed 800,000 workers of whom 150,000 were working at newly established looms in Bohemia. The great majority of the textile workers, however, did not yet operate in factories, but in domestic industries. As regards agriculture, statistics show that in the Prussian province of Kurmark the weight of the principal seeds sown (plus potatoes planted) increased in Frederick's long reign by 23.4%, which is not a considerable rise though crops probably increased by a larger percentage. In Saxony, where the peasants were mostly free, and economic policy more liberal, the results were better. The prominent historian Boettiger states that in 1755 6 millions Scheffel (bushels) of grain were harvested, and 17 millions in 1801, or almost three times more. Single years however are not comparable, because crops depend on the weather. The total weight of cereals, legumes and potatoes harvested in Saxony doubled from 1755 to 1799. The number of domestic animals, converted into units[9], increased in Saxony in the seven years from the average 1768-72 to the average 1786-87 by

[9] According to the usual key: 1 cattle equivalent to 2/3 horse or to 4 pigs or to 10 sheep.

40.6%. The silver output was 32,000 Mark in 1778, and 50,000 Mark in 1788. The movement of German trade is best indicated by the turnover of the Leipzig fair, which was the greatest market for the exchange of goods between the east and west of Europe. The Easter and Michaelmas fairs had in 1750 5,281 visitors, in 1775—9,062, and in 1800—10,487. A very important indicator of the movements of trade was the turnover of the Hamburg Giro Bank. It amounted in 1774 to 232 millions Mark Banco and in 1781 to 343 millions. This may have been typical for Germany's trade. But the increase to 900 millions in 1798, and to 1,506 millions in 1799, were not typical, since they were largely due to the fact that the political events compelled Dutch trade to move to Hamburg.

Many further statistics could be quoted showing that Germany's and Austria's output and trade were rising vigorously in the second half of the 18th century. But there also was much social misery. Masses of dismissed soldiers and other uprooted elements were roaming about living on begging, blackmailing, theft and robbery. Many peasants were hard hit by the consequences of militarism, fiscalism and mercantilism, and tried to emigrate. Labourers, women and children were much exploited in the new factories and cottage industries.

In the German and Austrian countries, however, economic progress had not enough time to unfold its long range political consequences undisturbed by war. After the Thirty Years' War and the long wars with Louis XIV and the Turks came the aggressions of Frederick II, and then those of the French Republic and Napoleon. Though war furthered the development of certain industries, it greatly hampered a sound economic evolution, a substantial increase of wealth, and a rise of the classes favourable to liberalism.

5

POLITICAL THOUGHT IN THE 17TH CENTURY

THE LEGACY OF THE PAST AND THE PROBLEMS OF THE AGE

THE political ideas of modern times have usually a very long history. Their origins can be traced to the Bible and the doctrines of the Church, to old Germanic traditions preserved in medieval laws or declarations, to the Greek and Roman writers and particularly to Roman Law, to the Reformation and the great struggles caused by it. All these sources contain important rules and observations forming the historical foundations for all the later political thought. Besides the general problems each age and each people has had its special ones demanding preferential treatment. For Germany the most urgent task was to rebuild the economic life and finance utterly devastated by the Thirty Years' War. It was not enough, however, merely to restore former conditions. The war had initiated a great intellectual revolution, the belief in old standards and authorities had broken down, and the intellectuals were longing for a new order based on reason and the law of nature. In addition the Peace Treaties had laid down a constitution for the Empire making the princes nearly sovereign and thereby weakening the central power still more. France had become the strongest power, and soon the reign of Louis XIV was to proclaim to the world the superiority of an unlimited monarchy. The revolutions in the Netherlands and in England, however, seemed to teach the opposite lesson. Many events, internal and external, demanded the creation of new forms of State, equipping the government with much greater powers than the former half-feudal régime had possessed. Standing armies and large bureaucracies were needed, costing vast amounts of money. The Estates strongly opposed these innovations, and often showed themselves less progressive than the princes. In many German territories this opposition brought about the decline of the Estates and the triumph of absolutism.

The defeat of the Estates often opened the road to a new organization of the administration which in some territories had been largely in the hands of the Estates. But there were also other forces exercising an authority competing with that of the government. In Catholic countries the Church formed a sort of state within the state. In Protestant territories the ruler was the head of the Church. But everywhere there was great ecclesiastical influence on matters of law, justice and politics. Many towns had great autonomy. The trade guilds claimed the right of determining who should be entitled to exercise their trade, and not seldom hindered economic development. The noble landowners had their feudal courts which often could even pass sentences of death. The opinion was widespread that the ruler had no right to interfere in old privileges concerning public powers. But in a modern state the government alone can hold public powers such as legislation, jurisdiction, taxation and so on. The development from the feudal to the modern state demanded a unification of these powers in the hands of one government, a task which only strong rulers could solve.[1]

THE RIGHT OF RESISTANCE TO DESPOTISM BY THE PEOPLE

The question of whether resistance to arbitrary government was permitted had formed the subject of fierce struggles in the past. It had already emerged in the middle ages in the conflicts between Pope and Emperor, and also played a great rôle in the strife between princes and Estates, between the religious parties after the Reformation, in the Dutch and English revolutions, and so on. Kurt Wolzendorff has written a masterly history of these controversies, and students of this problem are referred to this indispensible work. The arguments of the enemies of despotism were either based on historic statements of constitutional law, or on the idea of a law of nature and of the social contract in which a people was assumed to have transferred its power to a ruler, who was therefore an employee of the people. This theory is much older than Rousseau's version, it was put forward in the middle ages already by Marsilius of Padua, the

[1] In England, of course, the unification of the law, justice, currency etc. had already been achieved centuries earlier owing to the fact that William the Conqueror and his successors were legally the owners of the whole land by the right of conquest and the only overlord of the feudal forces. On the continent, and particularly in Germany, there were always a multitude of powers claiming public authority in their own right.

German monk Manegold of Lauterbach, and others. The Reformers tried to reconcile it with the words of the Gospel forbidding resistance. In many cases German Estates had, in concluding agreements with their prince, expressly reserved the right of resistance if he should break them. Many publicists further tried to define the cases of tyranny against which resistance was permitted, they discussed who was entitled to resist and how. Grotius found seven cases justifying revolt. Althusius' doctrine on this problem was particularly successful in being accepted by various writers. A frequently made point was that only Estates were entitled to start a revolt. Other authors denied the right of active resistance except in extreme cases.

The book by Wolzendorff gives the names and opinions of numerous German and other publicists who in the 17th and 18th centuries discussed the right of resistance. The great majority of them accepted this right. But it was very difficult, if not impossible, to define with juristic precision which conditions justified a revolt. The great German Peasant War and other risings had shown that even the revolutionary movements striving for rightful aims often resulted in anarchy and disastrous consequences.

IDEAS ON CONSTITUTIONAL QUESTIONS

The controversies on the right of resistance contributed much to thought on constitutional law. Jurisprudence alone could not solve all problems. The study of history, economics and politics was equally needed. In Germany the so-called Cameralists were particularly fertile in putting forward plans of reforms and discussing them from many points of view. Many of them were the counsellors of rulers, had a great practical experience in public affairs, and had studied conditions in foreign countries. But scholars versed in the philosophy and history of ancient Greece and Rome also had much to say about politics. The ancient thinkers had much discussed the merits and demerits of the different forms of state, and had often come to the conclusion that a mixed constitution combining elements of the monarchy, aristocracy and democracy would be the best one.

Christoph Besold (1577-1638), a Wurttemberger, was a famous professor of law and political science, distinguished by enormous learning. His conversion from Lutheranism to Catholicism made a great stir. He saw in the Catholic Church an institution moderating monarchical absolutism. He held that no form of state was the best in all conditions, but that it depended on the national character which constitution was best suited for a people. A republican constitution would appear to have the greatest merits and also to be the most pleasing to God. But it was like an instrument the playing of which was most difficult to learn, and which was most liable to get out of tune. Besold was therefore neither a republican nor a believer in monarchical absolutism. In all realms founded by Germans, he wrote, an unrestricted monarchy is abhorred. The Estates must have the right to decide on public finance and to control expenditure. Besold condemned 'the new politicians returning from Italy who are convinced that a prince is fully entitled to squeeze money from his subjects by any fraud, misusing for this purpose the teachings of Machiavelli.' He also had many sound views on economics and finance; he was, for example, against the exemption of the nobles from taxes, the misuses of the trade guilds, the prohibition of loans with interests, state monopolies, depreciating the currency, the formation of large estates at the expense of peasant holdings, and so on.

Among the writers on economics and finance Georg Obrecht (1547-1612), professor at the University of Strasbourg had a certain importance as a representative of the school of Regalists who laid great stress on covering the State expenses by other means than by direct taxes, requiring a vote of the Estates. This policy was naturally convenient to a régime of absolutism, and had been much developed in France. Obrecht wanted the government to direct all the activities of the economic organism, of which it formed the brain, and to charge fees for licences, to tax luxuries, to sell titles and offices, to make profits from trading, and so on. In particular, he proposed that the state should run a comprehensive system of insurances against many risks, which was useful to the common weal, and a source of revenue for the exchequer.

Another economist of repute was Jacob Bornitz, a Saxon who visited many countries of Europe studying economic conditions, later lived in Silesia and was a lawyer and imperial counsellor. In his books he points out that the perfection of a State depends on the right proportion between public and private income. He rejects the communism of Plato, Thomas More and others, but wishes to give the government wide powers to regulate all economic activities. The governments, however, should not manage industrial or commercial enterprises themselves, except in special cases. He strongly warns against the selling of offices and against depreciating the money without the utmost necessity and the assent of the people. Bornitz was a convinced mercantilist, and discusses many ways of increasing the amount of money within the state. Taxes should be moderate, and correspond to the income of those taxed.

The most important writer on finance was Kaspar Klock, who held high posts in North West Germany. In his work on taxes (1634) he defends the rights of the Estates. Every imposition of a new tax without the consent of the subjects is tyranny. He complains of the misuse of the Bible (I Sam. 8) to justify absolutism, and opposes the 'new politicians and Machiavellians' who want to give the ruler unrestricted powers. But the experience of the Thirty Years' War and the English revolution seem to have changed his opinions. In his last work, published in 1651, he shows sympathy for Stuart absolutism and calls Cromwell and Fairfax murderers of their father. The Puritan Revolution was followed with great attention in Germany, and the execution of Charles I aroused much indignation. But there were also many sympathizers with the revolutionaries, especially at the universities.

For a long time already the rising power of particularism had set students of public law wondering what were the legal positions of the Emperor and the Estates. In 1576 Jean Bodin had formulated the concept of sovereignty, or the supreme power in a state. He had also discussed the question in whom sovereignty resided, and had come to the conclusion that in France it was the King, in Germany the Estates. France was therefore a monarchy and Germany an aristocracy. This argument was taken up by the defenders of German particularism and a long controversy followed, which has been surveyed in Stintzing's learned History of German Jurisprudence.

Dominicus Arumaeus (1579-1637), professor at Jena, taught that sovereignty resided in the Reichstag, and came very near to the doctrine of the sovereignty of the people put forward by Althusius. Both scholars were Frisians, and strongly influenced by the spirit of the Netherlands. Arumaeus' most prominent disciple was Johann Limnaeus (1592-1663), who wrote the first systematic work on German constitutional law. His most distinguished opponent was Friedrich Reinking (1599-1664) who wrote in favour of the authority of the Emperor. But Reinking was by no means a defender of unrestricted absolutism. He even admitted a right of resistance to the Emperor if he violated the divine and natural law, or the constitution of the Empire, and if resistance was absolutely necessary. Both Limnaeus and Reinking were also practical statesmen, and men of the highest integrity.

Hermann Conring (1606-1681), a Frisian, was a scholar of stupendous learning. He was a professor at the University of Helmstaedt in Brunswick, where he lectured on medicine, law, politics, economics and history. Moreover, he became physician and privy counsellor to several kings and princes. His main achievements lay in the field of the history of law, and he criticized the exaggerated views concerning the validity of the Roman law, emphasizing the importance of legal doctrines of Germanic origin. Conring also tried to found a science of practical politics based on the study of many countries in a statistical and sociological sense. His historical mind made him a relativist. In his view it depended on the special circumstances of a country, and the national character, whether a political system proves good or bad. The supreme aim of politics is the public weal, which requires the maintenance of law, order and peace. Conring was often consulted about political questions by German and foreign rulers. He belonged to the school hostile to the Habsburgs and a strong emperorship, and defended the sovereignty of the princes. This brought him a considerable pension from Louis XIV; he was eager to defend the French King's policy, and wished that he might become Emperor of Germany, and King of Italy and Spain, too. The French government was even compelled to admonish him to moderate his zeal. But Conring was really convinced that the renewal of Charlemagne's Empire by the French king was in the best interests of Germany and Europe. He was not a glorifier of absolutism. The absolutist tendency in Roman Law was odious to him, and he wrote that as regards taxes it was on the whole unworthy of a Christian prince to strive for absolute power. But his relativism induced him to declare that it depended on the spirit of the people and the prince whether the right of taxation should be in the hands of the ruler, though he himself was favourably disposed to the rights of the Estates. Conring regarded it as unworthy of a scholar to write in any other language than Latin, since he had not to serve the interests of one nation alone but wrote for the international republic of scholars.

THE REASON OF STATE

The rise of absolutism was closely connected with the spreading of the idea of the Reason of State which in our age Meinecke has traced in an admirable book. Italy, France and England were the countries where it developed. In France the classical example was the massacre of St Bartholomew. In the Thirty Years' War monarchical absolutism made progress in Germany too, and with it the Reason of State. Wallenstein's assassination was its most striking example. However, long before it had been discussed in a book by Professor Arnold Clapmarius (Klapmeier) from Bremen, a Calvinist

His book on the Arcana of Politics (1605) gave rise to a whole
literature. Every state, he said, whether monarchical, aristocratic or
democratic is faced with specific dangers which it can often only
overcome by means which are not in accordance with strict legality.
Yet they should not be contrary to religion and morality. A people
striving for liberty or great power can only be kept in bounds by
giving them simulacra or phantoms of them. Further, certain
situations may justify the establishment of a legitimate tyranny or
dictatorship. Aristotle has shown how even in the democratic states
of Greece the aristocrats understood how to keep the power in their
own hands while the people believed that they were the sovereign.
The Roman Emperors too, as Tacitus and others showed, made the
people believe that they had the power, though in fact the power
was with the Emperor. In the defence of the security of the State
the ruler may disregard private rights. But he must in this respect
not go too far because otherwise his conduct would become
criminal. In particular, he must not apply illegitimate measures to
further his own private interests. In war he must not order the
poisoning of wells or weapons, or the killing of women and children, or the destruction of the enemy's property without necessity.
The murder of a tyrant is justified. These examples show that
Clapmarius was much more moderate in permitting illegalities in
the public interest than Machiavelli and most of his followers. He
deliberately avoided, however, discussing German constitutional
questions.

The arguments of the Reason of State and German Liberty were
put forward to defend particularism and Protestantism by Bogislaus
Philipp Chemnitz (1605-1678). He was of German origin, his family
had brought forth prominent Lutheran theologians, and in the great
war he served in the Swedish army. He later became Royal Swedish
Historiographer, and was ennobled by Queen Christina. In 1640 he
published, under the pseudonym Hippolithus a Lapide, a book
entitled 'The Reason of State in our Roman-German Empire'. This
book caused a great sensation. It contained the most vehement
attack on the policy of the House of Habsburg which then seemed
to have triumphed over its enemies. Chemnitz' authorship was never
openly admitted.

The author explains the term Reason of State in the title of his
book as the hidden and secret rules of policy, the true interests of
States, in contrast to the ideas of formalistic lawyers and believers
in political illusions. Human nature often makes it necessary to hide
the real motives of policy, for man is the most unruly of all
animals. The happiness of the citizens requires the maintenance and

the strength of the state, and this often cannot be secured within the limits of legality. Necessity knows no law. But the author stresses that the Reason of State must observe the laws of religion and morality. Chemnitz follows Bodin in rejecting the idea of a mixed constitution which is only a utopia. The practice of government is more important than the letter of the constitution. A monarchy, f.i., can be democratic if it admits citizens to all posts without discrimination. In Germany it is not the Emperor who is the sovereign, but the Estates of the Empire, the princes and Free Towns, assembled in the Reichstag. They can depose the Emperor if he is unworthy or ineffective. The Emperor is only an official of the Empire, the president of the Reichstag, who for the sake of prestige has been invested with a few trifling prerogatives. Chemnitz' ideal was the constitution of Poland where the King himself declared he was only the mouthpiece of the realm, the spokesman of the Estates. This was also the case in Germany. But the Estates were often not sufficiently aware of their rights and made undue concessions to the Emperor.

The Habsburg Emperors, Chemnitz continues, always tried to increase their power at the expense of the Estates, especially Ferdinand II, who was a real tyrant and a plague. They always used much cunning in order to undermine the Reichstag and to make it unpopular. One of their principal tricks was to represent the Turks as a danger for Germany and to demand the voting of great amounts of money for the defence of the Empire. Actually the Empire was not in danger at all. It was merely the wish of the Habsburgs to conquer Hungary which inspired this policy. They often provoked the Turks in order to have a pretext for obtaining financial help from the Reichstag. The aim of the House of Austria was that of enslaving the Estates and of establishing its despotism.

The old German liberty, the author concludes, can only be restored by expelling the Habsburgs from Germany and confiscating their lands, which should become the property of the Empire. Even if the Habsburgs had not committed countless crimes against it, however, they ought to be deposed and exiled because they are too powerful and therefore dangerous to German liberty. They are a brood of vipers or a festering sore on the body of the Empire which must be cut out. After their expulsion a new Emperor should be elected, but from a dynasty without much power, and no more than three successive Emperors should be of the same family. The author further proposes that the lands of the Catholic Church should also be expropriated and the profits from them used for keeping an army which, however, must be in the hands of the Estates. At the end he again praises the constitutions of Poland and Venice, which he regards as models for Germany.

In the eighteenth century J. St Puetter, the leading constitutional lawyer of his time, said of the appearance of this book: 'Hardly ever has a literary product had such an influence on state affairs'. A Reichstag was then assembled and many of its members were weary of war and not averse from accepting the policy of the Emperor. But Chemnitz' book brought about a great change.

IDEAS OF A CHRISTIAN STATE IN THE SPIRIT OF LUTHER

Luther was primarily a religious thinker, and has no more laid down a political system than the Gospel. His disciples showed very different political attitudes. But there also were some who, starting from his religious spirit, independently drafted the ideal of a state which made a great impression on wide circles.

Johann Valentin Andreae (1586-1654), a Wurttemberger, was the grandson of Jacob Andreae, the author of the 'Formula of Concord', the official creed of Lutheran orthodoxy. He engaged in very wide studies, particularly in mathematics, the ancient and modern languages and their literatures, history and theology, and spent many years on journeys to various countries. Then he became a clergyman and devoted himself to writing, education and social reform. During most of the time, the Thirty Years' War terribly devastated his home country, and in its midst he became court preacher and counsellor to its duke. In this position he had mainly to care for the Church and education in the turmoil of the war.

Andreae had gained great insight into the religious, political and social troubles of the time, which filled him with despair. He complained that the Churches were dominated by hypocrisy and intolerance, the governments by tyranny and the field of learning by sophistry and quibbling. The only remedy seemed to him a social organization realizing Christian love between all human beings. Though a great admirer of Luther he put Christianity above denominational differences anticipating thereby the ideas of the Pietists. In 1614 he published a book Fama Fraternitatis (News of a Fraternity) which relates of a small brotherhood of men wishing to bring about a general reformation religious and secular, to discover the mysteries of nature and to study men all over the earth. This aim seems to anticipate ideas of the Enlightenment. The book was received with the greatest enthusiasm and translated from Latin into Dutch, French, Italian and English. It seems to have had a great influence on Bacon's book New Atlantis. Andreae also wrote other tracts on the same subject. But his best known work is a utopia 'Christianopolis', published in 1619, which describes the institutions and the spirit of a communist republic called Christianborough. The author knew the utopias of Plato, More and Campanella but in many respects differs from them. The people of his republic hate war, slavery and corruption and regard peace, human equality and contempt of riches as their aims.

Andreae describes in detail the organization of Christianborough. In this republic the citizens choose councillors who vote laws and create a government consisting of three rulers. There is no hereditary aristocracy. All citizens are equal and are working under the direction of the state which provides the means of production, supplies, houses etc., carries on foreign trade, and educates the youth. It is a state of artisans, who work short hours, and are well educated. They are not merely working for material reasons, but are inspired by the wish to develop the little spark of divinity within them in creative work. Their great stimulus is the Christian religion. Its influence on the spirit of the community is visible in every respect, particularly in justice. Crime is rare and penalties are as mild as possible. Every effort is made to rescue an offender, instead of spilling his blood, and if he stubbornly resists he is expelled.

Andreae also describes the education which the children shall receive in his ideal state. His ideas contain principles which have become the foundation of modern paedagogics. In particular it is stressed that the pupils should not be compelled to learn by heart concepts, which they cannot understand, but should find the way to their understanding by the observation of nature and their environment, by experiments and performing manual work. They were to learn their mother tongue earlier than Latin, and should also be instructed in modern languages to be able to communicate with other peoples. Great stress is laid on natural science, mathematics, history, logic, ethics, solemn music and on religion. But the young people must also have exercises, sport and vacations. Andreae's ideas have greatly influenced later reformers of education. Comenius calls himself his admirer, disciple and pupil. He also much influenced the circles whose activities led to the foundation of the Royal Society of London.

Veit Luwig von Seckendorff (1626-1692) was a prominent scholar and statesman, who wrote a book fervently defending Lutheranism, and had a great share in the reforms of Duke Ernest the Pious of Gotha. Contemporaries called him the most Christian of all noblemen, and the noblest of all Christians. He also wrote a book called 'The State of a German Principality' which first appeared in 1655, and then in many revised editions. It was, for over a century, the principal textbook for political instruction at the German Protestant universities, and was re-edited as late as 1754. Many professors took it as the basis for their lectures.

The author starts with the confession that he was reluctant to use the new-fangled word 'State'—now so often employed to justify every perfidy, profligacy and recklessness in the name of the Reason of State. Seckendorff's ideal was a government in accordance with Christian morality and in his book he wanted to describe how a German principality ought to be ruled in the Lutheran spirit. But he was well aware that many rulers behaved in a very different and reprehensible way. He advises the rulers how first to acquire a detailed knowledge of their principality. They should not let themselves be deluded by the facile generalization of a people's character. Everywhere one finds intermingled good and bad men, wise and foolish, active and lazy, and it is not an innate character which forms the mind but education and environment.

The ruler has his authority directly from God, and is responsible to him. But this does not give him absolute power. The author thanks God that in Germany there is no unlimited power of the ruler for his own profit and according to his arbitrary will. The subjects are not slaves as in barbarian, un-Christian and tyrannical states. Dues, fees, etc., are legitimate as far as warranted by tradition and in extraordinary cases the Estates should meet reasonable demands, but their grants are voluntary and they alone can fix how much they want to pay. The prince must scrupulously fulfil his obligations to the Emperor and the Estates of his country and act in agreement with the latter, even when there is no strict obligation. In principalities without Estates the ruler must also avoid arbitrary decisions. Consultation with the Estates, however, is more in the old, free tradition of Germany. The prince must further try to find counsellors of the highest character and competence. In regard to other countries he should maintain the existing frontiers, and in the case of encroachments try peaceful means, such as negotiations, mediation and legal proceedings. In the last resort only should he turn to legitimate defence. The Empire is by its constitution designed for peace and quietude, and a German ruler should as a rule be peaceable. But he should not be ignorant of military science. Seckendorff strongly deprecates the employment of mercenaries and suggests a general militia. The people should for this purpose be trained in military exercises, which can be run in connection with popular entertainments.

The aims of government, Seckendorff continues, are peace, justice and the welfare of the people. The ruler should be a true Christian and not merely feign his belief in religion, as the for ever accursed Machiavelli suggests. He must shun extravagant expenditure, luxury, ambition and striving for glory, and be easily accessible to every subject. Immoderate indulgence in hunting is reprehensible and adequate compensation must be paid for damage to the fields. Special attention must be given to education, and all parents should be bound to send their children to school, which the government has to provide. An elaborate programme of measures to protect the poorer classes is given. No government can expect much from poor, oppressed, slavish and beggarly subjects, who feel no interest in the community. Unfortunately, arbitrary government contrary to the old freedom, has more and more spread in Germany too. This is largely due to the intrigues of courtiers and flatterers grovelling and prostituting themselves before the prince in order to obtain a dominating position. An arbitrary régime leads to all vices and ends in ruin. The princes are reminded that they were originally officials of the Emperor, and they should be content with their old rights and not hanker after more power.

Like all economists of the time, Seckendorff is convinced that a large population is a blessing for a country and he wishes a ruler to govern so well that many foreigners feel attracted to settle under his protection. He believes that every rank should abide by its traditional occupation. Though he feels as a nobleman, his sympathies go mainly to the peasants and artisans. The trade guilds are disapproved by him and he suggests their abolition. Many other abuses, too, are criticized, for example the sale of offices, state monopolies, alteration of the coinage for fiscal purposes, and so on.

It is significant that the strong advocacy of the rights of the Estates came from a conservative statesman. The liberals were then often in sympathy with the striving of the princes for the absolute power needed to overcome feudalism and to build modern states.

THE AUSTRIAN SCHOOL OF CAMERALISTS

The leaders of this school were not born in Austria, but had come there from western Germany. Their work showed the great hopes which Austria's rise to the leadership of a large group of States aroused in the other German countries. Johann Joachim Becher (1635-1682), born in Speyer on the Rhine, was largely self-taught, and became physician to a prince, and professor of medicine. But when he dissected the body of a woman who had been executed he had to leave the country, because at that time the mere touching of the hangman or an executed person made one an outcast. Becher was further engaged in alchemistic experiments in the course of time made valuable discoveries and inventions, and put forward a theory which was taken up by Stahl and which long dominated the thought of chemists. But he pursued as well the foundation of industries as economic reforms, and successively became adviser to several governments, though he nowhere stayed long. Lastly, he was the author of numerous books and tracts on natural science, economics and politics, philosophy, education and other subjects. The projects proposed to the governments were based on a very wide knowledge of facts and well devised. But their realization would have required many years and much money, caution and perseverance, and in these regards the conditions of the time and Becher's restless character were not propitious. He often greatly impressed leading personalities, but he always had many rivals and enemies, and his behaviour easily aroused the suspicion that he was an unscrupulous adventurer and could not be trusted. All his plans therefore failed, he was deep in debt, and spent the last five years of his life in Holland and England. In London Prince Rupert financed a laboratory for him, and the King and influential people were interested in his projects. But in 1682 he died, leaving his family in distress. Leibniz, who was on bad terms with Becher, nevertheless described him as a man of the highest genius, though without any self-control and in certain conditions capable of every crime.

Becher's active life fell into the time when Germany was utterly exhausted and impoverished by the Thirty Years' War, and exposed to new great aggressions. He was an ardent patriot, and was inspired by the idea of rebuilding the wealth and power of his fatherland. To this end, he proposed a policy of mercantilism and a planned economy which had just reached its classical form in Colbert's reforms. But Becher saw his ideal country in the United Nether-lands, which he visited several times, and which fascinated him. This country was then the greatest colonial and commercial power, and foremost in progressive ideas and in many cultural achieve-ments. It was the century of Rembrandt, Grotius and Spinoza. Becher wished that Germany, too, should take part in the develop-ment of colonies and overseas trade. This idea was shared by many German princes, especially by Elector Frederick William, who was advised by prominent Dutch seamen. Another personality working in this sense, but among the Catholic German powers, was a Spaniard, Bishop Christoph Royas y Spinola, who had great influence over the Emperor Leopold, and was employed by him in important diplomatic missions. He became the patron of Becher and supported him in many ways. His aim was to bring about an economic union of German states, to further their export, and to provide them with colonial territory, which Spain had in abundance. This would also have had great political consequences. Becher was inflamed by this idea, which was sponsored by the Emperor and several princes. He obtained from the Dutch East and West India Companies the offer of colonial territories, which were to be under German sovereignty and to be cultivated by German peasants. This induced France to offer colonial land also, in order to prevent a German-Dutch co-operation. But soon difficulties arose, which wrecked all the plans.

Becher's principal work was the *Political Discourse* (1668) which was dedicated to Emperor Leopold and had six editions. As he declares, he wrote it to further the common German fatherland. A small and poor State had no chance of development and survival. A true civil society demanded a large and wealthy population. The government was to be the servant of the people. No class could prosper alone, everything depended on a sound proportion and division of labour between the classes. In contrast to most other Mercantilists, who laid inordinate stress upon the abundance of money and the functions of commerce while neglecting agriculture, Becher considers the peasants as the most necessary class, and emphasizes the importance of consumption and employment. He even wants to forbid machines causing unemployment. Though he highly appreciates the functions of commerce, he denounces those merchants who import unnecessary foreign luxuries, or strive for a monopoly, or use practices suppressing competitors. The Jews are in this respect particularly harmful, but also the abuses of the trade guilds, and other privileges restricting competition are injurious. Everybody has the right to exist by honest work, and it is better that there should be many people of moderate wealth than a few big capitalists and a multitude of proletarians and beggars.

Holland and her internal free trade appear to the author as the model. But he soon has doubts whether this freedom does not go too far. It compels the workers to do good work at cheap wages, but keeps them in perpetual poverty. In consequence, Becher wishes that the government should interfere and regulate trade. The trade guilds should not be suppressed but reformed by prohibition of their abuses. The government should control prices and wages, supply and demand, export and import. For this purpose four institutions must be established: (1) In every district a store of provisions should be set up designed to prevent great variations in the prices of the principal foods, by buying and selling them at

D

fixed prices. (2) Workhouses should give work at good wages to unemployed, beggars and convicts. Why should a thief be hanged for having stolen fifty florins? He could earn four times this amount in a year if employed in a workhouse. When Becher later resumed his post in Vienna, he developed this idea further by making the workhouse an experimental institute for testing and teaching new industrial methods, with model workshops and laboratories. He also wished that almsgiving to beggars should be prohibited, but that there should be a special office to advise and assist the poor and helpless. (3) Wholesale trade was to be centralized in a number of privileged companies, located together in Commerce Houses. (4) A bank was to accept deposits and to give and supervise credit, but only for trade and commerce. It was not to lend money to the government for war or court expenses.

The central direction of these organizations was to be entrusted to a sort of Board of Trade, composed of merchants, manufacturers, lawyers and fiscal experts, whose vote was to be decisive. Economic policy therefore was not to be conducted by the bureaucracy alone, but experienced representatives of trade and commerce were to have considerable influence. The principal aim was to make the people wealthy, not the princes. These should draw their revenues mostly from their domains, and only in exceptional cases introduce new taxes.

Though Becher wanted to give the merchants much influence in his planned economy, this class was his bitter enemy. The businessmen neither liked his idea of restricting monopolistic practices, nor his programme of prohibiting the import of foreign goods which might be produced at home.

As regards the forms of government, Becher thinks monarchy has many good sides, but also the disadvantage of a leaning to causing war. An aristocracy was in some respects better, but suffered from party strife. Least suitable was democracy. The author recommends a constitution mixed of all three elements, as in the German Empire, but with the predominant influence for the Emperor. Yet he is strongly against monarchical absolutism with its Machiavellism, wasting of money on the splendour of the court, on building gorgeous palaces, and its exploitation of the people. In another place he remarks that republics always flourish more than monarchies. The ultimate aim of society is to make man more godlike and happy.

A book *Moral Discourse*, published by Becher in 1669, showed very radical opinions. All men were by nature equal and brothers, yet there was domination and servitude. Subjection to a government was right only if the latter had good aims. But governments usually led their subjects to war, like a butcher his sheep to the shambles. The peasants were the first and most important class, yet they were exploited and despised, and certain writers even defended the fleecing and squeezing of the poor. The peasants should be helped by emigration to colonies. The real origin of poverty, however, was money. It had an artificial value, was unnecessary, and should be abolished. Everybody should work, and non-workers ought to be despised. Money is the most pernicious pestilence in the world, and the bridle by which the devil governs it. The only people profiting from it are tyrants who want to have slaves and subjects. Becher wants to replace money by certificates showing how much labour had been performed. This requires a communist society, in which all goods should be in common, and equal work should be rewarded by an equal wage.

A tract *Foolish Wisdom and Wise Folly* written in 1680, on a sea journey to Scotland, is a sad retrospect on Becher's life. All his efforts had been in vain. He mentions here various projects and inventions made by him and others, among them forerunners of the telephone, aeroplane, submarine and the Suez and Panama Canals.

His last tract, *Psychosophia, or Wisdom of the Soul* (1682) again pleads for freedom and equality through a social organization on the model of the first Christians—small rural communities without private property, living in peace and concord. He wanted to found a society for the realization of this ideal, and Duke Gustavus Adolphus of Mecklenburgh-Guestrow offered him an asylum, but Becher died soon after the publication of this tract.

Philip Wilhelm von Hoernigk was a diplomat and brother-in-law of Becher, with whom he shared many opinions. In 1684 he published a book *Austria Above All If She But Wills*. This book at once became famous, had 16 editions within a century, and exercised great influence on Austrian policy and public opinion. Its aim was to show that the Austrian countries formed an economic organism, and had more than any other state the natural resources enabling them to become economically independent and wealthy.

Another German Cameralist who entered the Austrian civil service and achieved a great reputation was Wilhelm Baron Schroeder. His principal work appeared in 1686, dedicated to the Emperor, and was reprinted eight times. Schroeder was mainly inspired by his experience in the England of the Restoration. In 1662 he was elected a Fellow of the Royal Society, at the proposal of the famous scientist Robert Boyle. Hobbes' political views made a deep impression upon him, and he became a defender of monarchical absolutism, who in radicalism even surpassed his master. He also greatly admired Louis XIV's system. Schroeder studied England's industries and commerce and sought to introduce into Austria new technical methods used in England. But he also learned much from the English mercantilists, such as Child, Mun and Petty. In England it was, too, that he realized the value of banks in replacing cash transactions and creating credit, of commercial intelligence and journalism, and of statistics in our present sense. He applied all these and similar experiences to Austrian conditions.

POLITICAL THOUGHTS OF THE JESUITS

The most prominent representatives of Catholic views were the Jesuits, who in the seventeenth century exercised the greatest influence on many kings and princes. Their political opinions were dominated by the doctrines of great Jesuit scholars, in particular Roberto Bellarmino, Juan Mariana and Franciscus Suarez. They had based them on those of Thomas Aquinas and his idea of the natural law implanted by God in the mind of man. The scholastics and canonists of the Church had found the Greek and Roman concept of natural law in the writings of the Fathers, in ancient philosophers, and in Roman Law, and it accorded well with the Bible. They combined it with the thesis of the pre-eminence of the spiritual power of the Church over the temporal one. The Pope alone receives his power directly from God, a king, however, obtains it primarily by election of the people, guided or admitted by God. The philosophy of natural law stressed the equality of all human beings and the sovereignty of the people. The king appeared as an organ appointed by the people to safeguard law and justice, but if he himself gravely violated these, he became a tyrant and could be deposed. True, the Gospel seemed to bar every rebellion. Great thinkers of the Church, however, repeatedly argued for deposing a tyrant, and some even seemed to be not opposed to his assassination. It was natural that they should regard the Pope as competent to decide when a king became a tyrant. In the great religious struggles waged in the sixteenth century in France, both Catholics and Calvinists had used the natural law to defend the sovereignty of the people against the royal striving for absolute power. The most important Catholic theorists of this school were the Jesuits Mariana and Suarez. In these struggles, two French kings, Henri III and IV, were murdered as tyrants, besides attempts on others which failed. The murderers were Catholic partisans in touch with Jesuits. It was natural that the enemies of the Jesuits declared these as responsible and wanted to suppress them. Their accusations were, however, greatly exaggerated. The teaching of the Jesuits on tyrants was neither novel nor exclusively held by them. But Mariana had commented on the murder of King Henri III with obvious approval, and had called the murderer, J. Clement, the 'eternal ornament of France', though these words were omitted in the second edition of his works.

The course of history made the Church and the Jesuits the mainstay of absolutism in France and in other countries. But this may to a great extent have been adaptation to a development which they could not change. Monarchical absolutism not only tended to annihilate the freedom of the people, but also the privileges of the Church, and to reduce the latter to an instrument of the king.

Adam Contzen (1571-1635) was a Jesuit, prominent both as a scholar and as a statesman. After having held various posts, he became confessor to Duke Maximilian of Bavaria. This prince was Bavaria's most able and efficient ruler, a disciple and patron of the Jesuits, an indefatigable worker for reforms, and for the extermination of Protestantism. He initiated in his country the era of absolutism, though in a secret instruction of 1650 for his successor, he advised him to observe the privileges and liberties of the Estates, but not to enlarge them. This seems to show that the decline of the Estates in his reign was not so much due to a deliberate policy as to circumstances undermining their vitality and accustoming the public mind to absolutism. Contzen became the duke's principal adviser, and wrote various books. His most important work was called 'Ten Books on Politics' (1621). It shows very divergent features. Some of his propositions are very retrograde, others progressive. He lays particular stress on good finance. A prince with a full treasury can in a war buy peace with money, which is better than bloodshed. He should demand moderate taxes only, and obtain the consent of the Estates. The same freedom and form of state does not suit all peoples. Savage peoples at a low stage of civilization, such as the natives in South America or South Africa, need a mild king with unlimited powers. In general, however, the best form of state is a monarchy limited by a representation of the nobility, the towns, and the other occupations. Without their consent, no new taxes should be raised, nor new laws made, and questions of loans, war and peace, and the succession to the throne should not be left to the ruler alone. Contzen's work was much studied and highly appreciated even by Protestants. Another of his books dealt with court life in a very critical spirit. He condemned the pride, the laziness, and the luxury of the aristocrats with the sharpest words. All men were born equal, the poor and the king. Where noble descent is more appreciated than virtue, the state is bound to perish. The chase, with its exploitation of the subjects, is not the least reason why the nobles will be damned. The poor cry to heaven and God will hear them. Heavy drinking, too, is a terrible evil, which has perhaps ruined more German nobles than war. One of the reasons why so many Reichstags have had no result was the drunkenness of their members.

THE LAW OF NATURE

The idea of a natural law possessing a higher dignity than that of a law made by men is very old. Greek and Roman philosophers have devoted to it much of their thought. In particular, Stoic philosophy was imbued with it, and it was accepted by Roman Law and the Fathers of the Church. The Canon Law recognized it and in the twelfth century Gratianus put it at the head of his collection of Church Law, pointing out that it had priority over other law.

Various ways were tried of building a system of the Law of Nature. Many thinkers founded it on the precepts of God laid down in the Bible, particularly that we are to love our neighbours, and to treat them as we would like to be treated by them, or on the belief that all men are God's children and therefore essentially equal. It was also often pointed out that God had implanted in the human mind the voice of reason and of conscience and many philosophers undertook to deduce the natural law exclusively from reason. It had been observed that certain legal principles were accepted in the laws of most peoples and the conclusion was drawn that they must therefore be rooted in human nature. It also appeared self-evident to many that all men strive for happiness, peace, self-realization, freedom and equality. They then tried to conclude from such axioms how laws must be framed to correspond to human nature. The Law of Reason was often interpreted in a way leading to republicanism. But it also appealed strongly to the defenders of enlightened absolutism. Princes and statesmen striving to abolish the countless privileges hindering the establishment of a rational order in public affairs welcomed the idea of a natural law overriding all these privileges.

Luther had recognized that non-Christian peoples also had a natural sense of justice and morality, as the examples of heathen peoples, of the Jews and the Turks showed. God had given reason and conscience to them too though not sufficient ones. Mere human reason was not enough to reach salvation, which required divine revelation. But Luther deviated from the teaching of the old Church in strictly separating Church and State, religion and politics. He thought that the tasks of the two were different. If one were to govern the world according to the Gospel, this would lead to wild anarchy in the name of Christian Freedom. A true Christian would need no compulsory order such as the State. Luther in this way prepared a complete emancipation of political thought from religion, though he did not anticipate this. The Ten Commandments appeared to him as a natural law valid for all peoples, but all the other legal prescriptions in the Bible were only designed for the Jews.

Melanchthon tried to reconcile Lutheranism with humanism, and in civil affairs regarded Cicero as a better guide than the Bible. The natural law was to him not an outcome of man's animal instincts but an emanation of divine wisdom and justice in the human soul. Every form of government had its authority from God, but also derived its power from the people and must not act against its will. The right of governments is not absolute. It cannot, for instance, abolish private property as certain communist sects maintain.

Melanchthon's disciples, too, propagated his teachings on the natural law, especially Oldendorp and Hemming. Johann Oldendorp was born in Hamburg in 1480, became a famous lawyer who played an important role in municipal politics and in promoting the Reformation, and at last resided in Marburg as a professor and counsellor of Landgrave Philip. His book on the law of nature (1539) is based on Cicero, the Decalogue and Roman Law. He declares that it must be deduced from human nature as it was after Adam's fall. The attempt to derive it from his nature before the fall has led many to absurd views, such as communism. The book was written shortly after the communist régime of the Anabaptists in Muenster. Its fundamental principle is: don't do to others what you would not like others to do to you. Slavery, though permitted by Roman Law, is unjust, but serfdom is justifiable. Nicolaus Hemming, a theologian and professor of Greek in Copenhagen, wished to deduce the natural law not from the Bible but exclusively from human reason. He defined it as the science of the principles underlying positive law. Even the Ten Commandments were subject to the judgment of reason as to whether they were in agreement with human nature. The aim of politics was human happiness, a quiet, peaceful life. The most important of the early writers on the natural law was Benedikt Winkler, professor at Leipzig and later syndic of Lubeck. His book, published in 1614, bases the natural law on human nature prior to the fall, when there was no inequality among men. He lays great stress on the equality and liberty of all human beings. Even God cannot deprive man of moral liberty. The natural law is written in our hearts, it is eternal and unchangeable.

The political philosophy of Johann Althusius (Althaus), a professor of law and syndic of the town of Emden, a centre of German Calvinism in close touch with the Netherlands was particularly important. He lived from 1557 to 1638, and was a staunch advocate of Calvinism and municipal liberty against princes and nobles. His treatise on politics, published in 1603, is based on the ideas of the sovereignty of the people and the social contract. Society is not an agglomeration of atoms. It is an organic union, or as he says, a symbiotic community, composed of smaller groups. Man can only develop to a better life as a member of social communities and this requires a spontaneous discipline of the group in pursuance of the common weal, a sense of unity and solidarity making every member feel like a part of the people. Althusius thereby anticipated Rousseau's idea of the general will. Some communities are natural, such as the family, others artificial, such as corporations. They are integrated in the republic, and bound together by a consensus. In every state sovereignty or majesty is with the people. Against a tyrant it possesses the right of revolution or secession. In the social contract the citizens reserved for themselves a part of their original power. The people is represented by Estates which the author calls ephores (guardians) and which have supreme power. The chief of state is merely its highest official. As regards the German Empire Althusius regarded the Electors as the highest authority, not the Emperor. He criticized, however, the usual idea of a Law of Nature as too vague a concept. But his own thought was certainly not alien to it. He had many important disciples in Germany and the Netherlands and exercised considerable influence on political thought.

PUFENDORF

Samuel Pufendorf (1632-1694), a native of Saxony, came from a family of which most male members had for a long time been Lutheran theologians. After extensive studies he sought a post in Germany but without success. He obtained, however, employment by a Swedish diplomat abroad, and thereby connections with Sweden and practical experience of international relations. His writings aroused the interest of the Palsgrave Charles Lewis who in 1661 appointed him professor of natural and international law in the University of Heidelberg. It was the first chair of this kind. In 1667 he published his famous book on Germany's constitutional conditions under the mask of an alleged Italian nobleman Severinus de Monzambano. It aroused an enormous sensation, appeared in numerous editions and translations, and became the subject of violent controversies. The orthodox clergy of all denominations was up in arms against him. A few years later he became a professor in the Swedish University of Lund and published his classical work on the Law of Nature and Nations (1672). It was soon translated into many languages and was fiercely attacked by the orthodox. Pufendorf received great honours in Sweden, he was appointed a secretary of state, privy councillor and royal historiographer. But he also was faced with many influential enemies and the general antipathy against foreigners. In 1686 he accepted the offer of Elector Frederick William of Brandenburg to enter his service as councillor and historiographer. He wrote important works on the history of Sweden and Brandenburg, and other subjects. His last book pleaded for a union of the two great Protestant Churches. Shortly before his death he also was made a baron by Sweden.

Pufendorf's book on the constitutional and political conditions of the German Empire is a masterpiece of penetrating observation, wise judgment, and literary presentation. His conclusion was that the constitution was almost a monstrosity, and that it was largely responsible for the immense internal disunity, suspicion and jealousy between the rulers, ranks, classes and denominations. The origin of all this is traced back to the Italian policy of Charlemagne and the idea that Germany was the successor of the old Roman Empire. The result was the struggles between Popes and Emperors, the endowment of the German Church with vast possessions and excessive wealth, the decline of the Emperors' power and the rise of the princes. The Habsburg Emperors further acquired large dominions outside Germany which could easily form a separate Empire. They also often gave priority to their dynastic interest over their obligations to Germany. Their policy induced many princes to strive for aggrandisement without regard to Germany. The strength of the Empire was fatally impaired, and it sank to a sort of loose federation hardly able to defend itself. The greatest evil seemed to the author the position of the Catholic Church. Its wealth was wasted in idleness and luxury, and its power was used for fostering intolerance and internal strife.

Though Pufendorf judges the policy of the Habsburgs rather severely, he rejects the radical programme of Hippolithus a Lapide, who demanded their complete extermination as a German power. He shows that his proposals are partly impossible to realize, partly would have disastrous consequences. A well-ordered monarchy would certainly be the best form of state, but its realization would

D*

require enormous struggles which might easily end in the destruction of the Empire. The author recommends, therefore, a cautious
policy aiming at the restoration of internal concord by safeguarding
the rights of all the members of the Empire, and the status quo. The
Empire would best be transformed into a real federation with a
standing federal council controlling policy. He realizes, however,
that the House of Austria would hardly consent to this plan. But
an attempt should at least be made to persuade both the Emperor
and the Estates to abstain from actions to increase their power and
to decrease that of the others, and to avoid involving Germany in
war. In any case, religious toleration should be spread. It would
also be most desirable to secularize the ecclesiastical principalities,
and to drive out the Jesuits and the lazy lot of monks—but this too
can hardly be achieved because of the mutual jealousy of all rulers
grudging one another any increase of power.

It may be remarked that soon after the publication of this book
the House of Austria was compelled to enter into a series of great
wars with the Turkish Empire and with Louis XIV in which Emperor
Leopold I certainly defended vital interests not only of his dynasty
and his countries, but also of the German Empire. The Emperor's
efforts and achievements aroused enthusiasm in Germany. Pufendorf too seems to have been impressed since he altered certain passages in his book discountenancing Austrian policy. The edition of
1706, which appeared after his death, contains these alterations,[2]
and for the first time admits Pufendorf's authorship though it had
been known long before already.

Pufendorf's greatest work was his book 'The Law of Nature and
the Nations' (1672). It was preceded by a treatise 'Elements of
Universal Jurisprudence' and followed by an epitome for students
called 'The Duty of Man and Citizen According to the Natural Law'.
The main work is very extensive and shows the greatest scholarship.
Large parts treat the fundamentals of jurisprudence and civil and
criminal law. For the subject of this book merely the sections on
public law and political philosophy are of importance. But it must
be noted that Pufendorf and many other writers on natural law
have done much to further the development of new ideas in all
branches of law and justice. With the advance of enlightened
absolutism the time became ripe for great reforms and new codes
of law were elaborated, making use of these ideas. In particular.
law was emancipated from the influence of theological considerations. Pufendorf was foremost in demanding the separation of the

[2] The alterations are given in footnotes in H. Bresslau's excellent edition of
Pufendorf's book.

spheres of the State and the Church. His great merits as a thinker and teacher, however, lay not merely in the field of practical jurisprudence but also in the philosophy of law based not only on abstract reasoning but also on the universal study of human nature as shown by the history of all times and nations. In this regard he was a forerunner of Montesquieu. Like him Pufendorf thinks that the question which form of state is the best cannot be decided in general but only considering many circumstances, historic and social. These tend to create a certain mentality often called the people's character, with which the constitution must harmonize.

Pufendorf's political thought was closely related to that of his predecessors Hugo Grotius and Thomas Hobbes and he constantly refers to them. He agrees with Grotius that God had endowed men with a 'sociable' character in the sense of wishing to live together with others and of having a sense of right or wrong, however imperfect. On the whole man was peaceable and amenable to reason, and had founded states in order to end the prevailing state of insecurity, to satisfy his social instinct, and to attain a better life by co-operation with others. Hobbes, under the influence of English political conditions culminating in the Puritan revolution, had a quite different view of the nature of man. He appeared to Hobbes as thoroughly egoistic, violent and bellicose. Before states existed, there was a general war of all against all. Morality and justice were non-existent, since there was no inborn sense of them. In order to save their lives men therefore unconditionally subjected themselves to a supreme power, a sovereign. It might also be an assembly, but a king seemed to Hobbes to be the best holder of sovereignty. He repudiated a limited monarchy. Sovereignty could not be divided. The sovereign had not only to enact laws but also to decide about religion and morality, or rather about their outward profession. The sovereign had no obligations towards the subjects, and these had no right to resist him. The government, however, should not much interfere in the daily life of the people but only safeguard peace and order.

Pufendorf did not agree with these opinions of Hobbes. In particular, he denied that the people had unconditionally subjected themselves to a ruler. He believed that they had done so by a sort of contract, either stipulated or silent, expressing their aims in submitting to him. This would have obligated the ruler to comply with these conditions and would have entitled the people to demand their fulfilment. Pufendorf also rejected Hobbes' opinions of the life of primitive, stateless peoples. Reports of ancient writers and of contemporary explorers contradicted the view that they showed a wolfish character, were constantly engaged in a war of all against all, and had no sense of justice.

Though Pufendorf had based sovereignty on a pact with the people, he shows the greatest reluctance to allow the people any right of resistance if the ruler should infringe this pact. He points out that charges of tyranny against a ruler may often not be well founded because the subject may have no full knowledge of the state affairs concerned. But even if the charges are undeniable he fears that a revolt would bring about much greater evils than the ruler had inflicted upon the subject. The latter should therefore submit, or leave the country. The problem is treated in great detail, and we cannot enter here into a full discussion. Pufendorf admits, however, a limited monarchy which Hobbes rejects. He also accepts certain opinions of Grotius recognizing the right of resistance in special cases, and one may conclude from other passages that he would admit it in other extreme instances also.[3]

The duty of a ruler is clearly deduced from the purpose of states and rulers. He has to obey the supreme law to further the welfare of the people. He must therefore make himself as fitted as possible for this task and avoid anything likely to hinder him in its achievement. Pufendorf then describes in detail the different branches of a well-organized government and the aims which the ruler must have in mind. The belief in God is fundamental to the proper fulfilment of the duties of rulers and subjects. But the state must have the right to supervise the Church in order to prevent the rise of opinions leading to civil unrest. The idea that kingship reposes upon a special grant of dignity and wisdom by God is a superstition.

All men are naturally equal. Pufendorf emphasizes that the word 'man' implies a certain dignity, and that every man has a most sensitive self-esteem. It is therefore a precept of natural law that every man should esteem and treat another man as his equal by nature. From this equality derive other precepts, the observance of which has the greatest influence in preserving peace and friendly relations among men. The idea handed down from the Greeks that certain peoples are slaves by nature merits complete disapproval. Pufendorf bases on the principle of equality the general duties of humanity (chapter III). All nations, too, are equal, whether small or great. Backward nations, too, are protected by the Law of Nations, and must not be enslaved with the hypocritical argument that they are pagans or have a low morality.

[3] Cf. *Law of Nature* p. 1111. On p. 1103 it is said: 'The *lawful* commands of the sovereign should not be resisted. Another sentence (Elements, p. 13) says: 'When the subjects of a prince take up arms *unjustly* against him, it is rebellion.'

Aggression is against the law of nature and self-interest. The Romans paid for their ruthless aggressions with their own ruin. Even self-defence must not be driven too far. In minor points one should rather be forgiving and obliging. Before declaring war every effort should be made to settle the conflict by means of mediation or arbitration. The conduct of war should not transgress moderation or violate good faith, and the victor ought to use his triumph with humanity and generosity. Pufendorf professed that next to the weal of his fatherland he wished every happiness to all other peoples too. The Law of Nations is valid for all, and the duty of humanity links them together.

Pufendorf was a great forerunner of liberal ideas. He also appreciated democracy, which he considered the oldest and most natural form of state, but only suited to small communities not divided by wild party strife and pervaded by brotherly feelings. For his time a strong, enlightened and peaceable monarchy seemed to him preferable.

The subjects of Pufendorf's works were also discussed by numerous other scholars, whose writings cannot be surveyed here. Two of the most important writers were Samuel Rachel, who published a book on the law of nature and the nations (1676) and Johann Wolfgang Textor, the author of a synopsis of international law (1680). Their books have been reprinted in the series 'Classics of International Law', published by the Carnegie Endowment, and English translations and comments added.

THOMASIUS

Next to Pufendorf, the most important pioneer of the Enlightenment in the field of law was Christian Thomasius (1655-1728). He was born in Leipzig and came from a family which had brought forth many distinguished jurists and scholars. Christian, too, became a lawyer and a professor and defended Grotius' and Pufendorf's theory of the Natural Law. The fundamentals of law he deduced from human nature, not from divine revelation. This aroused the greatest wrath of the orthodox theologians, who accused him of atheism, though Thomasius was by no means a freethinker setting aside the essential Christian beliefs. But he made a clear distinction between theology and jurisprudence. The Church and the theologians had to care for man's happiness in heaven, while governments and their lawyers were concerned with his welfare on earth. Their laws, moreover, ought to restrict themselves to ensuring proper external conduct, in particular the maintenance of peace. But it had nothing to do with mere convictions and opinions of men, and governments should not interfere with them. This was the field of morality, and Thomasius laid stress upon separating it from that of justice. In 1688, he further caused a great stir by using the German language in his lectures instead of Latin—at the time a revolutionary step. A year later he began to publish a monthly journal, which he wrote himself, and which was the first magazine of its kind in the German language. It treated literary, scientific, moral and even political matters and often used a satirical style. Thomasius later published various other journals also.

One of the principal aims which Thomasius pursued was the liberation of higher education and intellectual life from academic pedantry, sterile scholastic speculations and the sanctimonious hypocrisy used to maintain the power of the orthodox theologians and to stifle common sense. This whole system was closely linked with the over-estimation of Latin and the suppression of the German mother-tongue in all learned matters and in the schools. Thomasius also despised metaphysics which, as he wrote, could corrupt a healthy man to such a degree that worms might grow in his brains. He therefore advised the Germans to follow the French in esteeming and cultivating their mother-tongue, in employing sound logic, and in scholarship. At that time Louis XIV's aggressions, especially his annexation of Strasbourg, had aroused a good deal of anti-French sentiment in Germany, and it required courage to swim against the stream. Yet Thomasius in academic lectures, later published, rejected every national prejudice on either side. Shortly before, the French Jesuit Dominique Bouhours had praised his nation for the wide diffusion of 'Bel Esprit' in the cultured classes, while the Germans, like the Muscovites, were, in his opinion, deprived of it because of their rough temperament and massive build.[4] This had aroused a heated controversy. The academician J. Barbier d'Aucour blamed Bouhours for disparaging whole nations, while other French writers supported him, and J. F. Cramer wrote a Latin tract in defence of the German name. Thomasius answered in a quiet and dignified way, remarking that Bouhours' national self-praise and slighting of other nations was not a sign of good taste. He himself pays great tribute to the many accomplishments of the French; in scholarship they are without doubt ahead of all nations. They also possess more vivacity than the others. The Germans have a cooler temper, and,

[4] Bouhours, however, relates a discussion between two friends of whom one puts forward the view of German inferiority while the other contests it. It has been remarked that Bouhours himself put his own opinions in the mouth of the latter. But in this case he must have expressed himself in a not very clear way since he was generally understood differently.

therefore, bring forth fewer men endowed with 'Bel Esprit', but on the other hand they show more patience. French vivacity and German patience should be combined, and this would make excellent scholars. In any case the Germans should take the French as models in all the good things in which they excel, not merely in fashion or cookery, but in serious matters, too. Thomasius particularly appreciates in the French their masterly translations of the ancient authors, their universality, clarity, fairness, honesty, fertility, good taste and manners, and so on. If the Germans would imitate them in these things, this would result in the appearance of really wise men fitted for important tasks in the world.[5]

Thomasius' liberal opinions in matters of law and religion were taken very ill by the adherents of Lutheran orthodoxy, and a great campaign against him started. His position became critical when courts also took offence at his teachings. The court preacher of the King of Denmark, H. G. Masius, had written that only Lutheranism secured the princes against rebellion, while the Calvinists and Catholics fostered it. Thomasius criticized this view in his journal and a controversy arose. He declared that the court preacher's striving to recommend his religion to the king with a non-religious argument was unworthy of a theologian. The idea that God directly created royal sovereignty was silly, unreasonable and contrary to history. The consent of the people was needed to make it valid. The Danish government had Thomasius' writing burnt by the hangman, and demanded from Saxony that he should be punished for the crime of lèse-majesté. Thomasius further aroused the anger of the Saxon court by defending a dynastic marriage between a Lutheran and a Calvinist. In 1690 he was forbidden to lecture, his publications were subjected to censorship, and he was threatened with prosecution. The zealots had succeeded in silencing their adversary and in depriving him of any means of earning a living. Thomasius thereupon left Leipzig and went to Berlin, where Elector Frederick III, who later became the first King of Prussia, granted him asylum, permitted him to give lectures at the academy of Halle and made him his counsellor. This was the starting point of plans which led to the foundation of the University of Halle. The spirit of these plans was expressed in the dedication of a book to the Elector in the sentence: 'If I shall say it in one word, it is unfettered freedom, yes, freedom, which is the very life of the spirit and without which human reason, in spite of any other qualifications, is as good as dead

[5] Thomasius' masterly dismissal of national prejudice has been reprinted in *Deutsche Litteraturdenkmale des 18. u. 19. Jahrhunderts*, ed. August Sauer, 1894.

and inanimate'. He also told the Elector that it was freedom alone which had given the Dutch and English, and formerly the French also, so many learned people. Thomasius also brought other scholars to the university of Halle, especially Francke. For some time Thomasius sympathized with Pietism and mysticism, but later became averse to them. The study of Locke had great influence on his thought. He was primarily an empiricist and utilitarian, and a man striving to realize practical reforms in the spirit of tolerance and humanity. His greatest merits lay in the field of jurisprudence, especially in his opposition to trials for witchcraft and to torture. Having had an orthodox and traditional education he long believed in both, but his growing experience induced him increasingly to reject them. It was largely because of his work that already in his lifetime both evils were reduced to a minimum in Prussia, and a few years after his death completely came to an end. King Frederick II later said that Thomasius had made the persecution of witches so ridiculous and had so incessantly raised his voice that one began to be ashamed of it. It is noteworthy that Thomasius also rejected prejudice against the Jews, such as the belief that they committed ritual murders.

As an academic teacher Thomasius opened a new epoch. The University of Halle became a seat of progressive thought largely owing to him, and he introduced many new ways of instruction. In his lectures and classes newspapers were read and discussed, and Prof Ludwig did the same. A considerable percentage of the students wanted to become civil servants, and among them young noblemen were numerous. In this way the university became the intellectual training ground for the officials of the nascent Kingdom of Prussia. There they acquired a belief in a rational law which guided them in their subsequent work. Imbued with this, they were enabled to get beyond their loyalty to the Crown to a realization of their wider duty towards the community as a whole.

Germany had, in the sixteenth century, been leading in the development of the ideas of a Law of Nature. Later she lagged behind other nations, but at the end of the seventeenth century Pufendorf and his school placed her in front again. How great her contribution was can be seen from a work on the Law of Reason by Adam Friedrich Glafey, published in 1732. It has a list of books on the subject, which fills 96 pages and comprises about 2,000 titles, mostly of books written by Germans. Yet the list was by no means complete.

6

G. W. LEIBNIZ

HIS LIFE AND WORK

THE greatest thinker of the early phase of German Enlightenment was Leibniz (1646-1716). He was born in Leipzig of Lutheran parents, studied jurisprudence, philosophy and mathematics, and became a counsellor of princes, first for five years in the service of the Archbishop Johann Philipp von Schoenburg, Elector of Mainz, and then for forty years in that of successive Dukes of Hanover and Brunswick, who belonged to the same dynasty. Research and diplomatic missions induced him to make many journeys, especially to Paris, London, Vienna, Berlin and Rome, and put him in touch with many rulers, statesmen and scholars all over Europe. Besides his posts at the courts of the House of Guelph, he was also appointed counsellor, and granted pensions, by Emperor Charles VI, Tsar Peter I, and Elector (later King) Frederick of Brandenburg-Prussia. Other rulers also and the Pope would have liked to win him for their services. Various very attractive propositions, however, foundered on Leibniz' refusal to become a Catholic since he feared that in this case his freedom of thought might be restricted. As an official he was not burdened with routine work, but could devote himself to the great questions of international policy, to planning important reforms, and to studies on the genealogy of the ruling dynasty and on the history of the country. This position naturally aroused the jealousy of the bureaucrats. Leibniz' fame, however, reposed mainly on his work as a philosopher and a scholar in many fields. The range of his scientific achievements was amazing. His main interest, however, was not merely the enlargement of knowledge but its practical utilization in order to increase human happiness. But the position of the philosopher as an official, and the abundance of his ideas, were not favourable to the publication of comprehensive presentations of his thought. Its fruits were largely scattered in secret memoranda, anonymous pamphlets and official manifestos, and in a vast correspondence. Two only of his writings became widely known in his lifetime, his most important philosophical work appeared fifty years after his death, and his greatest historical book had to wait a hundred and thirty years for publication.

LEIBNIZ AND LOUIS XIV

Leibniz' life coincided with that of Louis XIV, and he witnessed all his wars. The strongest longing of the philosopher was for universal peace and harmony, and the increasing aggressiveness of the King and his ministers therefore aroused his greatest opposition. On the other hand, he admired Louis' role as patron of arts and science, and his internal reforms. He had, moreover, often to take regard for the policy of the princes whom he served. Like many German princes, Johann Philipp, a ruler of great merit, saw in France mainly a counter-weight to Austria, needed to maintain the balance of power and the sovereignty of the princes. Moreover, he wished for good relations with France to avoid war. But the development of Louis' policy compelled him to change his policy. Leibniz shared this attitude. He wished that the Empire should make every effort to avoid being involved in war with France, but that a number of German princes should form a defensive alliance against possible aggressions. When the King prepared his attack upon Holland, Leibniz tried to avert him from it by directing his ambition to another enterprise which was rightful and much more profitable, namely the conquest of Egypt and other parts of the Turkish Empire. He pointed out that Egypt was one of the most fertile countries in the world. Its possession gave its ruler a dominant position commanding the whole East and, in particular, the commerce to India, which at that time was in Dutch hands. Its importance could be still further increased by digging a canal to connect the Mediterranean with the Red Sea. The Turkish Empire was rotten and easy to overthrow. The peoples oppressed by it would welcome the French liberators, and the European powers would be no hindrance. Leibniz later also suggested that France should undertake the conquest of the Turkish Empire in alliance with Austria, who seemed willing.

The Elector sent Leibniz to Paris to discuss the plan with the King, but he had no opportunity to do so, since Louis had already made up his mind to conquer Holland in alliance with England. But it remained Leibniz' ideal that all powers should give up waging war

against each other over a handful of soil in Europe and should rather
seek their aggrandisement overseas, where there was plenty of
space for every nation and where they could spread Christian
civilization. Men should use arms against wild beasts only, and
possibly against barbarians. Leibniz did not foresee that colonial
expansion too, would soon become a cause of great bloodshed
between the European nations. His idea of solving the Eastern
question by agreement between France and Austria, however, was
sound. The world would have been saved immeasurable misery if
this question had been settled two and a half centuries before its
final liquidation, and before Russia had become a great power.

Louis XIV's assault on Holland was followed by further aggressions against Germany, in which the King revealed ever more clearly
his limitless ambition, and his contempt of international law and
morality. This experience aroused Leibniz' sense of justice and
national sentiment and he wrote several anonymous pamphlets
vigorously denouncing the King's policy and exhorting the Germans
to the strongest resistance. The barbarous devastation of the Palatinate and the rape of Strassburg filled him with greatest bitterness and
he predicted that it would lead to further endless bloodshed. But in
spite of his deep resentment of the policy of the French King, he
did not let himself be carried away by national passion. He pointed
out that not all French were responsible for the doings of their
ruling classes, that the great mass of the French people themselves
were oppressed and exploited and lived in awful misery. Leibniz
always remained a great admirer of everything good in French
civilization and himself wrote his principal books on philosophy in
French. He also repeatedly thought of settling in France, and later
celebrated Louis as a great King, immortal owing to his patronage
of cultural life, and destined for still greater fame, if he would now
devote himself exclusively to a policy of peace and progress, and
to promoting the happiness of the world. But this hope was not
fulfilled. Soon the war of the Spanish succession broke out, in which
Leibniz defended the Habsburg cause.

NATIONALITY AND HUMANITY

The German Empire was held by Leibniz in high esteem. He
revived Dante's idea of the Emperor's mission to secure universal
peace, an international reign of law, and the maintenance of Christian civilization. The Christian nations appeared to him as a family
in which the Emperor was entitled to particular respect and trust,
and called on to be the mediator between rivals, and the leader in

common actions. The fact that the Empire was also the fatherland of the Germans appeared to Leibniz as a great advantage for its international mission. Germany's central position in Europe, its climate and resources, and the traditions of the German people qualified the Empire to maintain peace between the nations, to serve as a cultural mediator, and as a pioneer of progress. Leibniz pointed out the particular merits of the German tongue, which had a rich vocabulary in the scientific and economic matters first developed by Germans. The Germans had once been the pioneers in mechanical inventions and scientific discoveries. Other nations had learned from them, and had also taught the Germans much in religion, the art of government and philosophy. Now both economic life and art and science had so declined in Germany that the best scholars were compelled to leave it and seek employment in the service of foreign princes. Leibniz often wished to transfer his residence to a great city abroad. In a letter of 1696 he wrote that he felt cramped in a small German town without an intellectual life and would like to live in Paris or London, where there were numerous scholars from whom one could learn.

The Germans, as also the Dutch and English, Leibniz further wrote, loved freedom and hated the splendour of courts and the despotism of princes, while the French revelled in the prestige of their King like no other nation and excelled in all the arts cultivated at courts and in society. No nation should intervene in the affairs of others and impose its own manners and customs upon them, as the French were used to do. He defended the candidature of a German prince for election as King of Poland with the argument that Germany and Poland were both averse to an aggressive policy and threatened by the same powers, namely Russia and the Turkish Empire. Later, however, Leibniz also entered into close relations with Tsar Peter I of Russia, whom he met five times and for whom he elaborated plans of reform for Russia. National sentiment was not alien to the philosopher. But it was balanced by a strong and sincere love of humanity. He never wavered in the conviction that the ideal of humanity had precedence over that of nationality. In his first letter to Tsar Peter he said: 'I am not one of those who exclusively love their fatherland or some particular nation; but I aim at the advantage of the whole human race, for I consider heaven the fatherland and all well-meaning men its citizens. I should prefer to do the Russians a great deal of good rather than a little to the Germans or other Europeans, even if the latter should grant me any amount of honour and wealth, but without the possibility of doing much good to others for my inclination and my joy is to further the common weal.'

Leibniz often expressed his horror of war. The Chinese, he says, show much greater wisdom than the Europeans, for they detest war, while in Europe men behave like wolves against each other. It is a shame that the former are far superior to the Europeans in practical philosophy, in their system of government and in morality. It is the Chinese who should send missionaries to the Europeans to teach them the natural theology, while they could learn from the latter the revealed theology. Leibniz had a keen interest in China and was in correspondence with Jesuit missionaries who at that time held important posts at the court of the Emperor of China.

The ideal of perpetual peace and plans for an international organization to realize it were at that time widely discussed. Leibniz himself mentions plans by Emeric Crucé, the Landgrave Ernest of Hesse and the Abbé de St Pierre. When the latter put forward his famous plan of an international league of sovereigns to maintain peace, Leibniz expressed a great interest in it and agreed with the author in the idea that the Empire was a similar body and could serve as a model, though certain improvements were necessary. Yet he was sceptical whether the sovereigns would submit to an international authority. The essential point was the development of international rules of law out of the germs contained in international treaties and customs. Leibniz compiled a great collection of treaties concluded since the eleventh century. He rejected both the theory that there was no authority higher than the state, and the usual excuses for violating treaties such as honour, prestige or Reason of State. Inhuman ways of warfare such as the bombarding of towns were condemnable. The unrestricted rule of the military men would lead to barbarism and the destruction of civilization. Leibniz proposed a covenant between the states for outlawing all wars, except defensive ones, and for the establishment of an international reign of law. For this purpose an organization with a permanent senate presided over by the Pope and the Emperor should be formed for the amicable settlement of disputes between states.

THE RE-UNION OF CHURCHES

An aim which Leibniz embraced with the greatest fervour was the re-union of the Churches. It occupied him for more than thirty years. He cherished the ideal of religious unity for political reasons as well. The pacification of Europe appeared to him impossible without the reconciliation of the Churches. Moreover, in Germany the antagonism between the denominations was destructive of the very idea of a nation. Emperor Leopold I authorized Bishop Spinola, a Spanish Franciscan, to work for this aim, as he had privately already done for many years and Pope Innocent XI was also favourable to it. Spinola began by winning over the court of Hanover whose ruler, Duke John Frederick, was a Catholic. Leibniz became the moving spirit in this matter. Gradually many princes, theologians and statesmen, Catholics and Protestants, joined the movement. Negotiations started in which spokesmen of both sides showed much good will, and the preparedness to make great concessions. But later intransigent views were also voiced, and these eventually gained the upper hand. The real reasons why the negotiations failed were, however, political. Louis XIV had certainly no wish to further German unity, or international peace. It was in his interest that the strife between the religions should continue. In Hanover a Protestant ruler came to the throne who hoped to obtain the right of succession to the English throne too, and he could therefore no longer advocate a union of Protestantism with the Church of Rome since the latter was utterly detested in England. The plan was therefore frustrated. Leibniz tried at least to unite the Protestant Churches, but this, too, failed. His standpoint was that of absolute tolerance; he appreciated the good sides of other religions than his own too and e.g. often defended the Jesuits against disparagement. Each Church seemed to him to represent a different aspect of the truth. The struggles between them were largely about words. The doctrines and rites of the Anglican Church were, in his opinion, particularly suited as a basis for a general reconciliation.

THE PROJECT OF ACADEMIES OF SCIENCE

Another of Leibniz' great plans was that of an international association of societies for the advancement of science and learning, on the model of the London Royal Society and the two Paris Academies. They were to be composed of the best scholars, and possess all the necessary equipment, such as libraries, laboratories, museums etc., and the financial means for organizing and supporting research, and for publishing its results. Particular stress was laid on utilizing the progress of science for practical purposes, namely the development of agriculture, industries and commerce to improve the living conditions of the peoples. In his notes Leibniz also remarked that 'it must be the aim of such a society to free the manual worker from his terrible poverty'. Theology and jurisprudence were to be excluded. Yet missionaries highly qualified in science, medicine, etc., should spread in oversea countries both Christianity and civilization. The academies were to take special care of practical medicine by establishing anatomical theatres, chemical laboratories, microscopic investigations, etc. Leibniz hoped that these societies would become a sort of international republic of men of learning, a centre of the spirit of Enlightenment, designed to promote everywhere fruitful knowledge and to further international co-operation. The plan also had significance for German nationality since the German societies were to cultivate the German language, literature and history.

The first place where Leibniz took up the realization of his plan was Berlin. Elector Frederick, and still more his wife, were favourable to it, and a Society of Sciences was founded (1700). Leibniz became its permanent president. Three years later Elector Frederick August of Saxony, who was also King of Poland, wished to win Leibniz for his service in order to found an academy according to his ideas, and to have his advice for the education of his son. Leibniz elaborated the necessary plans, but their realization was frustrated by great wars which forced the Elector to flee abroad. A few years later Tsar Peter I took great interest in Leibniz' ideas and, besides other reforms, wished to found an academy in St Petersburg. Plans were worked out, but were realized only after the death of the Tsar and Leibniz. Lastly he seemed to have good prospects of achieving his great project in Vienna. Emperor Charles VI, Prince Eugene and many other highly influential personalities were convinced of its importance and had great admiration for its author. The Emperor in 1713 made him a member of the Imperial Aulic Council, and wished to have him in Vienna for other services also. He told the Hanoverian ambassador that he and Leibniz had already become very good friends. Yet the whole project was eventually foiled by the terrible financial exhaustion caused by the wars of Austria with France and Turkey. The Berlin Society was the only institution which Leibniz did establish. But it soon gave him much trouble; the King and the Queen who had carried out his plan died, and the successor, King Frederick William I, had no understanding for it at all. The board of the Society and the government treated Leibniz with ingratitude and lack of respect.

Leibniz' position in Berlin was also adversely affected by changes in the attitude of the Hanoverian government. Elector George Louis, since 1714 King George I of Great Britain, had not the wide outlook of his predecessors, who had realized Leibniz' greatness. To him he appeared merely as an official who neglected his duties chasing after the favour of other princes, staying abroad too much, without even asking for his permission. He treated him in a humiliating way, and Leibniz near the end of his life, after having served the House of Hanover for almost forty years, thought of settling in Vienna or Paris. Louis XIV had a high opinion of him. When, in 1715, Leibniz wrote to the French Jesuit Father Tournemine that he intended to live in Paris, the Father showed the letter to the King who ordered him to reply that he knew all the merits of Leibniz, would be pleased to see him at his court, and to make his residence as agreeable for him as he would be useful to France.

The attempt to found academies was only one of Leibniz' numerous projects to promote human happiness by cultivating science and learning. He was engaged in plans to establish new industries and to improve the machines in the state mines, he invented a calculating apparatus, and proposed a reform of the currency. Economic science seemed to him a particularly important branch of knowledge. He much admired Colbert, and accepted his mercantilism. In 1715 he combated in a pamphlet the view of the Tories in England that aggrarian and commercial interests were antagonistic. His view was that the progress of one branch of production was an advantage for the others too.

Jurisprudence too occupied Leibniz' thought, since he had read law at Leipzig to become a judge. He worked out a plan to unify the law, making use of the rules in force, and taking the natural law as the foundation. Justice seemed to him the reasonable love of all human beings from pleasure in their well-being. We should treat all others as we wished to be treated by them, and promote the welfare and happiness of everybody, just as we would our own.

LEIBNIZ' IDEAS OF THE STATE

Leibniz' ideas of the state are scattered in many of his writings and his correspondence. Professor Erwin Ruck has compiled them in an excellent book which is little known. He showed that the philosopher was entirely opposed to arbitrary absolutism, subordinated the ruler to the law and pleaded for freedom and equality, and for the predominance of the interest of the community over that of individuals. The state appeared to him as a moral personality able to have a common will. Neither the ruler nor the people are sovereign but form organs of the state personality. Right was not, as Hobbes thought, dictated by an omnipotent state. It was older than the state. Before its establishment the peoples formed loose communities based on family relations. The germs of the ideas of right and wrong were inherent in their social instincts and formed a customary law which later developed to a clearly formulated legislated law. Leibniz rejected Pufendorf's idea of a contract in which the people submitted to a ruler. The prince is merely the administrator of the state. Its aim is peace, security, intellectual and moral progress, and the happiness of the people. Leibniz wished that the English idea that the people was subject only to the law should spread to all peoples. He also pleaded for restricting the power of princes by Estates, though the rulers must have a certain scope for the exercise of their powers. Contrary to Hobbes' theory, he also admitted the right of the people to resist illegal actions of the ruler, though only in extreme cases, since otherwise resistance might lead to anarchy. Leibniz assumed that the peoples once lived in a state of common property, that later private property developed, but that in the end the trend will go back to common property again. He strongly stressed the necessity of the reign of law, and the duty of the state to care for the education of the people, and for public hygiene, to help the poor and to cultivate the sciences and arts.

LEIBNIZ' ATTITUDE TO POLITICS

In politics Leibniz sought, as in all other matters, to take the middle course between extremes and, if possible, to reconcile these. In 1710 he confessed to Thomas Burnet: 'The extremists only are reprehensible among the Tories as among the Whigs. The moderates of both sides will easily come to an agreement. The extreme Tories are Jacobites, and the extreme Whigs republicans. Tell me, Sir, whether the moderate Tories do not recognize that there are extraordinary cases when passive obedience comes to an end, and it is permitted to resist the sovereign, and whether the moderate Whigs do not agree that one should not recklessly, or without great reasons, proceed to resistance? It is the same with the hereditary right of succession, from which one should not deviate, except when the weal of the fatherland compels the people to do so. But the belief that these things are based on an inalienable divine right is a superstition.' Leibniz leaned more to the side of the Whigs. He had the greatest interest in English public life, and would have liked to follow his prince to London and to live there. But this proved impossible, largely owing to English public opinion hostile to Leibniz because of his controversy with Newton about the invention of the differential calculus. Newton had the priority, but Leibniz had later developed it, in another form, independently of Newton. Both were partly responsible for the rise of a quarrel poisoned by party passion.

Leibniz was well disposed towards parliaments, but he believed that a really enlightened monarchy would be the greatest blessing, though princes qualified to realize this ideal were rare. In his Essays on the Human Intellect he says that if once a great prince would come, a second Solomon, reigning in full peace, and striving to make men happier, more peaceable and possessing greater power over nature—what miracles could he perform in a few years! Surely he could achieve more in ten years than had hitherto been attained in a hundred or perhaps in a thousand.

The philosopher was constantly on the look-out for such a prince. He actually met several rulers sympathizing with his ideals, and impressed by his personality, who employed him in tasks congenial to his nature. But they were either princes whose power and means were much restricted, or great monarchs hampered by wars and financial straits from realizing his vision.

His genius was also much appreciated by princesses, such as the Electress Sophia of Hanover, her daughter Sophia Charlotte, Queen of Prussia and Elizabeth Charlotte, Duchess of Orleans, all of them descendants of Frederick V, the 'Winter-King' of Bohemia, and Elizabeth, daughter of James I. Sophia Charlotte was particularly interested in philosophical thought, and Leibniz often discussed the deepest problems with her. But he was also the confidant of Sophia in important political questions, such as the Hanoverian succession to the English throne. Both Sophia and her daughter died before Leibniz, and this weakened his position.

PHILOSOPHY AND THE SPIRIT OF THE AGE

Leibniz' philosophy could not directly influence the public mind since his speculations were too abstract for the average intellect. But its fundamental ideas were certainly related to the currents of his age and were later popularized by his disciples. In England and France the progress of physics and mathematics had promoted the spread of the idea that organic life, intellect and morality could also be explained in a mechanical, materialistic and utilitarian way. Morality appeared as a set of rules either dictated by those in power in order to hinder men from robbing or killing one another, or recommended by a self-interest aiming at the increase of the immediate pleasures of life. This easily led to very dangerous views on the relations between morality, right, power and utility. Leibniz did not fall into the error of connecting a false philosophy with the

personal ethos of its believers too closely. He admitted that material-
ists and atheists too had led an exemplary life. But their followers,
he thought, once they were liberated from religious and moral
scruples, or from far-sighted considerations of the interests of
posterity, were prone to give rein to their base passions. If they were
ambitious and hard-hearted they were able for their pleasure or
profit to set fire to the four corners of the world. It was not the
people which Leibniz mainly feared, but the rulers and particularly
the writers who were poisoning the public mind, and preparing a
great revolution all over Europe. People scoff at the love of the
fatherland, he wrote, and the care for the public weal, and won't
hear of dangers in the future. This state of things appeared to him
like a mental epidemic, which, if not healed, must lead to a revolution. Providence will then use this revolution to punish and reform
men because, whatever may happen, eventually the course of events
will turn out for the best. These words were written in 1704, and
the experience of the great wars of the epoch, and the terrible
misery caused by them, have certainly contributed to the predic-
tion. Many historians trace the French Revolution largely to the
power politics of Louis XIV. Leibniz, however, primarily feared the
prevalent moral nihilism which he regarded as the consequence of a
philosophy of materialism.

In Leibniz' own thought the world was not merely a mechanism
but an organism consisting of countless smaller organic beings
operating in harmony. He laid great stress on individuality, development, and the unfolding of internal forces. Morality and justice
were not arbitrarily dictated by governments, or merely sanctioned
by reasons of utility, but sprang from love and a sense of harmony
inherent in the human mind. He tried to justify God against Bayle's
scepticism by stating that this world, in spite of many evils, was
still comparatively the best one which God could have created. His
argumentation is largely theological and metaphysical. It provoked
Voltaire's mockery, put forward in his novel 'Candide'. The greatest
English philosopher of our age, Lord B. Russell, moreover, has in his
History of Philosophy added the comment that this view obviously
satisfied the Queen of Prussia, with whom Leibniz had discussed the
problem before writing his *Theodicy*. 'Her serfs continued to suffer,
says this eminent thinker, and it was comforting to be assured by a
great philosopher that this was just and right.' But Leibniz never
assured anybody that serfdom, or any other undeserved evil, was
just and right, nor would this have pleased the Queen. On the
contrary, four years before the appearance of the *Theodicy* the
King had decreed the abolition of serfdom on the royal domains in

Pomerania as contrary to the royal interests and detrimental to economic life. But it was made ineffective by the resistance of the bureaucracy and the nobility. His son and successor issued several other decrees in the same sense fulminating against the resistance, but with little success.

Leibniz thought that good on the whole prevailed, and that evil was largely due to the lack of enlightenment that it was often unavoidable and even useful, and that the world would gradually become better with the progress of knowledge and humanity. Leibniz was not the first thinker pointing out many cases in which an evil had a value, either as a deterrent, or as an incitement to improving bad conditions, and so on. Many happenings, regarded first as an evil, later turned out to be a blessing. According to the teaching of the Church, Adam's fall was the first evil and the source of all the further ones. But the Church also emphasized that without this fall Christ would never have appeared in the world, and a hymn sung in Catholic churches therefore praised Adam's sin. To Leibniz' arguments could be added that, from the standpoint of our age, Adam's fall was also a blessing because God condemned him to hard work. Without this there would have been no progress and no civilization. Man would still live on the most primitive level, without knowledge of good or evil, in conditions hardly considered human by modern opinion.

The *Theodicy* had the greatest success of all of Leibniz' books. It was eagerly read and discussed by the élite of all countries, except in England where one did not forgive him the conflict with Newton. The rather difficult metaphysical argumentation could hardly influence wider circles. But the book was very impressive as a confession of philosophical liberalism. Leibniz might, indeed, be called a liberal though not in the sense of the nineteenth century. True liberty was for him the force to follow reason. He stood for peace, toleration, the rights of man, and an international reign of law. He believed in spiritual freedom, and was convinced that the progress of enlightenment would make men free and happy. He had confidence in the possibility of reconciling all the conflicting ideals and interests and to bring them into harmony. Leibniz did not enter into the lesser quarrels of his day. He laid the philosophical foundations upon which Wolff was soon to build up his ideas of reform.

The closing years of Leibniz' life brought him bitter disappointment. He was out of favour with King George I, and this was the signal for the court and many others to give him the cold shoulder. The clergy were hostile to the man who never went to church, and held unorthodox views. Many scholars were jealous of his international fame. Personal faults, such as his irritability, aggravated the situation. Leibniz more and more became lonely. He suddenly collapsed and died and nobody attended his funeral except his faithful Jewish pupil Raphael Levi and his assistant Eckhart, a mean intriguer against his master.[1] A Scottish nobleman who was his admirer and who had just come to Hanover, wrote later he had been buried like a robber, not like the glory of his country. The Berlin and the London Societies of Science remained silent, but the Paris Academy honoured his memory by a famous obituary read by Fontenelle.

[1] Kuno Fischer (p. 299) states that it was not known where his grave was. But Johann Heinrich Voss relates in a poem that he visited the grave guided by Leibniz' pupil Levi

7

THE EPOCH OF LOUIS XIV AND THE RISE OF MONARCHICAL
ABSOLUTISM

THE ROOTS OF ABSOLUTISM

IN the seventeenth century many circumstances encouraged the rise
of monarchical absolutism. There had previously been times when a
strong king was desired by public opinion, but only now was the
idea spreading that an unrestricted central power was the best
possible form of government. An absolute king alone was expected
to be able to secure internal peace against the feudal and religious
parties which constantly threatened to excite rebellion and civil
war. He was to suppress odious feudal privileges and to increase
national prestige and power. In France these aspirations were particularly strong. Henry IV came to power owing to them, and began to
realize their aims. He wanted to crown his work by a great war
against the Habsburgs, which was to render France the leading
power in Europe. But this plan was frustrated by his assassination.
A glorious war was also considered by French statesmen the best
remedy against internal strife. An attack on the Habsburg dynasties,
ruling in Spain, Belgium, Italy and Germany, could easily be justified
before public opinion as aimed at breaking a dangerous encircle-
ment, and recovering countries which had once belonged to France.
Paris lay very near a possibly hostile frontier. Henry IV seems
further to have anticipated modern ideas of nationalism. He once
said that all the countries of the same language should be united in
one realm, and this should also apply to those of the French tongue.
According to another witness, however, he wished to extend
France up to the Rhine. This would have violated the former maxim,
since a great section of the peoples on the left bank of the Rhine
were German, Flemish and Dutch. Even Lorraine then contained a

large German element. The Duke of Lorraine in 1630 asked the General of the Jesuits to send him German fathers, because two-thirds and more of his subjects spoke German. Moreover, even the French speaking peoples left of the Rhine and in the Franche Comté were quite opposed to being annexed by the King of France. Where the nobles had the choice they preferred a weak central power to a strong one.

The foundations for Louis XIV's monarchy were laid by the Cardinals Richelieu and Mazarin. They broke the power of the unruly nobility, greatly strengthened the central authority and encouraged the growth of a national ideology. In internal policy, the Estates General of 1614 had already marked the beginning of a new epoch. The nobility at that time treated the bourgeoisie with the greatest insolence and contempt and thereby compelled it to set its hopes on the unrestricted power of the King. In external policy, an ideology was developed which became one of the strongest traditions of France. It proclaimed France's mission to break the Spanish-Austrian supremacy in Europe in the name of the balance of power, to protect the 'liberty' of the small states, especially in Germany and Italy, and to become the arbitrator of Europe. To this end the Habsburgs were themselves to be encircled by allies of France, religion was to be subordinated to politics, and even the infidel Turks and the Calvinists were welcome as allies against Catholic Spain and Austria. The Reason of State became the supreme maxim of politics, though Richelieu understood it also in the sense that reason implied regard to the King's reputation and the observance of caution and moderation. In this respect Louis XIV did not remain true to the principles of the great statesman.

LOUIS XIV'S SYSTEM AND ITS CONSEQUENCES

Louis XIV (1638-1715) came to the throne as a child, and began to reign himself after the death of Cardinal Mazarin (1661). His education had been rather neglected, but he possessed very considerable intelligence and will-power, and devoted much care and time to the tasks of government. Moreover, he was an unsurpassed master at representing the majesty of an all-powerful monarch. His wish was to decide every matter of importance himself, but in fact some of his ministers had great powers. Like many other despots he mainly employed ministers of bourgeois origin who were entirely dependent on his favour, and were rewarded with high rank and great wealth, but members of the high aristocracy were excluded from any real influence on policy. They might hold honourable and profitable posts in the army or the Church, and were expected to attend the court of Versailles, where they could easily be watched, but they were to have no opportunity of counter-acting the royal policy.

The regime was based on the absolute, unrestricted power of the king over everybody and everything. He regarded himself as God's representative, endowed with special faculties, and his admirers called him divine. This claim went much farther than previous arguments in favour of strengthening the royal power. Its earlier defenders, especially Jean Bodin, had assumed that the king was at least bound to observe the divine and the natural law, and the unwritten traditions of France. They laid the greatest stress upon the maintenance of a Reign of Law, on the security of person and property; the sanctity of contracts, and so on. But this condition was not always fulfilled in the reign of Louis XIV. As a rule, of course, the ordinary course of law was respected, and general security was even better safeguarded than before. The King even had powerful nobles executed if they broke the public peace. But in many cases the King himself disregarded fundamental principles of law and justice if this seemed to him appropriate. The extraordinary rise of absolutism was due partly to momentous developments in the public mind, partly to the unprecedented accumulation of power in the hands of Louis XVI. All the rival voices had been completely silenced. France had the greatest and best organized army, and her navy for a time surpassed those of England and Holland together. Her territory was protected, where necessary, by a threefold line of impregnable fortresses. The French revenues and economic resources were the greatest in Europe. Moreover, she was staking out claims to a vast colonial empire. In no other country did the central power thus dominate the whole life of the people. Louis XIV further had excellent ministers, diplomats and generals, and he disposed of vassals all over Europe. Lastly, French civilization had reached a splendour unparalleled in any country. No wonder that forces of this calibre also stimulated pride and ambition to the utmost.

A king, concentrating all these powers in his own person, seemed to be a super-human being, high above any moral responsibilities. This new godhead was surrounded by an almost religious ceremonial and adulation, celebrating his unique majesty. In magnificence and splendour the Court of Versailles eclipsed all other courts and dazzled the eyes of the world. Yet the King brought not only a new, most refined and gorgeous style of court life, but also a new idea of rulership for which this style was the symbol. It was the self-glorification of the new-born Power State.

This grandiose structure also had dangerous flaws, which were long obscured by the brilliance of its façade and ornaments. The suppression of every liberty created a festering sore. The cruel persecution of the Huguenots drove hundreds of thousands of France's best citizens abroad, enriched foreign countries, and aroused passionate criticism of Louis XIV's system. Taxation was extremely burdensome, and its full weight fell on the poorer classes, in particular on the peasants. The King's aggressive wars demanded enormous amounts of money and his extravagance in building, and his luxurious court were ruinous. In the first twenty-two years of his reign he had, in Colbert, a minister of finance and commerce of genius, who even tried to restrain his prodigality. In addition Colbert developed France's industries, foreign trade and colonies by a policy of mercantilism, based on the principle of economic power politics, especially on the belief that in trade the profit of one side was the loss of the other. Colbert's economic war against Holland contributed to Louis XIV's resolution to conquer the country. The promotion of France's economic strength, her independence of foreign countries, and her domination of the world market, were estimated as being much more important than the welfare of the masses. The interests of the peasants who formed the great majority of the people were sacrificed to those of trade and commerce, and also to that of the army, which had to be provided with cheap grain. And even Colbert's genius could not heal the wounds which many previous wars had already inflicted on France's financial system. The cost of war was the main reason which had induced the king to sell the posts of most judges and officials to people who could pay a high price. They became their property, which might be sold again or transferred to their heirs. The officials had, therefore, an interest in exploiting the people. Moreover, the collection of many taxes had been farmed out to financiers, who made excessive profits out of this business.

The great majority of the French peasants were free and their feudal rents and services were mostly not too onerous. But they were so oppressed by fiscal and capitalistic exploitation and by the consequences of mercantilism that they lived in awful misery. Absolutely reliable contemporary reports leave no doubt about this. This was the price which the French people had to pay for the warlike glory of their King. Louis XIV was not cruel or hard-hearted. He sometimes expressed sympathy for the lower classes, saying that there should be no destitution and begging, and that everybody should have his subsistence. But these benevolent feelings never led

E

to any effective social policy. Some attempts were made with work-houses and other relief, but on the whole the improvement was small. Power politics obstructed social policy both ideologically and financially. Richelieu had written in his Political Testament that all politicians were agreed that if the peoples were too well-off they could not be kept within the bounds of their duties. They were like mules which, accustomed to their burdens, were more spoiled by too much rest than by work, though the latter must not be excessive.

Mercantilism did not entirely neglect the interest of the workers. It stimulated industries, trade, shipping and building, fixed prices, wages and rates of interest, and so on. But the promotion of the welfare of the lower classes was very little developed. In the opinion of the time this was charity, and therefore left to the Church. Education too was regarded as its sphere. Pious congregations devoted themselves to the instruction of the poor. But all this was utterly inadequate with regard to the immense amount of destitution. Schools for the lower classes were scarce in the towns, and completely lacking in the country. Yet Richelieu had expressed the apprehension that there were already too many schools and that this was a danger to the state, mainly because educated people would refrain from becoming soldiers.

LOUIS XIV AND WAR

Louis XIV's ardent wish for ever more glory induced him to devote most of his energy to diplomacy and war. Almost two-thirds of his reign was taken up by war, and the rest with preparations for it. He declared himself that the striving for glory was his strongest passion, and that the most noble occupation for a king was war. His minister of war, Louvois, created an army of unprecedented power, often advocated new wars, and stood for the utmost ruthlessness in waging them. He thereby even came into conflict with the King, who would have preferred more humane methods, though mainly in order to win over the people attacked to submit to his rule. The King usually put forward legal arguments which were flimsy pretexts for his wars and he also began aggressions without any declaration of war. In his secret memoirs, written for his heir-apparent, he frankly admitted that at the beginning of his reign no state was able or willing to wage war against France, and that peace with his neighbours would probably have lasted as long as he himself desired. At the end of his life he even deplored that he had loved war too much. On his deathbed his last words to his successor, then a child, were the admonition to relieve the burdens of the people and therefore to avoid war as much as possible, since it was the ruin of the people. He continued : 'Do not follow the bad example I have given you in this matter. I have often too easily gone to war, and continued to fight from vain glory. Do not copy me, but be a peaceful prince and let your chief task be to render happier the lot of your subjects.'

France herself was not ravaged by Louis XIV's wars as were Germany, the Netherlands, Italy and Spain. Yet the financial burdens caused by them plunged the mass of the French people into the deepest distress. French historians most competent in this field agree in pointing out that the reign of this king was one of the most terrible times for the French people. There were many revolts of the peasants, which were suppressed with the greatest cruelty. During the whole eighteenth century the fear was widespread that a formidable revolution was in the offing. There is also no doubt that the system of Louis XIV had a great share in preparing the ground for the coming of the great revolution. Nevertheless the historians also agree that the King's wars were welcomed by 'public opinion', and that his warlike triumphs intoxicated the nation. Lavisse says in his masterly history of this epoch that the love of glory was 'the passion of the whole of France'. But he also adds what he understands by this term : It was three or four hundred thousand people, in particular the clergy, the nobles and lawyers educated by the Jesuits and at the universities. The figure given by Lavisse formed about 2% of the total population. This example illustrates the value of terms like public opinion, the nation, or the whole of the people.

The power and splendour of Louis XIV, however, not only fascinated that part of the French people who made public opinion, but also the corresponding classes of many other nations. Most European kings, princes and statesmen were at times Louis' satellites, and received from him subsidies and political directions. Besides financial and diplomatic reasons, the impression of the King's personality and system also contributed to this dominating position. Yet in the later years of the French King's reign developed in high circles and among intellectuals, an underground opposition to the fundamentals of his regime. A section of its followers wanted merely a restoration of the power of the nobility, but there were also those who were actuated by deep compassion for the sufferings of the people. Boisguillebert and Vauban criticized the injustices and faults of the economic and financial system. Fénélon, tutor of Louis XIV's grandson, the Duke of Burgundy, castigated, in his 'Télémaque', the bad kings who wage aggressive wars and sacrificed their peoples to their ambition. Many Huguenot refugees abroad published the most bitter attacks on the King's policy. In 1689, a tract appeared in Holland under the title 'Les soupirs de la France esclave qui aspire après la liberté'. Its author was M. Levassor, a former Catholic priest. It sharply denounced absolutism in France, and wished for a reform on the model of the English Parliament, the German Reichstag or the Dutch Estates.

THE KING, GERMANY AND EUROPE

The influence of Louis XIV on the German public mind in the course of his long reign showed great variations. There were times when he could in full peace march his troops deep into Germany to help one of his satellites, or when he could use German territories as a base for waging war, without losing his hold on many German princes. At the beginning of his reign most of them believed in his moderation and regarded his power as a counter-weight to that of the Emperor, and as a guarantee of 'German Liberty', namely the liberty of the princes from the central power. Mazarin's cautious diplomacy had created this confidence. Important German princes concluded a Rhenish Confederation (1658-67) which was joined by France and Sweden, and was directed against the Emperor. The plan was several times ventilated by French diplomacy that the German Electors should at the next election of an Emperor either vote for Louis XIV or for a candidate designated by him, and it was favourably received in Germany. This attitude was also shared by a considerable section of public opinion. Prominent German scholars and publicists were on the side of the King who generously granted them pensions for their services. A remarkable case was that of J. Frischmann, a German statesman, a brilliant publicist and a lover of universal peace. This sentiment made him an admirer of Louis XIV, and he was later appointed French envoy in Strasbourg. He gradually became a defender of French imperialism.

The first years of Louis XIV's reign were filled with military reforms of the greatest significance and with preparations for war. In 1667, the King attacked the Spanish Netherlands and won an easy victory, since Spain was unprepared. Five years later he waged war against the Dutch who were unarmed, except at sea, owing to the policy of appeasement followed by the ruling commercial classes. A great part of the country was overrun.[1] The Emperor, the

[1] The Jesuit Bouhours, a fashionable writer, celebrated the King's deeds in a poem saying he had conquered Lorraine in a day, the Free County of Burgundy in a week, Holland in a month, and it would take him only a year to conquer the whole of Europe.

Empire and a number of other states entered the war against the King. But by the Peace of Nimwegen (1679) he acquired very considerable aggrandisements. After the peace treaty the King continued his policy of annexations, under the pretext of 're-unions', and occupied German territories in Alsace, the Saar, Luxembourg and in the Rhinelands, and at last Strasbourg. The Empire protested, but was unable to renew the war. At that time Turkey, in collusion with France, made a great onslaught on the territories of the Emperor. The Empire was forced to conclude a twenty years armistice with the King. New threatening moves of the King induced several German and other rulers to make a defensive alliance against him. Thereupon he invaded Germany without a declaration of war, and terribly devastated the Palatinate, which he intended to annex. This war lasted nine years, and ended with the Peace of Ryswick (1697). Louis XIV's next great war was the War of the Spanish Succession (1701-13), which will be surveyed later.

The King's aggressions increasingly aroused public opinion against him and this also had considerable influence on the attitude of the German princes. This development was expressed in thousands of publications: when Louis began his warlike policy a French lawyer, Aubery, maintained in a book that the King was the legitimate successor of Charlemagne and that, therefore, the whole of Germany belonged to France. The King later, in his secret memoirs, put forward similar ideas, but at that moment Aubery's book embarrassed the government and he was for some time confined in the Bastille. François de Lisola, a prominent diplomat of the Emperor, answered in a book which became famous. In opposition to the policy of appeasement of his own government, he described Louis' policy as the greatest danger to European freedom and the international reign of law, and called upon all countries to resist it. He was a highminded and brilliant writer who published more than twenty major books and also inspired many other writers.

The trends of German public opinion as expressed in the pamphlets of the time have been analysed by a number of historians indicated in the bibliography. Noteworthy is that many of the writings show a national sentiment which Louis' aggressions had awakened. They often also pleaded for the strengthening of the power of the Emperor, but the ingrained particularism of the public mind made practical reforms very difficult. Prince Georg Friedrich von Waldeck, who had long been a staunch opponent of the Emperor, now proposed that his powers should be increased. In Brandenburg Gottfried von Jena wrote important pamphlets against Louis' policy.

Louis XIV's power rested not only on his military strength, but also on his consummate diplomacy. The Emperor was usually threatened by the King's allies from several directions. In the North, Sweden and Poland were long pillars of his power. In the South, the French King had the support of powerful princes and parties in Italy, Spain and Portugal. In the West, he not only had close relations with Charles II and James II of England, but also subsidized important members of Parliament. In the East, the Turks and the Hungarians often waited for his signal to attack the Emperor. The eventual decline of Louis XIV's power was partly due to the fact that he lost his principal allies. The Emperor defeated Turkey, and Tsar Peter I the Swedes. The most important change, however, was the expedition of William III of Orange-Nassau to England, which brought about the deposition of James II, the ally of Louis XIV. This expedition was made possible by several German princes, especially Frederick William of Brandenburg-Prussia and his successor, who sent troops in order to cover William III in the rear, otherwise Louis XIV could have invaded the Netherlands and cut off William from his base.

8

THE CONQUEST OF HUNGARY BY THE TURKISH EMPIRE
AND ITS CONSEQUENCES

ITS SIGNIFICANCE FOR OUR SUBJECT

THE fact that the Turkish Empire conquered the larger part of Hungary and was threatening many other countries of Europe was of the greatest importance for Austrian, German and international politics, and had considerable influence on the development of the public mind of the peoples concerned. The Austrian Empire was mainly formed for common defence against the Turkish menace, and since its principal countries were members, or close associates, of the German Empire, and the Austrian rulers regularly were elected German Emperors, the German people, too, was greatly affected by the questions springing from the situation in the large plains on the lower Danube. The Catholic Church and many nations saw in the Turkish hold over Hungary a terrible menace to Christianity and civilization, while France and other enemies of the House of Austria regarded the immense military power of Turkey as a most welcome ally. But also the intransigent Protestants in Germany and other countries often leaned more to the cause of the Sultan than to that of the Emperor. Lastly the attitude of the Hungarians also was often very hostile to the Emperor, against whom they revolted again and again, supported by the Turks.

An understanding of these complicated questions demands a closer study of the forces involved, and particularly of their mentalities. To this end, however, we must look back to the Turkish conquest of Hungary though it had happened more than a century before the beginning of the epoch forming the subject of this book.

HUNGARY'S SITUATION BEFORE THE CONQUEST

In the middle ages, the Hungarians rose from nomadism to life in a comparatively well-organized state, owing to the fact that the early kings from the Arpad dynasty, and some of their successors, possessed extraordinary prestige, power and wealth, forming a parallel to the Norman conquerors. The nobility were warlike, developed a sense of national unity and pride, and in the course of time obtained great privileges, particularly the right of electing the king, of resisting him, if he infringed their liberties, and of forming a kind of national assembly. In the fifteenth century, John Hunyadi won great fame as military commander against the Turks, and his son Matthias Corvinus, being elected king, sought to conquer the Bohemian and Austrian countries, too. His aim was largely achieved; the king resided and died in Vienna. He was the forerunner of the Habsburgs in creating a Danubian Empire. It is noteworthy that from the end of the Arpad dynasty to the Turkish conquest there were ten kings of foreign origin, and one of Hungarian extraction. Of the foreign rulers two were German Emperors too; Sigismund of the House of Luxemburg, and Albrecht II, a Habsburg, who both had to fight Turkish aggressions.

After the death of king Albrecht a great feudal reaction set in. According to dynastic pacts the Habsburgs should have followed. But the nobles did not want strong kings and moreover disliked the Habsburgs as Germans. There were no legal distinctions of rank among the nobles, but great royal dignitaries had titles, and a number possessed much land and great power, and were known as magnates. In this respect Hungary resembled Poland, in both countries the nobles alone formed the nation, and the trend went towards an aristocratic republic presided by a king without power. Leaders of the Hungarian nobles said they wanted a king whom they could hold by the tuft of his hair. Poland and Bohemia were the countries where the nobles were the real masters; therefore Wladislaw II, King of Bohemia and son of the King of Poland, was elected. He was a peaceable, good-natured man, but without any energy and unable to refuse a request. The nobles could do as they liked. He was in 1516 followed by his son Louis II, then ten years old, whose character showed promising features, although court life distracted him from serious work. Moreover, he was too young, and hardly possessed the capacity to stem powerful currents carrying the country to anarchy and ruin.

In this epoch great rivalries among the nobles prevailed, leading to the cleavage of the National Assembly into parties. The richest and most powerful magnate, John Zapolya, governor of Transylvania, nursed the ambition to become king himself. To this end he favoured the party of small nobles or knights, who were led by Stephen Verboeczi, a great lawyer and powerful orator. In those times most Diets could be attended by all nobles personally, though few did so, because of the expenses. Verboeczi encouraged personal appearance, since this enabled the knights to dominate the National Diet. Magnates and knights were not yet sitting in different assemblies. In the Hungarian conditions, the attendance of masses of excited, illiterate and armed knights, led by a gifted demagogue, was a great danger. Already before the age of Verboeczi, the nobles were unwilling to make sacrifices to the community and to strengthen the means of defence. Corruption and violence were rampant, and the strife of the parties paralysed any effective government. In 1514 a great peasant revolt broke out, which was suppressed by Zapolya with ghastly cruelty. The peasants were tied to the soil and depressed into hard servitude.

Since the end of the fourteenth century Turkey had conquered ever more countries and drawn nearer and nearer to Hungary. The Turkish Empire was a warrior state bound by its structure and tradition to constant aggression and expansion. Its military forces were more than half a million men, and manpower was practically inexhaustible. Luther, who was well informed about Turkey, thought that the whole of Europe was hardly a match for it. The Sultan had on the whole his troops firmly in hand and, unlike most European rulers, had not constantly to fear that his soldiers would revolt if their wages were not paid in due time. Owing to the tributes of the subjected peoples and the unrestricted power of the Sultan, the Turkish treasury had always plenty of money. The soldiers received their allowances and besides booty, slaves and extra gifts. The Janissaries formed a standing army of unparalleled training and fanaticism. Warfare was extremely ruthless, large sections of the people were massacred or carried away into slavery. But peoples who subjected themselves often had a tolerable life. They had to pay tribute, and in some countries to deliver a proportion of their children to become Mohammedans and Janissaries. As to their religion and nationality the Turks did not bother, and they were left a good deal of autonomy. The Turkish administration was not seldom better than that of Christian countries, and the common people among the Christians often hoped that a Turkish victory would relieve them from oppression by their feudal lords. The Turks had no nobility and privileged classes, and those Christians who became Mohammedans were equal to the Turks. The highest posts

E*

were even regularly filled with renegades. But even the highest dignitaries were considered slaves, and frequently put to death by order of the Sultan, merely to seize their property. The Turkish warrior-race despised trade and commerce, and Armenian, Greek and Jewish traders could grow rich. Before a court, however, Mohammedans alone were admitted as witnesses, and Christians were therefore practically without rights if they had a conflict with a Mohammedan. The spirit of Turkish policy is illustrated by the fact that it was held advisable for a Sultan at his accession to the throne, to kill his brothers and other relatives to prevent rivalries. Amurath III, for example, had his five little brothers strangled. His son, Mahomet III, inaugurated his reign by having strangled all his nineteen brothers. Moreover, ten pregnant women of his father's harem were drowned in the Bosporus.

In 1520 Solyman II ascended the throne and immediately set out to make great conquests. A year later, King Louis, then fifteen years old, married Maria, the sister of Archduke Ferdinand of Austria, who at the same time, married Louis' sister Anne. This double wedding implied a close alliance against Turkey. Besides, great efforts were made to obtain help from other Christian rulers, but with little result. The Pope, however, often gave considerable financial and political aid. Cardinal Campeggio was sent to Hungary as Legate and Baron Burgio as Nuncio. Their reports, edited by Fraknoy, give the most vivid picture of events. The Sultan sent an envoy to Hungary demanding tribute, but this was refused and his envoy was ignominiously maltreated. Soon, Solyman led a vast army towards Hungary and captured Belgrade and other fortresses, the gateway to that country. Yet he postponed his attack on it in order first to make other conquests. This gave Hungary still a few years' time to prepare her defence. But the party struggles became still fiercer, the financial situation was desperate, the fortresses dilapidated and were not repaired, and the military forces were at their lowest ebb. The currency was so bad that mercenaries refused to accept it. In 1523, Louis and Ferdinand made a military agreement to wage a preventive war against the Sultan. Louis was to contribute 60,000 men and 100 cannon, Ferdinand 21,000 men and 30 cannon. The German Reichstag was asked by Emperor Charles V to supply 20,000 soldiers, but granted only 10,000. Luther was strongly against the war, since the Pope advocated it. He called the princes, willing to vote supplies, miserable and blind, and declared that the Turks were ten times wiser and more pious than they. Ferdinand, however, wrote to his brother, the Emperor: 'The Kingdom of Hungary is in such a state that I believe, its promise will be like smoke. If the Turks come, the realm is lost and our countries, too.' This feeling was shared by all European rulers and contributed much to their reluctance to help Hungary.

The party of small nobles led by Verboeczi used the National Assembly of 1525 to seize power. The knights appeared in great numbers and in arms, and sent the king an ultimatum. Their demands, put forward by several deputations, were that all foreigners at the court, who were mostly Germans, should be removed and their posts given to Hungarians. The Ambassador of the Emperor was charged with having interfered in Hungarian affairs, and that of Venice of being a spy. Both, therefore, were to be expelled. The Fuggers, the great German bankers, were the main creditors of Hungary and possessed there important mines. Now it was demanded that their property should be confiscated, as well as the tithes of the Church. The Royal Treasurer, a former Jew, was accused of malversation and therefore should be burned. The Lutherans, too, should be burned at the stake. This was aimed at the queen and her circle, who sympathized with the Reformation. Lastly, Verboeczi was to become Palatin (Viceroy) and head of the government. The King was forced to comply with most of these demands, though he insisted on a form of legality. The Nuncio reported to the Pope that some of the knights even wished to murder him and make Zapolya King, with the result that this country would be still more oppressed and pillaged.

The menace of a Turkish invasion in 1525 seemed suddenly to disperse. The Sultan told the Polish Ambassador that he would grant Hungary peace, if she would permit him free passage to Italy, when he would be ready to receive Hungarian envoys for negotiations. He obviously intended to attack Charles V, as King Francis I of France urged him to do. King Louis was willing to enter into negotiations, but the ruling party of the knights was entirely oppose to it. They were filled with the illusion that they could easily defeat the Turks. The Estates of Croatia, however, threatened to negotiate themselves. If the King of Hungary could not protect them, they declared, they were entitled to seek another ruler able to do so.

Stephan Bathory, the former Palatin, whom Verboeczi had overthrown and replaced, had in the meantime been very busy forming a new party. He won over the middle strata of the nobles, resenting the domination of the poor and rustic knights. Magnates, too, joined it, and they engaged many knights for their service, who thereby became also political supporters of their patrons. The turn of the tide was so powerful that Verboeczi resigned the dignity of Palatin and fled to Zapolya. The National Assembly with enthusiasm hailed Bathory, declared Verboeczi to be a breaker of the peace and enemy of the country condemning him to the loss of his landed property. The resolutions of the former Diet were cancelled, and full powers were given to the King. Yet the financial aid voted was quite insufficient. The Estates exhorted the King to use his powers, else they declined any responsibility. The King answered, they greatly overestimated his revenues, they could not demand the impossible, and in the case of great danger arising, he too declined to be held responsible. The Papal Ambassador Borgio, who was present, noted in his report what a comedy they all played. The King's plight, he said, was so pitiful that he hardly had boots serviceable for a war. In this critical hour Borgio made desperate efforts to save the country. The Treasury was empty and the state had lost all credit. The Nuncio, however, spent great amounts of Papal subsidies for organizing the defence, recruiting soldiers, buying cannons, etc. Appeals to foreign powers had no result. Rich Venice wanted to maintain good relations with the Turks, Francis I was their ally, Henry VIII promised money but sent nothing. Germany was in 1525 in the midst of the great Peasant War, which threatened to become a general social revolution. The German princes had no standing troops and had to employ all their means to hire mercenaries, in order to preserve their existence. When the storm was over, the Reichstag resolved to send at once the ten thousand men promised two years before. But this resolution was passed only two days before Hungary's final catastrophe.

In Austria, Archduke Ferdinand was in the greatest anxiety. In spring 1526, he proposed to the Pope that he should entrust him with the defence of the whole of Hungary. But the Nuncio informed the Pope that great caution was needed because the Hungarians were most hostile to all Germans. The Croation Estates, however, resolved to place themselves under Austrian protection, and repudiated obedience to the Hungarian Crown. When the Sultan was already on the march to attack Hungary, she had not even a commander in chief, and quite contradictory strategical orders were given. The King asked Archduke Ferdinand to induce Count Salm, a very experienced German general and Austrian chief commander against the Turks, to accept this post. But Salm, too, realized that Hungary's internal conditions made effective defence impossible, and refused under the pretext of his old age and sickness. Three years later, however, he was to distinguish himself by successfully defending Vienna against a Turkish army six times greater than his own forces. At last, most nobles consulted advised the King to appoint Archbishop Paul Tomori, but he strongly protested declaring he was quite ignorant of conducting a great war. Nevertheless he obeyed, and the brother of John Zapolya was appointed second commander though he too was reluctant.

THE BATTLE OF MOHACZ

In the meantime, the Sultan had drawn nearer, and a battle was imminent. The army, which the King had assembled, was much smaller than the Turkish one, but could have been considerably reinforced had the battle been postponed. Zapolya, in particular, was quite near with forces surpassing those of the King. A council of war was held on whether the army should retire to delay battle till further troops had arrived. The knights, however, had been instilled with the illusion that the Turks, in previous wars, had lost their best fighters, and that the rest was but a cowardly rabble. When the King asked the Commander in Chief, Archbishop Tomori, how great the two armies were, he replied that the Sultan had 300,000 men of whom, however, 70,000 only were good fighters. The royal army, he said, had merely 20,000. He, too, however, was convinced that the battle should not be postponed. In the last moment some further forces arrived, and the final number of the Hungarian army was about 26,000, among them also Austrian, Bohemian, Moravian, Polish and Papal auxiliaries. The knights clamoured for a battle, they declared that victory was in their hands, and even threatened that if the King delayed it, they would go over to the enemy and fight against his evil advisers. Their terrorism silenced every counsel of prudence. The menace, however, showed that they were mainly actuated by political hatred against the party in power, which had the King's ear, and still hesitated to take the fatal decision.

The battle took place at Mohacz on August 28, 1526. The nationalistic blindness of the knights and other nobles even led to the neglect of elementary tactical precautions. The Hungarians furiously attacked and, at first, seemed to overwhelm every resistance. But the Turks had a tactical plan which worked well. Within one and a half hour, the Hungarian army was annihilated. The King, numerous bishops and magnates, and 22,000 warriors fell. Several thousand prisoners were decapitated before the eyes of the victorious Sultan. The country was terribly ravaged. Later, 25,000 peasants defending a fortified position, were wiped out, and the Turkish army marched homewards, driving 200,000 men, women and children with them to be sold on the slave markets of Turkey.

There is not the slightest doubt that the fundamental causes of

Hungary's fall were the weakness of the central power, ineffective-
ness of the executive, narrowminded nationalism, and violent party
strife. The last Diet had recognized this and had given the King
unrestricted powers, though denying him the necessary financial
means. But this came by far too late. In the ideology of the nobles,
in particular the lesser ones, the King was to be kept powerless since
otherwise he would threaten their liberty. To secure this principle,
the nobles insisted upon their unlimited right to elect the King,
though the real old tradition of the country was the right of
electing a member of the established dynasty, a combination of the
hereditary and the elective principles. The unrestricted right was
obviously leading to national suicide, as the fate of Poland and other
nations showed. It induced many candidates to compete for the
Crown, trying to win electors by bribes and favours detrimental to
the strength and welfare of the nation. The result was the fiercest
struggle between parties, the most shameful corruption, and the
disorganization of the executive. The execution of laws and local
administration were mostly in the hands of the counties dominated
by knights, except in the towns, where the administration was conducted by burghers, who were Germans. The counties, however,
very often could not be trusted to carry out a law. The nobles
further also clung to their right of resisting a King, infringing the
constitution, which had been guaranteed in the Golden Bull, and
had become an idol. But it had never been defined in a way preventing misuse and therefore could easily be invoked in order to serve
as justification of every rebellion and of anarchy.

AUSTRIA'S STRUGGLE FOR HUNGARY'S UNITY AND FREEDOM

Hungary's downfall exposed all the neighbour countries to a
terrible menace, in particular Austria, and it compelled some of
them to form a union for common defence. This was the first step
in the development of a great Danubian Empire. Archduke Ferdin-
and, Austria's ruler and brother of Emperor Charles V, whose
successor he later became, had claims to the throne in the Bohemian
and Hungarian countries on the ground of treaties between the
dynasties concerned. But he found it reasonable to stand as a candidate for being elected king by the Estates. In Bohemia he actually
was elected in 1526, and the other countries belonging to the
Bohemian crown, Moravia, Silesia and Lusatia, recognized him as
king on the ground of the dynastic pacts, without an election. In
Hungary, however, there were two parties which held separate

elections. The majority elected John Zapolya king who also was recognized by the kings of France, England and Poland, by Venice and some German princes. The other party elected Ferdinand who was also recognized by the nobles of Croatia. Ferdinand further took up arms, and defeated Zapolya who fled to Poland. Most of his followers left him and went over to his rival. Zapolya, however, succeeded in winning the favour of the Sultan who claimed to be the owner not only of Hungary but also of Austria, and declared that his 'slave' Zapolya should be king of Hungary by his grace.

Sultan Solyman undertook six campaigns in order to conquer Hungary and Austria, he could occupy most of Hungary, including the capital Buda, and twice invaded Austria with vast armies, but was unable to take Vienna by storm. We need not describe here the long wars with the Turks and the relations of Austria with Zapolya and other Hungarian vassals of the Sultan. When peace was concluded, it did not last long. The principal result of all the fighting was that the fertile plain forming Hungary's central part was occupied by Turkey, and gradually became a swampy waste. This territory amounted to 36 per cent of Hungary's soil. In the east Transylvania, amounting to 40 per cent, was a vassal state of Turkey, but had a good deal of autonomy, and the right to elect her ruler. The territories along the Austrian and Moravian frontiers, and in the Carpathian mountains, amounting to 23 per cent, were held by the Austrian rulers.

The Habsburgs were involved in many wars with Turkey for more than two centuries. Under Charles V they had split into two branches, a Spanish and a German one. The former ruled over Spain, the Netherlands, large parts of Italy and vast colonial territories. The heads of the German Habsburgs were hereditary rulers of the Austrian countries, elected kings of Bohemia and a part of Hungary, and elected Emperors of the German Empire. They often made great efforts to liberate Hungary from the Turkish yoke, but for a long time without success. The power of the Turkish Empire was much superior to their forces, it stretched from the Indian Ocean to a region not far from Vienna, as well as from the Sahara to Southern Russia, and was reigned by a ruler with unrestricted powers. The European states threatened by Turkish aggressiveness, however, were gravely disunited. The Habsburg rulers could not concentrate their forces to repel the Turks but also had constantly to fight many external and internal enemies, in particular France, the ally of Turkey, many German princes, and large sections of the nobles in their own countries. England was favourably disposed to Turkey because of their common enmity

towards Spain and the Pope, and because trade with her peoples was
very profitable. Commercial reasons also induced Venice to wish for
good relations with Turkey. Before the battle of Varna (1444) Venice
and Genoa had even transported the Turkish army from Asia
Minor to Europe, charging one ducat per soldier. The Habsburgs,
however, often received support from Spain and the Pope though
the latter was sometimes hostile to them too.

The circumstances under which the Austrian rulers had to wage
war against Turkey were therefore unfavourable. Even when peace
was concluded between the governments, the Turkish commanders
in Hungary did not respect it, but made frequent incursions into
Austrian countries, pillaging and devastating them, and carried
away thousands of men, women and children to be sold as slaves.
Many Hungarian nobles, further waged a guerilla war against the
Turks employing for this purpose subjects who were called hayducks, a mixture of mercenary, robber and patriotic fighter. Their
activities often served the Turks as pretext for their incursions.
Bloodshed therefore never came to an end. The standing Turkish
army, moreover, contained large numbers of well-trained and
seasoned soldiers and experienced commanders while their enemies
had no standing troops but had to engage mercenaries when war
broke out. Most of these soldiers were fighting merely for wages
and plunder, and mutinied when their pay was in arrear. The
Turkish Empire had vast resources. In 1571, its navy suffered a great
defeat in the sea battle of Lepanto, when Don Juan d'Austria commanded the Spanish, Venetian and Papal navies. But a year later,
Turkey had a new powerful navy, and won the war against Venice.

Austria's resources were limited, and she could not stake the very
existence of her peoples on a single chance. In her countries the
Estates kept the money voted for war, the recruiting, selection of
commanders etc. in their own hands, they sometimes delayed the
transmission of money for the maintenance of troops, and these
began to riot and to plunder the people. These conditions tended to
make great offensive operations unadvisable, and recommended a
wary, defensive warfare. To this end, the frontiers exposed to
Turkish attacks were fortified by many strongholds. On the borders
of Croatia, Slavonia and Dalmatia the population had been almost
wiped out by Turkish incursions, and a chain of fortifications were
built up, known as the Military Frontier. The empty land was settled
with Slav refugees from the Balkans who had mostly become
robbers and were now settled as peasants in favourable conditions
but with the obligation to defend the country. They were a particularly warlike kind of people who, later, became the hardiest

soldiers in the Austrian army though they were also feared for their wild customs.

The crux of the matter was the lack of money. The accounts of the Austrian Treasury for the time of Ferdinand have been published by Oberleitner and Huber, and their study is very significant. They show that the greatest exertions were made to raise money for repelling the Turks. The Estates of the Austrian countries introduced new taxes and everybody had to contribute according to his property. Great loans were raised, domains and Church treasures were sold or pawned, etc. Finance was also put in order in the part of Hungary ruled by Ferdinand. But in the period 1550 to 1554, for example, the Hungarian contribution available covered a sixth only of the cost of war in Hungary. Five sixths had to be paid out of the Austrian revenues. The Estates of the parts of Hungary under Habsburg rule sometimes voted considerable aids, but they were often not properly collected by the counties. Towards the end of Ferdinand's reign the Estates of his countries contributed annually about one million florins to the cost of war in Hungary, and this amount, later, still increased. The Estates of Styria, Carinthia and Carniola, moreover, paid also the cost of erecting the great fortress of Karlstadt in Croatia, those of Lower Austria contributed to the maintenance of the Hungarian fortress Raab, and Bohemia and Moravia to that of Komorn. Both the Austrian central government and the Estates were overburdened with debts. The German Reichstag and some of the Circles of the Empire also paid large amounts, which from 1594 to 1603 amounted to over twenty-four million florins. In 1572, the Emperor demanded contributions for fortifications in Hungary from the Bohemian Estates. They offered strong resistance, but at last voted six million Thalers, or nine million Gulden. The Pope, the King of Spain and other rulers, too, not seldom sent money or troops.

CONSTITUTIONAL AND RELIGIOUS STRIFE

In the course of time defence against Turkey was in Hungary much affected by constitutional struggles between the King and the Estates, and between Catholics and Protestants. Among the Hungarian nobles there had always been a strong nationalism regarding the foreign Habsburg dynasty with suspicion and aversion. They feared that the King and his organs would undermine their liberty and nationality. Ferdinand I and Maximilian II, however, had certainly no such intentions but they distrusted the Hungarian nobles, and not without reasons. In many of them the mentality which had led to the catastrophe of Mohacs was still alive and not a few were sitting on the fence, waiting to see from which side they might get a higher price for their allegiance. Many preferred Turkey, which was the strongest and richest power, and least hampered by moral scruples. On the other hand, the Hungarians, too, had some reasons to distrust the Habsburgs. Archduke Ferdinand had been born and educated in Spain, and when he came to Austria, then 18 years old, he was surrounded by foreign counsellors, such as Gabriel Salamanca, a ruthless representative of Spanish despotism. But Ferdinand soon emancipated himself from them. His counsellors were, later, mainly Austrians and Germans, and this was odious to a large section of Hungarians, dominated by hatred of all foreigners, particularly Germans. Ferdinand, however, employed also Hungarians in important missions, and was in general international-minded. He spoke Spanish, Latin, German, Italian, French, Hungarian, Czech and Croatian, and some of these languages perfectly. His marriage with his Hungarian-Polish wife was happy, and she bore him 15 children. The historian, Count Mailath, points out that he held in Hungary twenty sessions of the National Diet, more than any previous King, and that they made 671 laws. Under his reign the National Diet further assumed a form bringing it much nearer to that of a Parliament, and rendering it much fitter for useful legislative work. The former common meetings of all nobles, great and small, were separated into a House of Lords and a House of the nobles, and the latter was henceforth not to be attended by all the knights personally, but by elected deputies of the counties and of the fifteen Free Towns. The King placed more confidence in the Lords than the knights, who were on the whole less educated rustics, easily swept off their feet by demagogues, and intensely nationalistic. He gave also great care to reforms of the Hungarian law and administration, adapting them to modern conditions. A codification of the laws was elaborated by excellent Magyar lawyers but was not voted by the Diet because it provided that the Crown was hereditary and that the King was immune from trial.

The peasants had in 1514, after their revolt, lost the right to leave the land of their lords and had been depressed to hard servitude. In 1547, at the Diet of Tyrnau, their right was restored, on the initiative of the king, under heavy penalties for those hindering them. Their forced labour was reduced to 52 days annually, and later to 40 days, and further measures protecting them were enacted. But the law was not carried out since the executive was in the hands of the knights, who dominated the county sessions.

The National Diet had many grievances against the policy of the

Habsburgs. According to constitutional tradition, the King had to reside in Hungary and, if he was abroad, the Palatine acted as viceroy. But in a time when the King of Hungary was also German Emperor, King of Bohemia and ruler of many other countries, he could not regularly reside in his part of Hungary, which was always threatened by Turkish inroads. Ferdinand I stayed there for seven months after his coronation. Yet his regular residence was Vienna, which was quite near (about 37 English miles) from the Hungarian town of Pozsony, where the National Diet and the Hungarian government had their seat. The post of Palatine was for a long time not filled under the first Habsburg rulers, but the King appointed a governor assisted by a council, all of them Hungarians. That the post of viceroy chosen by the Diet for life was not acceptable to the King is not surprising, and it was doubtful whether his powers were in accordance with the requirements of the time. The question was later settled by agreement between King and Diet. A further grievance was that the foreign mercenaries in the frontier fortresses often plundered and manhandled the population, and the nobles frequently demanded that they should either be withdrawn or put under Hungarian commanders. But large contingents of these troops were raised and paid either by the Austrian, Bohemian or German Estates, or by foreign princes or the Pope, who made it a condition to nominate the commanders themselves. It is also a rule of international law, valid even in our time, that foreign troops sent to defend another country, are not subject to its government but to that which had sent them. Hungarian troops were mostly put under Hungarian captains, but Mailath says that nothing grieved the Magyars more than the fact that Ferdinand always appointed foreigners as commanders in chief, who were regularly unlucky because of their lack of qualities needed by a general. It is impossible, however, to say whether any Hungarians better qualified were available. The Hungarian nobles inclined more to dashing exploits, self-sacrificing heroism, or guerilla tactics than to a large-scale strategy.

One of the main recriminations of the Diet was, further, that the conduct of diplomatic, military and fiscal affairs affecting Hungary, was discussed by the King with Austrian counsellors and treated in Vienna Councils, in which Hungary was not represented. This complaint was certainly justified, but difficult to remedy. The imperial government paid most of the expenses for the troops stationed in Hungary as well as for the diplomatic service, and it was therefore natural that its organs gave orders to the commanders and envoys. The establishment of councils in which Hungary and other countries would have been represented was not acceptable to the Hungarian Estates who declined any transfer of part of their sovereignty. The right of different councils to decide might have had disastrous military consequences. Eventually, however, the Hungarians obtained the right for Hungarian counsellors, residing in Vienna, to advise the King in matters relating to their country.

In the sixteenth century and later, relations between the King and the Diet underwent many changes, which cannot be described here. The Magnates, especially their Catholic section, the Prelates in the House of Lords, and the towns inhabited by Lutheran Germans, tended to make concessions to the King, while the Calvinist knights usually were rather intransigent. But on the whole, before the reign of Rudolf II and the aggravation of religious antagonism, compromises were reached in almost all the important questions, though sometimes they did not last, and new dissensions broke out. The Hungarian statesman Count Andrassy comes in his History of Hungarian Liberty to the conclusion that the growth of the royal power was in itself salutary for the nation, and that the first Habsburg rulers neither desired to subordinate Hungary to a centralized system, nor to Germanize her, though the Kings, of course, also committed grave mistakes.

Towards the end of the century, however, two tendencies gained great influence in all the Habsburg countries. On the one hand, the Catholic Church had recovered power, and the Jesuits formed the vanguard in a great counter-attack on the Protestants. Religious tension therefore became ever more acute. On the other hand, in all these countries a fierce struggle between the rulers and the Estates broke out, each side claiming predominant power. Religion became a symbol of national and political aspirations. Great sections of the nobles fought for their ideas of liberty and nationality under the banner of Protestantism, and the Habsburg rulers allied with Catholicism. In the battle of Mohacs, seven of the ten Hungarian bishops and many prelates had fallen; there was no reign of law; moreover in the prevailing anarchy magnates and other noblemen had seized much ecclesiastical property. They had handed over the churches and schools to the Protestants and, where necessary, put pressure on their serfs to adopt this creed. The towns, too, had appropriated churches, made the new faith obligatory, and expelled the Catholic priests and teachers. From the legal point of view, these doings were acts of force, even if sections of the people had welcomed the new order and others submitted to it. Though the majority of the Hungarians had become Protestant, except in the royal part and in Croatia, the constitutional position was that

Hungary was a Catholic realm. The Prelates still formed the first Estate and had great rights and influence. Besides the nobles and towns, the Turks also had done much to wipe out the old Church. They had reason to regard the Catholic Church as their greatest enemy, and to prefer the Protestants. The principle of religious toleration was still rejected by all Churches and governments, except in Transylvania, where the Diet laid down that all the principal creeds were to be tolerated. It was therefore unavoidable that the Catholic Church, when she had recovered strength, made great efforts to reconquer the lost position by all means in her power. Her representatives argued that the confiscation of her churches and other property had been against the law, and when a nobleman had returned to the old faith, he had no hesitation in handing over the churches on his soil and under his patronage to the Catholic authorities, and to order his serfs to submit to them. The Protestants had previously acted in the same way.

The political and religious tensions came to a head in the reign of Emperor Rudolf II, a ruler grown up in Spain, and of unbalanced mind, verging on insanity. His actions aroused violent resistance, especially the addition of a clause to a law passed, prohibiting religious strife in the Diet. Precedents for the addition of a clause by a King could be quoted, but under existing conditions it was unwise, as also was the enforcement of the restitution of a Protestant church to the Catholics, and other acts. A great Hungarian revolt under Stephen Bocskay, Prince of Transylvania, broke out, its result was the Treaty of Vienna with the Hungarian Protestants (1606). This went far in granting them the political and religious liberties which they demanded, and its stipulations were repeated and reinforced in many subsequent treaties, such as the pacts of Nikolsburg (1621), Vienna (1624) and Linz (1645). The great struggles of this epoch, however, much aggravated resentment and animosities on all sides. The Thirty Years' War gave Emperor Ferdinand II so much to do elsewhere that he had not much occasion to exercise his religious intolerance in Hungary. It was fortunate that Turkey was at that time unable to continue her aggressions. The rapacious militarism and universal slavery of the Ottoman Empire, the reckless luxury of its Court, the intrigues between those in power, the limitless corruption of the administration as well as great uprisings, economic and financial events, etc., brought about a temporary decline of its forces.

A great change in Hungary's religious conditions was effected by Peter Pazmany (1570-1637). He was of the old nobility, his parents were Calvinists, but he early adopted Catholicism, entered a Jesuit

College, and became a Jesuit himself. Pazmany was equally great as a scholar, writer, preacher, statesman, reformer of the clergy and promoter of education. The impression of his personality was so overwhelming that nobody could withstand him. Within a short time he converted the majority of the magnates to Catholicism, and also many others. He became Archbishop, Primate of Hungary, and Cardinal. In politics he stood for moderation and compromise, and rejected forceful methods, also towards the Protestants, though he defended the right of the lords to decide which religion should be admitted on their land. Though he was a staunch advocate of the Habsburg regime, he was also a good Hungarian patriot, and, in particular, the first master in writing the native language. Pazmany further devoted his greatest care to founding colleges and schools, and the university of Budapest is the successor of the university which he had created in Tyrnau. Under the guidance of his spirit large sections of the people became Catholics again.

9

EMPEROR LEOPOLD I AND HIS POLICY

HIS PERSONALITY

TEN years after the Peace of Westphalia Leopold I was elected Emperor (1658-1705). Mazarin, then France's leader, had made every effort to prevent the election of a Habsburg, and to place a German prince subservient to France on the throne. At one time he had even thought of making Louis XIV Emperor. His diplomacy failed, but the electors at least put many further restrictions on the Emperor, especially the obligation not to take part in a war between Spain and France. Leopold had been educated for the priesthood, and had to give this up because his elder brother died. But he always remained ardently religious, and Pope Innocent used to call him the Holy Emperor. He was a mild, shy and most peaceable man, extremely righteous and moral, taciturn in speech and of melancholic temper. It was never his ambition to exercise a personal regime like Louis XIV. He regularly accepted the advice of the majority, or the most prominent, of his ministers, trying to bring about compromises between divergent opinions, and to reign more by conciliation than by force. If his counsellors sometimes won him for a display of force, he did not long abide by it. He had an aversion to great, risky actions, though in later years he overcame his wish for peace at any price, and preferred war if fundamental traditions of his house seemed to demand it.

The great French historian Lavisse ascribed Louis XIV's excessive pride and ambition to his Habsburg blood, but this thesis is not confirmed by Leopold's character. He was a close relative of the French King. Their mothers had been sisters, daughters of the Spanish Habsburg Philip III, and the monarchs married two sisters, daughters of Philip IV of Spain. In spite of this relationship Leopold had to struggle with Louis almost constantly. The Emperor's

greatest joy was music. He not only played it well but was a composer of numerous pieces, and he also was a great lover of books
and possessed considerable learning. He spoke Latin, Italian,
Spanish, French and German, did much to win foreign scholars for
Vienna, and an Academy of Natural Science bearing his name has
done very good work, and still exists. Foreign visitors were astonished to see how poor his residence looked in comparison with the
palaces of the great nobles. But no expense was too high for the
operas and concerts arranged at the imperial court.

The Emperor's religious zeal made him too dependent on his
confessors and ecclesiastical advisers, and this sometimes led to
great intolerance against Protestants. When Leopold, however,
realized the unfortunate consequences of such actions, he usually
stopped them, as examples will show. He also spent much money
on the Church and charity; when he was driven in a coach he was
surrounded by beggars to whom he distributed gifts.

Though the Emperor took his duties as a ruler very seriously, and
tried to exercise them with justice, mildness and moderation, his
personality did not enable him to dominate the conduct of policy as
Louis XIV did. His policy was rather the outcome of a complex
interaction of many forces and historic fate, and the court of
Vienna was the scene of the rivalry of different groups for predominance.

THE COURT OF VIENNA

At the head of the government there were mostly men of the
high nobility. The Secret Conference, comparable to a Cabinet,
towards the end of Leopold's reign, comprised thirteen members of
ministerial rank. There was, further, a wider council consisting of
164 privy councillors. All of them were lords with the title of prince,
count or baron. The lower nobility, the knights, were not represented and also in the ministries they formed the minority. Many
knights had, in the sixteenth and seventeenth century, played a very
active part in politics, striving to make the Austrian and Bohemian
countries a federation of aristocratic republics and to leave the king
only the shadow of power, as in Poland. They also wished for the
complete victory of the Reformation. But they had been defeated,
and a very great number of nobles had fled or emigrated to
Protestant countries. Those who remained had mostly become
Catholics, or had been so before. Nevertheless, lords and knights
still had power in the Estates of the autonomous territories of which
Austria was composed. The nobles who, in the Thirty Years' War,

had been on the Emperor's side had been rewarded by large tracts of land confiscated from the rebels and had risen to high rank. It was they and their descendants who formed the principal statesmen of the Emperor.

This nobility came from many countries. Besides Austrians and Germans there were many Czechs, Croats, Hungarians, Italians, Spaniards, French, Walloons, Irish, Scots, and so on. This mixture gave the Court of Vienna a most international character. Moreover, the stormy times provided a great opportunity for ambitious, gifted or unscrupulous men to rise to great wealth, power and honour. The Court of the Emperor therefore included statesmen and generals of special ability, though also many courtiers without any significance. The prospect of a great career in the imperial service attracted numerous men from most parts of Europe. French enemies of Louis XIV's régime, like Charles of Lorraine and Prince Eugène, set their hope on the Emperor. But men from the middle and lower classes too had great prospects if they had unusual gifts. Under Leopold's father, J. M. Prueckelmayer, the son of poor peasants, had become Court Chancellor—the highest post in the government. Later many lawyers from Western Germany rose to the highest positions solely because of their talent and qualifications, for example Hocher, Strattmann, Seilern and Bartenstein.

Among the lords surrounding the Emperor not a few had distinguished themselves in war and diplomacy, and also possessed great economic and cultural merits.[1] But the preponderance of lords also had disadvantages. It hindered centralization and the abolition of feudal privileges, and fostered financial recklessness. Many magnates held that a sumptuous style of court life was necessary to demonstrate to the world the majesty of the Emperor, and that parsimony was beneath his dignity. Even rulers personally averse to financial extravagance were forced by the atmosphere of their courts to lavish large amounts on festivities, ceremonial pomp and pensions or gifts to nobles.

Catholic prelates and confessors also had great influence. The Venetian diplomat Michieli in 1678 reported that they even had more power than the ministers, and not only in questions of conscience. About certain questions, however, they did not all have the same view. Some showed great intolerance towards Protestants, others were milder. Bishop Christoph Royas y Spinola, a Spaniard who was much in favour with the Emperor, even stood for universal peace between the religions. In general the members of the Court

---

[1] Adam Wolf has given most illuminating studies of the Austrian nobility in his book on Prince Lobkowitz and in other writings.

were split into different groups, partly serving personal ambitions, partly advocating different policies.

WAR AND PEACE

The countries of the House of Austria had very numerous enemies, both open and secret. They were actually threatened from all sides. But the most dangerous were France and Turkey, which had often co-operated in waging war against Austria and each of whom was stronger than she. It is therefore understandable that the Emperor and his statesmen strongly wished to avoid war, and, if this could not be achieved, they laid the greatest stress upon preventing war against both at the same time. Opinions, however, differed about which should be appeased at almost any price. For an Austrian or Bohemian the Turks were, of course, the more dangerous enemy, since they were much nearer than France. The Church too regarded the infidels as the principal foe. But the Emperor also had obligations towards the countries bordering on France and in fear of her. Spain, the Franche Comté, Belgium, Lorraine and others saw in Louis XIV their greatest danger. At the Viennese Court two groups of statesmen faced one another, the French and the Spanish party. They might also have been named the western and the eastern one. In the first third of his long reign Leopold had two Prime Ministers,[2] first Prince Auersperg, an Austrian, and then Prince Lobkowitz, a Czech. Both stood firmly for good relations with France, though the former had risen to his post through Spain's support. Lobkowitz was a statesman of great stature, an admirer of Louis XIV, and a fervent advocate of absolutism. Louis XIV's most energetic enemy was Baron Lisola from the Free County of Burgundy, and later Duke Charles of Lorraine and Prince Eugène of Savoy. Emperor Leopold did not intervene in the first aggressive wars of Louis XIV and even concluded a pact about the partition of the Spanish Empire with him. In 1673, at last, Lisola's policy triumphed and Leopold took up Louis' challenge. Yet Lobkowitz still worked for peace with France till he fell from power a year later. His successor was Bishop Sinelli, the son of a butcher, who was an intimate friend of Lobkowitz and opposed to the Jesuits and their intolerance against Protestantism.

The first war which Leopold had to wage was on behalf of Poland which had been attacked by Sweden, Brandenburg and Transylvania and was threatened with partition. The Emperor sent his best generals and troops to Poland, who fought for three years against

[2] Not in the modern sense, of course. The title was : First Secret Counsellor.

her enemies and he also supported her with a diplomatic campaign. His policy was completely successful.

The wars with France have already been mentioned in the preceding chapter, except the War of the Spanish Succession which will be treated separately. Moreover, we have to take account of the wars with the Turks and the Hungarian rebels. Before doing so, however, Austria's internal conditions must be surveyed, since they were of decisive importance for her wars.

ADMINISTRATION, FINANCE AND SOCIAL POLICY

Foundations for a civil service had been laid in Austria earlier than in most other countries of the Empire, and she possessed, therefore, officials of high training and experience. Yet administration was in certain respects not efficient, owing to the marked particularism of the Austrian and Bohemian countries. These were not just provinces of a centralized state but had a strong sense of their own individuality, clung to their particular laws and institutions and were reluctant to submit to the central government. The territorial administration was in the hands of the Estates of the territory and the local was largely managed by feudal authorities. The Estates had in great struggles lost many of their former powers, particularly in the Bohemian countries. But in reality they still had great influence because they had retained the territorial administration. Their common ruler in Vienna was as far as they were concerned not Emperor, but King of Bohemia, or Margrave of Moravia, or Archduke of Austria, or Count of the Tyrol etc. At his accession he visited his lands, received their homage, and pledged himself by oath to observe their privileges, including the right of territorial administration. He had certain revenues independently of them, such as old tolls and fees, returns of domains or mines etc., which were to cover the normal expenses of his government. But extraordinary taxes, especially for war, were subject to the consent of the Estates. These made energetic use of their control of the purse-strings as e.g. Pribram has shown in a study of the Lower Austrian Estates. Sometimes the government had to employ measures of doubtful legality to obtain the means for a war, but the Estates were watchful and usually more or less succeeded in safeguarding their rights. They assessed and collected the taxes voted, they recruited and equipped the troops, and demanded that only natives of their country should become officers. They also often sent money for the troops directly to the generals in the field. This system had great disadvantages, such as procrastination and corruption. The government received much less than the people had paid. Military operations of the greatest importance often came to a standstill because the Estates had not yet sent the money to pay the mercenaries and to buy supplies. The central government in Vienna therefore tried to build up an administration of its own and a standing army, and to restrict the rights of the Estates. After the Thirty Years' War some regiments were not dissolved and formed the nucleus of a standing army. The wars with the Turks and French then led to its constant increase. The Estates gradually had more and more to give way to the monarchical power.

In the course of this development the imperial administration also expanded and the number of their officials multiplied. But their salaries were not raised and were very low so that the officials could hardly live without gifts from the public. Finance was not sufficiently centralized. A number of independent treasuries had grown up between which there was much rivalry. Under the stress of long wars the government had the greatest difficulties in paying expenses. The Church and rich nobles often gave loans or made donations. The Estates too did what they could. Yet the Treasury frequently could not pay in cash but instead only gave assignments for the amounts which the Estates were expected to vote later. The risk of discounting them was considerable and very high interests were charged for it. The financing of war loans and the delivery of supplies was mainly in the hands of Jewish bankers and contractors, who for a time made ample profits but later often lost most of their capital. One of the richest was Samuel Oppenheimer. When he died in 1703 it was found that the liabilities were much greater than his liquid assets. The Treasury alone owed him 5 millions which it could not pay, and it raised counter-claims.

During the whole period many plans were made to reform finance. A bank was founded for taking over claims of the government to taxes voted. In 1705 it was transformed into Vienna Bank which was backed by the credit of the city of Vienna, enjoyed great confidence and prospered. A few years later a State Bank followed, but it was not successful.

The military strength of France and Turkey was largely due to their richness in resources which were much greater than those of Austria, and also to the fact that they could squeeze out of their peoples whatever they wanted without being hampered by Estates. In the beginning of the eighteenth century the total revenues of Leopold I were estimated at 12 million Gulden. The military budget had revenues of ca 8 millions. The French revenues were in 1683 reckoned at 215.6 million livres,[3] but they decreased after Louis XIV's wars. In 1733 they amounted to 140.3 millions. In 1702 the former Austrian ambassador in Paris reported that the ordinary revenues of France were 140 millions but could be raised to 187 millions. Voltaire in his History of Louis XIV reports that the King during his reign spent 18,000 million livres altogether, which made 330 million per year. The difference between expenses and revenues was covered by loans.

Austria's financial straits were aggravated by bad management. The Treasury (Court Chamber) was for 23 years presided over by Count G. L. Sinzendorf, who tried to cover the deficit by loans at increasingly unfavourable conditions. He was induced by adventurers to found state factories, and to engage in risky speculation. In 1680 he was accused of corruption and sentenced to lifelong imprisonment and loss of his whole fortune. The Emperor pardoned him before he died.

The financial misery, however, was mainly due to the endless wars, to ravages by the plague, to the economic backwardness of large areas and also to the trend of world trade which ever more shifted from the Mediterranean to the Atlantic. Austria being no sea-power could not take part in the colonial expansion of Holland, England and France, which brought them great riches, and when Charles VI tried to develop trade with the West and East Indies England and Holland forced him to abandon this plan by the threat of war.

Austrian statesmen were fully aware of the necessity to increase productivity by encouraging industries and trade. Excellent economic experts from western Germany entered the Austrian service and worked out plans for this purpose. The ideas of Johann Joachim Becher, Philip Wilhelm von Hoernigk and Wilhelm von Schroeder have already been surveyed. Hoernigk's book 'Austria Above All if She but Wills' had an extraordinary influence on the public mind and the various projects of these economists also became, for generations, the programme of the Austrian rulers. The economic policy of the western countries and its results were closely studied, all the means of Mercantilism were employed, and foreign industrialists, technicians and workers were offered great advantages if they would settle in Austria. Great highways were built, navigation was furthered by the improvement of ports and waterways, and even a plan for a ship canal between the North Sea and the Adriatic was taken in hand. When Hungary was liberated from the Turks the colonization of the waste parts was undertaken on a large scale.

[3] The value of the Gulden was at first 1½ and later 2 livres.

Social conditions, in particular the plight of the peasants, attracted the attention of the government. The oppression of the serfs by their lords caused serious riots in Bohemia, which were ruthlessly put down. But the Emperor also issued edicts blaming excessive demands of the landowners, restricting the amount of forced labour etc. The peasants were advised to put their grievances before the imperial district officers. But these decrees had little result. The lords were too powerful and the Emperor too much in their hands to make possible trenchant reforms. Moreover, great reforms could only have been carried out in times of peace and the incessant wars which Leopold I had to wage barred any such possibility.

As mentioned already, Jewish traders played a great part in finance and commerce. The Emperor and his ministers protected them but their Christian competitors hated them. When Leopold I married a Spanish princess she persuaded him, under the influence of her confessor, to expel the Jews of Vienna. In 1670 they had to emigrate and mostly settled in the Bohemian countries. But soon opinions in high circles changed. The Treasury, the Estates and other authorities wished them to be re-admitted, and after payment of a considerable sum this was granted.

HUNGARY'S LIBERATION AND AUSTRO-HUNGARIAN
RELATIONS

IN the second half of the seventeenth century, the Turkish Empire recovered its strength owing to able Grand Viziers from the family of the Kiuprili, and its aggressiveness was thereby revived. Prince George Rakoczy II of Transylvania had provoked the wrath of the Sultan, his overlord, and was deposed by him. The country was terribly pillaged and devastated, 100,000 inhabitants were made slaves and carried away by the Tartars, and it was about to lose its autonomy and become a Turkish province. Emperor Leopold was asked for help, and he intervened with diplomacy and the use of arms. This led to grave tension with Turkey, and the Emperor was compelled to make preparations to ward off an attack.

The recrudescence of the Turkish menace was still further aggravated by that of religious struggles. Owing to Pazmany's work, the House of Lords was now completely dominated by the Catholics, while the second Chamber was divided between Catholic and Calvinist nobles. The fifteen Free Towns, which were mainly German and Lutheran, had lost all influence since the nobles had restricted them to a single vote for all the towns together. The treaties of 1606, 1621, 1624, and 1645, had guaranteed complete religious freedom, though there was an ambiguous clause safeguarding the rights of the Catholic Church, which was used by the Catholics to undermine the Protestant position. Further, the nobles who had returned to the Catholic faith and were patrons of the churches on their lands, handed them over to the Catholic clergy and often put pressure on their peasants to become Catholics also. This aroused the violent complaints of the Protestants, though they were reminded that they had once done the same. Several times the kings had tried to settle this question by compromise. In 1662 the Hungarian Diet was again the scene of violent altercations, and the Calvinists declared that they would not vote any measures of defence before their religious grievances were redressed, since the freedom of the soul was more precious than that of the body. The Catholics accused their adversaries of favouring the Turkish cause. These eventually walked out hoping thereby to paralyse the Diet. But the Catholics continued the session and voted the proposed measures. Their leader, Count Niclas Zrinyi, Governor of Croatia, was a remarkable personality, cultured and an ardent nationalist. He wished the Hungarians to achieve their liberation by their own efforts and was very hostile to the Emperor's foreign generals, especially to Count Raimondo Montecuccoli. The latter had un-paralleled experience of warfare, and was also a thinker imbued with humanity. He belonged to the cautious school of strategy and was averse to wasting lives and staking everything on a very uncertain chance. Zrinyi stood for heroic deeds, for sacrificing everything to national freedom and greatness, without much calculating the risk and cost. His ideal was a national army, but under the existing conditions this was an illusion.

The Emperor still hoped that war with Turkey could be avoided. It was a terrible surprise when in the spring of 1663 a great Turkish army under the bellicose Grand Vizier Achmet Kiuprili advanced towards Hungary. The Diet proclaimed the Insurrection, the old feudal form of mobilization, obliging every nobleman to appear with his vassals and retainers. But it proved a failure, since the nobility, especially the Calvinists, were recalcitrant from hatred of the imperial generals. The Commander in Chief, Montecuccoli, could only slowly assemble mercenaries. The Emperor, with the help of the Pope and Spain, made the greatest efforts to bring together money and soldiers. Not only did the Estates of his own countries promise help, but also the German Reichstag, and a num-ber of German princes were ready to send considerable forces. Even the young Louis XIV, who had just begun to rule for himself, offered his help, though his aims aroused much suspicion.

In the meantime the Turks opened the war by conquering the important frontier fortress of Neuhaeusl, not far from Vienna. Tartar auxiliaries raided Moravia and Silesia and brought back 40,000 slaves. Soon floods of rain made the roads impassable, and the Grand Vizier let his army take winterquarters. This saved Vienna. Zrinyi proposed a winter campaign, and, though the Supreme War Council was against it, the Emperor accepted the plan, appointed Zrinyi Hungarian commander in chief and seconded to him 12,000 German and Austrian soldiers in addition to the 11,000 Croats, Serbs and Hungarians, which he had brought together. With these forces he harassed the Turks, set fire to a great bridge, and burnt down 500 Hungarian villages, carrying away 20,000 cattle, 3,000 horses and other booty. The siege of a fortress failed, because big cannons were not available. Zrinyi's exploits were celebrated by the Hungarians as magnificent achievements, and the Emperor and foreign kings also expressed their admiration. Montecuccoli doubted their military value. There had been many casualties, and the operation must have inflicted awful misery on the Hungarian peasants.

Gradually, the imperial army had been sufficiently built up, and the foreign contingents had arrived. Several armies were formed, since Turkish troops approached from different directions. North of the Danube, the imperial general, Count de Souches, a Huguenot, commanding imperial, Saxon and Brandenburg troops, won splendid victories over much greater Turkish forces. In the south, imperial, Rhenish, Bavarian and Hungarian troops, commanded by the generals Counts Strozzi, Hohenlohe and Zrinyi, were less lucky. Zrinyi had a conflict with the other generals, who found his strategic plans too risky, and left the army. The central army under Montecuccoli faced the Turks under the Grand Vizier at St Gotthard. The Turkish army comprised 120,000 men of whom half were well-trained and seasoned élite troops, the rest auxiliaries and train. On the other side stood 10,900 imperial troops, 8,300 Rhinelanders, and 5,250 Frenchmen,[1] altogether about 25,000 men. Montecuccoli won a complete victory.

A few days after this battle, peace was concluded at Vasvar or Eisenburg (1664). Its conditions were a cruel disappointment. Transylvania remained an autonomous realm, though under Turkish overlordship. The plan of making it a Turkish province had failed. But the other terms were unduly favourable for Turkey. It could certainly be said that the power of the Ottoman Empire was still formidable, that a continuation of the war was very difficult and a great risk, and that the general situation of European politics did not allow of a great war in the east, which might have paralysed the Emperor in the case of dangers from the west. Montecuccoli once expressed the view that even twenty victories over the Turks would not break their power, but that the Emperor might, by one defeat, lose everything. He was therefore against a long war with

[1] Ramsay Muir is wrong in saying that the Turks were only driven back by the aid of 30,000 French troops lent by Louis XIV to the Emperor. The total of the French troops was 7,000 to 8,000, but the number who took part in the battle was 5,250. The French fought splendidly, but also others were excellent, and the decisive factor was Montecuccoli's strategy.

F

Turkey. In addition, the imperial government was convinced that the Hungarian nobles could not be trusted, and that a great war with the Turks would give them an opportunity of siding with this power, if the Emperor should not grant them full independence.

HUNGARIAN CONSPIRACY AGAINST THE EMPEROR AND ITS CONSEQUENCES

The Hungarians also bitterly complained that their Estates had not been consulted in making peace. But if one remembers how, two years earlier, the Diet had behaved, it is doubtful whether its convocation would have been of any use. The diplomats of the aristocratic Republic of Venice often characterized the Hungarian nobility well. In 1661, Ambassador Molin reported that they always insisted the king should strictly observe the laws protecting their liberties. But they themselves did not keep the laws, and every magnate played a kinglet, regarding his subjects as slaves. The great Hungarian historian and ardent patriot Francis Salamon showed in his classic work on Hungary under Turkish domination that most nobles then did nothing, or very little, for the defence of the frontiers, because they were entirely engaged in party strife and opposition to the government, not seldom also because they were more on the side of the sultan than on that of their king.

This mentality contributed much to the rise of a powerful group at the Court of Vienna which saw the only solution of all difficulties in the establishment of a régime of absolutism. The two most prominent statesmen, Prince Lobkowitz and Chancellor Baron Hocher, were the heads of this party. They had great influence on the Emperor, who long hesitated, however, to resort to a strong arm policy. His peaceable character inclined much more to legality, compromise and conciliation. But the doings of a great section of the Hungarian nobles certainly strengthened the position of the statesmen advocating an authoritarian policy.

After the Peace of Vasvar, Leopold tried to appease the malcontents by convoking the Hungarian Councillors. They most of all demanded that the foreign mercenaries defending the Hungarian frontiers against the Turks, should be withdrawn; they occupied 88 strongholds, and their expenses were mainly paid by the Austrian Estates. These soldiers were, however, an unruly element, often committing robberies if they had not got their pay. Leopold could not promise the total dismissal of the foreign garrisons. But he replaced the foreign soldiers by Hungarian ones in a number of forts, retired a German general particularly odious to the nobles, and appointed an Hungarian, Count Franz Csaky, Chief Commander of the Upper Hungarian troops. The latter soon took part in the conspiracy presently to be discussed.

The discontent caused by the Peace of Vasvar and by real or alleged violations of the Hungarian liberties, permeated wide circles of the nobles and induced a number of magnates to make a conspiracy against the Emperor. Its soul was Stephen Vitnyedy, a lawyer and fiery representative of Hungarian nationalism and Protestant radicalism. He was capable of every crime to promote his political aims. The conspirators, however, were also largely actuated by personal ambition. Some wished to obtain high and profitable posts or to become princes of large parts of Hungary with the help of Turkey and Louis XIV, and were quite willing to recognize the Sultan as their overlord. As an alternative, they were also prepared to let Hungary join the German Empire, to overthrow the Habsburgs, and to become vassals of the French King. Furthermore, they also tried to induce Austrian nobles to revolt against the Emperor. After some time, Peter Zrinyi, the brother of Niclas, who had died, became the most active leader. Soon, however, many of the conspirators became afraid or changed their mind for some other reason. They confessed the plot to the authorities, and each of them tried to exonerate himself, and to put the guilt on one of the others. The Emperor accepted their apologies and pardoned them. But some soon relapsed into their treacherous intrigues, and in particular incited the Turks to invade Austria. Leopold I and his principal minister Lobkowitz, who was a close relative of Zrinyi's, had been for a long time very lenient, hoping that the conspiracy would fade out by itself. But the time came when this was no longer possible. Turkish troops had been assembled near the frontier and seemed to be waiting for the signal to march in. The Government now acted with energy. Zrinyi, two other magnates and an Austrian nobleman were arrested and put before a special court. The magnates argued that only the Hungarian Diet was competent to judge an Hungarian nobleman. But the Primate of Hungary, Archbishop Szelepcsenyi, stated that rebels might also be tried before another tribunal, and even outside Hungary. All four were convicted to death and decapitated (1670). The Emperor would have liked to pardon them, but his ministers insisted on justice being done as an example to many others.[2]

[2] A detailed presentation of the conspiracy and the trial is in A. Wolf, Lobkowitz, 1869. It clearly shows that the magnates were traitors and mainly inspired by personal egoism. Yet a well-known Oxford historian has expressed the opinion : 'Leopold inaugurated his rule by the judicial murder of several Hungarian patriots.' Cf. D. Ogg, *Europe in the seventeenth century*, sixth edition 1955, p. 487.

The conspiracy gave the ministers working for absolutism an opportunity to win the Emperor for their ideas, overcoming his aversion to deviations from legality and to forceful measures. Besides Lobkowitz and Hocher Montecuccoli, Margrave Herman von Baden, Count Königsegg and other important statesmen and generals also belonged to this group. It was maintained that the Hungarians were a guilty nation which had forfeited its liberties and should be governed like the Bohemians after their great revolt. They ought to be kept down by a strong military force, mainly consisting of Germans, and should be induced to adopt German customs and to learn the German language. One religion only should be tolerated, otherwise there would always be internal strife. The Hungarians ought to pay adequate taxes, to which the nobles should also contribute.

The first measure taken was the prosecution of accomplices of the conspiracy. Hundreds of nobles were arrested and arraigned before courts composed of Hungarian judges. Numerous others, however, had fled in time, mainly to Turkey. A great many of those arrested were soon set free on guarantees for good behaviour. Several death sentences were passed, but only one carried out. Others were condemned to loss of property, fines, imprisonment, etc. A special tribunal composed of Hungarian bishops, magnates and lawyers tried a great number of Protestant preachers and teachers. A passage had been found in the letters of Vitnyedy, who had died, saying that the whole Protestant clergy had been won for the planned uprising and that the Papist dogs would get their lesson. On this and similar evidence the accused were summarily condemned to death. But simultaneously the Emperor pardoned them on condition that they signed a confession of their guilt and pledged themselves to give up the profession which they had misused. Most of them signed these statements, many even became Catholics and others emigrated. But there was a hard core of intransigents who refused to be pardoned under these conditions. Bishop Kollonich sent 41 to Naples and others to Buccari to serve as rowers in the galleys. This aroused an outcry in many countries and several Protestant Governments intervened in their favour. Some of them, however, escaped, others died, and the rest were set free after a year. In the meantime, many Hungarian bishops and magnates directed a crusade against the Protestants. Their churches and schools were taken away from them or closed, their books seized and burned, and great numbers 'converted' to Catholicism. An exception was made with the army. The Commander in Chief, General Spankau, was a Protestant himself and, though the bishops

violently protested, the numerous Protestant soldiers retained their
preachers, churches and schools by order of the Emperor. The
persecution particularly hit the German Lutheran communities. The
Hungarian bishops and nobles not only deprived them of churches
and schools, but also used the opportunity to suppress the German
character of their towns. The town councillors were often forced to
adopt Hungarian costumes and language. All these doings naturally
aroused immense hatred against the Viennese Government, though
they were mostly the work of Hungarian Catholic fanatics, whom
the Emperor could not control because they were his main supporters in the Hungarian House of Lords. It is also probable that the
Emperor often had no full and clear knowledge of what was being
done. Even in Catholic circles, however, some disapproved of the
persecution, for example Bishop Emerich Sinelli, a Hungarian by
birth, who became an important Austrian bishop and statesman.[3]

The measures of political absolutism envisaged made little progress, except that the Diet was not convoked and taxes were introduced by decree. The appointment of a Governor of Hungary
remained a dead letter. Lobkowitz' whole policy was increasingly
criticized, and in 1674 he fell from power.

In the meantime, the measures taken in Hungary under his
régime had led to a rapidly spreading insurrection. Its leaders were
nobles, but the others were mainly hayducks, a mixture of robber
and soldier from the lower classes, who called themselves Kurucz.
The Emperor was involved in a war with France and had only weak
forces in Hungary. The rebels waged a wild guerilla war, favoured
by the mountainous character of Upper Hungary. The imperial
troops were hard pressed, and partisan warfare naturally led to
great cruelties being committed on both sides. The Viennese Government was willing to make concessions, if they would lay down their
arms. But they refused; violence and robbery were to the Kurucz a
very congenial and profitable way of life, and they received ample
subsidies from Louis XIV, and help from Transylvania and Turkey.
In 1678 Count Emeric Toekoely became their supreme leader. He
was a young magnate, gifted, rich, good-looking and ambitious. At
the head of 20,000 men he plundered the German mining towns
with their great stores of gold and silver. At last the imperial troops

---

[3] The temporary persecution of the Hungarian Protestants by the Hungarian Catholic zealots and their supporters at the court of Vienna has left a
very evil impression of Austrian policy in various countries, especially in
England up to our own times. As a rule no account is taken of later changes.
It is interesting however, to compare these persecutions with the treatment
of the Irish Catholics by England in the same period. Cf. Lecky, *History of
England in the Eighteenth Century*, vol. II, chapt. 6.

gained the upper hand, and an armistice was concluded, though it did not last.

The Emperor was now determined to abandon the authoritarian and anti-Protestant régime. In 1680 the Diet was convoked at Oedenburg. Toekoely too, was invited under a safe-conduct, but did not appear. Among the magnates the great majority were Catholic, and so were 66 of the 111 deputies of the other Estates. The King designated two Catholics and two Protestants as candidates for the post of Palatine (Viceroy) and the Diet almost unanimously elected Count Paul Esterhazy. The independence of the Hungarian Government, diplomacy and finance, from the imperial or Austrian institutions was restored. The taxes introduced by decree were abolished, and many other grievances redressed. As regards religion, the two parties still showed their intransigent fighting spirit. Each side submitted a long list of the most abominable atrocities committed against their co-religionists by members of the other Church. The Emperor thereupon proposed a compromise, settling all points in a careful way. But neither party was satisfied. The Protestants demanded more concessions, and the Catholics contended that too much had been conceded to them. Yet the Catholic majority could be brought to vote for the propositions, while the Protestants declared that they regarded them as null and void. The Government had, with these changes, definitely renounced its anti-constitutional policy. Pope Innocent XI, wishing to reconcile the Hungarians with the Emperor because of the impending assault of the Turks, used his influence to end the persecution of the Protestants.

Leopold made further efforts to appease Toekoely and the Turks, but in vain. Even many of Toekoely's followers now realized that he was largely actuated by his personal lust for power, and perhaps still more by the resistance of his captains to ending a civil war which had enabled them to rise from poverty to wealth, by the opportunity it gave them of taking booty. Toekoely therefore definitely took the side of the Turkish power, became a vassal of the Sultan, and was hailed by the Turks as King.

PREPARATIONS FOR DEFENCE AGAINST A NEW TURKISH ONSLAUGHT

Louis XIV was at that time engaged in annexing many German territories, in peace-time and under the most flimsy pretexts. In 1681, he seized Strassburg, the most important gateway to Germany, and Casale, a fortress commanding the access to Italy on the same day. In Turkey, the Grand Vizier Kara Mustapha was working for a new war. The Emperor was faced with a desperate situation. War might break out on all sides, since the French king had vassals in every part of Europe. How could money and men be raised for such an incalculable emergency? Should military preparations be made for war in the east or in the west? Fortunately, Pope Innocent XI was very helpful. His diplomacy made every effort to win the support of other rulers for Austria, or, at least, to secure their neutrality. Moreover, he was also ready to contribute great sums to the cost of defending Christian Europe against Turkey. The greatest achievement of the Papal diplomacy was that it paved the way for an Austrian-Polish alliance. It was not the first of its kind. Poland had, from 1655 to 1660, been involved in war with Sweden and her allies, and had been threatened with partition. To prevent this the Emperor had twice sent armies under his best generals to her rescue. Cromwell and Mazarin had at that time favoured the anti-Polish cause. But relations between Poland and Austria were very changeable, owing to the anarchic conditions of the former. In 1674, John III Sobieski, became King. He was on the French side, and favoured the Hungarian rebels against the Emperor. But Louis XIV offended the pride of John's French-born wife and committed other acts which angered him. Moreover, it was not yet known whether the Turkish armaments for war were directed against Poland or against Austria. The alliance of 1683 provided that if the Polish or the Austrian capital should be attacked by the Turks, each of the contracting powers should send an army to the other's rescue. Leopold I had further to pay great subsidies to John III for hiring and equipping his army, and to make other concessions. The Polish king later wrote to his wife from Vienna that the expedition had not cost Poland a penny. He had raised the army with the subsidies of the Emperor and the Pope. But the consent of the Polish Diet had also to be secured, and for a while the French and the imperial ambassadors in Warsaw vied in paying bribes to Polish noblemen in order to get their votes for the policy of France or Austria. At last the Austrian won.

A number of German rulers, resenting Louis XIV's annexation of German territories, promised the Emperor substantial contingents of troops if given adequate subsidies. Frederick William of Brandenburg, however, was only willing to do so if the Emperor ceded to the French wishes. Louis XIV put on the mask of neutrality, secretly hoping that Turkey should win. He would then have appeared as the defender of Christianity and as the head of Europe. England was on the French side and traditionally wished to remain at peace with Turkey, because of her profitable Levantine trade; many English, moreover, sympathized with the Hungarian Protestants. The Emperor, therefore, received no help from England. But Spain, Portugal, Venice, Italian princes, Sweden and the Netherlands favoured the cause of the Emperor, and some of them paid him substantial subsidies.

On the same day as the alliance with the King of Poland was concluded, on March 31, 1683, a Turkish army of 280,000 men, headed by Sultan Mohammed IV and his Grand Vizier Kara Mustapha, started marching from Adrianople to Belgrade, the gateway to Hungary and Austria. The Emperor had by the beginning of May assembled a main army of only 32,400 men under Duke Charles of Lorraine, an excellent strategist and personality of great character. Considerable Austrian forces were still on the Rhine watching the French forces. The imperial army also included 6,000 Polish mercenaries under Prince Lubomirski which the Emperor, with Sobieski's assent, had enlisted in Poland and which did not belong to the Polish army. Large forces were needed to defend a long line from Silesia to Croatia.

The advance of the Turkish army to Vienna forced Emperor Leopold and his pregnant wife to flee. On July 17th a Turkish army of 180,000 surrounded Vienna. The city was defended by 14,000 soldiers under Count Ruediger Starhemberg, and about 6,000 burghers, students and workers. For two months it was heavily bombarded, its walls were undermined in order to blow them up, the Turks tried eighteen times to take it by storm, and the beleaguered made twenty-four sorties. At last, Vienna was in greatest distress and near her fall. Sobieski with his army had been delayed, but some German contingents had arrived, and Charles of Lorraine already thought of attacking the Turks before Vienna without the Poles, when they appeared.

Since there have been many controversies about the share of the various allies in the battle, we give the figures which Wagner, whose work is the most reliable original source, has copied with much additional information from the diaries of Duke Charles, the Commander-in-Chief. They refer to the forces which took part in the battle of Vienna. The Imperial troops amounted to not quite 20,000, of which 8,400 were cavalry, 8,000 infantry, 1,500 Poles of the force Lubomirski, 600 Croatians, and some others. The Poles, under the command of their King, numbered 3,000 infantry and 12,000 cavalry. Wagner expressly stresses that certainly not more Poles than this took part in the battle.[4]

[4] Laskowski, the latest Polish biographer of Sobieski, speaks of 24,000 Poles, of which 14,000 were cavalry and 10,000 infantry. This book mentions, how-

Besides this, there took part in the battle 10,000 Saxons, 10,000 Bavarians, and 9,000 Swabians and Franconians, altogether 29,000 Germans from the Empire. The Bavarians and Saxons were commanded by their own Princes, and were therefore élite troops. Wagner puts the total army of relief at 64,500, of which 31% were troops of the Emperor, 23% those of the King of Poland, and 45% those of German rulers.[5]

The king, being the highest in rank, was in command, but the plans were mostly the work of Charles of Lorraine. Both were outstanding generals and they fully co-operated. On September 12, the allies attacked and after a long and fierce battle won a complete victory. The Turks had rapidly to retire to Hungary. Before taking flight, the Grand Vizier ordered all the women of his harem, all the Christian slaves and the animals of his menagerie to be killed. Enormous supplies and treasures had to be left behind.

The triumph over the Turkish power aroused jubilation all over Europe. But, as usual, discord soon broke out among the allies. Some of the princes thought that their merits were not sufficiently recognized. It was in the spirit of the time that every prince was extremely jealous about points of rank and etiquette, and the stiff ceremonial of the imperial court often made relations difficult. Most of the German troops, and a little later also those of the Polish king, returned home. The Bavarians, however, stayed longer. Shortly Frederick William of Brandenburg abandoned the French alliance and began to support the Emperor.

A war of sixteen years followed. The subject of this book does not require a detailed survey of the diplomatic and military events. The imperial army under Charles of Lorraine took up the liberation of Hungary, the Poles invaded Moldavia, though with little success, and the Venetians Morea. The Emperor concluded a twenty years' armistice with Louis XIV to free his hands for the war with the Turks. Their Empire still had vast forces and their warriors fought with ferocity and heroism. In the marshy plains of Hungary epidemics, too, cost countless lives. Hungary had to be reconquered

ever, that the main body of the infantry consisted of peasants, who were largely unpaid serfs. From Sobieski's letters to his wife we know that their tattered appearance and poor equipment astonished the German generals who saw them. This 'infantry' obviously did not consist of trained soldiers. This explains why their number is neither included in Wagner's figures, nor in the Polish report to the Pope, which puts the strength of the combatants at from 13,000 to 14,000 men. The lack of sufficient trained infantry induced Sobieski to borrow before the battle four regiments of Imperial and German troops from Charles of Lorraine.

[5] It is therefore incorrect for Ramsay Muir, in his excellent *History of the British Commonwealth* I. p. 522, to say that Vienna 'was only saved by the valour of the Poles'.

F*

step by step, and streams of blood were shed. The Emperor and the German Princes had constantly to raise fresh troops for Hungary. All Christian nations regarded the war as a crusade for religion, humanity and civilization, and great numbers of volunteers flocked to Vienna from all countries. They included also a great proportion of nobles, who were highly experienced in warfare. At the French Court the young nobles would all have hurried to Hungary if the King had not prohibited it. Some of them nevertheless got there, among them two Princes Conti, who fought with such foolhardiness that the Emperor told them he would have them interned in a fortress to save their lives. Many of the Emperor's best generals were Italians and Frenchmen. The greatest among them was Prince Eugène of Savoy. The German Reichstag and the Austrian and Bohemian Estates voted great amounts for the war, the Austrian Church sold parts of her lands for this purpose and the Pope and the King of Spain contributed large sums. The accounts of the imperial military treasury showed expenses of 137 million gulden for the war against the Turks and the rebels from 1683 to 1700, and this did not include the cost of the German troops. Max Emanuel of Bavaria alone later demanded 32 millions for his expenses from the Emperor.

In 1686 Buda, the capital of Hungary, was stormed and liberated from a Turkish domination which had lasted 145 years. Further victories followed. Duke Charles of Lorraine defeated the Grand Vizier Suleiman near Mohacs, where once Hungary had suffered the most terrible catastrophe. The fortress of Belgrade was conquered by Max Emanuel of Bavaria. This induced Louis XIV to break the twenty years' peace pact with the Emperor and to begin a war against the German Empire and the Netherlands. The Emperor was forced to send most of his troops under Charles of Lorraine to the Rhine, and Turkey was thereby saved from utter defeat.

The imperial troops, nevertheless, undertook expeditions deep into the Balkans and the Christian peoples under the Turkish yoke were called upon to revolt. If Louis XIV had not intervened, they probably would have been liberated and associated with Austria and the West of Europe, before Russia had become a great power. The two world wars of our age and their consequences might thereby have been avoided.

In Turkey, Grand Vizier Mustapha, another Kiuprili, efficiently reorganized the army and restored its strength. The Imperial Commander-in-Chief was then Margrave Ludwig of Baden, a very able general, but hampered by the insufficiency of his troops. There were serious setbacks, and the Grand Vizier re-conquered Belgrade. In

1691, however, Ludwig of Baden attacked a much stronger Turkish army at Szalankemen, and won a complete victory. Ludwig reported to the Emperor that it was the most bloody battle of the century, and that the Turks had fought like lions. How bitter the struggle was is shown by the fact that on the side of the enemy the Grand Vizier and eighteen pashas and most other officers were killed, and on the imperial side, too, many generals and colonels fell. But the Margrave had soon to leave Hungary in order to take over the command on the Rhine. The Eastern Command was now succes-sively entrusted to several generals of lesser ability, till in 1697 Eugène of Savoy, then 34 years old, became Commander-in-Chief. In the battle of Zenta on the river Theiss, the Turkish army was annihilated. Sultan Mustapha II observed the catastrophe of his army from the other side of the river and escaped, though ten women of his harem were captured. Here, too, the Turks had extraordinary losses, among them most of their commanders. The Grand Vizier, seeing his army crushed, sought death and found it. The losses of the imperial troops were small owing to Eugène's strategical genius. In the same year the war with France ended with the peace of Ryswick. When England and Holland had reached their aims, they entered into secret negotiations with Louis XIV, and thereby forced the Emperor, too, to make peace. The war with Turkey still went on for two years. At last, the peace of Carlowitz (1699) was concluded for 25 years. The Emperor received Hungary but without the Banate, further Transylvania, Croatia and Slavonia, Morea and Dalmatia were ceded by Turkey to Venice.

The breakdown of Turkish power in Hungary also had a great influence on Toekoely's Kurucz movement. When the Turkish army was retiring from Vienna, Leopold I proclaimed a general amnesty for the rebels who would submit. The longing to end the civil war was thereby much encouraged. Within a month, 14 magnates, 17 counties and 12 towns renewed their oath of loyalty to the King. Toekoely's answer was the most barbaric terrorism against those who deserted him or were suspected of intending to do this. Fifteen Hungarian nobles were killed by impaling, ten others were hanged, and ninety-six were decapitated. But all such cruelties could not prevent ever more of his followers from abandoning his cause and submitting to the Emperor. Even before the siege of Vienna and later, when Buda was beleagured, Palatine Esterhazy operated at the head of considerable forces of loyal noblemen, raised in the feudal way of insurrection, though they were long hampered by lack of supplies and by Toekoely's terrorism. As mentioned already, the long partisan war had fostered hatred, fanaticism and cruelty on both sides. Sobieski had formerly aided the Kurucz movement and shown sympathy to Toekoely. But after having experienced their activities in Hungary, he wrote to his wife that they were worse than the Turks. This feeling also inspired General Count Caraffa, a Neapolitan, who in 1687 was Commander in Upper Hungary, resident in Eperies. He was convinced that he was surrounded by dangerous traitors and conspirators still hoping that Turkey would win and a new rising would then be possible. He persuaded the Emperor to give him powers to investigate the conspiracy and to establish a special tribunal. The Emperor added the clause that the procedure must be according to Hungarian law, and that only those should be tried who had received his pardon but had again committed disloyalty and treason. The general proceeded with the greatest ruthlessness, arresting numerous persons who had supported Toekoely, or who had been denounced, even if no proofs were given. Torture was applied, and a number were sentenced to death and executed. The judicial records have not been preserved, and the extant statements on the trials come largely from Hungarian writers sympathizing with the rebels. Even the number of the persons executed is not exactly known and is given as eight by Wagner, as nine by Rinck, as twelve by Fessler, as six by Klopp and as seventeen by Redlich. The outcry of the Hungarians induced the Emperor to abolish Caraffa's tribunal and to appoint a commission for revising its sentences. Some of them were annulled and confiscated property was restored. Caraffa was replaced by another general. But he had not lost the confidence of the Emperor, who obviously regarded his doings as springing from an error of judgment.[6]

Leopold I had, in the first thirty years of his reign, held three sessions of the Hungarian Diet. The fanatical strife between Catholics and Protestant, between the radical Hungarian nationalists and their opponents, the striving of imperial statesmen for monarchical absolutism, lastly endless wars and rebellions, had frustrated normal constitutional relations. The great victories over

[6] Caraffa sometimes showed circumspection and moderation, in particular in his report of 1690 to the Emperor, concerning Transylvania. His advice was to win over public opinion there by mildness and toleration.—An interesting English counterpart to Caraffa's doings was the 'Bloody Assize of 1685, held to punish the Whigs of Southern England who had supported Monmouth's rebellion, which was absolutely insignificant in comparison with the Hungarian revolts. 320 Englishmen were sentenced to death and executed. For sheltering a refugee, an old woman was burned and another one beheaded. Nearly a thousand suspects were transported as slaves to the West Indies. This was the deed of the Chief Justice Sir George Jeffreys. Caraffa was only a soldier in a foreign and hostile country, not a trained judge in his native land.

the Turks, however, seemed likely to open a new era. In 1687, the Diet was convoked at Pressburg. The king proposed that the succession to the throne should henceforth not be by election of the Diet, but by heredity. The eldest son, or the next male relative in primogeniture was to succeed. Further, the right of every noble-man to resist by force of arms, if he considered that the king was acting contrary to his privileges, was to be abolished. Both demands were absolutely necessary. The later fate of Poland was to make this clear beyond any doubt and the great majority realized this and accepted the propositions. Further clauses guaranteed the religious and political liberties of the country, reserving a revision of obsolete customs by agreement between king and Estates. The king's oldest son, Joseph, was crowned king to reign in succession to his father. Later Transylvania also recognized Leopold's sovereignty, and the succession by heredity and the privileges of the country as well as the freedom of religion were guaranteed.

HUNGARY'S RESETTLEMENT AND A FURTHER REVOLT

The Turkish régime and the long wars had left Hungary in a state of utter ruin. Large parts had become a waste, covered with vast swamps, without roads, drinking water, population or cultiva-tion. The restoration of productivity required not only enormous amounts of money, labour and organization, but also the rebuilding of the administration and of a reign of law. To begin with the question of the money needed, it was clear that most of it would have to be raised in Hungary itself by means of taxation. Austria had for centuries made the greatest sacrifices in blood and wealth to liberate Hungary. Now she was bankrupt. The army, officers and men alike, had for a year received no pay, and the soldiery was driven to help themselves at the expense of the people. It was unavoidable that heavy new burdens had to be laid on the people, and this embittered it against the foreign rulers. Who should, further, direct the work of resettlement? A section of the Hun-garian nobles had supported the imperial cause, but a much greater one had either done nothing of this kind or even seriously hindered the liberation of their country by revolts and treason. It was diffi-cult to find enough able people who were also reliably loyal and acceptable to the majority of the Hungarians. These conditions made it necessary to employ in the reorganization of Hungary also foreigners, which aroused resentment.

After the liberation, numerous nobles demanded the restitution of their lands, which the Turks had confiscated several generations before. It was natural that their titles had first to be scrutinized and that they were asked to pay a contribution to the cost of recovering them. Should obdurate rebels also get back their lands? Had not those nobles who had remained loyal, and the officers and soldiers who had driven out the Turks, a better claim? Moreover, from where should one get sufficient peasants to cultivate the waste land? As in the Balkans, so in Hungary, the Turkish domination had induced a great proportion of the peasants to become Hayducks, i.e. robbers or mercenaries, averse to earning by work what they could get by violence. The free life of a Hayduck and the wild Kurucz spirit were to them more attractive than the laborious and poor existence of a peasant. The restoration and development of economic life therefore required the settlement of foreign elements qualified in agriculture or trade. Many German soldiers who had fought the Turks remained in Hungary and became her most progressive peasants or artisans. But also great numbers of Serbs, who had fled from the Turks, settled in Hungary. In the towns German craftsmen or traders had always formed the majority and their number now increased. All this was naturally irritating to Hungarian nationalists who saw that the foreigners settled by the Government became its loyal supporters.

Hungary was not only suffering from the consequences of Turkish domination and of the war of liberation, but also from many feudal usages which were obsolete and harmful, but were regarded by the nobles as the symbol of their freedom. Further, the course of history had bred the most bitter national and religious strife, paralysing the work of the Diet. The imperial Government would have liked to elaborate a great plan of resettlement in co-operation with responsible leaders of the opposition, and then to submit it to the Diet. But this proved quite impossible. A commission of experts was therefore set up which worked out a plan (1689). It was carefully avoided to propose any measures threatening the constitution or the rights of the Protestants, and the plan contained many reforms which would have been most beneficial for Hungary.

Nevertheless, the propositions of the Government were received by wide circles of the nobles with suspicion and hostility. Particular opposition was aroused by the plan to increase taxation and to oblige the nobles who had always regarded exemption from paying taxes as one of their most precious 'liberties' to pay an adequate part. Since the nobles resolutely rejected any reform, the Government had to decree it, though it declared that this was an emergency procedure which was not to become the normal one. Yet strong protests were voiced and the opinion gained ground that the Government was planning a régime of bare absolutism. This impression was still further aggravated by decrees laying down that the concessions to the Protestants were valid for those parts only, which had belonged to Hungary at the time of their enactment. From a legalistic standpoint this may have been right, but certainly not from that of far-sighted policy.

The shortcomings on the imperial side were paralleled by the ideas held by the radical Hungarian Nationalists. The very fact that Hungary had been liberated by the hated foreigners was to these nobles a new humiliation. The abolition of their right to elect the king and of resisting him by arms appeared to them an intolerable blow to their liberty'. It seemed to them equally outrageous that they too should pay taxes, not only their serfs, that the latter also had rights, namely to liberty from oppression, that other inhabitants than the Magyars might also claim liberty for their nationality, that the feudal 'insurrection' should be replaced by more modern forms of defence, that the executive power should be organized in a more efficient way than hitherto, when it was entirely dominated by the nobles, and so on. It is also evident that the Hungarian Diet had been so poisoned by party strife that it had lost the fitness to build a new and better Hungary alone, without the co-operation of the Emperor, his organs and peoples.

As early as in the last years of the seventeenth century the widespread discontent led to popular tumults and to a great increase in the gangs of hayducks, who roamed about, combining robbery with hatred of the foreigners. But a great rebellion broke out after the war of the Spanish Succession had begun (1701). The movement found a generally recognized head in Prince Francis Rakoczy, who became extremely popular, though the real leader was Count Bercsenyi. Louis XIV nourished the revolt with great subsidies, sent officers and technicians, and gave diplomatic support. The leaders succeeded in inflaming the national and religious passions of the great masses. Those who did not join voluntarily, or would have preferred a pacification, were compelled by ruthless terrorism to support the rebellion. Rakoczy also tried to induce many other powers to intervene, even Turkey and Russia. The maritime powers wished to end the revolt in order to make the forces of the Emperor free for the war in the West. They sent diplomats to Austria and tried to mediate. The English envoy was George Stepney, who told the rebel chief Count Bercsenyi that their cause was just and that God would not desert them. Apparently he said, God intended to ruin the House of Austria through the haughtiness of its ministers. Prince Eugene intended to demand that England should recall Stepney, but Marlborough persuaded him not to do so. The Slavs and many other non-Magyars stood on the side of the Emperor, whose Government and military commanders in general supported their striving for more freedom or social improvement. But the number of Hungarians loyal to the Emperor also gradually increased. He sought to appease the rebels by promising a great measure of national and religious freedom, a general amnesty, and other concessions. The revolt lasted eight years (1703-1711). Rakoczy was at last defeated and had to flee to Turkey, where he spent the rest of his days.

11

THE WAR OF THE SPANISH SUCCESSION AND ITS
CONSEQUENCES

THE BALANCE OF POWER

THE European cabinets had, for a long time already, been agitated
by the prospect that the Spanish Habsburgs would soon die out, and
that a great war about their heritage would then be waged between
the two main claimants, the dynasties of Austria and France. It was
not merely the interests of these powers, however, which were
concerned. England and the Netherlands, too, were keenly interested in preventing the enormous resources of the Spanish Empire
from falling, as a whole, into the hands of a nation likely to upset
the Balance of Power, and to damage their own economic interests
gravely. They had a great stake in the trade of Spain and her
colonies, and received most of the gold and silver from her overseas
possessions, since Spain's conditions rendered her unable to exploit
the possibilities of her world empire herself. But this state of things
would have completely changed if her resources had come under
the control of France, who was quickly becoming the most
formidable rival of the two maritime powers. She had colonial
settlements in three continents, which could be expanded over
vast open spaces, and her trade and shipping rose rapidly owing to
her policy of ruthless mercantilism. Without the War of the Spanish
Succession there would hardly have been a possibility of building
a world-wide British Empire.

It was further obvious that, if Louis XIV had obtained control of
the whole Spanish Empire, all the European nations would have
been gravely affected. The possession of the Spanish Netherlands,
or the present Belgium, would have enabled him to conquer the

United Netherlands, or Holland also. His power over Italy, France and Spain would have meant the domination of the Mediterranean Sea. In alliance with Turkey and the Hungarians he could have completely put down the House of Austria, and established his paramount power in Germany, Europe and the world.

It has sometimes been asked whether it would not have been better for Austria to renounce the Spanish heritage, to concentrate all her forces on the expansion and consolidation of her rule in the Danubian countries, liberating the nations under Turkish domination and building a great eastern empire before Russia had become a great power. This would certainly have been most desirable, but the idea was hardly more than a dream. If Louis XIV had completely triumphed, there would no longer have been a House of Austria, except perhaps as a French vassal. Yet it is true that a complete victory of this House would also have brought it and its peoples infinite difficulties. In any case the war was for Austria an enormous risk. At the Court of Vienna opinions on the policy to be adopted were much divided. Most of the statesmen were long opposed to a war with France.

The question was also considered whether the Spanish Empire should not be either accorded to a dynasty without much power of its own, or by agreement divided among the claimants. Both ways were actually tried, but failed. Louis XIV concluded various treaties about a partition in case the Spanish Habsburgs should die out, first with Austria in 1668, then with England in 1700. But even if the treaties had not been superseded by events, they were faced with the greatest opposition of Spain herself. She rejected any partition because it seemed to degrade her to a second-rate state. Spanish military power, however, was no longer great enough to defend her empire alone. This could be done only with the full support of a great military power, and France was certainly best suited to give this support, both for geographical reasons, and because of her strength. Spain's opposition to any partition also compelled the claimants to her crown to insist on getting the whole. They could not dare to make themselves most unpopular in Spain by being content with parts of it.

In 1700, the last Habsburg King of Spain, Charles II, was gravely ill and near his death. He had hitherto rather favoured the Austrian succession, but Cardinal Porto-Carrero put pressure on the king, lying in fever, concerning the salvation of his soul, and induced him to sign a prepared will leaving the whole empire to Louis XIV's grandson, Philip of Anjou, on the condition that Spain and France must never be united. It seems that the king later wished to revoke this will, but was hindered from doing so. Whether the will was legally valid is controversial. When the king had died, Louis XIV decided to accept the Spanish empire for his grandson, in defiance of his obligations to the maritime powers. Philip was crowned king, Spanish opinion welcomed him, and even the maritime powers recognized the new king. Louis XIV, however, at once showed that he regarded Philip merely as a puppet in his hands, and Spain a French vassal.

Austria was utterly exhausted by the long wars with Turkey. Most of the Emperor's statesmen stood for peace, and it might have been maintained if the French king had at least conceded to the Emperor the Italian provinces. But his insistence on letting his grandson keep the whole made war unavoidable. Leopold sent Prince Eugène to Italy to defend his rights. William III of England and Heinsius, the leading Dutch statesman, realized that the colossal increase in Louis XIV's power was a grave threat to their countries. But the English parliament with its Tory majority, and the commercial interests in both countries, believed in appeasement, and this greatly encouraged the French king in his policy. Even when he occupied the Belgian fortresses designed to defend Holland against French aggression and expelled the Dutch garrison, this was at first taken lightly by public opinion in England and Holland. The king could, with minor concessions, have secured the neutrality of the maritime powers. But his actions showed such contempt for their vital interests and of international law that they became alarmed and concluded the Grand Alliance (1701) with the Emperor. It was based on the principle of partitioning the Spanish Empire; the Emperor was to get the Italian parts and Belgium, Philip's claim to Spain was tacitly recognized, and the maritime powers reserved for themselves the right to annex Spanish colonies. In this moment James II, the exiled Stuart King, died, and Louis XIV recognized his son as king of England. This aroused a storm in England. Parliament was dissolved, and the Whigs obtained the majority. William died as the result of an accident, and the Alliance declared war on France.

THE POWERS, THEIR FORCES AND GERMAN OPINION

In Germany, the Emperor could make alliances with a number of princes, in particular with the newly created King Frederick of Prussia, the princes of Hanover, the two Hesses, the Palatinate, Trier and Mainz. The Western circles of the Empire, consisting of

numerous small rulers and towns much exposed to a French invasion, wanted to remain neutral, declaring that the Spanish Succession was merely the concern of the House of Habsburg, not of the
Empire. France had a special interest in their neutrality, because if
it was declared, the troops of the Emperor would have had great
difficulties in coming to the rescue of the Netherlands if attacked
by a French army. But the Emperor by clever diplomacy overcame
this attitude of the small territories. In the North, the princes of
Saxony, Holstein, etc., could not do much since they were involved
in a great war among the Baltic powers. Max Emmanuel of
Bavaria and his brother Joseph Clemens, Archbishop of Cologne,
sided with France and made war on the Emperor. The Duke of
Brunswick would have done the same, if he had not been stopped
in time by the military intervention of Hanover. When France
invaded Belgium and violated the territory of the Empire, the
Reichstag declared war on her. But of the contingents called up
only a third assembled and these were of a very low military fitness.

The Imperial party made much propaganda in order to win
German public opinion for the war. But the result was not great.
The public was not interested in the old rights of the Empire in
Italy, which many of the pamphlets emphasized. The Austrian
propaganda also often wavered between the demand for the whole
Spanish Empire and that for part of it. The mass of the people had
no national patriotism, as was soon to show itself in several cases.
That the princes were on the whole not much inspired by German
national feeling, was proved by many of their actions. But also the
Free Towns showed not much patriotism. A town like Frankfurt,
the financial centre of Germany, protested to the Reichstag in a
long legal argumentation that her monthly contribution to the war
had been assessed too high, namely at 800 Rhenish Gulden, which
was equivalent to 95 Pound Sterling. The town demanded that this
should be reduced to almost a third. Hamburg declared she would in
any case remain neutral, even if the Reichstag declared war.

The course of the war need not be related here. The French King
had the advantage of absolute power and a centralized government.
He could therefore mobilize much greater armies than the Allies.
In 1706 he had under arms the unprecedented number of 408,000
infantry, considerably over 60,000 cavalry, and 5,000 artillery.
France further had excellent generals and military engineers, and
was protected by very strong fortifications. The Imperial army
consisted, in 1705, of 85,000 infantry, 28,300 cavalry and 600
artillery. The maritime powers waged war partly with troops
raised in their own lands, but mainly with foreign mercenaries.

They made treaties with German and other princes, who were paid for the supply of troops. The mercenaries in the service of the maritime powers were mostly Germans; their number rose to 142,000 men. Some of the princes hiring out troops did so in the interest of their country and the Empire, others served mainly their personal interest, and this aroused much criticism. The Emperor was fighting for the position of his House, but no doubt also for vital interests of the Empire and the freedom of Europe, or, as it was called, the Balance of Europe. He did not lend troops for subsidies to other powers to fight under their colours and for their interests alone. But he raised by far most of the troops fighting for common interests and for this received loans from British and Dutch bankers, for which Austrian mines and other assets were pawned to them. In certain countries, however, in which the maritime powers had a special concern, they made great contributions to the maintenance of the troops. According to Braubach the loans from England to the Emperor amounted to 340,000 Pounds and those from Holland to 295 million Thalers.

England contributed most of the maritime forces towards the war. King William's Act of 1696, concerning the registration of seamen, was supplemented by Acts of 1706, but was repealed in 1710. This led to a great increase in the enlisting of sailors by the press-gang. Soldiers for the army were also largely brought together by compelling unemployed workers, prisoners, etc. to join. Marlborough's army, however, did not comprise more than 19,000 British troops, at Blenheim they numbered 8,500 out of a total of 52,000.[1] England's expenses for this war was stated by the Commissioners of Public Accounts to have been £65,85 million. The National Debt increased by £34,25 million.[2] Trevelyan, however, says that England's sacrifices, though great, were not out of proportion to her wealth and that 'she throve on the war' while Dutch commerce declined.

The greatest asset of the Allies was the strategic genius of Marlborough and Eugène, who showed also a rare willingness to co-operate. Great obstacles to successful co-operation arose, however, in the field of politics. The statesmen of the allies differed widely

[1] These figures are given by G. B. Hertz, *English Public Opinion after the Restoration*, 1902, p. 135.—T. W. Fortescue, History of the British Army, 1910, I, p. 556 states that the total British land forces reached their peak at 70,000 and that Marlborough's British forces wavered between 18,000 and 25,000.

[2] Cf. G. Chalmers: *An Estimate of the Comparative Strength of Great Britain*, etc. 1794, p. 85.

in their political interests and this led to many frictions and conflicts between them, which frustrated a complete victory.

Leopold I died in 1705, and his successor Josef I was a man of great talents and ambition, possessed an energetic and impulsive character and was opposed to religious intolerance and to the Jesuits. The young Emperor at once began centralizing reforms in his own realm, and in the Empire he stressed his authority over the princes. He also wanted to restore old rights of the Empire in Italy, which brought him into sharp conflict with the Pope. But he died in 1711 of smallpox, and his successor Charles VI held different views.

Marlborough's and Eugène's victories after long vicissitudes, brought Louis XIV to such a pass that he began to seek peace and was ready to make the greatest concessions, and also to return to Germany his recent annexations in Alsace. But the allies hoped for a total victory and the Dutch diplomats put conditions which the king could not accept.

THE PEACE OF UTRECHT

In 1710, the Whig party fell from power in England, and the leaders of the Tories began secret negotiations with France, though the Allies had pledged themselves not to do so. Josef's death, it was argued, had created the risk that his brother Charles would receive too many crowns, which would disturb the balance of power. The result was the Peace of Utrecht (1713), which gave Spain and her colonies to Louis XIV's grandson Philip, on condition that the French and Spanish crowns must never be united. Neither the French nor the Spanish Bourbons intended to keep this clause. Emperor Charles was to receive Belgium, Milan, Naples and Sardinia, and the Duke of Savoy got Sicily. Great Britain gained Gibraltar, Minorca, large territories in North America, and commercial advantages. The Emperor and the Empire refused to accept these terms, but later had to do so. The Emperor's finances were utterly exhausted.

The Austrian statesmen were well aware of the dangers implied in the acquisition of countries too far removed from their base of power, the Danubian countries. In Italy, Milan could still be defended, but Sardinia and Sicily were difficult to reach, since Austria was no naval power. Belgium was also far away, and it could be foreseen that France would continue her aggressive policy despite the barrier of fortresses which had been accorded to Holland and which had to be maintained at Belgium's expense. Austria therefore, in the eighteenth century, often made efforts to exchange Belgium for Bavaria, whose rulers mostly were quite prepared to make this bargain. But this plan was opposed by England, who wished that Belgium, which was dangerously near to her shores, should be defended against French aggression by a great power, and this could only be Austria. Moreover, Austria's striving to acquire Bavaria in exchange for Belgium was also opposed by other states, who wished to keep Austria as vulnerable as possible.

Germany, who had suffered most through the war, obtained no security against aggression. England and Holland received 'barriers' against it, but not Germany. Louis XIV had, before England's change of policy, offered to return Strasbourg and parts of Alsace annexed by him, and England and Holland had then declared that this was an absolute condition of peace. But in Utrecht the maritime powers were not inclined to do much for Germany's safety and integrity.

12

EMPEROR CHARLES VI

INTERNATIONAL POLICY

THE whole policy of Charles VI (1711-40) was dominated by his striving to secure the guarantee of all the powers for a statute called the Pragmatic Sanction, which laid down that the Austrian dominions should not be divided between heirs but should remain united, and also that female descendants should succeed in a certain order. It was made public in 1713, and was accepted by the Estates of all his countries. By means of considerable concessions the Emperor gradually also obtained the guarantee of the principal German princes and European powers.

Neither Charles VI nor King Philipp V of Spain had recognized the Treaty of Utrecht. Philipp, under the influence of his wife Elizabeth and his minister Cardinal Alberoni, both Italians, wished first of all to reconquer the Italian provinces lost to Austria. Spanish troops invaded them, but England and France concluded an alliance, soon joined also by the Emperor, Holland and Savoy; they stopped the war and brought about a settlement of the Austrian-Spanish conflict. Both sides recognized the Treaty of Utrecht and received territorial advantages.

In the meantime, Austria had also waged a war with Turkey, in which Prince Eugène won great victories, liberated the whole of Hungary from the Turks and took Belgrade. In the Peace of Passarowitz (1718) Austria received the Banate and great parts of Serbia, Wallachia and Bosnia. The Austrian Empire had thereby reached its greatest extension, but not for long.

Spain still had grievances, among them the recovery of Gibraltar and Minorca from England and claims to Italian territories, and since she could not get them redressed by the English-French alliance, she turned to the Emperor, trying to win him by plans of dynastic intermarriages, recognition of the Pragmatic Sanction and commercial advantages. In 1725 a pact was signed in Vienna concerning these points. The Emperor's favourite project at that time was the promotion of Austria's overseas trade by a commercial company trading to the West and East Indies, which was founded at the Belgian port of Ostend (1722).[1] Belgium had been burdened in the Peace Treaty and other pacts with very onerous conditions by Holland, designed to cripple her trade, and it was natural that the Emperor tried to give her the opportunity of taking part in the India trade, which made Holland and England rich. Spain now promised to grant to this company the same commercial rights as to England and Holland. The whole plan, however, aroused the fierce opposition of Holland, and later also of England, who saw their trade monopoly threatened.

Britain, France and Prussia countered the Spanish-Austrian pact by the Treaty of Hanover (or Herrenhausen), which was also joined by Sweden and Denmark. On the other hand, the Emperor obtained the aid of Russia and Prussia, who withdrew from the alliance of Hanover. King George I and Lord Townshend, the Foreign Secretary, believed in the existence of a secret treaty between Spain and the Emperor, hostile to Britain. This suspicion was entirely unfounded. Charles VI had promised nothing of this kind to Spain. But the Ostend Company aroused great animosity in the maritime powers. Spain had differences with the Emperor, abandoned the Vienna Agreement, and joined the Allies in the Treaty of Sevilla. The tension between the powers grew. In order to reconcile the maritime powers, Charles suspended the Ostend Company for seven years, but without result. These powers even authorized Spain to occupy Italian territories to which Queen Elizabeth of Spain claimed the succession, though her rights to them were contested, and their princes still living. This was a challenge to the Emperor, who had good reasons to fear a Spanish army on his frontiers. A great war seemed unavoidable. Both in England and in Vienna doubts were voiced whether this policy was reasonable, and whether a return to good relations between Britain and Austria would not be more recommendable. Townshend fell from power and was replaced by the peaceable Walpole. In 1731, a pact was concluded between the Emperor and Britain. Charles definitely sacrificed the Ostend Company and consented to the Spanish occupation of Parma and Toscana, as demanded from him. Britain, in return, guaranteed the

---

[1] Cf.: M. Huysmans, *La Belgique commerciale sous l'empereur Charles VI. La Compagnie d'Ostende*, 1902.

Pragmatic Sanction and promised military aid to defend Austria against aggression.

In 1733, Augustus II, King of Poland and Elector of Saxony, died. His son, also named Augustus, stood as a candidate for the crown, had the support of Russia, and also won over the Emperor by offering to guarantee the Pragmatic Sanction. France supported another candidate, much more popular in Poland, but Russian troops marched into this country and secured Augustus III's election. Austria did not send troops to Poland, but France in alliance with Spain and Sardinia took her diplomatic attitude as a pretext to wage war against the Emperor. Their armies were much stronger than the Austrian and they conquered most of her Italian possessions. On the Rhine, old Prince Eugène with a much inferior army was hard pressed and had to remain on the defensive. The Emperor appealed to England to honour her treaty obligations but Walpole, as a prominent English historian says,[2] on a flimsy pretext left him in the lurch, seriously damaging English interests thereby. In the Peace Treaty Austria lost her possessions in Southern Italy to the Spanish Bourbons, but increased her territories in the North.[3] Duke Francis Stephen of Lorraine, the husband of the Emperor's daughter Maria Theresa, had to cede Lorraine to France and received instead Toscana, a fief of the Empire, where the Medici dynasty had died out. France further guaranteed the Pragmatic Sanction.

The alliance with Russia had drawn Austria into this disastrous war, and it obliged her also to join Russia in her war against Turkey (1737), though the wish to make conquests contributed to the decision too. Prince Eugène, however, had just died and the generals succeeding him as supreme commanders were not equal to the task. The war therefore cost Austria great losses, was ruinous to her finance and ended with the loss of almost all the territories won in the Peace of Passarowitz.

The rise of the Austrian Empire to an expansion stretching from the North Sea to the Mediterranean, and from Belgium to the Balkans, aroused enormous jealousy all over Europe. But the imposing façade could not conceal its great weaknesses, such as its loose structure of many autonomous countries and nationalities,

[2] Cf. Basil Williams, *The Whig Supremacy*, 1939, p. 196. A German historian, Wolfgang Michael, thought that Walpole was right, but Williams points out that Michael himself admitted that the Polish question was merely a pretext and that France wanted to ruin the House of Austria.
[3] The Venetian ambassador and historian, Foscarini, says that Austrian rule was popular in Italy and that its breakdown was mainly due to the fact that the Austrian military authorities had dismissed most of the Italian troops. There are many other proofs that most Italians preferred the Austrian rule to the Spanish. Cf. Erdmannsdoerffer, vol. II, pp. 138, 227, 229, 230, 454.

the lack of territorial concentration and of financial strength.

The Anglo-French Alliance of 1716, later strengthened by the co-operation of the other Bourbon kings of Spain and Naples, had tended to arraign Britain against the Emperor and had led to the extension of Bourbon power in Italy at the expense of Austria. But in the thirties, the relations of the Bourbon courts towards England deteriorated and they began to make front against her. In 1739, Walpole, under the pressure of public opinion, declared war on Spain. Soon a series of great wars with France started, in which the question was at stake whether Britain or France should dominate the new world overseas.

INTERNAL POLICY

Within Germany the old antagonism between the Churches still led to many struggles, though in fact the motives were often more political than religious. Catholicism was gaining ground, and many members of Protestant dynasties, among them even ruling ones, became converts, besides numerous men of substance such as nobles, scholars and statesmen. Even the rulers of so eminently Lutheran countries as Saxony, Wurttemberg, Hanover and Mecklenburgh changed their religion, though they had to give strict guarantees to the Estates that they would not infringe the rights of the Protestants. The Rhine Palatinate, once a bulwark of Calvinism, passed by inheritance to a Catholic branch of the Wittelsbachs. Though here also the new rulers promised the Evangelical Churches the maintenance of their rights, they were in fact often harassed, as will later be shown. This led to strong protests and reprisals by Protestant rulers, both German and foreign ones. The Emperor often disapproved of the illegalities committed and tried to stop them, but he also rightly stressed that it was a matter for the High Courts of the Empire to take action against breakers of the law.

The worst case of Catholic fanaticism happened in Salzburg where, in 1731-32, more than 20,000 peasants were expelled by their ruler, Archbishop Leopold Anton Baron Firmian. Similar, smaller expulsions from various Alpine countries had occurred before. In all these territories a great proportion of the people was secretly Protestant. The Catholic rulers, priests and officials, partly closed their eyes as long as the Protestants made no trouble, partly were not aware of it. In the case of the Salzburg peasants the originator of the expulsion was the Archbishop's Chancellor H. C. von Rall, a harsh and cruel fanatic. He exaggerated the complaints of the peasants about vexations and represented them as a rebellion. Rebels, he maintained, had no claim to be granted an adequate term for settling their affairs before being expelled. This intrigue, however, did not succeed. For the Emperor the matter was most inconvenient, and he insisted on the observation of the law. Moreover, King Frederick William I of Prussia and other Protestant rulers threatened reprisals, the king invited the peasants to settle in East Prussia and promised the peasants his full support. In all Protestant countries great amounts were collected for the Salzburgers, and their migration to Prussia was like a triumphal procession. 20,694 Salzburgers set out for Prussia, and 13,944 reached Koenigsberg, since many found other asylums, some in America. They also received large amounts from the sale of their homesteads and land.

Charles VI laid great stress on legality, and often reprobated acts of intolerance conflicting with the law. He himself was very versed in law and liked to discuss difficult questions with experts. In the Austrian countries Protestantism was banned, especially exercising the cult in public. In certain territories, however, religious freedom was more or less granted, in Transylvania, and in parts of Hungary and Silesia. Protestants in other Austrian lands were often forced to migrate to Transylvania, or, if they refused, to become soldiers. These were granted religious freedom since it was unlikely that they should abuse religion as a pretext for political subversion. A few years after Charles VI's accession, in 1717, a public invitation was issued to foreign traders, industrialists and professionals, without distinction of religion, to settle in Austria. The result was a great influx of traders, largely from Protestant countries. It is significant that in 1675, Leopold I had decreed that in Vienna booksellers must be Catholics, but in 1736, the Archbishop complained that among the 13 Viennese booksellers three only were Catholic, and that there was a great number of Protestant manufacturers and traders attending religious services in the chapels of Protestant Embassies. Nevertheless from time to time cases of Catholic intolerance occurred. The Jesuits and other orders were the principal originators. The great success of their propaganda in high circles filled them with the conviction that they would achieve the complete triumph of their creed.

The Emperor often made attempts to settle the struggle between the religious parties. But the evil was so deeply rooted and widely spread that the results were not very great. He expressed his severe displeasure of Hungarian prelates and nobles, who encouraged hostility to Protestants, he warded off the persecution of the Moravian Brethren, and so on. The power of the Jesuits was restrained, numerous monastic abuses were forbidden, and ecclesiastical actions affecting the common weal or human rights put under state control. Count Seckendorff, an ardent Lutheran, became an intimate friend of the Emperor and his most important diplomat. In the second Turkish war, however, he proved a failure as Fieldmarshal and fell from power.

Besides the Emperor's sense of righteousness, political reasons also spoke for toleration. Though the grouping of powers often changed, on the whole the Catholic ones tended to be his enemies and the Protestant ones his allies. The former comprised France, Spain, Naples, Savoy and in Germany the Wittelsbachs of Bavaria, Cologne and Trier, and eventually also those of the Rhine Palatinate. The Protestant powers of Britain, Holland, Hanover, Prussia, Hesse-Darmstadt and Wurttemberg, were usually on the Emperor's side. The Emperor's hereditary countries were predominantly Catholic. He could not risk a policy resented by any of the religious parties.

The Emperor's greatest success was that after the end of the Rakoczy rebellion (1712) he understood how to pacify Hungary and to win the confidence of the nation. He pledged himself by oath to rule the country according to its own laws, to maintain her independence and integrity and to respect the historic rights of the Estates.[4] A great reorganization and resettlement of Hungary was initiated in this spirit. If the legislative realization of his pledges did not satisfy all wishes of the Hungarian patriots, this was not due to the Emperor, but to the opposition of powerful factors, namely the heads of the army, the Catholic intransigents who now dominated the Hungarian Parliament, the non-Magyar elements in Hungary, the Austrian upper bureaucracy, and many Hungarians with special interests. The Protestants still had grievances. But soon further concessions were made to relieve them. The resettlement got into its stride, and Hungary's population and production rose with extraordinary rapidity.

The Imperial Government also tried to further the national interests of the minorities in Hungary, but met strong resistance from the Magyar nobility. The Estates of Croatia resolved that they wanted their country to be perpetually under the dynasty ruling in Austria and rejected Hungarian protests against this independent action. The Hungarians too, however, accepted the Pragmatic Sanction. The Serbians were a more difficult problem. Under Leopold I great numbers of them had fled from Serbia and had

[4] Cf. the excellent chapter by Macartney in the *Cambridge Modern History*, vol. VII.

settled in Hungary, and the Emperor had guaranteed them autonomy and recognized them as a nation (Natio rasciana or illyrica). But their national aspirations aroused the apprehensions of the Magyars, and a national antagonism began to develop and was aggravated by the striving to make Hungary an entirely Catholic country. A section of the Serbians set their hopes on an intervention of orthodox Russia, or conspired with Rakoczi's partisans against the Emperor. But the great majority of the Serbians and other minorities remained loyal to the Austrian connexion.

The better relations between the dynasty and the Hungarians also enabled the Emperor to get the establishment of a standing army voted by their Estates. But he had to guarantee the freedom of the nobles from taxation as an unalterable, fundamental right. This formed a great obstacle to far-reaching reforms. They would all at first have cost much money and only later would have become profitable.

The Austrian army had in the long struggles with the Turks, French and others gathered much experience and training. Yet its organization had many defects. It had not enough officers and technical experts, and Charles VI reduced its strength for financial reasons. The dynasty itself was not martial, its members as a rule did not command troops themselves. Nor was the Austrian nobility imbued with warlike tradition as the French and later the Prussian. The greatest Austrian generals such as Montecuccoli, Charles of Lorraine, Prince Eugène and Loudon were not Austrians. The lords dominating the court had no need to choose the military profession to make a great career, and when one of them was made commander in chief through his influence in the highest circles, this generally did not have good results. The practice that colonels bought their posts was also habitual in Austria as in most other countries. This system was a survival of the time of the condottieri, who regarded warfare as a profitable business. It led to scandalous abuses; for instance a great part of the troops enrolled existed merely on paper but their pay flowed into the pockets of leading officers. Generals had a share in the profits of contractors and closed their eyes if provisions or materials of bad quality were delivered and high prices charged.

In spite of all the difficulties many reforms were planned and not a few succeeded. The Emperor was very anxious to develop trade, industries and shipping. An Oriental Company was founded in Vienna to trade with the East, and territories in India were acquired. Trieste and Fiume were made free ports, and the attempt

was made to create a navy. The ports were to be connected with
Vienna and other cities by great roads built in a modern way. The
Emperor was also interested in a project to connect the Adriatic
with the Baltic Sea by a canal. This idea had already occupied
Leopold I, and the work was begun, but soon came to a standstill.
The time was not ripe for solving the technical questions involved.
Charles VI also issued various decrees aimed at suppressing the
manifold abuses of the trade guilds, to create a wide market and to
protect new industries. Many new factories were founded. The
Emperor had great understanding for monetary questions and
finance. In 1717, he issued a detailed currency regulation declaring
that the welfare of a country mainly depended on a sound currency.
Moreover, reforms were achieved in banking and in taxation.
Tobacco was made a monopoly. The chronic deficit in the budget
temporarily (1724) disappeared almost completely. Emperor
Charles was also a great friend of arts and science. Under him the
greatest masterpieces of Baroque architecture were built in Vienna.

The government further considered changes in the administration
with fundamental political and social implications.[5] In 1714, Count
Gundaker Starhemberg, President of the Treasury, proposed that
the territorial Diets should send delegates to a central assembly to
discuss with the Government all the problems of administration,
and to create a better system of state finance. This assembly should
include also representatives of the common people. As Starhemberg
said, it had always been the principle of the House of Austria to
govern the people in the form of freedom.

Still more far-reaching plans were elaborated by the Counsellor
Christian Julius Schierendorff (1661-1726). In his youth he and his
brother, an Imperial Procurator, had in a legal case come into conflict with the Jesuits and had been compelled to flee abroad. But
Joseph I, who was an enemy of the Jesuits, gave him an influential
post in the civil service and was favourable to his plans. Schierendorff was particularly moved by the misery of the serfs in the
Bohemian countries. He described their terrible sufferings and
wrote that the ruler was, by the oath at his coronation, bound to
administer justice to everybody and therefore to protect the common man against his lord. He wanted also to give the people a
political representation. The principal territories were to form a
union with a central congress, in which not only deputies of the
Estates were to sit, but also several representatives of the common
man from every district. The assembly was to meet every year. A
sort of Minister of Social Welfare and in every district an Imperial

[5] Cf. A. Fischel, *Studien zur oësterreichischen Reichsgeschichte*, 1906.

Commissary were to be appointed to defend the interests of the mass of the people. In Hungary, in particular, the peasants must be liberated from the despotism of the aristocracy, if necessary, by encouraging their uprising. In this way their affection for the Crown would be won. But in all the other territories, too, the serfs should receive freedom and property.

AUSTRIA AND THE GERMAN PUBLIC MIND

The events described above in many ways influenced the development of political and social opinions in the peoples inhabiting the German Empire and the Austrian countries. On the one hand, the great military and political triumphs of the House of Austria aroused among the Germans also admiration and national hopes. A pamphlet of 1677 said that Austria alone was a 'majestic state' and should have the leadership to restore order and unity in Germany, and to remove the disastrous consequences of an exaggerated power of the territorial rulers. Moreover, German rulers, generals, statesmen and soldiers had contributed so much to defeating Turkish aggression and to frustrating Louis XIV striving for paramount power that a German national pride in these achievements was well justified. The liberation of Hungary, the further expansion to the South East, and the energetic promotion of economic progress opened great opportunities to German traders, industrialists and peasants, but also to lawyers willing to enter the Emperor's service. The part of the Empire to which the imperial policy particularly appealed were the numerous small territories of Swabia, Franconia and the Rhinelands. They had a surplus of ambitious intellectuals feeling cramped in their tiny homelands and yearning for a wide Empire and a great Court to unfold their talents. Many of the most prominent Austrian statesmen, officers, industrialists and scholars had migrated to Vienna from those parts of Germany.

But there were also wide sections of Germans who were averse to the Imperial policy. The striving of the Habsburgs for Spain, Italian territories, Hungary, etc., appeared to them as schemes of an exclusively dynastic character, which were alien to Germany's true interests. Protestant writers naturally saw the origin of the disastrous religious struggles in the connexion of the Habsburgs with Spain. It was also felt that the deep hostility of France to the Habsburgs was mainly due to this connexion. Among German scholars the view was held that the Italian policy of the old German Emperors had had fatal results for Germany. Was the Habsburg policy of collecting foreign crowns not a revival of this mediaeval Imperialism? Had they thereby not stimulated a similar ambition in many other German dynasties? Quite a number of them had already reached, or were near to reaching, the royal dignity in a foreign realm and this meant that the interests of a great foreign state had precedence of those of the small German homeland, and of the duties to the Emperor or Empire. The ascent of some noble families to royal rank aroused the jealousy of many others, too, and aggravated the German inclination to indulge in exaggerating questions of prestige, rank and precedence.

All these arguments attained their full development, and gave rise to great controversies, in much later times, but their germs can be traced earlier. In the age under review the argumentation on dynastic genealogical grounds was still prevalent. Various views of the origin of the House of Austria were put forward, which implied also different political outlooks.

The House of Austria was also the subject of many writings celebrating its deeds. Wolf Helmhard von Hohberg, a Protestant nobleman, wrote a long epic on their alleged ancestor Ottobert. He was a man of great knowledge, faculties and moral integrity, who later left his homeland and lived in Germany, in order to be free from the restrictions to which Protestants were subjected in Austria. Some writers sought to combine dynastic with national feelings, for example Jacob Wagner von Wagenfels, tutor in history to Leopold's son Joseph, the later Emperor. He wrote a book in honour of the Germans and their Empire, described their customs and traditions and stressed their virtues in contrast to France.

THE AUSTRIAN BAROQUE

Every nation devotes a sort of cult to features of the age which it considers the climax of its greatness. For Austria it was the age of the Baroque which was of particular significance in shaping her picture. The palaces of the nobility and the monasteries and churches of Austria comprise numerous beautiful buildings in the Baroque style, dating from the seventeenth and early eighteenth centuries. The term Baroque has later often ben extended from the sphere of fine arts to that of a philosophy of life. Austrian writers have gone far in identifying Austrian ideals with the Baroque. On the other hand, outspoken enemies of Austria, such as the historian Treitschke, have drawn a lurid picture of the degenerated Austrian character in contrast to the true German one, and Treitschke also expressed his contempt for the art of Baroque in a drastic way,

G

which today no expert would accept. All these speculations are of very doubtful validity.

The art of Baroque shows close connections with the spirit of the Counter-Reformation and the Catholicism of the Jesuits. It is the extreme opposite of the Calvinist view of religious service. The Baroque style appeals not to the intellect, but to the emotions, it employs every artistic means to impress man with the majesty of God and the grandeur of a heaven full of angels and saints, like the court of a great prince. It depicts not only the ecstasy of holy men and women, the fortitude of martyrs, the loveliness of the Virgin Mary, the piety of the priests, but also the despair of the condemned, the ugliness of the devil and his hosts, and so on. The public buildings and palaces in Baroque celebrate the heroes of mankind, both in war and peace, they show us the great thinkers of all times meditating on the deepest problems, and also princes and statesmen engaged in their God-ordained duty of ruling, the generals on prancing horses directing battles, and the peoples happy under the sceptre of their prince.

Art was therefore employed to impress upon the people the doctrines of the Church and the state, not in an abstract form, but by exhibiting the actions of the ruling powers and exciting intensive feelings. It is dramatic and often theatrical, making use of colour, movement and atmosphere to arouse awe, tension and the vision of a superhuman order. Heroism is its favourite virtue, though it may be that of the humble man, too. One of the most significant customs of the time was the wearing of large wigs or long hair, designed to express high rank, dignity or wisdom. It was said that a wig gave a person the appearance of a lion. Many nobles wore it even on the battlefield. In the battle of St. Gotthard, the French nobles attacked the Turks at full gallop, with their silken wigs fluttering in the wind. The Grand Vizier, seeing them approach, asked in surprise: Who are these girls? But they showed the courage of lions. The wearing of wigs was also obligatory for scholars or pastors, and it occurred that Christ was painted with a wig, or that on a picture of the resurrection the nobles emerged with wigs on their heads.

The Austrian public mind was moulded by many different forces. The rulers had as Emperors primarily to defend German interests, but as kings or princes of many countries and peoples, they had also to satisfy their aspirations. This double rôle often required compromise between different lines of policy. The Habsburg rulers usually spoke several languages and, moreover, Latin served as a universal language. At their Court there were always different parties, which often also represented the standpoints of different parts of the Empire. The Austrian nobility comprised men of all nations and was imbued with their civilization and traditions. The Church, too, was international, especially the Jesuits who in their schools educated the youth in this spirit. But the trading class, too, was to a great extent composed of foreign elements. Vienna was the meeting place of the West and the East, the North and the South. Under Charles VI about 20,000 Spaniards followed him when he left Spain, and among them were many grandees. Nobles from all parts of the Empire had their palaces in Vienna and employed great numbers of people. This had also considerable influence on the character of the Viennese. Many of them engaged in the production of luxuries and articles of taste and quality, laid great stress upon good food, sweets, coffee, etc., or aped the ways of high society. A certain cosmopolitan note was widely spread. Lady Montague describes the lax morality in high circles. The dynasty further cultivated music and theatre on the grand scale. The Habsburg Emperors were usually good musicians and even composers, they called the greatest musicians to Vienna and spent extraordinary amounts on the opera and concerts. Under Charles VI two famous Italians were made court poets, first Apostolo Zeno and later Pietro Metastasio, who spent most of his life in Vienna. Johann Strauss, the founder of the musical family, was partly of Spanish descent. Composers of genius moved to Vienna from many countries. The influence of Italy on Austrian culture and civilization was particularly great. But Italy also profited from the connection : a number of Italian historians emphasize that the Austrian connection was in many respects an advantage to Italy, since the Austrian rule was better than that in all other Italian states. Not seldom famous Italians, persecuted in their countries for liberal opinions, found a refuge under Austrian protection.

The Church also had great influence in shaping both policy and the mind of the people. The common people often showed intolerance or animosity to Protestants. After the misfortunes of the second Turkish war, public opinion raged against Fieldmarshal Count Seckendorff, a Protestant, accusing him of having betrayed the Austrian cause. The great preacher and writer Abraham a Santa Clara, a Swabian, in the age of Leopold I, castigated the vices of all classes, even of the high-born, in an original, drastic and witty way, and was immensely popular. The Jesuits had many enemies, even among other orders, such as the Capuchins and the Piarists. One of the most influential ministers of Leopold I, Prince Wenzel Lobkowitz, disliked the Jesuits and inspired pamphlets against them. The rivalries among the influential circles reached down to the lower classes. Rinck relates that in 1683, when the siege of Vienna by the Turks was imminent, much murmuring was heard among the common people against the Jesuits, who were made responsible for the fact that the Emperor's wish to appease the Hungarian rebels had been frustrated, and that no agreement with France had been achieved.

When the Turkish army retired from Vienna they left in their camp supplies of coffee, and this led to the opening of coffee-houses, which were soon to play a great rôle in Austrian life. The Benedictine F. Freschot from the Franche Comté, wrote in 1705 in a book about the Austrian Court that Vienna was full of coffee-houses, where literary men read journals and showed an incredible freedom in judging the policy of the ministers and even the life of the Emperor. It would be interesting to know more about these intellectuals, especially what was their profession. Vienna, as the seat of the Imperial Court and many embassies, and being visited by numerous important people, offered great opportunities of hearing valuable information, perhaps by bribing a person connected with the Court, or by winning his favour. The Court parties, diplomats, etc., had a great interest in influencing public opinion by inspiring tracts or spreading rumours. Such information was used in printed publications, or in confidential hand-written news-letters. In 1703 there appeared also the first issue of the Wienerische Diarium, which still exists under the title of Wiener Zeitung. An institution which attracted very many people was the Imperial Aulic Council, the High Tribunal of the Empire. Every German ruler, and many others, had their representatives in Vienna to deal with it, when necessary. Keyssler, who visited Vienna in 1730, estimated that this tribunal occupied almost 20,000 people, including not only its own personnel, but also all the solicitors, etc., of the parties concerned, and the clerks and servants. This seems incredible, though Keyssler was a very well informed writer. In any case, the Imperial Court formed the centre of a very large number of intellectuals of many nations. Keyssler also remarks that a great proportion was formed by Protestants and that many believed that one religion was as good as another.

13

THE PRINCIPAL GERMAN STATES UNTIL ABOUT 1740

BRANDENBURG-PRUSSIA

Elector Frederick William's Early Policy

IN 1640, Frederick William, known as the Great Elector, came to the throne of Brandenburg (1640-88). He was then twenty years of age and his long reign, extending over nearly half a century, gave him time to lay firm foundations for the greatness of his realm. As a boy he had been filled with enthusiasm for the personality of the Swedish King Gustavus Adolphus, his uncle, who was fond of him, wishing to make him his son-in-law, and the heir of his crown. The young prince had a good education and learned, besides German, Latin, French, Dutch and Polish as well. He stayed four years in the Netherlands, and was deeply impressed by the development of their commerce, sea-power and culture. The spirit of the House of Nassau-Orange, the implacable enemy of the Habsburgs, and the Calvinist atmosphere also moulded his mind, and he later married the grand-daughter of William the Silent.

After his accession the Elector made an armistice with Sweden, and the Brandenburg Estates at once pressed for the complete dismissal of troops. But when this had been carried out, the country was again ravaged by enemies. The Peace of Westphalia deprived Brandenburg of free access to the Baltic by the Oder, and put heavy Swedish tolls on her trade. Frederick William's paramount aim became to obtain the part of Pomerania annexed by Sweden, and to free Prussia from Polish overlordship in order to build a state on the Baltic shore, where trade and shipping could be developed on the Dutch model.

The Elector had to choose between the policy of loyalty to the Emperor traditional in his House, and that of the Calvinists, who considered the Habsburgs as the arch-enemy to be put down by every means. His mind harboured different tendencies; there were various parties among his statesmen, and his attitude to the Emperor and the Empire often changed under the influence of alterations in the international situation. He first joined the side of the Emperor, but soon turned to the other side, mainly under the influence of Count Waldeck, who advised the Elector to form a union of German princes, both Protestant and Catholic, assisted by France and other powers, and designed to overthrow the Habsburgs and replace them as Emperors by princes from other dynasties. Frederick William accepted this programme. Waldeck was in secret contact with Mazarin and a great war was planned, in which France was to conquer Belgium, while Brandenburg was to obtain large Rhenish territories. He admitted to Frederick William that the Empire might collapse in this war. But ne added that the Elector might then be able to get large parts of it for himself. The negotiations with German princes, however, had no considerable results, and the outbreak of the Nordic War gave the Elector's policy another direction.

In Sweden, Queen Christina, Gustavus Adolphus' daughter, had come to regard the crown as an intolerable burden. In 1654, she abdicated, went abroad and became a Catholic. Next to the throne was a German prince of half-Swedish descent, the Count-Palatine Karl Gustav, who became King Charles X. Sweden's army had found the war in Germany most profitable and craved for a new one. The Swedish Estates also saw in a foreign war a means of saving money, since the army could then live on the spoils of war, and the new king hoped that a victorious war would consolidate his position. The Estates deliberated against which country war should be waged, and it was decided against Poland. Between her and Sweden there was an old rivalry, other powers would probably support Sweden, and Poland's internal conditions seemed to promise an easy victory and rich booty, even a partition of the country between the victors. Polish and Lithuanian nobles invited the invaders and promised their help. But Sweden intended also to continue her drive for domination of the Baltic Sea and for acquisition of German and other ports. Russia, a rival both of Poland and Sweden, opened her own war against Poland in 1654, and a year later Sweden followed her example. Frederick William was in a difficult position, since the Swedish-Polish war could only be effectively waged by making use of his territories. Both parties therefore tried to obtain his support and made alluring offers, and later other powers also intervened, especially Denmark. The Elector, who was a vassal of Poland, first remained neutral, then fought on the side of Sweden and later on that of Poland, which, to secure his help, renounced the overlordship over East Prussia (1657). The Elector conquered West Pomerania but had to return it to Sweden because France insisted upon it (1660).

The Elector, the Emperor and Louis XIV

Louis XIV had then reached the summit of power. Frederick William, in the conflicts of the King with the Emperor, followed a policy primarily determined by the striving to win West Pomerania from Sweden. For a long time he remained loyal to the Emperor on the whole, though he sometimes, for good payment, also made treaties with France, which were detrimental to the German cause. In 1674 he was engaged, together with the Emperor, in war against France on the Rhine, when suddenly the Swedes at French behest attacked him in the rear, and invaded Brandenburg. He hurried back and defeated the Swedish army at Fehrbellin, and in the following year he conquered their part of Pomerania, and repulsed another Swedish attack in East Prussia. These victories, however, did not secure him the coveted price. France had at last remained victorious on the Rhine, and the Elector was forced again to hand back West Pomerania to Sweden, as France demanded (1679).

This outcome of all his struggles embittered Frederick William against the Emperor, whom he made responsible for it. The tension was increased by the fact that the Emperor refused his claim to certain Silesian territories based on family pacts. The Elector now tried to reach his aim in alliance with France, and in the following years concluded five pacts with her. In these he promised to permit French troops free passage through his territories, the protection of his fortresses and his support for the French candidate for the Polish crown. At the next election of an Emperor he promised to vote against a Habsburg, and to elect either Louis XIV or his son, or another candidate sponsored by France. Later he pledged himself to fight for France without questioning whether her cause was right or wrong. This obliged him to defend also the numerous French annexations of German territories left of the Rhine. Frederick William thereby became a vassal of Louis XIV, and received from him large subsidies, which he used to keep a great army. Shielded by the Elector, Louis XIV annexed Strassburg. He further gave his vassal grounds for hoping to obtain Pomerania through him, but in this the Elector was disappointed. He consequently began to turn to the Emperor's side again, and embittered by Louis' persecution of the Protestants, he completed this change of policy. Frederick William still hoped that the Emperor would recognize his claims to part of Silesia, but this was not the case. The Viennese cabinet distrusted him, and moreover the intolerance of the Austrian government towards the Protestants, especially their persecution in Hungary, greatly distressed Frederick William.

In his last days Frederick William took a warm and active interest in the plan of his nephew William of Orange to·make an expedition to England in support of the Protestant cause. He assembled an army on the Lower Rhine to protect his venture in the rear, against France. But the Elector died on May 9, 1688—six months before the Stadholder landed in England to become King William III.

Frederick William's tergiversations and his support of Germany's main enemy have often been criticized. They must, however, be judged against the background of the time. In the seventeenth century, German national sentiment was dormant and awakened only under great provocation. In any case the religious factor was much stronger. Frederick William's Political Testament of 1667, a secret memorandum for his successor, shows in many points how his whole mind was dominated by Calvinistic piety. At the same time he was far ahead of his age in religious tolerance. In politics, however, the Elector's one persistent enemy was Protestant Sweden, so that he was faced with the choice of siding either with Austria or with France, both powers intensely hostile to his creed.

The Testament advises his successor to hold the balance between them, and always to come to the rescue of that power, which at the moment was at a disadvantage. The general principle in foreign politics is said to be to have good relations with all powers, and alliances guaranteeing peace and security with as many as possible. In this Testament there is no trace of any aggressive intentions. In another secret memorandum of about the same time, the Elector reminded his successor of the indisputable claims of the Hohenzollern to Silesia, if the Austrian Habsburgs should die out in the male line, as then seemed probable. He had formerly thought, the Elector said, he should not enlarge the wide possessions which God had bestowed upon him, nor advise his successors to pursue a policy of aggrandisement. Now, however, he had changed his mind, since God willed that opportunities offered should be utilized lest they be used by others. This was also necessary to make safe the cause of the gospel. If therefore the question should arise who should succeed the Habsburgs in Silesia the then ruler of Brandenburg should not tolerate Saxony or Sweden getting a foothold there, but quickly take measures to assert his right and take possession.

Internal Policy

Frederick William aimed at the integration of his territories into a strong unitary state, which required a central government and a standing army. But the territorial Estates strongly opposed both plans, which threatened their own power. The Elector, however, succeeded, in breaking their resistance. In 1644 troops were raised of which a part was not dismissed. This was the beginning of a standing army. The Secret Council was in 1651 transformed from a Brandenburg institution to one for all territories. An important measure was the introduction of the excise, an indirect tax levied in the towns on many goods. It had first been developed in Holland and had the advantage that the consent of the Estates was not needed to levy it. In the rural areas a landtax was levied which mainly burdened the peasants, and was subject to the vote of the Estates. The nobility opposed the tax reforms, but in vain. To appease them, the Elector did not touch their rights to exploit the serfs. The fiercest struggle took place in East Prussia. The Estates were here very unwilling to come under the full sovereignty of the Elector, and did their best to maintain the suzerainty of the Polish crown. They refused to pay homage to the Elector as Duke of Prussia, and there were grave agitations and conspiracies, both among the knights and among the burghers of Koenigsberg. But Frederick William broke their resistance. The Estates, or committees of them, continued to meet, but lost much of their importance.

The Elector further took many measures to reform the administration in a centralizing sense, though only limited progress was achieved. But his most important work was the creation of a standing army of mercenaries, recruited by the government. This could only be realized by the subsidies which the Elector received from various foreign governments. In the first place it was France which contributed the money to lay the foundations of a Prussian army. The strength of the army rose from 4,000 to 30,000 men. The total revenues of the State amounted to 2½ million Thalers, of which more than a million were spent on the army.

Frederick William was his own prime minister; he carefully considered the opinions of his counsellors, but then decided himself. Most of the prominent ministers and diplomats were of middle-class origin. The nascent power of Brandenburg-Prussia was largely due to the fact that in selecting officials and officers, talent was decisive, not high birth. Frederick William was strongly influenced by his religious convictions in his policy. He believed that God had prescribed to a ruler his duties to the people, and inculcated in his sons that the aim of government was not the private interest of the ruler,

G*

but the welfare of the people. He twice refused the crown of Poland, because he would have had to become a Catholic. Though a fervent Calvinist, he rejected the belief in predestination. Any propagation of a creed by force was also declined by him. In wholly or partly Catholic regions, the Catholics, too, could freely exercise their religion, but not in purely Protestant ones. The realm became the asylum for all those persecuted because of their religion. When Louis XIV began his oppression of the French Protestants, Frederick William invited them to settle in his country and offered them valuable assistance. About 20,000 came, and in the towns they formed French colonies, enjoying a great autonomy. Many brought their wealth with them or founded new industries, and their contribution to the economic and cultural development of the country was very great. Protestants from many other countries were also received with friendliness and settled. The same welcome was accorded to the Socinians, expelled from Poland. This sect was particularly odious to the orthodox, and the Prussian Estates strongly protested, but in vain. In 1670, the Jews were expelled from Vienna. Many of them, too, found an asylum and opportunities to work and live in the lands of Frederick William. In East Prussia the Estates again vigorously protested, and the Elector had for a time to yield. But soon means were found to tolerate them, and in 1680, they even received permission to build a synagogue in Koenigsberg.

The Thirty Years' War had devastated and exhausted the country to the utmost. A large part of the population had died from plague and starvation, and wide tracts became a wilderness. The first task of the Elector was therefore to restore agriculture. Numerous measures were taken, and colonists called in, largely from Holland and Friesland. But the time was not propitious for freeing the peasants from servitude. On the contrary, the Elector was compelled to win the knights for his plans of building a new State by consolidating their position as masters of serfs. After the war there was much land without an owner as records had often been destroyed. The squires had therefore a good opportunity to enlarge their estates by putting forward doubtful claims, and by promising to make the waste land fertile again. As local justice was in their hands, their claims were easily proved.

The Elector did much also for the development of trade and communications. Roads, bridges and canals were built by him, the foundation of industries encouraged, a postal service introduced, and so on. The example of the Netherlands inspired him with the wish to develop overseas trade, to found a navy and to establish colonies. A Dutch shipowner and merchant, Benjamin Raule, became his main adviser in these matters, and was eventually appointed Director-General of his navy. An African Company was founded and a colony set up on the Gold Coast. The merchant navy rose to 30 vessels and the armed navy to 10.

In the towns the Elector furthered the interests of the lower classes against the patricians and against the narrow-mindedness of the trade guilds. Newcomers and people commonly treated as pariahs, such as sons of shepherds and other despised occupations, were enabled to become burghers and to make a living by trade. The edict of 1573, banishing the Jews from Brandenburg, was cancelled and also various other disabilities abolished. Yet Frederick William did not wish that the differences of rank should be obliterated; everybody should remain in his station.

In cultural matters the Elector showed much understanding. He furthered learning and higher education, and added a new university of the reformed creed to the two Lutheran ones. Nothing, however, was done for elementary schools. The Prince's interest was also roused by the plan of a Swedish scholar and statesman, Benedikt Skytte, to found an international university open to all nations, religions and sciences on the basis of equal rights and full autonomy, and designed to work for eternal peace. Frederick William gave the proposed institute accommodation at Tangermünde and in 1667 issued an invitation to all interested to come there. But the project could not be carried out. Of the Elector's cultural achievements there may further be mentioned the foundation of the Berlin Library, the beginnings of collections of art and of objects of natural science, the support given to the study of Oriental languages and the appointment of scholars such as Pufendorf, with whom he had much in common. In the long war the population of Berlin had sunk to about 7,500, but under the Elector it rose to 20,000, and he took special interest in the cleaning, lighting and paving of the roads, in public hygiene, protection against fire, and the embellishment of the town. In 1659, the first book-shop was founded in Berlin. Travelling abroad was, in 1686, made subject to a special licence to prevent young gentlemen from becoming debauchees, gamblers and despisers of religion. Duelling was strictly prohibited. On the other hand, it has to be said that the Elector's love of splendour, the chase and building cost much money.

Though the Elector regarded the unity and strength of his territories as his main aim, he was still under the influence of patrimonialism. His last will made his eldest son the heir to the bulk of his state, but accorded to the five younger brothers considerable territories, though not in full sovereignty. This might have led to the lasting diminution of the area of the state. But his successor, Frederick III, declared the will invalid, and compensated his brothers with money.

King Frederick I

Margrave Frederick III (1688-1713) was very unlike his father. He was a weakly, somewhat deformed person who enjoyed pomp and splendour, but left the conduct of government mostly to Prime Ministers. The first was his educator Danckelmann, who was a prominent statesman, but was, after eleven years, brought to his fall by a powerful clique at the court, and ignominiously treated. He was then succeeded by favourites of the Elector, who mismanaged the administration and caused great financial disorganization. Brandenburg joined the Grand Alliance of 1689 against Louis XIV, and later fought at the side of the Emperor, England and others in the War of the Spanish Succession. The Elector's loyalty to the cause of the Emperor contributed to the fulfilment of his greatest wish : the elevation of Prussia to a kingdom. After long negotiations Frederick could, at Königsberg, celebrate his coronation (1701). He was not a king made by the Emperor, as Prussia was outside the Empire, but himself set the crown on his head.

King Frederick I showed a great interest in art and science. His father had already engaged German and foreign scholars and artists, and the influx of the French Protestants brought many famous men to Berlin, who had a great share in creating a very active intellectual life. In 1701, a Society of Sciences was formed on the model of the London Royal Society. Its organizer and president was the great Leibniz. The Society soon played a leading part in furthering scientific investigations and learned enterprizes. Two tendencies formed a characteristic element in the mind of the intellectual élite of the new Kingdom. One was Pietism, the striving to overcome the narrowness of Orthodoxy by a freer and deeper piety centred not on arid dogmas but on Christian love of God and one's neighbours. The other was expressed in the school of public law founded by Pufendorf and Thomasius, which aimed at the liberation of the state and legislation from the fetters of theology and the Bible, and based them instead on natural law and on reason. These two doctrines, Pietism in theology and Rationalism in public law, were particularly cultivated at the university of Halle, which Frederick I founded (1692). The state, with a population of only about 1.5 million, now had four universities : two Lutheran ones at Königsberg and Frankfurt on the Oder, one reformed one at Duisburg, and one at Halle, which was to be free from theological fetters and work for the conciliation of all Christians.

The wife of Frederick I, Queen Sophie Charlotte, was the patroness of enlightenment and art. In her palace at Charlottenburg, later named so after her, she cultivated a refined social life. At her private theatre the works of the great poets and composers were given. Leibniz was her special friend, and she assembled thinkers of all religions to debate the most profound problems. The free-thinker Toland discussed his pantheistic Deism with her, and dedicated one of his writings to her. Shaftesbury too, visited Berlin and described his impressions with enthusiasm for Prussia.

King Frederick William I

The successor of the first King of Prussia was his son Frederick William I (1713-1740). His mother Sophie Charlotte planned a care-ful education for him in the modern spirit of high society. But the boy was wilful and obstinate, and easily flew into a rage. His mother-tongue was French, which then dominated the Courts, and he spoke it better than German. But he hated Court life, luxuries, frivolity, and also all learning without any obvious practical utility. When his tutor taught him the Calvinist doctrine of predestination, that God had for his own glorification damned the majority of men to eternal suffering in hell, he burst into the words : 'This God is the devil. I shall vex him and become a Catholic.' He remained, how-ever, in the Reformed Church, but always rejected predestination, and often showed himself amenable to Pietism, and its wish to help the poor and oppressed. His mother had given him Fénélon's charm-ing tale of Télemaque with its praise of a peaceable, benevolent ruler, and had told him to read it over and over again. Frederick William was indeed deeply impressed by it.

Like his grandfather, the King was very fond of the Netherlands, which he visited twice to study the conditions there. He learned Dutch, and when in later life he for some time thought of resigning his kingship, he was attracted by the idea of settling in the Nether-lands and engaging in mercantile business. When he called himself a republican, this obviously meant the opposite of an aristocrat. His idea of the state had nothing to do with liberty, but was founded on the equality of all men in subjection to the supreme authority which itself was subject to the commands of God, as he understood them. Privileges of rank or wealth were as odious to him as intel-lectualism or aestheticism. After his accession, his first act was to dismiss the Master of Ceremonies as a completely useless person, and to reduce the expenses of the Court to a fifth of what they had been. Frederick William lived like a burgher of modest means, using only inexpensive furniture, and he ordered the taking away of all the upholstered furniture, because it accumulated dust. The King liked also the company of burghers. Many of his officials, even high ones, were of middle class origin and he also rejected the view of the age that monarchs were above the normal rules of morality. He was completely faithful to his wife, who bore him fourteen children.

The King's aim was to make his country strong and respected and his people happy. But his choleric temper often induced him to treat a subject neglecting his duties, or in other ways arousing his anger, by brandishing his walking-stick and hitting the delinquent. If the royal children were naughty, they were also mercilessly thrashed. Once a Jew in his caftan seeing the King approaching tried to run away. The King had him stopped and asked why he had run. The Jew answered he had been afraid, and Frederick William rapped him and exclaimed: 'You shall not fear me, you shall love me.' Once, early in the morning, the King found that travellers were waiting before the house of the postmaster of Berlin, without whose order the coach to Hamburg could not start. When the King heard that the postmaster was still asleep, he intruded into the house and caned him out of bed, apologising to the passengers for the neglect of duties by an official. A soldier was once sentenced to death for a grave case of burglary by the High Court. This agreed with the law. But a general, wishing to save the soldier because of his tall stature and strength, reminded the king that the Court had recently not sentenced to death an official who had defrauded a much larger amount. The King was so enraged that he ordered that all the judges should at once appear before him. Four of them, who came first, were so beaten by the King that they soon fled with bleeding heads and with the loss of teeth.

Frederick William certainly wished to govern in a patriarchal spirit benevolent to the people. But great irascibility, vehemence, and inconsistency combined with ideas of autocracy and militarism, very often induced him to act in a way utterly opposed to his true intentions. The king's intimate confidant and minister General Grumbkow, many foreign diplomats and his nearest relatives often expressed the apprehension that the King was, or would become, deranged.[1]

The King's Policy

Continuing the policy initiated by his grandfather, the Great Elector, the King ruled autocratically. He disregarded the privileges

[1] Cf. Stenzel, III, p. 519, where proofs are given.

of the Estates, brushed aside their protests, and when they appealed
to the High Courts of the Empire, he refused obedience to their
decisions. The principal work of the king was the creation of an
army which was the marvel of Europe. It was out of proportion to
the smallness of his realm and placed it militarily in the rank of a
great power. In order to raise the means for it, the administration
was thoroughly reorganized. The autonomy of the towns and districts was much restricted and subjected to the control of royal
officials. These were under the strictest discipline and the smallest
offences were severely punished. Financial reforms and parsimony
resulted in a treasury overflowing with money. The demands of the
army stimulated the striving to develop the resources of the
country, and led to the foundation of various industries. Many
grain stores established for the army later also became an important
means of keeping the price of grain steady, by buying up corn in
years of plenty and selling it when the crops were poor. This served
the purpose of warding off both a famine and a glut of grain. The
army was therefore, also of great importance for economic life.
The soldiers were mostly mercenaries, and a large proportion consisted of foreigners, in order not to decrease the manpower of the
country for productive purposes too much. The soldiers regularly
got ten months' leave in order to be available for production. Many
of them were married and were encouraged to exercise some
handicraft or other productive occupation when they were not on
duty.

Despite the extraordinary size of the army, the King abstained
from waging war, and could therefore devote much time to economic and social problems. He regulated, with care and common
sense, countless questions in order to further the economic development of his country. His great interest in it induced him also to
found two chairs of practical economics at the Universities of Halle
and Frankfurt on the Oder, the first of their kind. The King wished
that officials, too, should thereby be trained in understanding
problems of economic life. His reforms mostly followed the principles of mercantilism, then dominating the spirit of the age. The
royal domains were much increased, and eventually comprised
about a third of the productive soil. The King reserved only 52,000
Taler (about £8,000) for his free disposition and this was the
amount designed to pay for his household expenses. The rest of the
returns went to the State and formed almost half of its income. The
enlargement of the army could therefore be carried out without
new taxes. The King, as his father had done, wished to abolish
serfdom, but was persuaded by the nobles and officials drawn from

their ranks, that this was unnecessary or impracticable. On the royal domains the burdens of the peasants were considerably alleviated. Towards the end of his life (1738) the King, who so often employed his stick for punishing subjects, issued a decree strictly forbidding the beating of peasants on his domains and threatening officials trespassing it with severe penalties, even hanging. But the peasants of East Prussia were excepted because they were 'lazy, godless and disobedient'. In other provinces lazy peasants might be punished with the stocks or forced labour, but had the right to complain if beaten.

Frederick William's greatest deed was the colonization of wide tracts of East Prussia. This country had been terribly devastated by foreign troops and by the plague. It had become a desert. The King settled there and elsewhere great numbers of foreign refugees from religious suppression, among them nearly 20,000 Salzburgers alone, but also many thousands of Rhinelanders, Walloons, Swiss Menonites, and so on. All were settled as free peasants with good rights of tenure. Their freedom was, of course, restricted at the king's pleasure. Emigration, for example, was strictly prohibited, even under the penalty of death. The just quoted edict on beating shows also that the king had then a poor opinion of the East Prussian peasants, probably because a section of them had disappointed him.

The king further founded a weekly intelligence journal, mainly designed for artisans and peasants, which he provided with economic news. Inn-keepers, Jews, clergymen, etc., were ordered to subscribe, and the post offices accepted advertisements. The profits went to the military orphanage, which the king had founded for children of soldiers. He also cared for sick, invalid and old soldiers and their widows, founded a large hospital and provided for the training of physicians, apothecaries, etc. Berlin grew during his reign from 24,000 inhabitants to 69,000, not including the garrison of 20,000 soldiers.

In religious questions the King was tolerant, as was the Hohenzollern tradition. When Catholic rulers oppressed their Protestant subjects, he took reprisals by taking the same measures against Catholics in his countries. Though he disliked Jews, he appeared with the Court at the opening of a synagogue in Berlin. But various happenings later increased his aversion, and he often treated them harshly. For science and learning he had no understanding, and he appreciated knowledge merely if it served practical purposes. It is characteristic of him that he found special pleasure in making rude fun of scholars. Some of them were even invited to the king's beer-parties, where they were often treated as court jesters. But he had much interest in founding schools for the common people, mainly under the influence of Pietist clergymen. His decree that all parents should send their children to school remained in most provinces a dead letter, since sufficient schools were lacking. But in East Prussia and Lithuania alone the king had 884 new village schools built and 454 others completely rebuilt in six years. Moreover, 322 were built by the landed nobility.

Frederick William I wished that in the courts of law everyone of his subjects should find sure and quick justice. The protraction of lawsuits and the many abuses aroused his anger, but he did not possess the knowledge and patience to understand the problems of law and justice. He hated the lawyers exploiting the people by pettifoggery and procrastination, and prescribed a costume for them to wear which was designed to make them ridiculous and to deter the people from consulting them. Yet many real improvements, too, were achieved, since the civil service comprised some outstanding lawyers, in particular Samuel Cocceji. Frederick I already had ennobled him for his merits, and Frederick William I promoted him to the rank of Chief Minister of Justice. The king's own innovations were sometimes a progress, such as the abolition of witch trials, but more often they deteriorated justice by great harshness and cruelty. Girls who had killed their new-born children had hitherto been decapitated, but the king replaced this by the former punishment of drowning them in sacks which they had to sew themselves. Girls who had borne illegitimate children were to be whipped and expelled. Gipsies over 18 years were all to be hanged, even if they had done no wrong. Sodomy, even if merely attempted, was liable to death by fire. The King issued numerous decrees setting excessive punishments on relatively minor offences, for example the death penalty for stealing small amounts. All grave criminal cases had to be put before the king, and he frequently increased the penalty or decided against the judgment of the Court: 'Shall Hang'. In some cases it was later found that an innocent person had been executed.

Power Politics

When the king came to the throne, the great Nordic War had already been going on for thirteen years. Russia, Poland, Saxony, Denmark and Sweden were taking part, and offers were made to Frederick William to win him as an ally. But he long remained neutral, declaring he did not want to do anything against his conscience. Later he entered the war, and in the Peace of Stockholm (1720) received Stettin and part of West Pomerania.

The king certainly had the ambition to acquire new territories, and sometimes wavered whether he should not let his troops march. The unrest in Mecklenburgh and East Friesland aroused his hopes of obtaining a footing there, as it did those of Hanover and other powers. He sequestrated various small territories, had an eye on Courland, and made efforts to assert claims to the Duchy of Berg. But the results of all these steps did not satisfy his ambition.

In certain respects the king made use of his power in the most ruthless way, particularly in enlisting soldiers by force. Other rulers, too, tolerated abuses in recruiting. But the agents of the King of Prussia proceeded with a brutality which became a European scandal. It often aroused riots, and he was induced to forbid the application of force, but this was not meant seriously. Force continued to be employed in a veiled form. Moreover, a certain number of recruits was legally enrolled by the introduction of a restricted conscription. Frederick William was further possessed by the craze to have particularly tall soldiers. In spite of his parsimony and conscience he was prepared to pay any price and to condone any crime to get hold of a giant. His recruiting officers searched for such persons all over Europe and often abducted them regardless of their citizenship, family, rank or profession. The greater the height of a soldier, the more was paid for him. Tall men were often allured by false pretences to come to Prussia and then seized, or they were even kidnapped in their own countries. The king spent enormous amounts on this sport, and in order to cover part of the expense, posts of officials were sold to applicants.

Even the Prussian diplomatic representatives abroad were compelled to take active part in this sordid business. The envoy in Hamburg, Evers, who failed to deliver the recruits promised, and probably had already received money for their acquisition, was recalled and sentenced to lifelong imprisonment. The Prussian ambassador in Britain, C. W. von Borcke, engaged a particularly tall Englishman, James Kirkland, as a lackey and sent him to Prussia, where he was forced to become a grenadier. The cost of getting this one man amounted to 9,000 Talers, which was then about £2,000. The British government declared that this diplomat could no longer be tolerated in the realm and advised him to depart. In Saxony, a Prussian officer was sentenced to death for the same offence, and Frederick William sent a minister to the Saxon Ambassador in Berlin to tell him that if this sentence was carried out, he himself would be hanged. A tall peasant was abducted from Poland in 1731, and when the Polish sheriff, who happened to be the lord of the peasant, arrested a Prussian sergeant, declaring he would be kept till the peasant was returned, a whole Prussian regiment marched over the frontier and devastated the estates of this lord, who retaliated in a similar way, though with a smaller host. Hanover was particularly affected by Prussian acts of violence. When numerous protests remained ineffective, several Prussian military persons were arrested on Hanoverian soil. This almost led to a war. King Frederick William assembled 44,000 men at the frontier of Hanover and King George II took counter measures. Two years later Hanover set a price of 50 Talers on the head of every Prussian recruiting agent, dead or alive, delivered to the police —just as a price was set on the head of wolves. Frederick William also once challenged King George II to a duel.[2]

Shortly after the acute conflict between Hanover and Prussia had been settled, there were negotiations between George II and Frederick William about a double marriage between their dynasties. The Prussian heir to the throne, later known as Frederick the Great, was to marry Princess Amelia, daughter of George I, and his sister Wilhelmina, the later Margravine of Bayreuth, was to be espoused to the Prince of Wales. England wanted in this way to obtain in Prussia a strong military ally. The negotiations seemed to succeed. But when the English special envoy, Sir Charles Hotham, was received by the Prussian king to convey to him a favourable message from his king, he also handed him an intercepted letter from his minister Grumbkow, whom English diplomacy regarded as an enemy, and wished to have dismissed. Frederick William was so enraged about this step that he did not read the letter but flung it at Hotham's feet, stamped upon it and left the room.[3]

The King's temper often induced him to commit the greatest brutalities against members of his family and others. He maltreated his son Frederick, then 18 years old, in the roughest way so that he tried to escape to England, but failed. The king was so enraged that he thought of having his son executed and also his daughter Wilhelmina, whom he suspected to have known of the attempt. The British Envoy at Berlin, Mr. Dickens reported: 'The King of Prussia went up to the Princess Royal's (Wilhelmina's) apartments, and after a great number of appellations, as I am ashamed to repeat, he

[2] In Droysen's great work a note of Frederick William is published in which he says it would greatly please him to begin a war with Hanover, and he would immediately be cured from an illness if he could see a few hundred Hanoverian villages burn.

[3] The most careful presentation of this episode, based on the archives of Berlin, Vienna and London is by Edith Cuthell, Wilhelmina, Margravine of Bayreuth vol. 1, 1905. This historian thinks that English diplomacy provoked the king to an outburst.

beat off her head clothes and twisting his hands in her hair, dragged her about the room, kicking and beating her about the head, face and breast, in so violent a manner that Her Royal Highness has been obliged to keep her bed ever since. The whole Castle was alarmed at her shrieks and cries and the guards, not knowing the reason of it, stood to their arms. If I am rightly informed, the Queen of Prussia herself had not been used much better.' Wilhelmina in her memoirs relates that, as she lay unconscious on the floor, the King redoubled his blows, and kicked and trampled on her.

Long and grave troubles occurred between Prussia and the Netherlands. In 1733, a Prussian recruiting officer was court-martialled and shot by the Dutch. This enraged the king to the utmost, he took reprisals, and again a great war threatened to break out. The Emperor at last brought about a peaceful solution. Both sides declared that the affair was settled. Yet the King was still so revengeful that a year later he had two Dutch sergeants hanged under a pretext. There were numerous similar frictions with other states.

On the other hand, foreign rulers and diplomats, wishing to win the favour of the Prussian king, knew that the best method was that of presenting him with men of high stature. Tsar Peter I sent him a hundred tall Russians every year, and most foreign governments occasionally followed his example. Frederick William treated his giant slaves well, and granted them many favours, though he sometimes attracted one by great promises, which he did not keep when he had him under his power.

The King and the Emperor

Relations between Frederick William I and Emperor Charles VI went through many vicissitudes. Their final outcome was a deep resentment of the king, who was convinced that the Emperor had broken his pledge to obtain for him the possession of the Duchy of Berg. This feeling prepared the ground for the aggression of his son Frederick II on Austria. In order to justify this action many Prussian historians, and others under their influence, ascribe its origin exclusively to Austria's ill-will towards Prussia, grudging her every aggrandisement in spite of promises and treaty obligations. It is true, and very understandable that the Viennese statesmen were imbued with deep distrust of the king, as also were most other powers. This was partly due to his extreme irritability and inclination to violent steps, to his striving for aggrandisement, his building up of a very powerful army etc., and partly also to his gross disrespect towards the authority of the High Courts of the Empire who acted in the name of the Emperor. Messengers of the High Chamber Court serving a writ were by order of the king man-handled, imprisoned and expelled. The king tried also to obstruct the jurisdiction of the Imperial Aulic Council. The diplomats of the Emperor remembered the policy of Elector Frederick William, which often showed tendencies quite incompatible with the duties of a German ruler. Though these conflicts had been settled, they could easily be revived as the actions of Frederick II were soon to show.

Nevertheless the existing conditions compelled the Emperor to make every effort to win him for his side. Frederick William par-ticularly wished to obtain a part of the territories of Jülich-Berg, namely the Duchy of Berg, when the ruling house of Pfalz-Neuburg should have died out, as could be foreseen. There were many claimants to this heritage and the question who had the best right was most complicated. The Emperor, too, had claims, since his mother was a Princess of Pfalz-Neuburg. In 1728, the Emperor con-cluded an alliance with Frederick William I, in which he declared his willingness to cede him his own claims to the Duchy of Berg and those to the Duchy of Jülich to the Prince of Pfalz-Sulzbach, provided that both agreed, and he promised to do his best to bring about this agreement. He also endeavoured to achieve this, but in vain.[4] Actually, Frederick William had by his policy and particu-larly by his forcible and brutal ways aroused or aggravated the hostility of all the princes and statesmen concerned. When Prince Eugène met the king in 1732, he told him quite frankly that he had no friends except the Emperor and Russia, and he could not demand that the Emperor should become involved in war with the whole world on his behalf.[5] It may also be mentioned that the Estates and people of Berg, who sympathized with the freedom of their Dutch neighbours, were quite opposed to becoming subject to a king of the

[4] Cf. L. Haeusser Geschichte der rheinischen Pfalz, II. p. 880. The Emperor made great offers to the House of Pfalz-Sulzbach, but they were rejected, and the result was that the powerful group of the Wittelsbach dynasties became enemies of the Emperor.

[5] Cf. Droysen, II, p. 164. Droysen and other great historians, also Ranke, who have formed the view of Frederick William I generally accepted by German historians, say extremely little of the king's brutalities and his repu-tation abroad. Droysen thinks that the reports of them were largely slander. Students reading only these classics therefore receive a very onesided impression, attributing the whole responsibility for the coming Austro-Prussian conflict to Austria. There was, however, a very distinguished and critical Prussian historian, who took full account of Frederick William's character, namely H. Stenzel, whose history of Prussia began to appear in 1830, and is still indispensable.

habits described. They had strongly resisted the attempt of Elector Frederick William to annex their country.

When the War of the Polish Succession broke out, Prussia officially took the side of the Emperor. The king even offered the Emperor to mobilize most of his army for him, but the Emperor refused this offer because otherwise all other German princes, even those hitherto friendly to him, would have become his enemies, and nobody doubted that Frederick William at the head of a big army would behave in a way incompatible with the obligations of the Emperor to protect law and order. The king therefore supplied only the contingent promised in the treaty of 1728, and this only after a long delay. These troops did not do much except devastating and ransacking the parts of Germany through which they marched or where they took quarters in the most awful way. Their behaviour was so barbaric that the whole of Germany regarded them with horror and detested them like the plague.[6] The king during this war, was practically sitting on the fence between the Emperor and France, willing to favour that side which would procure him the Duchy of Berg. The Emperor regarded this as contrary to the alliance and his attitude to the king became very cool. Frederick William was greatly offended. At last, France who won the war, made two treaties. She agreed with the Emperor that when the succession to Juelich-Berg should occur, the Prince of Sulzbach should provisionally occupy the country for two years to maintain peace and order, but without prejudice to the rights of others and to the competence of the High Courts of the Empire. At the same time France made a treaty with Prussia, promising to procure her the greater part of Berg by agreement with the House of Sulzbach, or, if this was not possible, to let Prussia occupy the territory. The consent of the Emperor to the first treaty has been represented by Prussian historians as a betrayal of the king which, as shown, is not true.

SAXONY

The Electorate of Saxony, situated between Brandenburg and Bohemia, had been particularly ravaged by the Thirty Years' War and had lost a very great part of its population. But it was soon increased by the acquisition of the large territories of Lusatia, ceded to Saxony by Austria as compensation for the cost of war, and by the influx of numerous Protestant refugees from Bohemia, Austria and later France. Nature, its situation and long experience made

[6] Cf. Seckendorff, Life, vol. II, pp. 71, 100, 136, etc

Saxony the most industrial and wealthy part of the Empire. The refugees now brought with them the knowledge of many further trades, valuable technical improvements, and also considerable capital. Many events showed that the country was ahead of most others in economic, administrative and cultural progress.

The Saxon dynasty of the Wettins had brought forth, besides insignificant rulers, some outstanding ones also, such as Frederick the Wise, Maurice and Augustus in the sixteenth century, whose work had been most beneficial. The dynasty, however, showed on the whole little striving for concentrating, increasing and expanding its power. It rather had the tendency of dividing into ever more branches and sub-branches, and thereby increasingly splitting up its territories, though these were mostly not entirely separated, but preserved a certain community. The Electorate itself was less affected than the attached territories of the Wettins, particularly Thuringia, which was largely in the hands of the Ernestine branch of the house. Towards the end of the seventeenth century, this small country was divided into thirteen duchies, and in the beginning of the eighteenth, it contained as many as thirty-four 'states' or fragments of such.[7] Many of them, however, soon disappeared again since most of the sub-branches quickly died out.

Saxony and the attached duchies also had Estates which had great influence on politics, though as a rule they were in good relations with the dynasty. In the sixteenth century, the nobles had greatly increased their power by indicting and executing Chancellor Crell, and since that time they occupied all the high and profitable posts in the government, though the actual work was largely done by their non-noble secretaries. The troubled times were ruinous for finance, and the Estates held the strings of the purse. The Saxon nobility was not warlike; many of them were well-educated, widely travelled and refined. They showed interest in art and literature, despised the money-grubbing burghers and regarded French court-life as their ideal. They more and more became a court aristocracy on the model of Versailles. The peasants were not serfs as in Brandenburg, most of them were legally freemen, but the power of the nobles nevertheless often depressed them to unfavourable conditions. Many towns prospered because of industries and enjoyed a wide autonomy. Since the Reformation Saxony had also become foremost in learning and education, it had three universities and excellent classical colleges, and many famous scholars, writers and musicians were born there, though the power of Lutheran

[7] Cf. E. Devrient. *Thüringische Geschichte*, 1907, pp. 115, 117.

orthodoxy compelled not a few of them to leave the country and to seek a living in a freer atmosphere.

The Wettins were usually loyal to the Emperors and supported them in their wars against the Turks and French. After the Thirty Years' War, they set up a standing army of mercenaries and the expenses were voted by the Estates. In 1683, the martial Elector John George III appeared with them before Vienna when it was besieged by the Turks, and contributed much to the splendid victory.

Towards the end of the century Elector Frederick Augustus I came to the throne (1694-1733). He is commonly known as Augustus the Strong, because of his extraordinary strength. He possessed in addition a majestic appearance, a brilliant and subtle mind, a refined taste, charm and a friendly character. He was free from any moral inhibitions, and his countless love affairs startled even his age, which was used to scandals. In politics he was inspired by high-flying ambitions, which almost ruined his country. In order to be eligible for the Polish crown, he became a Catholic, though full freedom was guaranteed to the Protestants. Frederick Augustus was elected King of Poland against a French and other candidates (1697). The bribes for the Polish nobility had cost him 11 million talers. But his ambitions soared much higher, he dreamed also of building a great Empire, or of becoming Emperor. His loyalty to Charles VI was sometimes doubtful.

Augustus II, as he was called in Poland, in alliance with Russia and Denmark, began an aggressive war against Charles XII of Sweden, mainly in order to deprive him of Livonia and Esthonia, which were also coveted by Russia. He had been made to believe that Livonia would at once rise against the Swedes, but nothing of this kind happened. The Polish Reichstag declined to support him, and the young Swedish King quickly beat one enemy after the other, even invaded Saxony and forced Augustus to resign the Polish crown, though a few years later he was able to recover it. Charles XII laid heavy contributions on Saxony, and when the nobility protested, referring to their privileges, he reminded them that he would not be in Saxony if they had done their duty in defending their country. Frederick Augustus' ambition cost Saxony a very high price. It has been calculated that the Elector had sacrificed 40,000 lives, 88 million Talers, and 800 cannons for the war against Sweden. This was, however not his only warlike adventure.

Already before Frederick Augustus' reign, the Court of Dresden had emulated Versailles in extravagant luxury. But now gorgeous pageants, masquerades, theatre performances, etc., formed an

almost uninterrupted chain of festivities, which were arranged with
artistic taste, and mostly could be attended gratis by every person
decently dressed. The King-Elector also spent money lavishly on the
erection of beautiful palaces, on collecting precious paintings and
other works of art, and on similar interests. This laid further heavy
burdens on the country. Yet the aristocracy dominating the Estates
voted the amounts required, for which the Elector granted them
further privileges. Dresden was often called the Venice or Florence
of the North, it was a centre of fine arts, and a meeting-place of the
high society of Europe. Kings, princes, aristocrats, adventurers, and
courtesans of all countries flocked there, and their expenditure was
a source of great profits to many industries and commerce. The
connection with Poland, too, opened them a wide market. Leipzig
was the greatest centre of trade with the East of Europe. The
recruitment of mercenaries was supplemented by a measure of
conscription which, however, was very unpopular, and was strongly
attacked in pamphlets.

Frederick Augustus was followed by his son of the same name,
who also became King of Poland. We shall later have to come back
to him. A few words, however, may be said about one of the many
smaller Saxon rulers, namely Ernest the Pious, Duke of Saxe-Gotha
(1640-75). In the great war he and four of his brothers valiantly
fought for the Protestant cause, and he then devoted himself
entirely to the spiritual and material welfare of his people, and of
other Christians, even in Russia and Abyssinia. In Gotha he created
a system of instruction, which became a landmark in the history
of education. His regime was the ideal realization of a peaceable
patriarchalism in the spirit of Luther. But his successors, Frederick
I, II, and III were very different. Two of them became satellites of
Louis XIV, and all three were imbued with his spirit. Their Court
was sumptuous and its extravagant cost was covered by trading in
mercenaries.

BAVARIA

Bavaria also had been particularly ravaged by the great war, and
her population had been reduced to almost half. Later the ambitious
and warlike policy of her rulers, and their excessive luxury, imposed further heavy burdens on the people. Foreign policy was
mainly determined by the old traditional rivalry with Austria. It
often induced the Bavarian Electors to conclude alliances with
France against the Habsburgs, and to receive subsidies, which were
used to build up a Bavarian army. But the Habsburgs sometimes

succeeded in winning over the Bavarian princes by holding out chances of aggrandisement, and these were thereby induced to support Austria in her wars with Turkey and in other questions. French diplomacy, on the other hand, encouraged their ambition to become Emperors. Both tendencies by turns reached their peak under the reign of Maximilian II Emanuel (1679-1726), a prince of great gifts and ambitions. First Austria succeeded in obtaining his alliance against Turkey and France by a marriage which opened to the Bavarian House prospects of inheriting the whole Spanish Empire, if the Spanish Habsburgs should die out. But these prospects were frustrated by unforeseen events, and when the war of the Spanish Succession broke out, Max Emanuel after some hesitation joined Louis XIV, who promised him Belgium. He was outlawed by the Emperor, but after the war received Bavaria back. His successor, Karl Albert, too, alternated in both policies, for and against Austria, and for a short time was even Emperor.

THE RHINE PALATINATE

The Rhine Palatinate was, after the Thirty Years' War ruled by Elector Charles Lewis (1649-80), the eldest son of the 'Winter-King' Frederick of Bohemia. During the great war he lived mainly in the Netherlands and England. His mother Elizabeth was the sister of King Charles I, and the English and Scots Puritans regarded the Palatine cause as demanding the intervention of their countries in the Continental war. When the English Civil War began, his brother Rupert joined the King's forces. Charles Lewis, however, was convinced that royal absolutism was doomed, he advised the king, in vain, to seek an understanding with Parliament, and was in close touch with the Puritans. There were circles wishing he should become king himself. Parliament granted him £8,000 yearly 'for his good affection to the popular cause'.

The Rhine Palatinate had been terribly devastated in the war and was empty of men when it ended. Charles Lewis devoted himself to making it a home for human beings again. He publicly invited men of every religion and nationality to settle in his country, especially in Mannheim, which he hoped to make a great Rhine port and commercial centre. His far-sighted economic and financial policy did much to heal the wounds of war and to restore the former wealth, but his work was often interrupted or destroyed by new warlike invasions.

The Elector had very tolerant views in religious matters, though the bitter strife between the Churches, especially the Lutherans and the Calvinists, compelled him to preserve many restrictions for the sake of peace. His own standpoint was demonstrated in the erection of a Church of Concord, designed for all three great denominations. He was also interested in movements to bring about the union of all Christian religions, or at least that of the Protestants. One of his favourite aims was the restoration of the University of Heidelberg to its former high rank. The prince made Pufendorf the first professor of public law, and it was said that he collaborated in his famous book on the German Empire. Spinoza was invited to become a professor of philosophy at Heidelberg. He refused, and Charles Lewis realized that, as conditions were, he was right. His sisters were enthusiasts for Spinoza and the Elector, too, found in the evening of his life peace in reading Spinoza's thought.

Yet the Prince, despite his enlightenment and common sense, was also a child of his epoch, actuated by a passionate wish to preserve the prestige of his house by obstinately clinging to antiquated forms. This involved him in much strife with other princes.[8] When, in the College of Electors, the Bavarian envoy made a remark critical of his house, he drew his sword and when prevented from using it, threw an inkpot at him.

His attitude to the Emperor and Empire exhibited an astounding fickleness, which characterized many other German princes also. Emperor Ferdinand III and his successor Leopold I had shown him sincere kindness and the wish for fruitful co-operation. Nevertheless he became a satellite of Louis XIV for the sake of high pensions, but soon astonished even the French diplomats by tergiversation. In consequence both sides did not trust him.

His successor, Charles, ruled for only five years. He excelled in Calvinist narrowmindedness and a luxurious court life. The Elector was the last of his House, and the right of succession lay with the Catholic branch of the family, the House of Pfalz-Neuburg. Charles made a pact with them, safeguarding the rights of the Protestants, but died before he could sign it.

Elector Philipp William of Neuburg also reigned for five years only. He was peaceable, good-natured and insignificant. The Protestants were assured that the pact in their favour would be rigorously observed. But in spite of the ruler's good intentions the Catholic orders made many proselytes and this led to frequent frictions and quarrels. Moreover, Louis XIV, disturbed by the great

---

[8] His quarrels about the right of 'Wildfang' at least aimed at a practical purpose, namely increasing the number of his subjects, but the demand for his 'Erzamt' aimed merely at an entirely useless title. Cf. Hauck, pp. 97, 104, 109, 126, Haeusser p. 618, etc.

victories of the Emperor against the Turks, began a new war in his rear and expressly gave order to devastate the Palatinate in a barbarous way (1688). The French army particularly maltreated the Protestants, forced them to become Catholics or to flee, and handed over all the churches with their lands, etc., to the Catholic communities.

When in 1697 peace was concluded at Ryswick, a clause dictated by France laid down that the religious changes enforced in the war had to stay. As intended, this clause led to endless new strife between the German religious parties, which at times threatened to become a civil war.

The Rhine Palatinate was now ruled by Elector John William (1690-1716), who was much under the influence of the Jesuits. Yet he began in a moderate way, promising religious freedom. But later he increasingly veered to a policy of discrimination against the Protestants. This induced many Protestant governments in Germany and abroad to protest strongly and to take counter-measures. Prussia took reprisals by the sequestration of Catholic chapters and monasteries. So the Elector issued more tolerant decrees and in 1705 a pact called the Religious Declaration was concluded, granting freedom of religion. But soon numerous quarrels flared up again. In 1715, the Reichstag enacted a statute, forbidding all religious invectives and the Imperial Aulic Council ordered the Elector John William to punish the Jesuit Professor Usleber, who, in an academic disputation at Heidelberg, had violently attacked the Calvinists. Before this was settled, however, the Elector died. His Court at Düsseldorf was exceedingly splendid, he built fine palaces, created a wonderful picture gallery and was a patron of art and science. But in the Palatinate great masses were living in misery and many thousands emigrated.

The Elector's brother Charles Philipp succeeded him. He had first belonged to the clerical profession, but had later left it for the military one. In the many campaigns against the Turks he had risen to the position of an Imperial Fieldmarshal, was later appointed Governor of the Tyrol and at last received the dignity of Elector (1716-42). His first decrees made him very popular, but soon others followed, which aroused bitter complaints from the Protestant section. A number of German and foreign rulers again raised protests and took reprisals, especially Prussia. Charles VI reprimanded both sides and ordered that a reasonable compromise should be accepted. These reactions to his challenge induced the Elector to withdraw his measures, but soon other conflicts developed. The Emperor continued his policy of impartial arbitration and the Protestant princes, too, kept a sharp lookout on the situation. In a few years the tension abated since public opinion had got tired of all these quarrels.

The House of Pfalz-Neuburg had for three generations been closely connected with the House of Austria and belonged to its most loyal followers. It seems surprising that it began to turn away from the Habsburgs and to join their enemies under Elector Charles Philipp of all people, the former Imperial Fieldmarshal and Governor. According to the greatest expert on this question,[9] 'it is certain that the Emperor's moderation in the ecclesiastical quarrels, his more judicial than partial procedure, had the greatest share in this change'. The Elector in 1724 concluded a family pact with the Elector of Bavaria, also a Wittelsbach, which stated that they and the Electors of Cologne and Trier, their close relatives, should keep troops and co-operate in certain questions, particularly in common defence. France backed this alliance. Its principal aim was to ensure common action when the succession to the throne of Juelich-Berg should take place. This powerful group soon began to show a hostile and treacherous attitude to the policy of the Emperor.

WURTTEMBERG

In Wurttemberg after the Thirty Years' War Duke Eberhard III continued to rule. The country was largely a waste, and needed reconstruction on the greatest scale. Numerous measures were taken to this end. In 1649, elementary education was made compulsory for every child. The Estates continued to oppose any step towards a standing army of professional soldiers. When Louis XIV's aggressive policy led to several invasions of Wurttemberg by French and Imperial armies, the country was practically defenceless and again had to suffer greatly. Eberhard Ludwig (1677-1733) at last overcame the resistance of the Estates against an efficient army. His successor Karl Alexander, an Austrian Fieldmarshal, became a Catholic and was dominated by a Jewish financier, Suess Oppenheimer, who understood how to raise money for military purposes without the Estates. This aroused their opposition, and the Duke planned to break their power. A grave conflict was brewing, but the Duke suddenly died. Suess Oppenheimer was arrested, tried and hanged.

HANOVER

The Dukes of Brunswick-Lueneburg, later called Hanover, achieved a spectacular ascent after the Thirty Years' War. The luxury of their Court was dazzling. They set up a standing army and

[9] Cf. Ludwig Haeusser, Geschichte der Rheinischen Pfalz, II, 1856, p. 879.

compelled the reluctant Estates to vote the necessary expenses. The possession of an army enabled them to play a rôle in international politics, and most of them supported the Emperor in his wars with Turkey and France. This service was rewarded by the elevation of Duke Ernest Augustus to the rank of an Elector (1692). In 1658, he had married a grand-daughter of James I of England and this in 1701 induced the English Parliament to declare the Hanoverian dynasty the legitimate successor to the reigning Queen. After her death Elector George Ludwig of Hanover became also King George I of Great Britain.

There were now six German princes who were also foreign kings. The union of Hanover with Britain was strictly personal. The King alone was common to both. British opinion was full of suspicion that the union might prejudice British interests, and the Act of Settlement contained many clauses designed to prevent this. George I visited Hanover five times and George II twelve times. These journeys caused much grumbling in Britain, and George III therefore never set foot on Hanover's soil. In spite of all British precautions, George I was much influenced in politics by Count Andreas Bernstorf, a Hanoverian statesman. This aroused great resentment and it was constantly complained in speeches and pamphlets that the interests of Britain were sacrificed to those of Hanover. But already sixty years ago a great English historian, Adolfus Ward, came to the conclusion on ground of close studies, that the charges against Bernstorf were either greatly exaggerated or were untrue, and that his policy served British interests well. He also pointed out that the personal union exposed Hanover to great risks and that Britain had therefore a moral obligation to defend her. But this was very difficult. Britain's great rival was then France. In a war with Britain France regularly sent a big army to conquer Hanover, and this country was subjected to terrible depredations again and again.

The personal union also often affected the relations of Hanover to the Empire. Before it the rulers of Hanover had for a long time been loyal supporters of the Emperor. After it they had to combine their duties to Britain with those to Hanover and to the Empire.

The memorable international agreements of 1716 and 1718, which secured Britain the leadership of Europe in the striving for peace were, as Ward has shown, the common work of British and Hanoverian statesmen. In 1725, however, the Treaty of Hanover placed the King-Elector in very strained relations to the Emperor, which nearly led to a war. The Hanoverian ministers had been completely against it but had to give way to the British Foreign Secretary, Lord Townshend. In the Seven Years' War Britain and

Hanover stood on the side of Prussia against the Emperor and the Empire.

The personal union had advantages and disadvantages for both countries. Hanover, however, probably had much more reason to feel aggrieved by it than Britain. Nevertheless public opinion in Hanover showed much pride in the connexion, while in Britain politicians constantly denounced it in the sharpest words. When Britain was, however, threatened by a foreign invasion in 1756, Hanoverian troops had to be called in and in the course of time they had to fight for British interests in many parts of the world[10] for example in Gibraltar and Minorca against Spain (1775-84), and in East India against French troops and Indian princes (1781-92). They fought in the wars of Britain against revolutionary France and served under Wellington in Spain (1808-14). After the dissolution of the Hanoverian army by Napoléon they formed the British-German Legion and took part in the battle of Waterloo.

HESSE

The territory of Hesse had been divided in the sixteenth century, and two dynastic lines had remained: Hesse-Kassel and Hesse-Darmstadt. The former became a leader of Calvinist antagonism to the Habsburgs, while the latter remained Lutheran and loyal to the Emperor. In the course of time the Calvinist line produced several very remarkable rulers who developed a real tradition. After the Thirty Years' War, a ruler of importance was Landgrave Charles who reigned for 53 years (1677-1730) and distinguished himself as a patron of science, art and technology. He admired progressive Holland, gave asylum to many refugees from religious persecution, but also established his personal rule on the model of Louis XIV, and had a splendid court and a standing army. In order to cover the expenses he began, in 1687, to lend troops to foreign states, especially Venice and the maritime powers. His successor, Frederick I, became, by marriage, King of Sweden. Hesse-Kassel became a military state and a main supplier of Britain when she needed troops. This business was very profitable and the princes could therefore spend large amounts on erecting beautiful buildings, buying precious works of art and maintaining a gorgeous court, which soon assumed an entirely French character. Calvinism showed itself more tolerant than Lutheranism and paved the way for enlightenment. Lutheran Hesse-Darmstadt was less progressive, but

[10] Cf. L. von Sichart, *Geschichte der kgl. Hannoverschen Armee*, 5 vols, 1866-98.

on the other hand spurned the traffic with soldiers. But as some of its princes were also rather lavish in expenditure, they soon got into long-lasting financial difficulties.

14

CHRISTIAN WOLFF AND ENLIGHTENMENT

LIFE AND TEACHING OF WOLFF

CHRISTIAN WOLFF (1679-1754) was the most effective teacher of the doctrines of Enlightenment in Germany. He was born in Brelau, and was the son of a man who had not been able to afford studies at a university, and had been compelled to become an artisan. But he had made a vow that his son should become a scholar. Christian studied theology but his indefatigable zeal to ascertain the truth induced him to study also many other branches of learning. As he later confessed he was from his youth inspired by the ardent longing to contribute whatever he could to the spread of human happiness, reason and virtue. Reason was to him the supreme authority. Nothing was to be believed without critical examination and conclusive proof. In 1706 he became professor of Mathematics, and later also of Physics, at the University of Halle, and lectured also much on philosophy. In order to influence a wider public he used mainly the German language, but later, in order to reach also other nations, he wrote mainly in Latin. He had the faculty to speak freely and convincingly, and he soon became the most popular academic teacher and writer of Germany. Wolff remained a pious Lutheran Christian and rejected atheism, deism, materialism and scepticism. Yet he taught that also atheists might be virtuous, that the Hottentots who did not believe in a God had many good sides, and that the Chinese who possessed no religion but lived according to the philosophy of Confucius were, in their classical time, models of pure morals and wise statecraft. He also cast doubts on miracles and on the need for revelation and said other things which aroused the defenders of orthodoxy. In 1721 an academic oration in which he extolled the morality and politics of the Chinese over that of the Christians led to a crisis. Some of his theological colleagues

H

denounced him to King Frederick William I of Prussia as suspect of atheism, and the king instantly dismissed Wolff and ignominiously expelled him from his realm. At the same time, orthodox Lutherans started a campaign against professors who were followers of Wolff at many universities. The expulsion of the philosopher caused a great stir all over Europe and was widely condemned as an act of bigotry and despotism. Wolff immediately obtained a much better post at Marburg, and universities, academies, rulers and statesmen of many nations bestowed great honours upon him. The oration condemned by the Lutherans at once appeared in two editions approved by the Catholic authorities, in the Acta Eruditorum, in an English edition, etc. Even King Frederick William later changed his mind and would have liked to have Wolff back. He was recognized as the leading philosopher in Germany and enjoyed world fame. His treatises were translated into many languages, used as textbooks by the universities and gave rise to numerous commentaries and popularizations. Most teachers of philosophy were his followers, and the journals propagated his teachings. Gottsched, the most prominent literary critic, was a great admirer of Wolff and spread his principles. A special patron of the philosopher was Ernst Christoph Count Manteuffel a Pomeranian who became a Saxon minister and later lived in Berlin. He belonged to a masonic circle and in 1736 founded in Berlin a Society of the Friends of Truth devoted to propaganda for Wolff's doctrines. It soon had many members of high rank and established branches in other towns. Since the upper classes preferred French to German, Wolff's ideas were also spread by books and lectures in French. Formey, an influential preacher and later Secretary of the Berlin Academy, gave French lectures on Wolff's philosophy, eagerly frequented by the high society of Berlin, and also published a popular manual on it under the title La Belle Wolfienne. In this way Wolff's ideas became the fashion of the day. Moreover, Manteuffel and his friend Reinbeck, a high-placed churchman, succeeded in winning many of the younger clergy, and they were instructed how to use their sermons for the propagation of Wolff's principles. Many pamphlets and satires, too, were published to this end.

Manteuffel further interested the heir to the throne, Prince Frederick, in Wolff's philosophy. In 1740 the philosopher dedicated to the Prince his work on the Law of Nature, and Frederick said in his answer: 'The philosophers must be the teachers of the universe and the masters of the princes. They ought to instruct the world by reasoning and we by example. They shall discover and we practise.' Shortly after, Frederick came to the throne and reinstated Wolff in his former post at Halle. His return was a triumphal progress accompanied by the jubilation of the students and the burghers. He also was made a baron of the Empire by the Emperor Charles VII and received other honours.

The king, however, soon abandoned Wolff's eclectic rationalism and adopted the ideas of English and French thinkers, first deism and empiricism, with an admixture of stoicism, and later material-ism and scepticism. The spirit of the time turned away from rationalism and Wolff was regarded as obsolete. The young people followed new prophets. Yet Wolff's contributions to intellectual progress were lasting. He has been called the schoolmaster of the Germans, for he had given them a rigid discipline in clear and critical thinking which bore rich fruit even after his name had sunk into oblivion. The Society of the Friends of Truth coined a medal with the images of Leibniz and Wolff and the motto: Sapere aude! Dare to think! This principle was, indeed, Wolff's lodestar. But he was also imbued with warm sympathy for all mankind and wished to make them free and happy by enlightenment. In this sense the famous French physicist Réamur gave him the name 'The Professor of Mankind', which Wolff proudly accepted.

As a philosopher Wolff reduced Leibniz and other's ideas to a system but modified it in various ways.[1] He tried to overcome the antagonism between rationalism and empiricism, and emphasized determinism. In his belief the power of reason had no limits. Man could be brought to tame his passions by a strict logical demonstra-tion of what was reasonable. Life's aim was the perfection of man, the harmonious development of all his faculties which leads to happiness. Man serves God best by becoming enlightened. The whole creation shows God's benevolence and wisdom. He has ordered all things so as to be most useful to man. This teleological utilitarianism was carried to such lengths that it could easily be ridiculed.

In his principal book on social and political questions Wolff puts forward the following principles: Man has an innate duty to follow the law of reason and to perfect himself, and to this duty correspond the innate rights of man. Since individuals in isolation, however, were unable adequately to realize their duties and rights, they founded societies and states by way of a covenant. The aim of society is the harmonious development of all human faculties and the happiness of the greatest number of individuals. The particular aim of the state is security and welfare, and the power of govern-

---

[1] He later denied that Leibniz had exercised a paramount influence on his thought and said that he owed to Thomas Aquinas more than to him.

ment does not extend farther than these aims require. In the state of nature all men were free and equal, and there was no private property. The course of social development caused many inequalities, but the fundamental laws of nature still subsisted and set limits to inequality. Wolff discusses in great detail the obligations and rights of man, and his principles often anticipate Rousseau, Bentham, and the Socialists. Though he was nothing less than a revolutionary and would have abhorred any unleashing of mass passions and violence, his principles had far-reaching revolutionary implications, which began to appear when the time was ripe. He was, naturally, well aware that the conditions of his time were not in accord with the voice of reason. But he considered it neither his task, nor necessary, to point out the discrepancies in detail and to devise practical steps to put them right. This was partly due to his optimistic views of the power of reason. To him the aim of social science was not primarily to show how things were, but how they should be. He was, furthermore, confident that once the rules of reason had been fully and clearly demonstrated, men would feel more and more compelled by their conscience and their true interests to abolish old abuses and create conditions in conformity with reason. Actually, his exposition of what should be, was, for everybody with eyes to see, a formidable criticism of existing conditions. His confidence, moreover, was not without some justification. The ruling circles of that time were, to a great degree, imbued with similar views or at least had the ambition to show themselves enlightened. Many of them sincerely believed in doctrines of rationalism and were convinced that they also coincided with the interests of their states.

Wolff assumed that men, by adopting the social contract, had given up their original status of freedom and equality, but that they had not thereby forfeited their rights of man. Every contract implied the reservation that the fundamentals of natural law must not be infringed. A characteristic example is Wolff's attitude to slavery: a man able to find his happiness in freedom must not be made a slave. But it is not unjust that men be made slaves until the time comes when they can reach their happiness in liberty. Slaves, moreover, must be well treated. The master must love his slaves and feel pleasure when they are happy. Not long before Wolff wrote this book, Britain had, by the Treaty of Utrecht, secured the monopoly of the import of slaves to Spanish America as a precious fruit of the war against Louis XIV. Wolff cannot have ignored the evils of these conditions. His remark that it was the duty of the masters to care for the happiness of the slaves implies his criticism of reality. In a similar way, Wolff takes little, or no, account of other existing inequalities. But his statement of the natural law indicates what he thinks of them.

The commonwealth or community—as Wolff calls state and society—is conceived as a large family. In this he followed the model of the Chinese, whom he considered the wisest of all nations and whose ideas of social life he identified with his own. The best commonwealth was that where the greatest number of men lived together in happiness and security. The various forms of the state and their advantages and disadvantages are set forth mainly according to Aristotle. Wolff does not declare any one constitution as the absolutely best; he admits that quite different governments might work well, from an unlimited monarchy to a free republic in which the wisest and most virtuous representatives of all ranks, from the highest to the lowest, formed the Estates. But the latter constitution could only work with a civilized people, and the common man was not fitted for it. New financial burdens should be laid on the people only with the consent of the Estates. This involved a considerable restriction of the power of governments, but a reasonable government would realize that this restriction was both in its own interest and in that of the community. Yet Wolff would not go so far as to say that this restriction must take place everywhere. His standpoint, therefore, was that as a rule new taxes had to be voted by the Estates, but that certain countries might form exceptions. Even an unlimited government, however, was bound to observe the fundamental laws implied in the social contract and the precepts of religion, and if a government broke its constitutional obligations and protests were ineffective, it might be restricted by the Estates. Yet Wolff also stressed that the people must obey even a bad government, except if its orders were against the natural law. In this case the people should offer passive resistance and patiently bear the consequences. If the ruler, however, violated the fundamental laws, even a civil war against him was legitimate. In another place Wolff says that since the people had transferred their sovereignty to the ruler, the latter could not arbitrarily change the constitution, but was bound by the fundamental laws. The people, however, could change them, provided that the legitimate rights of the ruler were not infringed. The right of the ruler had to be interpreted according to the will of the people at the time when the social contract was concluded.

At Wolff's time the Estates were, in general, losing in power, but in many German principalities they still had considerable influence. In others they had not been convoked for some time, but had not renounced their rights. In East Prussia, for example, the Estates had been assembled for the last time in 1704, and at the accession of Frederick II in 1740, they petitioned to be convened regularly. In these circumstances Wolff's thesis that the rights of the ruler ought to be interpreted according to the will of the people at the time the social contract was concluded might have been quoted in support of the historic rights of the Estates. But Wolff himself does not seem to have taken an interest in strengthening the position of the Estates. His heart was in the proclamation of the rights of man, and this cause had at that time certainly more to expect from enlightened monarchs than from Estates dominated by orthodox churchmen, backwood squires and burghers with a parochial outlook.

Great stress is laid upon the moral and intellectual qualifications of the prince, his advisers and servants. The prince must be a philosopher according to Plato's precept; he should receive a most careful education. His dignity requires the display of splendour by means of court life and of magnificent buildings, gardens, and so on, and he should cultivate the arts and sciences. But he must beware of wastefulness, to check which was the duty of the Estates. The interest of the community has always to have precedence over his private interest; it should be his highest glory to be called a Prince of Peace. Of the greatest importance was also the careful selection and training of the civil servants. In appointments no regard should be paid to rank, but only to competence, loyalty, justice and sense of duty. All the officials, and also the judges, must be subject to dismissal if they deserve it. Titles and distinctions should not be for sale.

Though Wolff was a pious member of the Lutheran Church, he was himself tolerant, stood in very friendly relations with Jesuits and also wanted the state to be free from bigotry and intolerance. His rationalism is characterized by his statement that religion is necessary for the commonwealth because the fear of divine punishment alone is a barrier to crime if there is no witness, and because men would otherwise lose their belief in the sanctity of an oath. Atheists should, therefore, not be tolerated in the community. But Wolff makes it clear that he only fears the danger that the atheists might make propaganda for their unbelief and stir up trouble, and that he would not bother about them if they kept quiet. Yet he is also much opposed to zealots denouncing as an atheist anybody who does not go to church and he advises the government not to tolerate such denunciations, which might do more harm than atheism itself.

The government, according to Wolff, has to care for every possible need of man, for his security, morality, instruction, employ-ment, material welfare, entertainment, and so on. Wolff's ideal of a commonwealth has much in common with the modern Welfare State. The commonwealth has to see to it that nobody suffered want of food, clothing and lodging, it is to enable everybody to find adequate work at reasonable, though not too high, wages and under healthy working conditions, and also to care for the provision of cheap supplies. To this purpose wages, prices and interests are to be fixed, working hours and other conditions of labour to be regulated, unemployment to be prevented by the control of the labour market, credit to be organized and, in brief, a system to be established which today would be called a planned economy. People living exclusively on interest or rent, though able to do useful work, cannot easily be tolerated in the commonwealth, and one should give them some useful task, but only if they were fitted for it. Wolff, therefore, proclaimed both the right of the worker to employment and the right of the community to demand that everybody should work. One of the most important tasks of government was education, and the philosopher deals in great detail with the various types of schools to be provided, with the training of teachers and the methods of teaching. His ideas on education are similar to those of Locke. There must also be schools for the children of the poor who could not pay any fees, and schools for teaching trades. At the top of the system was to be the Academy of Science, which was to organize scientific research and form an advisory body to the government. Wolff wanted to give this academy a very influential position and demanded full freedom of research. The Academy should also collect and compare the laws of all the nations and suggest how the laws of the country might be improved. An Academy of Arts, too, was needed to promote the arts.

The commonwealth has further to give every attention to the health of the people, to provide well-trained doctors, midwives, hospitals, to care for expectant mothers, to protect orphans and to prohibit drunkenness. Illegitimate children should have the same rights as legitimate ones in inheriting from their parents. There should be orphanages and poor-houses, and also work-houses with a severe discipline for the able-bodied poor. Duelling is to be strictly pro-hibited, as it is utterly absurd. Public health demanded the cleaning of the streets and the control of buildings, in particular the care for light and air in the houses, the prevention of dangerous vapours and measures against conflagrations. Fireplaces were to be built in a way securing adequate ventilation and the privies should conform to the rules of hygiene. Buildings and streets should satisfy the sense of

beauty. An important contribution to the furtherance of public
health is to be the encouragement of sports and gymnastics. Many
measures were demanded by reason in the interests of morality, for
example the prohibition of wastefulness or of pictures of nudities,
which might arouse lewdness. The government, furthermore, was
also to provide entertainment, such as theatres or museums. Music
and poetry might contribute much to the aims of society. On the
other hand, the authorities had to prohibit amusements in places
where they might have an unfavourable influence on students. But
coffee houses, like those in England, could become useful meeting-
places for people of learning. Among countless suggestions Wolff
did not forget to advise the government to protect nightingales and
other song-birds from any disturbance.

The economic policy of Wolff was the mercantilism of his time,
though he had no understanding of the power politics and commercial jealousy connected with this system. But he endorses the
striving for self-sufficiency; he dwells on the economic advantages
of a large territory and a sizeable population and approves of restrictions on emigration, though the subjects of a country should not
be treated as slaves. His precepts for increasing wealth are the
usual ones of mercantilism.

It is obvious that the realization by the government of all the
aims put forward by Wolff would necessitate a continual interference in the life of the subjects and their constant supervision. The
philosopher himself is aware of the dangers of too close a control;
he thinks that personal freedom should not be too much restricted
and that many things might be left to individual initiative.

The reform of law according to the rules of reason formed a
principal subject of Wolff's investigations, and he made proposals
concerning many problems though he was not a jurist. Only such
acts were to be punishable which diminished the public weal or
security. Error was not punishable, but the spread of errors was.
The aim of punishment was to deter the criminal from repeating
his misdeeds and others from imitating him. For this reason punishment had to be public. Wolff indulges in the most elaborate precepts
how to increase the deterring effect of an execution. The place
should be chosen in such a way that the greatest possible number of
people could see the execution well. There ought to be ceremonies to
make it more impressive, for example the criminal should wear a
special dress. The corpses should be left unburied and carcases of
animals should lie about to produce an evil smell and to increase the
deterring horror. And so on. In elaborating the principle of arousing
horror in order to deter from committing crimes Wolff even admits

capital punishment and breaking on the wheel for theft, provided that more lenient penalties have been ineffective. In criminal procedure he does not absolutely exclude torture, though he admits it in exceptional cases only; for example if a person has been arrested who is strongly suspected of a highway robbery, has the stolen objects on him, without being able to give an alibi or to explain how he got the objects, and provided he had a strong and healthy body, so that torture would not do too much harm.

On the other hand, Wolff is anxious to make the law more humane. The judge should be patient, friendly and helpful to everybody without distinction of rank. This should also be his behaviour towards a person accused of a crime, however great this may be, both during the trial and in pronouncing judgment. The judge must have pity even on a criminal. When he passes his sentence he should not do it in harsh words or in passion. He must not hate the criminal but show him sympathy and remain his friend, though he must hate his crime.

War appears to Wolff a great misfortune, to avoid which every effort should be made. It is only legitimate as a defence against an actual or intended aggression, or to realize a just claim when all other attempts to achieve it by negotiation, reprisals or mediation have failed. But mere advantage is no legitimate cause. A war undertaken for this purpose is inhuman and beastly. The mere fact that a nation becomes so powerful that it becomes a danger or upsets the balance of power is no justification for war, nor are reasons of religion or morality sufficient. In an unjust war killing is murder and seizing of things is robbery. In a war no greater damage must be inflicted than is absolutely necessary. The looting and killing of the civil population is against the natural law. No nation has further the right to expel another nation from its homeland in order to settle there. Wolff also points out that war should be waged without hostile feelings against the individuals. The subjects of a State are only obliged to military service in cases of extreme danger. The pressing of foreign subjects to become soldiers is a crime.

Wolff's opinions on international law culminate in his doctrine of the Civitas Maxima. He assumed that just as a state formed a kind of organism there was also an organic connection between all states, a universal society or republic of nations possessing the right to intervene in relations between nations and to establish rules in the interest of general security, justice and welfare. This society exists without a formal pact. This doctrine has aroused much criticism even among prominent disciples of Wolff's. But an international reign of law is hardly possible without it.

H*

EMERIC DE VATTEL

Wolff's ideas have exercised a momentous influence on numerous political thinkers,[2] jurisprudents and statesmen of his and later times. Emeric de Vattel (1714-1767) was the most important propagator of his doctrines on international law. He was born in the principality of Neufchatel which was ruled by the king of Prussia and also was a member of the Swiss Confederation. Vattel studied theology and philosophy at Geneva and became an ardent admirer of Leibniz and Wolff. Later he entered the service of the elector of Saxony and became one of his leading diplomats. As minister to Bern he wrote his principal work on the Law of Nations, which appeared in 1758, in which year he was also called to Dresden as Privy Counsellor. It was the time of the Seven Years' War, in which the country had much to suffer, and the burdens of his office contributed to his early death (1767).

Emeric de Vattel at first wished only to popularize Wolff's doctrines, as he relates himself. Wolff had laid them down in 16 or 17 big volumes written in Latin and in a difficult form. His disciple intended to make them understandable and attractive to the men who managed or influenced international affairs, to statesmen and the ruling classes. For this purpose he wrote in French, then the language of high society, and being an excellent stylist, he had great success. In the course of his work, however, he changed his original plan, and wrote a work of his own, following Wolff's ideas in the main, but modifying them, adding new points, and formulating the theses in felicitous sentences. He created a work which for almost a century formed the indispensable handbook of all statesmen dealing with international affairs. Scholars often criticized Vattel, pointing out that he was not an original thinker, that contradictory conclusions could be drawn from passages of his book, that he had failed to provide the Law of Nations with a philosophical sanction, and so on. We need not go into these controversies here, and wish only to say that they are largely inherent in the idea of a Law of Nations under actual conditions, and that in the two centuries which have passed since Vattel's work, mankind on the whole has not come nearer to the ideal of a real international reign of law, but in vital points has even lapsed into a more barbaric state.

In our age, Vattel's masterpiece has been reprinted in the Classics of International Law, edited by the Carnegie Foundation, and Albert de Lapradelle has given an excellent survey of his views there.

[2] Kant for a long time used Wolff's books as basis for his lectures.

Though Vattel adopted and elaborated most of Wolff's doctrines, he put the abstract theories of his master into a more concrete and less pedantic form, and in addition he also contributed important new ideas to the Law of Nations. In particular, he laid great stress on the liberty, sovereignty, and equality of nations. Even savages must not be civilized against their will, and still less should an advanced nation interfere in the internal affairs of another one. But every nation must assist others against oppression by a ruthless tyrant or unjust aggression, if this can be done without endangering its own liberty and security.

Vattel's liberal and democratic spirit renders him a forerunner of the ideologies of the American and French Revolutions. His bold theses can be deduced from the principles of his master. But what Wolff formulated in a cautious and inoffensive way, assumes in Vattel's book a revolutionary ring. His book had a success far surpassing any other work of its kind. The edition quoted gives a list of twenty editions in the original French, twenty-two in English, six in Spanish, and there were also other ones. In Germany it was mainly read in the French text, since the educated classes there universally understood French. Vattel was least appreciated in France. As Lapradelle, himself an eminent French scholar, says, international law was at that time mostly not taken seriously in France, and there was not a single chair for it at any of the numerous French universities. But in England and America Vattel exercised an enormous influence. The fathers of the American Revolution regarded Vattel as the greatest authority justifying their claim to independence. When, a century later, Cavour took steps to realize Italy's national unity and liberty, and the great Empires of Europe appeared to take concerted action against his policy, England supported him; Lord John Russell wrote a famous despatch, in which he declared : 'Vattel, that eminent jurist, has well said that when a people for good reasons takes up arms against an oppressor, it is but an act of justice and generosity to assist brave men in the defence of their liberties.' England agreed with this principle. This despatch was a fine tribute to Emeric de Vattel, but indirectly also to his master, the forgotten German professor.

Wolff's ideas on education played a great rôle in the development of modern pedagogics, and particularly influenced Basedow and his school. This will be discussed in a later place (p. 384). But a great educational factor was also a kind of journalism mainly inspired by Wolff's thought.

THE PROMOTION OF ENLIGHTENMENT BY JOURNALS

The ideas of enlightenment were largely spread by a specific type of journal written for the general public. Their task was not to print news or to give information of interest to certain professions but to publish articles critical of prejudices, harmful customs and obsolete institutions. The actions of governments could then not be criticized openly. There was no freedom of the press for discussing affairs of the state. But other wide fields were more or less open to criticism.

Apart from the newspapers reporting the news of the day a very great number of journals was published in Germany designed to discuss general or professional problems, most of them weeklies. Professor Kirchner has compiled a list of 3494 journals published in Germany up to 1790, and he gives many details about their aims, editors, circulation etc. in one of his books. Many of them appeared only for a short time, though a few had a longer life. The first ones appeared towards the end of the seventeenth century, following French and English models. Up to 1700, 58 journals had been founded in Germany, in the following ten years 64 more were added, and in the next ten years 119 further ones. It is significant that a large proportion, about 40%, were historical-political. They dealt not only with the past but also with current affairs, and while some were written for scholars, others tried to attract the general public by sensational stories. The most successful among writers for these journals was David Fassmann, who was both a scholar and a journalist, and had much personal knowledge of King Frederick William I and other high-placed persons. He published his periodical 'Talks in the Realm of the Dead' (1718-40) for twenty-two years, and also books on the princes of his age, which had a big sale. With the progress of time the number of journals grew rapidly. The first journals were published in the great commercial towns Leipzig, Frankfurt and Hamburg and in a few university towns such as Halle and Jena. Later journals were founded all over Germany, even in quite small places. But for a considerable time it was Protestant Germany which went ahead. The Catholic territories played almost no part before 1770.

A specific type of journal devoted to the ideas of enlightenment were the 'Moral Weeklies'. Their models were the English journals founded by Steele and Addison, especially The Spectator. The splendid rôle played by these two authors and their journals in

English life and letters is generally known. It was natural that they were much imitated not only in Britain, but also in other countries, and particularly in Germany. A study by Kawczynski gives a list of titles of moral weeklies which appeared in the eighteenth century in various countries. It comprises 220 English weeklies, 28 French and 511 German ones. But the German number must have been even greater since Jacobi found 91 in Hamburg alone, of which ca 40 were missing in Kawczynski's list. Yet conditions of publication were much less favourable in Germany than in England. The art of writing was much less developed, the German language had suffered a fatal deterioration in the long war and the upper classes preferred French. The public for such journals was also much smaller, and authors could hardly make a living by their pen alone.

Steele's and Addison's most important journals appeared between 1709 and 1714, and as early as 1713 an imitation came out in Hamburg under the title *Der Vernuenftler* (*The Rationalist*). But much more important was the foundation of *The Discourses of Painters* by Bodmer and Breitinger in Zuerich (1721). The title expresses the idea of giving the reader pictures of the human mind, its virtues and vices, ideals and customs in the form of discussions between members of a group. In 1724 a group of distinguished burghers of Hamburg, who had formed a Patriotic Society, sponsored the publication of a journal called *The Patriot* which soon sold 5,000 copies and was several times reprinted. A year later J. C. Gottsched in Leipzig started a weekly *Die vernuenftigen Tadlerinnen* (The rational lady critics), mainly designed for women, and a few years later another one entitled *Der Biedermann* (The Upright Man). In Goettingen the weekly *Der Buerger* (The Citizen) appeared in 1732. As mentioned already gradually very many similar moral weeklies were published and the movement reached its climax in the time before the middle of the century and then declined.

The moral weeklies were faced with many enemies such as the representatives of unenlightened despotism, orthodoxy and inveterate privileges. They therefore avoided or even opposed radical ideas regarding politics and religion and mostly followed the peaceable and moderate thought of Wolff and his school. The spirit of enlightenment also implied great differences—the unavoidable consequences of free thought—which soon led to sharp conflicts between various schools. The ideals common to all of them were freedom to unfold all human faculties and a life according to reason and morality. This presupposed the education of man to humanity, the refutation of countless prejudices, the refining of morality and taste, the development of patriotism and world-citizenship and their union, and particularly the study of the human mind. The moral weeklies criticized old customs which did not fit in with the new world, condemned things such as the despotic power of the father over his wife and children, the education of the young by harsh exercise of authority disregarding the psychology of the pupils, cruel and degrading superstitions, obsolete forms of law and justice, and also the dangers of radical free-thought such as the negation of a God and immortality. Fashionable follies of the higher classes were severely denounced, for example gambling, duelling, prodigality, idleness, boasting of titles and stressing of social distinctions, contempt for the mother tongue and the use of a German corrupted by the admixture of foreign words, reading of bad literature, exaggerated compliments, silly amusements, gossiping, servility towards princes and nobles, meanness towards servants and so on.

The higher classes distinguished themselves from the others by speaking French, the scholars mostly regarded Latin as the only language worthy of a learned man, the middle class largely did not know correct German, and the lower classes spoke dialects understandable to the people of their own region only. Without a common language, however, the Germans were not a people, and without a cultivated language they could not have a literature comparable to that of many other peoples. The elevation of the German language to the literary level and questions of literary criticism were therefore of great significance for the development of the Germans to nationhood and for cultural progress. Many of the moral weeklies dealt with these problems also. The Swiss 'Discourses of Painters' gave particular attention to them, and the controversies of their editors Bodmer and Breitinger with Gottsched on questions of how to improve both the German language and its literature prepared the ground for their rise to classical perfection.

The English models imitated by these German journals could discuss politics also. In Germany this was a great risk and most journals avoided it, though others sometimes did it with caution. The 'Patriot' which appeared in a Free Town, but others also, criticized princes and nobles in a general way. The 'Citizen' of Goettingen demanded that a citizen must actively further the common weal, mere passive obedience was not enough. Excessive wealth of a few idle people, the journal said, was detrimental, but the work of the mass of poor labourers made the community rich. The fatherland is there where one is well-off. Foreigners useful to commerce and to international understanding should enjoy greater rights than natives without these merits. Most weeklies showed an outspokenly cosmopolitan standpoint. *The Patriot* of Hamburg begins with a fervent confession of world-citizenship. Twenty-five years later *The Druid* appeared. It was published in Berlin during the reign of Frederick II, who had just waged, for eight years, his first great aggressive war. But the weekly shows no influence of the spirit of Frederick the Great. The editor relates (I, 18) that a town councillor of a Free Town had asked for his opinion on the great political events of the time. He finds this ridiculous. A private person could not judge politics, but must leave them to the government. He himself, he confesses, was inspired by love of the fatherland and all mankind. When a battle was fought he mourned for friend and foe, both of whom he regarded as brothers. He wished that his fatherland, the great and mighty Germany, should enjoy true and lasting happiness through the flowering of science, and of the useful arts, through true religion, good taste, the quietness and contentment of all citizens, through the wisdom and greatness of all rulers, and through its formidable armed forces. But he did not wish for the return of the times when all peoples trembled before the sword of the Teutons. In the last war he had felt no hatred of other nations. In another article (I, 48) he makes fun of the alleged virtues of the Germans and rejects national vanity. The article 'On Tyrants' (II, 83) complains that men have a slavish respect towards the terrible, and admire a pitiless, cruel tyrant. Miserable village squires (Dorfjunker) are brought up in a way which is bound to make them into raging tyrants. The chase, in particular, is an abominable torture of the hunted animals. The editor of this weekly never revealed his name, but it has been ascertained that it was J. G. Sucro.

The Moral Weeklies sprang mainly from the rising self-consciousness of the middle classes, and they also pleaded for groups suffering under prejudices such as women, servants, children and so on. They were often read by the father to the assembled family.

The emphasis was on education for a reasonable life, for women as well as for men, and on humanity for all. Their educational ideas often anticipated Rousseau and the Philanthropists. Most editors and contributors remained anonymous, partly to impress the readers by the appearance of a mysterious power observing their life, partly to escape persecution. Criticism of influential classes easily led to prohibition of the journal by the censorship. This happened to the *Vernuenftler*, the first of the moral weeklies, after it had published 100 issues—and this in Hamburg, proud of its 'republican freedom'! Most weeklies had only a short life owing to the smallness of the reading public. Moreover, most of the contributors were not yet highly qualified for journalism, though in the course of time this improved. The greatest merit of these weeklies was that they trained writers to write attractively for a larger public than a few scholars and thereby created an expanding number of readers. Most of the great authors of the classical period in their youth contributed to moral weeklies. But gradually these journals outlived themselves. Literary taste had become refined and fastidious, and prominent critics found the constant repetition of moralizing platitudes tedious. Moreover, the policy of Frederick II and Joseph II and the threatening rumbling of the coming revolutions raised greater problems. In the end the weeklies were replaced by other organs. Special journals were founded for literary criticism, education, social questions, and so on. Many newspapers began to publish supplements printing articles on subjects formerly treated by the moral weeklies.

The ideas of enlightenment were also spread by many other means as well as the journals. Professors put them forward in their academic lectures and in books. Preachers employed them in sermons, authors introduced them in novels, plays and poems. Societies were founded to cultivate the spirit of humanity. Freemasonry was particularly active among princes and the aristocracy, though it was not restricted to them. The educated classes were much influenced by the great French, English and Italian authors, and the Greek and Roman classics were also studied under new aspects. We have seen the great impression which the knowledge of Chinese thought, owed mainly to Jesuits, made on Leibniz and Wolff. Explorers and missionaries also gained knowledge of primitive peoples and thereby made a great contribution to the study of mankind. Montesquieu's masterpiece is based on materials collected in all parts of the world or gathered from the history of many nations. This expansion of the interest of scholars over the whole world fostered cosmopolitanism and led to further elaboration of the doctrines of enlightenment.

15

PRUSSIA BECOMES A GREAT POWER

FREDERICK II AND MARIA THERESA

IN 1740, Maria Theresa succeeded her father as the ruler of the
Austrian and Hungarian countries and Frederick II became King of
Prussia. Their long struggles and their internal reforms opened a
new epoch for Germany and for Europe, and the indirect consequences of them have in the highest degree determined world policy
down to our own days. In this chapter we shall give an outline of
the power politics which made Prussia one of the European states of
the first rank and in reaction gave the impulse to Austria's transformation towards centralization and absolutism. The personalities
of the rulers and their internal reforms will be treated separately.

Frederick, then 28 years old, was primarily actuated by his love of
fame and power. His extraordinary intelligence and energy were
entirely concentrated on the aim of building a mighty state and a
monarchical absolutism, which were to become a lasting monument
of his greatness. He was not only the model of a warrior king, but
also an acute thinker on the greatest questions, widely read in the
literature written in French, or translated into it. His knowledge of
cultivated German was very poor. From his youth onward he was
regarded by the intellectuals of many nations, especially the French,
as the flower of enlightenment. He himself wavered between quite
opposite ideals, but once he had decided to open his career by a
great war, he was bound to continue this path.

Maria Theresa was 23 years of age; she was as attractive and
temperamental as intelligent, very pious and imbued with strict
moral principles, including politics. She spoke German, French,
Latin, Italian and Spanish, and had had a careful education, though
no instruction or training in political matters. But she possessed a

great intuition in judging character, which enabled her to choose excellent statesmen, and a most successful way of overcoming opposition by tact, gentleness and firmness. In defending what she considered right, she showed unbending energy, even in the most desperate situations. Her husband, Francis Stephen, former Duke of Lorraine and now Grand Duke of Tuscany, was a pleasant man, who had administrative, economic and cultural ability, but no great faculties as a statesman. Their marriage was very happy and Maria Theresa bore him sixteen children in nineteen years. Her husband became co-regent and later Emperor.

THE OUTBREAK OF THE WAR OF THE AUSTRIAN SUCCESSION

Charles Albert of Bavaria protested against Maria Theresa's succession and claimed the crown for himself. The text of the family pact, however, put forward by him as his principal proof, turned out to be faked. The Elector, nevertheless, maintained his claim, and other dynasties asserted equally unfounded pretensions. Frederick II of Prussia assured Maria Theresa of his most friendly disposition, but secretly prepared for war, and two months after her accession to the throne, he invaded and overran the Austrian province of Silesia, which was occupied by a very small Austrian force only. The legal claims put forward by Frederick were a pretext. He did not believe in their validity, but used them to convince his people and others that his cause was just. Moreover, he disguised his aggression as an act of helpfulness, offering to protect Maria Theresa against all her other enemies, for which Silesia was to be the price. This, too, was a clever move to win public opinion. Frederick later confessed to friends, and in his writings, that he began this war seduced by the passionate desire for glory, wishing to read his name in the press and then in history.

The action of the king induced many other powers also to take up aggressive plans against Austria, and these got into their stride after Prussia had won her first battle at Mollwitz.[1] Nearly all of them had recognized and guaranteed the Pragmatic Sanction, laying down the integrity of the Austrian dominions and Maria Theresa's succession. But Frederick's example encouraged them to consider how they might make the greatest profit from Austria's weakness by robbing

---

[1] It was not Frederick, however, who was the victor. The Austrian cavalry attacked the Prussians with such vigour that Count Schwerin, Frederick's best general, regarded the battle as lost and entreated the king to save himself. He fled, but later received the message that Schwerin had won by making use of the iron discipline of the Prussian infantry.

her of territories. In France, the leading Minister, Cardinal Fleury, personally did not wish for war, but he was 87, and had to give way to the war party, led by Marshal Count de Bellisle whose aim was to shatter the Austrian Empire completely. The most valuable parts were to be divided between the three Bourbon dynasties of France, Spain and Naples-Sicily, other parts of the booty were to go to Bavaria, Saxony, Prussia and Sardinia, and Maria Theresa was only to retain Hungary and 'by the grace of France' Vienna and the surrounding territory. The French satellite, Charles Albert of Bavaria, was to become Emperor, and the structure of the Empire was to be changed in a way making France its perpetual arbiter and overlord. Bellisle expected that France would then have secured her predominance in Europe for ever. Actually, all the states who were envisaged as participating in this plan began diplomatic and military preparations, and at different times took up hostilities against Maria Theresa.

Austria's military and financial forces, which could be mobilized quickly, were much smaller than those of her numerous enemies and she had to defend frontiers widely removed from the centre and from one another. Maria Theresa was in a desperate plight and even most of her ministers lost hope of being able to resist. It was mainly her own fortitude and her trust that her cause was just which made it possible to overcome the most dangerous times and to gather forces. It was her luck that her enemies were not led by one will, but were often disunited.

BRITAIN AND AUSTRIA

Britain and the Netherlands had in 1731 guaranteed Austria's integrity and had received a high price for this pledge, namely the sacrifice of Belgium's colonial trade by the abandonment of the Ostend Company. The two maritime powers had obliged themselves to defend the Pragmatic Sanction with all their forces in the interest of the liberty and the Balance of Power of Europe. Britain, in particular, had promised to furnish 12,000 men, and, if necessary, more. But her leading minister Sir Robert Walpole had, in 1734, disregarded this treaty by leaving the Emperor in the lurch when attacked by France and Spain. This act went far in undermining the respect for the Pragmatic Sanction and increasing France's lust for further aggrandisement, which was now threatening Britain too. Walpole had long foreseen that France would become Britain's most dangerous enemy and had for years tried to win Prussia as an ally. Now Frederick's aggression was so patent, and British public opinion so aroused against him, that the minister was compelled to acknowledge Austria's right to British aid under the treaty of 1731. But he wanted to combine it with his plan of getting the King of Prussia as an ally against France, and it seemed to him right that Austria should pay the price for it by ceding to Frederick Silesia, or part of it. It was said for this policy that it might deter France and her satellites from waging war against Austria, which would otherwise be faced with the overwhelming power of her enemies, and that Britain alone was not able to save her. The Netherlands, as usual, were very reluctant to risk France's enmity by fulfilling their obligations towards Austria, and Russia, another guarantor, was threatened by a war herself. On the other hand Silesia was not an insignificant territory, but Austria's most industrial province, and her cession would not only have been incompatible with the Pragmatic Sanction, but also ruinous to Austria's prestige, her position in the Empire, and to the idea of an international reign of law. No great power has ever submitted to such a demand without having first appealed to arms. In Vienna, Maria Theresa's husband and co-regent Francis of Lorraine, and a few ministers would, nevertheless, have liked to negotiate with Frederick and to make concessions. But Maria Theresa and her trusted minister Bartenstein were for a long time entirely against it, especially as they still believed that France, another guarantor, would remain neutral.

In assessing the arguments of both sides it must first be considered that Austria still had great military resources which could be organized if time and money were available. Her trouble was that she was exposed to the simultaneous attack of many enemies from all sides when her army and her finance were particularly weak, owing to Charles VI's unfortunate trust that international treaties would be kept. Frederick II had not yet developed his full military genius, and for a considerable time his chance of success was very uncertain. The only state able and willing to give Austria aid was Britain. Parliament granted her, indeed, a subsidy of £300,000 and the support of 12,000 Hessian and Danish mercenaries hired by Britain. Walpole further at once began negotiations designed to induce Austria and Prussia to come to an agreement on the basis of a cession of part of Silesia to Prussia by Austria. Maria Theresa was three times compelled by British diplomacy to let Frederick have most of Silesia, but he broke every agreement if he believed it to be in his interest. The British aid, moreover, had a curious fate. The £300,000 were shipped to Amsterdam but it took ten months till they reached Vienna because of difficulties of transport. When they arrived Frederick had already broken the first agreement which Maria Theresa had been compelled by Britain to conclude with him and which left most of Silesia to him. The 12,000 Hessians and Danes were ready, but did nothing. King George II then ordered them to march to Hanover where he used them to build up, from various contingents, a 'Pragmatic Army'. But when a great French army appeared in Westfalia the king at once declared himself neutral and at the election of an Emperor voted for the Elector of Bavaria who was waging war with Maria Theresa.

In 1742, Walpole fell from power and Carteret became Foreign Secretary. He possessed much more understanding for Continental affairs than Walpole, followed a well-devised plan, induced the king to abandon Hanover's neutrality, granted Austria and other powers large subsidies, and achieved great success. But William Pitt in 1743 attacked him as being responsible for the fact that Britain 'this great, this powerful, this formidable Kingdom was considered only as a province to a despicable Electorate', and forced Carteret to resign (1744). The British army was so reduced that when in 1745 England was threatened by a Jacobite rising backed by France, Hessian troops, partly in the Dutch service, had hastily to be called in and had a great share in putting down the uprising.

Before outlining the general course of the war it must be said that the Pragmatic Army had no luck. Its first considerable action was the battle of Dettingen, in which King George II personally defeated a French army. It occurred 2½ years after Frederick's invasion of Silesia. The next substantial operation was the battle of Fonteney which took place two further years later, and ended in a defeat. Both the first British subvention to Austria and the military aid voted by Parliament therefore failed to help Austria in the first epoch of the war in which she was most in need of it, in order to have time to organize her military resources. Later British diplomacy and also financial and naval support were a considerable help, but could not prevent Frederick II's ultimate success. Walpole's 'Appeasement' of the aggressor had made world history.

THE COURSE OF THE WAR

In 1741 France undertook a great assault on Austria in alliance with Bavaria, Prussia, Saxony-Poland, and Spain. They all attacked Austria with great armies and occupied large parts of her territories. Maria Theresa convoked the Hungarian Diet, confirmed the national privileges and granted new ones, was crowned and aroused the enthusiasm of the nobles. They voted the formation of a large army. English diplomacy brough tabout an armistice between

Prussia and Austria, and Maria Theresa ceded Lower Silesia to Frederick. But he very soon began to wage war again and invaded Bohemia and Moravia. A year after Frederick's invasion of Silesia Austria began a counter-offensive. General Count Khevenhueller with about 16,000 men liberated Upper Austria from the French and Bavarian troops and soon conquered Bavaria just at the time when its ruler was in Frankfurt elected Emperor, and assumed the name of Charles VII. Austrian troops further forced the French and their allies to retire within Bohemia and later to leave it completely. Frederick had to move out of Moravia and fought a great battle at Chotusitz. The Austrians seemed to win and plundered the Prussian camp which gave Frederick the opportunity of gaining the upper hand. But his losses were so great that he was eager to make peace. His minister Count Podewils offered Lord Hyndford, Britain's special representative, 100,000 Talers if he would arrange this, but he replied that a British peer did not take bribes. Hyndford later negotiated the peace treaty of Breslau in which Frederick received Silesia and Glatz (1742). Carteret had just replaced Walpole, and the war with France and Spain continued. In Italy, Austrian and Sardinian troops had fought the Spaniards with great success. France offered peace, and Maria Theresa might have considered it, but Carteret was for a continuation of the war with the Bourbon powers and made great promises to her which, however, were partly not ratified by the British cabinet. Austria was to be compensated for Silesia by Bavaria and the Bavarian ruler was to receive Alsace and Lorraine or Italian territories instead. The Bourbon kings were to be expelled from Italy and Savoy-Sardinia was to be rewarded with Italian territories at the expense of the Bourbons. The Pragmatic Army won the battle of Dettingen, and Saxony made an alliance with Austria.

Hitherto France had waged war under the pretext that her action was not an official war but merely a defence of German liberty against the Habsburgs. But now she formally declared war on Britain and Austria. An Austrian army under Duke Charles of Lorraine crossed the Rhine and invaded Alsace, striving to reconquer Lorraine which France had seized nine years before. This expedition partly seems to have been made in order not to lose British subsidies. The Austrian countries were thereby deprived of an adequate military defence and Frederick II, in alliance with France, used this opportunity to attack Bohemia, hoping to gain part of it for himself and the rest for Charles VII. Charles of Lorraine hurried back, the Prussians occupied Prague, but were soon forced to retire from Bohemia pursued by the Austrians. Charles VII died, his son

made peace with Maria Theresa, and her husband Francis of Lorraine was elected Emperor. Frederick was able to repel the Austrian
army from Silesia and to occupy Dresden, the capital of Saxony. In
1745 the Austro-Prussian war was concluded by the Peace of
Dresden leaving Silesia in Frederick's possession.

The war with France and Spain went on. In Italy Austrian generals
fought successfully against Spanish and French armies, but on
Britain's demand had to attack southern France, an expedition
which failed. In the Netherlands British, Dutch and Austrian troops
were faced with a much stronger French army under the command
of Maurice of Saxe who was a master of strategy while the allies
had no great leader and were disunited. Britain and Austria made an
alliance with Russia who sent an army, but it came too late. Peace
was concluded at Aachen or Aix-la-Chapelle (1748). Besides small
territorial changes in Italy the powers guaranteed to Maria Theresa
the integrity of the Austrian countries and to Frederick that of
Silesia and Glatz.

With certain exceptions, the war of the Austrian Succession
showed that the different peoples of the Austrian Empire stood for
its maintenance and resisted its enemies. In many parts even the
peasants took up arms inflicting much damage on the invaders.
Frederick later wrote in his history of the war (Ch. X) that the
stupid Bohemian peasants under the influence of their government,
nobles and clergy, showed an insurmountable aversion to the Prussians, fled into the woods and did not sell supplies at any price. The
Austrian troops, he says, possessed the affection of the people and
were therefore informed about everything, while his troops received
no information. In Silesia a section of the Protestants sympathized
with Frederick and he took great care to win over the people. But
the conscription of recruits and other exactions caused a mass flight
of the population which the king tried to stop with the greatest
ruthlessness.

THE REVERSAL OF ALLIANCES AND THE SEVEN YEARS' WAR

The War of the Austrian Succession had lasted eight years and
had caused great losses to all powers engaged in it. Britain, in particular, had spent large sums on her own warfare and on subsidizing
allies, and the results were by no means satisfactory. No wonder
that public opinion got sick of it. Maria Theresa felt very bitter
about Britain's policy in forcing her to cede Silesia to Frederick, and
other territories to the King of Sardinia and to a son of the King of

Spain. Britain had at Aachen again made a separate peace with France, and then imposed it upon Austria, as she had done in previous common wars at Nimwegen and Utrecht. Various tensions contributed to an estrangement between Austria and Britain.[2] The principal contemporary English historian of the subject, William Coxe, whose great knowledge of the English diplomatic records still makes him indispensable for research, ascribes it also to 'the language held in the memorials and papers of the British Cabinet, who assumed a high tone of superiority, expatiated on their great and important services, which had saved the House of Austria from ruin, and imperiously demanded a return of gratitude.'[3] He also relates that the Emperor and the Empress complained to the British Minister in Vienna of 'the arrogant and peremptory style' of these messages, that this complaint was too justly founded, that the Minister often declined to deliver the haughty declarations and more than once incurred the censure of the king and ministers for his delicacy and good sense.

The principal difference, however, was the fact that Britain naturally regarded France as her main enemy and was thereby induced to expect from Austria military expeditions to the West on a scale which would have given Frederick an opportunity of dealing her a mortal blow in the rear, possibly in alliance with Turkey and the Tartars, as the king often planned. The English navy could not protect Austria against Prussia and as regards English participation in a land war, the tragi-comedy of the Pragmatic Army did not encourage one to rely on it again.[4] A real conciliation between Maria Theresa and Frederick was impossible, as both clearly realized. Even if neither directly wished for a new war, there were many circumstances likely to bring it about, in particular the inescapable race in armaments and in seeking alliances.

At the Court of Vienna opinions were greatly divided about the choice of a strong and reliable partner in the coming struggles. Emperor Francis and most of the ministers saw in the maritime powers, especially in Britain, their natural allies. The idea that France might become her principal ally seemed at first fantastic. For about two and a half centuries France had waged war against

[2] Cf. Sir Richard Lodge, Studies, pp. 345, 375, 381, etc.
[3] W. Coxe, *House of Austria*, vol. 3, p. 349.
[4] Even a very impartial historian like Keith Feiling remarks in his History of England (p. 666) that 'Maria Theresa would fight for ever at other people's expense.' His succeeding remark blaming Austria for the reversal of alliances is also incorrect. The Treaty of Westminster certainly came before the Treaties of Versailles.

the House of Austria again and again. But the idea was taken up by Wenzel, Count Kaunitz, a statesman of the first rank. He came from a Czech noble family of which several members had distinguished themselves in the imperial service. After extensive studies and travels, he was engaged in important diplomatic missions, and in 1753 became Chancellor. It was his fundamental conviction that Frederick would always be Austria's most dangerous enemy, and that Prussia therefore must be put down in a new war with the help of France and Russia. Silesia was to be recovered and Prussia's power was to be drastically reduced. But various attempts to win France for a rapprochement and an anti-Prussian policy were not successful, since France did not wish to abandon her alliance with Prussia. Russia, however, had already, in 1746, offered to Austria an aggressive pact aga'nst Prussia, but had obtained only a defensive alliance. In 1755, King George II made a treaty with Russia who for subsidies, promised to provide 50,000 Russians for the defence of Hanover if Britain should become involved in a war with France. This implied a threat to Prussia, though George II had certainly not intended this. Frederick countered the move by concluding the Convention of Westminster with England, declaring Germany as neutral (1756). His new policy greatly embittered France and made her willing to conclude a defensive pact with Austria, the first Treaty of Versailles. It promised to Austria French help against Prussian aggression. Further negotiations led to plans of an offensive character. For her support Austria was willing to cede to France the Austrian Netherlands, the later Belgium. But no definite treaty was concluded. France was still very reluctant to consent expressly to a partition of Prussia.

Frederick kept secret agents among the diplomatic officials of his enemies and received information of their plans. Moreover, their armaments revealed their intentions, though the opening of a war depended on a prior Prussian aggression. The king, however, regarded it as an advantage to start a war at once. He asked Austria for definite assurances, and when he did not obtain them he marched, without a declaration of war, into Saxony and attacked Bohemia. Saxony was on Austria's and Russia's side, but had not joined the alliances hostile to Prussia. Her invasion and occupation were therefore not justified. But Frederick wanted thereby to obtain the possibility of fully exploiting Saxony's manpower and wealth for his warfare, and there is hardly a doubt that, in case of a complete victory, he would have annexed Saxony and perhaps indemnified its ruler with Bohemia as he had envisaged in his Political Testament of 1752. The king was on principle against a war which brought no aggrandise-ment.[5]

Frederick incorporated the whole Saxon army, except the officers, in the Prussian army, believing that the common man did not mind under what colours he had to serve. In this he was greatly mis-taken, for the Saxon regiments later used every opportunity to desert and join the Austrian troops. Soon after, France broke off relations with Prussia, and Russia joined the coalition against her. William Pitt formed a cabinet and made a pact with Prussia to wage war against France. This induced France to conclude a new, offen-sive alliance with Austria. Prussia was to be smashed, Silesia res-tored to Austria, and Belgium to be transferred partly to France, partly to the Spanish Bourbon Don Philipp. France was further to send a great army to Germany and to grant large subsidies to Austria. Frederick received English subsidies only after the battle of Kolin had put him into grave danger. Sweden also joined the anti-Prussian alliance. The German Reichstag declared that Frederick had broken the peace, and raised an army against him, though it was not of much military value. The Protestant Estates, however, protested against outlawing Frederick, and a few Protestant powers connected with the dynasty Hanover-England, joined Prussia, while other Protestant Estates fought on the Austrian side. Prince Ferdin-and of Brunswick successfully defended Hanover and the adjoining Prussian territories against the French. Frederick had issued the slogan that this was a war to defend Protestantism, though he des-pised all religions as superstition. His propaganda slogan was, however, widely believed, including England, where the masses jubilated about every victory of Frederick's. The signboards of numerous English pubs were decorated with the inscriptions 'The King of Prussia' or 'The Protestant Hero'.

The strategic history of the war need not be related here. The anti-

---

[5] The king by his propaganda spread the view that he was only defending his country against Austrian aggression. This thesis also was accepted by the majority of German historians. But Count Hertzberg, the king's principal diplomat, in 1787 admitted in a lecture to the Berlin Academy that the agreements between Austria and France did not definitely aim at a war but made this dependent on Prussia's attitude, and that it was therefore question-able whether these powers would have attacked Frederick. In 1894, moreover, Professor Max Lehmann, a very distinguished historian, put forward the thesis that the king's principal aim was that of making new conquests and his arguments are very weighty. His Prussian colleagues treated him for this revelation almost like a traitor. After the downfall of the Hohenzollerns, in 1920, however, Frederick's Political Testament of 1752 was published, and showed that the king had contemplated in it the plan of conquering Saxony in Bohemia, as he formulated it. On the influence of the King's policy on the deliberations leading to the war of 1914 cf. 311 of this book.

Prussian coalition had greater forces, but was often weakened by lack of military or political co-operation. Pitt and Frederick, however, were much better fitted for working together than their enemies. Frederick's military genius aroused universal admiration. Yet Austria also had generals of the first rank, especially Daun, Brown and Loudon.[6] Both sides won great victories and suffered great defeats, and the fortunes of war swayed to and fro. Austrian troops twice occupied Berlin, once together with the Russians. When Frederick defeated the French at Rossbach, this aroused national pride in many Germans who belonged to the king's admirers.

In 1759 a new phase of the war began in which Frederick restricted himself to the defensive. After the battle of Kunersdorf he wrote to his Minister Finkenstein that he had no more resources, and that, to speak the truth, he believed that everything was lost. He would not survive the defeat of the fatherland and bade him: Farewell for ever! The king often thought of committing suicide and always had poison with him. He also said he feared his own troops more than the enemy. Sometimes, more than two-thirds of his soldiers were non-Prussians—partly prisoners forced to serve on his side against their own countries. In this situation he would have liked to make peace, but not by ceding Silesia. The war went on. In the meantime Pitt had lifted Britain's war effort against France to an unparalleled level, the British troops amounted to nearly 150,000 men, the fleet to 400 ships, and the national debt was eventually doubled. He also found great leaders for the navy and army. England was victorious in Canada and India, the West Indies and West Africa. But the spreading desire for peace and the accession of George III weakened Pitt's position, and the rise of Bute led to his fall. Frederick was in desperate straits. He could only continue the war by most disreputable financial transactions, he incited the Turks and Tartars to attack Austria and, if all should fail, intended to kill himself.

[6] Brown was of Scots origin and Loudon's family had also come from Scotland, though centuries earlier. Frederick wrote that the Austrian General Count Traun was the perfect model of a strategist and that he learned from him how to wage war. This referred to the War of the Succession. Traun died before the Seven Years' War. The king in his history also points out 'that the Austrian generals on various occasions, from exaggerated caution, omitted to give the deathblow to the Prussians, when these were in a desperate situation and near ruin.' Austrian strategy had, indeed, a defensive tradition founded by Montecuccoli though Prince Eugène and Loudon belonged to the offensive school. King Frederick was aggressive in diplomacy, strategy and tactics, which meant that warfare became much more bloody than before, as shall presently be shown.

In 1762, Empress Elizabeth of Russia, Frederick's implacable enemy, died and this saved the king. Her successor was her nephew, the Duke of Holstein-Gottorp, who became Tsar Peter III. He was an ardent admirer of Frederick, and at once concluded peace with him and then even an alliance. Shortly afterwards, however, he was murdered and his widow, Catherine II, became Empress and immediately recalled her troops from the war. Sweden, too, made peace with Frederick. At the same time as Russia withdrew from the war, his alliance with Britain came to an end. The English Cabinet wished Prussia and Austria to make peace and that Austria should then possibly wage war against France. To this purpose Bute urged Frederick to give up Silesia, which Austria and Russia had reconquered. But he definitely refused to do so, and when Bute suspended the subsidies, the king defiantly renounced them. Owing to the Russian withdrawal he could reconquer Silesia, but not Glatz and Dresden, which remained occupied by the Austrians. England made a separate peace with France, though the terms of her alliance with Prussia excluded this. Pitt, now Lord Chatham, denounced this peace in the sharpest words, declaring that America had been conquered on German battlefields. England's policy aroused Frederick's greatest resentment. Yet he had, on previous occasions, certainly had no scruples in disregarding the terms of an agreement. Moreover, there were arguments for the English policy too.[7]

The war was ended not by the force of arms but by financial exhaustion. Austria in particular was on the brink of bankruptcy and her government did not know where to get foodstuffs for the maintenance of the army, though the fertile plains of Hungary, Italy, etc. had not been devastated by the war. Frederick would, if necessary, have commandeered the last sheaf of corn for his army. But in any case his treasury was not as empty as that in Vienna. Saxony mediated between the enemies and in 1763 the Peace of Hubertusburg was concluded confirming the territorial status of before the war.

The Seven Years' War had not fulfilled Frederick's hope for great new conquests, but had definitely established his reputation as a warrior and diplomatist of the very first rank. But the price which Prussia, and the other powers involved, had to pay for the enhancement of Frederick's prestige was enormous.

THE COST OF THE WAR IN LIVES AND WEALTH

Frederick II has in his own history of the Seven Years' War stated the losses of all the belligerents. Their total amounted to 853,000

---

[7] Cf. J. Corbett, *England in the Seven Years' War*, II, p. 362.

soldiers. To this figure the king added 33,000 civilians killed by the Russians in the Prussian provinces invaded by them. But the indirect losses of Frederick's realm were much greater. He states that the population, inclusive of Silesia, declined by 500,000, or a ninth of the total and gives a terrible picture of the sufferings of his peoples and the general breakdown of civilization, which resembled that after the Thirty Years' War. The number of soldiers killed given by the king probably included those who fell in the war between Britain and France also. But the great majority lost their life in the war between Prussia and Austria and their allies.

In the Austrian countries a census of the civilian population was taken in 1754 and 1762, while the war lasted from 1756 to 1763. If we compare the sum for all countries excluding the Tyrol, Vorarlberg and the Vorlande, we find from 1754 to 1762 a decline of 1 million or about 17%, against 11% in Prussia. The losses in the War of Succession, which lasted eight years, were certainly not smaller than those in the Seven Years' War.

The fact that Austria was compelled to end the war from financial exhaustion while Prussia had still money to fight on, seems surprising. The natural resources of Austria and Hungary, such as grain and cattle, were certainly much greater than those of Prussia; she was also superior in industries and mines, though the country with the greatest industrial output, namely Silesia, had been annexed by Frederick, who could also exploit industrial Saxony which he had occupied. Bohemia and other parts were much afflicted by the war. But Austria still possessed the iron industries of Styria which in 1767 produced about as much pig iron as England. Wood and water-power, in which Austria was rich, were then much more important than coal. The reason why, nevertheless, Austria was financially weaker than Prussia was their different policy of defraying the cost of the war. According to Frederick himself the Seven Years' War cost him 125 million Reichstaler. Loehr has calculated that on the exchange rates of the time this was equivalent to 180 million Gulden. Austria's expenses were 260 million Gulden. Of this nearly two thirds, or 167 millions, were covered by loans and by the issue of paper money in order not to burden the people too much. The disadvantages of this method were inflation and the putting off payment to the future. Schmoller has calculated that taxation in Prussia per head of the population was double or three times the amount of that in Austria. Hungary contributed much less than she could have done since Maria Theresa was bound by her pledge to respect the Hungarian constitution and not to raise taxes without the consent of Parliament. Further

Frederick had squeezed very high amounts from Saxony and the other countries which he had occupied for this purpose, in disregard of international law. While Austria received about 20 million Gulden in subsidies from France, Frederick obtained, from Great Britain, 16 million Reichstaler and converted them by fraudulent mintage into 27 million Taler. He had secretly minted the money of many states, including neutral ones, at a much lower content of silver than the legal standard and used this faked money mainly for payments abroad.

If the king later wrote that in this war his people had to suffer almost as much as in the Thirty Years' War, he should have added that his financial ruthlessness was largely responsible for this.[8]

A few years after the Seven Years' War the Empress proposed to the king to reduce their armies in the same proportion and to oblige themselves not to increase them again. But Frederick declined.

THE FIRST PARTITION OF POLAND

Emperor Francis died in 1765 and his son Joseph succeeded him as Emperor and, in the Austrian countries, as joint ruler together with his mother. He was then twenty-four and a half years old and was soon faced with the problem of Poland. The existence of this aristocratic republic had for a long time already been threatened by the suicidal party strife among the nobles and the intrigues of Russia. The slogan of Polish liberty was used to justify the worst anarchy and corruption. The king was elected and had no power. About half of the population were not Poles but Red and White Russians, Lithuanians, Germans and Jews. A great section were non-Catholics and were grievously oppressed, which induced Russia to intervene and to undermine Poland's independence. The middle class of the towns had no influence. The numerous nobles possessed extraordinary privileges while the common man was hardly more than a slave. For a long time already far-sighted Poles had foreseen that this state of things would lead to a catastrophe, but any striving for reforms was hopeless.

The Polish question entered an acute phase with the death of

---

[8] A very strange interpretation of the events is given by G. M. Trevelyan, the most famous British historian living. According to him Frederick was 'a self-sacrificing, laborious king, his people's stern but careful tutor while against him were arrayed, with the blessing of the Pompadour, the self-indulgent eaters of the people's bread who presided over the decadent governments of the ancient régime upon the continent'. He also compares the lot of the Protestants in Austria with that of the Catholics in Ireland. Cf. G. M. Trevelyan. History of England, new edition, 1952, p. 544.

King Augustus III, who was also Elector of Saxony (1764). His successor Count Stanislaus Poniatowski owed his election to Catherine II of Russia, whose lover he had been. She had just concluded an alliance with Frederick II, largely referring to Poland. When the new king tried to introduce reforms she vetoed this and intervened ever more in Poland's politics. Russian troops occupied parts of Poland and committed many acts of violence. The situation was still more complicated by the fact that Turkey, provoked by Russia's violation of her frontier, declared war on her. But this war took a course very unfavourable for Turkey. The Russian army was victorious, and Empress Catherine even sent a navy to the Mediterranean in order to liberate the Greeks from Turkish domination. This was not achieved, but Catherine conceived far-reaching plans for expanding her power. It appeared that Russia would become an enormous Empire, incorporate Poland, the Crimea and the Balkans, or at least become predominant in these regions by means of the foundation of vassal states. This would have been a mortal blow for Austria, who had to fear the influences of Panslavism on her own Slavs and other peoples. Austria therefore intervened in favour of Turkey and concluded a treaty with her, aimed at preventing her dismemberment.

Prussia was allied with Russia and Austria with France. A great European war seemed unavoidable; since the balance of power was seriously threatened. Neither Maria Theresa nor Frederick II, however, wanted a war. Their countries had not yet recuperated from the devastation and losses of the last great wars. Frederick therefore suggested to Russia that she should rather annex parts of Poland than too much Turkish territory. This required compensations for Prussia and Austria to safeguard the balance of power. Empress Catherine was willing, but Maria Theresa regarded the despoiling of a state which had not committed any aggression as a flagrant violation of religion, morality and Austrian interest. Many of her utterances leave no doubt that she detested and rejected this policy. Joseph and Kaunitz long wavered between going to war for Poland's integrity and taking part in the partition planned by Frederick and Catherine. The international situation was unfavourable to Poland. Britain was not interested, and France had to fear a new war with Britain. The French Premier, the Duke of Choiseul, nevertheless sent Colonel Dumouriez to Poland to explore how she could be saved. But he found that nothing could be expected from the Polish party opposed to Russia's plans. Moreover, Choiseul soon fell from power and with him disappeared the possibility of an effective co-operation between France and Austria against Russia and Prussia.

King Frederick asserted that Austria had already taken the first step to partition Poland. The truth is this : the internal war in Poland extended to the Hungarian frontier and this induced the Austrian military authorities to draw a cordon along it. Its line included a number of towns and villages of the Hungarian county of Zips which, in 1412, had been pawned to Poland for a loan. Hungary had always claimed that they still belonged to her and were only under Polish administration till the loan was repaid. The districts concerned were enclaves in Hungarian territory and were populated by Germans who had settled there in the twelfth century and had received full autonomy from Hungary. The King of Poland had, through his brother, asked the court of Vienna to occupy these parts because the Polish rebels against his regime used them as a vantage ground. These rebels too were willing to recognize Hungary's rights for financial compensation. But the Hungarian governor appointed by the Viennese government believed that Hungary had further claims and with Joseph's consent occupied Polish districts while the archives were searched for documents on the historic frontiers of the territories in question. Now Poland protested, and Kaunitz, who was against the extension, assured her that her rights would be respected. Later Kaunitz and Joseph declared that Austria was willing to return the contested districts to Poland and to retain only the territories pawned. The loan would be repaid.

Kaunitz and Joseph further tried various ways to save Poland from her fate. They wished to obtain the support of other powers even thinking of waging war against Russia and Prussia. But it soon became clear that Austria would stand alone in such a war and that it would be a terrible risk for her. If Russia and Prussia alone had acquired new territories this would have made them still more dangerous to Austria. She had therefore to get a territorial compensation but hoped for some time to obtain it not at the expense of Poland, either by recovering Silesia from Frederick or in the Balkans. But all these plans failed. Maria Theresa, feeling tired and dispirited, had increasingly to give way to Joseph and Kaunitz. A partition of Polish territories between the three powers became unavoidable.

In the first partition of Poland she lost 35% of her territories of which percentage Russia received about half. In population, however, the Austrian part was the greatest. Prussia got the smallest part but the most valuable one. Empress Catherine pointed out that she had not annexed Polish land, but liberated the orthodox White Russians from foreign domination. Austria's share was Galicia whose population was at that time also predominantly non-Polish. Austrian statistics showed that two-thirds were Ruthenians or Ukrainians. Seventy-three years later, the Austrian census of 1846 showed 1,994,802 Poles, 2,441,771 Ruthenians, and 335,071 Jews in Galicia besides Germans and others. In the meantime a great Polish district (Cracow) had been added. West Prussia, annexed by King Frederick was mainly Polish though there were also Germans. It had been colonized by the Teutonic Knights but had been conquered by Poland in 1466. Frederick achieved the connection of East Prussia with his other provinces by this acquisition. Both Prussia and Austria extended their shares beyond the agreed limits by arbitrary interpretation of clauses of the treaty.

Maria Theresa had, as mentioned already, made efforts to prevent the partition but had at last to submit—much against her will. In a letter to her son Ferdinand she wrote : 'This unfortunate partition of Poland will cost me ten years of my life. How long have I struggled against it! It was merely a succession of disasters, blow after blow, which has induced me to enter into this unfortunate proposition, namely : the Turkish affairs, no support to be expected from France and England, and the risk of standing alone in a war with Russia and Prussia, with its misery, famine and loss of lives. It will be a stain on my whole reign! God forbid that this will make me much responsible in the other world. I must tell you that I cannot get over it, my heart is so afflicted that it worries and poisons my days, which are already sad enough.'[9]

The outlook of the Empress, however, was not in accordance with that of most of the 'enlightened' thinkers. The principle of self-determination was not yet recognized, and, moreover, it would in many cases hardly have spoken for Poland. Many people were living in this realm who were alien to the Poles in religion, language and tradition. The philosophy of enlightenment, which Frederick and Joseph accepted, assumed that the welfare of the people was the aim of the state. The idea, however, that the old Poland had served this welfare would have been absurd.[10] The luminaries of the enlightenment expressed themselves very unfavourably on Polish conditions. Abbé Raynal wrote that Poland was not a republic but merely a league of many small tyrants against the people. When

[9] Cf. *Briefe der Kaiserin Maria Theresia an ihre Kinder und Freunde* 1881, I, p. 151. Other characteristic utterances in eimann, Preuss. Geschichte, I, pp. 445, 448, 461.

[10] Professor D. B. Horn in his book on British Public Opinion and the first Partition of Poland shows that the Whigs were for an alliance with Russia, and that no voice was raised for Poland in either House of Parliament. The City was greatly interested in trade with Russia. Writers took little interest in Poland, though some regarded the partitioning powers with disfavour. English travellers to Poland had brought back most unfavourable views of her internal conditions. Coxe wrote that Polish liberty was the source of Polish wretchedness.

I

Empress Catherine sent her troops into Poland Voltaire celebrated this event as unique in history : an army coming to bring peace and to make men happy. World history, he wrote, had never before shown such a wonderful deed. On the partition he later remarked that if the house of a neighbour burns one may enter it and take measures for self-protection.[11] Rousseau, asked by the Poles for advice, wrote that the diminution of their territory would be beneficial for them.[12] Diderot was full of enthusiasm for Catherine II whose generosity he enjoyed. In the French Revolution the Jacobins soon took the view that oppressed peoples must be liberated from their tyrants, and that their countries must be annexed without a plebiscite.

It is hardly necessary to say that Poland's partition was an enormous disaster from the point of view of international law and European interest. The people living in the parts annexed by Austria and Prussia certainly received much better living conditions, and civilization, which also contributed to the development of their national feelings. Yet, these advantages cannot change the condemnation of the policy of partition.

FURTHER CONFLICTS BETWEEN AUSTRIA AND PRUSSIA

Before the partition of Poland Emperor Joseph and Chancellor Kaunitz had met King Frederick and had exchanged opinions, looking for possibilities of a rapprochement. But in spite of many polite diplomatic phrases the abyss of distrust could not be bridged. In 1777 the Elector Maximilian Joseph of Bavaria died, and his land fell to another line of the Wittelsbach dynasty, then represented by Charles Theodore of the Palatinate. The Emperor claimed certain parts of Bavaria, partly as escheated fiefs, partly on the ground of family pacts, and Charles Theodore recognized these claims. Austrian troops occupied parts of Bavaria. But Frederick II was determined to prevent any considerable aggrandisement of the Austrian power in Germany, he succeeded in winning several German princes for his standpoint and made efforts to array the great powers against Austria. The legal questions involved were very complex, and long diplomatic negotiations took place while great controversies on the validity of the claims were fought out by

[11] Voltaire has also expressed his views in a lengthy footnote to his play *Les Lois de Minos* which he was then writing and then sent to Catherine. Cf. G. Brandes, *Voltaire und sein Jahrhundert*, vol. II. p. 366.
[12] But Rousseau also sent them a plan for building a new state.

publicists.[13] Maria Theresa wished absolutely to avoid a war and opposed Joseph's intention of taking a strong line in dealing with Frederick. The king at last broke off the negotiations and with a great army marched into Bohemia. Here the Emperor himself and his two greatest generals Lacy and Loudon had strongly entrenched themselves. Maria Theresa had insisted that the war was only to be waged in a defensive way and Lacy was a master in this sort of strategy. Loudon, who preferred the offensive, was obliged to abstain from it. The war consisted merely in manoeuvres and small encounters. The king was in bad health, ill-disposed and not successful. His troops starved and plundered and maltreated the population in a barbaric way, encouraged by Frederick, who thereby wanted to put pressure on the Austrian government.[14] Many of his officers and men lost their trust in him, and thousands deserted to the Austrians. Maria Theresa, regardless of prestige, sent a diplomat to him, proposing peace. Joseph was in despair about this measure, but submitted to his mother. The war went on, and the Prussian army had to withdraw from Bohemia. At last peace was made at Teschen (1779). Austria received a small territory from Bavaria and various other territorial questions were settled. France and Russia guaranteed the peace treaty.

Maria Theresa died in 1780. Her last step in making peace had made her immensely popular. Gleim, who had sung the glory of Frederick the Great, now wrote a poem in adoration of the 'Holy Theresa'. Klopstock praised her as the greatest of her house because of her humanity. Matthias Claudius had, at the conclusion of peace, celebrated both the Empress and the king. Warlike glory and honour, he wrote, are but folly, goodness of heart, pity and generosity alone are real greatness. When Maria Theresa died he wrote one of the finest poems in the German language. It has only six lines:

> Sie machte Frieden. Das ist mein Gedicht.
> War Mutter ihres Volkes und ihres Volkes Segen.
> Und ging getrost und guter Zuversicht
> Dem Tod als ihren Freund entgegen.
> Ein Welteroberer kann das nicht.
> Sie machte Frieden. Das ist mein Gedicht.

[13] No less than 288 books were published about them. Cf. A. Wolf u. H. v. Zwiedineck, Aesterreich unter Maria Theresia etc., p. 171. Arneth Maria Theresia, v.10, E. Reimann, Gesch.d.bairischen Erbfolgekriegs. An important source is also the memoirs of C. W. v. Dohm, a prominent Prussian diplomat.
[14] For details cf. Dohm's memoirs.

JOSEPH'S EXTERNAL POLICY AND ITS FAILURE

Emperor Joseph could now pursue his plans of great reforms without being restrained by his mother's moderation. His measures will be related later. Though many of them were beneficial to the people, they also aroused much opposition and, in Hungary and Belgium, even revolutionary movements. Recent events had shown that King Frederick was still Austria's greatest enemy, and he was particularly dangerous through his alliance with Russia. Joseph therefore wished to win Empress Catherine as an ally and this move succeeded; Frederick was isolated thereby and greatly resented it. In the eighties a conflict developed between Joseph and the Netherlands, which in old treaties had imposed very onerous burdens on Belgium, in particular the closure of the river Scheldt. Their aim was to cripple the trade of Antwerp in the interest of Dutch commerce. The Emperor demanded the freedom of navigation but the Netherlands rejected it and, when the Emperor intended to enforce this right by military means they opened the sluices on the Scheldt, flooding wide tracts of Belgian and Dutch soil. The Austrian troops in Belgium were too small for immediate operations against Holland. France, who was allied with Austria, had at first consented to Joseph's demand to open the Scheldt, but later changed her attitude. The conflict was at last settled by French mediation. The Scheldt remained closed and the Belgians received an indemnity for the damage done to their land by flooding. There was general surprise that Joseph had yielded so quickly. Frederick wrote : 'I begin to suppose that this prince is very inconsistent and at once drops a project if he is faced with serious obstacles.'

This affair was connected with another of Joseph's plans, namely the exchange of Belgium for Bavaria. Austrian policy had for a long time already sought to acquire Bavaria and to compensate her ruler with Belgium and the title King of Burgundy. (The Austrian Netherlands were called the Burgundian Circle in German constitutional law.) Certain parts of Belgium, however, were to be used to acquire Salzburg by exchange also. Elector Charles Theodore of Bavaria-Palatinate was favourably disposed to this plan. Belgium was a much richer country than Bavaria and much nearer to his principal possessions on the Rhine. Austria would have been much strengthened by obtaining Bavaria and Salzburg, whereas Belgium was far away and difficult to defend. Empress Catherine supported Joseph and France was at first also on his side though her attitude later became uncertain. The project was, however, frustrated by King Frederick, who formed a great Confederation of German

Princes with the purpose of preventing any substantial augmentation of the Habsburg power in the Empire. A similar plan had already been considered by some princes before Frederick's intervention, as certain actions of the Emperor had aroused their apprehension. Gradually the majority of the princes joined this union, and Joseph had to abandon his project (1785). A year later Frederick died.

Joseph wished to put his principles into practice in Belgium too. But his anti-clerical measures such as the abolition of many monasteries and the granting of tolerance for the Protestants aroused the wrath of the Pope and the powerful Belgian bishops, who had extraordinary influence on the public mind, and used it to excite the masses against the government. Nuncio Zonzadari, the ambassador of the Pope, was expelled by order of the Emperor but this only increased the unrest. In 1787, moreover, Joseph issued edicts greatly interfering with the constitutional structure and the administration of the country. Numerous feudal and other privileges were abolished and the organization of public institutions thoroughly reformed. The alterations would certainly have been beneficial to the great majority of the people. But they violated old traditions of self-government dear to influential sections of the Belgians. The provincial Estates protested and in part refused to vote taxes. A democratic movement developed beside the opposition of the clerical, feudal and liberal parties. The radicals resorted to armed resistance and the government used troops to put down demonstrations. The tension therefore constantly increased and gradually turned into a revolution. Its inspiration partly came from nearby France where the revolution was on the point of breaking out. But Prussia and Holland also encouraged the Belgian movement. The Emperor was at that time far away, first in the Crimea on a political visit to the Empress Catherine of Russia and shortly afterwards with his army waging war with Turkey while in addition a revolutionary tension spread in Hungary. His directives to his officials in Belgium wavered, but by the end of 1789 he revoked all his edicts which had led to the movement. Yet this came too late. The Belgian Estates declared themselves independent and sovereign and the imperial troops had to withdraw.

The alliance with Russia which Joseph had concluded in order to draw her away from Frederick II and to win in her a strong ally against him, had in the meantime involved the Emperor in a great war with Turkey. Frederick had since died, but Prussia's attitude to Austria had remained very hostile. She also encouraged Turkey to provoke a war with Russia, which might give her a good opportunity for new actions at Austria's expense. Joseph would at that time have preferred to avoid a war, since he had to cope with many other difficult problems. But the alliance obliged him to take part in it, and he went himself into the field with a very large army. The supreme commander was Count Lacy who, probably because of his defensive warfare, was more sympathetic to the humane Emperor than Loudon, who excelled in an offensive strategy. But this choice proved unfortunate. The big army was for a long time deployed over almost 200 miles of difficult terrain and had to suffer terribly through epidemics. At last Joseph was compelled to appoint Loudon Commander-in-Chief; he took Belgrade and other victories also were won by the Austrians. The political situation, however, was very gloomy. Belgium was lost, Hungary was near a revolution, Prussia was preparing a new aggression, and the war had done great damage to the army, and ruined Austria's finances. The Emperor had been ill before this already but the fatigue of the war, the bad climate, and the failure of all his benevolent plans fatally aggravated his condition. He had to leave the army, in despair withdrew most of his reforms in Hungary, and shortly afterwards died, only 40 years of age (1790).

FREDERICK II, HIS PERSONALITY, THOUGHT AND WORK

FREDERICK'S YOUTH

FEW monarchs have aroused such admiration and reprobation and have agitated their own time and posterity so much as Frederick II, called the Great (1740-86). It has always seemed most astonishing how one man could shine in so many fields, in war, diplomacy and administration, but also in thought, literature and the arts, and how he could combine quite different moral standards. For almost half a century he dominated the political scene of Europe, and his fame spread over the whole world. His writings, his correspondence, his conversations and the literature about him make a library. How far his policy was, in the end, beneficial to his realm, to Germany and to the world, will always be controversial. But even his bitter enemies would not deny that he was a star of the first magnitude.

Frederick's father, the uncouth Frederick William I, wanted to make him a god-fearing, peaceable and conscientious ruler, a good soldier and honest man, unspoilt by the demoralizing culture and new ideas spreading in high society and among the intellectuals. He was to become a faithful husband and the thrifty head of his family, rear numerous children and soundly thrash them for any deviations from his commands, and he was to find recreation as a companion of other soldiers drinking beer, smoking, hunting, enjoying horse-play, and so on. But the boy was in every respect the opposite of what his father desired; he appeared to him lukewarm in religion, of lax morality, leaning to dissimulation, averse to the military spirit and to hunting, and instead wasted his time on art and literature. Frederick was already a young man of eighteen but his father still treated him for small offences with a brutality which made life intolerable to him. At that time (1730) negotiations began on a double wedding between the royal families of Britain and

Prussia which have already been mentioned. Frederick was to reside in Hanover as Governor of this Electorate. The realization of this plan, sponsored by Frederick's mother and ardently welcomed by him, would have changed the course of world history. Prussia would have become the most valuable ally of Britain in her coming struggle with France for a world Empire, and in this contest might have had great opportunities of expanding in the West towards the Rhine, instead of the East. She might have become a great power without attacking Maria Theresa and waging three wars for the conquest of Silesia. The plan was, however, wrecked by a particularly rude outburst of the king's temper. Frederick was in despair. He tried to escape to England, but his attempt was discovered and he was arrested. The King put him before a court martial and treated him with abominable harshness. The plan of an English marriage was now abandoned and Frederick soon had to marry a German princess whom his father had chosen and whom he did not love. He was further trained in practical administration, financial and military matters and then was given the estate Rheinsberg by the king, where he spent four happy years, which became decisive for his further development.

In previous years the prince had already shown keen interest in philosophy, science, literature and the arts. He had collected a large library, which he carefully concealed from his father in a private house. But in Rheinsberg, Frederick could devote himself to insatiable reading and developed his own critical thought. His cultural interests were exclusively French, and as his pastime he wrote elegant French verses, though his French never became quite correct. His German was always extremely poor, he read no German book and spoke it only when he could not avoid it. He knew some Italian but no English. His father had brutally stopped his learning Latin, but French translations also opened to him the study of Greek and Roman literature. Frederick now became a 'philosopher', which at that time meant a man of independent, critical thinking, especially on religion and the nature of man, and he also led a life embellished by spiritual pleasures, refined taste and friendship with men of similar inclinations. He particularly admired Voltaire and began the correspondence with him which, with interruptions, was continued throughout his life. In this way Frederick, already before his accession to the throne, became the idol of the literary world in France, which had great influence on the enlightened sections of high society.

Frederick's personality developed from the combination of fiery ambition and high faculties striving to unfold themselves in diverging and incompatible directions. His acquaintance with the French pattern of enlightenment destroyed the belief in all traditional values and inhibitions, and rendered him an intellectual for whom his own intellect was the supreme authority. He soon reached the stage of a man beyond good and evil and with a deep contempt for men in general. The ideological heritage of Louis XIV contributed to this development. Many observers of his doings later found that his predominant wish was to outshine everybody by the brilliance of his spirit, though he had too much taste to enjoy common flattery. Bismarck has in his memoirs (III. 10) characterized Frederick's craving for being admired even in small things, his vanity and exaggerated self-confidence. Yet he could also scoff at his glory and merits, declaring that it was all due to good luck. He was very far from any megalomania, and was certainly convinced that kings, too, were human beings with all their faults and weaknesses, and that his own power was an instrument to make his subjects happy. But he understood by happiness something quite different from the ideas of the great majority of them.

CONFLICT OF IDEALS

As a boy he had been inflamed by Fénelon's Télémaque, a book written in opposition to Louis XIV's warlike policy which painted the image of an ideal prince abhorring war and setting humanity above everything else. His ethos was then formed by the memory of Roman greatness and wisdom as celebrated by the French classicists, and most of all by Marcus Aurelius, whom he regarded as the model of a prince. In philosophy, Leibniz and Wolff interested him for some time, but later he was most impressed by Locke's empiricism, Bayle's scepticism, and Gassendi's materialism. The study of the ancients showed him two different schools, which both attracted him, that of Epicurus, recommending a retired life and the wise enjoyment of natural and spiritual pleasures in a small circle of friends, and that of the Stoics, praising an active life of duty and heroism in the service of humanity. He later often complained he was born to be a philosopher and compelled to be a king.

Internal conflicts and his reading made Frederick revolt early against dogmas and intolerance, and he became a freethinker. In particular, he rejected free will. Life after death, too, seemed to him an unacceptable myth. For some time deism impressed him. The purposeful order of the universe seemed to prove the existence of a God who had created it, but the course of the world seemed to show that he did not meddle in its operation. Human affairs appeared so

1*

infinitely small in comparison with the universe's immensity that it could not be imagined that God should take any notice of such trifles. These ideas struck at the roots of Christian beliefs, and the idea that man was morally responsible for his actions lost its sense. Under the influence of Voltaire's teachings, Frederick further came to look upon the doctrines and practices of all Churches with the greatest contempt. All religions were to him only absurd fables, invented by priests in order to dominate and exploit the people. But he believed that these superstitions were also useful since they prevented, by the fear of hell, the stupid populace from committing crimes. The common people were incurably blind and fanatical and it would be dangerous to enlighten them.

Though Frederick rejected the Christian dogmas, he professed to agree with Christian morality and even asserted that Christ and the Fathers had been deists. But any trace of Christian humility was obviously alien to his mind and incompatible with his striving for the glory of a superman. Neither can we find in Frederick's life much of Christian love; his ideology replaced it by the idea of humanity which, however, was not the same. In 1738, Frederick joined the freemasons, who regarded humanity as their highest aim. Frederick meditated much on morality. On the whole he identified it with enlightened self-interest, its aim was happiness and its path was restraining and refining of human passions by reason. It need hardly be said that the happiness principle, though not wrong in itself, was extremely vague and could be interpreted in many different ways. Who was in difficult questions to be the authority competent to decide which was the way to happiness? Conscience and the ethos of the Gospel were replaced by the commands of the government and the pressure of enlightened society. Further without freedom of will man became part of a machine to be run by the intelligence of its operator. The idea fitted well into the machine-state with an intellectual superman at the helm. In regard to the nature of man, Frederick often wavered between moderate optimism and the deepest pessimism. The higher classes, however, seemed to him at least capable of the feelings of honour and duty, while the lower and middle ranks could only be ruled by fear.

In the years immediately before he became king, the prince was agitated by conflicting urges. He believed that his realm needed aggrandisement for its consolidation, he was embittered by the policy of Austria in denying his house any expansion, even when he believed it to have good claims, and he foresaw that the death of Charles VI would unleash a great war in which he was ready to ally with France against the power of the hated Habsburgs. In the same

period, however, Frederick showed quite the opposite tendencies
also, he often condemned war and the lust of glory and dreamed of
devoting himself as king exclusively to the cultivation of peace, justice, humanity and the happiness of the people. These years show a
constant wavering between two attitudes, which both were strongly
rooted in his mind.

THE ANTIMACHIAVEL

Shortly before his accession to the throne Frederick wrote a book
in French called Antimachiavel using the French form of the name
Machiavelli. He sent it to Voltaire, who revised and published it.
Though the title page did not reveal the author, everybody knew
who it was and the book was eagerly read in all countries.

Machiavel, says the author, was to morals what Spinoza was to
religion. He had always considered Machiavel's 'Prince' one of the
most dangerous books, poisoning politics by advocating tyranny.
How had the power of princes originated? What could induce free
men to place a ruler above themselves? In olden times the peoples
wanted judges to settle their disputes, protectors against enemies,
and sovereigns to unite their various interests. For this purpose they
elected the wisest, the most just, the least egoistic, or the strongest
to rule them. The prince, therefore, is not the absolute lord of his
subjects, but their first servant. He must promote their happiness, as
they must work for his glory. A prince is only a man, his subjects
are equal to him. The only legitimate way of becoming a prince is
either succession or election by the people, where the latter have
this right, or the call of an oppressed people to liberate it, or conquest in a just war. The peak of glory would be to save a people
from oppression and then to grant it liberty. But we must not
expect too much from human beings. In Machiavel's time, arts and
sciences were not yet far advanced and reasoning power was undeveloped. The bloody glory of conquerors was therefore preferred
to mildness, justice and virtue. In our age, humanity is more
appreciated than deeds of violence. Conquests are of no advantage
for the peoples of the conqueror, and he, too, will not be happier,
because once his ambition has been aroused, he becomes insatiable
and strives for further conquests without ever being satisfied. His
conquests, therefore, are only of imaginary, not of real value. Mere
forces and skill without justice deserve no glory, which only those
earn who serve justice or who are compelled to become conquerors
not by temperament, but by necessity. A hero is like a surgeon, who

merits praise only when his operation saves a man from danger, but not when it is performed merely to show his skill.

Frederick further discusses the difference in the collective mind of nations, states and times, which are deeply rooted. Statesmen must take account of all these countless diversities, and there is no political system universally applicable. The most miserably governed states are those of the Church. The author shows in various places a particular appreciation of republics. He finds Machiavel's advice on how to subject a republic detestable. Why should free men be made slaves? The small republic of Holland is far superior in power, wealth and industry to the immense despotism of Russia. Frederick thinks that if any government of his day could be regarded as a model of wisdom, it would be the English one. In England, Parliament is the arbiter between people and king, and the latter has every power to do good, but none to do evil. England and Holland appear to him the two finest and richest countries in the world. No feeling is more inseparable from the human mind than freedom. It is the spirit of pride and independence that has produced many great men, and this spirit is cultivated in the republican system with its principles of liberty and equality. True, republics are threatened by internal strife and the ambitions of citizens and enemies, and after a time of flowering fall victim to despotism. But no political system can exist for ever, even the greatest monarchies are liable to decline and fall.

Machiavel's counsels to princes about how to strengthen their power even by the greatest crimes and to rule by arousing terror, are rejected with horror and contempt. His fundamental error lies in his view of human nature, which he regards as entirely bad, and therefore only apt to be ruled by force and fear. Frederick points out that there is also a conscience and reason. No doubt, few only are reasonable, the passions are very powerful, and even Christianity has been spread in Europe only by great bloodshed. The passions, however, must be tamed by reason. Machiavel is wrong when he says that in so vicious a world, goodness can only lead to ruin. He also errs when he wants a prince to be only a soldier. A ruler has primarily received rulership in order to be a judge, and if he is also a general, this is accidental. It is also wrong that most princes spend three quarters of their life on hunting. Of all entertainments, this is the least fitted for a king. The butchering of animals is a cruel and stupid sport, it trains only the body and holds the risk of the princes becoming as callous and brutal towards human beings as towards the hunted game.

A prince must first of all love the fatherland and strive to do

something great and useful for the state. To these aims he must
sacrifice his own interests and passions. The life of the subject is the
most precious good entrusted to the prince, and he must not sacrifice it without the direst necessity, while Machiavel counts it for
nothing. A king whose policy aims merely at making himself feared,
would only rule over slaves, unfit for great enterprises. Machiavel
further recommends perfidy as a means of policy. The author admits
that there are evil situations when a prince cannot avoid breaking
treaties and alliances. But he must inform all his allies in good time
and must only do so if the weal of his subjects and a very great
emergency force him.

A ruler should strive for glory, but for a real, not a false one. Bold
and successful enterprises are only praiseworthy if they are just. A
conqueror who plunders the subject nations is nothing but a thief,
as the Scythian envoys said to Alexander. Wars for religion, or
under its pretext, are also contemptible. A prince can obtain
aggrandisement either by the arms or by promoting the arts and
sciences, production and commerce, thereby making his states more
powerful and civilized. This way is better than the first. Kings
should reward and honour great artists and scientists. The wise men,
who enlighten the world, should also be its legislators. Princes must
further govern personally instead of letting their ministers rule.
Since self-love is the motive of virtue and public happiness, princes
must enthuse for glory, otherwise they would only indulge in
pleasures and become effeminate. But a good policy cannot ignore
justice.

Frederick now goes into the discussion of philosophical fundamentals underlying the ideas of justice, morality and a world order.
The defenders of free will seem to deny Providence and let the
whims of men govern the world. Those denying free will, however,
appear to make God responsible for all evils and to negate justice
and morality. We know that the author was primarily a determinist,
but here he does not openly declare himself. He compares the two
alternative answers with Scylla and Charybdis and comes to the
conclusion that we must try to apply reason, as far as we can, to
influence the course of events, but without forgetting that our fore-
sight is very restricted. Very often small accidents have, in politics,
incalculable consequences affecting the fate of states. A statesman
further largely depends upon the spirit of the time. Boldness has its
fascination, but involves great risks; prudence is less sensational,
but advances more steadily and may do more for the happiness of
the people. Now there are ages encouraging bold change and others

which favour a conservative policy. A ruler must be born at the right time to achieve greatness.

Great criminals are not great men, as Machiavel has tried to make us believe. The true wisdom of rulers consists in justice and acting for the benefit of mankind. The peace of Europe is mainly founded on a reasonable balance of power, when the preponderance of a state is checked by the united forces of others. The author discusses the ways conducive to this aim. The world would be very happy if the maintenance of justice and peace could be achieved by negotiation alone. Sometimes, however, war cannot be avoided. Wars are only justifiable if they are either defensive against aggressors or waged for just claims and for equality in the world, or if they are designed to forestall the danger of being overpowered by a state of overwhelming strength. The most contemptible ignominy, however, is the practice of those princes who barter the blood of their peoples and let out their troops on hire to the highest bidder. These little tyrants should blush for shame, they are selling the lives of the men whom they are bound to protect.

If kings and princes had enough imagination to visualize the awful misery a war brings to their peoples, they would not let themselves be carried away by their ambition. Every war is such a risk and misfortune that a ruler cannot think enough before he takes a decision. But the greatest atrocity is the waging of an unjust war. Princes must be most sparing with the lives of their subjects who are not their slaves but their equals and in some respects their superiors.

Many ideas in Frederick's book were not as novel as his uncritical admirers have often maintained, for example his much-quoted idea that a king was to be the first servant of the people. But the book was brilliantly written and its appearance was a momentous event. The fundamental idea was that a ruler was neither invested with a special divine authority, nor was he the owner of his country, entitled to do what he liked with it. The opposite theory had often been put forward, for example in an extreme form by King James I. He told parliament in 1609 that kings were justly called gods and that they had exactly the same powers as God in regard to their subjects. Louis XIV, too, regarded himself as the vicar of God, directly inspired by Him with superhuman wisdom and authority. He declared that royal power was a part of God's power and kings had full disposition of the goods of their subjects. This comes very near to the idea that they are the owners of the state. Frederick, however, often stressed that kings were only men, equal to all others, and that they held power only to serve the interests of the people or the state. He also pointed out that the state revenues must be spent in the public interests and that the king should claim only a very modest amount for himself, so to say as a salary for his services. This was in flagrant contrast with the luxury of Versailles.

The crucial question, according to Frederick, was, how far war could be said to be in the interest of the people or the state. The Antimachiavel abounds in the condemnation of wars waged by princes from lust of glory, it declares that only just wars are permitted and tries to define this concept. At the same time, however, as the book appeared, Frederick was starting an aggressive war against Austria, which caused many other wars and shaped the whole character of his reign and of Prussia.

Was the Antimachiavel, then, merely a Machiavellian trick to deceive public opinion about Frederick's policy? Plausible though this explanation may seem, it is hardly correct. Numerous utterances made by Frederick show that at that time two opposite forces were really contending in his mind. One of the best observers among those close to the king, Henri de Catt, reports that if the king tried, in conversations, to refute ideas, this was sometimes a sign that they were secretly working in his own mind. Frederick felt fitted to play the rôle of Télémaque as well as that of Caesar, and would have liked to combine them. This would have satisfied his ambition best. But in practice this could not be realized. Once he had chosen his part, he was bound to it. The Antimachiavel admitted that certain wars were just and the versatile mind of an intellectual could interpret the principles making a war legitimate in such a way that his own glory and the happiness of the people were in agreement. Was a war not just which sacrificed general happiness in our time to a greater one in the future? Was a great state not much more suited to realize the welfare of a people than a state without space and resources? And was a powerful and enlightened government of one man not better fitted for this aim than a nation torn by religious fanaticism, feudal anarchy or parliamentary party strife? Were not also the prestige and glory of a state a source of pride for the people? Lastly, should a ruler not assert the true interest of a people even if it in its short-sightedness was not in agreement with his policy?

The strange fact that Frederick could so easily change from one ideology into the entirely opposite one agrees with the characteristics of a specific type of intellectual for whom mere intellectual creation and the receipt of praise for it plays the main rôle. The king once said to H. de Catt that 'he should perhaps in his youth have made other studies of more practical value. But he then believed that a zealous cultivation of poetry, of belles lettres and philosophy would render him fitted for everything, and after all he thought that he was not so wrong'. He also reminded himself of the Sophists, who laid stress upon being able to defend first one attitude and then the opposite one. We may conclude that the writing of the Anti-machiavel had satisfied one of his two souls perfectly, and he could now proceed to satisfying the opposite one too, and thereby earn double praise. The co-existence of these two souls becomes very clear from Catt's reports of his doings in the midst of war. Even in the most dangerous situations requiring the utmost concentration on military matters, the king devoted part of his time to writing poetry, declaiming from memory passages from Racine, playing the flute—for his digestion, as he said—and to similar pursuits. He also showed that he wanted to impress others by these activities.

POLITICAL THOUGHT IN LATER YEARS

Frederick's youthful enthusiasm for the ideal of a peaceful, mild and just ruler, inspired by fatherly love for his people and devoted to making it happy, came early in conflict with, and increasingly gave way to, an entirely opposite set of ideas in which glory was the supreme aim and war the principal means. In the course of his wars he was often seized by horror of the immense sacrifices in blood and misery involved and he then longed again for the peaceful life of a philosopher. After the first two Silesian wars, the king repeatedly assured friends that he would henceforth never wage a war again, and that he was cured from his ambition. Already in 1742 he had begun to write memoirs exhibiting his internal con-flicts. After his later wars he continued them, and in his old age (1775) revised the text, calling it 'History of my Time'. In the preface he discussed the antagonism between morality and politics, and the problems of the Reason of State. 'I hope,' he wrote in 1742, 'that posterity for which I am writing, will distinguish in me the philosopher from the prince, and the man of honour from the politician.' Everyone drawn into European politics, he continues, finds it very difficult to preserve integrity and sincerity of character. He is always exposed to the risks of being betrayed by an ally, or left in the lurch by friends, or being crushed by envy and jealousy. He is thereby faced with the terrible alternative either of sacrificing his peoples or of breaking his word too. The fundamental law of all governments, the smallest and the greatest, is the striving for aggrandisement. If a prince were less eager to expand than his neighbours, he would be more virtuous, but would become weaker than they. In this general rivalry only farsighted sagacity can lead to success. But this art is often incompatible with private morality. It is guided by the morality of the princes who, by tacit agreement and according to countless historical examples, unfortunately have accorded themselves the prerogative of satisfying their ambitions at any price. All treaties are based on false and perfidious oaths.

He did not defend this statecraft, Frederick continues, but it had been sanctioned by the constant usage of the peoples. Every ruler is therefore forced to adopt this practice authorizing fraud and misuse of power. In consequence, he too had made up his mind to conform to this usage of the rulers. The geographical weakness of Prussia and its historical experience, in particular the humiliations inflicted by Austria upon her, are pointed out as motives for expansion. The political conditions at the time of his accession to the throne were favourable. His ambition, interest, and the wish to make a name were decisive, and he resolved to wage war.

These opinions of the king are also expressed in other writings of his. In many places he stresses his striving for glory as a main motive of his policy. What he says, however, about the general robber mentality of princes which had forced him to follow their example, is hardly convincing. It is true that the eighteenth century was a time of numerous wars, which sprang from dynastic ambitions and were often accompanied by very unscrupulous diplomacy. But this had special reasons, and did not apply to all dynasties. The Habsburg Empire had been formed in long wars with Turkey and France, in which quite predominantly these latter were the aggressors. Maria Theresa, in particular, certainly did not belong to the robber monarchs, in spite of Frederick's cynical sneer at her rôle in the partition of Poland.

FREEDOM AND AUTOCRACY

Every state had, in Frederick's view, a peculiar character, determined by nature and history, and laws and politics had to be shaped according to it. The rules valid for the particular case of Prussia were best put forward in his two Political Testaments of 1752 and 1768, which were designed only for his successors to read. The aims which he considered the best for his realm were more territorial expansion and a system of royal autocracy, a privileged position of the military and the nobility, a strict reign of law, and a far-going interference by the government in economic affairs. The great weakness of this system was the lack of spontaneous co-operation of the people in the tasks of government. The king was aware of this deficiency, but saw no effective remedy.

Though Frederick rejected effective parliamentary institutions for Prussia, he was not opposed to republicanism in other states. In the Memoirs of the House of Brandenburg he concludes from history that monarchies need more time to reach the peak of their develop-ment and maintain themselves on it for a shorter time than repub-lics. If it was true that a well-governed kingdom was the best régime, it was no less certain that republics fulfilled their task most quickly and maintained themselves best, for good kings die, but wise laws are immortal. Republics showed more unity, while in monarchies good kings are followed by bad ones, and the spirit of the people assumes no firm form. But neither the one nor the other lives for ever. In other writings Frederick also pointed out shortcomings of republics, such as the internal strife of parties, a weak executive, or neglect of defence.

Britain was considered by Frederick a republic, and he often judged her political system with understanding and sympathy, though not without objective criticism. His Ode to Liberty, addressed to Lord Baltimore (1739), is full of enthusiasm for English freedom, and the Antimachiavel shows the same spirit. A few years later the 'History of my Time' described Walpole's government with obvious sympathy for liberty, though the prevailing corrup-tion is mentioned. Holland, too, aroused Frederick's admiration. Sweden, whose constitution was predominantly republican, was weakened by party strife and parliamentary bribery; further the Swedes had preserved their old conquering spirit, though a republic must be peaceable if it wants to maintain its system. In a lecture to the Berlin Academy of 1749, Frederick discussed the causes of changes in legislation. He surveys the development of the British constitution from the beginning and comes to the conclusion that Britain has many wise laws which, however, are less observed than anywhere else. The rivalry between royalty and parliament leads to frequent changes in the law and to legal abuses, so that the law urgently requires reforms. This is illustrated by examples. His Epistle to the British envoy Mitchell (1761) regrets that the British restriction of royal power was not accepted by all countries, then there would be no war. In 1777 Frederick wrote an essay on forms of government, in which he maintains that the rule of the nobility easily leads to oppression, to revolts by the people and to loss of liberty. England was menaced with this fate if the House of Com-mons did not prefer the true national interests to the shameful corruption disgracing it. When Joseph II tried to cut down the rights of the Hungarian parliament, he thought it was unwise of him to act in this way against a nation accustomed to liberty.

The reason why Frederick refused his people any substantial participation in government was, besides his philosophy, the longing that Prussia should become a great power. This aim required the acquisition of links between the ten unconnected parts of the realm and its rounding off by neighbouring lands, the formation of a wide territory with strong frontiers, rich resources and a numerous population. In his secret instructions to his successors the king indicated as the most desirable objects of aggrandisement, Saxony, Polish-Prussia and Swedish Pomerania. He further thought of conquering Bohemia, if Austria should be attacked by Turkey, France and Sardinia, and of giving it to the Saxon dynasty as a compensation for the loss of Saxony to Prussia. His plans of conquest were therefore mainly intended at the expense of Austria who appeared to the king as the arch-enemy. Polish-Prussia and Swedish Pomerania were vital for defence against Russia. These countries should be won from Poland and Sweden preferably by peaceful means and piecemeal, either as the price for support or neutrality in troubled times, or by bribing Polish or Swedish senators. The king further declared in his Political Testament of 1752, a few years before the outbreak of the Seven Years' War, that he did not wish to begin a new war and that his ideas of expansion, which he designated as dreams or fantasies, should be achieved by his successors, in the course of generations, at times when favourable opportunities should offer themselves. Expansion was justified by the fact that all great kings were actuated by the mentality of robbers. Machiavelli was right in saying that a disinterested power among ambitious ones would be doomed. A prince must necessarily have ambition, but it must be wise, moderate, and guided by reason. Pacts should not be broken unless in quite exceptional cases. A ruler whirled in the floods of European power politics could not preserve his probity of character.

Later, Frederick was disquieted by the growth of a radicalism which in his view was bound to lead to the destruction of all institutions. Baron Holbach, a German living in France, was one of the spokesmen of this school, and the king wrote two tracts against him (1770). He opposed Holbach's detractions of monarchs, noblemen, priests and soldiers, and his attacks on war, privileges and religion. These were mainly directed against French conditions, and Frederick therefore warmly defends the French monarchy and its institutions. Though he largely agrees with Holbach's opinions on religion and priests, he points out that truth is only for the small number of those who can be enlightened. Man is in general more an emotional than a rational being and is strongly attracted by the mysterious. This is the origin of religions and leads to superstition and fanaticism. Most of all it is the great masses of the people who are unfit for reason, they must work to make a living and have no time for thinking. For the people prejudices take the place of reason and they cling to them. Every religion, including Christianity, has only won power by exterminating the former beliefs by fire and sword. If the philosophers want to win the masses for the reasonable, they would have to follow this example, which is not desirable. Though most human doctrines are founded on prejudices, error or fraud, they must be tolerated to prevent worse. It is not the kings alone who wage war. Republics have often been as warlike, or even more so.

GERMAN PATRIOTISM ALIEN TO FREDERICK

It is significant that in all his considerations Frederick cares only for his own realm, without the slightest regard for Germany as a whole. If he pretended to fight the House of Austria in order to protect 'German liberty' against Habsburg despotism, this was, of course, merely the old French slogan. In his Testament of 1768, he assumes that the German Empire will eventually fall to pieces, and he himself was prepared to hasten this process by making Prussia independent of the Empire. Steps were actually taken in this direction. France appeared to Frederick to be the natural ally of Prussia in fighting the Habsburgs, even at the expense of German interests. France had seized Alsace and Lorraine, he wrote, and Prussia had appropriated Silesia. They therefore had a common interest to stand together and to defend their conquests. Frederick declared to his successors that Prussia must never quietly look on if France were threatened with losing Alsace and Lorraine, but should take up arms against the Emperor. When in 1744, an Austrian army marched into Alsace, the king actually began a new war against Maria Theresa and invaded Bohemia, forcing her to give up the Alsatian campaign. The idea of a unified Germany under Prussian leadership never entered Frederick's mind. His brother Henry at times favoured a conciliation with Austria and a division of Germany into two spheres of influence: the North for Prussia, the South for Austria. Frederick, however, was quite opposed to such plans. To him, Austria remained the arch-enemy, against whom every opportunity must be used in order to damage her interests. He also often incited the Turks to attack her. This attitude naturally caused a permanent, deep cleavage in Germany, jeopardizing her security and vital interests. Frederick further rejected the aims of colonial expansion, which his ancestor, Elector Frederick Wilhelm, had pursued and also advised his successors in this sense. A colonial and maritime policy required a navy, and this would have meant cutting down expenses for the army. But as a navy was not needed to fight Austria, it was of no interest to the king.

FREDERICK'S AUTOCRACY

The king's system was called 'Cabinet Government', because he decided all questions of any importance, and many others too, while alone in his cabinet. His ministers were in principle only auxiliary and executive organs. There was no Council of Ministers. The king maintained that in Austria and France the ministers were the real rulers and that this led to constant rivalries between them, to financial corruption and oppression of the people. He substantiated his aversion to deliberations in council with his experience in a war council, where he realized that otherwise clever people began to talk nonsense when they were sitting and debating together. In this remark there is certainly some truth. In such a council every member tries, of course, to surpass others and for the sake of prestige they may even insist on a false view. Frederick's opinion that a powerful minister was likely to be corrupt was also not quite unfounded in the age of Count Bruehl and, moreover, it agreed with his suspicion that all officials could be bribed. But the king's attitude principally came from his belief in his own intellectual superiority and his preference for the military way of thinking. In a war a strictly unitary plan is usually better than a compromise between different points of view. It is often not so important what is ordered than the clinging to the order given. In jurisdiction and civil administration the situation is quite different. Account must be taken of various aspects which often require the deliberation of several experts. A wrong decision can be made good by an appeal to a higher authority. We shall see that in non-military matters the personal decisions of the king were often by no means as excellent as the legend contends. The enormous self-confidence of the king came, probably, from his early military triumphs. He did not discuss with others whether he should begin his wars because he knew that the great majority of his generals, diplomats and relatives were absolutely against it. His success proved him right—but at what a price in blood and suffering!

The king got up at a very early hour and read most important state papers himself. In the meantime, his secretaries made extracts from all the other letters, such as applications, petitions or reports. He then wrote or dictated his orders for the further handling of affairs as marginal notes to the extracts or in separate letters, laying stress upon answering every petition on the same day. In this way up to 200 cases a day were dealt with. Important matters of state were naturally treated with great care. But the remarks on private petitions frequently show more sarcasm and wit than sense of justice and humanity.[1] The king in these remarks often judged a case not on its merits, but because he had a bad opinion of the family or the profession of the applicant. The officials, in particular, are usually called blockheads, thieves, etc., and their petitions are treated accordingly. In many cases, including matters of principle, the king decided rather arbitrarily, actuated mainly by changing moods. He had a very nervous temper, and it depended on chance whether he decided in one way or its opposite. If a military interest conflicted with a civilian, it was naturally the former which was considered of much greater importance.

The Prussian patriotic legend, which was spread by numerous German, English and other historians, ascribes to the king the greatest personal merits in every field of justice and administration. He was certainly indefatigable in trying to develop the resources of his realm. In many cases he was certainly or probably successful. In many others, however, his dictatorial-militaristic ways were by no means suitable to achieve the aims intended as will later be shown. The king's administrative policy included both favourable and unfavourable tendencies. On the one hand he chose mainly former officers who had became disabled for military service for high posts in the administration, and this led often to considerable failures. He had further an injustifiable distrust of the professional officials and considered nearly all of them corrupt. The cabinet system, moreover, in principle degraded even the ministers to merely executive organs of the king. On the other hand Frederick had the gift of recognizing ability and often entrusted important posts to young men who became excellent administrators.

The Prussian civil service was already in a stage of development which provided the state with most conscientious and able functionaries. This was not primarily due to the 'Iron Rod' of certain rulers as the Hohenzollern legend seems to suggest. It had many causes among which the policy of former rulers, especially Elector Frederick William, played a great part. The principal causes were the early spread of religious toleration, the close connection with Holland, the influence of Wolff's rationalism and Francke's pietism, and the

[1] Cf. J. Borchardt's book, where a great many of these remarks are given.

reception of many refugees from religious persecution, especially
the French Huguenots. Frederick's personality, moreover, exercised
a great spell upon disciples of the Enlightenment of whom many
possessed extraordinary abilities and knowledge. Quite a number of
his best ministers and other high-placed officials came from other
countries, or from conquered Silesia. The king sometimes treated
them in a rather offensive way if they dared to contradict him. But
at last he usually restrained his temper and let them have their way.

THE KING AND THE ARMY

The cardinal points of Frederick's policy were the military
strength of his realm and the concentration of all power in his
person. First of all, he stressed, a king must lead his army personally.
This dictum obviously only suited rulers with military talent and
otherwise could be disastrous. But it certainly suited Frederick and
contributed much to his successes. A supreme commander who was
also the sovereign could act much more freely than any other
generalissimo. He was not threatened by the rivalry and criticism
of other generals and not dependent on the government at home. He
could act quickly, and in case of failure was not responsible to anybody. Though Frederick was a strategist of genius, he sometimes
made mistakes which would have ruined any general subject to a
higher authority. Many military experts of the highest rank have
blamed him for them, and the king himself sometimes confessed his
blunders and admitted that he was only saved by a stroke of luck.
General von Clausewitz, the author of the greatest classic of
Prussian strategy, wrote that Frederick was often a desperate
gambler and that, for example, the famous victory of Rossbach was
only due to the unbelievably foolish dispositions of the French
general commanding the enemy forces. Frederick's warfare excelled
because of the quickness of his planning and the carrying out of his
plans and his aggressive tactics, which necessarily cost much blood.
The troops had orders, in most cases, not to rely on shooting, but to
attack with the bayonet or the sabre, though this order could not be
maintained for ever. The Austrian generals clung much more to
Montecuccoli's tradition of cautious and defensive warfare, which
sought to outmanoeuvre the enemy without a pitched battle, to
capture or destroy his supplies and to exhaust and wear out his
troops. The generals Daun and Lacy were masters in this strategy,
while Laudon belonged to the opposite school.

The principle that military interests and outlook have absolute
priority over all other considerations forms the system of militar-

ism. Its pillars are the army officers. Frederick's predecessors had had great difficulties in overcoming the resistance of the landed nobility to the creation of a standing army and to taking service in its ranks. Frederick silently made definite peace with them by granting them a particularly honoured position. This preferment was not due to any belief in noble blood. The king often ridiculed or blamed kings and nobles for believing that they were by nature or by the Grace of God above other human beings.[2] He did not want a decorative court aristocracy of men with great titles, wealth and sinecures, but preferred men of low nobility and little wealth, such as most of the Prussian Junkers were, who, as French diplomats haughtily remarked, even accepted posts beneath the dignity of an aristocrat because of their poverty. Noble origin was in Frederick's eyes necessary for an officer or a high official, because only noblemen could have a sense of honour and duty, though he admitted that there were a few exceptions. Men of middle-class origin were seldom appointed officers, and only in quite exceptional cases reached a high rank. Yet noble birth alone was not enough. The king demanded much of his officers and paid them little. But he indemnified them with honours and great opportunities. The Junker class was left in the possession of their feudal prerogatives, such as power over their serfs, exemption from taxation, a special status in judicial matters, etc. The otherwise so parsimonious king could also show great generosity in succouring noble landowners who found themselves in money difficulties. He justified this because of the irreplaceable value of this 'race' for the defence of the country. Officers often received pensions or high posts in the administration when they had become too old for the army or had become invalids. But bureaucrats were seldom granted pensions, and the king mostly also denied them ennoblement, which was usual in France and Austria. For his favours, however, the noblemen had to serve him in war and peace, their whole way of life was closely watched, they were not permitted to marry beneath their rank, to engage in trade or to travel abroad without royal permission, which was seldom given. The English diplomat James Harris, later Lord Malmesbury, reported in 1750 that the whole realm of Prussia was in fact a prison. The character of the king seemed to him a strange mixture of barbarity and humanity.

The preference given by the king to the army may be illustrated by the following example. In 1774, the West Prussian Finance Office proposed moving the garrison from Marienwerder to another place, because of the scarcity of dwellings. The king replied: 'You are all

---

[2] He nevertheless rejected marriages of high-born with low-born people.

fools. If you think that, in the interests of a counsellor who is actually a thief and an accomplice of cheats, that for such a fellow I shall move a single dragoon you are quite mistaken. Among a hundred counsellors one can always with good conscience hang ninety-nine, for if one honest man is among them, it is much. More humility in face of the military!' The king's distrust of his non-noble administrative organs certainly went too far, and his trust in the integrity of his Junker officers in high positions was also exaggerated, as many cases showed.

The ranks of the army were partly composed of mercenaries, both foreign and native, partly of conscripted men, who were levied in the realm from the lowest classes of labourers and sons of peasants. Everybody with property, education or special skill was excepted. The king wished to prevent the productive population who paid taxes, from being diminished by military service. He even once ordered that two-thirds of the army should be foreign mercenaries, but this proved as ineffective as the prohibition to employ force in getting mercenaries. A great proportion was in any case foreign, and recruited largely in the small German states. The drill sergeant mostly treated the recruits with such brutality that many of them soon wanted to run away, and could only be prevented from doing so by the strictest supervision and the greatest ruthlessness in capturing and punishing deserters. When at home, the soldiers were occupied with military exercises for about two months every year, and for the rest were free to do agricultural or industrial work. Many of them were married. In peacetime they did not live in barracks, but were billetted on houseowners. Old soldiers sometimes got small posts, or, if they were invalids, were cared for in a home. But the number of these was, as Dohm says, very small, and the great majority of the invalids and their families lived in distress. Of the serving soldiers a great proportion welcomed the outbreak of a war, because they hoped that this would facilitate desertion. But on the march, the troops were constantly surrounded by hussars who were there to arrest deserters.

One of the statements made by the king characteristic of his system, was that the soldiers must fear their officers more than the enemy. Otherwise, he believed, they would abscond or refuse to fight. But he also often won their hearts by affability, friendly words, sharing their hardships, intrepidity in danger, care for their comfort, etc. On the other hand, he very frequently demanded from them the greatest sacrifices in enduring privations. Here again we find the two incompatible strains in Frederick's character. On the one hand, he wished to spare the people sufferings caused by war.

The peaceful citizen, he declared, should not suffer when the nation was at war. H. Hetzel has compiled numerous utterances of Frederick's from his writings and letters, which express his greatest horror of the sufferings caused by war and his desire for humanity, even between belligerents. They were no doubt sincere. Nevertheless the wars for which he was responsible brought about many scenes of terrifying barbarism. And Frederick ordered such acts to be carried out, too. He certainly did not find pleasure in cruelty, but he did not hesitate to apply it if it seemed to be in the military interest. Private humanity had to yield to the dictates of the Reason of State.

Countless anecdotes were told about the king, but most of them cannot be authenticated. There is no doubt that he was capable of actions of quite conflicting character. Like his father he possessed a highly irascible and passionate temper. But sometimes he showed astounding mildness and kindness.[3]

ADMINISTRATION

The structure of administration, which Frederick's father had built up, was little changed, except that a department of industries and trade was created for intensifying the policy of mercantilism. The ministries showed still a mixture of organization according to provinces and according to branches. The ministers formed no college, but within each ministry the Counsellors did. The king was not as averse to local autonomy as his father had been and restored and extended a limited measure of self-government. The landed nobility, in particular, proposed the Landräte (District Chiefs), and the king appointed them. In certain towns the burghers had some right of proposal for the magistracy. But on the whole the municipal autonomy was very small. Many towns were still subjected to feudal landlords, and the tax officials and police organs of the government, and also the military, often treated the town people with a very high hand. Frederick had to forbid his officers to beat up burghers. The Estates had no power, even where they still met, and in Silesia they came to an end altogether. The Civil Service was under a rigorous discipline, and the king not infrequently treated even high officials of merit with unbelievable harshness. Prominent posts were mostly given to noblemen, often former officers, except in branches where nobles with the necessary qualifications were not available. The King held the principle, as he himself wrote, of preferring clever officials of doubtful integrity to dull ones, whose honesty was

---

[3] Cf. the case reported by Dohm, vol. IV, p. 630 which is certainly true.

beyond doubt in the central departments. He also preferred unintelligent people as servants. A strange case was that of Frederick's valet Fredersdorf, a man of lowest origin and no education, but very handsome, who won his confidence and friendship to such a degree that soon after the king's accession he was ennobled, got very rich and had such influence that ministers and great lords crowded his ante-chamber.[4]

FINANCE

Finance was Frederick's special concern, since by far the greatest part of his revenues was needed for the army. His personal expenses and those for the court were modest. When the king died, it was found that all his shirts were in such bad condition that a court official provided one of his own in which the king was buried. But there were exceptions. After the Seven Years' War, when his people, according to his own words, was living in indescribable misery, the king spent very high sums on building a new palace just for reasons of prestige, in order to show that he still had money. In general, the king preserved the system of taxation which his predecessors had introduced, and he continued his father's habit of having sharp eyes and great ruthlessness for every fiscal misuse. It was, however, impossible, even for the highest officials, to survey the total finances, because there were various financial offices directly subordinated to the king. The alterations in the system made by him rendered this supervision more difficult.[5] In the predominantly peaceful period after the Seven Years' War, from 1763 to 1786, the average share of the military expenses in the total expenditure was 80%. In Austria the proportion was much lower. The special Prussian envoy in Vienna, Baron Fuerst, in 1755 reported to the king that the Austrian military expenses amounted to 35% in peacetime, and Biedermann states about the same for 1770.

Many writers praising Frederick quote figures given by his minister Count Hertzberg as a proof of the King's munificence in caring for the welfare of his people. Hertzberg stated in a lecture to the Academy that the extraordinary expenditure of the king for agriculture, industries, commerce, the arts, justice and the military

---

[4] As reported by Count Lehndorff, a high court official, in his diary (I, p. 359). Lehndorff says Fredersdorf had long played the rôle of a prime minister, ruling despotically. Another valet of the King, Glasow, was, however, his rival. The king showed him the greatest favours, but Glasow proved a thief and traitor and was arrested.
[5] Cf. Koser in FBPG vol. XVI 1903 and Behre, *Gesch.d.preuss. Statistik* pp. 82, 99.

amounted in the 21 years before his death to ca 40 million Taler, or almost 2 millions a year. Actually these figures are rather small in comparison with the terrible losses and damage caused by his wars. Moreover, they were by no means exclusively designed to support those people who were in need or wanted to develop their resources.[6] Hertzberg, in other lectures, gave a list of the items for which these subsidies were given. We find among them large amounts for military aims such as fortifications, barracks, pensions to officers, gifts to noblemen, but also reparation of damage due to fire or inundation, for relief in years of starvation, agricultural meliorations, new industries etc. The conversion of swamps into meadows or fields required the building of dykes which often burst and were repaired with the aid of subsidies. In any case, 2 millions a year for all such projects do not appear high at a time when the annual state revenues were about 22 millions, and the king accumulated a treasure of 51,3 million Talers, mainly as a safeguard against the sudden needs for a war.

The revenues were mainly increased by monopolies on salt, sugar, coffee and many other commodities, and by putting excise tax on almost every article. In order to enforce these measures, numerous French officials were engaged who employed the utmost ruthlessness in discovering and punishing any contravention. This aroused a general outcry and resistance. The number of smugglers and black-market traders multiplied and bands of them often fought the excise officials with open force and were supported by the people. Dohm says[7] that this system deprived the king of a great deal of the affection and esteem of his subjects, and many of them now saw in him a callous tyrant, planning ever more aggrandisement and extracting the means for this purpose from his people with the aid of foreign officials. The king himself wrote in his Political Testament of 1768: 'I have done nothing but good to my people, yet they believe that I want to put a knife at their throat whenever I intend to introduce a useful reform or a necessary change.'

THE KING AND THE PEASANTS

Frederick's predecessors had wished to abolish serfdom and to improve the lot of the peasants, but their striving had some success only on the crown domains. The extension of the reforms to the estates of the nobility was sabotaged by the nobles, who had a

[6] Mirabeau, I, p. 391, states that Frederick, in the last six years of his reign, spent 4,561.000 Taler on the embellishment of Berlin alone.
[7] Cf. Dohm, IV, p. 513.

strong position in the local administration and also in the central government. Frederick continued the attempts of his father, but had the same experience. In 1763 the king peremptorily ordered that serfdom was to be abolished at once, but dropped this when the Estates of Pomerania raised objections. He also often intervened in favour of peasants oppressed by their lords.[8] In theory he was certainly against serfdom but in practice did not find it opportune to undertake radical agrarian reforms. The nobles were the pillars of his army and his whole system. If serfdom had been abolished, the King would have had to pay them compensation, and the expenses for the army were so high that this was out of the question. Moreover, from the standpoint of his militarism, any loosening of the ties which bound the peasants to the lords seemed to him not advisable. The squires or their sons were mostly officers, and the King did not find it convenient to take the side of the peasants against their lords. Joseph II did this, but Frederick had a very different outlook. Among the leading officials there were also men of liberal opinions, who would have liked to emancipate the serfs, and who argued that a free worker was much more productive than an unfree one. But the king had little understanding for this view. His whole economic policy was built on the opposite principle; labour was to be strictly controlled from above.

Considerable improvements were, however, achieved in the territories annexed from Poland. Here the lot of the peasants was particularly miserable, and the king did not have to consider the feelings of the nobles, who were in any case his secret enemies. It was therefore possible to intervene effectively in the agrarian conditions in favour of the peasants. In Silesia, too, the king afforded considerable protection to the serfs, for similar reasons.

Serfdom was not the only obstacle to agricultural progress. The peasants were also much oppressed by the ravages of wars, by the requirements for the army in peacetime, by the fiscal policy and by the consequences of mercantilism. However, a great deal was achieved by the conversion of large tracts of swamps and waste land into fertile soil by drainage. The king settled great numbers of rural and urban people as free peasants on the land reclaimed and on the royal domains, altogether 57,475 families.[9] But it soon became clear that a large proportion of the colonists were of inferior calibre, who had not done well in their former occupations and now failed again. This was largely due to Frederick's autocratic

[8] Koser's admirable work on Frederick gives significant details, Cf. II, p. 94.
[9] Cf. A. Skalweit in FBPG vol. 24, 1911.

methods. Dohm gives many details,[10] and remarks that the king was only informed of the successes but not of the failures. He also showed great zeal in furthering the progress of agricultural methods and, for example, induced the peasants to cultivate new crops such as potatoes, hops or fodder plants. He did not hesitate to apply force if they were reluctant. Sheep farming was improved by the introduction of Spanish, English and African merinoes. The king also wished that every peasant should rear silkworms and plant mulberry trees. This proved a complete failure. More reasonable was his organization of credit institutes for the landed nobility though their operation gave often ground to sharp criticism. The province of Pomerania received 5½ million Talers in twenty years, of which the nobles got at least 4½ millions. One of the best experts, the Royal Agricultural Councillor Hering, wrote : 'These expenses for melioration, which the nobles owed to Frederick's generosity, have actually been entirely useless, and frequently even had the most disadvantageous consequences'. Proofs were given for this statement.

On the whole, Frederick's agricultural policy was not a success. The greatest agricultural expert of the age, A. Thaer, stated that so many of the good plans of the king came to naught, that he eventually seemed to give up the idea of making farming flourish, and devoted himself mainly to the promotion of industries, even at the expense of agriculture. A. F. Buesching, the leading statistician of the time, who had the closest knowledge of Frederick's policy and of economic conditions, judged in a book[11] that 'the poverty of the peasants increased from year to year' and 'one must confess that in most provinces the peasants increasingly became impoverished, mainly through the demands for military purposes'. Dohm comes to the conclusion (IV, p. 405) that the improvement of the peasants' social conditions did not sufficiently interest the king. He thinks that this is proved by the fact that the tenants on the royal domains, who formed a very great part of the peasantry, did not receive better conditions at all in Frederick's reign, though this depended merely on his will. G. F. Knapp, the famous economist, who has made a special study of the history of the Prussian peasantry, states that Austria was far ahead of Prussia in caring for their welfare.

[10] Cf. Dohm, IV, p. 390. For further details cf. W. Roscher, *System der Volkswirtschaft*, 7th ed. 1868, I, 571, note 7, and Schlosser, *Geschichte des 18 Jahrhunderts*, 1864, II, p. 248.

[11] Buesching, *Character Friedrichs*, 1788, pp. 83, 294. Cf. also Mirabeau, *De la monarchie prusienne* 1788, vol. III, p. 477. This work contains much valuable materials largely compiled by the prominent economist Mauvillon. It says that apart from some royal domains and a few estates of nobles the state of agriculture was wretched.

INDUSTRIES AND TRADE

At that time, all states practised the system of mercantilism which can be described as economic power politics. It fitted Frederick's general policy very well and he intensified it in many ways. There was a project which would have subjected the whole of economic life to direction by the government. To this end a number of monopolistic trade companies and a state bank were to form a giant trust. Frederick's chief adviser in this matter was an Italian financier, Calzabigi. The plan was not realized as a whole, but many highly privileged enterprises for certain branches were founded. The commercial circles and the liberal-minded bureaucracy had good reason to dislike these experiments. When a financial crisis broke out, several ministers submitted a memorandum critical of this suppression of every freedom of trade to the King. But Frederick not only showed himself blind to their arguments, but at once suspected that they had been bribed. He rejected their representations in the rudest and most insulting words, calling the ministers impertinent ignoramuses and the author of the memorandum a corrupt rogue. The author was a privy counsellor, Ursinus, an official of great merit and integrity, who was dismissed and sent to prison by the enraged king. The latter was very eager to collect economic information, and his memory was a storehouse of details about every trade. If nevertheless so many of his grand subjects failed or suffered great losses, this only showed that the task of mastering and deciding everything himself was too much even for an intellectual superman.

Frederick's deep distrust of his officials and his militaristic contempt of their civilian ways of thinking often induced him to put his trust in international adventurers and other unscrupulous types who cost the state much money. In order to introduce new manufactures the king granted, to persons who seemed suitable, large subsidies and privileges; in many cases they even received the whole capital needed, without the obligation of repaying it. The king's favourite plan was the foundation of a silk industry in and near Berlin. The raw silk, too, was to be produced at home. The amounts spent on this project were extraordinary. For some time the results seemed splendid, but this silk industry was like a hot-house plant. After the King's death it withered and in the end had largely to be wound up. Another example was the king's project of introducing into Silesia also the manufacture of damask, which flourished in Saxony. To this purpose Saxon weavers were abducted by force, settled in Silesia and induced by large subsidies to make damask.[12]

[12] Cf. Brentano, Ges. Aufsaetze, I, p. 584.

But in spite of all these efforts the enterprise failed. In a great many cases the king went so far as to command traders to buy otherwise unsaleable goods, and quartered soldiers in their houses if they disobeyed his orders. In order to make the salt monopoly profitable, every subject had to buy a certain quantity of salt, whether he wanted it or not.

At the same time, however, the lively growth of many industries took place in the most western provinces near the Lower Rhine, without any encouragement from the government. These provinces were regarded by Frederick almost as foreign countries, and the import of their manufactures into the central and eastern provinces was hindered by high customs duties and by prohibitions. Even in the latter provinces, however, a new industry developed and prospered, though it received almost no support from the state, namely the cotton industry.

Besides trying to make his realm independent of the import of foreign manufactures and to conquer foreign markets for Prussian goods, the king wanted to found a great international trade, shipping, insurance, etc. Industries and trade had spontaneously developed in some neighbouring states, such as Saxony and Hamburg, where conditions were favourable and trade less subject to state regulation. The Regent of Saxony, Maria Antonia, wrote to Frederick: 'Our great principle is the freedom of trade and the reciprocity of advantages', and she proposed concluding a commercial treaty in this spirit. But Frederick had no understanding for the value of economic freedom and refused. Instead, he waged a number of trade wars with Saxony, Austria, Hamburg and Poland, mainly using the position of his territories to impose high duties on transit trade and to strangle the exports and imports of competitors. The results were doubtful, because the traders often evaded Frederick's measures by altering the routes of trade. Breslau and Königsberg lost much of their international trade and suffered grievously.[13] Poland was forced to accept trade conditions which made her almost a colony of Prussia.

The rise of certain industries had partly been effected at the expense of the rural population. The prices of food and raw materials were kept down to foster the growth of manufactures, while the peasants had to pay high prices for industrial goods, often of inferior quality. On the other hand, Frederick William's policy of keeping great stocks of grain in all provinces for use in the case of war was employed by his son also to stabilise grain prices to a certain extent. In times of bad crops he was thereby able to provide

[13] Cf. the history of the great Silesian banking house Eichborn, p. 52.

the poor with cheap grain, and thousands of people migrated from the neighbouring countries to Prussia in order to escape starvation. Nevertheless, the masses of the people mostly lived in dire poverty and the number of beggars, tramps and robbers was very great.[14] Nor did the policy of forced industrialization create a class of wealthy industrialists, who might have formed a counterweight to the power of the Junkers. Apart from a few financiers, who profited from monopolistic transactions with the government, the middle class contained very few men of considerable means.

In the second half of the century the view that freer trade was necessary spread widely. The Physiocrats and Adam Smith were eagerly read in Prussia, too. But Frederick showed no understanding for the basic factors of economic prosperity such as individual initiative, competition and the formation of capital. The heavy expenses for military purposes weakened purchasing power and kept consumption down. The lack of wealth narrowed the market for luxury goods, such as silks and porcelain, on the production of which the king laid special stress. Roscher, in his classic work on the History of Political Economy in Germany, judges Frederick's economic views very unfavourably. In Austria, Joseph II, though also a protectionist, created a great customs union, while Prussia remained divided into many parts. Joseph showed much more economic and social understanding than Frederick in other respects also.

Town and country were not only separated by barriers of excise in Prussia. On principle, new crafts and industries were only to be founded in towns, while the rural districts were forbidden to compete with them. These mediaeval conditions were a great obstacle to the natural growth of industries. In most other countries modern industries, apart from the making of luxuries, developed first in rural areas, where labour and materials were cheap and where guilds intent on suppressing all competition did not exist. But the separation of urban and rural districts was deeply rooted in Frederick's system, though he made certain exceptions. The king wanted to preserve the old separation of the classes and the predominance of the nobility, which depended on the subservience of the peasants. He could therefore not favour the free penetration of the rural districts by urban, commercial and intellectual elements. The uncontrolled foundation of factories would have raised wages and prices, undermined the feudal spirit and spread new ideas, which might have made the peasants discontented and restless. Even the acquisition of knightly estates by rich burghers was much dis-

[14] Cf. Berlinische Monatsschrift vol. IX, 1787.

K

couraged, and, if it was permitted, the owners did not acquire the same privileges as noblemen.

Another fundamental condition of the natural growth of industries was good communications. Frederick had great merit in improving and extending the water-ways, which were connected with his great drainage operations. But he entirely neglected the building of highways, on the ground that they might be of advantage to enemies wishing to invade the realm. For the same reason he was against publishing good maps of the kingdom. The bad roads were further considered a useful weapon in Frederick's trade wars, since they increased the cost of transit transport. Prussia's roads were therefore left in a miserable state. At that time the beginning industrial revolution and the invention of the steam-engine encouraged a great rise in the use of coal. Frederick's realm was particularly rich in coal, both in Silesia and in the Ruhr district. But the bad roads were often an obstacle to its use and the king did nothing to promote it. Nevertheless, the minister Baron Heynitz succeeded in greatly raising its consumption and mining and metal industries in general expanded. Heynitz, a Saxon, had been minister in Brunswick and Saxony and was an expert of European fame. Frederick offered him the post of minister in Prussia and he accepted. But when Heynitz showed him that his fiscal innovations were entirely wrong Frederick replied very rudely. There were other conflicts and eventually the king dismissed Heynitz in spite of his extraordinary merits. His greatest disciple was Baron vom Stein.

The industrial revolution was already operating in many countries of Europe, including Prussia.[15] The number of factories and their output increased. Estimates of the value of industrial production in Prussia were published in Hertzberg's lectures and in the work by Mirabeau and Mauvillon. But they show great differences and are perhaps not comparable. Experts were doubtful whether the statistics submitted to the king were correct. Many were convinced that progress would have been much quicker and the increase of industries considerably greater but for Frederick's antiquated methods.[16]

---

[15] Heynitz sent one of his officials to England, who, in the disguise of a worker, spied out the construction of the newly-invented steam-engine. In 1783 the first engine was built in Prussia. On Heynitz cf. Steinecke in ADB, vol. 55.

[16] The most detailed contemporary criticism of Frederick's economic policy is given in the work by Mirabeau and Mauvillon, already quoted. For a reply cf. de la Hay de Launay and Zimmermann, *Fragmente*, vol. II. The latter book reposes on materials supplied by the ministers Baron von der Horst, Count Hertzberg and other organs of Frederick's administration.

LAW AND JUSTICE

When Frederick II came to the throne, he at once began to abolish cruel practices in penal justice. Torture and aggravations of the death sentence were abandoned, convicts sentenced to the wheel or the stake were first strangled, and only their corpse was broken or burnt.[17] The drowning of girls who had killed their new born children came to an end. The hanging of thieves was discontinued in Prussia, whilst it remained very frequent in France and Britain. Capital punishment only took place for murder, highway robbery and a few other very grave crimes, and death sentences were often commuted by the king into imprisonment. Many of the judges believed that his mildness went too far; he once declared that it was better that twenty guilty men should be acquitted than that one innocent man should be condemned. His Minister of Justice, Cocceji, further greatly raised the standards of the administration of justice by insisting upon very high juridical and moral qualifications of the judges and weeding out unsatisfactory ones. In 1746, Frederick ordered him to elaborate a comprehensive code of law, based merely on reason and the country's present constitution, not on the antiquated Roman law. But his draft was disappointing and was shelved.

Prussia, by these reforms, became for some time the vanguard of juridical progress, though we must not forget that the independence of the courts was not absolutely secured and that there was no jury. It is interesting to compare the conditions in Prussia with those in England.[18] In the seventies, for example, the annual executions of criminals per million inhabitants were three in Prussia and forty-seven in London and Middlesex, or more than fifteen times as much. This was mainly due to the fact that in England even petty offences against property were punishable by death and that this country had no police worth the name. As regards the prisons, we have detailed reports of the great philanthropist John Howard. His revelation of the terrible conditions in many English prisons moved Parliament to pass two bills of reform in 1775. He also visited the prisons and hospitals in all countries of Europe : in Berlin he found conditions favourable, except in Spandau prison. The great workhouse where petty offenders were kept, had his full praise.

A new era of reforms began in 1779, when Carmer became Lord Chancellor and resumed the work of comprehensive codification. He had excellent collaborators, especially the great jurists C. G. Suarez

[17] The strangling, however, was secretly done in order not to decrease the deterrent impression of the burning or breaking on the wheel.
[18] Cf. the excursus on this question after this chapter, page 312.

and E. F. Klein, who were the principal authors of the new laws. Only half the work was finished when Frederick died. He certainly had a share in the merits of the Prussian Code which appeared in 1794, eight years after his death. But the Code also contained very retrogressive clauses showing Frederick's insistence on aristocratic privileges. It even extends privileges hitherto reserved to the high nobility to the lesser nobles also. A nobleman, for example, cannot marry a woman from the peasant or lower middle class except with permission of the government, and even then he cannot provide his wife and children with the same rights as would be the case in a marriage with a noblewoman. This was called 'a marriage on the left hand'. The nobles further received exclusive rights, or priority, in regard to obtaining posts as officers or higher officials. On the other hand, they lose their title if they become artisans, retail traders or workers.

Suarez and his collaborators were much more progressive in reforming the law than was the practice of the king. Frederick's claim to his right to interfere in the course of a lawsuit, or to set the Reason of State above law and justice were the very opposite of their views. Their outlook can best be seen from the lectures which Suarez had to give after Frederick's death to the then crown prince, the future Frederick William III. They show an outspoken liberalism and advocate a good measure of liberty. The draft of the code, too, tended to eliminate the Reason of State, placing the welfare of the citizen and the rights of man above it, and vetoing any interference of the king in the course of justice. This was quite the opposite of Frederick's ethos; the king had in many cases superseded the normal judiciary procedure when state interests seemed to require it. Not a few men were executed or imprisoned for life, because the king was convinced that they were traitors or offenders against militarism. That he had the accused sentenced by a military court was not a guarantee of justice. Well-known cases are those of the Jesuit father Faulhaber, General Walrave, Baron von der Trenck, and the Privy Counsellor Ferber. Since in such cases the full circumstances which had aroused suspicion and the defence of the accused were not made public it is, of course, not possible to form a definite judgment.

The king had declared that he would not interfere in the course of justice, which, however, primarily meant in regard to Civil Law. But even this was not strictly kept. The most sensational case was that of the miller Arnold, a quarrelsome person, who was involved in lawsuits about the rent of a mill with his landlord. All the courts decided against the miller, but he appealed to the king. Frederick, always full of distrust of judges and officials, ordered a colonel to investigate the case. The latter left this to his military justiciary, a former advocate, who had been dismissed by the court concerned and now had an opportunity of taking revenge. He induced the colonel to report that the miller was right, and the king suspected that the courts had decided against him and for his landlord because he was only a common man. Full of indignation he wanted to have the judgment reversed and the judges punished and to this purpose he gave orders to the Court of Appeal and the Minister concerned, Baron Zedlitz. But both refused to do so, even when the king repeated his orders. The President of the Court pointed out that orders of the king could not influence judicial decisions. Frederick became furious and ordered the Lord Chancellor (Grosskanzler), Baron Fuerst, and the six judges of the Court to appear before him When Fuerst corrected a mistake made by the king, the latter shouted: 'Get out—your successor is already appointed!' The judges were removed from their posts, put into prison for a year and had to pay indemnities to the miller. There is no doubt that the law was on the side of the judges, and after Frederick's death his successor declared them not guilty. The incident made an enormous stir. The officials and the upper classes were enraged. Many of them demonstrated by calling on the dismissed Lord Chancellor to express their sympathy. But the common people acclaimed the king, believing that he was the defender of their interests against the aristocracy. The intentions of the king had certainly been well-meaning, but the belief in his own infallibility had caused him to commit a flagrant injustice.

TREATMENT OF THE PRESS

In former times Frederick was often praised for having granted unrestricted freedom of the press. But it has since been shown by historical research that this praise was undeserved. In the beginning of his reign the king actually granted freedom from the censorship to one newspaper, the Berlinische Nachrichten, but only for an unpolitical column, in order to increase its circulation and thereby to influence public opinion. This decree has been misinterpreted by countless writers as a general abolition of the censorship. This never took place. The king's policy showed many changes according to the political situation.[19] Scholarly books were as a rule censored very mildly, if at all, and this explains Kant's praise. The edict of 1746, however, prescribed that writings contrary to general principles of religion and of moral and civil order were not to be tolerated. Political literature and daily papers were censored by the Foreign Office.

[19] Cf. Koser, III, p. 464; F. Etzin in FBPG, vol. 33, 1921.

Any criticism of Prussian policy was out of the question, and even the publication of political news, or statistics, was greatly restricted. In times of war the king even tried to terrorize the foreign press. The editor of the Gazette de Cologne, Mr. Roderique, who printed only the Austrian war news, was beaten up by a hired ruffian on the king's orders, and was warned this might happen again. When the editor of the Gazette d'Erlangen, Mr. Gross, who was also on the Austrian side, dared to visit Berlin, he was arrested and publicly flogged. A Saxon journalist, too, who had reported a battle in a way different from the king's wishes, was later arrested and publicly humiliated. Lessing in 1769 wrote to Nicolai that the much-praised freedom of the press in Prussia consisted merely in the right to sneer at religion; but if someone in Berlin would try to write on other subjects as freely as Sonnenfels had done in Vienna, to tell the truth on the aristocratic rabble at court like the latter, to raise his voice for the rights of the people against exploitation and despotism, he would soon experience which country was the most slavish in Europe. Towards the end of his reign Frederick tolerated, however, the sale of writings satirical of his person, and even the expression of republican opinions.

RELIGIOUS TOLERANCE

The tolerance of the king in religious matters was celebrated by countless writers. In this respect he certainly had great merit, though in Prussia a good deal of religious tolerance had already been granted under his predecessors. Such abominations as still happened in France from religious fanaticism were impossible in Prussia. In the sixties, Voltaire aroused the horror of the world by revealing the judicial barbarities perpetrated by French courts on innocent Protestants. Even Frederick could hardly believe it when d'Alembert in 1763 told him that the Parlement or High Court of Paris had just forbidden inoculation against smallpox until the Faculty of Theology should declare it admissible. But it need hardly be mentioned that his tolerance largely sprang from lack of any concrete religion and from political reasons. The king often expressed his contempt for Christian beliefs in an extreme form, though such remarks were not designed for the common man, who was to retain his 'superstitions', which were even useful because they prevented him from committing crimes.[20] In Frederick's view the Churches

[20] He therefore laid stress upon religious instruction in the schools and ordered that a journal criticizing sermons should be suppressed. D'Alembert saw in this behaviour an objectionable opportunism and induced the King to order the Academy to arrange a public discussion about the question whether it was useful to the people if they were taught to believe in fallacies. Cf. Koser, III, p. 464.

were to be police organs and had to serve the purposes of the state. During his reign Frederick admitted many freethinkers to academic chairs and other posts, even to high posts in the Protestant Church. Many others who had been persecuted by zealots in their homelands received asylum in Prussia, among them Rousseau. The king also used his influence to promote peaceful relations among different Churches. There was a large Catholic population in Silesia. He was tolerant towards them in religious matters, but ruthlessly suppressed pro-Austrian tendencies among the clergy and used every means to subject the Church to his full control. Even the Jesuits seemed to him useful instruments, especially in the field of education. The papal edict dissolving the Jesuit Order was not recognized in Prussia, and the king made use of their services, though he preferred to employ French Jesuits who had no Austrian sympathies. Religious tolerance was also useful for getting mercenaries from Catholic countries. But the tolerance of the king did not go as far as to treat Catholics on exactly the same footing as Protestants and to give them high posts in the state service. For Lutheran soldiers a special military Church was formed. The pastors appointed by the king were to a great extent men of little education. One of them even intended to baptize in the name of the king. To become a field preacher the patronage of a sergeant-major was more important than the knowledge of theology.

<h2 style="text-align:center">THE JEWS</h2>

The Jews were considered by the king an undesirable and harmful element. He treated them harshly and subjected them to onerous restrictions. Many occupations were entirely closed to them and special care was taken to prevent their increase. Yet Frederick made great use of the services of individual Jews, particularly for his shady financial transactions, such as his debasement of the currency, which enabled him to pull through the Seven Years' War. But his policy of industrialization was also to a great extent carried out by Jewish financiers and manufacturers. In the Christian middle classes suitable people were rare, while Jewish businessmen possessed the necessary adaptability. The silk and cotton industry in particular was largely in Jewish hands and this contributed much to the social rise of the Jews, preparing the way for their emancipation. In Frederick's time the Jews of his realm brought forth a number of excellent thinkers and scholars, such as Moses Mendelssohn, Salomon Maimon and Marcus Herz. But the king took no notice of them. Nor did he think of liberating the Jews from their humiliating

and demoralizing position and opening the way to higher civilization to them, as Joseph II did.

As a philosopher, Frederick often praised the benefits of education, especially in the second half of his reign. Several of his writings
and letters put forward the commonplaces of the school of enlightenment about the necessity of overcoming superstition, of
making the people thinking and civilized beings and improving their
morals. Yet many believers in enlightenment harboured doubts
whether the vulgar people were able to be enlightened without great
danger. Would they not lose every morality when they heard that
they would not be tormented in hell if they had committed crimes
without being found out by the police? Frederick shared these
doubts and sometimes expressed them in a drastic way. In the Seven
Years' War, however, he was struck by the fact that a soldier needed
some education to qualify as a sergeant and this induced him to
give more attention to schools. He also became interested in providing invalid soldiers with posts as teachers instead of a pension,
though they usually had very little knowledge themselves and could
only live by carrying on some trade besides teaching. When he later
acquired Polish territories, where schools were entirely lacking and
the people utterly ignorant and miserable, he had a further reason
to have schools built. Yet he was never interested enough as to provide sufficient amounts of money for building schools, where
needed, and training an adequate number of real teachers. This
money could only have been raised by cutting down expenses for
the army, and this was utterly opposed to his general policy. He
would even have liked to save the moderate educational expenses
which he had, by leaving the instruction of the people to the Church
—a strange idea for a philosopher imbued with the greatest contempt for religion and the clergy. But the ecclesiastical department
of the government prevented this.

In spite of these dispositions of the king, progressive elements
were not lacking among the officials of the government who had to
do with education, especially members of the Consistory and
practical pedagogues. Their leaders were Protestant clergymen
inspired by pietism, but the tradition of humanism and the influence
of Rousseau and Basedow contributed to their plans and their zeal
as well. J. J. Hecker, a clergyman and headmaster of a technical
school, in 1763 elaborated a reform scheme for the evangelical
schools, which the king approved and decreed. It was based on the

edict of King Frederick William I of 1717, with its principle of
compulsory education for all children from 5 to 13 or 14 years. The
realization of the principle depended on the number of schools and
teachers available and on their quality, and Hecker was indefatigable in proposing helpful measures. In Silesia, a similar decree was
issued for the Catholic schools in 1765, worked out by Abbot J.
Felbiger.

The personal interest of the king showed variations. He had
signed Hecker's scheme, but it was doubtful whether he had read
it,[21] because he later showed himself ignorant of essential clauses. In
1771, the Church department in the government received a new
head, the minister Baron Zedlitz, who was an enthusiastic school
reformer and advocate of a classical education. The idea of lifting
the masses of the people to a higher intellectual level had many supporters and many enemies. Not a few squires disliked it, especially
if they themselves were illiterate. But there were noblemen inspired
by humanitarian ideas also, who wished to help the people and
founded model schools for them. Prominent figures among them
were Friedrich Eberhard von Rochow and Counsellor Scheffner.
They both soon found that most peasants were hostile to the idea of
instructing their children, who, they said, would do better helping
their parents by working in the fields. As Buesching wrote, the
greatest obstacle to the spreading of education was that the peasants
became constantly poorer and could not let their children have
sufficient time for learning.

The king's own opinion was expressed in a decree of 1779,
addressed to Zedlitz. He wished children to learn religion and morals
in order to prevent them from becoming thieves and murderers.
Besides, in the country it was enough if the children learned a little
reading and writing. If they knew much, they would run to the
towns and want to become secretaries and what not. The minister
himself was convinced that primarily obedience must be inculcated
in the common man, and that he should not receive too much
philosophy or enlightenment. When Professor Sulzer tried to convince the king that Rousseau and Basedow were right in teaching
the fundamental goodness of human nature, he replied: 'Alas, you
don't know the accursed race to which we belong sufficiently well'.

The opinions expressed by the king on questions of higher educa-

[21] Cf. F. Vollmer, *Die preuss. Volksschule unter Friedrich d. Gr.*, 1918. This
author shows how little interest the king took in the education of the people.
Koser, III, p. 467, is of the opposite opinion.

K*

tion often show an astounding lack of understanding.[22] If he sometimes laid stress on the study of Latin and Greek, he merely echoed
what Zedlitz had told him on the educational value of these
languages. He himself knew nothing of them, and his ample reading
of French translations of ancient writers does not seem to have
resulted in a real understanding of Greek cultural life. His attitude
to questions of science and learning was, of course, partly influenced
by his own knowledge of them, though he also asked experts for
advice, which, however, was not always accepted. In this respect,
the diary of Lucchesini, who in his later years was his confidant and
regular companion at table, are very informative. In his table talk
Frederick was against learning languages because it was better to
read translations. This opinion was probably influenced by the fact
that he himself had a very restricted knowledge of languages. Even
his French letters, if not corrected, showed grave faults, and his
German was dreadful. What a difference from the knowledge of
languages, also of the German tongue, on the part of the Habsburgs!
Frederick's understanding of the ancient culture is illustrated by the
fact that he preferred the contemporary French writers to the Greek
and Roman ones, and, in particular, put Voltaire's 'Henriade' above
Homer, and disliked Plato, Horace and Aristophanes. Lucchesini also
noted that the king knew little or nothing of natural science,
mathematics, geometry, physics, astronomy, the geography of
Asia, etc. But he often sought to palliate his ignorance by declaring
that this or that science was of no value, or that everything know-
able had already been discovered, or by disparaging great scholars
of whose merit he had no idea. When once a zoologist asked him
to procure him some information about a rare species of fish found
in one of his provinces for a book he was writing, he refused, saying
that everything worthwhile was already known about fish and
nobody would therefore buy the book. Yet, influenced by Fredersdorf, he seems to have shared some of the astrological superstition of
the time. The king had a particularly bad opinion of the medical
profession and dabbled much in medicine himself. He had a predilection for fat and spiced dishes, which were very harmful for

[22] Cf. Koser on the king's attitude to the universities (in his *Aufsaetzen und
Vortraegen*, 1921). He mentions that Frederick particularly despised economic
science, theology and public law. A theologian appeared to him as 'an
animal without reason'. In his *History of my time*, 1746, he blamed the
custom that young nobles had theologians or lawyers as tutors who sometimes were sons of tailors or cobblers and therefore imbued with the gross
vulgarity (bassesse grossière) of their descent. He also regretted that noble
students read public law instead of poetry and fiction (belle littérature). In
1748 and 1788 he decreed that Prussian subjects must only study at Prussian
universities.

his health. When his doctor once warned him against eating them, he dismissed him in an ignominious way.

THE BERLIN ACADEMY

The king from the beginning cherished the plan of founding an Academy which was to become the greatest centre of science and letters and the most powerful factor for propagating the spirit of enlightenment in the higher classes. A number of highly cultured aristocrats and statesmen had already formed such a circle, and it was then fused with the old Academy, which had much declined under Frederick's father. The king tried to engage Wolff, but the latter was sceptical and preferred to teach at the University of Halle. He then secured the collaboration of the great French physicist Maupertuis, who became President, and obtained the services of the most prominent scholars of Europe as corresponding members. Frederick prescribed that the Academy should publish all its papers in French and wrote a number of articles himself, though he never appeared in the Academy. The most important scientific contributions came, however, from German and Swiss scholars and were translated into French.

The Berlin Academy enjoyed full freedom in scientific matters, while that of Paris was restricted by regard for the Court and the Church. In Paris, an investigation could only be published when two doctors of theology had approved it, and every session of the Academy closed with a prayer for the king. Frederick and Voltaire had thought of using the Berlin Academy as an instrument also for undermining the Church. But the members were mostly not as hostile to religion as to indulge in such activities. The scientific research done was very important, especially in the natural sciences and mathematics. After Maupertuis' death the Swiss, Euler, directed the work,[23] and more Germans were admitted, among them Lessing, who was equally great as a scholar and as a poet. But the king disapproved of this, did not confirm Lessing's election and henceforth appointed new members himself. He tried to win the famous mathematician d'Alembert as President, who did not accept since he did not wish to leave Paris, but became the main adviser of the king in all scientific matters. Frederick became Vice-President and from 1764 onwards ruled the Academy autocratically, though always consulting d'Alembert. Sometimes he appointed members

[23] Euler was one of the greatest mathematicians. He worked 25 years in the service of the Academy and thereby lost his eye-sight. But Frederick treated him with ingratitude all the same.

who were unworthy of this honour. In the following twenty-two years, till Frederick's death, almost no Germans were appointed, and when the Academy proposed the excellent Jewish scholar Mendelssohn, he was turn down by the king. At the time of his death only five Germans were members. Herder won prize contests of the Academy three times, but did not become a member since he was too proud to apply to the king for it. Friends of Winckelmann, the greatest living authority on ancient art, tried to induce the king to appoint him director of his library and his collection of antiques. Frederick was almost won over, but when a salary of 2,000 Talers was suggested he decided : 'One thousand are enough for a German'. It aroused general surprise that the post went to a hitherto unknown French Benedictine, A. J. de Pernety. Later it became known that the king had made a mistake and taken him for his uncle of the same name, who had written a book. The man whom he had appointed was not at all fitted for the post, and was in addition very superstitious.

After d'Alembert's death Frederick chose Condorcet as his chief adviser. Both were also successively secretaries of the French Academy, so that the Academies of Paris and Berlin were actually under the same guidance. The king's attitude to the various branches of learning, however, went through different stages. Theology, naturally, was superstition to him, medicine was only humbug and jurisprudence was also suspect. In the end he looked very sceptically on the natural sciences too, except as far as they served practical purposes. His main interest became the education of man to a morality founded on enlightened self-interest.

GERMAN LITERATURE

Frederick's attitude to German intellectual achievements is also shown by his famous essay on German literature. It discusses the backwardness of the Germans in literary taste in comparison with other nations, especially the French, but ends with the hope that this will gradually become better owing to nascent national ambition, and said that German literature had a great future. The king saw the main reason for the low level of the fine arts in Germany in the fact that the German language had never been unified, subjected to firm rules and refined. Instead of one cultivated language, every province had its separate half-barbaric dialect, which was often unintelligible in other parts. In his view the superiority of French was largely due to the care bestowed upon it by French kings and statesmen. But Frederick in this point did not imitate the French

model. His Academy did nothing to refine the German language or
to stimulate German literature. The king's essay also shows that he
himself had no knowledge and understanding of German literary
development, which in this very period entered its greatest epoch.
His mind was completely dominated by the rules of French classicism, which even made him blind to the merits of those French
writers who did not belong to this school. For Rabelais and Mon-
taigne, therefore, he had only the greatest contempt, while inferior
classicists received high praise. He expressed disgust at the enthusiasm of the German public for the 'abominable plays of Shakespeare', those ridiculous farces, 'worthy of a Canadian savage', and
he calls Goethe's 'Goetz' 'an awful imitation of the bad English
plays' composed of 'tasteless platitudes'.

German literature, philosophy and learning at that time showed
a galaxy of illustrious names. But Frederick had no idea of this
flowering of the spirit, and when someone tried to interest him in
reading a German poet, he refused. Nevertheless his feeling of
intellectual superiority was so great that in his essay he undertook
to teach the German poets and scholars what they must do to reach
greatness. In Vienna, Joseph II showed much more understanding
for them, and though he mainly read the Italian poets he wrote
German well and did much for German literature, particularly by
means of the theatre. When Frederick met Gottsched, he told him:
'I have read no German book since my youth. I speak German like
a coachman, and now I am an old fellow of 56 years and have no
more time for it.' He reached an age of 74.

It was obviously not the lack of time or opportunities that prevented the king from gaining knowledge of German achievements,
but the fact that the spirit of the great thinkers and writers of his
age was alien and opposed to the fundamental tendencies of his
mind. Frederick's admirers point out that the sense of duty, which
he implanted in the Prussian mind, was the realization of Kant's
'Categorical Imperative'. Actually Frederick's materialism and
eudaemonism are the very opposite of Kant's philosophy. The King
regarded both human nature and the state as machines operated by
egoism, fear and illusions. He did not believe in moral forces in the
human soul, but conceived morality merely as well-understood self-
interest. He certainly wanted to improve the lot of his subjects and
devoted much time and energy to protecting them against unlawful
oppression and to furthering their interests. But this sprang less from
love of his fellow men, whom he despised, than from the conviction
that a reign of law and contented subjects were absolutely necessary
for making Prussia a powerful and rich state. His sense of duty was

actually the outcome of his striving for the glory of being the founder of such a state. Duty implies the idea of responsibility. But to whom was the king responsible? His Deism denied a God interested in the course of human affairs. A duty to the people, springing from the original pact of submission? If compared with the king's actual policy, this appears as a very poor phrase which the king would certainly not take seriously. He has pointed out his sense of duty towards the state, but this state was merely a machine in which the subjects were passive parts operating according to the plan of its builder. Can the builder of a machine have duties to it? Kant, in particular, has postulated that a human being must never be used merely as a means to an end and that a moral rule must be valid for all. This excludes both the ideas of human machines or a machine state, and that of a super-man above ordinary morality. No sophistry can reconcile Kant's principles with most of Frederick's philosophy and policy. Yet there were points in which Kant highly appreciated Frederick's work, namely the granting of freedom of thought and the press, and the maintenance of internal peace and justice. This judgment, however, does not refer to a complete freedom of the press, which did not by any means exist. Kant did not think of freedom for political journalists or soap-box orators, but of that for scholars and serious writers on great questions, such as philosophy and religion. He was convinced that if one could speak freely on these problems, the spreading of enlightenment over all branches of civilization could no longer be stopped, and that the principles of government could then not be excluded from free discussion and practical transformation either.

Kant has further laid down an opinion which was a shattering blow for Frederick's system. He said that it was not to be expected that kings would think like philosophers or that the latter should become kings. But more than that: it was even not desirable, since the possession of the power in a state must unavoidably corrupt the free judgment of reason.

In literary questions, too, the great German writers of the epoch did not see eye to eye with Frederick. The type of intellectualism which inspired him and his circle implied blindness to their aspirations. The king only knew of literature what his French companions had brought to his notice. That they had no understanding for the new German poets is not surprising. When Sulzer tried to interest Voltaire in Klopstock's 'Messiah' he received the characteristic answer that a second Messiah was not necessary since even the work of the first one was not read by anybody. The German poets, moreover, were opposed to the spirit reigning in French literature, while they enthused for Homer, Ossian, Shakespeare and the German past, and thus formed the vanguard of Romanticism. All these ideals were alien to Frederick. He despised Shakespeare, and the Nibelungen Saga seemed to him not worth being unearthed from the dust of centuries. He only appreciated clarity of reason, firmness of will, polished form, sparkling wit, irreverence of the past; he scorned everything mysterious and sentimental and disbelieved in natural goodness and probity. The idea which the Romanticists formed of a German character rooted in the traditions of their past, in particular that of 'Gemuet', would have appeared ridiculous to the king. Goethe rightly found that those things which had made Frederick so efficient, imposing and fascinating, he had learned from the French.

In spite of this attitude of the king it has often been asserted that he had given the impetus to the glorious unfolding of German classical poetry. Utterances by Goethe are quoted as proof. But these were probably not meant in the sense ascribed to them.[24] Moreover, they are open to critical objections. An exposition of the real reasons for that development would require an analysis of the literary and social history of the age, not merely in Germany, which is impossible in this place. A few observations, however, will be made later.

THE IMPRESSION MADE BY FREDERICK'S PERSONALITY ON HIS TIME

The impression which Frederick made on the public mind of all nations depended to a great extent not on an objective appreciation of his policy, but on the fascination exercised by his personality. Many observers pointed out that his character was composed of surprising contrasts, that it defied a definite classification and remained a riddle. His temper was nervous and restless and was often still more exasperated by the excessive drinking of coffee, by painful illnesses and insomnia. Frederick could fascinate visitors by the greatest kindness, generosity and fairness, he often admitted that his enemies had a good case also, or that his own successes were largely due to good luck. But he could also be hard, jealous and ungrateful, even to men to whom he owed much. He liked to show off his intellectual powers, to dominate the conversation, to jeer at people of other opinions, and to humiliate persons who had given him no cause. His particular pleasure was to hold up Christian beliefs to mockery, even before people who were much hurt by

[24] Cf. W. Mommsen, politische Anschauungen Goethe's p. 78, and F. Mehring, Lessing Legende.

this. It was mostly done in a witty and original way, but often violated justified emotions and good taste.[25] When Lisbon was destroyed by an earthquake (1755) with great loss of life, Maria Theresa prohibited all carnival festivities. But Frederick scoffed at the Empress, saying it was better to die in a domino, as worn at masquerades, than under the crucifix.

Frederick's court differed from most others by the lack of pompous ceremonies and gorgeous festivities. There were neither highborn courtiers to enhance the splendour, nor favourites pulling strings, nor mistresses dabbling in politics. The language of the court was French. Voltaire once wrote home that he had found Paris in Potsdam; only French was spoken and German was merely for the soldiers and the stables. The king's brother Henry once advised a nobleman to learn French, since surely he did not want to be taken for a German beast. The king's recreations were writing verses, history, satires, and papers on many subjects, playing the flute, composing and hearing music, and in sparkling conversation. He had a number of highly cultured companions, mainly Frenchmen and Italians, who lived with him, talked with him about literary, scientific or artistic subjects, but had no political influence. In this circle the 'bel esprit' reigned, and Voltaire was its most brilliant star. With short interruptions he was in lifelong contact with Frederick, either personally or by correspondence. Though each knew the dark sides of the other's character and they sometimes became estranged, they soon became friends again. Voltaire was the most effective herald of Frederick's greatness, but also spread malicious and poisonous stories about him. At certain times the king described Voltaire's character with the greatest contempt in his letters.

The king's fame among the intellectuals of all countries was enhanced by the fact that he gave asylum to many freethinkers, who had either had to flee their homeland or at least did not feel secure there. Voltaire himself believed that he could not write freely in France on certain subjects, and his collected works had to be printed in Germany and smuggled into France. When he died the clergy denied him a decent burial, but Frederick praised his memory in a lecture held in the Academy. For some time, one of the king's companions was Julien Offray de la Mettrie, a physician and witty writer, who by his denial of any morality had made himself impossible in every country. When he died of indulging too much in the pleasure of the table, Frederick wrote a speech of commemoration which was read to the Academy. His close relations to d'Alembert

[25] Cf. Thiebault, I, pp. 28, 36, 39, etc.

have already been mentioned. The latter thought of transferring the publication of the Encyclopédie to Berlin when the effect the first two volumes had in high circles seemed to make it dangerous in Paris. The King once sent him his portrait, and d'Alembert answered: 'I shall perpetually bear it with me and at night I will hang it up at the head of my bed, where believers place their crucifix and their stoup of holy water'. The other editor of the Encyclopédie, Diderot, also extolled Frederick's greatness in the article on Prussia in this work. But their political opinions differed too much to allow much sympathy between them. Rousseau, too, censored Frederick very severely. Yet when he was persecuted by the clergy in France and Switzerland, he fled to the then Prussian possession of Neufchâtel and put himself under the king's protection.

An interesting problem arises if we compare Frederick's achievements with his fame. It will not, of course, be denied that he was a great man according to the generally accepted standards. But his fame was so immense in so wide a part of the world, that to many contemporaries he seemed to outshine all the other kings living, or even those of all times. Johannes Mueller was a Swiss, an ardent follower of Rousseau and an historian of very great knowledge, who was widely regarded as the greatest historian of the time. His enthusiasm for Frederick was so great that he declared the king had put the rest of history in the shade, except Caesar; but the latter had suppressed liberty, while Frederick had strengthened it, in the Empire and in Europe. On the whole the king's glorification was less marked in Germany than in other countries. Most of all it flourished in France, but during the Seven Years' War England was also seized by the greatest enthusiasm for 'the defender of Protestantism and liberty'—though Frederick regarded the whole Christian religion as an absurd Oriental fairy tale, as he often declared, and liberty is not the principle which we should associate with his name. In England, however, this enthusiasm later subsided and largely gave way to aversion. Nor can his popularity have mainly been the result of Frederick's propaganda, since it was also great in countries where he could hardly exercise influence on public opinion. In 1740 already Voltaire assured the king: 'The French are all Prussians', and d'Alembert wrote 30 years later: 'The philosophers and men of letters, and in particular those of the French nation, have long regarded you as their leader and model' and on another occasion he wrote him that he was as universally admired as perhaps never a monarch before. Even in the Seven Years' War, during which France and Prussia officially were enemies, French public opinion soon saw its idol in Frederick again. In Switzerland Sulzer wrote: 'The whole of Protestant Switzerland is more Prussian than the Prussians themselves . . . there are many people here who fall sick with anger when matters go not as well for the king as they wish'. In Italy, King Charles Emanuel III of Sardinia regarded Frederick as the greatest hero and statesman since the beginning of the world. The majority of the Romans were on his side, and even several Popes, such as Benedict XIV and Clement XIV, expressed great admiration for the king, who in his Political Testament of 1752, wrote that Catholicism was the most ridiculous of all religions. Venice was split into two parties, the friends and the enemies of Frederick, who showed the fiercest hatred of each other. The friends, however, were stronger and they raised the slogan: 'Whoever is not a good Prussian is not a good Venetian'. Further examples could be adduced from the Scandinavian countries, from Spain, Turkey and from German states.[26] In 1780 a Prussian merchant-skipper, J. Nettelbeck, saw some wax-works in Portugal, in which the affair of the miller Arnold was illustrated, glorifying Frederick's justice. When he disclosed that he was a Prussian he became the object of great ovations by the people, who cheered him and his great king endlessly. A Dutch captain, Klock, whose ship carried the Prussian flag, was shipwrecked on the coast of Morocco and feared that he would be sold as a slave. But the Prussian flag induced the Emperor Muley Ismael to express his greatest admiration for King Frederick and to release Klock with rich gifts. The captain made a sworn statement of this event before a court in Amsterdam. Archenholtz assures us that Frederick's name was pronounced with veneration even in India and China.

In Germany, too, the king was celebrated by many writers of minor stature, though it must not be overlooked that they were mostly the king's subjects or in his service. Others had some special reason. When Frederick formed the League of Princes to defend the independence of the princes against the Emperor, this naturally aroused patriotic feelings in many small 'fatherlands', and he was praised as the protector of their liberty. Among South Germans, the best-known writer who was full of enthusiasm for Frederick was the Swabian poet D. Schubart. But the great German poets and scholars of the time mostly regarded the king with mixed feelings. Goethe, in particular, admired his demonic personality, like those of Peter I and Napoleon, but his policy left him indifferent and often

---

[26] The examples quoted are taken from Volz' excellent work *Friedrich d. Gr. im Spiegel seiner Zeit*, where many others, too, are given.

aroused his aversion.[27] Lessing, too, considered Frederick a great man, but judged his policy with bitter sarcasm. Herder long detested the king and his work, but when after his death his correspondence was published he received a new impression of the king's personality. He now felt pity for him as a king whose noble intentions had been perverted by political necessity, and admired his zeal in improving the living conditions of the people. Klopstock first celebrated Frederick in an ode, but when his hope of gaining the king's favour failed and it became obvious that the King despised German poetry, his attitude changed. Winckelmann has condemned Frederick in the sharpest possible words as a tyrant, butcher of men, and so on. More polite was Wieland who wrote: 'King Frederick surely is a great man, but God save us from the good fortune of living under his truncheon or sceptre'. One of the foremost publicists of the time, who was also a statesman, F. K. Moser, judged him very critically. He also remarked that the Germans would one day say of Frederick what Tacitus had said of Caesar: 'It would have been better if he had never been born, or if he had never died'. It was suggested to Schiller that he should write an epic on Frederick, but he declined on the ground that he could not love the king's character. His opinion of Frederick's military State was expressed in an essay on Lycurgus' legislation: Schiller described the institutions of Sparta and came to the conclusion that such a state was utterly reprehensible and that nothing could be more unfortunate than if all states would follow this model.

THE ATTITUDE OF THE PRUSSIAN AND GERMAN PEOPLE

It was not primarily German or Prussian public opinion which elevated Frederick to the greatest of all kings, though many of his subjects, and also many other Germans, felt more or less flattered when such views spread over the world. In the beginning the king's policy had little support, even in the inner circle of his statesmen and generals. The people were bewildered, but the mechanism of the state left them no choice. G. S. Roetger, a distinguished pedagogue and great admirer of the king, says in his memoirs that in the first half of the reign he was much less esteemed and loved by his subjects than was later assumed. The burghers and peasants did not

[27] Koser (vol. 3, p. 548) quotes unfinished verses by Goethe to a ruler whose name is not given, but which are widely regarded as his homage to Frederick. W. Mommsen (p. 76) finds this doubtful and thinks that they might more probably refer to Joseph II.

see at all why his wars and the high taxes caused by them were necessary. The clergy and the lawyers shook their heads. The soldiers alone were proud of the victories, yet this did not exclude a hidden aversion to war. Count Lehndorf reports that General von Winterfeldt was unpopular in the army because he was considered an instigator of the Seven Years' War and an opponent to making peace. K. L. von Knebel, known as Goethe's friend, said that as a Prussian officer he had grown up in gloomy admiration and fear of Frederick the Great, bowing to his superior might and insight, but the king, he says, was not loved. A very similar opinion was expressed by G. H. von Berenhorst, who was on the king's personal staff and knew him intimately. In the second half of the Seven Years' War, he relates, Frederick was neither loved nor esteemed, nor even feared by the officers of his entourage. They nicknamed him the 'gravedigger', and in their conversations always referred to him as 'the Digger'. Berenhorst later became a great hater of war and militarism. The foremost Prussian historian of Frederick's time, W. Gercken, wrote on April 15, 1780 : 'The constant enlargement of the army renders us all slaves and beggars. I am easily able to predict the end : eventually a great revolution will give the state another form.' This was written nine years before the French revolution and six years before Frederick's death.

There were certainly times at which a great many Prussians and other Germans hailed the king with enthusiasm. But this soon changed again, particularly under the influence of the financial burdens which the king laid on his people. We have already noted how this affected the feelings of the people towards the king.

The results of Frederick's reign of nearly half a century could satisfy only those who appreciated military prestige more than anything else, or who belonged to the privileged class of the landed nobility, and even among the latter there were many who were very critical of Frederick's system. The great mass of the peasants had certainly no reason to feel satisfied, nor the majority of traders, who saw that their interests were sacrificed to foreign adventurers. The middle class, had in the king's view, no sense of honour and duty. The backbone of the Prussian state was its class of judges and administrative officials, of whom very many were excellently trained, were inspired by justice, and did their best for the common weal. Yet the king very frequently expressed the opinion that they were all thieves and cheats, and in many cases treated them in the rudest way.[28] According to him scholars and men of letters were not worth much if they were not French; the clergy were swindlers or

[28] Cf. p. 287, 290, 293, 442 of this book; further Koser III, p. 526.

simpletons, the lawyers pettifoggers and the physicians charlatans. These opinions of the king were no secret, and it is improbable that the groups concerned felt very pleased about them.

Farther-looking people also had grave doubts whether the king's autocratic régime could lay the stable foundations of a prosperous community. There were many who realized that his personal despotism might have disastrous consequences—for who would be able to run the enormous state-machine after the king's death? Frederick himself seems to have been rather pessimistic regarding the future of his state. Four years before his death he wrote 'Considerations on the Political State of Europe', which ended on a very sombre note. He feared that his successor, the later Frederick William II, would let things go to rack and ruin and that in thirty years' time Prussia and the Hohenzollerns would no longer count, but that the Emperor Joseph would have swallowed every rival power and would have made Germany an absolute monarchy like France. He could not foresee that Joseph would die a few years after him and that his system would by then have largely collapsed. Frederick's opinion is, however, interesting because he assumes, however unwillingly, that Germany was capable of unification by an energetic emperor. The usual defence of Frederick's policy of preventing such a development and weakening the imperial power is that the Empire was merely a rotting corpse and that he was right in destroying it in order to make way for a new Empire under Prussia's domination though Frederick himself had harboured no such plans. Whether Joseph, had he lived longer, would have been able to satisfy the yearning for one German fatherland, which Herder expressed in a fine poem addressed to him, is a matter of speculation into which we need not enter.

When the old king died a feeling of relief pervaded a wide section of the people. Count Mirabeau, then staying in Berlin on a secret mission from the French government,[29] later wrote : 'I still shudder and am roused to indignation by the spectacle which Berlin offered to my amazed eyes on the day of the death of the hero who had struck the world dumb with astonishment or had made it voice its admiration. Everybody was sombre, but nobody sad; everyone was serious, but without showing any affliction. No regret, no sigh, no word of praise! This then is the end of so many victorious battles, so much glory, of a reign of almost half a century filled with

[29] Mirabeau related that it was apprehended in France that Austria might create a united Germany which France would not be able to tolerate. The best means of preventing this was an alliance between France and Prussia. It is significant that the same apprehension was felt in France as Frederick had expressed in the memorandum just mentioned.

marvels. One felt sick of it, even to the extent of hating these people. . . .'

The Russian diplomat Count Rumjanzow reported to his government from Berlin that the news of the king's death had not made the stir which one would have expected. In the town there was no agitation and the regret seemed to be extremely small. The indifference of the troops appeared to the diplomat particularly surprising. On the other hand H. von Boyen, who later became a famous Prussian general, relates that the news aroused general stupefaction, hard men wept like children and that even the opposition to the king who used to blame him anxiously asked what would be the consequences of his death. According to Mirabeau two clergymen in Stettin declared from the pulpit that the devil had fetched the king. A distinguished modern historian and admirer of Frederick, Professor Hans Prutz, says in his History of Prussia that wide sections of the people had silently longed for a change in the rulership and that Frederick's end was therefore almost joyfully welcomed, as a release.[30]

THE VERDICT OF HISTORY

Twenty years after Frederick's death the battle of Jena and Auerstaedt cast the final judgment on his system. The core of his policy was the hostility towards Austria, which bred an irreconcilable antagonism between the two great powers. The result was that both were defeated by Napoleon and that the Empire collapsed and had to be dissolved. Prussia was for many years subjected to French domination and exploitation and the German princes became vassals of Napoleon and had to supply him with large contingents of troops in order to fight for his ambition of becoming the Emperor of Europe or the World. The men who then worked for, and achieved, the restoration of Prussia and Germany, in particular Baron vom Stein, did not follow Frederick's example. They created a new Prussia whose spirit was very different from that of Frederick and who for a long time played a rightfully much admired cultural rôle. Yet this Prussia too could not overcome the fateful evil of German particularism and other legacies of the past.

In anticipation it may be remarked that Frederick's policy in some respects initiated a development fatal to the German people, in particular the rise of Russia to the position of the strongest power in Europe. Frederick himself had foreseen it with anxiety. But this did not by any means induce him to seek a real reconciliation with

[30] Cf. also L. Geiger, *Berlin, Geschichte des geistigen Lebens*, vol. I, p. 312.

Austria. On the contrary he continued until the last to aggravate the antagonism. Poland, who might perhaps have been integrated into a common defensive front against Russia, was destroyed. The possibility that Austria might liberate the Balkan peoples from the Turkish yoke and win parts of them for herself before Russia had become too powerful, was frustrated. This was the starting point of the rise of Russia's might and of Panslavism. Its results to-day form not only Germany's fate but also the greatest menace to all free nations in the world.

Russia's ascent was the natural consequence of the mortal enmity between Prussia and Austria which was Frederick's work. Each of the two states was compelled to do everything to win Russia's favour and alliance. Austria temporarily succeeded in outstripping Prussia, but this cost her very dear.

A further disastrous heritage of Frederick's policy was the claim of the army and of military considerations to predominance in the state. Prussia was certainly not the only power cultivating militarism, and Prussian militarism was not at all times a menace to peace. But it cannot be denied that, with other factors, it played a most disastrous part in bringing about the outbreak of the First Great War of 1914. At that time the idea was widely spread in Germany that she was encircled by enemies and most influential men, in particular Emperor William, asked themselves: What would Frederick the Great have done in such circumstances? They looked back to the situation before the Seven Years' War. Frederick had then decided for war and had marched into neutral Saxony in order to squeeze it to the utmost. The German General Staff of 1914 marched into neutral Belgium in order to strike at France's heart— Paris. This was not only a crime against the law of nations but was also the greatest possible error from a diplomatic and strategic point of view. A defensive war against the Pan-Slav menace in the East could certainly have been won by Germany and Austria. Russia, indeed, was defeated in spite of all the help given by her allies. But the invasion of Belgium implied an aggressive war against the West and made the intervention of Great Britain, America and other powers unavoidable. Without this invasion it would certainly not have happened.

None of the peoples involved in this war were, as a whole, guilty of the catastrophe. But those who had cultivated the legend of Frederick the Great and had praised him as a model had prepared the ground for it. Yet the question remains open whether Frederick himself in similar circumstances would have gone to war.

Excursus to page 291

CAPITAL PUNISHMENT IN THE EIGHTEENTH CENTURY

According to Frederick's II letter of October 11, 1777 to Voltaire the average number of convicts executed was from 14 to 15 a year. Professor Eberhardt Schmidt has found this in agreement with the figures for 1775 to 1778 in the Archives in Berlin. According to Lucchesini's diaries, the king stated in 1783 that the annual number was about 17. The total population of his realm was according to the census of 1786 5,277,281. If we assume that the annual average of executions was 16 in the last decade of the king's reign, these figures would work out at 3 cases of capital punishment per one million of the population.

For England, the first data were published in the British Parliamentary Papers, XVII, 1819, and the figures given there for the eighteenth century refer only to London and Middlesex. In the seven years 1776 to 1782, which roughly correspond to the period, to which the Prussian figures refer, the annual average number of the capital convictions was 95, and that of the actual executions 39. A Census was first taken in 1801, and the population of London including Middlesex etc. was then 865,628.[31] The Census Commissioners, further, made an estimate of the total population of England and Wales, based on the number of baptism, for 1780, and the share of London etc. in the number of houses taxed was 10.4%.[32] We can, therefore, estimate the population of London for 1780-81, and the number of annual executions per one million of the population works out at 47, or 15.5 times more than in Prussia.

These statistics correspond to the number of crimes which were liable to the death penalty. Professor L. Radzinowicz says in his admirable work on the History of the English Criminal Law from 1750-1948 that in old times the number of crimes punishable by death was low in England but that a great increase occurred in the eighteenth century. As late as 1668 it amounted to about 50 offences only, in 1765 Blackstone put it at 160, in 1786 Romilly observed it had since greatly increased, and in 1819 Buxton found it had risen to 223. Even in the nineteenth century it sometimes happened that children were sentenced to death for a trifle, for example in 1833 a boy of nine for stealing some printer's colours worth 2 pence. In 1814 five children between 8 and 12 years were convicted to death,

[31] Cf. Thomas Pennant, Some Account of London, 5th ed. 1813, p. 642.
[32] Cf. G. R. Porter, The Progress of the Nation, 1847, p. 25, and G. Chalmers, An Estimate of the Comparative Strength of Great Britain etc., 1794, p. 216.

and in the same year a boy of 14 was hanged at Newport for stealing.

In France conditions were unspeakably cruel. At the time of the outbreak of the revolution there were 115 crimes punishable by death. Cf. E. Hertz, Voltaire und die franzoesische Strafrechtspflege im 18. Jahrhundert. Even Napoleon's Code of 1810 was written in blood.

In Prussia Frederick II abolished the death penalty for theft in 1743, except if connected with the attempt to murder. Later it was restricted to murder, poisoning, highway robbery, killing of a child, arson, and inducing a soldier to desert.

The Austrian Code of 1787 abolished the death penalty, except for the leaders of a rebellion under martial law. The Code of 1803 restored capital punishment for high treason, murder, robbery with manslaughter, arson, and the gravest cases of falsifying banknotes, but convicts for high treason and falsification were pardoned almost always, as statistics show.

17

MARIA THERESA, JOSEPH II, THEIR PERSONALITY, THOUGHT AND WORK

MARIA THERESA'S PERSONALITY AND PRINCIPLES

MARIA THERESA entered the political scene imbued with rather conservative opinions, a distrust of innovations and a bias in favour of existing conditions. Before she became ruler she had had no instruction in politics. But she had strong religious and moral convictions and the belief that their observance was also the best policy. The aggressions of the King of Prussia and others, however, at once forced her to plan great reforms to prevent total collapse. The Empress later wrote a secret memorandum pointing out that the main cause of the initial weakness of the state was the great power of the nobles, who put their particular interests above those of the community. They dominated both the assemblies of the Estates in the territories and the central government. The taxes needed for defence were voted and collected by the Estates who also managed the returns, recruited troops, bought the supplies etc. This system was wasteful and corrupt. The nobles in the Vienna ministries too were often influenced more by the interest of the territories in which they possessed extensive lands than by the safety of the whole state. The poor peasants alone had to pay the taxes voted by the Estates.

It was in the vital interest of the State to create a centralized administration, a better military and financial system and a fairer distribution of the burdens of defence. Maria Theresa declared in her memorandum that it was not the longing for more power and glory which made these aims paramount, but the striving to safeguard the existence of the state against the rapacity of many foreign powers. She was convinced that the aims of government were justice and the welfare of the people, which were higher than glory or honour. If her successors should ever disregard these aims, she wrote, it would be a thousand times preferable that a foreigner or even an enemy who cared more for the people should become the ruler. If the rights of the Estates were as well founded as they asserted, and if their administration had shown more justice than the monarchical one, she would not have hesitated to submit her authority completely to theirs, since the happiness of her peoples had to have precedence over that of her house.

The repulse of Frederick's aggression was to Maria Theresa not merely a struggle for power but a fight for the reign of justice in the world. She wrote that if she had not always been pregnant nothing would have prevented her from going to the front herself to fight the perfidious enemy. Frederick's warfare embittered her because of its ruthlessness also. When he forced subjects of hers, in the territories occupied by him, to serve in his army, the War Ministry proposed retaliating by taking the same measure against Prussian subjects, but Maria Theresa vetoed this.[1] She wrote to Field-marshal Count Khevenhueller that she did not intend to exercise such atrocities against innocent subjects since her inherited Austrian mildness prohibited it. The traditional Austrian strategy was defensive and sparing of the lives of the troops and the people. The Austrian recruiting officers too had a good reputation in comparison with the Prussian. Frederick II wrote in his history of his wars that on various occasions the exaggerated caution of the Austrian generals prevented their complete victory. It was, of course, not always possible to realize humanitarian principles in a great war. When Frederick started his aggressive wars Austria was in the greatest need of troops and accepted the offer of the officers Menzel and Baron von der Trenck to raise Free Corps at their own expense. These were recruited among the warlike Slavs on the Turkish border, who mainly joined to make booty. They were a wild people, though not quite as savage as the Red Indians fighting on the French and English side in North America. The Austrian generals tried to check them. Baron von der Trenck, who from the military point of view had shown the greatest bravery and had fought with much success was put before a court martial because of rape and violence

[1] Maria Theresa also rejected any compulsory levy of troops from the Austrian people since it appeared to her as enslavement. Frederick made large use of it even in foreign territories which he invaded for this purpose. Later necessity compelled also the Austrian government to employ a very limited conscription. Cf. M. Lehmann, *Friedrich der Grosse und der Ursprung des siebenjaehrigen Krieges*, 1894, p. 11.

in warfare and was sentenced to death. A second court martial changed this to life imprisonment.

In Prussia the military possessed a higher rank than the civilian authorities and were not subject to them. In Austria this was not so, except in strictly military matters, as the following case shows. In 1760, Austrian and Russian troops occupied Berlin, and General Count Esterhazi took a few objects belonging to King Frederick II for himself and sent them to Vienna. But the Austrian customs became aware of this and confiscated the booty, which had not been declared to their officers. The general appealed to the grace of Maria Theresa. The Financial Council (Bancorat) proposed that this application should be refused. The matter was laid before the State Council. Here Field-marshal Count Daun, the highest ranking commander, supported the proposal of rejecting Esterhazi's appeal. It was necessary, he said, to set an example to show that the military were not exempt from declaring booty to the customs. The Chancellor, Count Kaunitz, moreover, considered the appropriation of the objects contrary to international law and custom and moved that they should be returned to King Frederick. The Empress decided in this sense. It is also noteworthy that when the Vienna cabinet received information of a plot to murder King Frederick they informed him of it, regarding it as inadmissible to participate in a crime, even against their greatest enemy.

In later years Maria Theresa became ever more averse to any war, and in 1778 she wrote to General Count Lascy that she would prefer her countries to form only a second-rate power to making her people unhappy by waging war. The striving of Joseph for aggrandisement was a torture to her and she condemned it in the sharpest way. In Frederick she saw a monster, a cruel tyrant, and in Prussia a slave state. She was deeply worried by the fact that Joseph seemed to have been impressed by Frederick's ways and in certain respects even followed his example. The Empress also gave great attention to public opinion, quite contrary to Joseph, and she complained that Frederick always had public opinion on his side. He even made the public believe that he was fighting for religion and right, though he was devoid of any religious or moral scruples. Actually, the majority of German Protestants believed that the Prussian king was waging war to save Protestantism and this had some share in shaping Maria Theresa's attitude towards them.

The conservative outlook of the Empress showed itself in the clinging to differences of rank and social station, though this habit was greatly mitigated by her humanity and kindness towards everybody. She also for a long time maintained the belief in obsolete and harmful institutions, such as the laws denying tolerance to Protestants, cruelty in the penal law etc. She appreciated old traditions and distrusted the power of the reason of individuals and the validity of abstractions, and early admonished her son not to indulge in intellectual coquetry, in showing off his power of arguing and in ridiculing opponents, of which means the fashionable philosophers of enlightenment made great use. And Joseph's extreme rigorism in fulfilling his duties and demanding the same from others seemed to her inhuman also: 'One must not demand too much from human beings' was her advice. In her younger years she was fond of splendid entertainment, played cards for high stakes, made great gifts to ministers and generals of special merit and so on. The expenses of the court were high.[2] But she won the affection of the nobles and even of great sections of the people, especially the Viennese, by this.

CENTRALIZATION AND THE ESTATES

The first war with King Frederick showed that the rights of the territorial Estates to vote taxes for the army, to exercise the collecting of taxes, to recruit soldiers etc., resulted in a slow and inadequate raising of troops and that this system was responsible for many of the shortcomings of the army. Maria Theresa therefore consented to the proposition made by Count Haugwitz to induce the Estates to vote higher taxes for ten years in advance and to transfer their administrative functions to the government. In most territories Haugwitz succeeded in winning the Estates for these reforms and where there was opposition in overcoming it. The freedom of the nobility and clergy from taxes came to an end, though they were taxed at a lower rate than the peasants, and the distribution of taxes was improved by a new cadastral survey.

Subsequent reforms aimed at decreasing the influence of the Estates on justice and administration and, as far as possible, to create a centralized organization in order to bring about a quick, just and effective realization of the functions of government. This could only be carried through gradually since enough trained officials and sufficient experience had to be available first. The Estates were not

[2] In studying the expenses of the court it must, however, be remembered that they included the cost of the ministries, the diplomatic service and other items which to-day are not accounted as court expenditure. The Staatsarchiv, Vol. IX, part 34, contains authentic data on the expenses and income for 1776 in the Austrian countries which belonged to the German Empire. The total income was 52.8 million florins and the expenditure for the Court 535.309 fl. or 1%, which is really low.

consulted, though they could exercise influence, since some of the leading statesmen were on their side. The result was the establishment of several central offices with ministerial functions. Diplomacy, war and the finance needed for them were affairs common to all territories and were managed by Austrian offices. The Austrian and Bohemian countries received a common ministry comparable to a Home Office. Hungary, Belgium and the Italian territories had quite separate institutions as did the affairs of the Empire. The centralization of the administration in the Bohemian and Austrian countries, however, was not completed. The landed nobility retained jurisdiction in smaller affairs though under control of the government. The meagre rights of autonomy left to the towns shrinked further. The Estates, too, lost most of their rights, which were taken over by territorial governments subject to the central ministry in Vienna. With the progress of this centralization it became possible to carry out great reforms in the interest of the people, which formerly would never have worked owing to the resistance of the Estates and their organs. At the top was a Council of State composed of a number of statesmen of the highest experience but without the power of decision. It had to discuss all important questions, to criticize faults in the administration and to submit propositions to the Empress. Its members were mostly progressive and their authority was so great that the Empress, despite her conservative views, regularly accepted their advice.

Owing to the reduction of the power of the Estates the system of government became more absolutist than before. Yet the Empress followed a way of ruling entirely different from that of the Prussian king. Frederick was an autocrat, he decided everything which appeared to him as important himself. His ministers had, in principle, only to carry out what the king had ordered. But in Vienna the high officials had great influence on legislation and administration. Maria Theresa remained true to the Habsburg tradition of accepting, as a rule, the proposals of competent ministers. Only when the ministers could not agree did she decide herself. Frederick's habit of issuing 'Machtsprueche', namely of deciding judicial matters without or even against the decision of the competent court of justice, was entirely alien to her. In this respect, Joseph II came near to Frederick's autocracy, though in a quite different spirit.

The Empress had also a closer circle of advisers, the most prominent of whom were at first Bartenstein and Haugwitz and later Kaunitz. In cultural matters Gerhard van Swieten, a Dutch scholar who was her physician, also had great influence. Count (later Prince) Wenzel Anton Kaunitz came from an old Czech family which had already given Austria several prominent statesmen. He first served the Empress in various important posts and in 1753 became Chancellor. He remained the leading statesman for 39 years. Kaunitz possessed the highest diplomatic skill, a wide outlook, refined culture and great humanity. He set the interest of the state and its people above that of the aristocracy. When in 1763 it was proposed that the power of the Estates should be restored, he wrote to the Empress that, though he was a nobleman and landowner himself, he could not advise her to consent. The measure proposed would frustrate all hopes of progress and would militate against her power and the common weal. The strength of a state reposed upon the mass of the people. Yet the common man was grievously oppressed and deserved special assistance. Kaunitz was not a strict absolutist. He once suggested that deputies of the people should be admitted to the Hungarian parliament, and when the French Revolution broke out, he for some time sympathized with it. Though primarily minister for foreign affairs he also played a great part in internal policy. He possessed Maria Theresa's full confidence, in spite of the fact that he was a great admirer of the French writers whose opinions on religion she detested.

JOSEPH'S PERSONALITY

Maria Theresa's eldest son, Joseph had a careful education, based on the detailed instructions of his mother, which were full of psychological insight and educational wisdom. He also had some excellent teachers, especially in public law, political science and history, and he spoke Latin, German, French, Italian, Czech and Hungarian. According to the Habsburg tradition he also had to learn a handicraft and chose to become a printer. As a boy and young man he was often difficult to manage because he clung to his own opinions obstinately. His gospel was the Law of Nature, he hated privileges and believed in the equality of all human beings. This creed often made him disregard the power of irrational motives in human nature, the awe of the mysterious and the clinging to old traditions, in particular national peculiarities. Joseph also had an impetuous temper which frequently caused him to offend others unintentionally. Though he was imbued with deep humanity and the passion to make his people happy, even against their will, his intellectualism sometimes led him to draw conclusions from general principles which were revoltingly harsh.

In 1765 Maria Theresa's husband, Emperor Francis I, died. She had loved him with all her heart and in deepest grief mourned for him until her death. Her energy decreased, and she also lost the help of some prominent men who died at about the same time as her husband. Joseph became Emperor, and in the hereditary lands co-regent of his mother. He was then 24 years old. A new generation of statesmen came to the fore most of whom shared Joseph's opinions. Kaunitz, however, always remained paramount.

Joseph's personality now reached its definite shape. An important factor was that his first wife, whom he had loved dearly, soon died, as did his only surviving daughter, and soon afterwards his second wife whom he had only married for dynastic reasons. He did not marry again, and had no family life. The Emperor's day was filled with strenuous work from five or six in the morning. His father had left him a vast private fortune, largely made by business, but he handed it over to the state treasury in order to relieve the public finances. At court he abolished the pompous ceremonial and cut down unnecessary expenses. Great parks hitherto reserved to the court were thrown open to the people. Joseph's own life was austere. His meals were very simple, he did not drink wine, disliked playing cards and practised hunting merely for reasons of health. Otherwise, he once remarked, it was a waste of time and often harmful to the peasants. After the death of his father he slept on straw, covered with a stag's skin and a sheet, and only in his last illness could the doctors persuade him to use a mattress and to take a little wine.

It was an old Habsburg tradition to be easily accessible, especially to the poor. Maria Theresa practised it too. But Joseph went much farther; he kept constantly in touch with all classes. Everybody could enter his palace, walk to the corridor where his working room was and speak to him. He often came out of his room and talked with the people waiting, or took some into his room. There was no doorkeeper, for the Emperor opened and closed the door himself. Bowing of knees was prohibited, as incompatible with human dignity. Many anecdotes relate the humanity and justice of Joseph, but also show his stern and pitiless intransigence when public interests were at stake. When a noble lady complained she could not live on the meagre pension left her by her husband the Emperor advised her to let her daughter become a servant, as he himself also was a servant.

Hardly any other ruler of a great Empire has ever cared so much for observing the social conditions of his and other peoples with his own eyes as Joseph did. He made numerous journeys and visited not only all parts of his dominions, but also most other countries of Europe. These journeys were mostly made incognito, often on horseback, without a great following and sometimes under considerable hardship. Joseph declined great receptions, displays of loyalty, or festivities and, if possible, refused to stay in the mansions of the great and preferred to sleep in an inn or hotel, in order to be free to mix with people of all classes and to explore how they were living and what they needed. His reports and jottings of his observations are full of details concerning living conditions, and plans of future reforms. When he found that officials or nobles had misused their powers, oppressing the people, he at once stopped this or helped the victims with gifts or in some other way. On travels to advanced countries, such as France or the Netherlands, he laid stress on seeing welfare institutions and visiting philanthropic reformers. In Paris he had long talks with Turgot and Necker, the foremost advocates of liberal reforms. But he by-passed Voltaire's country house where he was eagerly awaited, and also showed little interest in other famous writers. Frederick II and Catherine II showed these men their greatest favours and were amply rewarded for doing so by their praise which was read by the intellectuals of all countries. Joseph, however, made an unexpected visit to Rousseau, the apostle of equality and democracy. He was also versed in political literature. His secretaries read all important journals and marked passages of interest, especially those criticizing him. The Emperor's greatest recreation was music and the theatre. He played several instruments well and encouraged great composers and German dramatic art. Joseph later himself arranged Schiller's republican drama *Fiesco* for the stage of the Viennese theatre and once performed in a public concert in Naples, singing an Italian air with much spirit and expression, as the press reported.

MARIA THERESA'S AND JOSEPH'S JOINT RULE

The Empress and her son reigned together for fifteen years. The epoch was filled with great reforms, mainly due to Maria Theresa and her advisers. Joseph was at first primarily occupied with military and financial questions, but soon extended his influence and pressed for more radical reforms. This led to great tension with his mother and Joseph repeatedly offered to resign his co-regency. The army had undergone a great improvement previously to this already, and conscription was increasingly introduced. It was restricted almost entirely to sons of peasants and labourers and was extremely unpopular. Joseph devoted much zeal to reforming military matters but he was neither warlike nor a good general. He once ordered the soldiers to shoot only at the horses of the enemy's

L

cavalry since the riders were innocent of the outbreak of war. His principal care was the lot of the common soldier and he preferred their company to that of the officers, who much resented this. As mentioned already he sacrificed large parts of his fortune to the state and was most economical. The deficit in finance decreased and temporarily disappeared. But new wars and apprehensions of war soon caused the financial situation to deteriorate again.

Maria Theresa created a Ministry of Justice, which was to work out new codes of law. In 1769 a new penal code was published which, however, contained so antiquated and cruel stipulations that Kaunitz was horrified and at once induced the Empress to withdraw her sanction. But he was told by the jurisconsults that the code had merely the aim of abolishing contradictions between existing laws. He therefore dropped his opposition. Every grave case had in any case to be submitted to the Empress who was inclined to mildness and in 1776 ordered that the number of executions must be reduced. The centralization of capital justice, moreover, was a great step forwards because a very large number of local and feudal courts whose jurisdiction had hitherto been particularly antiquated were thereby abolished. Maria Theresa, towards the end of her reign (1776), abrogated torture and restricted capital punishment. This was due to Joseph's influence.

Furthermore, the Empress was greatly concerned about the miserable conditions of the peasants in the Bohemian countries. She wanted to improve them but the noble landowners offered stiff resistance and even tried to prevent the government from obtaining a true knowledge of the existing conditions. In consequence a commission was sent to Bohemia in 1750 which had to visit all estates and to investigate the state of the serfs. Nobles who had treated them very badly were severely punished. The continuing resistance of the nobles to reforms led to uprisings of the peasants in 1775 and several measures decreed by the Empress sought to decrease their burdens. On the imperial domains the land was let to the peasants on favourable conditions; forced labour and the tying of the peasants to the soil were abolished. Maria Theresa had originally not wished to set the peasants completely free from their lords, but only to improve their conditions. But the stubborn resistance of the landowners brought her to the conviction that the peasants must be completely liberated.

Trade and industry too were encouraged by many measures of the government and increased considerably. In 1775 most of the Austrian countries became a common customs area. In this large space trade was set free and this made possible a most beneficial division of labour between the various regions. Minister Count Cobenzl had declared even before the appearance of Adam Smith's Wealth of Nations that the best thing would be international free trade between all nations.

In religious matters Maria Theresa long clung to the principle that in the Austrian countries Protestants, with certain exceptions, were not to be permitted the public exercise of their religion. Offenders had to migrate to Transylvania where the freedom of religion was law. Joseph often protested against this practice and in 1773 he succeeded in changing his mother's mind. Protestants and their cult were henceforth tolerated.

Both the Empress and her son were devout Catholics, but they were strongly opposed to the existence of an ecclesiastical state within the state and to privileges of the Church harmful to the common weal. The Church was deprived of her power to punish offenders against her laws by imprisonment, to excommunicate people without consent of the government, to grant asylum to those accused of a crime, to charge too high fees for ecclesiastical actions, and to increase her wealth by inheritance and by the acquisition of land without control by the government. The Church too had to pay taxes. Many holidays and long pilgrimages were forbidden in order to increase production. The foundation of new monasteries and becoming a monk or nun required the consent of the government. In Lombardy the government closed many monasteries and founded new bishoprics. But the most important event was the downfall of the Jesuits. This order had many enemies, not only among the adherents of Enlightenment but even within the Church. Various other great Catholic orders were bitter rivals of them. The Jesuits were rigid defenders of orthodoxy, exercised the censorship, and dominated the universities and most other schools. Their great wealth also aroused much hostility. But the Order still contained great scholars and writers also. Gerhard van Swieten and others induced the Empress to reduce their power over the censorship and the universities considerably. This encouraged the spreading of intellectual freedom. The suppression of the Order, however, was the work of France and her satellites. They treated the Order with considerable disregard of justice and with brutality and eventually forced Pope Clemens XIV to dissolve it (1773). Maria Theresa was personally friendly to the Jesuits, but was won for their abolition by the wish to maintain good relations to France and to wed her daughter to the heir to the French crown. In Austria the dissolution was carried through with fairness, the great possessions of the Order were used to found a fund for educational purposes. The former Jesuits received pensions and many of them continued to excel as scholars, teachers and writers.

The universities were of special interest to G. van Swieten who laid the foundation for the rise of the university of Vienna to a leading rôle in medicine. In the field of jurisprudence the professors Martini and Riegger were the most prominent authorities and in political and economic science Sonnenfels. All these also had great influence in advising the government. Maria Theresa's greatest achievement, however, was the foundation of schools for the people and the introduction of the obligation of all parents to have their children educated (1774). This great reform was organized by Abbot Felbiger. All children had to be instructed from the sixth to the twelfth year, and, if possible, to the thirteenth, with refresher courses up to their twentieth year. The method of teaching, the training of teachers, the question of text books etc., were regulated in a very practical way. The parents had to pay very little, the poor nothing, and gifted pupils were to receive scholarships to visit higher schools. Within a few years thousands of schools were founded or re-organized, and the number of pupils attending school multiplied. But there were also many who were hostile to the universal spreading of education. Many landed nobles, especially in Galicia, feared that their serfs would become too independent, clerics saw in it a danger for religion, and numerous peasants did not wish that their children should become better educated than they and should sit in school instead of working in the fields. Among the Slavs some apprehended that the schools would lead to the Germanization of the people. But under Maria Theresa this fear was unfounded. If the schools were called German, this meant non-Latin. The Empress reprimanded ecclesiastical schools in Bohemia because they taught only Latin and neither Czech nor German. In 1763 she ordered that Czech should also be taught and that every official in the Bohemian countries should understand it. Textbooks were also issued in Czech. The other vernaculars too were cultivated. Great stress was laid on the learning of German as a language of communication. But it was emphasized in the State Council that nobody should be forced to learn it.

MARIA THERESA AND HUNGARY

In Hungary the nobility preserved their power over legislation and administration, as Maria Theresa had again solemnly promised at her coronation. The Hungarian claim to independence from Austria was on the whole fulfilled, except in foreign policy, the army, and their finances. These were common affairs and dealt with by Austrian ministries. But the Hungarian Diet had the right to decide Hungary's contributions to wars and usually granted less than needed. There were Hungarian standing troops which in the case of war were supplemented by the personal levy of the nobility, the so-called Insurrection. Many magnates provided, voluntarily, a great number of hussars. This system worked slowly and unsatisfactorily. It would have been better to replace it by a financial contribution. But the Diet was absolutely opposed to this, complaining that Hungary was poor because her exports were subject to high Austrian customs. Austria replied that her customs on Hungarian imports were necessary because Hungary paid little in taxes.

The Hungarians often asserted that the Vienna Government treated their country like a colony, trying to prevent its industrial development, to the profit of the Austrian industries. Actually the system of mercantilism followed the principle that industries were reserved for the leading state while economically backward countries should primarily supply raw materials in exchange for industrial products. The policy of Great Britain towards Ireland and the American colonies was a well-known example. But Maria Theresa also contributed very much to Hungary's economic development, in particular by bringing large areas into cultivation, by the drainage of swamps, by making the rivers navigable, by improving the means of transport, and removing customs between different parts of Hungary, by the settlement of peasants and artisans, by loans, and so on. The Venetian ambassador in Vienna in 1769 reported to his Government that in the last 25 years Hungary had made incredible progress. Villages had become populous towns and many trades, of which formerly there had been no trace, were flourishing.

When Hungary was liberated from the Turks many territories associated with her were treated by the Austrian army as autonomous, partly for military, partly for political reasons. Their population was predominantly not Hungarian but Slav, Wallachian or German. Among these territories were Transylvania, Slavonia, Croatia and the Banat. Parts of them formed the Military Frontier, a fortified zone against Turkey. Maria Theresa in the course of her government united most of these territories with Hungary. She also joined the towns of the Zips to it, as well as Fiume, which became Hungary's port on the Adriatic. Hungary therefore owed her a considerable expansion.

A question which Maria Theresa had particularly at heart was the improvement of the conditions of the peasants. Their situation was largely very poor, though certainly there were also cases of patriarchal relations between lords and serfs. But the peasants were tied to the soil, their judge was the lord of the manor and there was no appeal against his verdict. A serf could not sue his lord, nor could he be witness against a nobleman. Their situation was therefore extremely precarious and depended exclusively on the character of the lord.[3] The improvement of the lot of the peasants was also in the interest of the state, because they alone paid taxes, while the nobles were exempt. Maria Theresa wished that the relations between lords and peasants should be regulated by the Diet of 1765. But when a bishop raised this matter there was general laughter and nothing was done. The queen, however, considered this as a question of conscience. She told a magnate that she would not endanger the salvation of her soul because of a few Hungarian noblemen. After this event she convoked no more Diets. Councillor von Raab who had already carried out great agrarian reforms in Austria, worked out a law which Maria Theresa enacted by decree. The peasants were no longer bound to the soil, they could let their children choose what ever occupation they liked without needing the consent of the lord, they could rise to every dignity and were represented by an official lawyer in the courts. They could also appeal against the judgment. Their obligations to the landowner were fixed and moderate. Maria Theresa thereby abolished serfdom in Hungary earlier than Joseph II did in the Bohemian and other countries. But it is questionable how far the Hungarian administration carried out the decrees of the queen, for the judges and officials were elected in each county by the noblemen.

In ecclesiastical questions Maria Theresa introduced in Hungary reforms similar to those in Austria. She proceeded in this matter in agreement with the Pope. However, she sometimes exhibited great intolerance against Protestants,[4] probably under the influence of the Hungarian clergy. Later her attitude became more olerant.

The queen was very popular in Hungary, not only owing to her policy but also because of her personal attitude. She surrounded herself with Hungarians, treated them with great distinction and

[3] Marczali's contention that their conditions were favourable appears to me not well substantiated. This Hungarian historian admits himself that the peasants expected an improvement of their conditions not from the Diet or from the nobility, but from the king, and he finds this 'to be regretted'. Cf. H. Marczali, pp. 175, 191, 245. A Hungarian peculiarity was the great number of agricultural workers and peasants who had titles of nobility. K. H. von Lang relates in his memoirs (I, p. 128) that, when he lived with an aristocratic family in Hungary as a tutor, the servants too were nobles, even the herdsmen. They wore sabres, and it was not permitted to beat them. Many of the common people spoke Latin.

[4] Cf. Mailath, IV, p. 48.

gave or loaned large sums to many of them. Joseph had Hungarian tutors as a boy and learned the language and history of the country. Many Hungarian magnates lived more in their palaces in Vienna than on their estates in Hungary. They also frequently intermarried with the Austrian and Bohemian nobility. It was primarily the magnates who became loyal servants of the dynasty, while the Calvinist lesser nobility kept aloof.

JOSEPH AS SOLE RULER

After the death of his mother Joseph continued her reforms but also tried to realize his own ideas, which showed a much more radical tendency. During the time of little over nine years during which he reigned alone he issued more than 6,000 decrees or more than two every day concerning countless reforms, great and small. Such an expansion of the activities of the state would have required many more officials to deal with them. But the Emperor instead dismissed or pensioned numerous employees in order to save money. He hoped to make good the decrease in manpower by better organization and an increase of the zeal of the officials. To achieve this Joseph issued most impressive exhortations, decreed excellent measures, and also improved the working conditions of the civil servants. Their amount of work was rigorously checked and every neglect was severely punished. The Emperor for some time harboured the plan of dividing his countries into three groups, an Austrian, a Bohemian-Galician and a Hungarian one. The first would have been predominantly German, the second Slav and the third Hungarian, though each with national minorities. Each group would have had its separate government and Estates. But the State Council raised objections and the plan was abandoned. Joseph also wished to enhance the feeling of responsibility of ministers and other leading officials by ceasing to bind them to the decisions passed by the majority of their counsellors. The model of Frederick II induced him to imitate his ways of autocracy. He became extremely overworked by the accumulation of business, his health suffered and his nervous temper led him to many precipitate actions. Decrees were often issued which had at once to be changed or withdrawn. Since the Emperor, moreover, was so easily accessible he often received complaints and gave orders to relieve them, when it became obvious that matters were quite different from what he had been led to believe. His chief fault was that he wanted to reform too much too quickly, and in too radical a way.

Joseph also demanded too much from the officials, was therefore frequently disappointed and became distrustful and sometimes unjust. But he never went as far as Frederick, who regarded most of his officials as cheats and corrupt and often unjustly treated them as criminals. The Emperor always showed them respect.[5] Neither was he imbued with Frederick's contempt for men in general. Though an autocrat, he wished to educate his subjects to become thinking beings. His decrees therefore had long introductions explaining that the common-weal demanded the measures prescribed. Strict absolutists blamed him for this procedure.

Maria Theresa had already mitigated the censorship, and Joseph now abolished it except for worthless books of an obscene kind or hostile to religion. Objective criticism of the government was permitted and welcomed. When the censor prohibited writings attacking the Emperor the latter annulled this. The freedom granted, however, was much misused. A spate of writings appeared which were merely designed to arouse sensation and distorted the truth to make money. In consequence a few restrictions were decreed, in particular a stamp duty. The book trade was also set free; everybody might sell books. However no copyright was granted to books printed abroad, which was unfair.

Under Joseph's reign many reforms of the law and justice were also enacted. The criminal code of 1787 abrogated the death penalty except for instigators of a rebellion under martial law. Imaginary crimes like witchcraft or sorcery disappeared from the law. Offences against religion and morality were treated mildly. Joseph repealed capital punishment not merely for reasons of humanity, however, but rather to increase its deterrent effect. He believed that a criminal would be more deterred by the prospect of a long imprisonment than by quick death. Criminals had further to expiate their crimes by doing hard and useful labour. In the case of particularly grave crimes imprisonment was to be made more rigorous by additional penalties such as solitary confinement, a hard sleeping-place, branding, shackles, by making convicts tow barges etc. But this had the result that penalties sometimes became so cruel as to arouse opposition, including that of Kaunitz in the State Council. Joseph occasionally intervened in law cases to make a punishment more severe.

One of the strongest convictions of the Emperor was that all men should be treated equally without consideration of rank or religion. Under him the Aulic Council condemned even princes of the Empire to long imprisonment. The criminal code stipulated that noble birth

---

[5] He also addressed all officials with the polite 'Sie' while Frederick even addressed generals and ministers with 'Er', like servants.

was an aggravating circumstance, since the offender had not acted under the influence of a depressing environment. Cases are known in which Joseph seemed to have been biased against offenders of noble origin.[6] The nobles were furious when nobles were sentenced to humiliating penalties such as to be placed in the pillory or to have to sweep the streets. Money fines were rejected by Joseph because they were too mild for the rich, and too hard for the poor. A court of justice was to consist of two representatives of the local population as well as the judges which implied an approach to a jury. In civil law marriage was declared a contract which under certain conditions could be dissolved, the marriage between persons of different religion was permitted, discrimination against illegitimate children was abolished etc.

In economic matters Joseph continued the policy of mercantilist protection of industries, but also showed himself influenced by physiocratic ideas. Within the Austrian Empire complete free trade was eventually to reign though for the time being Hungary was still left outside. All privileges impeding trade were to disappear. The variety of currencies, weights and measures was also to end. The import of all goods not indispensable for the people was burdened with high tariffs. To give a good example all foreign wine in the imperial cellars was distributed among hospitals. The high tariffs, however, were often circumvented by bribing the frontier guards who were very poorly paid. Joseph also continued his mother's policy of settling colonists in territories where there was plenty of uncultivated soil. In the Banate alone 50,000 were settled under very favourable conditions, and large numbers in Galicia, the Bukowina etc. Agriculture, trade and industries were promoted by many means and with good results. The statistics show that the number of factories and workers, and their output, rose rapidly.[7] Though the government granted loans and subsidies both Joseph and his advisers knew that private entrepreneurs and companies of the right kind were needed to achieve real progress. Austrian conditions encouraged numerous able industrialists, merchants and technical experts from many countries to found and manage large enterprises in the Empire. The export trade rose considerably, especially to the Near and Far East.

When Joseph had become the sole ruler he issued several decrees completing the reforms of agrarian conditions begun by his mother. The peasants now no longer needed the consent of their lords to

[6] Cf. Hock and Bidermann, p. 151.
[7] Cf. the statistics in J. de Luca, Krones IV, pp. 461, 492 etc., Mayer, II, p. 579, and the bibliography.

L*

leave their farms, to marry, to take up a trade, etc. Their fields were protected against stags, boars etc., and the chase, they were liberated from many onerous burdens, their children were no longer obliged to serve the lord, and feudal jurisdiction was further restricted. In case of a suit with his lord a peasant received free legal advice and representation by an advocate. The noble landowners, however, remained obliged to support the peasants in case of illness, or natural catastrophes. Joseph's final aim was to make the peasants free owners, or tenants, of the land tilled by them. His premature death and world events frustrated the full achievement of this aim. The long wars with revolutionary France and Napoleon created a reactionary atmosphere and the last remnants of serfdom were only abolished in 1848. Yet the peasants' obligations were restricted to a reasonable measure and their rights of tenure were improved by Joseph's reforms.

In 1789 Joseph further decreed that the peasants should pay not more than 30% from their gross returns to the lord, of which 12.3% was land tax and 17.7% was rent. In territories where the conditions of the peasants were particularly wretched, as in Galicia, special measures were taken to assist them. It was also prohibited that the peasants should bow deeply before the lord or his stewart, or kiss their hands, since this would be incompatible with freedom.

The Emperor also founded many welfare institutions which were most beneficial and aroused great admiration. Among them were hospitals, maternity clinics, lunatic asylums, homes for the deaf and dumb, for incurables, foundlings, old people, orphans, and juveniles needing special care. District physicians and trained midwives were appointed and the poor were to receive medical treatment and medicine gratis. In order to improve the treatment of wounded soldiers Joseph founded an academy for military surgery at his own expense.

Special care was further devoted to the protection of children working in factories. At that time child labour was encouraged in many countries. The economist Justi stated in 1780 that in Holland and England children were often employed at an age of between four and six years. As a rule children were lodged in dormitories at the factory. In Austria the children had also to attend school up to their 12th year. In 1785 the Emperor visited a silk factory and was greatly shocked by the condition of the working children. He therefore issued a decree in 1786 ordering that no child under nine should be employed, unless in case of urgent need, that boys and girls had to have separate dormitories, and that every child must be washed and combed and receive fresh shirts and underwear at least once every week, and that every month the bedstead must be cleaned and fresh bed-linen supplied. Every six months the district physician had to examine the children's health and give the necessary orders. The local magistrate and parson were to report every three months to the government about the children's health and take scrupulous care for it. Mises states in his study on this matter that in Austria the number of factory children under 12 years was insignificant. This was obviously due to the regulations about attending school. It is interesting that Joseph's decree of 1786 was issued 16 years before Sir Robert Peel's first Factory Act concerning 'pauper apprentices' in the cotton mills. This Act, moreover, was much less comprehensive and effective than the Austrian regulations.

In handicrafts the guild regulations usually fixed the age of a learner at above twelve years and the masters were against child labour. Joseph further ordered that the juvenile apprentices must not be employed to do the domestic work or be treated harshly. In regard to all workers the paying of wages in goods (Truck system) was made illegal. The provincial government in Vienna also had a factory inspector on its staff.

Immediately after he had become sole ruler Joseph issued a Patent granting tolerance to Protestants and Greek Orthodox. In order to prevent clashes with Catholics, however, their churches should not have open access from the street, nor have bells. All civil discriminations against non-Catholics were removed. They could acquire houses and land, become burghers, masters of guilds, officials, doctors etc. Cemeteries and other institutions should be open to all. The Patent had the consequence that the number of Protestants much increased. Many of them had already secretly been Protestants before. Moreover, many sectarians appeared, though sects had not received toleration. Most of them were peasants who usually held odd opinions based on falsely interpreted sentences of the Bibles. Many believed themselves to be inspired by God. Some demanded community of property and women, some wished to live in poverty and refused to work and to pay taxes. The Adamites followed Adam's example in going about naked. Not a few declared themselves to be Jews as prescribed in the Bible. The Emperor was first for drastic measures. He ordered them to be given 25 strokes on the backside because they were talking nonsense. He even sent some to Transylvania or put them in the army. These orders were severely criticized by many writers in Germany, but Joseph soon reconsidered the matter and ordered that they should be left in peace.[8]

The Jews too received tolerance and civic rights. The clergy and officials had to tell the people that the Jews were fellow citizens and should be treated accordingly. The obligations to wear a special costume or badge, to live in a ghetto, to pay toll at town gates, etc., were abolished. Jews could send their children to Christian schools or to their own ones, and talented children were to receive scholarships. The universities, all occupations and every post was open to them, except certain activities which might arouse public opinion against them. The Jews could also serve in the army, have Christian domestics and visit public entertainments. But foreign Jews were only to be permitted to settle if they brought a new trade and paid a special tax. Poor Jews were to get relief. They also had to adopt family names and to keep their accounts in German. Joseph even granted some Jewish bankers and traders titles of nobility.

The Emperor regarded most monasteries as seats of superstition, a lazy life and obscurantism. He intended to tolerate only those doing work useful to the community such as preaching, hearing confession, attending the sick, teaching, research, and so on. Many monasteries were closed and their number decreased within five years from 2163 to 1425. The former monks and nuns received small pensions. The property of the dissolved monasteries was used to form a fund for building churches, the foundation of new parishes, charity etc. This policy was largely beneficial. But in many cases it was not carried out with sufficient care.[9] The sale of the large estates, buildings and other objects was a difficult task which could only have been properly carried through if sufficient time was available. But Joseph urged the officials entrusted with it to sell them quickly because he wanted the money for other plans. Moreover, he tended to underestimate the merits of certain orders in learning, charity and other respects.[10] It also happened that officials

[8] The complaints of the Catholic Church later induced the Emperor to issue regulations designed to settle certain points. The intolerant section of the Catholic clergy often abused these decrees to make the change of religion difficult.

[9] Cf. Hock and Bidermann, p. 394.

[10] The Trinitarian Order aimed at liberating Christian slaves, mainly in Turkey and the Barbary states, by paying ransom. Counsellor von Born, who played a great part in the campaign against the monks, jeered at them as 'dealers in human flesh'. Other enemies argued that the former slaves were mostly old and a burden on the state after their return. If their owners would realize that ransom was no longer paid, they would no longer carry away Christians but only rob goods. Cf. S. Brunner, Joseph II, p. 200. M. Buchberger, Lexikon fuer Theologie und Kirche, vol. X, 1938, says that the Trinitarians had liberated 900,000 slaves and paid one-third of the ransoms out of their own property. In modern times they have also worked for the emancipation of negro slaves in America etc.

made profits by buying valuable objects which had belonged to a monastery at a cheap price themselves. Neither the Emperor nor most of the civil servants employed had understanding for historic monuments or documents. Objects of art were sometimes sold as scrap metal. Previously when the Jesuit Order had been dissolved its archives, which were of the greatest value for historical research, had been sold as waste paper to a Jewish trader for a pittance.

Joseph continued his mother's policy of restricting the power of the Church, but went much farther than she, for he also interfered in matters which were purely ecclesiastical. The priests had hitherto mostly been trained for their profession in monasteries. Now Joseph founded special schools where they were to be educated in the new spirit, not merely to be good priests but also to be organs of state designed to teach the people their civic duties. Many of his reforms were certainly in the ecclesiastical and public interest, for example the prohibition of multiple livings in one hand. Numerous clerics of every rank welcomed the reforms and supported them though others bitterly opposed them.

Holidays were still farther reduced in order to increase production, as were processions and pilgrimages. The cult of relics, the ringing of bells to avert hail, the over-rich ornaments of certain churches etc., were forbidden. A solemn high mass with music was only to be held on Sundays and holidays. The number of candles burning at mass was restricted, superfluous ornaments, precious vestments on statues of saints, and similar things were removed. Poor churches received objects from the possessions of rich ones. Money collections in the church were regulated. The family vaults of the nobles were closed, since the dead are all equal. Even coffins were to disappear in order to save wood. Corpses should be put into sacks naked and covered with unburnt chalk as a disinfectant and to expedite decay. The priests should not deliver speeches of praise at funerals or weddings nor accompany the dead to the grave. Persons allegedly possessed by demons were not to be subjected to exorcism but sent to a lunatic asylum for treatment. Protestants, Jews and suicides were no longer to be buried outside the cemetery but should rest side by side with Catholics. The Emperor also founded new bishoprics and appointed the bishops himself.

Pope Pius VI protested against Joseph's innovations, but in vain. He therefore travelled to Vienna in 1782 in order to induce him to change his policy. He was received with great honours but could not achieve anything of importance. The following year Joseph visited Rome. There were rumours that he wanted to make the

German Church quite independent of Rome. But nothing of this kind happened.

Many of the Emperor's reforms must certainly be approved of. Others were well meant, but aroused great resistance in wide sections of the people. Some had to be withdrawn at once, as for instance the decree concerning corpses. It sometimes happened that Joseph's policy was attacked from two sides. To some it seemed to go much too far while others found it was not radical enough.

Maria Theresa's educational policy was carried on, but with alterations. Academies for the education of young nobles for the civil service were closed down. At the universities, Joseph stopped many lectures held in Latin but increased those in German. The schools for commercial and technical instructions were specially supported. Wealthy parents had to pay high school fees which were used to grant scholarships to poor, gifted pupils. Whether the pupils were to go to confession or take communion was left to the decision of the parents. The social status of the teachers in elementary schools was to be raised.

JOSEPH AND THE EMPIRE'S NATIONALITIES

Maria Theresa had treated the numerous nationalities in her Empire with great tact and thereby avoided tension. In the Austrian and Bohemian countries the Estates had lost important privileges but were not abolished. In Galicia Estates were even introduced. The Hungarian Diet was no longer convoked. Yet the privileges of the nobility, and their county assemblies continued. As regards language, Latin remained the tongue of the law courts and the administration in Hungary. It was also spoken by wide circles of non-scholars, though it was usually not very good Latin. In the Bohemian countries and in Galicia the judges and officials mostly used the German language which everybody of any education understood. German was also widely spoken in Hungary. Many Hungarian nobles even no longer understood Hungarian, but spoke Latin, German or French. The vernaculars of the Hungarian nationalities were taught in the schools where necessary.

In Maria Theresa's time a movement began in Bohemia for the cultivation of the Czech language and literature. Its pioneers were Jesuits and Piarists and other clerics who were supported by highly cultured noblemen. In 1775 a chair for the Czech language was founded at the University of Vienna and in 1791 another at the University of Prague. This movement greatly increased under Joseph. In the nine years of his reign more Czech books were published than in several previous generations. The granting of freedom of the press and other reforms furthered this revival of Czech literature. The liberation of the peasants and the universal obligation to attend school laid the foundations for the rise of the Czech people to nationhood. The pioneers of Czech nationality were therefore fervent adherents of Joseph's reforms.

When he became the sole ruler, however, his policy showed some momentous new features. Joseph did not let himself be crowned anywhere, obviously in order to evade the coronation oath to maintain the old privileges of the Estates, so that he would have a free hand. Soon he began to make territorial changes in his countries. The Hungarian crown was sent to Vienna which aroused great unrest in Hungary. Joseph apparently aimed at the integration of all his countries in a great Empire without respecting their peculiarities and privileges. In Hungary the counties, the bulwark of aristocratic power, were replaced by a new organization and Austrian laws were introduced there. Latin was superseded as the official language by German. All officials and members of the Diet had to learn the latter within three years. In the Bohemian countries the Czech language ceased to be used in the law-courts, the administration and the schools. Joseph certainly did not wish to suppress the vernaculars but only to introduce German as the general language of communication and the state. He referred to the fact that in Great Britain, France and Russia there was an official language besides the other languages which were not employed by the government. In Great Britain various Celtic languages were spoken, in France, Breton, German and Provencal and in Russia a multitude of languages. Joseph expected the introduction of a common language in his countries to help to unite all the nationalities in brotherly love.

Actually these and similar measures had exactly the opposite result. A violent nationalism developed in Hungary directed against Joseph and everything German. It reached its peak when the king decreed a new cadastral survey in order to subject the nobles to taxation and thereby to abolish their most highly cherished privilege of freedom from it. Much bad blood was caused by the outbreak of a rebellion of Walachian peasants against the Hungarian nobility. The peasants erroneously believed that Joseph approved of their movement. Wide circles of the nobility thought of rising against the king with the help of Prussia and electing another one. These events coincided with others which hit Joseph severely, in particular the revolution in Belgium. He became very ill and shortly before his death he issued orders revoking most of the decrees which had caused the discontent in Hungary.

Joseph's policy towards Hungary aroused much criticism from progressive publicists who otherwise shared his ideals, especially in Germany. It was easy to see that Joseph's policy was rash and risky. The Hungarian events revealed the terrible antinomy between political rationalism and nationalism which became the crux of all troubles in the Austro-Hungarian Empire and eventually the cause of its break-down. Whatever one may think of Joseph's ways of procedure, his aims were rational, and if they could have been realized Hungary and other Danubian nations would probably not have lost their freedom completely and become Russian satellites in our time.

The feudal 'liberty' of the Hungarian nobility which Joseph wanted to abolish was certainly incompatible with the modern ideas of freedom, equality and nationality. A considerable section of the Hungarian nobility, especially among the magnates, realized this, and they occupied the most important posts in the Hungarian administration in Joseph's reign.[11] They probably approved the abolition of antiquated and harmful feudal privileges, hoping that then a way would be found to a reformed constitutionalism. It was mainly the lower, less cultured nobles who indulged in the wildest nationalism against their king. That the latter too committed great errors should not be ignored.

JOSEPH AND PUBLIC OPINION

The reforms of the Emperor naturally aroused great gratitude and the warmest affection in wide circles, especially among the peasants and the intellectuals. Most of the great thinkers and poets of Germany, such as Lessing, Klopstock, Schiller, Goethe, Herder, Wieland, and others paid homage to him, and, of course, numerous Austrian personalities did so too.[12] But his innovations conflicted with the interests of many owners of privileges and adherents to old customs. It is understandable that a large proportion of them set their egoism above the common weal and bitterly resented his reforms. These classes also had a great influence on public opinion. Moreover, not a few of those who had profited from the reforms were for various

[11] Cf. the judgment of the great Hungarian historian Fraknoi quoted in German translation by Wendrinsky p. 300. Even Marczali, who usually sympathizes with Hungarian nationalism, admits in his history of Hungarian Constitutional Law, that a great proportion of the nobles were won over by Maria Theresa's policy and regarded the constitution as antiquated or 'Hunnish'.

[12] Cf. examples in Wendrinsky, p. 384, and Engel-Janosi, p. 300. Herder wrote the most moving lines on the tragedy of his life. Cf. *Briefe zur Beförderung der Humanität*, I, 10.

reasons not satisfied with them, and showed themselves cool or hostile to Joseph. A widely read pamphlet of 1787 enumerated Joseph's reforms beneficial to the people and after each reform came the words: 'and yet the people does not love him.'[13] A factor which brought discredit to the Emperor was also that many of his actions in foreign policy failed. His last war against Turkey was most unpopular and at his death Austria was in a desperate situation. The Emperor was well aware of the existence of these tendencies hostile to him. He said that his tombstone should bear the inscription: 'Here lies a prince who despite his best intentions could realize nothing of his plans.' On the deathbed he told a minister that he did not miss the power he had had, that he was at rest, but somewhat worried that, despite all his work and trouble, he had rendered so few men happy and so many ungrateful.

[13] Cf. Brunner, p. 130.

THE SMALLER GERMAN STATES IN THE AGE OF
ENLIGHTENMENT

VARIOUS TRENDS OF ENLIGHTENMENT

In the second half of the eighteenth century the ideas of enlightenment gained ground all over Germany, though not in all classes. It was mainly the rulers, the aristocracy and the intellectuals who became imbued with this ideology, while the majority of the common people and also large sections of the middle classes remained alien to it. It was by no means homogeneous but comprised very different trends. The models of enlightened rulers were Frederick II and Joseph II, who had much in common, but also differed widely. Not a few princes took humanity very seriously, while for others it was nothing more than a fashionable phrase. The smaller princes included therefore the most different types. Many of them have left a bad record of their reign, which mainly consisted in squandering the public means on extravagant luxury and in gratifying their passions and whims in a despotic way. In a large state forces usually existed checking such tendencies to a certain extent: the tradition of great rulers and statesmen, who had laid the foundations of the state's eminent position, a certain national feeling and sense of responsibility towards the country among the leading classes, and ample means permitting considerable expenses for the splendour of the court. But the smaller a state was, the more everything depended on the character of the prince, or of those dominating him. We have shown in Chapter II, how the two High Courts of the Empire very frequently cancelled arbitrary decisions of small princes, and even punished them. In some cases, they were deposed.

But there also were always princes who took the duties of a ruler very seriously, had had a careful education and possessed the gift of choosing excellent men as counsellors and ministers. Under these circumstances, a small state offered great opportunities to further the welfare of the people. The enormous historic and structural evils of the Empire's institutions and traditions could, of course, not be changed by the good intentions of a small ruler. Nevertheless, fruitful work could be done in financial, economic, educational and cultural questions. Many princes and statesmen were eager disciples of Wolff, Pietism, Freemasonry, Frederick II and Joseph II but also of Voltaire, Rousseau and the Physiocrats.

SOUTH GERMANY

In 1742, Elector Charles Albrecht of Bavaria had, by the grace of France, been elected and crowned Emperor Charles VII, but he had hardly more than the bare title and soon died. His son Maximilian III Joseph (1745-1777) made peace with Austria (1745). Bavaria had suffered enormous damage through the wars and wastefulness of his predecessors and had been overburdened with debts. The young prince was very kind-hearted and helpful, though he had not the faculties of a great ruler. One of his tutors, Johann Adam (later Baron) Ickstatt, the son of a blacksmith and a great jurist, was a disciple of Christian Wolff, and filled Max with enthusiasm for the ideas of enlightenment and for the necessity for reforms. This ruler, therefore, decreed, or planned, an extraordinary number of major and minor reforms in almost every field.[1] The only point which Max did not dare to touch was the problem of toleration. The power of the Church and the prejudice of the people was far too great to expect them to consent to equal rights for Protestants. Bavaria was to remain an entirely Catholic country. Nevertheless, many laws were made restricting the privileges of the Church. Another field in which progress was made was the codification of law. This was due to W. X. Baron Kreittmayr, a prominent jurist, whose codes of law brought many improvements, but his criminal law was not distinguished by humanity, and the number of death sentences remained very great.

Max III Joseph, Ickstatt, and his pupil Lori and other enthusiasts for enlightenment did their best to carry through their plans for the benefit of the people. But they were often faced with the resistance of the privileged classes and the indifference or distrust of the peasants, and many of their efforts failed. Great reforms, if they

[1] Cf. the long list in M. Döberl, *Entwicklungsgeschichte Bayerns*, 1912, II, p. 262.

were to succeed, required time and patience, and could not simply
be decreed from above. The leaders of the progressive party founded
an Academy of Sciences in Munich which was to become the organ
for the elaboration and propagation of the ideas of enlightenment.
It did much valuable work and in particular cultivated a refined
German language and literature, such as had developed mainly in
Central Germany. Many Bavarians regarded them still as 'Lutheran'
and preferred to speak their own dialect. But the golden age of
German literature was near, and it was definitely decided that German as spoken in Leipzig and Frankfurt was to be the common
language.

The greatest stress was laid upon improving education at all its
levels, from the university to the elementary school. In 1771, it was
decreed that everyone was obliged to send his children to school,
though in practice it was found impossible to carry this through in
many Alpine districts where communications were difficult. When
the Jesuit order was dissolved, its great school system and rich funds
were taken over by the government and devoted to education. The
people largely deplored the dissolution; and in spite of it the Jesuits
retained many influential posts.

The Elector Max III Joseph was widely beloved by the people,
who called him Father Max. When, in 1770, a great famine broke
out, he gave his last jewels to buy grain and had the game in his
forests killed. He later fell ill of smallpox and his physician ordered
him to swallow, as a medicine, a little picture of the Virgin. Nevertheless he died, and was much mourned by the Bavarians.

His successor was Charles Theodore of the Palatinate (1777-99).
He belonged to another line of the dynasty, had no great affection
for Bavaria and was prepared to cede it to Austria for Belgium, but
Frederick II twice foiled this plan. His reign was characterized by a
relapse of court life into extravagant luxury and by the revival of a
narrow-minded clericalism. This led to widespread underground
propaganda for the ideals of radical enlightenment, which was
carried on by secret societies, mainly the 'Illuminati'. When this was
betrayed, the government persecuted their members. But the prince
undertook beneficial reforms also, though they found little recognition.

Wurttemberg was, for almost half a century, governed by Duke
Charles Eugène (1737-93). Till 1744 he was a minor and the government lay in the hands of a regency. Later he devoted himself
exclusively to his pleasure, lived much abroad, and left the government to the leading officials, who were very well qualified. The
prominent historian L. T. Spittler wrote that the people perhaps

never enjoyed so happy a time as that from 1737 to 1757. But then the behaviour of the Duke changed. He himself began to govern in a despotic way and to lead a life of the worst libertinage. Charles Eugène had great gifts and was inspired by ideas of enlightenment, but under the influence of favourites became a tyrant. His favourite, Count Montmartin, induced the Duke to adopt the French practice of selling the posts of officials and to commit other grave financial abuses. The money raised by such means was squandered on the most sumptuous court life and every kind of extravagance and licence. The whole administration was infected with corruption.

Nevertheless Charles Eugène took certain duties of a ruler seriously, giving great attention to administrative matters and receiving everybody, however humble. He also helped many subjects in need and therefore became popular in wide circles. On the other hand, great sections of the people were grievously oppressed. The reputation of the Duke is characterized by the fact that in his capital Stuttgart the Freemasons refused his application for membership of the lodge. The despotic rule of the Duke brought him in grave conflict with the Estates of Wurttemberg. They appealed several times to the Imperial Aulic Council, and also to the three powers, Britain, Denmark and Prussia, who had guaranteed the rights of the Estates. In 1770, the Duke and the Estates concluded a pact restoring all constitutional rights. Yet the Duke violated them again.

In the second half of his life Charles Eugène to a certain extent moderated his excesses under the influence of Franziska von Hohenheim, who was first his friend and whom he later married. She was much influenced by pietism. In particular she induced the Duke to appoint as a leading minister, a man who was an excellent administrator. The character of the ruler was a strange mixture of good and evil—Lavater told Goethe that his personality combined heaven and hell. In 1778, on his 50th birthday, Charles Eugène issued a proclamation to the people which had to be read from the pulpits of all churches. In it the Duke confessed that he had been a great sinner, but promised henceforth to improve himself. This promise was often not kept, but nevertheless increased his popularity. In his later years the Duke devoted himself mainly to building up a college, for which he engaged prominent professors. Its most famous pupil was Friedrich Schiller.

Baden was a very small country before Napoléon's favour increased it tenfold. Her princes for a long time lived in a very simple and patriarchal way. But this changed when the sun of Versailles began to shine and to dazzle the German princes. Margrave Charles

III William (1709-38) was a benevolent ruler, and one of the greatest horticulturists of his time. He surrounded himself with a corps of 160 pretty girls, who were not only his gardeners, but also his life-guard, hussars, court staff, ballet, and partly his harem, too. His successor was his grandson, Margrave Charles Frederick, who reigned for 73 years (1738-1811). He was closely related to the princes of Nassau-Orange, studied at Swiss and Dutch universities, and greatly appreciated the liberties of Holland and Britain. He was an excellent ruler, did not indulge in libertinage, and enjoyed great popularity. Torture, the death penalty and serfdom were abolished in his reign, full religious tolerance was granted, and the censorship was mild and reasonable. The prince believed in the system of physiocracy, and wrote a book about it, full of humane suggestions. The physiocratic experiments which he undertook in his country were not successful. But his state was considered a model by the intellectual élite of Europe.

CENTRAL GERMANY

In Saxony Elector Frederick Augustus I, known as Augustus the Strong, was succeeded by Frederick Augustus II (1733-63), who, like his father, was also King of Poland. He was good-natured, greatly interested in art, but politically indolent. Under him, therefore, Count H. Bruehl became Prime Minister and the real ruler, using his powers largely for his personal profit. The country had to suffer exceedingly because of the great wars between Austria and Prussia, especially when Frederick II, at the beginning of the Seven Years' War, invaded the neutral Saxony and squeezed it to the utmost. Nevertheless, Saxony's economic and cultural resources were so great that she could soon recover. Her industries, commerce and agriculture were unsurpassed in Germany. Leipzig was already the centre of Germany's learning and commerce, particularly also of the book-trade; it was widely called Little Paris. Dresden, the seat of the court, was one of the most splendid centres of art and music. The administration, too, was well ordered. Frederick Augustus II was followed by his son, who died soon afterwards, then Frederick Augustus III came to the throne (1763-1827), who was then a minor, and did not begin to rule for himself until 1768. He was one of the best princes of his time, his actions were distinguished by a strong sense of justice and humanity, and the unflinching rejection of any aggrandisement achieved by violating the rights of another state. He also abstained from expanding his power at the expense of the Estates, who in Saxony always had considerable influence on politics. Posterity has called him Frederick Augustus the Just.

The older line of the Saxon dynasty of Wettin, called the Ernestinian, reigned mainly in Thuringia, and by the end of the seventeenth century it had divided into thirteen branches, each possessing a little duchy. Other dynasties too, possessed parts of Thuringia. In consequence this little territory, which was not much larger than the counties of Devonshire and Somerset together, contained 27 courts and governments, a Prince Bishop, two Free Towns, and four possessions belonging to states outside its borders. Not a few of these princelings lavished their money on a luxurious court life, covering the expenses by lending troops to foreign powers. Poaching in the ducal forests was subject to barbarous punishments. In the time of the Enlightenment, however, conditions improved. This was often due to the influence of the princesses, who created a new intellectual atmosphere of high cultural aspirations, active humanitarianism and devotion to the people's welfare. In Gotha it was Louise Dorothea, in Weimar Anna Amalia, and in Meiningen Charlotte Amalia who fulfilled this rôle. Their little courts became centres of the most brilliant intellectual life and reformatory zeal, and they educated their sons in this spirit. Charles Augustus of Weimar, his cousins Charles and George of Meiningen, and Ernest II of Gotha were brought up to be very good rulers. A similar part was played by Henrietta Caroline of Hesse-Darmstadt; Goethe called her 'the great landgravine'; Wieland wished to be all-powerful for a moment so as to make her the Queen of Europe; Frederick II, though no friend of women, called her the ornament and the admiration of her century. She had grown up in the entirely French culture dominating most courts, and did not know much German; yet she was in close contact with the greatest German writers of the time and supported their strivings.

South of Thuringia were the principalities of Ansbach and Bayreuth, belonging to the Franconian line of the Hohenzollerns. Margrave Charles Frederick William of Ansbach had on his desk a marble bust of Voltaire, but this did not prevent him from committing abominable acts of violence. In 1769 his principality went by inheritance to his relative Charles Alexander of Bayreuth. This prince was much criticized because he supplied troops to England for the American War, and was dominated by his English mistress, Lady Craven, whom he later married. She hated everything German and induced the Margrave to sell his country to Prussia and to live with her in England. Schiller was inspired by some of these events in writing his tragedy 'Kabale und Liebe' which paints a terrible picture of the depravity of a small court. Yet, it is doubtful whether the régime deserved this castigation. Some of the most prominent and best informed champions of Enlightenment, Nicolai, Dohm and Schloezer, praised the prince as a noble-minded man and the model of a ruler, and also appreciated his ministers very highly.[2] Even a critic of them, L. von Hess, admits that the prince's judgment and intentions were good, and that the people liked him sincerely, and puts the responsibility for faults on Lady Craven. A contemporary book[3] gives a detailed account of his policy which shows that the money received for the troops hired out was exclusively used for paying back heavy debts burdening the country, not for the prince. Since he had no children, his country would after his death in any case have fallen to his Prussian relatives.

In the house of Anhalt a martial character was predominant. One of its princes was Leopold of Dessau, who under the first three Prussian kings created the Prussian army. He was a rough soldier with uncouth manners and despotic habits; Prince Eugène of Savoy called him a bulldog. Like other princes of his house he married a woman without rank, the daughter of a chemist, but had mistresses also. His grandson was Prince Frederick Franz, who still lives in the memory of the people as Father Franz. He was a most high-minded man and a ruler very beneficial to his country. The prince was in close touch with the progressive thinkers and reformers of his time, trying to ennoble mankind and to make it happy. His special enthusiasm was devoted to philanthropism, (Cf. Ch. XVIII). Duke Charles Augustus of Weimar and his companion Goethe were special friends of Prince Franz. Charles Augustus wrote in a letter that Franz had one of the most beautiful souls he knew, that he had never met anybody whose mere presence spread so much benevolence, probity and love of mankind, and that personal contact with him gave one the feeling of improving oneself. Prince Franz reigned for 66 years. Napoleon passed through Dessau and met the old prince after the battle of Jena. The Emperor was much impressed by his personality, ordered that his country should be free from exactions and invited Franz to visit him in Paris.

Quite a number of princes who reigned over little territories had been deeply influenced by pietism, by the Herrenhuter and other sects, especially the houses of Lippe, Reuss, Stolberg, Isenburg, Wittgenstein and Saalfeld. Their courts cultivated a sincere piety and strict morality. F. K. von Moser, who knew the small courts and bitterly criticized many of them, expressed the greatest praise of

[2] Cf. Nicolai, *Reise durch Deutschland*, I, Dohm in Deutsches Museum, 1781, and Schloezer in Staatsanzeigen, part 3. Hess' criticism is in Vehse, vol. 40, p. 144.
[3] Cf. *Gemaelde aus dem aufgeklaerten 18. Jahrhundert*, 1786, I, p. 101.

the house of Lippe. Count Wilhelm von Schaumburg-Lippe was particularly remarkable. He was not only a famous general, and a ruler full of zeal for promoting the welfare, education and self-government of his people, but also in close touch with the most prominent thinkers and authors of his time. Moses Mendelssohn characterized him as 'the most refined Greek soul in a rugged West-phalian body.' He was a staunch enemy of any aggressive war and wished to frustrate it by developing the art of defence and a national militia instead of mercenaries. In order to propagate these principles, he founded a military academy. His greatest disciple was Scharn-horst who later, together with Gneisenau, reformed the Prussian army into a national and liberal sense. As Gneisenau said this work was entirely based on the ideas of Count Wilhelm.

Hesse-Cassel was an important factor in international affairs, owing to her close family relations with Britain, Denmark and Sweden. When the war of the Austrian Succession broke out (1740), the Landgrave of this country, Frederick I, was also King of Sweden and resided there, while his brother, William VIII, was his deputy in Hesse-Cassel. The latter was a martial ruler who for some time was also general in the Dutch army. In the traffic with soldiers he showed businesslike impartiality, supplying, in 1743, 6,000 mer-cenaries to King George II of Great Britain, who was an ally of Maria Theresa, and after the Union of Frankfurt (1744), 6,000 to Charles VII, who was her enemy. The Hessians formed a great part of the Pragmatic army, both under the British and the Dutch flag. When, in 1745, Britain was threatened by a Jacobite rising backed by France, 5,000 Hessians under Prince Frederick had a great share in putting it down. In the Seven Years' War Hesse-Cassel fought on the side of Britain and Prussia. In 1756, King George II informed Parliament that, as France threatened an invasion, he had sent for a body of Hessian troops again. Both Houses addressed him to let Hanoverian troops and artillery come to England as well, though Hanover, too, was menaced by France. The expected invasion, however, did not occur.[4]

[4] The attitude of British public opinion towards the German troops called to defend the country has been described by Smollett in this way: 'As the fears of an invasion subsided in the minds of the people, their antipathy to these foreign auxiliaries emerged. They were beheld with the eyes of jealousy, suspicion and disdain. They were treated with contempt, reserve and rigour. The ministry was execrated for having reduced the nation to such a low circumstance of disgrace, as that they should owe their security to German mercenaries.—In a word, the doubts and suspicions of a people naturally blunt and jealous were inflamed to such a degree of animosity that nothing would have restrained them from violent acts of outrage but the most orderly, modest and inoffensive behaviour by which both the Hanoverians and Hessians were distinguished.' Cf. *History of England*, 1804, III, p. 495.

Frederick II of Hesse-Cassel (1760-85), was educated in Geneva, where he also attended the university. His mother Maria, a daughter of George II of Great Britain, was highly cultured and had a very noble character. She exercised great influence on his education, and he was in fact humane, tolerant, knowledgeable and amiable, and was considered the paragon of enlightenment. As early as 1749 he secretly became a Catholic. When this later became known, his father was furious, and all Protestant rulers of Europe concluded a pact guaranteeing the rights of the Protestants in Hesse-Cassel. The Estates were to have the right to ask for their intervention should these rights be threatened. But Frederick never thought of doing so. He had excellent ministers and enacted many humane or advantageous reforms, greatly embellished Cassel, engaged famous scholars and artists, kept a splendid court and had numerous mistresses. He also was a great patron of Freemasonry, and his son Charles, who was a perfect scholar, a wise thinker and a good general, made efforts to win all rulers for it, in order to secure perpetual peace and universal happiness. Frederick wrote a 'Catechism for Princes', which received Voltaire's greatest praise. The long wars, however, in which the country was involved, and the great expenditure caused by them exhausted the finances. Their balance was restored by the trade in soldiers, in which this country was foremost among the German states.

Hesse-Cassel was traditionally the greatest supplier of troops to Britain. When the War of American Independence broke out, Frederick made a pact with George III, promising to supply 12,000 soldiers. This was particularly hateful to the people, because, in 1762, restricted conscription had been introduced. Thousands of Hessians emigrated in order to escape military service. A part of the price paid by Britain went, however, to Hesse's public finance, and Frederick too became rich through it.

William IX (1785-1807) continued the policy of reforms to a certain extent, but he was primarily a soldier and financier, and very parsimonious. He also carried on the lending of troops for subsidies, and had a very able court banker, Mayer Amschel Rothschild. When the prince was deposed by Napoleon and had to flee, his fortune was left in the custody of Rothschild, who managed it so well that both the prince and his banker became immensely rich.

Prince Frederick Augustus of Anhalt-Zerbst, the brother of the Empress Catherine of Russia, was also one of the princelings who made money by hiring out mercenaries to Britain and other governments; in the Seven Years' War he left his country and henceforth lived almost exclusively abroad, mainly in Basle. He authorized officials to carry on the government and instructed them that he did not want to be bothered with it.[5] Quite different was the House of Waldeck. Its princes had a martial tradition. Many of them commanded foreign armies. But some of them were also good rulers, especially Charles, who died in 1763, is highly praised by K. F. Moser as a true father of his country. The latter also described several princes of Nassau as excellent rulers.

<h3 style="text-align:center">NORTH GERMANY</h3>

Hanover's ruler was the king of Great Britain. The administration was entirely in the hands of the nobility who dominated the Estates. Hanover's greatest contribution to enlightenment was the work of the university of Göttingen, which will be discussed in another place.

Brunswick was, in the epoch surveyed, first governed by Duke Charles I (1735-80). Like many of his ancestors he was a well-meaning and humane ruler and very popular, but greatly hampered by the bad state of the finances, mainly brought about by great wars in the past.[6] He enacted and planned many reforms, but was faced with the opposition of the Estates even to promising projects. The state was saved from bankruptcy by treaties with Britain and Holland about the supply of troops for subsidies. The Estates consented to these agreements. It was later laid down that only foreigners should be enlisted as mercenaries. Charles' son Ferdinand later became his co-regent, and then his successor (1780-1806). He was regarded by European public opinion as a model of liberalism and also as a great general. Ferdinand was in close touch with the luminaries of enlightenment in many countries. He granted the Estates greater rights, and did much for the development of the school system. We will have to come back to his rôle later.

In Mecklenburg there had for a very long time been great struggles between the Dukes and the Estates, which were ended in 1755 by a settlement (Erbvergleich). The knights agreed that the Duke should have decisive power within his domains, which comprised two-fifths of the country, while the Duke left the nobility the power in the remaining three-fifths. This meant that he could not protect the peasants against the landlords. Mecklenburg had to suffer terribly in the Seven Years' War, since King Frederick of Prussia did not

---

[5] A. Crome, a very conscientious and well-informed writer, says in his autobiography (p. 108) that he was somewhat odd but very just and humane if the truth was known to him, and gives an example to prove this.

[6] Some historians call him a wastrel, but this is denied by P. Zimmermann in the *A.D.B.*

respect the neutrality of the country, but exploited it to the utmost. Duke Frederick I (1756-85) was a pietist and ruled in a just, mild and benevolent way. His successor, Frederick Franz (1785-1837), was also a good ruler. He had been educated in Switzerland and was filled with philanthropic ideas. At the same time he loved pleasure and was lavish in his expenditure but was exceedingly popular.

There were close dynastic relations between Denmark and the German countries of Holstein and Oldenburg. In 1488 the Estates of Denmark, Sleswick and Holstein elected Count Christian of Oldenburg their king, and a few years later Sweden and Norway did the same. His descendants still reign in Denmark. Oldenburg had mostly separate rulers, of whom Anton Guenter may be mentioned. He ruled in the seventeenth century for 65 years in a benevolent way, and skilfully kept his country out of the Thirty Years' War. From 1667 to 1773 Oldenburg was under the Danish Crown, and, like Holstein profited much from the reforms of the two Ministers Bernstorff. It then came to the Dukes of Holstein-Gottorp, a sideline of the Danish dynasty. The Dukes Frederick Augustus and Peter Frederick Ludwig were excellent rulers. Justus Gruner, a prominent statesman of liberal convictions describes the countries' conditions in his *Westphalian Pilgrimage*. He found there a most happy state of freedom, social equality, wealth and cultural accomplishment.

THE ECCLESIASTICAL STATES

Enlightenment also greatly affected the numerous ecclesiastical states. On the whole here too the princes, the nobles and the intellectual élite were to a great extent imbued with its ideas, while the lower clergy, the Jesuits and the masses of the people were opposed to them, often with fanaticism. The ruling archbishops, bishops and abbots usually belonged to the nobility and were elected by noble canons. There was, however, a great difference between those who took their religious duties and enlightenment seriously, and those who regarded the latter merely as a fashion and felt neither obliged to care much for the people nor to lead a life different from that of most princes or nobles. The Archbishopric and Electorate Cologne, together with other bishoprics, for example, was from 1583 to 1761 always in the hands of a Wittelsbach prince. They were usually neither beneficent rulers nor good priests, but led a dissolute life and carried on a policy hostile to the Emperor. This changed when, in 1761, Archduke Max Franz, a brother of Emperor Joseph II, was elected Archbishop of Cologne. He was a true Christian, a priest, ruler and patriot, who regarded his subjects as brethren equal to himself. Like his brother Joseph, he was an enemy of feudal and clerical privileges, and stood for equal right for all. He was opposed to the tradition of reserving high posts to noblemen, and insisted upon admitting non-nobles against the protest of the aristocracy. Georg Forster, the later leader of the Rhenish republicans, relates that he once saw him helping a poor woman to carry some heavy burden, and calls him a real human being in the most noble sense of the word. He did much for the welfare of the people. The new university of Bonn developed under his reign to the centre of enlightenment for the catholic countries on the lower Rhine.[7]

Many other prelates too tried to combine Christianity and enlightenment and have left a good record as rulers. Of the archbishops and electors of Mainz Emmerich Joseph belonged to them. Knigge, a great fighter against despotism, wrote that his subjects adored him. But the adherents of the old régime, especially the Jesuits, opposed him, and his successor Friedrich Karl returned to the tradition of a luxurious and sensual court life, and the maintenance of privileges. Yet he too professed enlightened principles, and introduced progressive reforms. High society was then dominated by the spirit of the Illuminati, preferred Voltaire to the Gospels, and flirted with republicanism. The Archbishop's coadjutor and successor was Baron Dalberg, a noble representative of enlightenment among Catholics, who was called the German Fénélon. In Trier, Archbishop and Elector Johann Philipp and his successor Clemens Wenzel, were both benevolent rulers. Other distinguished disciples of enlightened Catholicism were the Prince-Bishops of Bamberg Adam Friedrich, and his successor Franz Ludwig.

The Archbishop of Salzburg, Hieronymus Count Colloredo, was an outspoken follower of the doctrines of enlightenment. The busts of Voltaire and Rousseau stood in his study. He was very intelligent, industrious and economical, though the money which he saved partly increased his personal wealth. The reforms which he introduced in the Church agreed with those of Joseph II in Austria. The seminary for priests received a director who was an ardent disciple of Kant and held that religion and morality were identical, a view which the Archbishop shared. In spite of his numerous reforms in the interest of his country, he was not popular. The people resented the abolition of many holidays and old customs. Both the canons and the Estates brought an action against him at the Imperial Aulic Council, one of the High Courts, opposing his financial reforms. Hieronymus was an autocrat and bureaucrat, and very close-fisted.

[7] Cf. Braubach's excellent books about the last electors of Cologne and the first university of Bonn.

Mozart was in his service, was very badly paid, and had to dine at a table with the archbishop's valets. When he asked for a higher salary, the Archbishop refused, and his lord chamberlain turned him out of the door with a kick.

The Prince-Abbot Frobenius Forster of St. Emmeran was a famous scholar and former professor, who even when he had become a prince used to lecture to his subjects on the philosophy of Leibniz and Wolff, also issued an excellent edition of Alcuin's works, and was a great student of natural science. In Fulda Prince Bishop Henry VIII reigned, a scion of the barons of Bibra, whom F. K. Moser, a sharp critic of the ecclesiastical states, called the model of a humane and enlightened ruler. He was a father to his people and a most venerable personality. In particular, he improved the schools and homes for old people, and also cared for the Jews in his country by founding schools for them and in other ways. His relative Baron Siegmund Bibra was the head of the government and also edited a very progressive paper, the 'Journal from and for Germany' which will be discussed later. Other enlightened rulers of ecclesiastical states were the Bishop of Constance, and that of Hildesheim and Paderborn. There also were churchmen who aroused much criticism by anti-liberal decrees, for example Augustus, Prince-Bishop of Speyer. He was very intelligent, but impetuous and despotic, though he also did much for humanitarian purposes such as homes for old people, orphans and widows, hospitals etc. which he founded at his own expense.[8] Numerous high dignitaries belonged to Freemasonry though this movement had been condemned by the Pope. As examples may be mentioned the Prince-Bishops Count Schaffgotsch of Breslau, Count Welbrueck of Luettich, and Count Waldburg-Zell of Chiemsee. Many other cases of princes more or less guided by the spirit of the age could be adduced, but this is hardly necessary. It is obvious that the principles of enlightenment were widely spread in the ruling circles of Germany. The adoption of those principles alone was, of course, not enough to determine the character of a régime. It was only one factor among a great many which influenced the policy of a ruler.

[8] Cf. Gemaelde, I, p. 78. His conflict with Schloezer will be related later.

19

POLITICAL IDEAS IN THE AGE OF FREDERICK II AND
JOSEPH II

THE intellectual revolution brought forth by the Enlightenment entered a new phase about the middle of the century. Many events successively increased its momentum. The political climate was in many ways influenced by the fact that enlightened princes came to the throne. Though many of them ruled autocratically their reforms and plans not seldom brought about revolutionary changes in the public mind. Moreover the period was actually filled with revolutionary movements, which successively broke out in America, Holland, Belgium and France. Some of these movements kindled enthusiasm in Germany. But events in the field of political literature nourished such sentiments also. Montesquieu's greatest work, which became the Bible of liberalism, appeared in 1748. It was soon followed by the Encyclopédie, by the works of Rousseau, and by many other great writings. In Germany poetry and philosophy entered their Golden Age.

At the same time momentous social changes took place. The torchbearers of the new ideas were members of the liberal professions, especially professors, civil servants, and noblemen. In Germany these classes were particularly numerous owing to the multitude of states, governments and universities. The commercial and industrial middle classes too, increased and gained weight, though they could not compare in wealth with the merchants of London or Amsterdam. Many of the burghers of Hamburg, Leipzig and Frankfurt were helpful to the intellectuals, they bought their books, attended their plays and assisted them in publishing books and journals. The efforts of many literary critics to refine the

German language, literature and taste, the study of the great French
and English writers and the increase in the demand for good books
had the result that the number of authors rapidly rose. Up to the
sixties or longer it was hardly possible to live by writing alone.
Even a classic like Lessing was worried by grave financial troubles
all his life though he had a post as well. But the expansion of the
market for books enabled the publishers to pay better fees[1] and
writing became financially attractive, especially for officials and
professors who had another income besides. A journal of the time[2]
complained of the 'mania for writing', and attributed it to several
causes, particularly to the fact that the salaries of civil servants had
not been increased for a hundred years while the cost of living had
risen by the half. The increase in the number of writers is shown in a
periodical handbook which was founded by professor Hamberger
and continued by professor Meusel. It gave the names, addresses
and writings of the authors. Their number was between 2,000 and
3,000 in the sixties, a little over 3,000 in 1771, over 4,300 about 1776,
over 5,200 about 1784, nearly 6,200 about 1788, ca 7,000 in 1791,
ca 8,000 in 1795, 10,648 at the end of the century, and ca
11,000 in 1806. This publication also showed the distribution
of writers according to the various branches of literature and to the
regions in which they lived. The increase in the number of writers,
partly also was due to the growth of the reading public. The improvement of education, the exciting events of the time, and also the
increase in general wealth contributed to this rise. In many places
reading societies were founded, where the members could read the
latest books and journals. The fact that many German governments
and ecclesiastical authorities had for a long time already taken care
of the people's education had the result that sections of the lower
classes also increasingly became readers. Books of practical value
for peasants or artisans sold in very large editions. But poetry and
scientific books, too, were often read by people of the lower classes.
Gellert's poems were particularly popular.[3] In Saxony there were,
for instance two peasants who seriously studied astronomy, J.
Pahlitzsch and J. Ch. Gärtner. Pahlitzsch became famous when, in
1758, he was the first to observe a large comet through his telescope.
In the Tyrol a peasant, Peter Anich, aroused a sensation by the

[1] On the fees paid by publishers, and other relevant facts, cf. the books by
Krieg, Goschen and Goldfriedrich listed in the bibliography.
[2] Cf. *Journal von und fuer Deutschland*, vol. VII, 1790, p. 498.
[3] There were also writers of poetry from the lower classes. A real peasant,
Isaak Maus, who lived in the Harz region, often published poems in intellectual journals like the Deutsche Museum. Meusel mentions in his Gelehrtes
Deutschland a farrier, Johann Kaspar Wilke, whose poems were after his
death published by his friends.

scientific working out of the most accurate maps of his country. He was assisted by another peasant, Blasius Hueber, who was also scientifically instructed. When Anich died in 1766, at the age of 43, the government of the Tyrol set him a marble monument. Its Latin inscription said that he was equally excellent as a peasant, turner, cosmographer, astronomer, geographer, geometer, engraver and mechanic. Ulrich Bräker, a poor Swiss weaver, was deeply moved by Shakespeare and wrote a fine appreciation of his works, and also an autobiography. It is surprising how many men of the lower classes, such as small artisans, traders or peasants, wrote remarkable reminiscences of their life in the eighteenth century, sometimes revealing high cultural aspirations.[4] Some of them had considerable libraries. Besides the numerous lending libraries the number of bookshops was also comparatively great. In Hanover, for example, then a town of hardly 20,000 inhabitants, there were six or seven bookshops, and G. C. Brandes, a leading Hanoverian statesman, commented on 'the mania of the lower classes for reading'. Even the servants, he remarked, had their own reading society.

CONTROVERSIES ON THE IDEAS FATHERLAND AND NATION

Many political, social and intellectual events contributed to the rise of strong interest in political questions of basic importance. The defenders of enlightened absolutism increasingly destroyed the old ideological foundations of state and society, and declared that their aim was the happiness of the people and that men were essentially equal. Progressive rulers actually did much to promote social and intellectual liberty and equality, a reign of law, toleration and welfare. Political liberty, however, made no progress, except by the gradual relaxation of the censorship. Yet the self-consciousness of wide circles, in particular the young intellectuals, increased, and was vented in bitter criticism of despotism and the demand for political liberty.[5]

The words 'fatherland' and 'nation' became symbols of this striving. The idea of the fatherland was derived from the political and historical writers of antiquity and had been taken up by the humanists and their successors. The word nation had had a long history and its sense had gone through many changes till it

---

[4] Prof. R. Stadelmann has surveyed them in a most valuable book which, after his premature death, was finished by Prof. W. Fischer.

[5] Goethe has in his autobiography (book 12), given his views of how this feeling originated, and his statements should be read in the original.

M

approached the meaning of a sovereign people.[6] These watchwords, however, remained largely restricted to theoretical controversies. Political movements for their realization could hardly develop, mainly owing to the extreme German particularism. A striving for national freedom, in the sense of a wide participation of the people in functions of government, was impossible as long as the Germans were split into countless territorial and social groups between which there was very little unity, but much discord. There were exceptions which have already been mentioned. But on the whole particularism and other factors frustrated German national unity and liberty.

A certain movement towards these aims might have been possible when Germany had recuperated from the ravages of the Thirty Years' war and the aggression of Louis XIV, and when the ideas of enlightenment began to gain in strength. But just at this moment Frederick II began a policy rendering the two great German powers mortal enemies and thus barring any development of national unity and freedom. Frederick's militarism was based on the absolute autocracy of the king, and it forced Austria to suppress the rights of the Estates in order to have a free hand in increasing her military forces. Leopold II restored these rights and even planned a real parliamentary system. But he died too soon, and the French Revolution and twenty years of war with France gave complete predominance to the forces of conservativism and reaction.

It has been shown in earlier chapters that ideas of political freedom were discussed by German writers at all times. In the heyday of enlightenment, however, the discussion spread from academic circles to a wide public, largely owing to the influence of some brilliant French writers, who found many enthusiastic disciples in Germany. But as regards the fundamental German problem of particularism, their ideas were hardly helpful in finding a solution. Most of them praised little communities and regarded the small state as alone capable of true liberty. When the argument was raised that a small state could not defend itself against strong aggressors, they recommended the remedy of a federation, and pointed out that the German Empire actually was a federation. Rousseau praised the Empire as a bulwark of European peace also. A large state appeared to most of these authors as disposed to aggression and fitted only for a monarchy, though Montesquieu thought it might be tempered by the division of power, and regarded the English constitution as the model for this. Voltaire, too, had sympathies for small peaceable communities and for the English constitution, but in practice pre-

[6] I have described this development in the *Jahrbuch fuer Soziologie*, Erster Ergaenzungsband, 1927.

ferred a large monarchy, such as France, where a splendid cultural
life had developed, which in his view was unattainable in a small
republic. The physiocrats, in particular Quesnay and Turgot, advocated large states and an enlightened monarchy for reasons of
security and economic progress. The Swiss physiocrat Iselin, town
clerk of Basel, believed that only a large monarchy could guarantee
a reign of law and general welfare.[7]

The idea of a fatherland also became the subject of much discussion. It implied a protest against a system in which the prince
arrogated the exclusive right of governing. In Wurttemberg an
official once had a dispute with Duke Charles Eugen and pointed out
to him that he also had duties towards the fatherland. The Duke
thereupon exclaimed: 'What? I am the fatherland!' This idea,
however, was not only opposed to autocracy, but also to cosmopolitanism: the idea of a nation could imply both opposition to
monarchical absolutism, and to the sentiment of citizenship of the
world. Aristocratic writers, such as Count Oxenstierna, treated the
idea of a fatherland in a sarcastic way. Leibniz wrote that too many
people shared Thomasius' opinion that the duties to the fatherland
were only a chimera invented by pagans. In his view the fatherland
was to be dear to the heart of good men. The editor of the Hamburg
journal 'The Patriot', which was several times reprinted and translated into French and Dutch, declared in its first issue that he
regarded the whole world as his fatherland, even like a single city,
and himself as a co-citizen of all human beings. The idea admitted,
however, of different interpretations. Jaucourt, an editor of the
Encyclopédie, later contended that without political liberty there
could be no fatherland and no patriotism. Voltaire, in his Philosophical Dictionary (1764), came to the conclusion that only some-
body who possessed a part of the national soil, or other property,
and political rights, was a member of the community and had a
fatherland. He also found that the larger the fatherland the less one
could love it: a too numerous family whose members one hardly
knew could not arouse warm love; Patriotism, moreover, often made
men enemies of all others, since to wish for the greatness of one's
own country meant to wish for the misfortune of one's neighbours.

Voltaire's objection that the love of the fatherland, or patriotism,
might easily become national hatred of other nations was also put
forward by other writers. J. G. Zimmermann, a Swiss, in 1758,
published a book on national pride which was very widely read. He
had a great reputation both as a physician and as a writer, and was
British-Hanoverian court doctor and medical consultant to the

[7] Cf. E. Sieber's book, where interesting details are given.

Empress of Russia and many other royal persons. In the first edition of the book he maintained that love of the fatherland could only be found in republics, but in the following editions he admitted that in enlightened monarchies also the people might be proud of their nation.[8] Zimmermann was a great admirer of Frederick the Great, who consulted him in his last illness. His book, however, introduced a new subject into the discussion, namely the nature of nationalism, though he does not use this term. He begins with the statement that almost every nation wears on its nose the falsifying spectacles of national self-love and haughtiness. There are praiseworthy exceptions, and one must not make a whole people responsible for the faults of some. Nevertheless, the typical attitude is almost everywhere, the boasting about national virtues, real or imaginary, the looking down on other nations, and an exaggerated feeling for the national honour. The national self-love is only a specific case of a much wider sentiment. Almost every group develops self-praise and contempt of other groups. The Greeks regarded all foreign peoples as barbarians, and modern nations show very similar views. Zimmermann illustrates his psychological observations with numerous examples. Though he had the greatest admiration for the English and the French he finds that contempt of foreigners is very outspoken with them. The English despise the French, whom they regard as slaves, most of all. If they wish to insult a foreigner, they call him a French dog and men dressed in an un-English way are assumed to be French and are pelted with mud. The French regard themselves as the first nation of the world and other peoples as inferior, though their politeness induces them not to say this frankly. Zimmermann admits that there is also a justifiable national pride which may be most valuable in inspiring the young people of a country to emulate the great men of their nation, and to follow its praiseworthy traditions. But even this noble national pride may degenerate to detestable barbarism.

A French critic asked why Zimmermann had said nothing unfavourable about the Germans. He replied that this had good reasons. He himself was not a German but a Swiss, and there certainly was much social haughtiness among Germans, but no feeling of national supremacy. Quite the contrary, the Germans on the whole showed no national pride, but considered everything foreign as superior to their own achievements. This view was confirmed by many other writers.

Zimmermann's book incited Thomas Abbt to write a book on

[8] I have used the 4th edition of his book (1768) which is much larger than the former ones, and greatly improved.

dying for the fatherland (1761). The author was a Swabian, who from enthusiasm for Frederick the Great had gone to Prussia and had become a professor there. Later, however, he became a counsellor and professor in the little principality of Schaumburg-Lippe. He was a writer of great gifts but died when only 28 years old. The book mentioned was written at a time when the Seven Years' War had taken a very bad turn for Frederick. Abbt's intention was to induce students and other young people to join the Prussian forces. It was generally assumed, he wrote, that only republicans had reason to be proud of their fatherland and that in a monarchy it was merely empty talk, a meaningless phrase. This may be true in an arbitrary despotism, and a republic is in fact apt to bring forth a greater passion for the fatherland than a monarchy. But there were also bad republics which were really subject to a dictator; Rome lost the character of a fatherland through her exaggerated lust for wars of conquest. A monarchy which did not restrict the liberty of its citizens more than was necessary for the common weal, was a fatherland too. Patriotism ennobled the mind of a people. The honour of the monarch and that of the people coincide. Abbt had the success that many students joined the colours—and a great proportion of them lost their lives. But when the war was over, most of those who had become officers and were not nobles were soon deprived of their rank, because the king considered officers of non-noble descent as unfit for the army. He believed that only noblemen had a sense of honour, though he admitted that there were exceptions. This was not at all what Abbt had had in mind. In 1779 the king himself wrote his Letters on Patriotism to show that Prussia was not a despotism. It was the law that reigned, the people had some share in the government, and all owed much to the state.

Klopstock's poetry, which will later be discussed, is full of enthusiasm for the fatherland and for freedom. The poet himself was a republican, as were many of his disciples. Yet in 1775 Heinrich Fuessli, a Swiss, spoke with bitter contempt about patriotism and the whole German exaltation about the fatherland. If he were at least a Swiss! But a German fatherland did not exist. It reminded Fuessli of a servant proud of his livery.

Joseph von Sonnenfels also wrote an essay on the Love of the Fatherland (1771). He starts with the observation that in the ancient world patriotism was a passion which we cannot fully understand. Our hearts remain cold when the word 'fatherland' is pronounced. Merely feeling satisfied with one's fatherland does not yet amount to patriotism which is not impartial, but an emotion exalting our own nation and state as the best. Even the most primitive nation believes itself to be better than all the others. Actually the love of the fatherland is a kind of self-love. Sonnenfels tried to trace the conditions either promoting or counteracting this feeling. The Romans punished any insult against a Roman by war : the possession of Roman citizenship was a privilege maintained against the whole world. Raynal was right when he remarked that, in modern times, the English were the first who proclaimed the majesty of their nation. Cromwell said he wished to bring it about that the English name was honoured as much as the Roman had once been. He set up the principle that, even in foreign countries, an Englishman could only be judged by Englishmen. The author makes many shrewd comments on national sentiment. As an Austrian he obviously recognized the elementary passion slumbering in national emotions. But he probably could not carry his observations to their conclusion since they might have conflicted with the policy of Joseph II. Sonnenfels published the second, enlarged edition of his treatise, which we have used here, just at the time (1785) when the Emperor began a policy which aroused fierce national passion in Hungary. This conflict disclosed the tragic antagonism between enlightenment and nationalism, which has become world-wide in our time.

A criticism of Sonnenfels' essay appeared in a Frankfurt journal. Its author was the young Goethe, who was an editor and principal reviewer of the journal.[9] The critic objected to the constant complaint that in Germany there was no fatherland, no nation and no patriotism. 'If we find a place in the world,' he asked, 'where we can live quietly with our belongings, if we have a field which nourishes us and a house which gives us shelter—have we then not got a fatherland? But the patriotism of the Romans'—he continued—'God forbid!' This review needs the comment that Sonnenfels certainly did not wish for a patriotism like that of the Romans.

Of the German classics C. M. Wieland had a particular interest in politics. In 1739 he wrote : 'In my childhood I was told much of my duties, but the duty of being a German patriot was so alien to the age that I cannot remember ever having heard the word German pronounced in an honourable sense, and the word Deutschheit (German nationality) was entirely unknown. In 1780, a project for a German Academy was published, which Wieland criticized in an article. He expressed the opinion that the words fatherland and

---

[9] In his splendid book on Goethe's political opinions, Wilhelm Mommsen has expressed doubt of Goethe's authorship of this review, but without giving any reasons. To me the reviewer seems exactly to express Goethe's views; three years before he had rejected Gleim's war-songs with the words that he was not interested in German victories at all. Cf. A. Bielschowsky, *Goethe*, 30th edition, 1917, p. 150.

patriotism certainly sprang from good intentions, but easily led to madness. Germany was so divided that all idea of achieving great aims by united action would for ever remain a patriotic dream. All the disadvantages of this lack of unity, however, were greatly out-weighed by a sole, inestimable gain, namely the fact that because of it no great and civilized people in the world enjoyed a greater measure of human and civic freedom. The multitude of political forces within Germany resulted in an equilibrium favourable to the freedom of the spirit and the unfolding of all talents. Germans should be proud of such a constitution, and patriotism could only consist in its preservation and improvement. It was the Palladium of the nation on which its freedom, strength, fame and wealth depended.

Though particularism had plunged Germany into catastrophes like the Thirty Years' War, and other disasters, it had not thereby become discredited in the eyes of the German peoples. Even thinkers of the greatest experience in politics left no doubt that they pre-ferred the multitude of small states to one strong Germany. If they pleaded for German unity they meant concord between these states, not their disappearance or their depression to mere provinces. If they wished for an influential central authority, they did not think of power politics but of the promotion of culture, as Herder's poem to Joseph II shows. There also was much pride in Germany's achievements in learning. spread of education and enlightenment, and the wish to reach a similar position in poetry. The disadvan-tages of excessive particularism were sometimes complained about, especially the misgovernment of the rulers of small states, but on the whole the majority obviously believed that particularism had more good than bad sides. Even Franz Karl von Moser, the most ardent defender of the idea of German national unity, in 1759, expressed the wish that the old custom of partitioning a state between heirs should be restored, because many small states were better than one strong one.

It is very significant that the opponents of a political unification of Germany by strengthening the power of the Emperor often laid great stress upon the fact that this kind of unity would make Ger-many the strongest military power, would disturb the European balance of power and was therefore inadmissible. This was, for instance, a principal argument of Johannes Mueller, the greatest historian of the age, and of S. Puetter, the most prominent expert in public law. Both Justus Moeser and Immanuel Kant would have liked Germany to be a federation of many small states of a republi-can character.

If the average inhabitant of Germany felt more allegiance to his little homeland than to the idea of a great, united powerful Germany this was the emotional tradition formed by many centuries. The absence of a strong central power was widely regarded and defended as 'the German Freedom'. And if great thinkers and citizens of the world, like Goethe and Wieland, deeply distrusted the idea of one German fatherland or nation they also had a foreboding of the evils of nationalism and imperialism spreading to Germany. These evils were already operating in the existing national states. A short while later the French Revolution bred a frenzy of French nationalism which deluged the world with blood. What these thinkers desired was a peaceable, gradual evolution of freedom, respecting that of the individual and of other nations, and setting cultural values above the power and prestige of the state.

The demand for freedom was also faced with the fact that there were so many different sorts of it. The most prominent political philosophers of antiquity had found that a mixture of monarchy, aristocracy and democracy would be the best form of state to safeguard freedom. Montesquieu had advocated a balance between the legislative, executive and judicial powers to this end. Moreover, the demand for freedom referred to many different fields such as internal and external politics, religion, economics, morality, social relations, education and so on. Experience showed that freedom in one field did not necessarily foster freedom in another field, too. A republic based on political freedom might be less willing to grant religious, social or educational freedom to the people than an enlightened monarchy. History contains numerous examples confirming this observation.

THE UNIVERSITY OF GOETTINGEN

At the beginning of the epoch of Enlightenment it had been the University of Halle which, soon after its foundation, had become the centre of this movement. Thomasius, and later Wolff, continued Pufendorf's rationalism in elaborating the principles of natural law. Francke cultivated pietism which often consisted in criticizing the same obsolete powers as rationalism, though under an entirely different aspect. Both schools laid the foundation for great reforms leading to a new era.

Forty-five years after the University of Halle that of Goettingen was founded (1737). Its originator was the Hanoverian Minister Gerlach Adolph von Münchhausen, who induced King George II as Elector of Hanover to sanction his plans. Münchhausen had himself studied at Halle, and also at Utrecht and Jena. For thirty-three years, until his death (1770), he had decisive power in all questions regarding the University of Goettingen, and by his talents and character he was qualified for this task to the highest degree. His great plan was to create a university where, besides other students, the rulers and statesmen of the coming generation should be instructed in the political sciences and in the lessons of history, imbued with an enlightened spirit and trained in the practical application of what they had been taught. The best professors available were to be entrusted with this task. Goettingen was further to be emancipated from the predominance of clerics which still prevailed in other universities. Orthodox theology, scholastic philosophy and antiquated ideas of law and morality were to be avoided. But natural science, medicine and other branches of learning too, should be cultivated in a modern, empirical spirit. The students had no longer merely to memorise certain prescribed textbooks, but were to learn by observation, experience and discussion. The new university received a large library, an operating theatre, clinics, an observatory, etc. Moreover, Münchhausen succeeded in winning numerous scholars of the highest rank as professors, of whom a few will be treated later in detail. All this made the university the first modern one, which served as a model for all the others.

It was characteristic of Goettingen that the greatest stress was laid on pragmatism, or the value of studies for the welfare and moral improvement of mankind. Hitherto a learned man had been expected to know countless details which had no significance for practical tasks at all. This tendency was, for example, particularly marked in history and classical philology. Now, the scholars of Goettingen developed a spirit in many branches of learning which exemplified what Pope had meant by his words : 'The proper study of mankind is man'. The decisive question now became : what can we learn from certain facts about human nature, the spirit of individuals and nations? Historical research ceased to be merely an accumulation of dynastic details and was directed to the development of civilization, thought, economics, social conditions, and so on. Moreover, it was extended from one's own people to all other nations, and became universal history. The principal aim was thereby to approach a deeper insight into the spirit of the nations, to find out the causes of its development and variations. Was it the climate or other geographical factors, which formed it? Or was it the outcome of the mentalities of peoples, or of the initiative of great men, or of religion or the forms of state or economics? Did intellectual enlightenment also bring about moral improvement?

M*

What was the rôle of war and peace? Was historic development due to chance or was it guided by an inherent law towards a goal such as freedom or happiness?

A deeper study of the past raised many such questions. The Goettingen historians, influenced by Hume, Ferguson, Montesquieu, Herder and others, contributed much to the elaboration of a new concept of history. But in other fields also the principles of empiricism, universalism and pragmatism were exceedingly fruitful and led to the development of many new disciplines, such as anthropology, sociology, technology, and so on.

Münchhausen's aim of attracting to Goettingen young men who one day would be rulers of states, or their ministers was amply fulfilled. Great numbers of them, from abroad also, assembled in the lecture rooms and institutes. They not only increased Goettingen's reputation but were also very welcome from the financial point of view, since students of high rank had to pay much larger fees than commoners, were usually accompanied by tutors and valets, and had money to spend. Owing to their example the behaviour of the students was also much more civilized in Goettingen, than in other universities. Münchhausen selected mainly scholars with progressive opinions to become professors. Since the Elector resided in London, Hanover was practically an aristocratic republic like Great Britain. Many professors admired the British constitution, while others saw their ideal in Switzerland or Holland. The young princes and nobles heard a good deal about the evils of despotism and aristocratic privileges from many professors. The students were also instructed in the politics of the day and attended courses in which newspapers were read and discussed. Goettingen not only opened a new epoch in the history of German learning, but also did much to spread the seeds of Enlightenment in the ruling circles.

THE TWO MOSERS AND THEIR FIGHT
AGAINST DESPOTISM

Johann Jacob Moser (1701-85) came from a family which for centuries had supplied Wurttemberg with excellent civil servants and Lutheran clergymen, and which had been ennobled, though he himself made no use of his title. At the age of 19 he began his career as a professor of law at the University of Tuebingen, but soon he was attracted by the imperial court in Vienna where many Swabians had reached the position of leading statesmen. The young man, although without connections, was at once received by the Vice-

Chancellor of the Empire, Count Frederick Charles Schoenborn, who was impressed by his talents and introduced him to other ministers. Emperor Charles VI, too, several times granted him audience. Moser could have made a great career in the imperial service if he had become a Catholic, and even without this condition great opportunities were offered to him. But he refused them and went back to his homeland where he entered the service of the ruling duke as counsellor, and married. But soon he returned to Vienna, where he stayed for two years and worked for the Imperial Aulic Council, one of the two High Courts of the Empire.[10] In 1726, however, he was in Stuttgart again and in the following years he occupied various posts as counsellor to the government and as professor of jurisprudence in various German states. These changes were mostly due to his rigorous sense of justice and his unwillingness to submit to the spirit of despotism then prevalent in many governments. He early achieved fame as an outstanding expert on German public law, and was frequently consulted about difficult legal questions, which he also treated in his numerous writings. In 1748 he founded an Academy of Political Science to train princes and statesmen for their future occupation. But his experience of the ruling circles, manifold intrigues against him and painful illness induced him to withdraw temporarily from the world. In his youth theological studies had destroyed every religious belief in him, but later the writings of the English theologian, Derham, on the purposeful structure of the universe, restored in him belief in a God and he came very near to the spirit of pietism. Yet aberrations of this movement, in particular Zinzendorf's excessive emotionalism, repelled Moser. Nevertheless, he lived several years in a small community of friends inspired by quiet piety, and also educated his children in this spirit.

In 1751 the Estates of Wurttemberg offered him the post of counsellor in legal questions, which he accepted. The full Estates were at that time not assembled, but had nominated a committee to represent them. Moser endeavoured to safeguard the parliamentary rights of the Estates, to maintain good relations between them and the ruling Duke, Charles Eugen, and to promote the introduction of important legal and economic reforms. His proposals for reforms, however, found more understanding with the Duke than with the committee, which was averse to any innovation. But soon Moser came into the sharpest conflict with the Duke.

[10] Moser wrote an autobiography, which appeared in 1768. His experience in Vienna and other important news were added in a separate volume to the 3rd edition which appeared in 1783.

Charles Eugen had received subsidies from France on condition that he put troops at her disposal on demand. In the Seven Years' War France made this demand, but the Duke had squandered the money on his own pleasures, and so he raised the soldiers by means of press-gangs. This was against the constitution and aroused an outcry. Moser drafted energetic protests on behalf of the Estates and advised measures of resistance. The Duke and his leading minister, Count Montmartin, saw in him the soul of the opposition. In 1759 he was arrested and imprisoned in a fortress where he was not permitted to receive any visitors, to possess any books except the Bible, or to have the means for writing. This harsh internment lasted for more than five years. The Estates tried to have him released, but in vain: Moser's opposition to the illegal raising of troops seemed to be against the military interest of the powers which were involved in a great war with Prussia and England. Justice was therefore silenced. When the war had ended, however, the Protestant powers which had guaranteed the rights of the Estates, namely Prussia, Denmark and England, intervened in Moser's favour and the Imperial Aulic Council ordered the Duke to set Moser free immediately. Charles Eugen had also changed his mind and endeavoured to make good his despotic violation of justice by granting a pension to Moser and various favours to his family.

Besides his official activities, Moser was indefatigable in writing works on German public law, defining the rights and duties between governments and between them and their subjects. He became the greatest authority in this field of learning. In his autobiography he gives a list of 227 books published by him and a number of others which were not printed—and many of his works had numerous volumes. His unfinished German Public Law (1737-53) runs into 52 parts in 27 volumes, and the revised edition (1766-75) is equally large. His Reichs-Fama, a periodical which printed legal documents, had 23 volumes. Moser's biographer, A. Schmidt, estimated that he wrote between 500 and 600 volumes, treating historical, economic and other subjects besides public law. He also wrote about a thousand religious poems.

For Moser the most urgent task appeared to be the protection of the rights of all sections of the people. He did not consider the existing laws satisfactory, and thought that a major revolution might break out, which would, perhaps, lead to better conditions. Yet he was convinced that one should not work for a revolution, but should preserve the existing order and try to improve it in a legal way. This order, he believed, contained provisions which, rightly interpreted and used, could have good results. He expected this largely from the supreme judicial authority of the emperor, who should most energetically resist the striving of the territorial rulers for unlimited, arbitrary power, and protect the rights of the Estates and of all groups and individuals. Even in the countries where the Estates were no longer convoked by their princes, they still existed legally and could assert their rights. The question was whether they would dare to do so and whether the emperor would be strong enough to secure their rights. But though Moser stood for a strong central power, he did not wish for an all-powerful one. He wanted the maintenance of the numerous small states and saw in their existence a guarantee that Germany would not become a strong war-like empire breeding militarism and despotism. Germany, he said, was under existing conditions most unfitted for war and the emperor should not enter one except in extreme necessity. Moser once expressed his political ideal in the words, 'It would be best if all nations of the world were like the Swiss'.

His eldest son, Frederick Charles Moser (1723-98), was inspired by the same principles as his father and had to suffer for them in a similar way. He was both an active statesman and the author of numerous books, mostly written at times when he was not occupied with official duties. His reading was enormous and his writing pithy, brilliant and fearless. In his youth he had been imbued with the spirit of pietism, and he always clung to the conviction that politics should conform to the spirit of Christianity. Moser deplored that many adherents of enlightenment tended to abandon the religious foundations of morality and to regard it merely from utilitarian aspects, thereby opening a road to the most arbitrary conclusions. But he was filled with enthusiasm for true enlightenment. Montesquieu's greatest work became his gospel, but he also highly appreciated Rousseau, whose principal works appeared shortly after his own. It is astounding with what facility Moser wrote books substantiated by great learning and practical experience, and most impressive in style. In historical, juristic and political argumentation he smashed all his opponents; he could rise to the height of pathos to waken conscience, was a master of satire, and also wrote poetry. Goethe, who knew him, says in his reminiscences that Moser's writings had a very important influence upon him; he describes him as a fine character, pleasant, versatile and tender, but of a restless temperament, never satisfied and therefore often compelled to change his post. Nearly all of Moser's writings are directed against despotism and militarism, which he regarded as the greatest plagues of mankind, and he never minced his words. In spite of his frankness, his books were not prohibited by the censor, nor did they hinder his rise to the highest dignities. But conditions in Germany were most unfavourable to the full unfolding of his genius. The highest post which he achieved was that of prime minister of a state with less than 300,000 inhabitants. If Moser had lived in England, he could have become a Burke.

Moser's official career consisted in his employment by different rulers of the House of Hesse, which was split into several branches. For a short time he was also in the imperial service. He acquired an intimate knowledge of conditions at the small courts, and was revolted by the moral depravity and the disregard of justice and honesty which was characteristic of many of them. There were exceptions, but the general picture was disheartening. In the Seven Years' War, Moser became a diplomat of Landgrave Louis VIII of Hesse-Darmstadt. This prince indulged in excessive hunting and was overburdened with debts, partly the outcome of great wars in the past and partly due to the extravagance of his predecessors. He was on the Austrian side. His son, the later Louis IX, also had an expensive hobby : he kept a regiment of specially tall grenadiers whom he drilled to perfection personally. Hesse-Darmstadt did not lend her troops for money to foreign powers as did Hesse-Cassel. The prince lived aloof from the capital, in an armed camp; he was an ardent admirer of Frederick II. His wife, Henriette Caroline, was one of the most highly cultured and distinguished women of her age, greatly admired by the intellectual élite. She acted as a patron to F. C. Moser and hoped that he would save the country from bankruptcy and make it the model of a progressive state.

Moser had already written many books before he entered the Hessian service, but the book which made him famous was 'The Master and the Servant', that is, the prince and his principal minister. It appeared in 1759, while the Seven Years' War was raging. In the preface Moser says that he had been encouraged to write it by a highly-placed person who wished to have a picture of how a good government should be organized. This probably refers to Henriette Caroline. The author begins by pointing out that every government has its tradition and the most important factor in forming it is the personality of its rulers. The so-called great kings are mostly great evils for their peoples. True, there was at present a king (Frederick II) who was certainly a great man by his outstanding intelligence, energy and character; it was a pity, however, that he had not a world for himself alone. Peoples in general were too much disposed to think the best of their princes and to exculpate them from their misdeeds. True, here and there one finds princes deserving the name

of father of their people, but there are also many tyrants, a perpetual shame for their country. Few princes do not misuse their
powers. In former times a prince was educated in his youth for his
task and then introduced into public affairs, but to-day this has
mostly ceased. Many young princes are told by the courtiers surrounding them that serious studies and work in general are beneath
their dignity, and they spend their youth in shameful laziness,
debauchery, hunting, gambling, drinking or playing at soldiers. The
introduction of primogeniture has aggravated the evil, since now the
younger sons must become soldiers. It is doubtful whether it is a
blessing for Germany to have a few powerful princes instead of
many of lesser power.

The primarily military education of a prince, Moser continues,
leads to great evils, such as the harsh treatment of subjects, ignorance concerning the real tasks of a ruler, a disposition to violate the
most sacred obligations to the Estates, and so on. This system
originated in France, where the warlike nobility demanded that a
nobleman must have taken part in wars to deserve esteem. The
restless French temperament also required an outlet in war. Frederick William I imitated the French example and from Prussia the
French military system spread over all the German countries. The
military training of a prince may also have advantages, for example
discipline, but if it lasts too long it accustoms him to neglect his
other duties. He commands his ministers like military persons and
demands from them and others a blind, unconditional obedience
like that imposed upon soldiers in the field. Such princes spurn
careful, patient deliberation and think that a country can be
governed like a regiment on the parade ground. In a war, violence is
above right, it suppresses humane feelings and the mind becomes
insensitive to the misery, poverty and distress of the people. The
idea gains ground that a prince is only great if he has a great army.
This plunges a country into financial ruin and induces princes
to take subsidies from foreign powers for delivering troops to
them.

Even in our times a minister must dare to tell a prince to his face
that he should respect the voice of God and of his conscience.
There were formerly rulers who did so, but this has changed since
Richelieu in his Political Testament gave the poisonous counsel that
a ruler or statesman must not let himself be induced by qualms of
conscience to act against the interests of the state, but must harden
himself against having scruples. Despotism is now defended by the
maxim that a ruler is responsible to God only, and this phrase is

used to stop the people from complaining. God will certainly punish princes who are inflated with the lust for unlimited power, alleged fathers of their people, who allow their children to be murdered to gain foreign money; but the lickspittles in their cabinets and unworthy court preachers do not remind them of this. Examples of conscientious rulers are today all too rare.

Moser then discusses many specific consequences of despotic principles. The cases mentioned, without names, obviously refer to well-known happenings. He speaks, for example, of a prince searching all countries from Norway to Naples to find a particularly tall fugleman for his troops, ready to pay ten thousand florins for him. Such actions were habitual to the prince who was soon to become Moser's own ruler and under whom he served as prime minister. After describing and condemning the aberrations of despotism, the author deals in great detail with the ways of organizing a good government. In opposition to the cabinet system, the basis of despotism, he recommends the nomination of a prime minister who must not only have the confidence of the prince, but also enjoy the trust and love of the people. Moser's observations show great psychological penetration.

The book caused a sensation not only in Germany, but all over Europe. Soon 10,000 copies were sold. It was reprinted and translated into various languages, twice into French and even into Russian. Other books appeared supporting or criticizing Moser. He became the hope of the progressive intellectuals. Many princes were furious with him but did not dare to show this publicly. His severe criticisms of princes and governments, therefore, did not hinder his further career. He was even appointed to a high diplomatic post in the service of Hesse-Cassel.

When Frederick II waged his first aggressive war, Moser believed his propaganda slogan that he was fighting for Protestantism and German liberty against the sinister plots of the Habsburgs and Jesuits. It took some time before he saw through this falsehood. Though he was deeply impressed by Frederick's personality, he abhorred his militarism and despotism, and the more he pondered the questions involved, the more Frederick's policy appeared to him as the greatest danger to German unity and freedom. The Seven Years' War seemed to him a civil war and a fratricidal struggle. When Joseph II was elected Roman king (successor to the emperor) and in 1765 became emperor and his mother's co-regent, Moser was filled, instead, with enthusiasm for him. It had always been his guiding principle that politics must be in agreement with morality and the existing laws. This idea had been elaborated by Veit Ludwig von Seckendorf in the spirit of an enlightened Lutheranism, and laid down in a classical book which Moser appreciated very highly. Gradually, however, the influence of Montesquieu and Moser's own experience enlarged his vision and made clear to him that the national spirit was also of significance. It was not enough that the prince and his ministers should heed the voice of the Christian conscience. The whole people has to be educated to active participation in political life and to be filled with a desire for solidarity and co-operation. But the idea of an active national spirit went much farther and implied incalculable consequences. Moser was, in this question, much influenced by Isaac Iselin, a Swiss statesman, patriot and thinker with whom he was in frequent correspondence and whom he greatly admired. Iselin worked for the education of Swiss youth to a new patriotism, and was inspired by the ideas of the philanthropists, who propagated a system of natural education. Hitherto Moser's patriotism had been predominantly particularistic. Every little homeland was, in his eyes, the fatherland of its citizens. He also wished for a strong central authority, but merely to defend peace and the reign of law. Now, however, Moser became increasingly imbued with a wider feeling of patriotism towards the German fatherland, though he rejected any exaggerated national self-love and animosity against other nations.

These ideas were put forward in several writings, of which the little book *Of the German National Spirit* (1765) was particularly successful. The Germans, Moser proclaimed, were one people, having in common their language, customs, laws and institutions. Yet they had for centuries been a riddle, disunited and powerless, and therefore the victims of aggression and the objects of contempt. All these troubles were due to an excess of territorialism, the lack of a common national spirit, religious hatred, ignorance of the national history and laws, and the spreading of despotism and militarism. Reform must begin by educating the young people to a new patriotism, which recognizes duties towards the common fatherland.

This pronouncement caused a great controversy in which Moser was severely criticized by those defending the unlimited rights of the territorial princes, most of all by the admirers of King Frederick II. Moser replied, elaborating his ideas in further books and tracts. He stressed that only a free people could have a fatherland, praised England as the country of freedom, and declared that in Germany the Estates represented the people and must take part in the government. But his ideas on the details of constitutional reform were never stated fully and clearly, probably because a far-reaching reform could not have been achieved by peaceful means, but only by great wars and revolutions, which Moser detested. Germany's extreme decentralization in any case made her quite unfitted for a revolution, and the example of the French Revolution was soon to show that exciting mass passions could only lead to anarchy, and at last to a new and ruthless militarism and despotism. Moser sharply attacked Frederick's system. His militarism, he declared, was incompatible with human dignity and degraded men to the level of beasts or machines. The German national spirit could not but consist in the striving for freedom, as its history showed, until the influence of Louis XIV brought about the rise of despotism and militarism in Germany too.

Moser had come to the belief that the House of Austria alone could lead Germany to nationhood. As early as 1766 he had published a book defending it against the usual denigrations with very convincing arguments. The partisans of the Prussian cause replied in a flood of pamphlets attacking Moser with vicious aspersions. Moser went to Vienna, where he was enchanted by Joseph II's personality. He was particularly impressed by the fact that the Emperor knew long passages from Montesquieu's books by heart and was determined to carry out his proposals. In 1767 Moser obtained the high post of a member of the Imperial Aulic Council. The Emperor also renewed the old nobility of the Moser family and made him a baron. Yet relations between him and the Emperor were soon disturbed. Moser found that Joseph was imitating Frederick and often fell into despotic ways, though his aims were high and he was benevolent to the people. Other reasons, too, made Moser feel unhappy. In 1770, the Emperor complied with his wish to be relieved of his duties in Vienna, and he appointed Moser administrator of the county of Falkenstein, which was near Hesse.

In the meantime, Louis IX had become the ruler of Hesse-Darmstadt, and he and his wife, Henriette Caroline, urged Moser to enter their service again and to become president of the government, with wide powers. The prince and the country were in the greatest financial straits. Moser accepted the post (1772) and his name alone went far in restoring confidence and procuring credit for the country. He succeeded in settling the financial difficulties in a satisfactory way. Moreover, he introduced and planned great reforms in the interest of the common weal. But his great success in restoring sound conditions had made him many enemies among the courtiers and bureaucrats, and they endeavoured to bring about his fall by accusing him of having misused his powers. Their intrigues greatly wounded Moser's sensibilities and he resigned voluntarily. The prince knew what he owed to him and he declared in an edict that he was completely satisfied with his services and that it must be said to his everlasting fame that he had rescued him from a labyrinth, which previous ministers had been unable to achieve. Yet Moser's enemies redoubled their efforts and their machinations had the result that he fell into disgrace (1780). It may be that they directed the attention of the prince to the numerous passages in Moser's writings condemning and ridiculing princes who played at soldiers and wasted money on it. In any case the new ministry published the worst defamations against the former head of the government, without giving him any opportunity of defending himself. He appealed to the Imperial Aulic Council as the High Court, which ordered the prince to make good the injury to his honour and to compensate him for the damage suffered. Yet his enemies raised juristic objections and continued the persecutions, even sequestrating his property. The High Court issued further injunctions against this illegal procedure, but it was still carried on in a new form. In 1790, however, the prince died and his successor, Louis X, had an excellent character. He at once stopped the proceedings, compensated Moser for all losses and granted him an adequate pension.

After his resignation, Moser resumed his literary activities. The first to appear were his letters to Iselin dealing with Necker, whose plans for solving France's financial distress were then in the foreground. A book dealing with Luther's opinions about rulers and governments, which closely agreed with Moser's own views, followed. Then appeared one on the ecclesiastical princes of Germany, discussing the reasons why their states were not as happy as they could be. This is mainly ascribed to the lack of intellectual freedom, so Moser proposes to secularize these states, to compensate the bishops, and to give the states new secular rulers to be elected by the Estates. It is significant that the author, though a Protestant, recognizes many of the good sides of the ecclesiastical states also. Many of their rulers were enlightened and doing their best for the state's welfare, so that on the whole the old saying still held good : 'It's a good life under the crozier'. Moser's next publication was a history of the papal legates in Germany. Leaving aside various other books, we must mention the book 'Political Truths' (1796) which contributes further material to Moser's unceasing war against despotism and militarism. From 1784 to 1790 he also edited a periodical entitled Patriotic Archives which served the same cause, and in particular published many historical records of good and bad rulers and statesmen, which had not been printed before, but were copied from the originals in the archives. When the last issue appeared, the French Revolution had just broken out and Moser printed on the front page a picture of the Rhine and its banks. On the French side the sun was rising in all its glory and there was one word above it: 'Endlich . . .' (at last). The whole of intellectual Germany was inspired by this feeling. But in a few years the scene had completely changed. The French liberators had become conquerors and the whole of Europe was involved in unending wars. At the end of his life Moser became imbued with deep pessimism. Once Poland was completely partitioned between the great powers, he remarked, it would be Germany's turn. In 1798 Moser died.

THE STRIVING FOR ECONOMIC AND SOCIAL FREEDOM

As mentioned before, political freedom, in the conditions of the age, did not necessarily imply social or economic freedom too. A republican system was mostly connected with the rule of privileged classes under which large sections of the people were greatly oppressed and deprived of social freedom though they may have been legally free. Economic policy was long everywhere dominated by the principles of mercantilism, the monopolistic position of the craft guilds and other institutions denying, or much restricting, the freedom of the individual in making a living. Mercantilism was in particular an onerous burden on agriculture, and the craft guilds often hampered the development of industries. But the policy of enlightened rulers with absolute power tended to uplift oppressed classes and groups, and to comply with the demand for social equality and freedom.

The belief in a natural order, and other factors, led also to theories propagating economic freedom. A great school of economic thought advocating it was founded by Dr Francois Quesnay, physician to King Louis XV and Madame de Pompadour. His disciple Dupont de Nemours gave it the name of the physiocrats, and their principal publications appeared from 1756 to 1778. Physiocracy means the Rule of Nature. The system was based on the maxim that society was subject to a natural order, and the conclusion was drawn that it was the best if the government would not interfere in economic life but leave it to the operation of the laws of nature, and to the initiative of the individuals. We cannot go here into the very ingenious doctrines of this school. They were partly misleading, but nevertheless had great merits by laying the foundations of the new science of political economy. Adam Smith admired it, and said he would have dedicated his fundamental work Wealth of Nations to Dr Quesnay if he had not died three years before its publication.

The core of the doctrines of the physiocrats is their opposition to mercantilism and state interference in general, their advocacy of internal and external free trade, their idea of a single tax on the net product of agriculture, and their belief in the blessings of free competition. In politics they were strict monarchists and opposed to parliaments, which seemed to them unavoidably liable to corruption. Their economic ideas made a great impression on some rulers inspired by the striving to improve social conditions. Frederick II had no understanding for the advantages of economic freedom. But Joseph II and Leopold II were interested and tried to make use of some of the new ideas. Count Cobenzl, Joseph's minister of commerce, united the principal Austrian territories to a large area with common customs and internal free trade. He also expressed the opinion it would be the best if trade between all nations would be made free. Margrave Charles Frederick of Baden wrote a book in favour of physiocracy and tested the idea of a single tax in some of his villages. The theories of the physiocrats were also much discussed by German writers. Their most important defender was J. A. Schlettwein, who became a counsellor of the margrave and later a professor in Basle and Giessen. He wrote numerous books and pamphlets, also on political questions of the day, edited journals and contributed articles to many others. Schlettwein was a polyhistor, inspired by the ardent wish to promote justice, humanity and general happiness. Another prominent writer of this school was J. Mauvillon, whom Roscher regarded as the most ingenious of the German physiocrats. He supplied Mirabeau with the materials for his great work criticizing Frederick II's whole system. Mauvillon was an officer and became a professor of tactics and politics at the Academy of Cassel. Yet he was very critical of professors and even proposed that teachers salaried by the government should be replaced by such not controlled by anybody. There were enough lawyers who could lecture on law and enough clergymen able to teach theology. The physiocratic principle, to replace state activities by private ones, was here extended to education.

Adam Smith's Wealth of Nations appeared in 1776, and was at once translated into German. Several reviews highly appreciated it, but mostly emphasized its parallels with the physiocratic theories. The predominance of these among the German economists for some time seems to have hindered the full appreciation of its importance.

Its full understanding by students of economics had therefore to wait till the nineties. At that time Garve published a much better translation than the first one, and great scholars, such as Professor Christian Jacob Kraus, and Georg Sartorius as also many others, became enthusiastic followers of Adam Smith's doctrine. Economic and political liberalism thereby received a powerful representation in Germany's learned circles, and through them also among statesmen. But this development took place at the end of the period treated in this book and its full consequences appeared later.

H. G. VON JUSTI

Both the old and the new doctrines had their representatives and not a few tried to combine them, or taught first one thesis and later a different one. The most widely read author on political and economic science was Heinrich Gottlob von Justi (1720-1771). His life had many vicissitudes. As a student he was expelled from the University of Jena, became a Prussian soldier and was made a prisoner by the Austrians. In 1750 he was appointed professor at the Academy Theresianum in Vienna and received the nobility. But later he entered the higher police service in Saxony and Hanover, became a professor in Göttingen and then Inspector of Colonies in Denmark. In one of his writings he criticized Frederick II's system and particularly condemned his practice of issuing false money in war-time. For this he was imprisoned in Prussia, but later he dedicated a book to the king and was made Superintendent of the Prussian State Mines. After some time he was suspected of irregularities and imprisoned again. He died before the final sentence, and probably was not guilty.

Justi had wide knowledge not only of political and economic science, but also of chemistry and metallurgy. He was a very prolific and often acute and brilliant writer, and his handbooks on the administrative and economic sciences were considered the best there were. But many of his writings also show signs of very hasty writing. His ideas correspond to the transition from mercantilism to the new doctrines of freedom, and he sometimes wavers between them. But his admiration of Montesquieu and the influence of Hume and the physiocrats are marked. Adam Smith's greatest work only appeared several years after his death. Justi regards the English constitution as 'perhaps the wisest which men can devise', though he is aware of the party strife and corruption connected with it. But he blames Europeans for looking down on the inhabitants of other continents and does not hesitate to declare like the physiocrats, the Chinese constitution for the most reasonable. Justi often shows such variations of judgment. On the one hand, he regards the people as the source of all power and the ruler as obliged to follow the united will of the people who strive for happiness. A ruler forfeits his rights when he breaks the constitution. Yet he also thinks that, under existing conditions, an absolute monarchy can more quickly realize the aims for which states exist, namely the welfare of the people. This welfare requires most of all the increase of the population and of agricultural output by the emancipation of the peasants, the partition of many of the large estates among them, and the introduction of the improved methods of farming devised in England. Further, commerce is the best way to promote the wealth of a people. Justi praises the splendid rise of English trade. He remarks that it presupposes a good constitution with a proper balance of power, and that commerce is favourable to the abolition of despotism. Yet he also approves many mercantilistic trade restrictions which, however, were then also in force in Britain.

JOSEPH VON SONNENFELS

Joseph von Sonnenfels (1733-1817) was one of the most prominent spokesmen of the Enlightenment in Austria. His father, the son of a Berlin rabbi, had settled there; he was then converted to Christianity, and became a teacher of Oriental languages in the University of Vienna. For unknown reasons he was also raised to the rank of a knight and given the title Sonnenfels.[11] His son Joseph was compelled by financial difficulties to enter the army, where he only reached the rank of corporal but had the opportunity of reading widely. After five years he left the army and studied law in Vienna. But he changed his profession, when he found that literary critics in Germany, such as Nicolai, looked down upon Austria as a very backward country in literature and that in Vienna correct German was suspect as a sign of Protestantism. Sonnenfels, who knew nine languages, had the ardent wish to contribute to the spread of literary culture, particularly in Austria, and he joined a society of scholars and other prominent people devoted to this purpose, where he soon became the chairman. He intended to become an author and professor of literature, and he also edited in succession several journals on the model of the moral weeklies. Some of them appealed particularly to women, since he assumed that they were most important for the reforms which he had in mind.

[11] There was a rumour that in the war with Prussia he had been in the Austrian secret service and had done valuable work.

Sonnenfels' extraordinary abilities, high aspirations and impressive personality were greatly appreciated by scholars and aristocrats of influence, who recommended him to the highest circles. In 1763, he was appointed professor of political science at Vienna University and later also at two Academies where young noblemen were educated to become useful citizens and good civil servants. At the Savoy Academy he said, in his inaugural address that a haughty noble, proud of his birth but without knowledge, belonged to the mob, and he reminded his hearers of the sufferings of the downtrodden serfs. Soon every student at the university wishing to become a judge, an official or a parson, had to attend his lectures. Later, six further chairs of his science were founded at provincial universities and academies, and pupils of Sonnenfels' were made professors there.

Besides his academic activities, Sonnenfels also had great merits as a writer on politics, economics and cultural questions. He pleaded for many reforms in the spirit of humanity. In particular, he was foremost in arguing for the abolition of torture and for at least the utmost restriction of the death penalty. The resistance of the conservative jurists and public opinion to these propositions was very strong and the co-operation of many forces was needed to overcome them. Sonnenfels had certainly a great share in converting powerful personalities to his views. A statue of him stands to-day before the Town Hall of Vienna, the broken instruments of torture at his feet. In his journal 'The Man without Prejudice' he described the misery of the peasants oppressed by their lords. His ideal was a free peasantry. Abuses in the Church and evils in monastic life were also criticized. In consequence, he was much hated by men of great influence who defended the old order, and they often tried to silence him. But the progressive section of statesmen, in particular G. van Swieten, Baron Gebler and Prince Kaunitz considered him a valuable ally and frustrated the intrigues of his adversaries.

Sonnenfels was employed by the government in various posts. He became a censor of books and plays, using his powers in a liberal way. Then he was appointed an Aulic Counsellor and entrusted with important administrative tasks. Official work took so much of his time that he restricted and eventually gave up his academic lecturing, though his influence on the universities remained strong. He later became Rector of the University of Vienna, where his bust still commemorates his merit. Sonnenfels' great interest in art, poetry and music also had valuable results, such as the foundation of the Academy of Arts, of which he became secretary and later president. Like Joseph, he believed that the theatre was not merely an entertainment, but an important means for educating the taste and character of the people. In this belief he wrote critical observations, striving to ban vulgar and obscene comedies and to promote dramatic art of high value, such as Lessing's plays. A small incident led to tension between him and Lessing, but farther-going rumours were unfounded. Sonnenfels also played a great part among the freemasons, and was in correspondence with many German scholars and writers. After the outbreak of the French Revolution he was much attacked by the enemies of the Enlightenment. But his merits were so great that his position remained unaffected. Sonnenfels received many honours and also became a Baron of the Empire. But when he died, he left only a very modest sum, which showed again that he had devoted the work of his life to his ideals and duties alone.

As a writer, Sonnenfels was very productive. He belonged to the school of Justi, and his main work, the 'Principles of Administrative, Commercial and Financial Science', had many editions and remained the basis of instruction in all Austrian and many other universities until the middle of the nineteenth century. His extensive knowledge, wide observation, the study of the principal writers in several languages, together with his acute judgment and aversion to extremes, enabled him to create an excellent textbook which contributed much to giving the Austrian bureaucracy a high level of efficiency as Roscher remarks, his doctrines were widely accepted and exercised great influence. Here only a few ideas can be singled out from his writings.[12]

In his interesting study *On the Love of the Fatherland* (1771) Sonnenfels also appreciates the value of a democratic and aristocratic constitution, but agrees with Pope's words: 'For forms of government let fools contest, Whate'er is best administered is best'. Just at the time when he wrote this tract a tragic event showed that it was not the form but the spirit of a constitution which was decisive: the republic of Poland became the victim of its unbridled aristocratic liberty. Sonnenfels' ideas of liberty show the influence of his study of Montesquieu and Rousseau, of Blackstone and Hume, and many others. The aim of the state is to him the welfare of the people, and he believes that the government must not merely leave it to individuals to care for their own welfare, but must actively promote it; most people have not the ability to achieve it alone. The state envisaged by Sonnenfels is therefore a welfare state. This idea includes external and internal security, a reign of law, the right and

---

[12] An excellent analysis is given by Louise Sommer, vol. II. Cf. further Kopetzky's and Müller's biographies and Prof. Lustkandel's discourse.

duty for everybody to work, and favourable working conditions. The principal conditions of ample productivity is a great number of people employed in useful work; the government has in many respects to create or facilitate production, and to this end has absolute power. But Sonnenfels is on the whole not in favour of compulsion. He proposes many ways of furthering productivity by encouragement, such as premiums, lower taxes, and so on. In order to increase manpower, he suggests the prohibition of emigration and the replacing of the death penalty or expulsion with making the convict do useful work. Marriages should be promoted, young girls pregnant with illegitimate children should not be shamed, but cared for in maternity homes and even receive a money present for the gift made to the state by giving birth to a child. Unemployed workers should be assisted, and everybody should do useful work. The author would restrict the number of unnecessary servants in the palaces of the lords and proposes to end the difficulties put in the way of the freedom to work by the selfishness of the trade guilds. If a landowner does not cultivate his land, or uses it for unproductive purposes, the government should claim it and make it available for peasants. Large estates should, to a great extent, be divided up between peasants, whose work is more productive. Machines should not be tolerated if they cause any unemployment which cannot be remedied quickly. Sonnenfels admits the fixing of prices and wages, if necessary, would discourage too high rates of interest and organize cheap credit by a national bank. He rejects state monopolies and state factories. No class must have inordinate wealth or power at the expense of the others. The author also sees great disadvantages in too large towns and recommends that the growth of many smaller towns be promoted instead.

When Sonnenfels laid the main stress on the idea of the welfare state, he included in it a strict reign of law and the protection of every citizen against arbitrary actions of the police. After the French Revolution he also advocated the restoration of the rights of the Estates which were not merely to consist of representatives of the privileged orders but also of such of the middle class and the peasants. He also continued his opposition to an inordinate extension of the powers of the police, and in a time of increasing political reaction tried to protect the rights of individuals.

IMMANUEL KANT AND LIBERALISM

Kant's philosophy contains powerful arguments for freedom though it is not easily understandable to the great majority of people. This is proved by the fact that even countless scholars, Germans and others, have identified Frederick the Great's ethics with Kant's Categorical Imperative, which is an indescribable absurdity. (Cf. above p. 301). Actually, Kant was the master-exponent of true liberalism—not the wide-spread sham liberalism regarding as its aim the most comfortable life for as many people as possible without creating much trouble to those already enjoying it. It was natural that he also shared certain shortcomings of liberalism.

The philosopher had a great interest in politics, not only from an academic point of view but also with warm sympathy for the cause of liberty and justice. He was a constant reader of newspapers, discussed the political news with intimate friends and was well informed about them. Rousseau, Montesquieu and Hume exercised great influence on his political opinions. His enthusiasm for the American and French Revolutions is very characteristic of his views. But he also harboured a strain of pessimism concerning human nature, and was well aware of the danger that a revolution might lead to anarchy. Most of his writings on politics came out soon after the French Revolution (1793, 1797), but they had, of course, originated in his mind much earlier.

The type of state which Kant, in his writings, regards as the ideal, is the 'Rechtsstaat', the state guaranteeing the reign of justice, and thereby to everyone the greatest possible measure of freedom. For justice is, according to Kant, the demarcation between the liberty of the individuals, which enables everyone to enjoy equal freedom without detriment to that of others. The aim of the state is liberty, which is the same as the maintenance of the laws freely enacted by the will of the citizens. In this point Kant deviated from most other thinkers on political philosophy who assumed that the aim of the state was the 'happiness', or in our language the welfare, of its members. Kant rightly remarked that wellbeing might also be enjoyed by savages not yet possessing a state, or by the subjects of a benevolent autocrat.

According to Kant the only just form of state is a republic in which the laws enacted by the will of all citizens are supreme, while the ruler has merely executive power and the judges deal with the administration of justice. This was Montesquieu's theory of the distribution of the three powers and of the balance between them. Kant, however, did not understand by 'citizens' all members of a people, but distinguished active and passive members. The former alone were to be full citizens possessing the franchise. The passive members should enjoy equality before the law but not the right to make laws. The reason is, according to Kant, their inability freely to form a will in matters of legislation, because of their sex or their social position. Women appeared to him too dependent on others to become legislators. But he also considered domestic servants, journeymen and classes of tenants closely dependent on their land-lord, etc., unfit for the franchise. Yet they should at least have opportunities to ascend to the status of full citizens endowed with the vote. Kant was opposed to the frequent habit of denying freedom to serfs or others because 'they were not yet ripe for it'. He pointed out that one could not become ripe until after one had been set free, though he admitted that conditions might make it necessary to postpone full emancipation. The distinction between active and passive members of the people was for a long time the doctrine of the liberals. In the French Revolution it was the law until in 1793, the Jacobins introduced manhood suffrage. Before this time most workers and other poor people had no vote in France.

Kant laid great stress both on a representative constitution and on the division of power. He was critical of the English parliamen-tary system, not only because of its corruption and the striving of the parties to employ their power in parliament for their private profit, but also because it united the legislative with the executive power, which in his view necessarily led to corruption. In this respect he followed Rousseau's opinion. The fathers of the American Republic also held this view and therefore, in framing the constitu-tion, stressed Montesquieu's principle of the separation of powers, instead of adopting the English example of a fusion of powers. In justice, however, Kant recommended the English system of the co-operation of judge and jury.

The philosopher has been much blamed by his commentators because he declared any active resistance to violations of the con-stitution by the executive power as unlawful, except by vote of Parliament, in particular by the rejection of treasury bills. It seemed to them illogical that Kant, the admirer of the American and French Revolutions, rejected any right to make a revolution. It was, how-ever, very difficult, if not impossible, to formulate such a right. It would certainly have been misused, and the result would have been anarchy and despotism, and a great increase in the injustice com-mitted by both sides.

It was, however, not only an internal reign of peace, justice and liberty in one state, which Kant regarded as the highest aim of politics. He clearly recognized that it could not be achieved without extending it over the whole world. He abhorred war, though he admitted that sometimes it was still an unavoidable evil and might even ennoble the mentality of a nation by inducing its members to sacrifice their lives. Yet it was his most ardent wish that war should be abolished. To this end various conditions were to be universally recognized : no war was justifiable but in self-defence against a threat to the existence of a people, and with the consent of its Parliament; a people must never be forced to make war; it must not be waged to punish, exterminate or subjugate another people, nor should treacherous or vile means be used such as spying, murder, looting of civilians, etc. The passions of fear, or hatred between the nations concerned must not be spurred on, and nothing should be done in a war which might deteriorate relations between them, thereby making the restoration of peace impossible. Standing armies are a principal cause of war and efforts should therefore be made to achieve disarmament.

A lasting peace, however, can only be secured by the conclusion of a great confederation between the peoples, a League of Nations. For this purpose all nations should receive a constitution decreasing the motives making for war, namely a republic. Many reasons are put forward which render the establishment of a League of Nations absolutely necessary, not merely the longing for perpetual peace and freedom, but also the demands of economic self-interest. Commercial and money interests always work for peace. The achievement of a true and effective League of Nations guaranteeing a reign of law between all peoples appeared to the philosopher as the highest aim of politics. Yet he was well aware that this problem was extremely difficult to solve. Its complete solution even seemed to him impossible since 'man was made of such crooked wood that nothing quite straight can be made out of it.'

Kant has put forward many other interesting views concerning politics. Some of them will be discussed in a later place. As regards criminal law he was against the theory of deterrence but for the preservation of capital punishment. He fully recognized the threat of nationalism, which received fatal momentum through the French Revolution and its consequences. He regarded national pride and national hatred as blind instincts which in the past may have been useful for the development of nations and their rivalry, which brought about a certain progress. But they are illusions and must be superseded by rules given by reason. 'The national mania', says Kant, 'must be exterminated, and replaced by patriotism and cosmopolitanism.' He also had interesting opinions concerning the so-called national character. The English nation appeared to him, in their internal affairs, as the most estimable people. But the English state in relation to other states seemed to him most pernicious, violent and domineering, and the greatest warmonger of all. He also regarded the English as particularly nationalistic and even suggested that they did not look upon foreigners as human beings. Yet he also credited them with favourable features. His picture of the French character is elaborately drawn in the brightest colours. As regards the Germans, Kant mentions their sense of order, caution, discipline, accuracy, industry, honesty, pedantry, fondness for titles, pride of rank, etc. He likes their cosmopolitanism, lack of national animosity and their habit of learning many languages and rejects 'the babble encouraging them to show national pride'.

At that time the interest in the peculiarities of nations was very wide-spread and gave rise to countless descriptions. It is not possible to take up this problem here, but the frequency of its discussion had at least to be mentioned.[13]

WILHELM VON HUMBOLDT

The idea that the aim of the state was to be not so much the welfare of the people but the freedom of every individual had already been put forward a little while before Kant by Wilhelm von Humboldt in his essay 'Ideas on how to determine the limits of state activities'. It was written in 1792, three years after the outbreak of the French Revolution, but was not caused by it. Humboldt wrote it in opposition to the political system of Emperor Joseph II, who wanted to make the people happy by governmental measures even against their will. The state, Humboldt says, is not an aim in itself; it should serve the full and harmonious development of the individual towards an integrated personality, and should therefore restrict its activities to the maintenance of security and justice, for the forces of the individual will best develop in freedom. Humboldt was afraid that the policy of trying to make the people happy by decrees of the government would foster the growth of a vast bureaucracy putting forms above everything else and restraining individual freedom by countless regulations. The existence of this risk is undeniable. But Humboldt went too far when he wanted to leave popular education, physical welfare and decisions regarding marriage and morality exclusively to the individual. His arguments seem to describe the state merely as a necessary evil. They overlook that the individual was in many respects faced with obstacles to the development of his personality which he could not overcome by his own abilities in particular poverty, lack of education and pernicious

[13] I have given an outline of some of these writings in a study in the *Archiv für Sozialwissenschaft und Sozialpolitik*, vol. 54, 1926.

traditions. Of Humboldt's essay, fragments only were published in his lifetime and the whole text was discovered and published long after his death. John Stuart Mill praised it in his essay 'On liberty' (1859).

FREEDOM AND EDUCATION

The ethos of the Enlightenment sprang from a many-sided longing for freedom : freedom from the tyranny of old beliefs, customs and institutions contrary to truth and justice, but also freedom from one's own base passions and blindness. The positive aim was a life according to reason, which the philosophy of rationalism conceived of not merely as the faculty of thinking but also as the source of morality and justice. Human nature was regarded as essentially reasonable, and the word humanity designated a morality inherent in the nature of man and developed by reason. The spirit of the age was imbued with the ideas of a natural religion, morality, law, economy and literature and this tendency led also to the demand of an education free from unreasonable and unnatural features such as mechanical memorizing, learning under the threat of the cane, the cult of obsolete traditions, the neglect of empirical observation, of the forming of clear concepts, of physical exercises, and so on. Bold reformers envisaged an education in freedom. The mind of the young was not to be forced but helped to develop its natural faculties and it was hoped that this would lead to the formation of a mind fit for freedom in all fields of life.

The ideas of a new education, according to the rules of nature, had already been put forward by bold thinkers of many nations long before the age of Enlightenment, but their realization had met great difficulties everywhere.[14] In Germany Wolfgang Ratke, called Ratichius (1571-1657), was an ardent champion of an education based on nature and reason. In a memorandum to the Reichstag (1612), he said that such an education would bring about concord in language, religion and politics in the whole Empire. Several Free Towns and rulers supported him. He also had great influence on the Czech pedagogue Amos Comenius who was a pioneer of modern education. Erhard Weigel, a mathematician and physician, also was a radical defender of these ideas, and through his pupil Christoph Semler he contributed to creating the non-classical secondary school. Several schools and regulations for schools accepted points from the reformers' programme. Education was then still a matter of the Church, though the governments controlled it in the Protest-

[14] Cf. particularly Paul Barth's work.

ant countries of Germany. Pietism and similar movements worked for improving the schools and for extending elementary education to the whole people. It has already been shown that even at the peak of the period of Enlightenment it was educationalists influenced by their spirit who were the pioneers of progress such as Hecker, Semler and Buesching in Prussia. On Austria Catholic priests played a leading rôle in introducing obligatory attendance at schools for the whole people.

The idea of a 'natural' education further received a great impetus through Rousseau's novel *Emile* (1762). Though Rousseau took up many ideas of the heralds of reason he was primarily a romanticist, appealing not so much to the intellect as to the emotions. If he praised nature he understood by it not so much logical thinking as following the dictates of the heart, the natural sentiments not corrupted by the development of a society and civilization based on private property and class privileges. But he did it with such a magical power of persuasion that he entranced and aroused even the coolest thinkers. His novel 'Emile' describes the education of a boy whose rich and noble parents had died, and whose tutor uses the opportunity to bring him up in a very unconventional way, namely according to the rules of nature. Rousseau himself had no experience as an educator since he shunned the trouble of rearing his children and preferred to deposit them in a foundling hospital. The publication of his novel at first aroused against him a wave of persecution. The University of Paris condemned it, the parlement (High Court) had it burnt and ordered his arrest; when he fled to Holland and to Switzerland he suffered the same fate there, till at last he found an asylum in Neuchâtel whose ruler was King Frederick II of Prussia. Even here the clergy incited the people against him, and he fled to England.

JOHANN BERNHARD BASEDOW

J. B. Basedow (1723-1790) was born in Hamburg, and devoted himself to the theory and practice of pedagogy. He was a rationalist of the school of Wolff, and was influenced by the Deists and by the writings of Ehlers. Rousseau, however, aroused his enthusiasm for a natural education, and he elaborated a system based on the idea that the principal aim of education was not the accumulation of knowledge but the cultivation of the heart or the emotions towards the love of mankind, probity and a moral and happy life. The children were not to be educated by compulsion, reprimands or punishments but in a way pleasing to them, by games, by arousing their interest and ambition, by encouraging them by little gifts and so on. Languages should be learned by conversation not by cramming the children with rules of grammar. The mother-tongue had to receive adequate attention and also French and Latin. The pupils were not to be instructed by the inculcation of concepts which they did not understand and which were to them mere words. They were to observe real things and happenings and form clear concepts of them with their own minds. Manual labour and sport were also important as means of education. As regards religion the young people were at first to be taught certain general principles common to all great religions but no doctrines peculiar to any denomination, and they were not to be instructed in the Christian beliefs until they had reached the age of fourteen.

Basedow was a good propagandist and received assistance from princes, nobles, ministers and educationists, Goethe was acquainted with him and in his reminiscences has given us a not very attractive portrait of his personality. Prince Leopold Friedrich Franz of Dessau called him to his country and gave him the means to found a school according to his principles, which was called Philanthropinum (1774). The Prince sent his own son to this school. Basedow explained the name of the school in the words that it was designed to educate philanthropes (Friends of Mankind), or Cosmopolitans. After two years a public examination of the pupils was held, attended by educationists from various parts of Germany who were invited to put questions. The results were very favourable. Basedow's own daughter, named Emily after Rousseau's novel, proved a youthful prodigy. One of the questions was where little children came from, and the pupils showed themselves well-informed about the birth of a baby. Kant set great hopes on this experiment in education and the Prussian minister of education, Baron Zedlitz, was also greatly impressed and furthered Philanthropism in various ways. By the year 1790 63 other schools of this type had been founded in Germany, though most of them did not live long. The school at Dessau was closed in 1793, when Basedow quarrelled with his collaborators and withdrew. There were also controversies between the educationists about questions of method.

The Philanthropists aimed at educating children in freedom and cheerfulness to be human beings happy and useful to the community. A great number of the higher and intellectual classes were inspired by enthusiasm for this aim. Many princes and aristocrats actively supported the movement. But it soon became obvious that the realization of their ideals was much more difficult than expected. A number of the Philanthropists, among them Basedow

N

himself, lacked certain faculties necessary to be a really good teacher, and the theory and practice of education were only in their beginnings. Gradually, however, many excellent teachers appeared whose experiences laid the foundation for the development of pedagogics. Some of the prominent pioneers were Ch. G. Salzmann, J. H. Campe, E. C. Trapp, and most of all Johann Heinrich Pestalozzi (1746-1827), a Swiss, who was the greatest personality of them all. The Dessau Philanthropinum had been mainly frequented by children of nobles and merchants who had to pay considerable fees, though scholarships were provided to poor children of talent. But Pestalozzi ardently longed to lift the poor people out of their misery by procuring them education and work.

The striving for the expansion and improvement of education assumed many different forms. On the one hand, the conviction spread that the whole people had a natural right to receive education, and opinions on its scope expanded from the three R's to many other things necessary for the individuals and the community. In particular, it increasingly seemed important that the pupils also should be instructed in matters needed for earning a living. It was hoped this would overcome the resistance of many parents to the duty of letting their children attend a school, and would improve the working ability and living conditions of the people. On the other hand, much thought was also devoted to the question what education could do for the development of a professional and cultural élite. The neo-humanistic movement saw the best way to the unfolding of all intellectual, moral and aesthetic faculties of man in the profound study of the Greek and Roman culture and their languages. There were also scholars and statesmen who demanded that all classes of the people should be educated to good citizens and patriots. In France, the physiocrats claimed that their system should be taught in all schools because it alone expressed the laws of nature. The Marquis de Mirabeau, the father of the politician, was a physiocrat, and discussed the question of education in his correspondence with Margrave Charles Frederick of Baden and King Gustavus III of Sweden. In Germany, Dohm and others wished that the whole people should be instructed in political and economic fundamentals.[15]

SECRET SOCIETIES FOR PROPAGATING
THE NEW IDEALS

The development, cultivation and propagation of the new ideals

[15] Cf. Edelheim p. 86, and Deutsches Museum, 1777, p. 97. Dohm was an editor of this journal.

led to the foundation of organizations which assumed the character
of secret societies. The most widely spread movement was Freemasonry. It consisted of numerous fraternities primarily devoting
themselves to the education of the brethren in the spirit of
humanity. This required the overcoming of old prejudices and the
cultivation of fraternal sentiments for the whole of mankind. To
this end the Freemasons also practised much charity and gave
personal assistance to people suffering. This meritorious activity
was veiled by the cloak of secrecy and mystery which exercises
great attraction on most human beings, as is shown by all religions.
Actually Freemasonry does not possess secrets, except certain
symbols and rites which have for a very long time been disclosed to
everyone in numerous books. The awakening of brotherly love for
all men, however, can hardly be explained by the arguments of
enlightened self-interest which Frederick II considered the only
possible source of morality, so this may indeed be regarded as a
mystery. Christianity derived brotherly love from the fact that it
considered all men children of God and therefore brothers and
sisters. A certain seclusion and organization according to the grade
of enlightenment sprang from the nature of things. Between the
brethren there was to be no difference of rank, religion or nationality. All men were regarded as free and equal. Freemasonry
demanded belief in a supreme Being but without any dogmatic
obligation. Solemn rites were performed, intended to lift up the
soul to the contemplation of ideals, following the model of the
Churches.

Freemasonry originated in England, where in 1717 the English
Grand Lodge was founded. From there it quickly spread to other
countries undergoing variations in its course. In Germany the first
Lodge was founded in Hamburg (1737), and soon Lodges were
established in almost all parts of the Empire. It is very significant
that princes and aristocrats were the pioneers of this movement.
This shows that the spirit of enlightenment spread earlier among the
ruling and upper classes than in the lower ones. Duke Francis
Stephen of Lorraine even became a Freemason before the first
Lodge was founded in Germany. In 1731, a deputation of the Grand
Lodge of England received him into Freemasonry at the Hague.
Four years later he married Maria Theresa and in 1745 became
Emperor. Frederick II of Prussia, when crown prince, secretly joined
the movement as early as in 1738 and after his accession to the
throne he actively supported its propagation. Though the Pope
condemned it, it made rapid progress in the ruling circles and
numerous German princes, both secular and ecclesiastical, and

members of the high aristocracy, became Freemasons. Emperor Joseph II, however, refused to join it and expressed his dislike of certain masonic ceremonies, though he tolerated the movement because of its charitable work. Besides the princes and aristocrats a great proportion of the intellectual élite also assembled in the lodges, such as leading officials, great scholars, poets, industrialists, and so on. With the exception of Schiller all the classical poets of Germany, Klopstock, Lessing, Herder, Wieland and Goethe, were members and served the movement as writers and speakers. Mozart dedicated enchanting music to it.

The wide diffusion of Freemasonry, however, was not entirely beneficial. History shows many examples of lofty aspirations which became platitudinous or were fatally mismanaged through obtaining too many followers. A large section of the freemasons were really inspired by high ideals. But a great many others joined the movement mainly because it was fashionable, or hoping to derive some pecuniary profit from it. Great dissensions broke out about questions of ceremonial, symbols, the high degrees etc. Adventurers and swindlers found entrance, the original ideals were adulterated by mystical nonsense or egoistic strivings, for example the attempt to make gold, and this led to great scandals.[16]

Even among the true believers in humanity, however, opinions differed about the attitude of Freemasonry to certain questions. Many thought that it should adopt a more active position towards politics. Lessing too was of this opinion. Actually in certain lodges the masters and certain members often exercised a political influence, though officially Freemasonry was unpolitical. Under the reign of Joseph II, for example, leading statesmen who were masters of Vienna lodges also were pillars of the Emperor's policy towards the Church. Among them Ignaz von Born, who was also an excellent scientist, was particularly prominent, and wrote a violent satire against the monks. This was, at that time, certainly a political question.

The wish for great social and political reforms led to the foundation of the Order of the Illuminati in 1776. Its originator was Adam Weishaupt, a young professor of constitutional law in Bavaria. It was the year of the American Declaration of Independence, when German progressive opinion was jubilant over the successes of the republicans and enraged against German princes who had furnished troops to England to fight against them. Weishaupt was greatly

[16] King Frederick seceded from freemasonry a little while before the Seven Years' War, because swindlers had misused it, and he also ordered those of his ministers who were freemasons not to attend the meetings of the lodges.

influenced by Rousseau, and for the organization of the new order made use of ideas developed by the Jesuits and Freemasons. The 'brothers' of the Order called one another by new names, and Weishaupt himself adopted that of Spartacus, the name of the leader of the greatest uprising of slaves in ancient Rome. This was significant for his ideas, though he himself was by no means fitted for the rôle of a revolutionary leader, nor intended to excite the masses to a bloody uprising. The original freedom and equality of mankind, he taught, had been destroyed by the rise of states, nations and the ownership of property. Jesus Christ's teaching had aimed at freedom and equality but had been falsified by Churches and states. Yet the progress of enlightenment could make princes and states superfluous.

The Order was at first restricted to Bavaria. In 1780, however, Marquis de Constanza was sent to Protestant Germany in order to found branches there too. He met Adolph Baron Knigge, a fiery and ambitious freemason, who seized on the idea with enthusiasm, received full authority from Weishaupt, and within a short time won a great number of members for the Illuminati, among them many important people. Even ruling princes and heirs to the throne joined the Order as well as aristocrats, statesmen, scholars and writers. Goethe, Herder, Pestalozzi, Sonnenfels and other great men became members. But soon conflicts broke out between the leaders and Knigge was so disgusted that he left the Order and made up his mind never to join a secret society again. He was also a popular writer of novels, plays, didactic literature etc. and a great enemy of despotism.

In 1784 the Order was denounced to the Bavarian government as the seat of subversive activities. The government dissolved all secret societies and persecuted some of their members. The next ruler, however, at once made Count Montgelas, a former Illuminate, his leading minister, who, together with others of the same description, transformed Bavaria into a modern state, though he dropped the original Utopian ideas. A similar society as the Illuminati was the League of the Euergeten in which Ignaz Fessler, an important writer, played the leading rôle. It is typical that this organization also was paralysed by long disputes between its leaders whether they should first work for a higher morality or resolutely begin with politics.

THE POLITICAL IDEAS OF POETS AND WRITERS

Political ideas were also often expressed in the works of poets and other writers and not seldom the magic of their words made a great impression on the public mind. The greater, however, an author is, the less will he make use of the political slogans and arguments coined for the understanding of the masses. His stand-point is higher than that of the party member and differs also from that of the scientific student. The main field of a poet is his inner life and the variety, complexity and contradictions of human nature. The more important a poet or philosophical observer of the world is, the less is it possible to record his political feelings and views in a few words.

Literary currents not infrequently interact with political and social ones. French classicism let only gods, heroes and princes appear on the stage, and excluded the common people; its back-ground was the age of Louis XIV. Its domination in Germany was largely broken by the intrusion of English poetry, which brought a more popular spirit and prepared the soil for romanticism. The young people of Germany were seized with enthusiasm for Shakes-peare and enraptured by the ideas of nature, genius, and freedom. The German writers, however, were often greatly hampered in the expression of their feelings by the censorship and the police, the social structure and the narrowness of the conditions in which they lived. They longed for English freedom. Satirical writers like Christian Ludwig Liscow and Gottlieb Wilhelm Rabener attacked the evils of Germany's social conditions. But they had to be cautious. Liscow was imprisoned for his frankness. The most popular writer of satirical and moral literature was Christian Fürchtegott Gellert, who was very critical of war, oppression and social abuses, and was widely read by the lower classes too.

Literary life was much enriched by the appearance of Frederick Gottlieb Klopstock (1724-1803). His inspiration was religious and national. Though an admirer and lover of England, he dared to rival her poets in order to show that Germans, too, could worthily treat the most lofty subject. The first part of his *Messiah* (1748) aroused, in all parts of Germany, an enthusiasm as never a poetic book before. Klopstock regarded the whole of Germany as his fatherland. Yet he lived nineteen years in Denmark, where the king and his Minister Count Bernstorff were his patrons. In Copenhagen he became acquainted with Scandinavian mythology and mixed them with Celtic and Anglo-Saxon elements and Tacitus' relation of Germanic conditions to a phantastic picture of the old Teutonic beliefs and life, which became the background of his further poetry. His idea was thereby to revive a German national spirit, but this had no success. Youthful poets ecstatically hailed him as their master and he was also much respected for his idealism and for his real services to German literature and language; but his Teutomania remained alien to wider sections of the people and was ridiculed by competent critics. One of Klopstock's most moving odes is that on Maria Theresa's death. In another poem he praised Joseph II for three deeds: he made the priests followers of Christ again, he allowed the Jews to become human beings by loosening their shackles, and he set free the oppressed peasants. In other poems he warns against the over-estimating of foreign models and declared the German language as particularly fitted for poetry because it is unmixed.

Klopstock was a republican, a democrat and hater of despotism. He admitted, however, that freedom also could exist in a monarchy, but he meant Denmark under her enlightened King Frederick V. He used to contrast him with Frederick II of Prussia whom he hated because of his atheism, wars of conquest and contempt of German achievements. War appeared to the poet the greatest disgrace and horror inflicted upon mankind, except a war for freedom. His Teutomania was closely connected with his love of freedom, since he believed that the Teutons had been a people of free peasants and their community a democracy. In the seventies, when Klopstock had returned from Denmark for good, a number of young poets formed a circle, often called the Hainbund, in which they expressed their devotion to Klopstock and his ideals. They celebrated the alleged virtues of the old Teutons such as faithfulness, simplicity, contempt of luxury and lack of corruption. The French appeared to them to personify the spirit of despotism and immorality while they praised the English for their liberty and love of nature. Their antipathy to the French was largely caused by the fact that many princes and aristocrats, in particular King Frederick II, greatly preferred everything French to persons and things of German origin.[17]

Klopstock was convinced that Germany too would once become a free republic, but he also thought that the struggle for freedom would still take a century and cost blood. His disciples believed that the killing of a tyrant could bring about the outbreak of a revolution. The poet Johann Heinrich Voss, describes in a letter a discussion on freedom between the Hainbund members which became so excited that they all would have been prepared to commit a great heroic deed, even the murder of a prince. Two of Klopstock's most fiery disciples were the Counts Friedrich Leopold and Christian von

[17] Frederick even engaged hundreds of French as fiscal officials who were particularly qualified to squeeze money out of his subjects. This would have been absolutely impossible in a national state.

Stolberg. Frederick wrote a poem in which the spilling of the blood of tyrants was so drastically described that critics said he waded in it. When they visited Goethe's mother, she served them the best red wine in her cellar as 'tyrant's blood' on condition that they stopped speaking in her house about murdering tyrants.

With Klopstock and his followers began the great revolt of emotionalism against rationalism, which reached its height in the Romantic Movement. Contrary to widespread belief, it was by no means peculiar to Germany. Romanticism actually came from the Romanic countries and spread in England earlier than in Germany. Rousseau later became its greatest herald. Sentiment, imagination and intuition were set above cool reason; unselfish love and heroism contrasted with utilitarianism; religion and old traditions vindicated against the sneers of a Voltaire; the fatherland and nationality were praised instead of an abstract cosmopolitanism, and freedom was regarded as a higher aim than the happiness cultivated under enlightened absolutism. Early Romanticism was mostly coupled with republican, radical and democratic opinions, and only later, in opposition to the terrorism and anarchy of the French Revolution, became partly conservative and reactionary. Rationalism and emotionalism were not entirely antagonistic. Most great writers combined them in various forms and degrees. The cult of feelings and passions was often indulged in eccentric forms in literary circles. A certain extremism was perhaps the result of the narrowness of German conditions. Young intellectuals liberated from the fetters of orthodox opinions wanted to express their emotions and thirsted for action and distinction. In England, many ways were open to such ambitions which in the German environment did not exist. This repression intensified their feelings and they revolted against society, the world order and God—at least in fiery poems, daring dramas, bitter critical tracts, or in the circle of like-minded comrades.

Gotthold Ephraim Lessing (1729-1781) was a great scholar, a profound thinker on art and literature, and a poet of classical rank. His belief in freedom and truth rendered him a valiant fighter. From his youth onwards he wrote and planned dramas showing his enmity to tyrants of every kind. This early made him famous, but was not favourable to his career. He constantly had financial worries and had to make his living mainly as a freelance writer, journalist, theatre critic and translator until he obtained a poorly-paid post as librarian to a duke fairly late in life. It is significant for German literary conditions of the time that in 1767, when he was already famous, he received no payment for the comedy Minna von

Barnhelm, one of his best plays, which is still performed to-day. Three years before he had been offered the post of a professor of rhetoric at the University of Koenigsberg. He had declined it because it involved the obligation of delivering a speech in praise of the king every year. Lessing also had much to contend with the hostility of the orthodox Protestant theologians, because he stood for the freedom of research into the Scriptures.

As regards German literature Lessing's greatest merit was that both by means of his criticism and of his plays he liberated it from the shackles of French classicism. The Greek, English and Spanish dramatists seemed to him better models for the Germans. But he was not an enemy of the French though he blamed them for looking down on the Germans, and thought highly of Molière and Diderot. Lessing was a staunch citizen of the world. In his letters he said that the reputation of being an eager patriot would be the very last he would wish to possess and that the love of the fatherland appeared to him at the most an heroic weakness which he was glad to be without. He abhorred war, though he had many friends among Frederick's officers and for a time was a secretary in the service of a Prussian general. He recognized that Frederick was a genius and a great king, but was not blind to his many faults.[18] He reminded Lessing of a 'bloody tiger', and his sneering at religion disgusted him. In a letter he declared that Prussia was the most slavish state of Europe, and had Frederick in mind when he wrote that a great, very active king was worse than an inactive, dull one, and that a king should not have wit because it mighe be exercised at the expense of justice.

Lessing's political convictions made him grieve about the fact that the Germans had lost their old liberty. This was, as he said, due to the facts that the princes everywhere established standing armies of mercenaries and that the Estates accordingly lost power. The decline of the Emperor's authority had also contributed much to it and the fact that the princes won the nobles by maintaining their privileges and granting them favours. But, Lessing continues, should we not at least continuously protest in our writings against these unjust proceedings instead of flattering and excusing the rulers and justifying their actions? Lessing also said once that he wished Germany had only one ruler.

In his 'Talks for Freemasons' Lessing discusses political fundamentals. His ideal was a community without coercive power and government, though this could not be realized entirely. The state

---

[18] Mehring has in his *Lessinglegende* refuted the view that Lessing was enthusiastic for Frederick and Prussia. Cf. also Stahr's book.

N*

existed only for its citizens. The fatherland too was merely an idea. Every other thesis was conducive to tyranny. Even the best state had, moreover, bad sides too. National and social conflicts could not be avoided. But in each state there should be men above national prejudice and willing to mitigate the unavoidable evils as much as possible. This seemed to him the task of the Freemasons.

Lessing dedicated this tract to his ruler, Duke Ferdinand of Brunswick. He was Grand-Master of all German lodges and a prince famous all over Europe for his enlightenment. But his attitude to Lessing was odd. He behaved towards him with great politeness and kindness but probably suspected him of being a republican and holding revolutionary views. Lessing certainly had republican sympathies though he did not make propaganda for a republic or a revolution. In any case, the Duke asked Lessing to promise him not to continue the work just mentioned without his consent. Lessing agreed. At that time the American Revolution was near its victory and the Duke had delivered soldiers to England. Among the German Freemasons there were many, as Lessing wrote, who wished 'to fight for America in Europe'. Some even believed that the American Congress was a Freemasons Lodge and would found a state according to masonic principles by armed force. But the great majority of masons regarded Lessing as a dreamer and had no understanding for him. Few only defended him, among them Herder, Hamann, Campe and Claudius.

Lessing's last play Nathan the Wise was one of the most splendid contributions to the cause of humanity. His friend Moses Mendelssohn was the model for the wise Jew who formed the central figure of the play. It prepared the way for the civil emancipation of the Jews and pleaded for universal tolerance between all religions, nations and races.

Soon after Lessing died. There was no money available for his burial and he was interred at public expense like a pauper. The place of his grave fell into oblivion and was only re-discovered at a much later time. I. Engel, a contemporary poet, wrote that if Lessing had been a Briton, his coffin would have been set beside the graves of kings and a monument would have been erected in his honour.

Lessing's personality rendered him the centre of a large circle of congenial writers and admirers. In this place Moses Mendelssohn only may be mentioned. He was a small, weakly and deformed Jew who, in his youth had to struggle with much distress and was faced with difficulties in learning literary German and acquiring a higher level of education. But he overcame all obstacles by sheer diligence and frugality. The study of Wolff and the English philosophers inspired him to write a number of books, which made him famous. Hettner says of him that nobody had hitherto treated philosophical questions in such a beautiful way. His personality exercised a charm which nobody could resist and his correspondence shows that many of the most prominent men were his friends. Though greatly influenced by the English deists he remained a pious Jew. He induced Dohm, one of Frederick II's best diplomats, to write a famous book which contributed much to the abolition of the oppressive and humiliating regulations prescribed for Jews.

A further German poet who reached the rank of a classic was Christoph Martin Wieland (1733-1813). The forces of pietism and rationalism, enthusiasm and frivolity, puritanism and lust for life, struggled for predominance in his mind. He possessed a rare grace of language and sparkling wit, took both the French and the English as his models, and was the first to translate most of Shakespeare's works into German. His strong cosmopolitanism and his imitation of French writers aroused the greatest wrath of Klopstock and his followers, who detested him as the opposite of their ideals. Wieland further had much interest in politics and, when he had obtained a stable position at the court of Weimar, he began to edit a quarterly *The German Mercury* (1773-1810), which, because of its excellent literary and political articles, became the favourite journal of enlightened society. He also liked to express his views on the state and society in novels likely to attract more readers than political tracts. This also had the advantage that he could veil bold opinions in a satirical form. The principal work of this kind was the *Golden Mirror* (1772), in which he described the reforms of an enlightened Oriental ruler whose portrait was obviously modelled on Joseph II. He would have liked to enter the Emperor's service as a professor. In his youth, Wieland was a republican; he enjoyed his residence in Switzerland and the freedom there, then he became town clerk of Biberach, a small Swabian Free Town, near which he had been born. But the experience of these small oligarchic republics induced him to see his ideal in an enlightened monarch of a large State.[19] The

---

[19] Iselin, town clerk of Basle, came to the same conclusions. Lessing condemned the despotism of the patricians in the Swiss republic of Bern in his unfinished tragedy *Henzi*. Wieland ridiculed the philistine mentality of the burghers of a small town republic in his satirical masterpiece 'The Abderites' which was largely inspired by his experience in Biberach and similar places. The journal *Deutsches Museum* of 1776 printed a reply from the burgomaster of such a town who admitted that its laws and customs were intended to prevent what was usually called economic and cultural 'progress'. But their aim was to maintain thereby a state of things in which there were no deep cleavages among the burghers—no rich or poor, no highly educated or quite uneducated, no foreigners, Jews or freethinkers, and so on.

Golden Mirror became the textbook for the education of princes, and this was in fact Wieland's task in Weimar.

Wieland was a liberal who hated war, despotism and intolerance, was opposed to extreme views, and stood for compromise and gradual progress. He had much in common with Erasmus, whom he venerated. While Voltaire raised the slogan 'Ecrasez l'infame' and undermined all religious beliefs, Wieland thought that even the worst religion was still better than none at all. Rousseau's attack on social injustice impressed him strongly, but he did not share his views that civilization was a pernicious aberration and that small, primitive communities were the best. He believed that the happiness of the individuals should be the only aim of the state and that peace, freedom, the rights of man and the welfare of the people formed the right way to it. A great state fostered the progress of civilization, while small ones gave no scope to great personalities and led to cultural stagnation, poverty, a petty, mean spirit, prejudices, egoism and despotism. Monarchy was better than a republic, but it was to be restricted by unalterable fundamental laws. Wieland was no uncritical admirer of representative institutions. He found that even very clever people behaved unreasonably when they formed an assembly. They tended to misunderstand one another, to lay stress on inessential points, liked to waste time by superfluous speeches and put their private interests above the public ones. Nevertheless, Wieland wanted provincial Estates, in which the peasants should also be represented, and which should have the right, if they had a two-thirds majority, to annul decrees of the monarch found incompatible with the fundamental statutes. They should also be entitled to express their wishes, and grievances must be put right. Wieland went further in advocating parliamentary rights after the outbreak of the French Revolution, and this change in his attitude will be discussed later. But as early as the time of the American insurrection he stood on the side of the rebels. His aversion to a pure democracy was largely nurtured by his study of the ancient world. Solon's mixed constitution, in which the influence of different classes was carefully balanced, inaugurated Athens' happiest time, but Pericles increased the power of the common people and thereby paved the way for Athens' fall. Other Greek republics, too, were ruined by demagogues and mob rule. A democracy, Wieland believed, was only suitable for small states. Larger ones required a monarch for reasons of defence, civilization and social reform. A German political nation appeared to him impossible. Like all the classic writers of Germany he was a very pronounced citizen of the world. In 1798 he wrote: 'To what levels

of perfection and wealth could the peoples of Europe lift themselves
up if they would for ever forsake that shameful remnant of old
barbarism, cannibalistic national hatred, the miserable prejudice
that the good luck of others is detrimental to our own, and all the
contemptible tricks of swindlers and gangsters formerly called
politics which cannot deceive anybody, in order to found a permanent League of Nations, regardless of the essentially unimportant
differences of the forms of states, and thereby to organize a lasting
European community.'

The problems arising from nationalism and humanity were pro-
foundly meditated upon by Johann Gottfried Herder (1744-1803).
He was born in East Prussia, near the German-Russian frontier, and
the contact between different nationalities in the Baltic countries
may have made him see clearly the importance of nationality. He
first became a preacher in the German town of Riga, then the
principal clergyman in a small north-German state, and in 1776 the
head of the Lutheran Church in Weimar. The latter post he owed
to Goethe, on whose development he had exercised momentous
influence at Strasbourg a few years earlier.

Herder's achievements were of the greatest possible significance
for German poetry, thought and the study of man.[20] On various
occasions he showed the wish to take part in public life in order to
promote great reforms in the interest of the people, either in Livonia
or in Russia or in Germany. But this proved to be impossible and it
is also questionable whether he was fitted for active politics. He
chose, however, the profession of a preacher hoping that this
would enable him to speak to the people and to work for raising it.
He was an ardent disciple of Rousseau and also owed much to
Hume, Montesquieu and other English and French political thinkers.
His whole heart was with the ordinary people of every language,
while he did not agree at all well with princes and nobles. Many
passages in his works show his inclination to republican ideas,
especially to those of Rousseau. His greatest hatred was directed
against war, despotism, conquest and militarism. King Frederick
and his Prussia were long judged harshly by him. However, when
Frederick died and his correspondence was published, Herder's
attitude changed. He now regarded Frederick's military policy
largely as the consequence of circumstances suppressing his
humane feelings, and appreciated much of his peaceable work, his
justice, sense of duty and lack of prejudice. The personality of
Joseph II was more sympathetic to him, but he blamed his warlike

[20] I hope to be able to publish a comprehensive study of Herder in another
place.

actions, his disregard of traditions and national individualities and his autocratic tendencies. When Herder wrote his greatest work, the *Ideas on the Philosophy of the History of Mankind* (1784-1791) and came to the exposition of his political views, he met stiff resistance from the government about its publication. Minister von Goethe declared that not a word of it could be left unrevised and Herder had to re-write the text four times till the government was satisfied that it was not subversive. Herder's attitude to the French Revolution confirmed the suspicion that he had great sympathies for republicanism.

Though it is here not possible to discuss his ideas of the philosophy of history in detail, they must at least be mentioned in outline since they form the basis of his political attitude. Herder was deeply impressed by the diversity of the character of nations, and he sought to find its causes. He conceived the bold plan to write a history of the development of the human mind, and, though he could not pursue this work to its end, he made very valuable contributions to knowledge on this field. The diversities are explained by the effects of the environment, the dynamics of the movements of peoples and by the force of tradition. But Herder declines the assumption that a hereditary racial character exists and clings to the unity of the human race. The development of numerous, different nationalities seems to him beneficial because it obstructed the striving of conquerors to form great empires and maintained freedom by the balance between many nations. (Montesquieu had first put forward this view.) Herder was further convinced that only the individualities of numerous nations put together were able to evolve the fulness of possibilities dormant in human nature. His fundamental idea was that the development of mankind led to the gradual unfolding of humanity. He understood by this word the striving for truth, goodness and beauty, or of the divine spark in the human soul. In sharp contrast to the assumption that there were superior and inferior races and peoples justifying the subjection and exploitation of the latter by the former, Herder found that all peoples, even the most primitive ones, showed in many ways, especially in their songs, that they too possessed the spark of humanity. He translated many of the folksongs of tribes, undeveloped in civilization, in a masterly way. But the peoples with a high civilization too show national peculiarities which are valuable and must be respected. Every people has to make a contribution to the evolution of humanity. This should be furthered by the study of foreign languages and literature, the exchange of cultural achievements and the mixing of peoples.

The problem of national peculiarities is discussed by Herder in a most impartial and instructive way against a large historical and anthropological background, and with a penetrating psychology. He had peoples which had been hindered by their environment or history to reach an advanced stage of civilization particularly at heart, and was one of the first in western Europe who thought highly of the Slavs and predicted that they would have a great future. The heralds and champions of the Slav renaissance therefore celebrated Herder.

His political conclusions were that a state ought to be based on nationality, the consciousness of forming a great family-like, close community with a common language, religion and historical tradition. In Herder's view language also was interrelated with the thought of a nation since it reflected its historic experience and social structure. He hated states formed by conquest and subjection of peoples. Free nations, he was convinced, would not act in this way but would fraternally live side by side. It need hardly be said that the history of nations exhibits a different picture. The foundation of great nations was largely the work of conquerors who integrated many small peoples into a large state which became the cradle of a nation. National languages developed out of the usage practised by the royal chancellery (The King's English). Nor were free nations always imbued with fraternal feelings against one another. Herder obviously thought of conditions in the future when the historic rivalries and enmities created by conquering kings had been appeased by the democratic idea of self-determination.

Herder castigates and condemns national vanity, the striving for warlike glory and the domination of other peoples, in short what is called nationalism to-day.[21] A person proud of his nation appears to him a perfect fool just as someone proud of his noble birth. He wrote : What is a nation? A large unweeded garden, full of plants, good and bad. It is an accumulation of follies and faults as well as virtues and excellent traits, and one should not defend all these features without distinction against other nations. Let us contribute to the honour of the nation, and defend it if it is unjustly attacked —but praising it professionally is self-praise without any value. National glory is a terrible illusion, and the national mania is described as a sort of most dangerous plague.

As a philosopher of history and as a poet, Herder has made a great

---

[21] It is rather misleading if many American and English scholars speak of Herder as the founder of nationalism. His warm interest in the cultural individualities of all peoples was the very opposite of the nationalism of prestige and power which is in our age the greatest menace to culture.

contribution to the understanding of human nature, its countless variations and yet essential unity. Many new fields of study were opened by his work. The ideals which had guided him were well expressed in three words on his tombstone in Weimar, which he had chosen himself. They were : Light, Love, Life.

The greatest of all German poets, Johann Wolfgang Goethe (1749-1832) was the least political. Klopstock's enthusiasm for the liberty of the old Teutons appeared to him absurd, and even upon Herder's preaching of the gospel of humanity he looked with some irony. He did not feel called upon to become a preacher or politician, but a poet, and in poetry he wanted to express his own, personal experience exclusively. What interested him were not the collective actions of parties or masses, but the feelings of individuals and the achievements of great men, like Frederick and Joseph, and most of all of Napoleon. Simple men and women, too, had his warm sympathy when they filled their small sphere well, and he wanted them to be protected against oppression, and their welfare to be promoted. But Goethe did not wish to grant the people political rights. The art of government was not given to every ignoramus. Political nationalism was quite alien to him. Even German unity did not appeal to him if it threatened to encroach upon the independence of the small states. Goethe had further the greatest interest in the cultural achievements of all nations, which seemed to him to be the common patrimony of mankind. This whole outlook of a cultural aristocratism and an enlightened, patriarchal conservatism was determined by many factors, such as the conditions and course of his life and by countless experiences. It is impossible to imagine Goethe as a political partisan. Even so universal a genius was, however, sometimes not free from bias, and it is strange that he did not find much to criticize in the German public conditions of his time. But his greatness consists in the fact that he has demonstrated that in the cultural sphere the spirit can rise above party slogans and strife among nations.

An entirely different attitude to public life is shown in the dramas and other writings of Friedrich Schiller (1759-1805). They boldly attack tyranny and praise freedom. Schiller regarded the theatre as the most effective institution for educating men to a higher morality, which was needed for political freedom, and to give the people a national character. But nationality was to him not a political idea and not directed against other nations. He was most emphatically a world citizen. While Goethe was a realist, Schiller called himself an idealist and found his enthusiasm for freedom strengthened by Kant's philosophy, though he modified it. Both

Schiller and Kant enthused for Rousseau. Schiller's poetry and Kant's philosophy became the gospels of the liberals.

The age brought forth many minor poets and thinkers, too, of whom not a few were remarkable, but cannot be treated here. In dramas and poems terrible pictures were drawn of the depravity of princes and noblemen, misusing honest persons of the lower classes for their profit or to satisfy their desires. They echo Rousseau's mighty voice for freedom and equality. But some writers understood by freedom mainly the shaking off of all fetters of law and customs. Wilhelm Heinse, in his novel *Ardinghello* (1787) preached unbridled licence as the highest law of nature. The only crime is weakness, the greatest virtue is power, the highest good is beauty. Ardinghello, the hero of the novel, at last founds a communistic state, the characteristic features of which are free love, female suffrage and the worship of the elements. This author was librarian and reader to the Archbishop-Elector of Mainz, who appreciated his art. F. M. Klinger, after whose drama *Storm and Stress* a school of writers was named, could not sufficiently vent his dynamism in his numerous poetical works alone, but wanted to be a man of action and a soldier. He first wanted to join the American revolutionary army, and when this failed, he first entered an Austrian Free Corps, and then the Russian army, in which he became a general and nobleman.

The German writers often formed groups, usually assembled around a predominant personality. Their members edited journals, wrote articles for them and advised one another in literary matters. But political movements with concrete aims did not exist. German conditions made them almost impossible. But in addition the extraordinary number of intellectuals and authors was not favourable to their formation. There were too many different opinions and a great deal of mutual jealousy. The predominance of intellectual interests, particularly also of abstract thought, hindered activities for political aims. The middle classes were critical of abuses of the upper classes, and there were many who declared that their existence was not justified. But one cannot speak of a movement for the abolition of the nobility. Wieland wrote in 1793 that the most zealous defenders of the position of the nobles were non-nobles, and the most ardent democrats were of noble origin.

NEWSPAPERS AND JOURNALS

For a long time books and periodicals were subjected to the censorship which in most countries was very severe. Governments did not want any public discussion of their affairs, and in many places the Church too had influence in deciding whether the printing or selling of a publication was permitted. There were, however, always exceptions which increased in the course of time. Scholarly books were often censored by a professor of the university to which their author belonged, in some countries the censorship was mild, or did not exist. But even in places where it was severe, authors and booksellers not seldom knew ways to circumvent it. Writers sometimes castigated an imaginary oriental despot for his deeds, but the public knew who was meant. In certain Protestant countries one could speak very frankly about the Catholic Church, and in Catholic countries attacks on Protestant institutions were tolerated. Rulers were pleased if some other prince whom they disliked was shown in an unfavourable light. A great many books appeared with a fictitious place of publication on the title-page, but the booksellers knew very well how to procure them. F. W. von Taube, a senior Austrian official wrote also scholarly books which the censor did not pass. He confessed, however, to friends, that books prohibited by the censor, and printed abroad, had double the sale than else, and the booksellers liked them because they could charge a higher price for them. Nevertheless, the censorship was in many cases a grave obstacle to intellectual freedom.

With the progress of enlightenment the restrictions relaxed, and a new era may be said to have begun approximately in 1775. Emperor Joseph proclaimed a far-reaching freedom of the press in 1781, and in many countries the rulers or their ministers did not wish to appear less liberal than the Emperor.

In the later part of the century the number of the newspapers and journals increased considerably and every town soon had its own paper, or even several. The great majority were only of local significance, and a few only were widely read. The greatest German newspaper was the Hamburgische Unparteiische Correspondent, which had numerous foreign correspondents, and enjoyed an outstanding international reputation. In 1780 nearly 30,000 copies were printed and in 1803 50,000. A discussion of the political attitude of the German newspapers, however, is not possible here, and would hardly be fruitful for our subject. The time when they dominated, or made, public opinion, had not yet come. It was monthly or weekly journals which became the pioneers of the public discussion of politics.

From 1757 onwards, Friedrich Nicolai, a bookseller and publisher, founded several journals and he also wrote books himself. His most successful periodical was the Allgemeine Deutsche Bibliothek which appeared from 1765 to 1806. Nicolai was a close friend of Lessing and Mendelssohn, and the most prominent writers and scholars contributed to his journals. He was widely regarded as the head of the school of enlightenment and its disciples were called Nicolaites. Nicolai was a great admirer of Frederick II and an opponent of religious orthodoxy. In his later books he attacked Goethe, Kant, Fichte and the early Romanticists, and thereby provoked controversies which diminished his literary reputation. Of his works may be mentioned his *Travel through Germany*. He had made it in 1781, and later published a relation of it in twelve volumes containing a good deal of valuable information collected by him. He was very critical of Austria and Southern Germany, and in Catholic countries scented the pernicious influence of Popery and the Jesuits everywhere. Though he was often right, he also fell into exaggerations, which even prominent Protestants like Lavater and Garve refused to accept. His criticism aroused great resentment and showed again how deep the antagonism between Prussia and Austria, the Protestants and the Catholics still was.

Of the Journals published by Nicolai the *Berlinische Monatsschrift* (Berlin Monthly) was particularly significant for the political opinions of his followers. It was edited by two Prussian officials, the headmaster Friedrich Gedicke and the Royal Librarian Johann Erich Biester and appeared, with some modifications, from 1783 to 1811. Biester had formerly been secretary to the excellent liberal minister Baron Zedlitz, with whose portrait the first number of the journal was decorated. The editors maintained close relations with him and with the minister Count Hertzberg, also a far-sighted statesman. Biester knew how to win the most prominent scholars and writers as contributors and the journal was read by numerous intellectuals. The editors fervently admired Frederick II, especially his promotion of spiritual liberty, better justice and economic progress. Yet they often showed a great independence of opinion, even during the reign of Frederick. The very first volume of the journal printed a poem by a professor who signed with his initials J. F. H. - -l. He celebrated the victory of freedom in America and visualized the glorious day when the peoples of Europe, too, would break their chains and chase away their princes to flourish in freedom and happiness. But the poet awakes from his dream because of the clanking of the iron chains fettering him; they remind him that he is a German. Schloezer, a liberal, but opposed to the American revolution, parodied this poem in his journal and its editors replied in a declaration showing that they agreed with the poem. Two years later the journal published an article treating the majority of German princes with bitter sarcasm and advising them to acquire immortality by resigning and giving their peoples republican freedom, after having trained them in self-government. Other articles sought to spread understanding for the political spirit of England. Justus Moeser suggested that the German nobility should be transformed according to the English model. The journal often pleaded for the interests of the common people and Zedlitz himself made proposals on how to reform the schools. In 1786 an article pointed out that reading societies were spreading political discontent among the lower middle class and servants.

The passages quoted show that even under Frederick's reign, and before the French Revolution, republican sympathies could be put forward in Prussia unhampered by the censorship. It was obviously assumed that the expression of sympathies would not disturb the public order. In the case of this journal the fact of its close connection with two ministers may have been considered a guarantee that it would not make a subversive propaganda.

Several influential political journals were founded and edited by Wieland, Schubart, Weckherlin, Schloezer and Moser. All these writers were born in Swabia. This region had an old republican tradition, numerous Free Towns, and in various parts parliamentary institutions. In the time before the French Revolution Wieland's journal, *Der Deutsche Mercur* (1773-1810), put forward the same ideas as his books, already discussed, treating public questions in the form of novels. It was the spirit of humanity and the belief that a benevolent constitutional monarchy was best fitted to govern in this sense. The journal appeared in Weimar which was then the leading literary centre, and it published many conributions by the foremost poets and philosophers and also comments on current politics.

Quite different was the journal *Deutsche Chronik* which Christian F. D. Schubart founded in 1774 in Augsburg and later transferred to Ulm. Schubart had studied theology, but led the life of a Bohemian who was more at home in the beer-house and in the company of women than in church. He was, however, an excellent musician and forceful poet, and after various projects had foundered turned to journalism, for which he was very well fitted. He hated despotism in every form and detested the servility of most journals, which indulged in the flattery of princes and in descriptions of court festivities instead of castigating the vices of the ruling class. His sentiments were decidedly republican, he admired Switzerland and envied England for her freedom of the press. Yet he admitted that most republics were badly governed by small cliques, and that the opinion might be right that there was more freedom in a good monarchy. He celebrated Frederick and Joseph, but attacked bad princes in violent verses and with biting sarcasm. The corrupt clergy, too, were sharply criticized, though Schubart clung to Christian beliefs and deplored Frederick's attitude to religion. He was one of the first writers who wished that Prussia should obtain leadership in Germany. Yet he was not hostile to Austria and ascribed to her a great mission, especially in Eastern Europe. Sometimes he advocated conciliation and co-operation between the two great powers, but then wavered again. Would this not be detrimental to freedom? He deplored that the Germans had no national self-esteem and sometimes voiced a strong German nationalism. But he also had a lively Swabian patriotism. English liberty was his ideal, and he contrasted it with German servitude. The English were to him 'the first people in the world', and he called himself 'one of the most ecstatic admirers of Britain'. The outbreak of the American insurrection, however, changed this, and he now ardently took the side of the Americans and even prophesied that America would become the legislator of the world. His national pride was hurt by the fact that the British looked with cold contempt upon all the other peoples, in particular the Germans.

The journal, which appeared twice a week, was eagerly read even by people who had never before taken an interest in politics. But its editor, by poignant satire, offended various governments and princes, among them Duke Charles Eugen of Wurttemberg, and the Duke ordered one of his officials to lure Schubart to his territory, where he was arrested. For more than a year he was kept in a miserable dungeon and later in light confinement. Since his hope of a speedy release failed, he wrote scathing poems against despotism which aroused the wrath of the Duke again and prolonged his imprisonment. He was detained for ten years. His fate aroused many protests from German liberals. At last the Duke changed his mind, wished to make good all the harm he had inflicted on the unfortunate Schubart, and appointed him director of his theatre and music. He was also permitted to edit his journal again, and its circulation even rose to twice its former figure. But Schubart was a broken man and died in 1791, only 52 years old.

Soon after Schubart had been silenced by imprisonment, another Wurttemberger, Ludwig Weckherlin, aroused sensation as a journalist. From 1778 to 1788 he edited a journal of which the title was twice changed. It was best known under the name *The Grey Monster*. Previously he had lived in Paris and Vienna, where he had many friends among diplomats and writers. In Vienna he seems to have been secretary of the French ambassador, Duke of Rohan, and to have received the title of a French Counsellor of Legation. But, when he published gossip about the Viennese aristocracy he was expelled. He then described his impressions on a journey through Upper Germany, where he was particularly struck by the decay of the Free Towns under the rule of their patricians. Here, too, he got into trouble with the authorities and then retired to the small territory of Prince Ludwig of Oettingen-Wallerstein, who admired him and granted him his protection. Weckherlin edited here the journal already mentioned, and showed himself a brilliant, fearless writer and an excellent satirist. Moreover, the journal had many prominent contributors. Unlike Schubart Weckherlin was a pronounced cosmopolitan and imbued with a strong predilection for French life and literature. Against German detractors of the French he liked to stress that the French were still the first people in the world, that Germany owed them a great deal and was in many respects still inferior to them. His journal often criticized cases of violations of justice and humanity. For example, he castigated the Swiss canton of Glarus, where a woman had been accused of being a witch, sentenced to death and executed. The canton Glarus tried to get hold of him by summoning him to appear before their court, and when the Prince declined his extradition, they tried to bribe Weckherlin to disclose the person who had informed him about the witch-trial. When this, too, failed, they ordered that Weckherlin's journal should be publicly burned by the hangman, and its editor sent the republic of Glarus his portrait, suggesting that they should burn it instead of himself.

Weckherlin did not believe that there was an ideal constitution suitable for all peoples. He rejected every despotism, whether monarchical or republican. The king was to be responsible to the nation, which might judge or depose him. His power was to be restrained by Estates consisting of nobles, burghers and peasants. Yet he was not an admirer of parliaments in general. The alleged balance of power of the English constitution, he thought, was an illusion. Whoever dominated the parliament also had power over the executive and judicature. Small republics seemed to him liable to corruption, and great ones easily became victims of leaders aiming at dictatorship. Weckherlin had a great antipathy against the bourgeoisie, which appeared to him to be marked by callous egoism and lack of any national spirit. He had a better opinion of the nobility, though he was against caste seclusion and hereditary privileges. But Frederick, he believed, was right in thinking that only the nobility had a strong sense of honour, devotion to great aims and patriotism. At least the rule of honour was better than that of money. A democracy tended either to fall under the power of the moneyed interest or under mob rule.

The views put forward by Weckherlin were often daring and opposed to public opinion. He denied that Christianity had furthered civilization, though it had improved morals. Positive religion was to-day merely an instrument of tyranny. War was a terrible evil, but sometimes it had its good side too and promoted progress. A long peace could be ruinous for society by bringing about a decay of energy and internal dissolution. War, therefore, was something natural, a disease of the organism, but also a means of purging and strengthening it. Civil freedom was impossible without political liberty, and the latter reposed upon harmony among the three powers of government. Criminal justice was in opposition to humanity and reason: there were no criminals, only socially diseased persons; the prisons ought to be converted into reformatories. In foreign relations he defended the partition of Poland and rejected the plan of dividing Turkey, since she was needed for the balance of power. The American revolution was judged unfavourably. The state which the Jesuits had built in Paraguay and which had a socialist character was praised. The author regarded the group mind, or esprit de corps, as poison. Even good-natured men became malevolent when they belonged to an organized group. The idea of a national character was nonsense, for social factors had everywhere the same effect on the mind of peoples. Like Schubart, Weckherlin had very free opinions on sexual relations. He defended polygamy or free love, wanted the State to build 'temples of love' where intercourse between lovers should be permitted, and proposed that illegitimate children should be named 'children of the Fatherland' and brought up at public expense.

Though Weckherlin was a friend of freedom and humanity, he was too sharp an observer of the reality to believe that there was a simple panacea for making men happy. In particular, he realized that the power of property might be as dangerous to true freedom as the privileges of princes and aristocrats.[22] Weckherlin did not primarily write to make money or to become famous, but had a sincere wish to contribute to the improvement of the world. The journal was soon read everywhere, and the publisher could not print enough copies of it. Schloezer wrote that it rose like a comet over Germany.

[22] Forerunners of socialism therefore greatly esteemed Weckherlin. There were many contemporary writers who raised the demand for social freedom and equality. A survey of this literature is given in E. Weller, *Die Freiheitsbestrebungen der Deutschen im 18. und 19. Jahrhundert dargestellt in Zeugnissen ihrer Literatur*, 1847. The author seems to have been a socialist or communist.

When the French Revolution broke out, Weckherlin founded a newspaper on Prussian territory and had the support of the government. But the people regarded him with distrust, and when the rumour spread that a French invasion was threatening, the mob attacked him as a French spy and secret Jacobin. His nerves could not withstand the shock and he died on November 24, 1792.

Another journal of importance was founded and edited by Leopold Friedrich von Goecking under the title *Journal von und fuer Deutschland* (1784). Goecking was a landowner and Prussian official, and also distinguished himself as a poet. He wished to create a journal in order to make people from different parts of Germany better known to each other. His frank criticism of governments abusing their powers aroused, however, the anger of a ruler who complained to the Prussian government in whose service Goecking was. The government of Frederick the Great thereupon demanded in a harsh way that he should resign as an editor. This aroused an outcry against the violation of the freedom of the press. But Goecking retired from the editorship, which was taken over by his friend Baron Siegmund von Bibra, the president of the government of the ecclesiastical state of Fulda, which was then ruled by his relative Prince-Abbot Heinrich von Bibra.

It is rather astounding that the highest official of a principality was the editor of a journal very critical of every despotism. In an article he called himself a 'journalist', and wrote that he did not care if certain people looked down upon this activity. He also pleaded for freedom of the press, and compared bad princes and their counsellors to blood-sucking leeches on the bodies of their peoples. Goecking once even remarked, though not in the journal, it was a disgrace for the German nation that not a single of their princes had as yet been hanged or broken on the wheel. The journal laid the main stress upon publishing facts from which political conclusions could be drawn without going far into theoretical discussions. It printed decrees of rulers, judgments of the High Courts, important speeches, statistics, and other valuable information. The readers were encouraged to write letters illustrating conditions in their countries. In religious matters the journal stood for absolute toleration, for friendly relations between men of every religion, and for elimination of superstitious elements from the rites. It also provided much information on schools, care of the poor, social and educational reforms, promotion of economic progress, and so on. It even admitted that the peoples of the Catholic ecclesiastical states were in many respects not as well off as they could be. A price contest was arranged for the best inquiry into the causes of this state of things, and of the measures apt to improve it. The price was won by Joseph von Sartori, and his was published in vol. IV in 1787. It is a most illuminating and impartial exposition of the conditions which hindered the ecclesiastical states from reaching a much higher level of general welfare, and makes proposals of reforms.

A. L. SCHLOEZER

The most important periodical before the French Revolution was the journal edited by August Ludwig Schloezer (1735-1809). He was the son of a village pastor in Swabia and after the study of theology and many other subjects he spent eight years in Russia where he became a professor of history. In 1769 he was called to the University of Goettingen as a professor of statistics, politics and history. Statistics then meant the description of all the resources of a country. He lived in Goettingen for almost forty years and rose to great fame. His activities as a scholar and a publicist will be appreciated together here.

As an historian Schloezer was somewhat hampered by his manifold interests and by his agile, pugnacious temperament from concentrating on one field and producing a masterpiece. His most important work was on Russian history, and it has won him the credit of having initiated critical research in this field. He also wrote on universal history, on the trade and navigation of the ancients, and on Nordic, Scandinavian, Turkish, North African and Transylvanian history, besides works on political science and other writings. His cosmopolitan outlook induced him to learn fifteen languages, to visit many countries and to plan scientific expeditions to Asia. He also was one of the founders of comparative philology. In his writings the idea of world history was extended from that of a few leading nations to include also those hitherto neglected and thus to comprise the globe. Moreover, he thought that history consisted not only in the narration of wars and other political events, but should also include economic and cultural development. In Schloezer's view the introduction of the consumption of tea, coffee, sugar and tobacco had effected more momentous revolutions than the greatest wars. History, he said, was statistics in motion, and statistics was history become static.

One of Schloezer's main interests was education. His students were trained in political judgment in seminars in which the latest newspapers were discussed, and in classes on foreign countries. The latter were particularly designed for young aristocrats, who, after their studies, used to make the grand tour to the principal European countries. The Professor's aim was to educate his students to independent, critical thought on politics and to break the yoke of 'dull servilism'. But Schloezer also wrote an elementary introduction to history for children and other similar books, which went through many editions and were translated into other languages. These books preached the gospel of equality. The children were reminded that men were all descended from Adam, who was a simple man without a title, and that 'heroes' such as Alexander or Caesar were great villains and tyrants. The later King Frederick William III of Prussia had to read this book as a child and much enjoyed its gibes at kings.

The wish to spread political enlightenment also induced Schloezer to found and edit a periodical, which began to appear in 1775 received its definite title of *Staatsanzeigen* (State News) in 1783 and was then regularly published till 1793. This journal printed many secret official documents with critical comments and thereby shed light on the actions of government which hitherto had escaped any criticism. Sympathizers in high circles, ministers, diplomats and even ruling princes provided him with material. The journal defended the rights of man against arbitrary and oppressive measures. It castigated denials of justice, cases of religious intolerance and harmful superstition, wastefulness and corruption in the public finances, unfair privileges, the oppression of the lower classes and the Jews and similar abuses, and wished to spread better international understanding and good will, especially towards France, for whom Schloezer had particular admiration and sympathy.

The main seat of maladministration and petty tyranny were certain small territories of Germany where the princelings sometimes behaved as if their 'state' was their private property. It was natural, therefore, that Schloezer's criticism was mostly directed at them. In regard to powerful states, and those in close political relation with Hanover or England, he had to be cautious. Yet the greater rulers too were sometimes not spared. Though he highly admired Emperor Joseph II, Schloezer sharply blamed his harsh measures against sects in Bohemia. The first partition of Poland took place before the appearance of the paper, but the second partition between Russia and Prussia was strongly reprobated. In Hanover the censorship was mild, and professors were altogether exempt from it. Moreover, Schloezer could to a certain degree count on sympathizers in the ruling class. When he attacked the Prince Bishop of Speyer, a ruler of great influence, the Bishop twice wrote to King George III demanding that his impudent subject should be silenced. But the king declined the request. The bishop then tried to organize a protest of the Reichstag and a boycott of the University of Goettingen, but both moves failed. A number of influential princes, however, continued to urge the king to take measures, and in the end Schloezer had to submit his journal to the government of Hanover for perusal before it came out. This did not cause much harm, because he had powerful friends in the government.

The journal reached a sale of 4,400, for that time a high circulation. Schloezer obtained a great reputation and influence, though he made no use of it. Maria Theresa and her son, Joseph II, were regular readers and greatly appreciated the paper. It has been authenticated that the Empress once vetoed a decision of her Council of Ministers with the words: 'No, impossible—what would Schloezer say of it?'

Schloezer hated war and called the great conquerors robbers, murderers, barbarians, butchers, etc. The army should be merely a police force. Nobody had the duty to sacrifice his life for the fatherland, though one might erect monuments to those who did so voluntarily. Conscription, therefore, would be a cruelty. Yet Schloezer said he would approve of a war by Russia for the liberation of the Balkan peoples and he could not understand that the other powers objected on the ground of the balance of power. Like many liberals, Schloezer had no great interest in foreign policy. His heart was in internal reforms, in the peaceful progress of civilization. The great lesson of natural law, he thought, was the essential equality of men, though the striving for security and progress had brought about restrictions of the original equality. The rights of man, however, were sacrosanct. The serfdom of the peasants appeared to him absolutely inhuman, and he pleaded for its abolition. When the junkers of Mecklenburg enclosed land rented to their tenants, he compared them to the Mongols who had wanted to make China a sheep pasture. Racial discrimination against coloured people and the division of a people into different classes with unequal rights, he called disgusting and a disgrace for humanity. The oppressive privileges of the nobility should disappear, but the nobility itself should not be completely abolished. Schloezer also demanded equality for women, and denounced the usual reference to the Bible to justify the tyranny of the male sex over the female as a blasphemy. His daughter Dorothea was educated accordingly and at the age of seventeen she took the degree of doctor of philosophy, and became a most charming and brilliant woman.

The state was regarded by Schloezer not as an organism but as a machine for the promotion of progress and happiness. He also compared it to an insurance company, but this did not mean that the state should only care for security. Welfare, education and progress were also aims which it had to further. Schloezer shared Montesquieu's preference for mixed constitutions and for the English system. Sovereignty was with the people, but this did not imply unrestricted democracy. Patriarchal absolutism, the monarchical claim to be ordained by God, aristocratic oligarchy and democratic mob rule were all dangerous aberrations. The best was a system in which the three elements of monarchy, aristocracy and democracy were mixed and prevented each other from abusing their power. The peculiar conditions of each country, too, were of great importance. In a great and backward empire, such as Russia, an enlightened monarch was obviously the best ruler. In a small and primitive country pure democracy was possible because everybody could easily understand the issues of policy. In a great and advanced realm, however, public affairs were too complex and difficult to understand for the common man, and a mixed constitution, therefore, was advisable. Schloezer agreed with Montesquieu in the view that a great state had much better chances of progress and civilization than a small one. On the one hand, therefore, Schloezer condemned conquerors, on the other he praised the advantages of great empires which were the historic products of conquerors.

Rousseau had praised small states, which alone were able to be republics. Many German writers had accepted this view, which also agreed with the wide-spread predilection for the existing 'Kleinstaaterei'. Schloezer's view, therefore, was contrary to the opinion of most writers. One of the greatest weaknesses of small republics, he pointed out, was their inability to co-operate for common defence and other purposes. The Greek city states ruined each other by internecine strife, and the much vaunted Athenians were particularly aggressive and ruthless. Their freedom bordered on anarchy. Schloezer much preferred a large, well-ordered empire, such as the Persia of Cyrus or republican Rome. In modern times Switzerland and the Netherlands were examples of small states forming loose confederations but unable to attain real unity because they were too much separated by local interests and oligarchical egoism. Like most of the progressive thinkers of his time on the Continent, Schloezer did not think highly of the existing Estates, which were too much inspired by aristocratic class interests to be able to abolish oppressive privileges. Enlightened monarchs seemed to him much better fitted to realize civic equality than diets dominated by noblemen or plutocrats. In the Dutch republics the rich merchants were the rulers and they merely defended their vested interests. The Swiss republican system, too, was really an oligarchy. Schloezer was particularly aroused by the tragic fate of parson Waser in Zurich, who had contributed an article to his journal, criticizing the financial policy of the oligarchy dominating Zurich. When this was discovered the local rulers had him sentenced to death and he was executed (1780). True, he had also committed another offence, but the death sentence laid the main stress on the contribution to Schloezer's journal. Another case was that of the poor girl from Glarus who was executed for witchcraft in 1782. Such cases induced Schloezer to declare that the Swiss cantons were among the most backward states.

The freedom of the press seemed to the professor the most effective instrument of progress. He set the highest hopes on the development of newspapers and demanded the abolition of every censorship, though he also wanted a law against libel by the press. The crime of lese-majesty, torture, capital punishment, etc. should be eliminated from penal law. The Jews should be emancipated, though they should first be educated to promote their assimilation.

In economic policy Schloezer was essentially a mercantilist and an adversary of the physiocrats, but he sometimes also leaned to freedom of trade. A trade policy directed by the state appeared to him to be a useful instrument of planning in order to secure full employment for every worker. The accumulation of wealth in the hands of a few was a social danger. In the last 200 years, he wrote, many of the most sanguinary wars had been caused by commercial rivalry, and world trade had, on the whole, been much more of a curse than of a blessing. He declared: 'One capitalist (Geldmensch) renders a million people immoral'. Schloezer's liberalism sometimes seems to give way to feelings of social revolt. 'An able-bodied man,' he writes, 'unable to find work, is entitled to suspend the whole social contract and consequently also the seventh commandment.'

Like most liberals of his age, Schloezer was very bitter against the Papacy and the Jesuits, whom he accused of keeping the people in a state of stupid submissiveness. But he esteemed Catholicism as a religion. The Churches should be subordinated to the state, and religion should be based on a rational interpretation of the Bible, eliminating miracles. In regard to nationality, Schloezer scoffed at the 'physical love of the fatherland', which reminded him of a cow accustomed to her stable. A thinking man could venerate his fatherland and king only on grounds of utility, because they secured him peace and public order. Germany's lack of political power, therefore, did not worry the staunch cosmopolitan. In his youth he once wrote in a letter that it would be best if Germany were under one ruler, whoever he might be, and that the king of Prussia would be best fitted to achieve this aim by means of conquest. This astounding anticipation of the distant future was not, however, an outcome of nationalism, but the consequence of the conviction that large states were much more likely to pursue a policy of enlightenment and progress than dwarf territories under a patrimonial ruler or a local clique. Later, however, especially after the French Revolution, Schloezer saw in Germany's division into several hundreds of states a benefit rather than a drawback. In spite of all the oddities and faults of the constitution of the Empire it seemed to him, on the whole, partly already conducive to the welfare of the people, partly capable of being reformed in a gradual way without convulsive changes. If a prince abused his power, there was the possibility of appealing to a High Court of the Empire which could declare his acts invalid and punish him. Schloezer was proud of the cultural achievements of the Germans in which they often surpassed other nations. Enlightenment, he wrote, was in Germany not restricted to the upper classes as in France but more evenly spread among all classes. In consequence, there was no abyss between the classes and no danger of a sanguinary revolution. Every reform could be achieved in a gradual and peaceful manner.

In spite of his preference for quiet evolution, Schloezer did not entirely reject the right of the people to rise against intolerable oppression. He also changed his opinion on the advantages of enlightened absolutism. Joseph's despotic way of dictating reforms aroused his bitter comments, and he said Joseph reminded him of the Stuarts; measures by Frederick William II were also criticized. Already in 1772 he declared that only a monarchy limited by popular representation had a healthy constitution, and he abided by this conviction. A nation, he said, which permitted itself to be governed without such representation was like 'stupid sheep'. The opposition of the Estates against reforms was the lesser evil, compared to their suppression because of their unwise policy. The further fate of Schloezer's journal was determined by the French Revolution, and will be dealt with later.

JUSTUS MOESER

Enlightenment had almost reached its peak when a very different spirit made its appearance in the writings of Justus Moeser (1720-94). He lived in the small Westphalian territory of Osnabrueck which,

according to the Peace of Westphalia, was to be governed alterna-
tively by a Catholic and a Protestant bishop of whom the latter had
to belong to the House of Hanover. Moeser became a barrister, then
syndic of the knighthood, and soon afterwards a civil servant also.
In the latter position he was for a long time the leading statesman of
his country, enjoying the greatest trust of the ruling circles and the
love of all classes of the people. A stay in England increased his
admiration for English conditions.

Moeser had a most original personality distinguished by integrity,
humanity, learning, humour and skill in dealing with people of
every kind. His best known writings consisted in articles written
for a local journal which were later collected under the title
Patriotic Phantasies (1774), through them he wished to inform the
people of public affairs and to further their welfare and political
thinking. Already as a barrister he had been indefatigable in defending the poor and helpless against oppression. Yet his articles often
arouse the impression that he was a defender of the most antiquated
prejudices and abuses, in a way contrary to the demands of the
school of enlightenment. Many of the articles dealt with the questions of serfdom which still existed in a mild form in the country,
though many of the peasants were freemen. He showed that it had
originally often been created in the interest of the peasants and even
now was preferred by many tenants to full freedom. His aim was a
reform to take place by agreement between the nobles and the
peasants. Moeser was in the curious position that he was both the
representative of the knights in the Estates, and of the government
which depended on their financial aid. He had therefore to make
concessions to the feudal interest if he wished to maintain the confidence of the nobles.

But this was not the only cause of his attitude to old privileges
and customs. He also wrote a history of his country which, like
many of his articles, showed that he had considerable feeling for
the middle ages and sympathy for the peasantry. The believers in
Enlightenment regarded mediaeval laws and customs as the results of
universal ignorance, clerical superstition and feudal barbarism. In
their view the new despotism with its officials and soldiers, should
abolish these antiquated institutions, where they still existed, and
replace them by others based on reason. Moeser, however, was quite
opposed to the spirit of autocratic centralization demolishing
ancient institutions with their wide autonomy. He tried to show
that they were based on reasonable grounds and that even their bad
sides were often outweighed by good ones. He idealized the free
yeoman of the old Germanic past and the peasant of his own time

even appeared to him to be more valuable than aristocrats, bureaucrats and intellectuals. Every local or social section of the people
had its individuality, tradition and honour. This diversity based on
organic growth seemed to him better than the general Rights of
Man, equal rights not rooted in reality but in abstract speculations.
His heart was in the small homelands, the attachment to the
native soil and historic development. Moeser found much that is
good in mediaeval institutions, such as the differences of rank,
armed self-help, dispersal of powers etc. Feudalism, it seemed to him
was marked by virility, independence and a pugnacious love of
freedom and honour.

But Moeser did not merely look backwards. He advocated a constitution on the English model, stressed the right of the nation to
make their decisions in Parliament and on the juries, appreciated
English education, and wished that the German nobility should be
reformed according to the model of the English. He deplored that
the egoistic policy of many emperors and princes had prevented the
German burghers from laying the foundations of national freedom.
If this had been done, he said, it would not be Lord Clive who gives
commands on the Ganges but an alderman from Hamburg. Moeser
draws a fascinating picture of the English character which, under
the influence of freedom, promotes the constant activity of all
individual forces, while in Germany despotism paralyses them. In
England the whole nation was always in movement, inspired with
enthusiasm for the common weal. Even the lowest man regarded it
as an aim for which to strive. This free and forceful life created great
ideas and bold initiative. In Germany this spirit was lacking, the
state was nothing but a mechanically operated machine and the
subjects could only acquire honour in its service or in scholarship.
In consequence the French called the Germans industrious pedants,
the English regarded them as pitiable slaves, and the Italians looked
upon them as wretched boors.

Though there is certainly much truth in what Moeser says he
curiously ignores the connection between national unity and political liberty. England's free institutions had only been made possible
by the early achievement of a considerable measure of national
unity. This was largely the work of kings who were exceptionally
strong by right of conquest and who combined centralization with
local autonomy. But Moeser clings to territorial and social particularism. He overlooks the fact that the egoism of the German
towns had much contributed to the frustration of German national
liberty. His ideal would have been a Germany composed of
numerous small republics and free associations between them. He

also wished for a kind of German customs union. Sometimes he also pointed out that Germany too had valuable institutions. A Habeas Corpus act, for example, existed in many German states.

The state appeared to Moeser as a sort of private association comparable to a limited company. Members of the nation were only the legal successors of the original freeholders of land and those who had been admitted to partnership. The members of the nation were, so to speak, shareholders and the shares were the land. The new-comers without land had no share in the national sovereignty except in so far as the possessing class had voluntarily granted them political rights. This practically corresponded to the ideology widely held in England, even by Burke. Moeser's predilection for mediaeval institutions too had parallels in England, where many statutes of the middle ages were still in legal force though they had more or less fallen into desuetude. Moeser's criticism of many of the principles of enlightenment sound very reactionary. Yet we may assume that its real aim was not to restore mediaeval conditions, but to draw attention to the over-simplified onesidedness of the modern ideology, and to plead for a compromise with the natural instincts of man, which otherwise threatened to assert themselves despite all the rational and humanitarian laws. Moeser had been greatly impressed by Rousseau's doctrine that all true virtues sprang from great passions. He also came near to the view that morality was differentiated according to characters and circumstances. English politics and life were full of irrational and inhumane forces and yet realized more freedom, happiness and greatness than the reasonable regulations of the German police state. Moeser, however, was not entirely antagonistic to the principles of the Enlightenment and even sometimes fell into the error of judging things from a too rationalistic and utilitarian point of view himself.

Besides the journals discussed here, there appeared in the seventies and eighties a great many others which cannot be dealt with here for reasons of space. They also greatly differed in value though some of them had excellent editors and contributors. On the whole, they all condemned despotism and stood for the principles of Enlightenment. With the outbreak of the French Revolution a new epoch began, and journalism, too, showed new features which will have to be surveyed later.

THE AMERICAN REVOLUTION AND GERMAN OPINION

In 1763 the Seven Years' War ended, and Britain received Canada

o

and other possessions in America from the French. The colonies of Britain were thereby relieved from the fear of French or Spanish aggression and from the need to rely on the protection of the British navy. Almost at once a constitutional conflict broke out between Britain and the colonies. It was followed by war; in 1776 Congress voted the Declaration of Independence and the insurgents, supported by France, were victorious. The Treaty of Paris (1783) acknowledged the independence of the United States.

The American Revolution aroused lively interest in Germany, and was much discussed. Britain had many supporters, owing to her personal union with Hanover, and to her relations with other German states. Six German princes had, in all supplied her with 29,875 soldiers for the war in America. This fact was bitterly resented by large sections of German youth who clamoured for liberty. Thousands of Germans, however, were also fighting on the American side, namely in the regiments composed of Germans which the French government sent to America. Their officers were mostly German noblemen,[23] who largely sympathized with the fighters for freedom. At an even earlier date Baron Johann Kalb had joined the American insurgents, who at once made him a Major-General in their army. He was the son of a German peasant, had served for about 35 years in the French Army and had become a general and baron. It was further of inestimable value for the American cause that Baron F. W. von Steuben, merely from enthusiasm for democracy, offered his services to George Washington. He had once served in the Prussian Army and had the greatest experience in military matters. He at once became Inspector-General in the American Army and trained it to perfect efficiency. Many French aristocrats, too, took part in the war as members of the French forces and not a few of them were thereby inspired with sympathy for republican ideas. This was later of significance for the outbreak of the French Revolution.

Goethe wrote in his autobiography *Dichtung und Wahrheit* that people in Germany wished the Americans every good fortune, and he himself thought for a moment of going there, though not for political reasons. Schiller, however, intended to emigrate to America because of his enthusiasm for freedom. An American historian, H. Gallinger, has made a careful study of the opinions expressed in the principal German journals of the time. He shows that most of the writers took the side of the insurgents. Schloezer disagreed with them arguing that Britain had not oppressed the colonists and that

[23] The French army at the middle of the eighteenth century contained 19 battalions of German infantry with 525 German officers.

the rebels practised terrorism against the loyalists which was contrary to liberty. The American revolution did much to further
republican ideas in Germany.

20

THE FRENCH REVOLUTION

GERMAN PUBLIC OPINION CONCERNING IT
AT ITS OUTBREAK

THE outbreak of the French Revolution aroused unprecedented jubilation among the German educated classes. Thousands of voices welcomed the revolutionary events, numerous Germans hurried to Paris to take part in them, or to imbibe their spirit. The young people, in particular, were exuberant in their joy and many who in later years became leaders in the fight against the ideas of the revolution were then the most fiery believers in the new gospel. Almost forty years later, Hegel, now an enemy of democracy, in his Philosophy of History, remembered the outbreak in the words: 'It was a glorious sunrise. All thinking beings celebrated this event. A sublime emotion reigned over the epoch, the world was thrilled with spiritual enthusiasm as if the Divine had now really conciliated itself with the world.'

Not only the young were overwhelmed with joy but also mature men of great experience of the world. Klopstock, who was 65, wished to have a hundred voices to sing hymns to the triumph of liberty. It seemed to him the greatest action of the century, more beautiful that the bloodstained laurels of a Frederick. Though he detested war, he passionately welcomed the French challenge to the monarchs. He wished to be a French citizen, and the National Assembly indeed conferred on him, Schiller and other Germans the French honorary citizenship. Wieland, too, expressed his joyous approval and in his journal now eagerly defended plans of a free constitution. Kant, who was as old as Klopstock, was one of the most ardent and lasting friends of the revolution. The fiery Fichte soon had the reputation of being a dangerous revolutionary. As newly found letters show he wished to become a French citizen and a professor in a German university under French rule in order to work for a revolution in Germany too. The young writers who were to become the leaders of the Romantic movement were almost unanimous in hailing the victory of freedom. The great scholar Schloezer wrote that the angels must be singing Te Deum in heaven. Schubart, who from German patriotism had been hostile to France, changed his mind and became her fervent admirer.

Nowhere was the revolution hailed with greater joy than in Prussia. The very worshippers of Frederick the Great were convinced that his principles were essentially the same as those of the French revolutionaries. This belief may seem odd to us, but was quite sincere. In theory, of course, Frederick had proclaimed the equality of all men, though his practice was different. His attitude towards religion was similar to that of many revolutionaries in Paris. Moreover, they certainly agreed with his hatred of Austria, and most of them also shared his opinion that France and Prussia were natural allies, and only temporarily separated by Kaunitz' diplomacy. Frederick also was extremely popular among the French intellectuals because of his relations to Voltaire, d'Alembert etc. As mentioned already, towards the end of Frederick's reign a certain republicanism had further spread in Berlin's intellectual circles. This tendency was now vented by various writers. Jenisch published an ode in Wieland's journal, celebrating the revolution. The tyrants were advised to flee from their shaking thrones since the thunder of freedom was roaring, and the Germans were grimly gnashing their teeth. In Austria and South Germany the Berlin intellectuals were soon called the German Jacobins. Many Prussians flocked to Paris, among them Count Schlabrendorff a highly cultured and rich nobleman, who became a member of the Jacobin Club and played a very honourable rôle. Some Prussians found that the French revolutionaries were not progressive enough. The president of a high court of law, Morgenbesser, blamed the Jacobins because they were sparing private property. Andreas Riem, who came from a distinguished family in the Palatinate, became a clergyman in Prussia. He showed a fervent republicanism, got in touch with the Jacobins, and made propaganda for an alliance of Prussia with France, which was to bring about a united and free Germany under Prussia's hegemony, while France was to receive the territories left of the Rhine. But the Prussian government expelled him and he went to Paris.

Some men of letters, however, maintained towards the revolution an attitude of reserve and distrust, among them Goethe. The French

Revolution appeared to him as a natural phenomenon which had its deep-lying causes, but which reasonable men could only dislike as they would have disliked an earthquake. In such political struggles rights and wrongs were on both sides inextricably mixed, and politicians were not exclusively actuated by ideal motives but also by the lust for power. Every radical breach with the past and every intoxication of the masses with slogans threatened the evolution of the minds of the individuals to freedom, culture and happiness.

THE RISE OF RADICALISM AND OF ANTI-REVOLUTIONARY TENDENCIES

The revolution had not started in a spirit of excessive radicalism. The great majority of the deputies were long for a constitutional monarchy, and a régime directed by the wealthy, and educated classes. How it came that France was swept into a régime being the very opposite of the ideals proclaimed as the rights of man and citizen need not be related here. Nor could healthy social and financial conditions be achieved, and the alleged war for universal liberty, begun by France, soon assumed the character of a war of conquest and spoliation. With the increase of violence and bloodshed in France the enthusiasm of the German admirers of the revolution gradually vanished. Many liberals long hoped that this phase would pass. Schloezer wrote that cancer could not be cured by rose water. Klopstock was in despair because the revolutionaries did not keep their pledge to renounce a war of conquest. Wieland followed the events with anxiety. His ideal now was a constitutional monarchy according to Montesquieu's ideas, but he early foresaw that the anarchy created by the revolution would end in a military dictatorship. While he had previously treated German conditions with sarcasm, he now found that the Germans could be well satisfied with their constitution, which secured them valuable liberties, a firm reign of law and a flowering of culture. In France, he wrote, the acute antagonism between the social classes aroused an exaggerated demand for equality, and this must also lead to the striving for economic equality. A great capital like Paris now appeared to him as an evil which Germany should be glad to lack. He hoped that better education would render the people fitter for liberty, and wanted talented children of the lower classes to be enabled to acquire higher qualifications by state scholarships. The idea that political liberty required first the moral education of the individual also inspired Schiller, who saw an important instrument for it in art, in particular dramatic art. Herder's warm sympathies for the Revolution changed after the king's execution. Kant was more steadfast; he condemned acts of violence but still believed that the noble principles of the revolution would at last prevail over temporary aberrations. In 1794 he said to a friend that all the evils of the Revolution were not as great as those of despotism and that the Jacobins were most probably right in everything they did. The Romanticists, like Friedrich Schlegel, L. Tieck and others, were not deterred by the execution of the king. Schleiermacher was shocked by it, not because he was a monarch, but because policy was no justification for the murder of an innocent man.

The censorship became ever more rigorous in most German states and democratic authors had to be very cautious to evade persecution. Nicolai was suspect to the Prussian government of being a person of subversive tendencies. He found it advisable to publish his journals no longer in Berlin but in a state where the censorship was still tolerable. Schloezer had already begun to criticize French politics sharply. But this did not prevent the enemies of a free press from accusing him of having paved the way for a revolutionary movement. He had hitherto been free from the censorship, but in 1793 he was subjected to it, and three years later the publication of his journal was prohibited under a pretext.

The unexpected change in the character of the Revolution and the war aroused a mighty wave of reaction against the liberal tendencies of the Enlightenment in many countries. Though Frederick II and Joseph II had been against granting influence to the Estates, or representation in them to the middle class, some of their statesmen had already in their reign, before the Revolution, suggested such reforms[1] and after its outbreak more ministers and high officials did so. But the rise of aggressiveness and a reign of terror put an end to plans of political reforms. Emperor Leopold was convinced of the necessity of a real parliament, but found it quite impossible to undertake so revolutionary an innovation at a time when his state was threatened on all sides with the greatest possible dangers.

The French propaganda for a revolution in all countries also brought about the appearance of German journals directed against its slogans and combating subversive tendencies. Various pamphlets

---

[1] Minister Count Hertzberg in 1784, in a lecture to the Berlin Academy, proposed Estates with representatives of the peasantry, though it seems that he was thinking of consultative Estates only; Cf. Hertzberg, Huit dissertations, etc. 1787, p. 141. In Austria, Minister Count Zinzendorf in 1787 declared that only an assembly of representatives of all landowners could decide about the reform of direct taxation. Cf. Hock-Bidermann p. 169. This assembly would have become States General as assembled two years later in France.

of this kind were published in Vienna by Leopold Alois Hoffman, a professor who had been, before, a radical defender of Joseph's policy. He had the support of Emperor Leopold, and from 1791 to 1792 he edited the 'Wiener Zeitschrift'. The journal had, however, difficulties in finding able contributors and sufficient readers and, when the Emperor died, it came to an end. Another journal of this kind was then edited by Hofstaetter, a former Jesuit.

In Germany the journal *Eudaemonia* played a rôle as a sort of central organ of the circles opposed to the revolution and there were many other publications of this kind. Valjavec states that these conservative movements were mostly not furthered by the governments, which rather hindered and even sometimes suppressed them. Nor were their leaders fanatics of reaction. Most of them were neither for revolution, nor for monarchical absolutism, but for a middle way. In Austria and Bavaria the government for some time prohibited any writings for and against the Revolution.[2]

A school of moderate liberalism on the English model, and based on Montesquieu's ideas, developed in Hanover. Two civil servants, Ernst Brandes and August Wilhelm von Rehberg, each published a book on the French Revolution from this point of view. Brandes's book appeared almost at the same time as Burke's *Reflections on the Revolution* (1790), while Rehberg's came out two years later and was already strongly influenced by Burke. Both, however, had already admired Burke before and were in personal contact with him. All these writings agreed in emphasizing the importance of historical continuity and national traditions in contrast to revolutionary innovations on the grounds of abstract principles. The nation appeared to these writers as an organism composed of classes with organic functions. The national constitution was deeply rooted in the past, and could not be changed simply by a vote of the present majority of the people. Brandes and Rehberg, however, were more liberal than Burke, and regarded his fanatical attacks on every act of the Revolution and his enthusiasm for royalty, the Church, the aristocracy and the good old days, as going too far. Burke's *Reflections* were at once translated into German. Two different translations appeared in Vienna and a third in Berlin. The latter was by Friedrich Gentz, who became the most zealous propagandist for Burke's ideas and the leading publicist in the fight against the Revolution and France. Burke's campaign for war against France aroused much opposition in Germany, and even many of those who were against the Revolution criticized his

---

[2] Cf. F. Valjavec, *Die Entstehung der politischen Stroemungen in Deutschland. 1770-1815.* This is the best exposition of the subject.

extremism. Fichte violently attacked Burke and Rehberg. An enlightened Catholic priest in Salzburg, Lorenz Huebner, wrote in his
journal that Burke, in recommending the British constitution to the
French, had made no allowance for the French national character,
which differed from the English. Regarding Burke's contempt for
the National Assembly because it included so many solicitors and
village parsons, Huebner remarked that these knew better what the
people needed than young noblemen who had learned only how to
indulge their own pleasures. The discussion of Burke's ideas
awakened the interest of the German conservatives for England,
while the liberals mostly turned to France. Kant, in particular, was
strongly on her side against Britain. The German Romanticists,
however, later adopted Burke's ideas, and Adam Mueller, in particular, found in him his gospel.

The Revolution in the following years effected great changes in
the press. Many new writers came forward and new journals were
founded, while others disappeared. Here we must restrict our-
selves to a few remarks. A prominent liberal writer was J. W. von
Archenholtz, a Hanoverian nobleman, who had served under
Frederick II and later travelled widely. He was long an ardent
admirer of England, lived there for six years and published various
books and periodicals designed to inform the Germans about
English politics and life. But the French Revolution filled him, too,
with enthusiasm. He dismissed Burke's attacks as pitiful and
settled in Paris. The reign of terror, however, was a great shock to
him, he left Paris and later lived mostly in Hamburg. He founded
the journal *Minerva* (1792), which became a main organ of liberalism. It also criticized revolutionary excesses, but was entirely
opposed to any German intervention in France and worked for
friendship between the two nations. Another journal hailing the
Revolution was the *Braunschweigische Journal* edited by Joachim
Heinrich Campe, who also distinguished himself as an educationist
and scholar. Campe was for some time fascinated by the events in
Paris but later was disillusioned. His articles against military intervention in France induced Prussia to protest strongly to the Brunswick government; but the Duke, himself a liberal, left Campe free
from censorship, though warning him to be more cautious in future.
Johann Friedrich Reichardt was a famous court conductor and
composer with many high connections. He was filled with
enthusiasm for the Revolution, and later founded two journals,
one called *Deutschland*, the other *Frankreich*, which preached
republicanism and close relations with France. Quite the opposite
tendency was represented by the influential *Hamburgische Poli-*

o*

tische Journal founded in 1781 by Gottlob Benedict von Schirach, who edited it till his death in 1804. This journal was, from the beginning, hostile to the Revolution. Since it had a very good news service, it was widely read and in 1790 boasted of having the largest circulation of all German political journals. When Napoleon started to rise to power, new journals and writers emerged, and also new ideas developed.

WHY WAS THERE NO REVOLUTION IN GERMANY?

The question was often raised why no revolution broke out in Germany too, and opinions were put forward making the German character responsible for this. Certain German traditions certainly contributed to it, but there also were strong emotional forces counteracting them. The hatred of the evils of despotism and republican opinions were widely spread in Germany's educated classes. And it was these classes which started the outbreak of the revolution in France, not the masses of the people. France was threatened by a financial catastrophe and the States General, after a pause of 175 years, were convened to prevent it. The disastrous financial situation was the result of endless wars and the wastefulness of the old régime. France's latest war in support of the American insurgents against English rule had been particularly expensive. Moreover, many officers and soldiers in the French troops sent to America had acquired sympathies for republicanism.

In 1789 the French national debt amounted to 4,467 million livres, there was a large deficit, and the financial system suffered from deep-rooted evils such as the privileges of the Church and the nobles in regard to taxation, the fact that most posts in the state service had been sold to people as inheritable property, and the farming out of the collection of taxes to financiers who made vast profits out of it. In the principal states of the German empire finance and administration were in much better order than in France.[3] The

[3] One of the reasons was that many German states did not wage so much war as France, and contributed little to the wars of the Empire. The Imperial Aulic Council, as High Court, often intervened in the financial affairs of states to prevent bankruptcy or other abuses, and put the finance in order. J. J. Moser, Vom reichstaendischem Schuldenwesen, 2 vols. 1774 discusses 58 cases of this sort. K. von Lang, a bitter critic of the abuses of small princes says in his memoirs (I. p. 105) that these rulers had become extremely anxious and scrupulous in financial matters wishing to prevent thereby their subjects from bringing an action against them at the Imperial Aulic Council. Many rulers and governments also made great profit from hiring out mercenaries to foreign states. Lastly many princes had large domains and very remunerative rights to tolls and similar dues which did not depend on a vote of the estates.

Austrian Empire's population was approximately five sixth of that of France, but the French state debts were more than six and a half times larger than the Austrian, which were already considered unusually high.[4] Prussia had no debts at all, but had accumulated a treasure which was equivalent to between 150 and 200 million livres. Hesse-Cassel had splendid finances, mainly owing to her traffic in soldiers. From many states it was reported that they had discharged all or most of their debts. Saxe and Hanover had still debts from the Seven Years' War, but they were rapidly paid back. Mecklenburg had bad finances. Bavaria-Palatinate had larger debts, but they were not excessive. Some German statisticians maintained that the lot of the peasants was worse in France than in Germany.[5] This cannot be proved. But that the burden of taxation and of interests on debts was more oppressive in France than in the Empire is very probable.

The revolution was, in fact, brought about by the nobility, the rich bourgeoisie and the intellectuals who wanted to obtain a share in the government, either for idealistic or egotistic reasons. In Germany a class comparable to the French bourgeoisie did not exist. There was a number of wealthy patricians, merchants, bankers and manufacturers, but they were content with a respected position in their home town, and had no ambition to play a political rôle in Germany. The German nobility was numerous, but the majority was not rich. The soil was, on the whole, less fertile in Germany as in France, and it was mostly poorly worked by the stewards of the nobles, and by the serfs. In some German states the knights had ceased to attend the Diets because of the expenses. Many nobles, however, had remunerative positions at the expense of the state or the Church.

In France the demand for a real parliament had probably more adherents in the middle and upper classes than in Germany, though a considerable section of the nobles would have preferred a system like the old States General. But this difference was largely due to the fact that France was a unitary, national state while particularism prevented national unity in Germany. Under the conditions of particularism, the German nobles and substantial burghers had hardly any reason for being discontent. They, or their representa-

---

[4] According to F. von Mensi in the *Oesterreichisches Staatswoerterbuch*, vol. IV 2. ed. 1909 p. 438 the Austrian debts amounted to 338 million Gulden in 1789. Two livres were equivalent to a Gulden. On the finance of the German states cf. F. L. Brunn, *Deutschland* etc., 1819, 3 vols., and T. B. Clarke, *Statistical View of Germany*, 1790.

[5] Cf. J. P. Suessmilch, *Die goettliche Ordnung in den Veraenderungen des menschlichen Geschlechts* etc., 3. ed. 1765 I pp. 347, 438, II p. 433.

tives, had seats in the Reichstag and in the territorial diets. The Free Towns, moreover, possessed an almost republican self-government. In most of them the patricians ruled, but there were also some where the guilds of artisans nominated a number of the town councillors, and in some diets the peasants too were represented. The whole system had, of course, grave inadequacies, but the classes indicated could hardly complain about them, as long as they clung to particularism.

The French aristocrats were, on the whole, richer and more cultured than the German, but in political rights the latter were in a much more privileged position. About 1,800 German nobles, from kings down to the Free Knights, had the rights of rulers, and in the ecclesiastical states there were 4,000 noblemen who were eligible to 64 posts of princes, or to those of numerous, well-paid canons who had to elect these. Their status was certainly higher than that of a deputy to a national assembly, and they had hardly a reason to covet such a post.

In a revolutionary movement it is usually the intellectual classes which play the leading rôle. In this respect, there were considerable differences between France and Germany, though perhaps less in the numbers of the individuals concerned than in their tradition and social status. Owing to the multitude of governments and universities in Germany, the number of officials and professors was very large in this country. But they were very numerous in France, too. In the states of the Empire, however, they were greatly dependent on their governments, and could often be dismissed without a good reason, though in some states, at least, they were rather safe, and also the Supreme Courts of the Empire protected their rights in certain cases. In France, however, the judges and officials had bought or inherited their posts and could not be dismissed. The members of the High Courts, called parlements, considered themselves guardians of the unwritten constitutional laws. The free professions, such as the lawyers or the authors, also had great independence and a high status.

The lower middle classes and the industrial workers were much more numerous in France than in the Empire because industrial and capitalistic development was farther advanced in the former. They also were more settled in, or near, big towns in France, while the great majority was rural in the Empire. French manufacturers sold luxury- and fashion-goods to the courts, nobles and rich of the whole of Europe. These industries were settled in towns such as Paris or Lyon, near their customers. In the Empire, many governments tried to establish such industries at home, but the results were mostly not great. Industries developed in Germany and Austria first in mountainous regions where agriculture was stopped for a long time during the winter, and the people could only earn a living by other work at their homes, such as weaving, carving, plaiting or grinding. These places also were often rich in wood, ores and water-power, which before the age of coal and railways were the most important foundations of industries. Big towns also demanded numerous trades supplying the population with food, clothes etc. In Germany, particularism tended to disperse trades in numerous small towns. For many reasons therefore the industrial workers were less numerous and less concentrated in large towns in Germany than in France.

Small traders, craftsmen and industrial workers, particularly the unemployed, formed a considerable part of the masses which the demagogues of the French Revolution used to seize power, and to establish a reign of terror. The fact that Paris and other French towns contained a large number of them had therefore considerable influence on the course of events. In German towns there was a proletariate, too. But its number was much smaller than in certain French towns, and, moreover, the antagonism between the classes was less fierce. Vast riches, excessive luxury and the abuse of wealth were certainly much more frequent in Paris than in any German town, and the cases of abject poverty as well.

The most important fact was the unique position of Paris. The party which dominated Paris was likely to have power over the whole country. In the Empire there was no town comparable to Paris in this respect. Moreover, it also must be considered that the outbreak of the Revolution, and its course were partly due to the inadequacy of many leading persons, especially of the king. If France had had a king possessing the ruthless energy and shrewdness of Frederick II, the people probably had hailed him, as they later acclaimed Napoleon.

At various times considerable proportions of the French population either hailed the Revolution, or were more or less for a Republic. With the great changes in the character of the Revolution, however, the opinions of great sections changed too. Whether the majority of the people was ever revolutionary-minded is very doubtful. In the first years the franchise and the indirect way of voting were by no means democratic, the poorer people were excluded from voting and from becoming deputies. But even of the 'active' citizens, possessing the franchise, nine-tenths soon did not go to the polls.[6] In 1793 a democratic constitution was submitted to a

[6] Cf. Lefebvre p. 150.

plebiscite in which every male adult could vote. In spite of the terrorism of the ruling Jacobins three-quarters of the electors abstained from voting. Two years later anti-democratic elements had seized power, and submitted a very reactionary constitution to a plebiscite. It was accepted with a majority of 95.5% of the votes cast. But when Napoleon's star was rising great masses, who had never voted before, began to flock to the polls. At the plebiscite rendering him hereditary Emperor he received double the votes which in 1793 had been cast for the democratic republic. This seems to indicate that national prestige was much more cherished than liberty, which did not exist under Napoleon.

The origin of the war, from which most of the evils of the revolution sprang, appears to confirm this diagnosis. The legend that the war was the work of the monarchs, and that the French revolutionaries fought for the liberation of the peoples oppressed by them, has been discarded by responsible French historians more than a century ago. The deviation of the revolution from its original, excellent intentions was mainly due to the fact that, as Lefebvre, the greatest scholar in this field, said, the representatives of the people were not able to compel the French people to pay taxes and to obey the law. The government was therefore forced to flood the country with paper money, and inflation, with all its social consequences followed. Large masses were deeply disappointed, and the king's attempt to escape disastrously aggravated the tension. The Girondists, a bourgeois group, resorted to the old trick of stopping internal strife by the triumphs of a successful war. They worked up national pride and the lust for the glory to liberate all the peoples oppressed by their tyrants, the kings and aristocrats. Their real aim was to maintain and increase the power of their party. To this end they preached a warlike nationalism in the name of world freedom. A group of royalists, too, set hopes on a war, and unreasonable steps of the monarchical powers added fuel to the flames. The radicals were then absolutely against a war because they rightly foresaw that it would lead to a military dictatorship. But the Girondists were principally responsible for the outbreak of war. Their leader Brissot exclaimed: 'The war will be beneficial to the nation. The only disaster would be if there was no war.' When the French parliament declared war, the deputies were so intoxicated by this ideology that only seven of them voted against it.

The war initiated a period of unlimited violence. The reign of law increasingly gave way to terrorism and bloody anarchy. Different factions raged against each other with fanaticism, risings of large sections of the people in the provinces were suppressed with a cruelty comparable to the worst deeds of modern totalitarianism,[7] and when the leading demagogues had been massacred by their enemies, an anti-radical reaction set in. The red terror was followed by a white terror, the Directory began its reign, and movements directed against the ruling clique were put down by General Bonaparte.

Napoleon once expressed the opinion that the chief reason why the French king had been overthrown was the battle of Rossbach. This implied the view that the striving for liberty was a lesser motive in bringing about the revolution than the feeling that French prestige had suffered and must be restored. France's prestige had indeed decreased through various military and diplomatic misfortunes as Ranke has shown in a famous essay. In the age of Louis XIV France had been the strongest power of Europe, and could look forward to the development of an enormous French colonial empire too. Since that time England, Prussia, Russia and Austria had achieved a great expansion of their territories, largely at the expense of France's prestige. The battle of Rossbach was the symbol of the decline of her position,[8] and the continuation of the alliance with Austria, which had led to this defeat, discredited Louis XVI and his Austrian wife. The wish for new glory, the hatred of Austria, and the hope for an alliance with Prussia, the 'natural ally' of France, went far in arousing the feelings which brought about the

[7] At the beginning of the war a Prussian soldier was killed by civilians from Verdun. To prevent severe punishment according to the custom of war, the people of Verdun sent 15 women to King Frederjck William of Prussia who offered him flowers, and begged for pardon, which was granted. When the Prussians had retired, the Jacobins had 13 of the women guillotined, the two youngest, who were only 15 years old, were sentenced to 20 years imprisonment, and had to stay six hours at the guillotine. At another occasion the Convent resolved that English, Hanoverian and Spanish soldiers should not be made prisoners but should be killed.

[8] Nicolai quotes a pamphlet which appeared in Paris in 1792, in which the battle of Rossbach is represented as a French victory. Frederick's army, it says, contained numerous French deserters, who decided the result of the battle, since French soldiers can be vanquished by other French soldiers only. These statements are, of course, completely untrue. Cf. Nicolai, *Anekdoten* etc., vol. VI, p. 203.

The rise of French nationalism also induced leading Jacobins to propagate the extermination of the non-French languages spoken in France, namely Breton, Basque, German and Italian. Cf. the speeches by Barrère and Gregoire delivered in the Convent on January 27 and June 4, 1794. These languages were denounced as 'barbarous jargons and rude dialects' which only served the purposes of counter-revolutionaries. The Alsatians were accused of sympathizing with the Germans and of being traitors. St. Just, Monnet and other Jacobins demanded the most ruthless measures against them, even mass deportation of all Alsatians who did not speak French and the settlement of French revolutionaries in their stead, who also were to receive their possessions.

revolution.[9] In the mind of many revolutionaries it may have been an unconscious motive. All nationalists pretend to fight for liberty, but actually are striving for prestige and power.

One of the reasons why there was no revolution in Germany obviously was the fact that there was no German nation or nationalism. Any policy aiming at the creation of a powerful German nation would have been faced with the overwhelming resistance of other Germans. If one of the German peoples had started a revolution for liberty, the other Germans would probably have remained indifferent, or would even have become hostile, if their particularism was menaced. The neighbouring princes would naturally have come to the rescue of the prince afflicted by a popular rising, but the peoples would not have been able to overcome their traditional jealousies in order to support other Germans in the fight for national sovereignty. The main reason why Germany had no revolution was therefore lack of national unity and sentiment, and the strength of particularism. The intellectuals expressing enthusiasm for liberty and unity, but detesting any strengthening of the central power were involved in a vicious circle. National unity has always been achieved by a strong central power. Some Germans, however, realized that particularism was the deadly foe of German liberty. A pamphlet of 1791 said: 'We have as many nations, as many divergent national interests, and as many grievances, as we have princes. There is no common centre, no mutual solidarity and there will always be Germans willing to march to subjugate other Germans.' Johann Gottfried Seume, a staunch democrat, wrote in verse that hatred and strife reigned between the German peoples, unity alone could save them from ruin, and yet they were trying to escape unity like a plague.

[9] Cf. S. Skalweit, *Frankreich und Friedrich der Grosse* etc., 1952.

21

THE END OF THE EMPIRE

EMPEROR LEOPOLD II AND HIS LIBERALISM

JOSEPH II was succeeded by his brother Leopold. Before he became Emperor, he was Grand Duke of Tuscany where he was a model of a liberal ruler and introduced many beneficial reforms. Yet he, too, experienced ingratitude. The people, at the instigation of the priests, were opposed to progressive innovations and the nobles kept aloof. In contrast to Joseph he was in favour of respecting the rights of the Estates and disapproved of his brother's measures against them in Hungary and Belgium, though he did not attempt to influence him. When in 1789 the States General were assembled in France, he welcomed this event. He wrote to his sister Maria Christine that a constitutional régime was much to be desired: the only aim for which a government existed was the happiness of the people, and no government, however enlightened, could know better what suited the nation than the people itself and its representatives. He continued 'France will become the most powerful state in Europe. The French will at last have a fatherland and it will be generally loved and enjoy great loyalty. France's regeneration will become the model which all sovereigns and governments of Europe will be compelled by their peoples to imitate, voluntarily or involuntarily, and this will everywhere lead to unlimited happiness, to the end of injustice, wars, conflicts and revolts.' The first outbreaks of violence in Paris aroused his fear that anarchy and despotism might arise. Yet, on January 25, 1790, in a letter to his sister, he laid down his principles in a detailed way. 'I believe, he wrote, that a ruler, even a hereditary one, is only a delegate or official of the people, for which office he is destined, and that he has to devote to them his care, efforts and vigilance. . . . In every country there should be a fundamental law as a contract between people and ruler, limiting the latter's authority and rights. If the ruler does not observe this pact he in fact renounces the principles on which his position is based, which has only been given him under the above conditions, and nobody is then any longer obliged to obey him. The executive power belongs to the ruler, but the legislative power belongs to the people and its delegates. At every change in rulership the people can establish new conditions. The ruler must neither directly nor indirectly interfere in civil or criminal justice. . . . He must give account of the use made of the public revenues and the state of finances and is not entitled arbitrarily to raise taxes, dues or fines. Only the people have this right when the ruler has explained to them the requirements of the State, and when their delegates have recognized these as just and reasonable. The ruler has also to report all changes in the system and the law, in pensions and emoluments, and obtain their approval before publication. His decrees become valid only by the consent of the Estates. The military shall only be used to defend the country but never against the people. Nobody shall be arrested or judged without the order of a law court and then only in the usual forms and publicly, never on the basis of an arbitrary order, not even one decreed by the ruler. Lastly I believe that the ruler must rule according to the law only; his authority comes from the people, which cannot tacitly give up the imprescriptible, natural law, nor be deprived of it. The people appoint a ruler, i.e. gives him prerogatives in order that he should create their happiness and welfare, not according to his will, but according to the will and feelings of the people, for the only purpose of states and governments is the happiness of the individual.' These principles, often called Leopold's Creed, formed a carefully elaborated system of liberal parliamentarism. He also tried to introduce a representation of the people in Tuscany, but the plan, elaborated by his counsellor Giani, did not become law.[1]

When Leopold arrived in Vienna to succeed his brother he found the Austrian Empire in a most serious condition. The war with Turkey had not yet been ended, and had gravely deteriorated the financial situation. Belgium had declared herself independent, and in Hungary a great revolt was brewing. The events in France stimulated a revolutionary spirit, which spread over wide areas. Prussia was trying to ally herself with other enemies of Austria,

[1] Leopold published also a statement of his activities as a ruler of Tuscany which he considered the account owed by the ruler to the people. He further wrote propositions for the reform of criminal law. The death penalty and the crime of lese-majesty were to be abolished and people having become victims of an error of justice were to be indemnified.

and preparing for a new war. The feudal and other classes, whose interests had been hit by Joseph's reforms were in a bitter mood against the government. With great skill, patience and moderation Leopold and his ministers managed to appease this dangerous situation, as will later be shown. Belgium was brought back under Austrian rule and Leopold became Emperor. In internal politics some of Joseph's reforms which were particularly unpopular were revoked. Some of the improvements in the conditions of the peasants also had to be abandoned because the landlords offered strong resistance which, under the existing circumstances, could not be broken.

The nobles tried to use this favourable opportunity not only to restore their former privileges, but even to increase them. In particular, they insisted upon the re-establishment of their powers in the Estates and the administration, and Leopold was compelled to recognize their rights in principle. But the urban middle classes, too, and the peasants, raised claims for seats in the Estates, and showed great energy in striving for this aim, especially in Styria and Carinthia. In Bohemia the peasants also demanded to be admitted to the Estates. The nobles opposed these claims, but several Austrian ministers, and Sonnenfels too, supported them. In Bohemia the nobles went far in their demands for political power, but could only recover the status they had had in 1764. They further claimed that Joseph's measures of Germanization should be revoked and the Czech language be more widely used in the schools and the administration. In this respect they received valuable concessions.

In Hungary the aristocracy contained a strong faction which planned a revolution with Prussia's support. But Leopold succeeded in preventing this and he guaranteed the nobles their rights. They also were compelled to moderate their intransigence, because the national minorities in Hungary, in particular the Serbs, demanded national rights, too. Leopold satisfied their claims, and was crowned king.

KING FREDERICK WILLIAM II OF PRUSSIA

In Prussia Frederick II was succeeded by his nephew Frederick William II who was, in every respect, his opposite. He was a friendly man without his uncle's intellect and energy, more devoted to women than to strenuous work, who largely left the government to favourites. The former king's harsh fiscalism, especially the monopolies of coffee and tobacco, and their French management, were universally hated, and the new government tried to make itself popular by abolishing the most odious fiscal institutions. Frederick's autocracy had also aroused much resentment, particularly among the officials, and the new government therefore introduced various reforms tending to convert the administration from an autocratic into a bureaucratic régime. Judges and officials were no longer to be deposed by the king's will, but only by the judgment of a court or by the majority vote of the state council respectively. The legal code worked out by Svarez and Klein was made law. Frederick's contemptuous attitude to German cultural achievements was not continued. The Academy was transformed from a French into a German institution, German scholars, authors and artists were encouraged and the German theatre was cultivated.

The king was a member of the secret Order of the Rosicrucians who was opposed to the Enlightenment and practised mysticism and occultism. He was much under the influence of two Rosicrucians, Johann Rudolf von Bischoffwerder, an impressive personality, and Johann Christoph Woellner. The latter had for several years lectured to Frederick William on political science and the art of government. Woellner was a sharp critic of Frederick's system, had adopted the theories of the physiocrats, and pleaded for economic freedom. The serfdom of the peasants was to be abolished, the royal domains and the estates of the nobles and the Church to be partitioned into peasant farms, the aristocracy should be subjected to taxation, and a progressive tax on property and luxury taxes should be introduced. Woellner further regarded Frederick's attitude to religion and the decline of Christian orthodoxy as the cause of demoralization and grave evils. The Rosicrucians exercised the greatest influence on the King's mind. They also tried to restrain his sexual licence and actually induced him to give up intimate relations with his mistress, the daughter of a musician, who later became Countess Lichtenau. The King, however, though married later twice took second morganatic wives. The Church authorities gave their consent referring to Melanchthon's acceptance of the double marriage of Landgrave Philip of Hesse.

Bischoffwerder and Woellner became the real rulers of Prussia, and the latter was generally called the Viceroy. Their projects of social reform were faced with the resistance of the landed nobility and had to be shelved. But trade and industry profited from the relaxation of Frederick's rigorous mercantilism, and intellectual and artistic life flowered. Woellner further began to combat free-thinking in the Protestant Churches, though within certain limits. The Edict on Religion (1788) expressly laid down the principle of toleration, which under Frederick had only been an unwritten maxim. But the Lutheran clergy was obliged to abstain from preaching or practising deviations from the creed as formulated by Luther. This clause evoked protests from free thinking theologians and had little effect. Woellner, though greatly worried by this, did not want to enforce it. Yet Frederick William II demanded strict measures against clergymen critical of orthodoxy. The censorship became very rigorous and even Kant had to undertake not to write anything more on religion. The Jews were treated in a liberal spirit and made progress towards social recognition.

PEACE WITH AUSTRIA, WAR WITH FRANCE

The influence of various parties at court, as also the King's own vacillations, rendered foreign policy unstable. At first Count Hertzberg possessed the decisive influence. He embodied Frederick's traditions and therefore was convinced that Austria would always remain the arch-enemy and must be hindered from increasing her power. A great war with Austria seemed imminent, but Leopold II averted it by approaching the King in a way which made him change his mind. The treaties of Reichenbach and Sistova maintained peace between the two German powers, Austria concluded peace with Turkey, and Hertzberg was replaced by Bischoffwerder. While Hertzberg had wanted to win even revolutionary France as an ally against Austria, his successor and the king wished to march with Austria against France. The French aristocrats who had fled to Germany made the greatest efforts to induce the German rulers to wage war on the revolutionary régime. Their actions went far to deteriorate relations by provoking French apprehensions and resentment and by misleading the German powers concerning French conditions and opinions. In particular they seem to have been responsible for the fact that diplomatic notes from the German powers were sometimes couched in terms liable to increase the tension. Yet there is no doubt that the overwhelming rsponsibility for the war fell on the Girondists, the French war party. Emperor Leopold did what he could to avoid it while the king of Prussia was eager to wage war. Moreover, Catherine of Russia wanted to have the two powers involved in war with France in order to have her hands free for a new spoliation of Poland. But the king did not wish to let Russia to be free to obtain all the lands coveted by her. He, too, wanted his share and he wavered whether to send his troops mainly to the west or to the east. This was soon to have dire consequences.

Emperor Leopold died suddenly in 1792. He had reigned for two years only and reached an age of forty-five years. His successor was his son Francis II, whose political views were to develop in a direction very different from that of his father. Two months after Leopold's death, on April 20, 1792, the French government declared war on the King of Bohemia and Hungary, though not on the German Empire. The war was stated to be a crusade for liberty, and the slogan was raised: Peace for the cottages, war on the palaces! France pledged herself to renounce any conquests and to leave the peoples full freedom to decide their own fate. But all these good intentions were soon thrown to the winds. Within France the war led to a dreadful reign of terror, and in the invaded countries the promised liberation soon turned into open or veiled subjugation and ruthless financial spoliation. In reaction to the French propaganda, instigating peoples to revolt, the menaced governments resorted to restrictions of freedom; plans for reforms were dropped and the cause of political and social progress everywhere suffered a severe setback.[2]

Shortly after France had begun the war the Austrian Chancellor Prince Kaunitz resigned, in order as he said, to save his reputation. He deeply distrusted Prussia as an ally, and the events showed that he was right. His successor, Count Cobenzl, was soon replaced by Baron Thugut, a man of low birth but great gifts, though his diplomacy was open to criticism. It was a great misfortune that the potential strength of revolutionary France was long considerably underestimated. The French aristocrats who had fled abroad spread the illusion that her army was completely disorganized, that her people would welcome the invaders, and that her government could be intimidated by a threatening language. They also proposed that France's currency should be ruined by printing false paper money. Emperor Francis ordered that this 'infamous project' should be rejected off-hand. But Napoleon and Pitt later employed this stratagem on a great scale. The first war lasted five years and swayed to and fro. The rise of a reign of violence in Paris, the threat to England inherent in the conquest of Belgium and Holland, and the execution of Louis XVI induced Pitt to break off relations with France, and the latter answered by a declaration of war (February 1, 1793). Britain formed a coalition with Austria, Prussia,

[2] When Leopold still reigned his former tutor Andreas Riedel submitted to him the plan of a democratic constitution but the Emperor found it impossible to realize Riedel thereupon planned a revolution in Germany which, however, was discovered and frustrated. Under the reign of Francis II various real or alleged conspiracies were disclosed in which men of rank took part. Some were sentenced to death or life imprisonment, others were dismissed.

the Empire and other states. But she herself waged war mainly at sea and occupied the French and Dutch colonies. The British navy also sought to destroy French trade, and its proceedings aroused strong protests from the neutrals, some of whom formed an alliance to ensure the freedom of the sea.

The main burden of the war on land fell on Austria, who in the following twenty-three years had to conduct six great wars against France. In the war of the First Coalition she had, at first, the support of Prussia. The other German states gave her little aid, if any. Geography was again against Austria; she had to defend Belgium, a country remote from her and difficult to reach. She had tried to exchange it for Bavaria many times, but Prussia and France had hindered this in order to keep her vulnerable. England too laid the greatest stress upon Austrian rule over Belgium, in order to prevent her from falling under French domination, which would have threatened England's security. Austria had further to provide for possible complications in Italy, Poland and the Danubian countries. Previous wars had exhausted her resources and she was soon in dire financial distress.

The French army had by no means lost its efficiency as the noble refugees declared. It had still a good organization, equipment and tradition, and many of its noble officers had remained on their posts. Now also non-nobles could become officers, and some of them distinguished themselves. Moreover, the army soon obtained a national character while the troops of the allies were largely mercenaries.

In the first year of the war the French armies conquered Belgium and the German territories left of the Rhine, as well, but by the middle of 1793 they had lost these conquests again. After this time, however, the fortune of war turned, and the French armies could soon reconquer the countries mentioned and occupy large other territories in addition. This primarily was the work of Lazare Carnot, an engineer officer, who had been trained under the old régime, and was a genius of organization. He created many armies and developed new tactics emphasizing mass offensive. Besides he selected able generals, worked out the plans of operation and himself directed battles. Enormous war industries were established, and everyone had to serve the war effort. Numerous volunteers flocked to the colours, inspired by a morale which made possible dispersed fighting. The Convention decreed a mass levy, which furnished more than a million soldiers, and the Directory enacted conscription. Carnot also had the principal share in overthrowing the Jacobin régime, which was discredited by its policy of terrorism and mass murder, and in establishing the system of the Directorate which was based on the ideology and the forces of the bourgeois class. Lastly, this development was crowned by the rise of Napoleon Bonaparte.

The monarchical states could not keep pace with this increase of France's military power, especially as Prussia was more interested in making conquests in Poland, than in defending Belgium and the Rhinelands. Austria wanted to follow the example of the enemy, and call up masses of the German people, but Prussia protested. Within Austria later large numbers of volunteers joined the forces. If the Allies had erred in believing that the French people would receive them with open arms, the French, too, were quite wrong in their confidence that everywhere the peoples would enthusiastically take their side and rise against their rulers. In Germany, in particular, there were a few minor riots, but nowhere did the masses show the wish for a revolution on the French model, nor for being 'liberated' as the invaders understood it. Most of all the peoples wanted peace and they distrusted the intentions of the foreigners. In some places, especially in the Rhinelands, the French armies were welcomed by groups of intellectuals and young people inspired by enthusiasm for the new ideals. But even many of these friends of the revolution were soon bitterly disappointed. The French political leaders were for some time divided in their views whether to annex the countries left of the Rhine, or to make them satellite states, but at last the aim prevailed to extend France to her 'natural frontier' of the Rhine. The dictators in Paris laid down that a people which did not wish to be liberated in their fashion thereby showed that it was an enemy of freedom and a partisan of the old régime and should be treated accordingly. The military commanders were ordered to demand heavy contributions and the revolutionary rulers began ruthlessly extorting vast amounts from the 'liberated' peoples, a system which Bonaparte later brought to perfection. Besides the large sums exacted as war contributions the peoples were subjected to requisitions and were paid for supplies in French paper money of little value.[3] The new administrators, moreover, were arbitrary and often trying to enrich themselves. The peoples

---

[3] The French armies also invaded German states which were not in a state of war with France. Large sections of the troops had no uniform but only tattered clothes and very bad shoes. Many of them had been unemployed workers and had volunteered for military service. In Coblenz the French Commander asked the inhabitants to appear on a large square. They were then invited to take off their shoes, and to give them to the military. The Commander told the people that each of them had certainly a second pair at home and could therefore give one pair to the troops. They could then go home without shoes.

in the countries occupied by the French armies also resented the attitude of the French revolutionaries towards the Church.

In Poland, a year before the outbreak of the war, a constitutional reform had been voted by the Estates which aimed at placing the state on a stable basis. Kaunitz who then was still the chief of Austrian diplomacy, and Emperor Leopold, were greatly in favour of it and supported the Polish reform party. But soon after France had begun the war against Austria and Prussia, a big Russian army invaded Poland and conquered the larger part of it. Prussia shifted large forces to the east, and eventually made an agreement with Russia about annexing parts of Poland: the Second Partition. Austria was unable to prevent this since she depended on Prussia's military and diplomatic assistance. Baron Thugut, who followed Cobenzl as Foreign Minister, went even farther. He laid great stress upon obtaining territorial compensation for Belgium which had been conquered by France. This led to the Third Partition of Poland between Russia, Prussia and Austria.

All these transactions were not only utterly contrary to international law and morality, but also had a disastrous influence on the war in the west. The French politicians who had begun the war, had always reckoned with Prussia's hatred of Austria and hoped to win her as an ally. Prussian and French officers had secret talks and expressed their hatred of Austria. The Austrians even feared that their ally Prussia might attack them in the rear. It is significant that the Prussian Field-Marshal von Moellendorff informed the French of an important strategic move planned by the Austrians which he had promised to support, assuring the French that the Prussians would do nothing. It was the Prussian army which began to negotiate a separate peace behind the back of their king.

On April 5, 1795, this peace was concluded at Basle, and supplementary pacts followed. North Germany was neutralized, and the left bank of the Rhine, which, including Belgium, was inhabited by 3.3 million people was abandoned to France. Prussia was to be compensated for her possessions left of the Rhine by territories right of the river.

The Peace of Basle was passionately discussed in numerous pamphlets and articles. In Prussia and other German states public opinion seemed to be in full agreement with it, and both in Berlin and in Paris influential circles were for an alliance between Prussia and France. Prussian historians have later made efforts to put the responsibility for the abandonment of the Rhinelands on Austria. But the publication of the documents and their critical study did not confirm their views. The shortcomings of Austrian diplomacy were very minor in comparison with Prussia's policy.

On the Austrian side the most brilliant publicist was Karl Friedrich Glave, a Pomeranian. He had been a Prussian judge and was a victim of Frederick's cabinet justice. The King was convinced that Glave had abused his authority as a judge and condemned him to two years' imprisonment with hard labour. Glave was chained to a barrow full of gravel and had to drag it around for more than four months. After Frederick's death the High Court revised the sentence acquitting Glave of any grave charge, and the government came also to the conclusion that he had not committed a defamatory offence. He then played a rôle in Poland and was ennobled. Henceforth he was known as Glave-Kolbielski. In the two years 1795 and 1796 alone he wrote twenty-two pamphlets under various names. He called on the Germans to become 'nationalists' and to rally round the Emperor, who alone could make them a nation. He pictured the grave political and economic disadvantages and dangers of Germany's excessive particularism and pleaded in fiery words for national unity. For this purpose, he said, it was absolutely necessary that Germany should have a House of Commons; the power of the princes must be curbed and the Emperor's authority restored. The greatest enemy was Russian despotism, and the partition of Poland was a crime that must be made good. The author further demanded that Europe should be transformed into a League of Nations in order to guarantee a lasting peace. No European State should be allowed to use force against another, and offenders should be outlawed by the League. Besides Glave other writers too defended the cause of Austria and pleaded for strengthening the imperial power and national unity. But the writers following the tradition of Frederick the Great and Particularism were more numerous and vocal.

THE RISE OF BONAPARTE

In 1796 the Austrian army under Archduke Charles won great victories and pushed the French back over the Rhine. Had the Austrians not kept a large army on the Silesian frontier watching Prussia they would have been able to deal a decisive blow to the French. A wave of patriotism rose in South Germany, and the Imperial government now took energetic steps against German princes who saw in France their protector against the Emperor. Prussia protested against these measures. All hopes were, however, shattered by the great victories of General Bonaparte in Italy. This country had for many centuries already been a main object of the rivalry between the French dynasty and the House of Habsburg. Napoleon saw in it primarily the stepping stone to the realization of his personal ambitions, the defeat of England and the acquisition of an Oriental Empire. The leaders of the French Republic had various aims in mind when they consented to the expedition. On the one hand, it would weaken the Austrian front on the Rhine, and threaten Vienna which was much nearer to Italy than to the Rhine. On the other, France herself had through the Revolution been plunged into dreadful misery. Bonaparte received from Paris the characteristic order: 'Carry away from Italy everything movable which could be useful to us in any way'. He acted accordingly. On March 27, 1796, he issued a proclamation to his troops:[4] 'Soldiers! You have no clothes and are starving. The government owes you much and cannot give you anything. Your patience and courage among these rocks are admirable but they do not provide you with glory and splendour. I shall lead you to the most fertile plains of the world. Rich provinces, great cities will fall under your power. You will find there honour, glory and riches. Soldiers, should you be missing courage and perseverance'.

This appeal and Bonaparte's military genius worked wonders. The army naturally saw in the proclamation a licence to acquire wealth by force and the country was grievously plundered.[5] Many generals, commissariat officers, contractors etc. made vast profits. Bonaparte imposed heavy contributions upon the Italian states and sometimes confiscated the silver in the churches and the jewels deposited in banks. Many Italian states had no quarrel with France and wished to remain neutral, but some pretext was easily found to make them pay large amounts. The simplest way was to 'liberate' them from their 'tyrants'. This was certainly worth the price of some millions. Moreover, Bonaparte everywhere forced the Italians to hand over to him the greatest art treasures, the most precious antiques, manuscripts etc. On February 19th he reported to the Directory that this action had had good results in many places and, when also the art treasures from Rome should have arrived the army would have

[4] The following is the official text published in Napoleon's correspondence. Actually he spoke to his soldiers in the same sense but in slightly different words. Thousands of soldiers had really no boots, rifles, etc. and received their wages in worthless paper money, if at all.

[5] The French historian Paul Gaffarel, *Bonaparte et les republiques Italiennes*, 1895 p. 12 says: 'A real fever of theft and pillage possessed the army. The generals themselves gave the example'. It may be mentioned that in the beginning of 1798 a French army seized Rome, and the Treasurer of the army called on Pope Pius VI and told him to deliver his valuables. He stripped two precious rings from his fingers himself and did not forget to put the Pope's tobacco into his own pocket.

together everything beautiful existing in Italy except a small number of objects in Turin and Naples. By these methods the general could not only raise the means to pay the whole cost of his large army, but also to send 30 millions in good money to the French treasury, and priceless works of art to the Paris Gallery, not to speak of the vast amounts which flowed into the pockets of generals, politicians, etc. All this, however, could not save France from bankruptcy. In 1797 the French paper money amounting to about 60 milliards was completely annulled and the state loans reduced to 1/3. The remaining third lost at once 80% of their value.

Bonaparte's military successes were brilliant. He defeated all his enemies and gained control of Italy. Various Italian republics were established and Bonaparte visualized the development of Italy to a unitary nation though he was aware that it would take time. In his correspondence with the French government he points out that at present the great majority of the Italians was against him, and that the republicans amongst them would be killed by the people if the French army were no longer to protect them. His triumphs were partly due to the fact that the Austrian strategy was still the traditional one of cautious manoeuvres while the French applied the method of reckless attack. France could afford great losses owing to the general conscription. The Austrian soldiers were still partly mercenaries. The Austrian generals were old men, Wurmser was 72 years old, Beaulieu and Alvinczy both 71. Bonaparte was 27. Yet in his correspondence Bonaparte speaks with great admiration of Wurmser, and his troops. He also warned his government repeatedly not to underestimate Austria. He reported that her government was mild and popular and that masses of volunteers were joining the Austrian army.

The French army penetrated deep into Austria, and an armistice was concluded. Bonaparte's triumphs naturally strengthened the section in the French government which demanded the cession of large territories by Austria. After long negotiations peace was made at Campo Formio (1797). Austria lost Belgium and Lombardy, and received Venice, Istria and Dalmatia. Peace with the German Empire was to be concluded later at Rastatt and the Emperor had to consent to the French annexation of large parts of the left bank of the Rhine. The attitude of the German princes made a further defence of the integrity of the Empire impossible. Thugut, however, regarded the peace merely as an armistice and a few days after its conclusion approached Britain with proposals for a new alliance.

At the Congress of Rastatt French diplomacy had an excellent opportunity of winning many German princes to its side by permitting them to annex numerous ecclesiastical states, which hitherto had been the main part of the Estates supporting the Emperor in the Reichstag. The countries left of the Rhine were ceded to France. Bonaparte made his expedition to Egypt.

In 1798 England, Russia, Austria and other states formed a new coalition against France. At first it had great successes, but later its luck turned, the Allies quarrelled and Russia withdrew from the alliance. Bonaparte returned from Egypt, seized power under the title of First Consul and defeated Austria in Italy, while General Moreau won decisive victories in Germany. The peace of Luneville (1801) confirmed the agreements of Campo Formio and Rastatt with certain modifications. The Rhine definitely became the frontier between Germany and France. Prussia and, with few exceptions, the other German states had remained neutral and had thereby helped France to win the war. This attitude was now richly rewarded by Bonaparte. Under his influence, the Reichstag, represented by a small committee called a deputation, handed over to the pro-French princes almost all the ecclesiastical principalities, forty-one Free Towns and other territories. Most of the major princes owed their aggrandisement to Bonaparte and thereby became his vassals. A year later he elevated himself to the dignity of hereditary Emperor, and had this confirmed by a plebiscite.

The position of Emperor of the Holy Roman Empire had before this already lost every significance. Francis II therefore proclaimed his Austrian dominions an Empire and assumed the title of Emperor of Austria (1804). In this capacity he is known as Francis I. Soon a new coalition was formed against France by Britain, Russia, Austria and Sweden, while Prussia and the other German states again remained neutral. This war ended with the French victory of Austerlitz and the peace of Pressburg (1805). Austria had to cede large territories in the South and West. At the court of the Emperor Francis there was a strong party favourable to great military and political reforms; it included three brothers of the Emperor, the very popular and gifted Archdukes Charles, Johann and Joseph. But they were faced with the resistance of a group which, terrified by the French Revolution, stubbornly clung to the past and which the Emperor found congenial. Nevertheless Count Stadion now became the leading statesman, a man of enlightened views and great energy. In his reform programme of 1806 also he proposed to give the middle classes political rights. Archduke Johann, in 1810, suggested that both the urban middle class and the peasants should be represented on the diets. He and other high-placed persons had great sympathy for Britain and her institutions.

Prussia had, in the last ten years, followed a policy of strict neutrality. King Frederick William III (1797-1840) regarded peace as his highest aim and set internal reforms in the interest of the lower classes above glory and power, and Germany's national security. The needs of the army were neglected and its equipment and spirit deteriorated. The king, a good-hearted and righteous man of mediocre gifts, hoped that this attitude would secure permanent friendship with France, but he only aroused Napoleon's contempt. During the war with Austria the Emperor sent a French army through Prussian territory in order to attack the Austrians in the rear. This provocation aroused even the peaceable Frederick William. Prussia planned an armed mediation between the belligerents, but she came too late and Napoleon manoeuvred her into a position which made her almost completely dependent on him. Hanover was promised her as reward and she had to close her ports to Britain. This induced Britain to wage war against Prussian ships and trade, which suffered terribly.

Napoleon's vassals in South Germany and on the Rhine received further great favours. They were permitted to annex the lands of numerous small neighbours and were compelled to secede from the German Empire and to join a Confederation of the Rhine under Napoleon's protectorate. Emperor Francis of Austria, therefore, laid down the German imperial crown. This was the end of the Empire which had begun with Charlemagne's coronation a thousand years before. In the history of the German public mind, however, the formal dissolution of the Empire was not an event of great importance. With few exceptions it was accepted in a spirit of resignation or indifference. Napoleon's star was still ascending.

PRUSSIA'S FALL

Now Prussia's turn came. Her neutrality had paved the way for Napoleon's triumphs. But gradually the sentiment spread that the French Emperor could not be trusted and that his policy was a deadly menace to Prussia. A warlike Prussian patriotism began to awake and the subjection of Germany to a foreign conqueror aroused in certain circles a German nationalism. Public opinion demanded energetic measures, and diplomacy acted accordingly, though in an ill-considered way. Prussia mobilized and in an ultimatum requested Napoleon to withdraw his troops from her frontier and to consent to the foundation of a North German Federation, a plan which he himself had suggested a little while previously, but which he now seemed to discountenance. War broke

out and Prussia's defeat at Jena and Auerstaedt shattered her military power (1806). The French army quickly overran the country
and the king and the government fled to the East. The war continued
since Frederick William set hopes in his ally Russia, whose army
was approaching. Napoleon, however, hoped to defeat Russia and
then to use the forces of the whole continent to conquer
Britain. From Berlin he issued a decree ordering a blockade against
British products, which was to operate throughout the countries of
Europe. In this way, he hoped, Britain's export trade would be
destroyed and the country ruined. It would thereby be made ripe
for internal convulsions and an invasion. Britain was the traditional
enemy of France, and the Emperor's propaganda convinced wide
circles in all countries that she was also the greatest enemy of the
whole of Europe. She was described as a 'Vampire' who had always
exploited the world out of commercial greed and had for this
reason also instigated all wars among the European nations.
Enormous amounts were squeezed out of Prussia to maintain the
Emperor's armies and to prepare for further conquests. The first
great battle with the Russians remained undecided and Prussia and
Russia concluded a pact to continue the war and to make no
separate peace. But in the battle of Friedland the Russians were
beaten; Napoleon met Tsar Alexander I and won him over to his
plans. The agreement of Tilsit (1807) implied the division of world
domination between France and Russia. Alexander was to be free to
annex Finnland and to conquer large parts of the Turkish Empire,
which was in a state of anarchy. Napoleon would then be able to
muster all the forces of Europe to destroy Britain's power and to
seize her colonial empire. Prussia was now granted peace but was
reduced to half her former territory and remained indefinitely
under French occupation and exploitation, since she could hardly
raise the amounts which had to be paid before the occupation was
to come to an end. The western parts of Prussia were used to create
a kingdom of Westphalia under Napoleon's brother Jerome. Another
brother, Joseph, was already King of Naples and was later made
King of Spain, and Napoleon's Marshal Murat then received the
crown of Naples. A third brother, Louis, was made king of Holland,
but later this country was united with France. All these kings, however, remained subject to the Emperor. Portugal, too, was seized. In
Sweden the French Marshal Bernadotte was adopted by the Swedish
king and designated as his successor. Many French generals received
principalities, the title of duke, etc., or large domains in the conquered countries. Switzerland was also under French domination.

In 1810 the Confederation of the Rhine comprised thirty-nine

German princes, among them four kings. They had to place large contingents of troops at the disposal of the Emperor whenever he demanded this. Further large parts of Germany were directly united with France, among them the Rhinelands, Oldenburg, Bremen, Hamburg and Luebeck. In five years General Bonaparte had reached the position of Emperor, and in another four years almost the whole of Europe was at his feet. Apart from Austria the only independent powers were Britain and Russia, and the latter was now France's ally. The Emperor had achieved his miraculous rise not only by his genius as a strategist, diplomat and organizer, but also by the exploitation of the deep divisions among his adversaries and by his skill in posing as the champion of peace. Great sections of his own and many other nations were convinced that Napoleon wanted peace and that only the egotism and wickedness of England prevented its realization. He further adopted many of the beneficial reforms of enlightened absolutism and the revolution. This rendered him popular, not only in France but also in wide circles of Italy, Germany and other countries. The abolition of feudal privileges and obstacles to progress, the recognition of the principle of human equality in civil life, great reforms in law, administration and economic matters created an atmosphere of prosperity. The blockade against British manufacturers protected the continental industrialists against the superiority of their English competitors and led to the development of industries. But the blockade also caused great hardships and enormous corruption among the French customs officials. In the long run the grievous burdens of militarism and economic protectionism, the suppression of political liberty, of the freedom of the press and of public discussion and other features of the régime, aroused great discontent, which all the measures of the secret police, all the glory and all the unscrupulous propaganda could not prevent. Under Napoleon's rule, in spite of constant wars and high prices, France's budgetary expenses were comparatively low. The cause was that Napoleon made the conquered peoples pay for the cost of his wars, and exacted even more than it, in order to prevent discontent in France.

Napoleon further made much use of another power developed by the revolution, namely nationalism. He himself confessed that as a usurper he could only maintain his régime by constantly satisfying French national pride and that this hindered him from making concessions which might offend it. He also appealed to the national feelings of the Italians, Poles, etc., and promised them liberty, though at the same time he wrote of them in confidential letters with the greatest contempt saying that they were quite unfit for freedom. In the conquered countries Napoleon pursued a policy designed to denationalize and frenchify the peoples, though not by force, which would have aroused resistance. The strongest factor which owed its origin to the French Revolution and Napoleon was modern nationalism. Certain forms of nationalism had already existed before, but the development of a specific ideology and phraseology characteristic of modern nationalism was mainly their work.

When Napoleon was at the summit of power the nationalism of the conquered peoples began to stir and to revolt against his rule. The armed resistance of the Spanish people against foreign domination was inspired by a violent national sentiment strengthened by religious fanaticism. The Spaniards soon received great military support from Britain, and their long war became a festering sore in Napoleon's system which did much to prepare its ruin. The example of Spain revived the hope of liberation and courage to work for it in many other countries. In Prussia Stein and others undertook military and social reforms with the aim of strengthening the forces for the day of liberation. In Austria the reform party under the minister Stadion and the Archduke Charles worked in the same direction. In 1809 Stadion considered the time ripe, though Charles warned against precipitating a war. The Austrian government addressed appeals to the oppressed peoples of Europe to rise against the dictator and firmly hoped that Prussia would join its efforts. But Prussia was not yet ready, the Tsar dissuaded the King, and Austria had to fight alone. At Aspern Archduke Charles inflicted on Napoleon the first defeat of his life, but at Wagram the Emperor remained victorious. Austria was not beaten down and could have continued the war, but Emperor Francis would not take the risk and concluded peace, which cost heavy sacrifices in territories. The people of the Tyrol had followed the Spanish example, driven out the foreign conquerors and even fought on when the Emperor was compelled to abandon them. In North Germany, too, there were several armed risings undertaken in the hope of support from the peoples and governments.

GERMAN OPINIONS

When troops of revolutionary France first invaded the Rhinelands, they were enthusiastically welcomed by many intellectuals who had already under the reign of their princes formed republican opinions. Among them were many professors of the enlightened universities of Mainz and Bonn, lawyers, physicians and even

P

officers and wealthy bourgeois. In co-operation with the French generals, they founded societies for propagating the new principles among the people, and for establishing a republican régime under French protection. The French troops showed themselves friendly and helpful in order to win the Germans for their cause. Yet the great majority of the people were neither inclined to choose a union with France, nor to set up republics of their own. Some of the intellectuals made every effort to overcome this resistance, but in vain. They continued, however, to work either for a union with France, or for close relations with her, or became French citizens taking part in the politics of the republic. Georg Forster, a famous scholar went to Paris, but the conditions which he found there were so distressing, and opposed to his ideals, that he lost every hope, and soon died. Eulogius Schneider, a former Franciscan monk, professor and poet was not deterred by the reign of terror; he even became public prosecutor in Strasbourg, and caused numerous enemies of the Republic to be sentenced to death. But in spite of his zeal, he was guillotined himself, for unknown reasons. Quite a number of other Germans in France had the same, or a similar, fate as these two men. More fortunate was Andreas Rebmann, a judge and prolific writer, who because of his republican conviction settled in Paris. But he was distrusted by the terrorists, and was forbidden to live in Paris; later he made a honourable career as a judge under Napoleon's reign, and after his fall in his native land, the Palatinate.

The war with France was extremely unpopular in Germany, and this feeling was expressed in many ways. In Hanover an influential nobleman, Baron Berlepsch, moved a resolution in the Diet of Calenberg condemning the policy towards France of the ruler, who also was king of England. and demanding that his country should not take part in the war. When the government thereupon deprived him of his positions as a judge and administrator, he appealed to the Reichskammergericht, one of the two High Courts, which decided in his favour cancelling the decree of the government.

The opinions of the German democrats about revolutionary France and the war are expressed in the memoirs of Friedrich Laukhard, a deserter from the Prussian troops, who for some time lived in close touch with the French army. His description of the mentality and actions of the French is very favourable to them, and discreditable for the Prussian and imperial troops. Though his statements sometimes may be tendentious, they contribute to our knowledge of opinions on both sides, the French and the Germans.

With the development of the revolutionary régime to a dictatorship, which changed its character several times, German opinions also changed. Anti-revolutionary ideas spread, which have already been described, and which were strongest in Austria, who had most to suffer because of the war. In certain parts of Germany particularly affected by the war various opinions and sentiments made their appearance. In some places the peasants had great losses owing to French depredations and reacted violently. In others the French armies were welcomed by groups of intellectuals of republican opinions. But the great mass of Germans had not any active national feelings; they wanted peace at any price and had no means of effective resistance to French encroachments. Sympathy for the ideals of the revolution, appreciation of Napoleon's reforms and admiration for his genius contributed to this attitude. Lastly, many German princes expanded their territories, and obtained the rank of king or grand-duke, by Napoleon's favour, and many of their subjects felt pride and could expect advantages from these measures. They did not anticipate that they or their sons would in consequence be sent to Spain or Russia as cannon fodder for Napoleon's glory. The rise of the new Caesar particularly fascinated the intellectuals. Goethe admired his demonic personality as he had that of Frederick. Hegel saw in him the personification of the world-intellect, the man of destiny. Both believed that his Empire would last and bear beneficial fruits, that it would enforce universal peace and bring about the victory of reason over prejudice and promote the progress of civilization. Even so outspoken a republican and pacifist as Kant hoped that Bonaparte would obtain supreme power in Europe and use it to end war. He also sharply condemned England's war policy though he admired her parliamentary constitution. As mentioned before he was glad that the Germans were cosmopolitans and had no national pride.

When the First Consul assumed the title of Emperor there was almost no opposition in the three sections of the French Legislature. One of the very few opponents was Carnot, who had created the army and the conditions enabling Bonaparte to achieve his triumphs. In Germany Beethoven had just finished his grandiose Eroica Symphony, which he intended to dedicate to Bonaparte. The news of his step, however, induced him to tear up the front page on which his name was written exclaiming: 'So, he, too, is like the others. . . . Now he, too, will tread under foot all the rights of man and only indulge in his own ambitions. He will place himself over everybody and become a tyrant.'

Schiller and other great German authors had already felt so disillusioned and repelled by the raging of violence that they withdrew from politics altogether and dedicated themselves exclusively to the cultivation of the spirit by creating masterpieces of art and thought. Schiller had come to the conclusion that the character of the people must first be liberated from the power of base passions before true political liberty was possible. After the peace of Lunéville, when the Empire was already falling to pieces, he planned the writing of a poem 'Germany's Greatness', but later gave it up. Only fragments and sketches were found in his papers long after his death. Schiller consoled the Germans for their political downfall with the idea that the culture and character of a nation were much more important than power and wealth. The liberation of the spirit and the integration of the cultural achievements of all nations in one supra-national harmony was the task of the Germans.

The Romanticists, in particular the brothers A. W. and F. Schlegel, Hardenberg (Novalis) and other remarkable men of letters, also clung to cosmopolitanism for a long time. Yet the collapse of the old Empire, and the triumph of Napoleon's imperialism aroused in them national feelings and turned their thoughts back to the middle ages and Germany's glorious past. The poet Novalis, though a Protestant himself, saw in the Reformation the origin of the destructive rationalism of the age and of the unending strife among the Germans. Some of them admired the efforts of the House of Austria as defenders of the Empire, and set their hopes on its policy.

As Napoleon's rise was made possible because Prussia left Austria in the lurch, the Prussian ideology based on the tradition of Frederick the Great aroused much criticism. Georg Heinrich von Berenhorst was the son of Prince Leopold von Anhalt-Dessau, the famous organizer of the Prussian army under Frederick's father. In 1796-98 he published a book on the art of war in which he described Frederick, on whose staff he had served, as an ambitious and egotistic conqueror without any respect for human rights, and said that he certainly had great gifts, but that his extraordinary fame was mainly due to good luck and to the exaggerations of his admirers, who formed public opinion. Prussia was not a state possessing an army, but an army possessing a state. Berenhorst expressed the greatest possible hatred of war and was glad that in Prussia and the whole of Germany ever more people preferred civil professions to military ones. He wanted the abolition of all large armies and of conscription, and pleaded for small defensive armies which could be reinforced by a call-up of the people when an enemy invaded the country. The author also early realized Bonaparte's real character and warned against the prevailing Prussian policy towards him. He was one of the few Prussians who wanted true reconciliation with Austria and close co-operation between the two powers. His book caused a great sensation. One of Berenhorst's best friends was Dietrich von Buelow, a former Prussian officer and brilliant writer, who shared his views and served as a volunteer in the armies of the Belgian and American revolutions. It is remarkable that even Scharnhorst, who later created Prussia's new army, abhorred war and wrote to his wife: 'I am not born to be a soldier'. Baron vom Stein, too, was very critical of Frederick's system. Ernst Moritz Arndt in 1805 published the first part of his 'Spirit of the Time', in which he sharply attacked Frederick as a curse for Germany. His machine state appeared to Arndt as absolutely opposed to the German character. The Hanoverian statesman Rehberg, too, put forth a devastating criticism of Frederick's political system and, particularly, denounced his lust of conquest and his overcentralization. Austria, on the contrary, had earned the love of many German peoples. Hegel preferred Austria to Prussia mainly because she granted rights to the people.

Berlin was the centre of many political authors of talent whose mind had been inflamed by the revolution and who mostly combined a staunch cosmopolitanism with pride in Prussia's enlightenment, love of France and hatred of Britain and Austria. Many of them edited journals, wrote for them, and thereby exercised influence on public opinion. A great number of them saw in Napoleon their idol and they trusted that his world domination would bring about a new order in which England's commercial greed and warmongering could no longer disturb peace. Friedrich Buchholz was a particularly influential writer in this sense, and his book 'The New Leviathan' (1805) aroused sensation. The greatest opponent to this outlook was Friedrich Gentz, who in 1802 took residence in Vienna. He defended the Austrian and British policy of the Balance of Power against Napoleon's striving for a world empire.

The downfall of Prussia came as something quite unexpected, since the Prussian army had been considered invincible and the administration of the country superior to that of any other state. The catastrophe opened the gates to a spate of controversies about its causes. Certain writers believed the cause to lie in deviations from Frederick's maxims and in the decline of the military spirit. Others maintained that it was the very clinging rigidly to Frederick's system which had brought about Prussia's and Germany's fall.

Fichte, Arndt, Jahn and others began to preach a gospel of national rejuvenation. Stein, Hardenberg and Scharnhorst worked for liberation from the foreign yoke and for the foundation of a new Prussia and Germany. These aspirations got into their stride when Napoleon approached the zenith of his power. They operated mostly beyond the limit of time set to this study, and belonged to the beginning of a new epoch.

The epoch discussed in this book began with the Peace of Westphalia (1648) which put an end to the Thirty Years' War. The Empire was in a state of utter devastation, depopulation and cultural decline, which it required generations to make good. The peace tried to terminate the bitter struggles between the religions by establishing compromises, and prescribed a constitution which definitely reduced the central power to a minimum, and barred the way to national unification. The result was a system of political and social separatism and of lose federalism, which was later called particularism and was entirely in contrast to the idea of a unitary national state obtaining in England and France. It determined Germany's further development and her peculiarities in many respects.

The great war, and the tasks of reconstruction, furthered the rise of many intellectual and emotional currents which belonged to the spirit of the age, such as religious toleration, enlightenment, monarchical absolutism, pietism, mysticism, the baroque, preromanticism, nationalism and cosmopolitanism. These currents appeared in all nations which had reached a certain level of development, but in different varieties, degrees and combinations. The war had thrown back Germany for almost a century, and it was natural that her ruling circles and intellectual élite saw their models in France, England and Holland which showed a vigorous development in many fields. However, it is a widespread error to assume that all their progressive ideas were drawn from foreign sources, or that they exercised lesser influence on Germany's public mind than in other, comparable nations. The ideas of the law of nature and nations, which were the roots of liberalism and internationalism, developed spontaneously in Germany also, largely inspired by the Stoic philosophers, Roman law and Christian doctrines, and enriched by the influence of foreign thinkers. The German scholars, however, for a long time wrote their treatises on politics mainly in Latin, and could not compete with Voltaire's wit and Rousseau's fire.

The principal achievement of the epoch was the growth of the modern state which was farther advanced in England and France. Even at the end of the seventeenth century a political thinker like Seckendorff saw in the word 'State' a strange, new-fangled and uncanny term arousing the evil spirits of the 'Reason of State' and

Machiavellism. The lack of a strong central power in Germany had preserved the mediaeval idea of a patrimonial pluralism and this was still very widespread. The Church, feudal lords, town councils, trade guilds etc. claimed public powers 'in their own rights' which were often regarded as something like private property, and exercised accordingly. In a modern state public powers are its monopoly. This concentration of power had great implications for the public mind.

In the seventeenth century the idea of monarchical absolutism was in the ascendancy in many countries. Wide sections of the middle classes and the intellectuals were convinced that a powerful ruler alone would be able to curb the fanaticism of the religious parties, establish a reign of toleration, and suppress the privileges and claims to power of the warlike aristocracy. The most splendid personification of such a king was Louis XIV. He became the model of many German princes too, and these actually were his vassals. The Prussian army was built with the help of Louis' subsidies, and his most successful disciple (except in religious matters) was Frederick the Great. The rise of absolutism caused the decline of many German territorial diets, although they preserved some of their influence in many German states. These diets had their merits and their vices, they often fought abuses of power by the princes and refused to vote taxes in order to enforce their protest. But they were very frequently strongholds of feudal, local and religious privileges also. In liberal writings of the eighteenth century it was often pointed out that the situation of the peasants was worst where the nobles dominated the diets, and it was demanded that also the peasants must have representatives in them, which in some diets was the case.[1]

On the whole, however, the friends of progress for a long time, expected more from enlightened and benevolent princes than from the Estates. In fact, some German rulers carried out reforms in the interest of their peoples, which were not achieved in any other country of Europe. Joseph II was convinced that in states with a representative assembly dominated by the nobility no substantial social reform in favour of the common man was possible. His death and the conditions of the time prevented the accomplishment of his work. His successor, Leopold II, harboured the ideal of a parliamentary constitution but this plan could not be realized owing to the French Revolution and to his premature death.

In the old Empire there was representation of certain sections of

1 Conf. the article by Johann Georg Schlosser, a senior official and brother in law of Goethe, in the journal *Deutsches Museum*, 1777, II. 1. 97.

the people, as in the Reichstag, the territorial diets and the communal councils of the Free Towns, but their activities were mostly unsatisfactory. The two High Courts of the Empire, however, were an important institution for the protection of the rights of the people. Every subject, even serfs and other lowly people, could sue their prince there, not only for personal injuries or denial of justice, but also for infractions of political rights, for example taxation without consent of the Estates. Such actions were very frequent and in numerous cases they achieved success; arbitrary decisions by the princes were annulled, the rulers had to pay penalties, or in some cases were condemned by the courts to long imprisonment, or were even deposed. This institution gave the Emperor, in whose name both High Courts administered justice, great power to enforce the reign of law and it could also have been employed to bring about far reaching reforms if conditions had been more favourable. In the nineteenth century and later, however, there was a school of historical research, which regarded any reform of the old Empire as impossible, and also tended to disparage the two High Courts as much as possible. This was the Prussian historical school which comprised many important scholars, who had great merits but also were imbued with the tendency to glorify Frederick II, 'the Great', beyond measure. In consequence they defended his policy and tradition, which brought about the ruin and end of the old Empire and thereby opened the way to the 'glorious' foundation of a new Empire by the Hohenzollerns. This book throws a good deal of light on the legend of Frederick the Great though it is not denied that he possessed extraordinary gifts and effected some reforms which deserve to be recognized.

Particularism has contributed a great deal to the development of German peculiarities, both in a good and in a bad sense. In the eighteenth century, it was, in particular, an obstacle to the rise of national sentiment. From the present point of view this would appear as a fatal misfortune, and German history contains countless instances confirming this judgement. But it is not the intention of this book to pass a general judgement on the merits or demerits of particularism or national sentiment. These studies, however, have clearly shown that the great poets and thinkers of the age, and the wider circle of the intellectual élite, not merely accepted particularism but greatly preferred it to the idea of a unitary political nation. They desired concord and friendship among the Germans, and among all nations, they sought to refine the German language and its literature and to promote the rise and spread of culture in every way. But they rejected the idea of uniting all Germans in a large powerful nation and of a strong central power. When they put forward the desire for national unity they thought, with few exceptions, of the realm of culture, not of politics. In the years 1795-96 Goethe and Schiller jointly wrote a book of verse called *Xenien* in which they expressed this opinion in the words:

Zur Nation Euch zu bilden, Ihr hofft es, Deutsche, vergebens Bildet, Ihr könnt es, dafür freier zu Menschen Euch aus!

(Germans, vain is your hope to unite as a nation, therefore it is open to you instead to develop to true human beings.)

BIBLIOGRAPHY

Books referring to all, or many chapters:

B. Gebhardt, *Handbuch der deutschen Geschichte*, 8. ed. ed. by H. Grundmann, vol. II, 1955 (contains the most up-to-date bibliography)
The New Cambridge Modern History, vols. V to IX, 1957 etc.
The Cambridge Modern History, vols. V to VIII, 1902-1912
Historia Mundi, ed. F. Valjavec, vol. VIII to X, 1952 etc.
Peuples et Civilisations, ed. L. Halphen and P. Sagnac, vol. X-XIII
Günther Franz, *Bücherkunde zur deutschen Geschichte*, 1951
Dahlmann-Waitz, *Quellenkunde zur deutschen Geschichte*. 9. ed., 1931
Fritz Valjavec, *Geschichte der abendlaendischen Aufklaerung*, 1961
K. Biedermann, *Deutschland im 18. Jahrhundert*, 5 vols., 1854-80
M. v. Boehn, *Deutschland im 18. Jahrhundert*, 2 vols., 1921-22
Universal Lexikon published by J. H. Zedler, 64 volumes and 4 supplementary vols., 1732-54
Allgemeine Deutsche Biographie, 56 vols., 1875-1912 (abbreviated: ADB)
Neue Deutsche Biographie (not yet finished) 1953 etc.
H. Roessler and G. Franz, *Biographisches Woerterbuch zur deutschen Geschichte*, 1952
H. Roessler and G. Franz, *Sachwoerterbuch zur deutschen Geschichte*, 1958

CHAPTER I

THE EMPIRE, ITS FRONTIERS AND STRUCTURE AND THE SPIRIT OF PARTICULARISM

THE EMPIRE'S CONSTITUTION

F. Hartung, *Deutsche Verfassungsgeschichte vom 15. Jahrhundert bis zur Gegenwart*, 1950
C. Bornhak, *Deutsche Verfassungsgeschichte vom westfälischen Frieden an*, 1934
A. Zycha, *Deutsche Rechtsgeschichte der Neuzeit*, 1937
S. Puetter, *Histor. Entwicklung der heutigen Staatsverfassung des Teutschen Reiches*, 3 vols. 1788 (also Engl.)
J. J. Moser, *Teutsches Staatsrecht*, 1737-54. 52 vols. and Register
J. J. Moser, *Neues Teutsches Staatsrecht*, 1766-82, 23 vols. and Register
C. F. Haeberlin, *Handbuch des Teutschen Staatsrechts*, etc. 3 vols., 1797

DESCRIPTIONS OF THE EMPIRE

A. F. Büsching, *Neue Erdbeschreibung*, 7. ed. 1789-92, vols. 7-10
H. Berghaus, *Deutschland vor hundert Jahren*, 2 vols., 1859-60
J. G. Meusel, *Literatur der Statistik*, 1790, 2. ed., 1806
H. M. G. Grellmann, *Staatskunde von Teutschland I*, 1790
H. Grellmann, *Histor. Statistisches Handbuch von Teutschland*, 2. vol. 1801
F. Brunn, *Deutschland in geographischer, statistischer und politischer Hinsicht* etc. 2. ed. 3 vols. 1819
Thomas B. Clarke, *Statistical View of Germany*, 1790
E. W. A. Zimmermann, *A Political Survey of the Present State of Europe*, 1787
O. Behre, *Geschichte der Statistik in Brandenburg-Preussen bis zur Gruendung d. kgl. Statist. Bureaus*, 1905
Ignaz von Luca, *Geographisches Handbuch von dem österr. Staate*, 1792
Andreas Demjan, *Statist. Gemälde der österreichischen Monarchie*, 1796

C. H. von Römer, *Staatsrecht und Statistik des Churfürstentums Sachsen*, 4 vols., 1787-1803

THE ESTATES

F. L. Carsten, *Princes and Parliaments in Germany from the Fifteenth to the Eighteenth Century*, 1959
H. Christern, *Deutscher Ständestaat und englischer Parlamentarismus am Ende des 18. Jahrhunderts*, 1939
Walter Grube, *Der Stuttgarter Landtag, 1457-1957*, 1957

CHAPTER 2
THE EMPEROR AND THE ESTATES

Cf. also literature to chapter 1

CONSTITUTIONAL QUESTIONS

F. Hartung, 'Die Wahlkapitulationen der deutschen Kaiser und Könige' (*Hist. Zeitschrift*, 1911)
H. Zwingmann, 'Der Kaiser im Jahrhundert nach dem Westfälischen Frieden, 1913' (*Hist. Zeitschrift*, 1913)
H. Kormann, 'Die Landeshoheit in ihrem Verhältnis zur Reichsgewalt im alten Deutschland seit dem westfälischen Frieden' (*Zeitschrift für Politik*, vol. 7, 1914)
H. Feine, 'Zur Verfassungsentwicklung des hlg. Römischen Reiches seit dem westfälischen Frieden' (*Zeitschrift der Savigny Stiftung für Rechtsgeschichte*, vol. LII, 1932)
K. Gmeiner, *Geschichte der öffentl. Verhandlungen des zu Regensburg noch fortwährenden Reichstages*, 3 vols. 1794-96
A. Berney, 'Der Reichstag von Regensburg 1702', etc. (*Hist. Vierteljahrsschrift*, 1929)

THE JUDICATURE, THE HIGH COURTS

E. Doehring, *Geschichte der deutschen Rechtspflege seit 1500*, 1953
R. Smend, *Das Reichskammergericht*, I, 1911
O. v. Gschliesser, *Der Reichshofrat* etc. 1942
K. Perels, *Die allgemeinen Appellationsprivilegien für Brandenburg-Preussen*, 1908
(J. J. Moser), *Alte und neue Reichshofrat Conclusa*, 4 vols. 1943-45
F. K. v. Moser, *Reichshofrathsgutachten*, 6 vols., 1752-69
J. M. Hoscher, *Sammlung merkwürdiger am Reichskammergericht entschiedener Fälle*, 1791
R. Smend, Brandenburg-Preussen und das Reichskammergericht (*Forschungen zur brandenburg. und preuss. Geschichte*, vol. 20, 1907)
P. Hohenemser, *Der Frankfurter Verfassungsstreit 1705-32 und die Kaiserlichen Kommissionen*, 1920
H. Huebbe, *Die Kaiserlichen Kommissionen in Hamburg*, 1856
J. J. Moser, *Von dem Reichs-Staendischen Schuldenwesen*, 2 vols., 1774-75

CHAPTER 3
RELIGION AND ENLIGHTENMENT

Die Religion in Geschichte und Gegenwart, ed. H. Gunkel and L. Zscharnack, 5 vols., 1927-32
Realencyclopaedie fuer protestantische Theologie u. Kirche, ed. Herzog and Hauck, 24 vols., 1896-1913 (prot.)
Lexikon fuer Theologie u. Kirche ed. M. Buchberger, 10 vols., 1930-38 (cath.)
Kirchengeschichte ed. Kirsch, vol. III, 2, by Eder, 1949, vol. IV by Veit, 1931-33 (Catholic)

Handbuch d. Kirchengeschichte, ed. G. Krueger, vol. IV by Stephan u. Leube (Protest.)

K. Hagenbach, *Kirchengeschichte*, 3rd ed. vol. V, part 2; VI, part 1, 1871

F. Nippold, *Handbuch der neuesten Kirchengeschichte*, 3rd ed., 1889, vol. I

G. Loesche, *Geschichte des Protestantismus im vormaligen und im neuen Oesterreich*, 3rd ed., 1930

G. Mecenseffy, *Gescnichte des Protestantismus in Oesterreich*, 1937

A. Tholuck, *Der Geist d. lutherischen Theologen Wittenbergs im Verlauf d. 17. Jahrhunderts*, 1852.

A. Tholuck, *Vorgeschichte des Rationalismus*, 1853

G. Franck, *Geschichte d. protestantischen Theologie*, 4 vols., 1862-1905

J. A. Dorner, *Geschichte d. protestantischen Theologie besonders in Deutschland*, 1867

E. Hirsch, *Geschichte d. neueren evangel. Theologie im Zusammenhang mit den allgemeinen Bewegungen d. europ. Denkens*, 5 vols., 1949 etc.

W. Elert, *Morphologie des Luthertums*, 2 vols., 1931-32

E. Henke, *Calixtus u. seine Zeit*, 2 vols., 1853-60

G. Leube, *Kalvinismus u. Luthertum im Zeitalter d. Orthodoxie*, 1928

Soldan u. Heppe, *Geschichte d. Hexenprocesse*, revised ed. by M. Bauer, 2 vols., 1912

Johann Weyer's life by C. Binz, in *Allgem. Deutsche Biographie*

A. Ritschl, *Geschichte d. Pietismus*, 3 vols., 1880-86

H. Stahl, *A. H. Francke*, 1938

Der Deutsche Pietismus, ed. W. Mahrenholz, 1921

H. Bruns, *Ein Reformator nach der Reformation* (Spener), 1937

W. Gruen, *Spener's soziale Leistungen und Gedanken*, 1934

E. Bartz, *Die Wirtschaftsethik Francke's*, 1934

E. Bunke, *A. H. Francke*, 1938

H. Stephan, *D. Pietismus als Traeger d. Fortschritts* etc., 1908

J. Klepper, *Der Soldatenkoenig (Friedrich Wilhelm I) u. d. Stillen im Lande*, 1938

H. Renkewitz, *Zinzendorf*, 1939

O. Uttendoerfer, *Zinzendorf's Lebensideal*, 1940; *Zinzendorf d. d. Jugend*, 1923

W. Fullerton, *Zinzendorf*, 1932

S. Nielsen, *D. Toleranzgedanke bei Zinzendorf*, 1952

H. W. Erbe, *Zinzendorf u. d. fromme hohe Adel* etc., 1928

(Graf zu Lynar) *Nachricht von d. Ursprung u. Fortgang der Bruderunitaet*, 1781.

H. Erbe, *Bethlehem, eine kommunistische Kolonie d. 18. Jahrhundert*, 1929

W. C. Towlson, *Moravian and Methodist, their Relations in the Eighteenth Century*, 1957

E. Seeberg, *Gottfried Arnold*, 1923

G. V. Lechler, *Geschichte d. englischen Deismus*, 1841

John M. Robertson, *A Short History of Freethought*, 2 vols., 1914-15

P. Sackmann, *Bernard de Mandville* etc., 1897

M. von Geismar (Bruno Bauer) *Bibliothek der deutschen Aufklaerer des 18. Jahrhunderts*, 5 parts, 1846-47

J. Semler, *Lebensbeschreibung*, 2 vols., 1781

A. Buesching, *Eigene Lebensbeschreibung*, 1789

C. H. v. Bogatzky, *Lebenslauf*, 1781

W. Mahrholz, *Deutsche Selbstbekenntnisse, ein Beitrag zur Geschichte der deutschen Selbstbiographie von der Mystik zum Pietismus*, 1919

B. Groethuysen, *D. Entstehung der buergerlichen Welt-u-Lebensanschauung in Frankreich*, 2 vols., 1927-30

P. Hazard, *La crise de la conscience européenne*, 1680-1715, 3 vols., 1935

E. Cassierer, *Die Philosophie der Aufklaerung*, 1932

H. Hettner, *Literaturgeschichte des 18. Jahrhunderts*, 3 parts in 6 vols., 6th edition, 1913

J. Huber, *Der Jesuiten Orden*, 1873
H. Boehmer, *Die Jesuiten*, 1913
B. Duhr, *Geschichte d. Jesuiten i. d. Laendern der deutschen Zunge*, 4 vols., 1927-28
P. v. Hoensbruch, *Der Jesuitenorden*, 2 vols., 1926-28
L. Koch, *Jesuitenlexikon*, 1934
G. Schnuerer, *Kathol. Kirche u. Kultur i. d. Barockzeit*, 1937; *Kathol. Kirche u. Kultur im 18. Jahrhundert*, 1941
L. Veit und L. Lenhart, *Kirche und Volksfroemmigkeit im Zeitalter des Barocks*, 1956

CHAPTER 4
GERMANY'S SOCIAL STRUCTURE AND ECONOMIC CONDITIONS

SOCIAL HISTORY

F. Luetge, *Deutsche Sozial—und Wirtschaftsgeschichte*, 1952
H. Sieveking, *Grundzüge der neueren Wirtschaftsgeschichte*, etc. 5th ed., 1928
H. Bechtel, *Wirtschaftsgeschichte Deutschlands vom Beginn des 16. bis zum Ende des 18. Jahrhunderts*, 1952
Handwörterbuch der Staatswissenschaften, 4th ed. 1923-29, and the new edition, *Handwörterbuch der Sozialwissenschaften*, 1952
W. Sombart, *Der moderne Kapitalismus*, 6 vols., 1928
G. Steinhausen, *Geschichte der deutschen Kultur*, 3rd ed., 1929
G. Freytag, *Bilder aus der deutschen Vergangenheit*, vol. 3 and 4
Die deutschen Staende in Einzeldarstellungen, ed. by G. Steinhausen, 12 vols., 1899-1905
Handbuch der Kulturgeschichte, vol. 5 : W. Fleming, Barock, vol. 6
E. Ermatinger, *Aufklaerung*, 1935
K. Biedermann, *Deutschland im 18. Jahrhundert*, 2 vols., 1854-80
M. von Boehne, *Deutschland im 18. Jahrhundert*, 2 vols. (without year)
W. Bruford, *Germany in the 18th Century*, 1935
G. Franz, *Der Dreissigjaehrige Krieg und das deutsche Volk*, 1943

AGRICULTURE.—THE PEASANTS

C. Fraas, *Geschichte der Landbau—und Forstwissenschaft*, 1865
Rockstroh, *Leben Schubarts*, 1846
W. Simons, *Albrecht Thaer*, 1929
Th. von der Goltz, *Geschichte der deutschen Landwirtschaft*, 2 vols., 1902
S. von Frauendorfer, *Ideengeschichte der Agrarwirtschaft und Agrarpolitik im deutschen Sprachgebiet*, Band I von den Anfaengen bis zum ersten Weltkrieg, 1957
Werner Conze, *Quellen zur Geschichte der deutschen Bauernbefreiung*, 1957
Werner Conze, *Agrarverfassung im Handbuch der Sozialwissenschaften*
J. von Rozwadowski, 'Die Bauern des 18. Jahrhunderts und ihre Herren' (*Jahrbuecher fuer Nationaloekonomie und Statistik* 1900)
O. Hoetzsch, 'Der Bauernschutz in den deutschen Territorien vom 16. bis zum 18. Jahrhundert' (*Jahrbuch fuer Gesetzgebung, Verwaltung und Volkswirtschaft*, 1902)
F. Luetge, *Die mitteldeutsche Grundherrschaft*, 1934, *Die bayrische Grundherrschaft*, 1949
G. F. Knapp, *Die Landarbeiter in Knechtschaft und Freiheit*, 1891
J. Kramer, *Die Grafsihaft Hohenzollern, Ein Bild sueddeutscher Volkszustaende*, 1873
G. F. Knapp, *Der Bauer im heutigen Wuerttemberg*, 2 vols., 1919
Th. Ludwig, *Der badische Bauer im 18. Jahrhundert*, 1896
W. Wittich, *Die Grundherrschaft in Nordwest-Deutschland*, 1896
F. Grossmann, *Ueber die gutbaeuerlichen Verhaeltnisse in der Mark Brandenburg*, 1890

K. Gruenberg, *Die Bauernbefreiung und die Aufloesung der gutsherrlich baeuerlichen Verhaeltnisse in Boehmen, Maehren und Schlesien*, 1893-94
W. Medinger, *Wirtschaftsgeschichte der Domaene Lobositz*, 1903

TRADE, FINANCE

E. F. Hekscher, *Der Merkantilismus*, 2 vols., 1932
A. Beer, *Allgemeine Geschichte des Welthandels*, vol. II, 1862
F. Fischer, *Geschichte des deutschen Handels*, 1792, vol. III-IV
E. Hasse, *Geschichte der Leipziger Messen*, 1885
K. Pribram, *Geschichte der oesterr. Gewerbepolitik von 1740-1860*, 1907
W. Treue, 'David Splitgerber, ein Unternehmer im preussischen Merkantilstaat' (*Vierteljahrsschrift fuer Sozialeund Wirtschaftgeschichte*), 1954
H. Kellenbenz, 'Wilhelm Treue und Wolfgang Zorn, Aufsaetze ueber Entstehung des Unternehmertums' (in the same journal 1957)
Max Barkhausen, 'Staatliche Wirtschaftslenkung und freies Unternehmertum etc. im 18. Jahrhundert' (in the same journal, 1958)
H. Rachel und P. Wallich, *Berliner Grosskaufleute und Kapitalisten*, vol. II. Die Zeit des Merkantilismus, 1938
H. Proesler, *Das gesammtdeutsche Handwerk im Spiegel der Reichsgesetzgebung*, 1954
W. Fischer, *Handwerksrecht und Handwerkswirtschaft um 1800*, 1955
R. Stadelmann und K. Fischer, *Die Bildungswelt des deutschen Handwerkers um 1800*, 1955
H. Sieveking, 'Die Hamburger Bank, 1619-1875', in *Festschrift fuer Melle*, 1933
K. v. Eichborn, *Das Soll und Haben von Eichborn & Co. in 200 Jahren*, 1928
H. Schnee, *Die Hoffinanz und der moderne Staat*, 3 vols., 1935
G. Schmoller, 'Der deutsche Beamtenstaat vom 16. bis zum 18. Jahrhundert (im Jahrbuch fuer Gesetzgebung, Verwaltung und Volkswirtschaft, 1894)
G. Schmoller, 'Staatenbildung und Finanzentwicklung' (in the same journal, 1909)

RANKS AND CLASSES

E. Vehse, *Geschichte der deutschen Hoefe* etc., 48 vols., 1853 etc. (contains many materials about the nobility)
F. Zoellner, *Einrichtung und Verfassung der fruchtbringenden Gesellschaft*, 1899
F. Barthold, *Geschichte der fruchtbringenden Gesellschaft*, 1848
A. Wolf, *Geschichtliche Bilder aus Oesterreich*, 2 vols., 1878-80 (on the Austrian nobility)
J. Falke, *Geschichte des fuerstlichen Hauses Liechtenstein*, 3 vols., 1868-82
O. Brunner, *Adeliges Landleben und europaeischer Geist*, 1949
F. Martiny, *Die Adelsfrage in Deutschland vor 1806*, 1938
Heinrich Benedikt, *Franz Anton Graf von Sporck*, 1923
J. Landau, *Die Arbeiterfrage in Deutschland im 17. und 18. Jahrhundert bei den Kameralisten*, 1915
F. Schulze und P. Szymank, *Das deutsche Studententum*, 1910
F. Paulsen, *Geschichte des gelehrten Unterrichts an den deutschen Schulen und Universitaeten*, 3rd ed. 2 vols., 1919/21
D. Haberle, *Auswanderung und Koloniegruendung der Pfaelzer im 18. Jahrhundert*, 1909
O. Beneke, *Von unehrlichen Leuten*, 1863

THE JEWS

G. Herlitz u. B. Kirschner, *Jüdisches Lexikon*, 5 vols., 1929
M. Philippson, *Neueste Geschichte des juedischen Volkes*, 3 vols., 1907-12
J. Elbogen, *Geschichte der Juden in Deutschland*, 1935
G. Liebe, *Das Judentum in der deutschen Vergangenheit*, 1903
S. Hensel, *Die Familie Mendelssohn*, 3 vols., 1879, New Ed., 1929
Die Juden in Prag, festgabe der Loge Praga, 1927

S. Mayer, *Die Wiener Juden, 1700-1900*, 1917
Franz Kobler, *Juedische Geschichte in Briefen aus Ost und West*, 1938
Franz Kobler, *Letters of Jews through the Ages*, 2 vols., 1952

CHAPTER 5

POLITICAL THOUGHT IN THE SEVENTEENTH CENTURY

R. Stintzing und E. Landsberg, *Geschichte der deutschen Rechtswissenschaft*, 5 vols., 1880-1910
O. v. Gierke, *Das deutsche Genossenschaftsrecht*, vol. IV, 1913
E. Wolf, *Grosse Rechtsdenker der deutschen Geistesgeschichte*, 2nd ed., 1951
R. Stammler, *Rechts-u. Staatstheorien der Neuzeit*, 1925
W. Roscher, *Geschichte der Nationaloekonomik in Deutschland*, 1874, reprint 1924
P. Joachimson, *Der deutsche Staatsgedanke -von dem Anfaengen bis auf Leibnitz und Friedrich den Grossen*
J. Bluntschli, *Gesch. d. allgemeinen Staatsrechts u. d. Politik*, 1867
Hinrichs, *Geschichte der Rechts-und Staatsprincipien seit dem Zeitalter der Reformation*, 1849-52
J. Puetter, *Literatur des Teutschen Staatsrechts*, 4 vols., 1776-91
Algemeine Deutsche Biographie, 65 vols., 1875-1912
G. Lenz, *H. Conring u. d. deutsche Staatslehre d. 17. Jahrhunderts* (*Zeitschrift fuer die gesammte Staatswissenschaft*, 1926)
O. Stobbe, *H. Conring, D. Begruender der neueren deutschen Rechtsgeschichte*, 1870
F. Meinecke, *Die Idee der Staatsraison i. d. neueren Geschichte*, 3rd ed., 1929
H. Hegels, *A. Clapmarius u. d. Publizistik ueber die Arcana Imperii*, 1918
Hippolithus a Lapide, *Dissertatio de Ratione Status in Imperio Romano. Germanico*, 1640 (Germ. edit. by Carrach 1761)
V. L. von Seckendorf, *Teutscher Fuerstenstaat*, 1656
J. V. Andreae, *Christianopolis, an Ideal State of the Seventeenth Century*, transl. and ed. with an Historical Introduction by F. E. Held, 1916
C. Besold, *Synopsis policiae doctrinae*, 1623
A. Contzen, *Politicorum libri X*, 1629
B. Duhr, *Geschichte d. Jesuiten i. d. Laendern d. deutschen Zunge*, vols. II und III, 1913
H. Dietze, *Johann Oldendorp als Rechtsphilosoph und Protestant*, 1933
F. Fries, *Lehre vom Staat bei d. protest. Gottesgelehrten im 17. Jahrh.*, 1912
A. Lang, 'The Reformation and Natural Law' (in : *Calvin and the Reformation*), ed. W. Armstrong, 1909
F. Arnold, *Zur Frage des Naturrechts bei Luther*, 1937
E. Cassirer, *Naturrecht und Voelkerrecht im Lichte der Geschichte und der systematischen Philosophie*, 1919
V. Cathrein, *Recht, Naturrecht und positives Recht*, 1909
K. Zielenziger, *Die alten deutschen Kameralisten*, 1914
Louise Sommer, *Die oesterreichischen Kameralisten*, 2 vols., 1920-25
H. Hassinger, *Johann Joachim Becher*, 1951
K. Wolzendorff, *Staatsrecht und Naturrecht in der Lehre vom Widerstandsrecht des Volkes gegen rechtswidrige Ausuebung der Staatsgewalt*, 1913
O. v. Gierke, *Johannes Althusius u. d. Entwicklung der naturrechtl. Staatstheorie*, 1902 (English by E. Barker, 1934)
Severinus de Monzambano (S. Pufendorf), *Verfassung d. deutschen Reiches*, transl. and prefaced by H. Bresslau, 1870
In the 'Classics of International Law', ed. Carnegie Endowment for International Peace (Latin and English) :
S. Pufendorf, *De jure naturae et gentium*, 2 vols., 1934 Elementorum jurisprudentiae universalis libri duo, 2 vols., 1931. *De officio hominis et civis juxta legem naturalem*, 2 vols., 1927

Hans Welzel, 'Die kulturphilosophischen Grundlagen der Naturrechtslehre S. Pufendorfs und ihre kultur-historische Bedeutung' (*Deutsche Viertel-jahrsschrift fuer Literaturwissenschaft und Geistesgeschichte*, 1931, Bd. IX
M. Fleischmann, *Christian Thomasius*, 1930
R. Liebenwirth, *Christian Thomasius, sein wissenschaftliches Lebenswerk*, 1955
L. Neisser, *C. Thomasius und seine Beziehungen zum Pietismus*, 1928
Debitsch, *Die staatsbuergerliche Erziehung an den deutschen Ritterakademien*, 1928
A. White, *Seven Great Statesmen in the Warfare of Humanity with Unreason*, 1910 (contains a chapter on Thomasius)

CHAPTER 6
G. W. LEIBNIZ

G. W. Leibniz, *Saemmtliche Schriften und Briefe*, herausgegeben von der Preussischen Akademie der Wissenschaften, 7 vols., 1923-50
Leibniz, *Deutsche Schriften*, her. von Schmied-Kowarzik, 2 vols., 1916
Leibniz' two most important works also have appeared separately in German : Leibniz, *Neue Abhandlungen ueber den menschlichen Verstand, ins Deutsche uebersetzt, mit Einleitung, Lebensbeschreibung und erlaeuternden Anmerkungen von C. Schaarschmidt*, 2 Aufl., 1904
Leibniz, *Die Theodicee*, uebersetzt von Kirchmann, 1879
G. E. Guhrauer, *Leibniz*, 2 vols., 1842, *Nachtrag*, 1946
K. Fischer, *Leibniz*, 1902
E. Pfleiderer, *Leibniz als Patriot, Staatsmann u. Bildungstraeger*, 1870
E. Ruck, *Die Leibnizsche Staatsidee*, 1909
R. Meyer, *Leibniz and the Seventeenth Century Revolution*, 1952
K. Huber, *Leibniz*, 1951
Hildebrandt, *Leibniz u. d. Reich d. Gnade*, 1953
Daville, *Leibniz historien*, 1909
P. Schrecker, 'Leibniz, ses idées sur l'organisation des relations internationales' (*Proceedings of the British Academy*, vol. XXIII)
G. Jordan, *The Reunion of the Churches, a Study of Leibniz and his Great Attempt*, 1927
F. Kiefl, *Der Friedensplan Leibniz' zur Wiedervereinigung der Kirchen*, 1903
Leibniz, Zu seinem 300 sten Geburtstag, her. von E. Hochstetter, 1946-52
E. Benz, *Leibniz und Peter der Grosse*, 1947

CHAPTER 7
THE EPOCH OF LOUIS XIV AND THE RISE OF MONARCHICAL ABSOLUTISM

R. Koser, 'Absolutismus' in *Staat und Gesellschaft d. neueren Zeit*
F. Hartung, 'Die Epochen der absoluten Monarchie' (*Hist. Zsch.*, 1932)
R. v. Albertini, *Das politische Denken in Frankreich zur Zeit Richelieus* (1951)
Philippe Sagnac, *Louis XIV*, 3rd ed.
Louis André, *Louis XIV et l'Europe*, 1950
E. Lavisse, *Histoire de la France*, vol. 6, *Louis XIV*, 1905
A. Rambaud on Louis XIV in *Histoire de la Civilisation Française II* (1916)
Sir Ch. Petrie, *Louis XIV*, 1938
M. Philippson, *Das Zeitalter Ludwigs des Vierzehnten*, 1879
Philippe Sagnac, *La formation de la société française moderne*, 2 vols., 1946
W. Heinecker, *Die Persönlichkeit Ludwigs XIV's*, 1915
H. Gillott, *Le règne de Louis XIV et l'opinion publique en Allemagne*, 1914
A. Pribram, *F. P. von Lisola u. d. Politik seiner Zeit*, 1894
B. Auerbach, *La France et le St. Empire Romain Germanique*, etc., 1912

G. Zeller, 'La monarchie et les frontières naturelles' (Revue d'histoire moderne, 1933)
A. Schulte, Frankreich u. das limke Rheinufer, 1918
J. Haller, Die deutsche Publizistik 1668-1674, 1892
G. Mentz, Die deutsche Publizistik im 17. Jahrhundert, 1897
F. Kleyser, Der Flugschriftenkampf gegen Ludwig XIV, 1935
H. v. Zwiedineck-Südenhorst, Die öffentliche Meinung in Deutschland im Zeitalter Ludwigs XIV, 1888
P. Havelaar, Der deutsche Libertätsgedanke und die Politik Wilhelms III, 1935
P. Wentzke, J. Frischmann, 1904
F. Meinecke, Die Idee der Staatsraison in der neueren Geschichte, 1924
J. King, Science and Rationalism in the Government of Louis XIV, 1949
P. Clement, Histoire de la vie et de l'administration de Colbert, 1846

CHAPTER 8

THE CONQUEST OF HUNGARY BY THE TURKISH EMPIRE AND ITS CONSEQUENCES

Cf. also the handbooks of Austrian history listed in the bibliographical notes to the next chapter
J. Szekfue, Der Staat Ungarn, 1918
J. Graf Mailath, Geschichte der Magyaren, vol. II, III, 1852-53
E. Csuday, Geschichte der Ungarn, 2 vols., 1900
M. Horvath, Geschichte der Ungarn, vol. I, 1851
H. Marczali, Ungarische Verfassungsgeschichte, 1910
A. v. Timon, Ungarische Verfassungs-und Rechtsgeschichte, 1904
Count J. Andrassy, The Development of Hungarian Liberty, 1908
G. D. Teutsch, Geschichte der Siebenbuerger Sachsen, 4 vols., 1852 etc.
W. Fraknoi, Ungarn vor der Schlacht bei Mohacs, 1886
F. Salamon, Ungarn im Zeitalter der Tuerkenherrschaft, 1887
A. Lefaivre, Les Magyars pendant la domination Ottomane en Hongrie, 2 vols., 1902
A. Wolf, Geschicht, Bider aus Oestereich, 1880
H. Meynert, Geschichte d. K. K. oesterr. Armee, 1852
H. Meynert, Geschichte d. Kriegswesens etc., 4 vols., 1868
K. Oberleitner, 'Oesterr. Finanzen u. Kriegswesen unter Ferdinand I' (in Archiv fuer Kunde oesterr. Geschichtsquellen, vol. 22, 1860)
A. Huber, 'Studien ueber die finanziellen Verhaeltnisse Oesterreichs unter Ferdinand I' (Mitteilungen d. Instituts f. Oesterr. Geschichtsforschung, 1893, Ergb, 4)
J. Koenig, Lazarus v. Schwendi, 1934
J. Mueller, Zacharias Geizkofler, 1938
J. Schwicker, P. Pazmany u. seine Zeit, 1888
J. Kornis, Le Cardinal Pazmany, 1937
J. Schwicker, Geschichte d. oesterr. Militaergrenze, 1883

CHAPTER 9

EMPEROR LEOPOLD AND HIS POLICY

F. Krones, Handbuch der Geschichte Oesterreichs, vol. III, 1878
O. Redlich, Oesterreichische Grossmachtbildung in der Zeit Kaiser Leopolds I, 1921
F. M. Mayer, Geschichte Oesterreichs, mit besonderer Ruecksicht auf das Kulturleben, vol. II, 1909
H. Hantsch, Geschichte Oesterreichs, vol. II, 1951
K. u. M. Uhlirz, Handbuch der Geschichte Oesterreichs etc., vol. I, 1927
B. Erdmannsdoerfer, Deutsche Geschichte vom westfaelischen Frieden bis zum Regierungsantritt Friedrichs d. Grossen, 2 vols., 1892

H. v. Zwiedineck-Suedenhorst, *Deutsche Geschichte im Zeitalter der Gruen-dung des preussischen Koenigtums*, 2 vols., 1890-94
F. Wagner, *Historia Leopoldi Magni* etc., 2 vols., 1719-31
E. G. Rinck, *Leopolds des Grossen Leben und Taten*, 2nd ed., 4 parts, 1709
The Life of Leopold, Emperor of Germany, 1706 (Germ. trsl. by Mencken)
C. Freschot, *Relation v. d. Kayserl. Hof zu Wien*, 1705
A. F. Pribram, *Franz Paul Frhr. von Lisola u. d. Politik seiner Zeit*, 1894
A. Wolf, *Geschichtliche Bilder aus Oesterreich*, vol. II, 1880
A. Wolf, *Fuerst Wenzel Lobkowitz*, 1869
K. Th. v. Heigel, *Beitraege zur Charakteristik Leopold I in Geschichtliche Bilder*, 1897
Esaias Pufendorf, *Bericht ueber Leopold I* etc. ed. Helbig, 1862
A. F. Pribram, *Die niederoesterreichischen Staende u. d. Krone in der Zeit Leopolds* (MIOeG, 1893)
F. v. Mensi 'Oesterr. Finanzgeschichte' in *Oesterr. Staatswoerterbuch*, ed. Mischler u. Ulbrich, vol. II, 1906
M. Doeberl, 'Das Project einer Einigung Deutschland's auf wirtschaftlicher Grundlage etc.' (in *Forschungen zur Geschichte Bayerns*, 1898)
H. Schwarz, *The Imperial Privy Council*, 1943
O. Brunner, *Adeliges Landleben und Europaeischer Geist. Leben und Werk Wolf Helmhards von Hohberg*, 1949
Heischmann, *Die Anfaenge des stehenden Heeres in Oesterreich*, 1925
F. Loidl, *Menschen im Barock. Abraham a Santa Clara ueber das religioes-sittliche Leben in Oesterreich*
D. Kaufmann, *Die letzte Vertreibung der Juden aus Wien*, 1889
A. Coreth, *Oesterreichische Geschichtsschreibung in der Barockzeit*, 1950
G. Loesche, *Geschichte des Protestantismus im vormaligen und im neuen Oesterreich*, 3rd ed., 1930
G. Mecenseffy, *Geschichte des Protestantismus in Oesterreich*, 1937

CHAPTER 10

HUNGARY'S LIBERATION AND AUSTRO-HUNGARIAN RELATIONS

J. Szekfue, *Der Staat Ungarn*, 1918
H. Marczali, *Ungarische Verfassungsgeschichte*, 1910
J. Graf Mailath, *Geschichte der Ungarn*, vol. II and III, 1952-53
E. Czuday, *Geschichte der Ungarn*, 2nd ed., 1900, vol. II
F. Salamon, *Ungarn im Zeitalter der Tuerkenherrschaft*, 1887
A. Lefaivre, *Les Magyars pendant la domination Ottomane en Hongrie*, 2 vols., 1902
Adam Wolf, *Fuerst Wenzel Lobkowitz*, 1869
H. v. Zwiedineck-Suedenhorst, *Die Schlacht von St. Gotthard* (MIOeG, 1889)
Bela Obal, *Die Religionspolitik in Ungarn nach dem Westfaelischen Frieden waehrend der Regierung Leopolds I*, 1910
O. Klopp, *Das Jahr 1683 u. d. folgende grosse Tuerkenkrieg*, etc., 1882
R. Lorenz, *Tuerkenjahr 1683, Das Reich im Kampf um den Ostraum*, 1934
'Das Kriegsjahr 1683,' in *Mittelungen des Kriegsarchivs*, 1883
W. Fraknoi, *Innocenz XI u. Ungarns Befreiungv. d. Tuerkenherrschaft*, 1902
O. Laskowski, *J. Sobieski, King of Poland*, 1944
Lettres du roi Jean Sobieski à la reine, 1826
G. W. Lochner, *Ueber den Anteil Johann III Sobieskis, Johann Georgs III und ihrer Heere an dem Ersatz von Wien*, 1831
A. von Arneth, *Prinz Eugen*, 3 vols., 1864
H. Oehler, *Prinz Eugen in Volkslied und Flugschrift*, 1941
H. Oehler, *Prinz Eugen im Urteil Europas*, 1944
M. Braubach, *Geschichte und Abenteuer. Gestalten um den Prinzen Eugen*, 1950

CHAPTER II

THE WAR OF THE SPANISH SUCCESSION AND ITS CONSEQUENCES

Cf. also the literature to Chapter 8
C. v. Noorden, *Europaeische Geschichte im 18. Jahrhundert*, Part I
Der Spanische Erbfolgekrieg. 3 vols., 1870-82
A. Gaedeke, *Die Politik Oesterreichs in der Spanischen Erbfolgefrage*, 2 vols., 1877
Ph. Sagnac et A. de Saint-Léger, *Louis XIV*, 3rd ed.
E. Lavisse, *Louis XIV*, 1905
O. Weber, *Der Friede von Utrecht*, 1891
W. Churchill, *Marlborough*, 4 vols., 1938
M. Braubach, *Die Bedeutung der Subsidien im Spanischen Erbfolgekrieg*, 1923
A. Berney, Der Reichstag von Regensburg 1702-04 (*Hist. Viertegahrschrift* 1929)

CHAPTER 12

EMPEROR CHARLES VI

Cf. also the literature to Chapters 8, 9 and 10
O. Redlich, *Das Werden einer Grossmacht, Oesterreich von 1700 b. 1740*, 1939
P. A. Lalande, *Histoire de l'Empereur Charles VI*. 6 vols., 1743
Schirach, *Biographie Karls VI*, 1776
The New Cambridge Modern History, vol. VII. The old Regime 1713-63, ed.
    J. O. Lindsay, 1957. Chapter 17. The Habsburg Dominions by C. A.
    Macartney, and other chapters
P. Muret et Ph. Sagnac, *La preponderance anglaise* (1715-63)
Schmidt-Millbiller, *Teutsche Reichshistorie*, vol. IX and X
G. Turba, *Die Grundlagen der pragmatischen Sanktion*, 2 vols., 1911
H. Bidermann, *Geschichte der oesterr. Gesammtstaatsidee*. 2 vols., 1867-89
H. Hantsch, *Reichsvicekanzler F. K. Graf Schoenborn*, 1929
F. v. Mensi, *Die Finanzen Oesterreichs 1701-40*, 1890
A. Beer on finance under Charles VI in vol. I of *Der Oesterreichische
    Erbfolgekrieg*, ed. Kriegsarchiv, 1896
Versuch einer Lebensbeschreibung des Feldmarschalls von Seckendorf, 2 vols., 1792-94
J. G. Keyssler, *Reisen durch Deutschland*, 2nd ed., 1751
G. Mecenseffy, *Karls VI spanische Buendnispolitik*, 1934
J. F. Chance, *The Alliance of Hanover*, 1923
G. C. Gibbs, 'Britain and the Alliance of Hanover' (*Engl. Hist. Review*, 1958)
B. Williams, *The Whig Supremacy*, 1939
W. Michael, *Englische Geschichte im 18. Jahrhundert*, 5 vols., 1896 etc.
J. G. Droysen, *Geschichte der preussischen Politik*, Part IV, vol. 2, 1869
M. Huisman, *La Belgique commerciale sous l'empereur Charles VI*. La
    Compagnie d'Ostende, 1902
H. Landau, *Die Entwicklung des Warenhandels in Oesterreich*, 1906

CHAPTER 13

THE PRINCIPAL GERMAN STATES UNTIL ABOUT 1740

O. Hintze, *Die Hohenzollern und ihr Werk*, 1915
L. v. Ranke, *Zwoelf Buecher preussischer Geschichte*, 3 vols, 1930
H. Prutz, *Preussische Geschichte*, 4 vols, 1900 etc.
G. A. Stenzel, *Geschichte des preuss. Staates*, 5 vols., 1830-54
O. Hintze, *Geist u. Epochen d. preuss. Geschichte*, 1943
M. Philippson, *Der grosse Kurfuerst*, 3 vols., 1897-1903
A. Waddington, *Le Grand Elécteur*, 2 vols., 1905-08
F. Schevill, *The Great Elector*, 1947

A. Berney, *Friedrich I und das Haus Habsburg*, 1927
C. Hinrichs, *Friedrich Wilhelm I*, vol. I, 2nd ed., 1947
F. v. Oppeln-Bronikowski, *Der Baumeister des preuss. Staates, Friedrich Wilhelm I*, 1934
J. G. Droysen, *Geschichte d. preuss. Politik*, 14 vols., 1855-86
C. Jany, *Geschichte d. preuss Armee u. d. Reichsheeres*, 5 vols., 1928-37
L. Tuempel, *Die Entstehung d. brandenburgisch preuss. Einheitsstaates im Zeitalter des Absolutismus*, 1915
Graf Seckendorff, *Lebensbeschreibung*, 4 parts, 1792-94
F. Giese, *Preuss. Rechtgeschichte*, 1920
G. Schmoller, *Umrisse und Untersuchungen zur Verfassungs-, Verwaltungs- und Wirtschaftsgeschichte, besonders des preuss. Staates im 18. und 19. Jahrhundert*, 1898
F. Vollmer, *Friedrich Wilhelm I und die Volksschule*, 1909
G. Kuentzel und M. Hass, *Die politischen Testamente der Hohenzollern*, 1919
Forschungen zur brandenburg-preuss. Geschichte (periodical)
R. Koetzschke u. H. Naumann, *Saechsische Geschichte*, 2 vols., 1935
Boettiger-Flathe, *Geschichte d. Kurstaats u. Koenigreichs Sachsen*, 3 vols., 1867
O. Kaemmel, *Saechsische Geschichte*, 1905
P. Haake, *August der Starke*, 1927
E. Schneider, *Wuerttembergische Geschichte*, 1896
K. Weller, *Wuerttembergische Geschichte*, 1909
S. Reizler, *Geschichte Bayerns*, 8 vols., 1878 etc.
M. Doeberl, *Entwicklungsgeschichte Bayerns*, 3 vols., 1906-12
L. Haeusser, *Geschichte der rheinischen Pfalz*, 2 vols., 1845
K. Hauck, *Karl Ludwig, Kurfuerst von der Pfalz*, 1903
O. v. Heinemann, *Geschichte Braunschweigs und Hannovers*, 3 vols., 1884-92
A. W. Ward, *Great Britain and Hanover*, 1899

CHAPTER 14

CHRISTIAN WOLFF AND ENLIGHTENMENT

Ch. Wolff, *Eigene Lebensbeschreibung, her. von H. Wuttke, mit einer Abhandlung des Herausgebers*, 1841
A. F. Buesching, *Beytraege zu der Lebensgeschichte denkwuerdiger Personen insonderheit gelehrter Maenner*, vol. I, 1783

WOLFF'S PHILOSOPHY

K. Fischer, *G. W. Leibniz*, 4th ed., 1902
W. Windelband, *Geschichte der neueren Philosophie*, 7th ed., 1922
E. Cassirer, *Die Philosophie der Aufklaerung*, 1932
F. Jodl, *Geschichte der Ethik*, 2nd ed., 1906, vol. I, p. 528
H. Hettner, *Literaturgesch. d. 18. Jahrhunderts*, part 3, vol. I, 6th ed., 1913, p. 199
W. Arnsperger, *Ch. Wolff's Verhaeltnis zu Leibniz*, 1897

WOLFF'S SOCIAL AND POLITICAL THOUGHT

Ch. Wolff, *Vernuenftige Gedanken von dem gesellschaftlichen Leben der Menschen* 1721 (here used is edition of 1754)
Ch. Wolff, *Jus Gentium methodo scientifica pertractatum* (Latin and Engl. tr. in the 'Classics of Internat. Law' ed. Carnegie Foundation)
Ch. Wolff, *The Real Happiness of a People under a Philosophical King* etc., 1750 (Engl. tr. by Mr des Champs, first published in 1772)
W. Frauendienst, *Ch. Wolff als Staatsdenker*, 1927
G. Namslau, *Rechfertigung des Staates bei Ch. Wolff*
Th. Link, *Die Paedagogik des Philosophen Ch. Wolff*, 1906
F. A. Brown *On Education, Locke, Wolff and the Moral Weeklies*, 1952

E. de Vattel:
Droit de Gens etc., 1758 (used is the edition in the 'Classics of International Law' ed. Carnegie Foundation)

JOURNALS FOR THE PROMOTION OF ENLIGHTENMENT
AND OTHER AIMS

J. Kirchner, *Das deutsche Zeitschriftenwesen* etc., I, 1942
J. Kirchner, *Die Grundlagen des deutschen Zeitschriftenwesens*, 2 parts, 1928, 1931
L. Lindenberg, *Leben u. Schriften D. Fassmanns*, 1937
K. Kaschmieder, *D. Fassmann's Gespraeche im Reiche der Toten*, 1934
L. Salomon, *Geschichte d. deutschen, Zeitungswesens*, vol. I, 1899
P. Merker und W. Stammler, *Reallexikon der deutschen Literaturgeschichte*, 1925-26. Articles on Moralische Wochenschriften by J. Wiegand and on Deutsche Gesellschaften
Denkschrift zum 200. Geburtstag. J. J. Bodmers, 1900
E, Reichel Gottsched, 1908/12
M. Kawczynski, *Studien zur Literaturgeschichte des 18. Jahrhunderts, Moralische Zeitschriften*, 1880
M. Stecher, *Die Erziehungsbestrebungen der deutschen moralischen Wochenschriften*, 1914
E. Umbach, *Die deutschen Moralischen Wochenschriften und der Spectator, von Addison und Steele*, etc., 1911
E. Milberg, *Die Moralischen Wochenschriften des 18. Jahrhunderts*, 1881
Der Patriot, 4th ed., 3 vols., Hamburg, 1765. *Der Buerger*, Goettingen, 1732
Der Druide, Berlin, 1749
H. Boos, *Geschichte d. Freimaurerei*, 1906
F. J. Schneider, *Die Freimaurerei u. ihr Einfluss auf die geistige Kultur Deutschlands am Ende des 18. Jahrhunderts*, 1909
L. Keller, *Die deutschen Gesellschaften des 18. Jahrhunderts u. die Moralischen Wochenschriften*, Vortraege und Aufsaetz d. Comenius Gesellschaft, 8. Jahr, Stueck 2.

CHAPTER 15

PRUSSIA BECOMES A GREAT POWER

Cf. also the literature to chapters 8, 12, 15 and 16
R. Koser, *Friedrich der Grosse*, 4 vols., 7 ed., 1925
A. von Arneth, *Geschichte Maria Theresias*, 10 vols., 1863-79
A. Wolf und H. v. Zwiedineck-Suedenhorst, *Oesterreich unter Maria Theresia, Josef II und Leopold II*, 1884
(Further literature on Frederick II, Maria Theresa and Joseph II is indicated in the lists to the two succeeding chapters)
F. Wagner, *Kaiser Karl VII und die grossen Maechte*, 1938
Preussische Staatsschriften aus der Regierungszeit Friedrichs II. 3 vols., her. v. R. Koser u. O. Krauske, 1877-92
Preussische und Oesterreichische Akten zur Vorgeschichte des 7 jaehrigen Krieges, her. v. G. Volz u. C. Kuentzel, 1899
Oesterr. Erbfolgekrieg, her. v. k. k. Kriegsarchiv, 9 vols., 1896-1914 (contains also political and financial chapters)
A. O. v. Loehr, 'Die Finanzierung des 7 jaehrigen Krieges'. (in *Numismatische Zeitschrift*, 1925)
R. Waddington, *La guerre de sept ans*, 5 vols., 1899 etc.
E. Reimann, *Geschichte des bayrischen Erbfolgekrieges*, 1889
J. Ch. Adelung, *Pragmatische Staatsgeschichte Europas* etc. 9 vols., 1762 etc.

The New Cambridge History, vol. VII, 1957 (various chapters by different authors)

M. Lehmann, *Friedrich d. Gr. und d. Ursprung d. siebenjaehrigen Krieges*, 1894

H. Butterfield, *The Reconstruction of a Historical Episode: the History of the Enquiry into the Origins of the Seven Years' War*, 1951

Sir R. Lodge, *Studies in Eighteenth Century Diplomacy*, 1740-49, 1930

Sir R. Lodge, *Great Britain and Prussia in the Eighteenth Century*, 1922

D. B. Horn, *Sir Charles Hanbury Williams and European Diplomacy*, 1930

Basil Williams, *The Whig Supremacy*, 1939

William Coxe, *History of the House of Austria*, 1807

J. Corbett, *England in the Seven Years' War*, 2 vols., 1907

D. B. Horn, *British Public Opinion and the first Partition of Poland*, 1945

L. v. Ranke, *Die deutschen Maechte und der Fuerstenbund*, 2 vols., 1871

A. Brabant, *Das heilige Roemische Reich teutscher Nation im Kampfe mit Friedrich d. Grossen*, 3 vols., 1904-31

A. Beer, *Die erste Teilung Polens*, 3 vols., 1873

Rousseau, *Considerations on Poland*, Engl. trs. in Pol. Works, ed. Watkins, 1955

CHAPTER 16
FREDERICK II. HIS PERSONALITY, THOUGHT AND WORK

The name of King Frederick II (or the Great) is here often given abbreviated to F. The principal periodicals are the 'Forschungen zur brandenburgischen und preussischen Geschichte' (abbreviated FBPG), the 'Historische Zeitschrift' (HZ), the 'Historische Vierteljahrschrift' (HV) and the 'Hohenzollern Jahr-buch' (HJ).

Cf. for this chapter also the literature given for chapter 15.

The works of F. are available in the original (French) edition in 30 volumes, and his political correspondence in 46 volumes, and there are in addition many volumes of his correspondence with relatives, other rulers and friends. The most important works and letters have also been translated into German. The most modern edition is the German one in 10 volumes, edited by G. B. Volz, 1912-14, with introductions, portraits, etc. A most valuable source is F.'s Political Testaments, translated by Oppeln-Bronikowski, 1922. Of the numerous contemporary memoirs and similar sources the most important ones are:

MEMOIRS, ETC.:

C. W. v. Dohm, *Denkwürdigkeiten meiner Zeit*, 5 vols., 1814-19; the last volume contains a list of many other reminiscences, with Dohm's comments.

Graf Lehndorff, *30 Jahre am Hofe F.* 3 vols., 1907

D. Thiébault, *Mes souvenirs de vingt ans de séjour à Berlin* etc., 2 vols., 1860

H. de Catt, *Memoiren und Tagebuecher*, herausg. v. Koser, 1884

Marchese Lucchesini, *Tagebuch, herausg.* v. Oppeln-Bronikowski und Volz, 1926

Wilhelmine von Bayreuth, *Memoiren*, 1920

Edith Cuthell, *Wilhelmina, Margravine of Bayreuth*, 1905

Karl von Hessen-Kassel, *Denkwuerdigkeiten*, 1866

Voltaire, *Briefwechsel mit F.* 4 vols., 1908-17

F. im Spiegel seiner Zeit, herausg. v. Volz, 3 vols., 1926-27; (contains excerpts from many less known memoirs)

A. F. Buesching, *Charakter F. II*, 1788

Buesching, *Zuverlaessige Beitraege zu der Regierungszeit F. II*, 1790

C. Garve, *Fragmente zur Schilderung des Geistes etc. der Regierung F. II*, 2 vols., 1798

Graf Hertzberg, *Huit Dissertations*, etc., 1787

Sir A. Mitchell, *Memoirs and Papers 1756 to 1771*, ed. by Bisset, 2 vols., 1850
H. Comte de Mirabeau, *De la monarchie Prussienne*, etc., 7 vols., 1788
H. Reissner, *Mirabeau u. die 'Monarchie Prussienne'*, 1926
Mirabeau-Mauvillon, *Von der preussischen Monarchie unter F. d. Gr.* 4 vols.,
    1793-95 (This is a revised and enlarged translation of Mirabeau's work,
    edited by Mauvillon and, after his death, by Blankenburg)
Ritter v. Zimmermann, *Fragmente ueber F.*, 3 vols., 1790
de Launay, *Justification du systéme d'écon. politique et financiére de
    Frédéric II*

BIOGRAPHIES:

J. D. E. Preuss, *Lebensgeschichte*, 4 vols., and documents, 1932
R. Koser, *F. d. Gr.*, 4 vols., 1912 (the present standard work, indispensable for
    all questions)
A. Berney, *F., Entwicklungsgang eines Staatsmanns*, 1934

SHORTER APPRECIATIONS:

G. Ritter, 1936, W. Elze, 1936, Gaxotte, 1941, G. Gooch, 1947

CRITICS

O. Klopp, *F. von Preussen und seine Politik*, 1867
W. Hegemann, *Fridericus*, etc., 1926

SYSTEM OF GOVERNMENT

Acta Borussica, *Denkmaeler der preuss. Staatsverwaltung im 18. Jahrhundert*,
    herausg, v. d. *Akademie der Wissenschaften* (numerous volumes treating
    the administration and the economic policy of F.II and his predecessors),
    1892-1926
On the Estates and the Administration in the Prussian provinces cf. Dahlmann-
    Waitz, *Quellenkunde*, 9th ed., 1931, p. 768 seq.
G. Borchardt, *Die Randbemerkungen F.'s*, 1936
H. Meisner, *Das Regierungs- u. Behoerdensystem Maria Theresias und der
    preuss. Staat*, FBPG 1941
F. Etzin, *Die Freiheit d. oeffentl. Meinung unter d. Regierung F.* (FBPG, 1921)

ARMY AND WAR

C. Jany, *Geschichte d. kgl. preuss. Armee bis 1807*, 3 vols., 1928-29
D. Graf Schwerin, *Feldmarschall Schwerin*, 1928
G. Volz, *Winterfeldt* (HJ, 1907)
G. Winter, *Zieten*, 2 vols., 1886
F. Graf v. Schmettau, *Lebensgeschichte*, 2 vols., 1806
Tagebuch d. preuss. Musketiers Dominikus, :891; *Preuss. Soldatenleben in
    der Fridericianischen Zeit*, herausg. R. Steinert
E. v. Petersdorff, *F.'s Kriegsphilosophie*, 1918
H. Hetzel, *Stellung F.'s zur Humanitaet im Kriege*, 1885
R. Koser, *Zur preuss. u. deutschen Geschichte, Aufsaetze u. Vortraege*, 1921

POLITICAL THOUGHT

F. Meinecke, *D. Idee d. Staatsraison*, 1924
J. v. Prott, *Staat u. Volk in den Schriften F.'s*, 1937
H. Jacobs, *F. u. d. Idee d. Vaterlands*, 1939
E. Cauer, *F.'s Gedanken ueber die fuerstliche Gewalt*, 1863
H. Pigge, *D. Staatstheorie F.'s in Festgabe fuer H. Finke*, 1904
E. Madsack, *D. Antimachiavell*, 1920
F. Luckwaldt, *F.'s Anschauung von Staat und Fuerstentum, in Festgabe f. A.
    Schulte*, 1927
Dock, *D. Souveraenitaetsbegriff von Bodin bis F.*, 1897
F. Klassen, *Die Grundlagen des aufgeklärten Absolutismus*, 1929

RELIGION, EDUCATION

R. Koser, *Friedrich d. Gr. und die preuss. Universitaeten* (FBPG 17)
C. Rethwisch, *Der Staatsminister Frh. v. Zedlitz u. Preussens hoeheres Schulwesen unter Frdrch d. Gr.*, 1886
F. Vollmer, *Die preuss, Volksschulpolitik unter F.*, 1918
Cochenhausen, *F.'s Gedanken über Erziehung, in Festschrift fuer Spranger*
W. Schneider, *Kirchenpolitik F.'s, in HV*, 1937
F. Hanus, *Church and State in Silesia under F.*, 1944
H. Pegge, D. *religioese Toleranz F.'s*, 1899

ECONOMIC AND FINANCIAL SYSTEM:

Cf. Mirabeau-Mauvillon quoted before
H. Rachel, *Der Merkantilismus in Brandenburg-Preussen*, FBPG, 1927
H. Rachel, *Handels-, Zoll- und Akzisepolitik Preussens, in Acta Borussica*, 1929
U. Froese, *Kolonisationswerk F.'s*, 1938
G. Rhode, *Siedlungspolitik F.'s*, 1939
G. Arndt, *Grundsaetze der Siedlungspolitik F.'s*, 1934
A. Zottmann, D. *Wirtschaftspolitik F.'s*, 1937
F. Matschoss, *F. als Befoerderer d. Gewerbefleisses*, 1912
G. Schmoller u. O. Hintze, D. *preuss. Seidenindustrie im 18. Jhrh.* etc., 3 vols., 1892 (in Acta Borussica)
W. Naudé, D. *Getreidehandelspolitik d. europ. Staaten vom 13. bis zum 18. Jahrhundert* (in Acta Borussica)
B. Schulze, D. *preuss. General-Chausseebau-Department*, FBPG, 1935
K. v. Eichborn, *Das Soll und Haben v. Eichborn & Co in 200 Jahren*, 1928
L. Brentano, D. *feudale Grundlage der schlesischen Leinenindustrie, in Gesammelte Aufsaetze*, vol. I, 1899
R. Koser, *Die preuss. Finanzen v. 1763-1786*, FBPG, vol. XXI
R. Koser, D. *Finanzen im 7jaehrig. Krieg*, FBPG, vol. XIII, 1900
S. Skalweit, *Die Berliner Wirtschaftskrise von 1763* etc., 1937

LAW AND JUSTICE

H. Thieme, *Das Naturrecht u. d. europ. Privatrechtsgeschichte*, 1947
H. Thieme, 'Die preussische Kodifikation' (*Zeitschrift der Savigny Stiftung, german. Abteilung*, 1937)
E. Wolf, *Grosse Rechtsdenker der deutschen Geistesgeschichte*, 1951 (ch. 11 on Suarez)
E. Schmidt, *Staat und Recht in Theorie u. Praxis F.'s*, 1936
E. Schmidt, *Einfuehrung in die Geschichte d. deutschen Strafrechtspflege*, 1947
A. F. Berner, *Die Strafgesetzgebung in Deutschland von 1751 bis zur Gegenwart*, 1867
J. Howard, *The State of the Prisons*, etc., 4th ed., 1792

FREDERICK AS PHILOSOPHER. THE BERLIN ACADEMY

A. Harnack, *Geschichte d. kgl. preuss. Akademie der Wissenschaften zu Berlin*, 3 vols., 1900 (abbreviated edition in 1 vol., 1901)
E. Haeber, *Geistige Stroemungen in Berlin zur Zeit F.'s*, FBPG, 1943
W. Gent, *Die geistige Kultur um F.*, 1936
W. Dilthey, 'F. u. die deutsche Aufklaerung' (in *Ges. Schriften*, vol. 3, 1927)
H. Fechner, *Philosophie F.'s*, 1891
E. Zeller, *F. als Philosoph*, 1886
E. Spranger, 'D. Philosoph von Sanssouci' (*Abhandlung d. Preuss. Akademie*, 1942)
E. du Bois-Reymond, *F. u. J. J. Rousseau*, 1879
G. Beyerhaus, *F. u. d. 18. Jahrhundert*, 1931

PUBLIC OPINION ABOUT FREDERICK, AND HIS
INFLUENCE ON IT

W. Bussmann, 'F. im Wandel der Zeiten', in *Rothfels Festschrift*, 1951
E. Allard, *F. in der Literatur Frankreichs*, 1913
S. Skalweit, *Frankreich u. F.*, 1952
H. Marcus, *F. in der englischen Literatur*, 1930
K. Schwarze, *Der siebenjaehrige Krieg i. d. zeitgenoessischen Literatur*, 1936
F. Ziehen, 'F. in der Schweiz', in *Die Schweiz u. d. deutsche Geistesleben*, 1924
G. Volz, *Prinz Heinrich als Kritiker F.'s.* HV, 1927
E. Cauer, *Flugschriften F.'s*, 1865
V. Heydemann, *Staats-u. Flugschriften aus dem siebenjaehrigen Krieg*, FBPG, 1928

CHAPTER 17

MARIA THERESA AND JOSEPH II. THEIR PERSONALITY, THOUGHT AND WORK

F. Krones, *Handbuch der Geschichte Oesterreichs*, vol. 4, 1879
A. Wolf, u. H. v. Zwiedineck-Suedenhorst, *Oesterreich unter Maria Theresia, Josef II und Leopold II*, 1884
A. Wolf, *Geschichtliche Bilder aus Oesterreich*, vol. II, 1880
F. M. Mayer, *Geschichte Oesterreichs*, 3rd ed., 1909, vol. 2
H. Hantsch, *Geschichte Oesterreichs*, 2nd ed., vol. 2
C. v. Hock u. H. Bidermann, *Der oesterr. Staatsrat*, 1868-79
A. v. Arneth, *Geschichte Maria Theresias*, 10 vols., 1863-79
Maria Theresia und Joseph II. ihre Korrespondenz samt Briefen Josephs an seinen Bruder Leopold, ed. Arneth, 3 vols., 1867-68
Biefe der Kaiserin Maria Theresia an ihre Kinder und Freunde, ed. Arneth, 4 vols., 1881
Fuerst J. Khevenhueller-Metsch, *Tagebuecher*, 7 vols., 1907-25
H. Kretschmayr, *Maria Theresia*, 2nd ed., 1939
E. Guglia, *Maria Theresia*, 2 vols., 1917
G. P. Gooch, *Maria Theresa and other Studies*, 1951
G. Dorschel, *Maria Theresias Staats-u. Lebensanschauung*, 1908
M. Moffat, *Maria Theresa*, 1911
O. Ch. Graf v. Podewils, *Diplomat. Berichte, F. d. G. und Maria Theresia*, 1937
L. v. Ranke, 'Maria Theresia, ihr Staat und Hof. Aus den Papieren des Gross-kanzlers v. Fuerst', 1875 (in *Zur Geschichte von Oesterreich u. Preussen* etc.)
G. Kuentzel, *Fuerst Kaunitz-Rittberg als Staatsmann*, 1923
A. Novotny, *Staatskanzler Kaunitz als geistige Persoenlichkeit*, 1947
Graf W. Bentinck, *Aufzeichnungen ueber Maria Theresia*, ed. Beer, 1871
A. Beer, *Die Staatsschulden und die Ordnung des Staatshaushalts unter Maria Theresia*, 1895
H. L. Mikoletzky, 'Der Haushalt des kaiserlichen Hofes etc.' 1956
H. v. Zwiedineck-Suedenhorst, 'Geschichte der religiosen Bewegung' in *Inner-Oesterreich im 18. Jahrhundert*
K. Schuenemann, *Oesterreichs Bevoelkerungspolitik unter Maria Theresia*, vol. I, 1936
J. Frh. v. Helfert, *Die Gruendung der oesterr. Volksschule durch Maria Theresia*, 1860
G. Strakosch-Grassmann, *Geschichte des oesterr. Unterrichtswesens*, 1905
Joseph II u. Leopold von Toscana, ihr Briefwechsel, ed. Arneth, 2 vols., 1872
Joseph II, Leopold II, und Kaunitz, ihr Briefwechsel, ed. A. Beer, 1873
Correspondances intimes de l'empereur Joseph II avec Cobenzl et Kaunitz, ed. S. Brunner, 1871
P. v. Mitrofanov, *Josef II*, 2 vols., 1910

A. Gross-Hoffinger, *Geschichte Josef II*, 4 vols., 2nd ed., 1847
H. Meynert, *Kaiser Josef II, ein Beitrag zur Wuerdigung des Geistes seiner Regierung*, 1862
J. Wendrinsky, *Josef II*, 1880
J. Pezzl, *Charakteristik Josefs II*, 1790
J. G. Meusel, *Ueber Kaiser Joseph II*, 1790
S. Padover, *The Revolutionary Emperor. Joseph II*, 1934
S. Brunner, *Joseph II*, 2nd ed., 1885
S. Brunner, *Joseph II als Kirchenreformer*, 1893
S. Brunner, *Joseph II als absoluter Beherrscher etc.*, 1892
F. Maass, *Der Josephinismus, Quellen zu seiner Geschichte*, 4 vols., 1951 etc.
G. Holzknecht, *Der Ursprung der kirchlichen Reformideen Joseph II*, 1914
A. Menzel, 'Kaiser Josef und das Naturrecht' (*Zeitschr. f. oefftl. Recht*, 1920)
Fellner, Kretschmayr u. Walter, *Die oesterreichische Zentralverwaltung* (many volumes of documents)
M. Graefin Calice, *Deutscher Nationalstaat u. oesterr. Reichsidee Die Grundlagen ihrer Entwicklung in der Regierungszeit Joseph II*, 1936
F. Valjavec, *Der Josephinismus, Zur geistigen Entwicklung Oesterreichs im 18 und 19 Jahrhundert*, 2nd ed., 1945
E. Winter, *Der Josefinismus und seine Geschichte*, 1943
E. Gruenberg, *Die Bauernbefreiung und die Aufloesung der gutsherrlichen Verhaeltnisse in Boehmen, Maehren u. Schlesien*, 2 vols., 1893-94
E. Murr Linke, *The Emancipation of the Austrian Peasants*, 1949
W. Lustkandel, *Die Josephinischen Ideen*, 1890
W. Lustkandel, *Sonnenfels und Kudler*, 1891
F. Kopetzky, *J. und F. v. Sonnenfels*, 1882
W. Mueller, *J. v. Sonnenfels*, 1882
H. Marczali, *Hungary in the Eighteenth Century*, 1910
Aus dem josephinischen Wien, Gebler's und Nicolai's Briefwechsel, 1888
I. *Fessler's Rueckblicke auf seine 70 jaehrige Pilgerschaft*, 2nd ed., 1851
H. G. von Bretschneider, *Denkwuerdigkeiten aus seinem Leben*, 1892

CHAPTER 18

THE SMALLER GERMAN STATES IN THE AGE OF ENLIGHTENMENT

Cf. the histories of the smaller German states indicated in literature to chapter 12

FURTHER:

K. Biedermann, *Deutschland im 18. Jahrhundert*, 5 vols., 1854-80
Max von Boehn, *Deutschland im 18. Jahrhundert*, 2 vols., 1921-22
E. Vehse, *Geschichte der deutschen Hoefe seit der Reformation*, 48 vols., 1853
K. H. von Lang, *Memoiren*, T vols., 1841
K. von Raumer, *Der Ritter von Lang und seine Memoiren*, 1923
Gemaelde aus dem aufgeklaerten 18. Jahrhundert, 2 vols., 1786
Karl Eugen von Wuerttemberg und seine Zeit, ed. Wuerttberg. Geschichtsverein, 2 vols., 1907-09
M. Schmitz, *Die Grafen und Fuersten von Hohenzollern*, 1895
J. Kramer, *Die Grafschaft Hohenzollern, Ein Bild sueddeutscher Volkszustaende, 1400-1850*, 1873
F. Martin, *Salzburgs Fuersten in der Barockzeit*, 2. Auflage, 1952
F. von Weech, *Badische Geschichte*, 1890
A. Kleinschmidt, *Karl Friedrich von Baden*, 1878
Geschichte des Rheinlandes, herausgegeben von der Gesellschaft fuer Rheinische Geschichtskunde, 2 vols., 1922
1000 Jahr deutscher Geschichte und deutscher Kultur am Rhein, herausgegeben, A. Schulte, 1925
M. Braubach, *Kurkoeln*, 1949

M. Braubach, *Die vier letzten Kurfuersten von Koeln*, 1931

M. Braubach, *Die erste Bonner Universitaet und ihre Professoren*, 1947

F. G. Schultheiss, *Die geistlichen Staaten beim Ausgang des alten Reiches*, 1895

Joseph von Sartoris, *Statistische Abhandlung ueber die Maengel in der Regierungsverfassung der geistlichen Wahlstaaten und von den Mitteln, solchen abzuhelfen*, 1787

Friedrich Karl von Moser, *Ueber die Regierung der geistlichen Staaten in Deutschland*, 1787

A. F. W. Crome, *Selbstbiographie*, 1833

J. Sauer, *Finanzgeschaefte der Landgrafen von Hessen-Kassel* etc., 1930

Lord Mahon, *The Forty Five*, 1951

G. Mentz, *Weimarische Staats- und Regentengeschichte vom westfaelischen Frieden bis zum Regierungsantritt Carl Augusts*, 1936

F. Hartung, *Das Grossherzogtum Sachsen unter der Regierung Carl Augusts*, 1923

Lady E. Craven, *Memoirs of the Margravine of Anspach*, 2 vols., 1826

O. Klopp, *Geschichte Ostfrieslands*, 1856

G. Loening, *Ostfriesische Geschichte*

H. Witte u. E. Boll, *Mecklenburgische Geschichte*, 2 vols., 1909-13

L. Keller, *Graf Wilhelm von Schaumburg-Lippe*, 1907

S. Stern, *Karl Wilhelm Ferdinand, Herzog zu Braunschweig und Lueneburg*, 1921

G. Schnuerer, *Katholische Kirche und Kultur im 18. Jahrhundert*, 1941

H. E. Feine, *Die Besetzung der Reichsbistuemer von*, 1648-1803

M. Buchberger, *Lexikon fuer Theologie und Kirche*, 2nd ed., 1934-38

Allgemeine Deutsche Biographie

CHAPTER 19

POLITICAL OPINIONS IN THE AGE OF FREDERICK II AND JOSEPH II

GENERAL LITERARY DEVELOPMENT

Hermann Hettner, *Literaturgeschichte des 18. Jahrhunderts*, 6 vols., 7th edition, 1913

Wilhelm Scherer, *Geschichte der deutschen Literatur*, 1917

Ferdinand Josef Schneider, *Die deutsche Dichtung vom Ausgang des Barocks bis zum Beginn des Klassizismus*, 1924

Kuno Francke, *A History of German Literature as Determined by Social Forces*, 1895, 10th impression, 1916

Wilhelm Wackernagel, *Geschichte der deutschen Literatur*, vol. II, 2nd ed., 1894

J. Goldfriedrich, *Geschichte des deutschen Buchhandels*, vol. II-IV

W. Krieg, *Materialien zu einer Geschichte der Buecherpreise und des Autoren-Honorars* etc., 1953

Johann Georg Meusel, *Das gelehrte Deutschland*, 4. und 5. ed., 1796-1812, 8 vols. and 8 supplements

J. de Luca, *Das gelehrte Oesterreich*, 2nd ed., 1777-78

J. Grossinger, *Berlin und Wien, in Betreff der Gelehrsamkeit* etc., 1784

A. M. Kobolt, *Baierisches Gelehrten Lexikon*, 1795 (new edition 1825)

L. Geiger, *Berlin, Geschichte des geistigen Lebens*, 1688-1840, 2 vols., 1892

M. S. Lowe, *Bildnisse jetzt lebender Berliner Gelehrter mit ihren Selbstbiographieen*, 1806

FATHERLAND, NATION, FREEDOM

Woldemar Wenck, *Deutschland vor 100 Jahren, Politische Meinungen und Stimmungen*, 2 vols., 1887, 1890

René Hubert, *Les sciences sociales dans l'Encyclopedie*, 1923

Eduard Sieber, *Die Idee des Kleinstaates bei den Denkern des 18. Jahrhunderts in Frankreich und Deutschland*, 1920

M. Boucher, *Le sentiment national en Allemagne*, 1947

Leonard Krieger, *The German Idea of Freedom, History of a Political Tradition*, 1957

J. G. Zimmermann, *Von dem Nationalstolz*. 2nd ed., 1760

A. Bouvier, *J. G. Zimmermann, Un Représentant Suisse du Cosmopolitisme Literaire au 18, siècle*, 1926

E. Ziehen, 'Die deutsche Schweizerbegeisterung in den Jahren 1750-1815' (in *Deutsche Forschungen*, Heft 8)

Thomas Abbt, *Vom Tode fuer das Vaterland*, 1761

O. Claus, *Th. Abbts histor. politische Anschauungen*, 1906

F. Brueggemann, *Der 7 jaehrige Krieg im Spiegel der zeitgenoessischen Literatur*, 1935 (reprints of the just mentioned tracts of Zimmermann and Abbt, and poems by other authors)

Josef von Sonnenfels, 'Ueber die Liebe des Vaterlands, 1771', 2nd ed., 1785 (reprinted in Sonnenfels, *Gesammelte Schriften*, 1785, vol. VII)

D. Jenisch, *Geist und Charakter des 18. Jahrhunderts*, 3 vols., 1800-01

Adolf Wohlwill, *Weltbuergertum und Vaterlandsliebe der Schwaben* etc., 1875

Fritz Valjavec, *Die Entstehung der politischen Stroemungen in Deutschland (1770-1815)*, 1951

THE UNIVERSITY OF GOETTINGEN

Goetz von Selle, *Die Georg August Universitaet zu Goettingen*, 1937

W. Buff, G. A. Freiherr von Muenchhausen als Gruender der Universitaet Goettingen, 1937

Ernst Schaumkell, *Geschichte der deutschen Kulturgeschichtsschreibung*, 1905

JOHANN JACOB MOSER AND FRIEDRICH KARL VON MOSER

J. J. Moser, *Leben von ihm selbst beschrieben*, 3rd ed., 4 parts, 1777-83

A. Schmidt, *Das Leben J. J. Mosers*, 1868

O. Waechter, *J. J. Moser*, 1885

A. Adam, *J. J. Moser als wuerttembergischer Landschaftskonsulent*, 1887

H. Kaufmann, *F. C. von Moser als Politiker und Publicist*, 1931

K. Witzel, *F. C. v. Moser's Beitrag zur hessen-darmstaedtischen Finanz- und Wirtschaftsgeschichte*, 1929

B. Renner, *Die nationalen Einigungsbestrebungen F. K. v. Mosers*, 1919

F. C. von Moser, *Der Herr und der Diener, geschildert mit patriotischer Freiheit*, 1759

F. C. Moser, *Von dem deutschen Nationalgeist*, 1756

F. C. Moser, *Was ist gut kayserlich und nicht gut kayserlich?*, 1766

F. C. Moser, *Ueber die Regierung geistlicher Staaten in Deutschland*, 1787

F. C. Moser, *Patriotisches Archiv fuer Deutschland*, 10 vols., 1784-1790

F. C. v. Moser, *Politische Wahrheiten*, 2 vols., 1796

JOHANN HEINRICH GOTTLOB VON JUSTI

(a full list of his writings is in the *Handwoerterbuch der Staatswissenschaften*, 4th ed. by Meitzel)

Justi, *Staatswirtschaft* etc., 1755

Justi, *Grundsaetze der Polizeiwissenschaft* etc., 1756

Justi, *Vollstaendige Abhandlung von den Manufakturen und Fabriken*, 2 vols., 1758-61

Justi, *Die Chimaerre des Gleichgewichts von Europa* etc., 1758

Justi, *System des Finanzwesens* etc., 1766

Roscher, *Geschichte der Nationaloekonomie* p. 444-465

L. Sommer, *Die oesterreichischen Kameralisten*, vol. II, p. 170-318

E. Kaeber, *Die Idee des europaeischen Gleichgewichts in der publizistischen Literatur*, 1907

JOSEPH VON SONNENFELS

Sonnenfels, *Gesammelte Schriften*, 10 vols., 1783-87 (A list of his numerous writings and of the writings about him is in the *Handwoerterbuch der Staatswissenschaften*, 4th ed. by J. Jahn)
Franz Kopetzky, *Josef und Franz von Sonnenfels*, 1882
Willibald Mueller, *Josef von Sonnenfels*, 1882
W. Lustkandl, *Sonnenfels und Kudler*, 1891
Roscher, *Geschichte der Nationaloekonomie*, p. 533-52
L. Sommer, *Oesterr. Kameralisten* II, p. 319-444

IMMANUEL KANT

Kant, *Metaphysische Anfangsgruende der Rechtslehre*, 1796
Kant, *Zum ewigen Frieden*, 1793
Kant, *Grundlegung zur Metaphysik der Sitten*, 1785
Kuno Fischer, *I. Kant und seine Lehre*, 2 vols., 4th ed., 1898-99
Kant, *Briefe, ausgewaehlt von F. Ohmann*, 1911
Karl Vorlaender, *Kants Weltanschauung aus seinen Werken*, 1919
I. Kant, sein Leben in Darstellungen von Zeitgenossen. Die Biographien von Borowski, Jachmann u. Wasianski, 1912
J. Bluntschli, *Geschichte des allgemeinen Staatsrechts und der Politik*, 1867, p. 328
F. Meyer, *Ueber Kants Stellung zu Nation und Staat* (H.Z.), 1925
Theodor Litt, *Kant und Herder*, 1930
Wilhelm Metzger, *Gesellschaft, Recht und Staat in der Ethik des deutschen Idealismus*, 1917
Rudolf Kress, *Die soziologischen Gedanken Kants im Zusammenhang seiner Philosophie*, 1929

FREEDOM AND EDUCATION

Paul Barth, *Die Geschichte der Erziehung in soziologischer und geistesgeschichtlicher Beleuchtung.* 1920
Theodor Ziegler, *Geschichte der Paedagogik*, 4th ed., 1917
Karl von Raumer, *Geschichte der Paedagogik*, 3rd ed., 3 vols., 1857
A. Pinloche, *La reforme de l'education en Allemagne au 18. siecle, Basedow et le Philanthropisme*, 1889
J. Rammelt, *J. B. Basedow, Der Philanthropismus und das Dessauer Philanthropin*, 1929
A. Heubaum, *J. H. Pestalozzi*, 1910
H. Jahnke, *E. v. Rochow oder die Schule von Reckahn*, 1905
A. Wiedemann, *J. J. Hecker's paedagogisches Verdienst*, 1900
J. Leyser, *Joachim Heinrich Campe*, 2 vols., 1877
J. Edelheim, *Beiträge zur Geschichte der Sozialpädagogik*, 1902

SECRET SOCIETIES

Allgemeines Handbuch der Freimaurerei (Neubearbeitung von Lennings Encyclopaedie der Fr.), 2 vols., 1900
Ferdinand Runkel, *Geschichte der Freimaurerei in Deutschland*, 3 vols., 1931-32
Ferdinand Josef Schneider, *Die Freimaurerei und ihr Einfluss auf die geistige Kultur in Deutschland am Ende des 18. Jahrhunderts*, 1909
Gustav Kuess und Bernhard Scheichelbauer, *200 Jahre Freimaurerei in Oesterreich*, 1959
Karl Goedecke, *Adolph Freiherr von Knigge*, 1844
Reinhold Grabe, *Das Geheimnis A. von Knigges*, 1936
Frh. von Knigge, *Der Roman meines Lebens*, 4 vols., 1805
Leopold Engel, *Geschichte des Illuminaten-Ordens*, 1906

POETS AND POLITICS

B. Litzmann, *Liscow in seiner literarischen Laufbahn*, 1883
E. Reichel, *Gottsched*, 1908-12
A. Stein, *Ch. F. Gellert*, 1901
Franz Muncker, *F. G. Klopstock*, 2nd ed., 1900
H. Kindermann, *Klopstocks Entdeckung der Nation*, 1935
Adolph Stahr, *G. E. Lessing*, 7th ed., 1873
Erich Schmidt, *Lessing*, 2 vols., 4th ed., 1923
Franz Mehring, *Die Lessing Legende*, 1893
Oskar Vogt, *Der Goldene Spiegel und Wielands politische Ansichten*, 1904
H. Wolffheim, *Wielands Begriff der Humanitaet*, 1949
V. Michel, *Wieland*, 1938
H. Wahl, *Geschichte des Deutschen Merkurs*, 1914
Rudolf Haym, *Herder*, 2 vols., 1880-85
Eugen Kuehnemann, *Herders Leben*, 2nd ed., 1912
Walter Goeken, *Herder als Deutscher*, 1926
R. Ergang, *Herder and the Foundations of German Nationalism*, 1931
A. Bielschowsky, *Goethe*, 2 vols., 31st ed., 1917
F. Gundolf, *Goethe*, 10th ed., 1922
Ottokar Lorenz, *Goethes politische Lehrjahre*, 1893
Wilhelm Mommsen, *Die politischen Anschauungen Goethes*, 1948
R. von Campe, *Der liberale Gedanke in Goethes Weltanschauung*, 1931
Karl Berger, *Schiller*, 2 vols., 7th ed., 1912
Eugen Kuehnemann, *Schiller*, 6th ed., 1920
Otto von Guenther, *Schiller ueber Volk, Staat und Gesellschaft*
Benno von Wiese, *Schiller*, 1958
A. Ruhe, *Schillers Einfluss auf die Entwicklung des deutschen Nationalge-
fuehls*, 1887-92
Heinz Kindermann, *Entwicklung der Sturm- und Drangbewegung*, 1925
Roy Pascal, *The German Sturm und Drang*, 1953
C. Stockmeyer, *Soziale Probleme im Drama des Sturms und Drangs*, 1922
Hermann Korff, *Die Dichtung von Sturm und Drang im Zu sammenhang der
Geistesgeschichte*, 1928
Wolfgang von Wurzbach, *Gottfried August Buerger*, 1900
E. Weller, *Die Freiheitsbestrebungen der Deutschen im 18. u. 19. Jahrhundert
dargestellt in Zeugnissen ihrer Literatur*, 1847
Wilhelm Herbst, *Johann H. Voss*, 3 vols., 1872-76
Carlo Schmidt, *Vom Reich der Freiheit, Schillers Vermaechtnis*, 1955
Ludwig Kahn, *Social Ideals in German Literature*, 1770-1830, 1938
Carlo Antoni, *Der Kampf gegen die Vernunft, Zur Enstehungsgeschichte des
deutschen Freiheitsgedankens*, 1951 (translated from the Italian)
Anton Friedrich Buesching, *Beytraege zu der Lebensgeschichte denkwuerdiger
Personen insonderheit gelehrter Maenner*, 6 vols., 1783-1789

JOURNALS

Ludwig Salomon, *Geschichte des deutschen Zeitungswesens*, vol. I and II, 1906
A. Buchholtz, *Die Vossische Zeitung*, 1904
L. von Goeckingk, *F. Nicolai's Leben u. literarischer Nachlass*, 1820
F. Nicolai, *Beschreibung einer Reise durch Deutschland etc.*, 12 vols., 1783-96
J. Beutler und J. Gutsmuths, *Allgemeines Sachregister ueber die wichtigsten
deutschen Zeit- und Wochenschriften*, 1790
(Johann Kaspar Risbeck) *Briefe eines reisenden Franzosen durch Deutschland*,
2 vols., 1784
Erich Schairer, *Christian F. D. Schubart als politischer Journalist*, 1914
Gottfried Boehm, *Ludwig Wekerlin, Ein Publizistenleben des 18. Jahrhun-
derts*, 1893
F. W. Ebeling, *Weckhrlins Leben*, 1869
Weckhrlin jun., *Geist Weckhrlins*, 1823

Johanna Schultze, *Die Auseinandersetzungen von Adel und Buergertum in den deutschen Zeitschriften des 18. Jahrhunderts*, 1925

Josef Hay, Staat, *Volk und Weltbuergertum in der Berliner Monatsschrift*, 1913

Journal von und fuer Deutschland, ed. by Goecking and Bibra, 1784-1792

Deutsches Museum, ed. by Boie and Dohm, 1776-1788

Ephemeriden der Menschheit, ed. by Iselin and others, 1777

AUGUST LUDWIG VON SCHLOEZER

Ch. von Schloezer, *A. L. von Schloezers oeffentl. und Privatleben*, 2 vols., 1828

F. Fuerst, *A. L. von Schloezer*, 1928

Berney, *Schloezers Staatsauffassung* (H.Z. 1925)

F. Frensdorff, *Ueber Schloezer* (Abh. GW Goett, N.F.11, 1909)

Schloezer, *Briefwechsel etc.* (1777-82)

Schloezer, *Staats-Anzeigen*, 1782-93

Schloezer, *Allgemeines Staatsrecht und Staatsverfassungslehre*, 1793

Schloezer, *Theorie der Statistik nebst Ideen ueber das Studium der Politik ueberhaupt*, 1804

JUSTUS MOESER

Justus Moeser, *Saemtliche Werke*, 10 vols., 1842-43

L. Rupprecht, *J. Moesers sociale und volkswirtschaftliche Anschauungen etc.*, 1892

O. Hatzig, *J. Moeser als Staatsmann und Publizist*, 1909

P. Klassen, *J. Moeser*, 1936

P. Poettsching, *J. Moesers Entwicklung zum Publizisten*, 1935

THE AMERICAN REVOLUTION AND GERMAN OPINION

Herbert Gallinger, *Die Haltung der deutschen Publizisten zu dem amerikanischen Unabhaengigkeitskriege*, Diss Leipzig, 1900

Friedrich Kapp, *Der Soldatenhandel deutscher Fuersten nach Amerika*, 2, ungearbeitete Auflage, 1874

F. Kapp, *Leben des amerikanischen Generals F. W. von Steuben*, 1858 (engl. trsl. 1859)

F. Kapp, *Das Leben des amerikanischen Generals J. Kalb*, 1862 (engl. trsl. 1884)

F. Kapp, *Friedrich der Grosse und die Vereinigten Staaten von Amerika*, 1871

Frh. von Werthern, *Die hessischen Hilfstruppen im nordamerikanischen Unabhaengigkeitskrieg*, 1895

CHAPTER 20
THE FRENCH REVOLUTION AND GERMAN PUBLIC OPINION

Georges Lefebvre, *La Revolution Francaise*, Nouv. Redaction, 1951

Crane Brinton, *A Decade of Revolution*, 1934

Martin Goehring, *Geschichte der grossen Revolution*, 2 vols., 1950 etc.

G. P. Gooch, *The Study of the French Revolution* (in *Studies in Modern History*, 1931)

Eva Hoffmann-Linke, *Zwischen Nationalismus und Demokratie, Gestalten der franzoesischen Vorrevolution*, 1927

Ernst von Aster, *Die franzoesische Revolution in der Entwicklung ihrer politischen Ideen*

Daniel Mornet, *Les origines intellectuelles de la Révolution francaise*, 1933

R. Redslob, *Die Staatstheorien der franzoesischen Nationalversammlung*, 1912

M. Boucher, *La revolution de 1789 vue par les ecrivains Allemands ses contemporaines*, 1954

G. Rudl, *Interpretations of the French Revolution*, 1961

E. Sauer, *Die franzoesische Revolution in deutschen Flugschriften*, 1896
Alfred Stern, *Der Einfluss der franzoesischen Revolution auf das deutsche Geistesleben*, 1928
D. Halevy, *Histoire d'une histoire* etc., 1939
George P. Gooch, *Germany and the French Revolution*, 1920
Jacques Droz, *L'Allemagne et la revolution Francaise*, 1949
Fr. Ruof, *J. W. v. Archenholtz*, 1915
Friedrich Bock, *J. W. v. Archenholtz*, 1915
Karl Vorlaender, *I. Kant*, 2 vols., 1924
H. Sieveking, G. H. Sieveking, *Lebensbild eines Hamburgischen Kaufmans aus der Zeit der franzoesischen Revolution*, 1913
Frieda Braune, *Burke in Deutschland*, 1917
Fritz Valjavec, *Die Entstehung der politischen Stroemungen in Deutschland, 1770-1815*, 1931
Kurt Lessing, *A. W. Rehberg*, 1910
Martin von Geismar (Bruno Bauer) *Deutschland im 18. Jahrhundert*, 1851
Golo Mann, *Friedrich von Gentz*, 1947
N. v. Wrasky, *A. Rebmann*, 1907
M. Braubach, *Die Eudaemonia* (H.Jb. 47, 1927)
G. Krueger, *Die Eudaemonisten* (HZ 143, 1931)
A. G. F. Rebmann, 'Lebensbeschreibung,' in ADB
N. von Wrasky, *A. G. F. Rebmann*, 1907
H. Brunschwig, *La crise de l'état Prussien a la fin du XVIII siecle et la genèse de la mentalité romantique*, 1947

CHAPTER 21

THE END OF THE EMPIRE

A. Sorel, *L'Europe et la revolution Francaise*, 8 vols., 1885-1906
K. Th. v. Heigel, *Deutsche Geschichte vom Tod Friedrichs d. Gr. bis zur Aufloesung des Reiches*, 2 vols., 1899
Sidney Biro, *The German Policy of Revolutionary France*, 2 vols., 1957
H. Frh. Langwerth v. Simmern, *Oesterreich und das Reich im Kampf mit der franzoesischen Revolution, 1790-97*, 2 vols., 1880
J. Venedey, *Die deutschen Republikaner unter der franzoesischen Republik*, 1870
A. v. Vivenot, *Herzog Albrecht v. Sachsen-Teschen als Reichsfeldmarschall*, 2 vols., 1864-66
Otto Tschirch, *Geschichte d. oeffentl. Meinung in Preussen* etc. 2 vols., 1933
A. F. Pribram und E. Fischer, *Ein politischer Abenteurer* (Glave-Kolbielski) 1937
W. Wendland, *Versuch einer allgemeinen Volksbewaffrung in Sueddeutschland waehrend der Jahre, 1791-94*, 1901
R. Lorenz, *Volksbewaffnung und Staatsidee in Oesterreich*, 1926
C. Th. Perthes, *Politische Zustaende und Personen in Deutschland zur Zeit der franzoesischen Herrschaft*, 2 vols., 1861
G. Lefebvre, *Napoleon*, 1935
August Fournier, *Napoleon*, 3 vols., 1926
P. Gaffarel, *Bonaparte et les republiques Italiennes*, 1895
Napoleon, *Correspondance*, 32 vols., 1858-70 (many supplements)
Ausgewaehlte Korrespondenz Napoleon I. uebersetzt von H. Kurz, 3 vols., 1870
H. v. Srbik, *Das oesterr. Kaisertum u. d. Ende des Reiches* (in *Archiv fuer Politik und Geschichte*, 1927)
Adalbert Schultze, *Kaiser Leopold II und die franzoesische Revolution*, 1899
Leopold II u. Marie Christine, Briefwechsel, her. v. A. Wolf, 1867
I. Zimmerman, *Das Verfassungsprojekt. Leopolds von Toscana*, 1907

Q

A. Wolf und H. v. Zwiedineck Suedenhorst, *Oesterreich unter Maria Theresia, Josef II, und Leopold II*, 1884, part IV

R. Kerner, *Bohemia in the Eighteenth Century*, 1932

Ernst Wangermann, *From Joseph II to the Jacobin Trials*, 1959

Huber A. *Die Politik Josefs II, beurteilt von seinem Bruder Leopold*, 1877

Andreas Th. Preuss, *Ewald Friedrich Graf v. Hertzberg*, 1909

Hertzberg, *Huit Dissertations* etc. 1787 *Memoire sur les revolutions*, 1791

E. Guglia, *Friedrich v. Gentz*, 1901

G. Mann, *Friedrich von Gentz*, 1947

J. Hansen, *Quellen zur Geschichte des Rheinlandes im Zeitalter der franzoesischen Revolution*, 4 vols., 1931-38

L. Engerand, *L'opinion publique dans les provinces Rhénanes et em Belgique*, 1919

A. Conrady, *Die Rheinlande in der Franzosenzeit*, 1922

Quellen zur Geschichte des Zeitalters der franz. Revolution, herausgegeben von Hueffer u. Luckwaldt, 3 vols., 1900-1907

Bailleu, *Preussen und Frankreich, 1795-1807*, 2 vols., 1881-87

W. Langsam, *The Napoleonic Wars and German Nationalism in Austria*, 1930

A. v. Vivenot, *Zur Geschichte des Rastadter Congresses*, 1871

Freiherr von Thugut, *Vertrauliche Briefe*, 2 vols., 1872

G. Just, *Als die Voelker erwachten, Literarische Bewegung und Zeitstimmung vor Beginn des Feldzuges 1809*, 1907

Hellmuth Roessler, *Oesterreichs Kampf um Deutschland's Befreiung (1805-1815)*, 2 vols., 1940

Theodor Bitterauf, *Die Gruendung des Rheinbundes und der Untergang des alten Reiches*, 1905

INDEX

GEORGE ALLEN & UNWIN LTD

London: 40 Museum Street, W.C.1

Auckland: 24 Wyndham Street
Sydney, N.S.W.: Bradbury House, 55 York Street
Cape Town: 109 Long Street
Bombay: 15 Graham Road, Ballard Estate, Bombay 1
Calcutta: 17 Chittaranjan Avenue, Calcutta 13
New Delhi: 13-14 Ajmeri Gate Extension, New Delhi 1
Karachi: Karachi Chambers, McLeod Road
Madras: Mohan Mansion, 38c Mount Road, Madras 6.
Mexico: Villalongin 32-10, Piso, Mexico 5, D.F.
Toronto: 91 Wellington Street West
Sao Paulo: Avenida 9 de Julho, 1138-Ap. 51
Buenos Aires: Escritorio 454-459, Florida 165
Singapore: 36c Prinsep Street, Singapore 7
Hong Kong: 1/12 Mirador Mansions, Kowloon
Ibadan: P.O. Box 62
Nairobi: P.O. Box 12446